Items should be returned on or before the last dat
shown below. Items not already requested by oth
borrowers may be renewed in person, in writing o
telephone. To renew, please quote the number or
barcode label. To renew online a PIN is required.
This can be requested at your local library.
Renew online @ **www.dublincitypubliclibraries.**
Fines charged for overdue items will include posta
incurred in recovery. Damage to or loss of items w
be charged to the borrower.

Leabharlanna Poiblí Chathair Bhaile Átha Clia
Dublin City Public Libraries

Lot OPL 13/9/17

Dublin City
Baile Átha Cliath

Central Library, Henry Street,
An Lárleabharlann, Sráid Annraoi
Tel: 8734333

Date Due	Date Due	Date Due
08. MAR. 06.	17. APR 0	2 2 NOV 201
27. NOV	23. FEB 12	2 5 JUN 2014
	07. AUG 13	- 8 NOV 2014
	25. MAY 15	
		- 9 DEC 2015

IRISH STONE BRIDGES: HISTORY AND HERITAGE

Irish Stone Bridges

History and Heritage

PETER O'KEEFFE

AND

TOM SIMINGTON

IRISH ACADEMIC PRESS

This book was typeset for Irish Academic Press,
Kill Lane, Blackrock, Co. Dublin.
by Seton Music Graphics Ltd, Bantry, Co. Cork

British Library Cataloguing in Publication Data
O'Keeffe, Peter
Irish stone bridges : history and heritage.
I. Title II. Simington, Tom
624.209415

ISBN 0 7165 2465 1

Printed in Ireland by Colour Books Ltd., Dublin

Contents

To St Benezet and St John Nepomucene

SPECIAL ACKNOWLEDGMENT

The publication of this book
has been made possible
by a grant in aid from
the Department of the Environment.

Foreword

Ruskin, following the introduction of the railway system, concluded that "all travelling becomes dull in exact proportion to its rapidity". Since the turn of the present century the continuously increasing concentration required for driving leaves little scope for viewing the landscape; as a result we now seldom hear about the handsome, picturesque, or beautiful masonry arch bridges that featured so prominently in travel coach literature. Perhaps this explains the current lack of interest in the history and characteristics of these precious man-made elements of the environment. This indifference is not peculiar to Ireland as evidenced by an editorial in a recent edition of the Council of Europe publication *A Future for our Past* which states that bridges, even those dating from the distant past, have not been given the attention they deserve as components of the European historic and cultural heritage.

In 1988 when Peter O'Keeffe, on the occasion of his retirement from An Foras Forbartha, announced that he intended to write a book on the history of road bridges in Ireland, in collaboration with Tom Simington, I was glad to be able to assure them of my full support in bringing the work to fruition and in getting it published. I had no doubt that the outcome would be a thoroughly researched work which would fill a glaring gap in the knowledge of Ireland's environmental literature. Both authors are past Presidents of the Institution of Engineers of Ireland and have demonstrated their flair and enthusiasm for the subject in many papers and addresses published by the Institution and other learned bodies. Decades of public service as engineers with various local authorities have enabled them to bring first-hand experience of the design, construction and maintenance of roads and bridges to bear on the work and this is indeed reflected in the quality.

The book has been structured and written in a manner that opens up this specialised topic to everybody. Students, teachers, antiquaries, historians, architects and archaeologists will find in it a framework and methodology as well as base-line information which will enable those interested to search and hopefully find more surviving medieval bridges and also to date thousands of later ones of uncertain origin. They are to be found in almost every townland throughout the length and breadth of Ireland, North and South. The authors rightly draw attention to the vast storehouse of information contained in 19th-century provincial newspapers which can be accessed through the microfiche copies in most county libraries. The collapse of a bridge or the construction of a new one always were and still are newsworthy items.

Apart from the cultural aspects of bridge history there is little doubt about the attraction of historic bridges large and small for the tourist. However, too often we find beautiful pictures and postcards of them in tourist literature with no information on their history—illustrative of the gap in environmental literature mentioned above. There are many examples among the many articles in Part II of this book which show how the information can be searched out and presented in a succinct historic perspective. Many towns in Ireland will be surprised to find in this book that they have, hitherto unidentified, rare examples of historic arches under their streets or in their hinterlands. Last year two of the bridges described by the authors, St Mary Magdalen's, Duleek and Babes Arch on the Boyne, were selected by the famous French bridge historian, Marcel Prade, for inclusion in his book on remarkable bridges of Europe published in 1990.

As an engineer, I have no hesitation in also commending this book to all of my colleagues and others who are involved in the maintenance and rehabilitation of Ireland's considerable stock of surviving masonry arch road bridges. In it they will find a fund of information relevant to their work, in particular the criteria by which rare and ancient survivors may be identified and dated. The book also draws attention to problems still to be solved in the rehabilitation of arches such as strengthening without obscuring the joints and stone facings on the arch soffits. These are difficult questions because bridges, unlike most other historic buildings, have to withstand forces from heavy axles above and the scouring, leaching and erosion of flood below. However, the overall number that require special treatment because of their antiquity is small.

Finally, as the readers will discover, there is an ethical dimension to bridges reflected in the many simple, humble and modest but nonetheless aesthetically pleasing small arches of earlier centuries. Today there is a growing concern about man's moral responsibilities to nature but this can often be forgotten in the face of demands for gigantic and spectacular structures. Hopefully in Ireland we will always keep in mind the historic bond between the ethical and the aesthetic when designing the bridges of the future using the best materials and techniques of the day.

L.M. McCumiskey
Director
Environmental Research Unit
Dublin

18 April 1991

Preface

Pride in and respect for our rich heritage of national monuments was something ingrained in most primary-school children in the decades following national independence. This was evidenced by the national inventory carried out through the schools in 1937. In Borris-in-Ossory boys' school, where my father was the master, each pupil in the senior classes was assigned an artifact—in my case an old forge—to investigate and record. The findings from all over the country are now in the archive of the folklore department of University College, Dublin. In my own family, we made periodic outings to Clonmacnoise, Aghaboe, Roscrea, etc., and we had some important books, notably a full set of Joyce's *Irish Names of Places* and Canon O'Hanlon's *History of the Queen's County*, which I still have and which were invaluable in the research for this book. Bridges, however, were never considered ancient, presumably because the survivors were in active service.

Concrete and steel were the civil engineer's materials we learned about in UCD when I was there from 1944 to 1947. The pride and joy of Professor Pierce Purcell was Kenmare reinforced concrete bridge, but he also told us about keeping the line of thrust in masonry arches inside the middle third. It was the Local Authority (Works) Act of 1949 that provided me and many of my contemporaries in the local authority service with the opportunity to learn more about masonry arch bridges, because the "works" included "in particular" the widening and deepening of "watercourses". The late Christy Byrne, with whom I worked at the time in Co. Wicklow, had learned about the dangers of scour from his former colleagues in the Office of Public Works and always insisted on deep foundations, for both new bridges and the underpinning of old ones.

In 1967, after sixteen years working with local authorities and in the Department of Local Government, mostly on roads and road construction, I moved to An Foras Forbartha, the National Institute for Physical Planning and Construction Research, as head of its roads research division. I experienced difficulty in obtaining information about the history of road bridges in Ireland, and began recording bits of relevant information, mainly from secondary sources, in a notebook, as I came across them. In August 1985 the archives committee of the Institution of Engineers of Ireland, of which I had been an active member for many years, invited Tom Simington along for a discussion on bridge records. Tom, as professed in his presidential address to the Institution in 1961, had been an avid "pontist", to use his own word, since he qualified as a civil engineer in 1927, and worked largely on bridge and marine structures until retirement in 1972. The morning after the meeting he called to see me and proposed that we pool our information and write a joint book on the history of Irish bridges, a proposal I instantly accepted.

It so happened at that time there was a growing concern about the effects of the increasing weight and volume of heavy goods vehicles on roads and bridges. Responding to this the roads division of An Foras Forbartha organised a series of seminars and courses on the assessment of the condition and load-carrying capacity of bridges. The findings highlighted the dearth of information on the ages and historical importance of a diminishing stock of ancient ones. This afforded me an opportunity to explore these aspects in greater depth. Encouragement came from everyone, in particular Andy O'Connell of the City and County Engineers' Association and Bill McCumiskey, the chief executive officer of An Foras Forbartha. Information was hard to find because most early mentions of bridges are incidental. The search however was greatly facilitated by Maurice Curtis, of the Central Catholic Library, who gave me access to its "Irish Room" which has a superb collection of diocesan histories, annals, archeological journals etc.

When the announcement of the abolition of An Foras Forbartha came in September 1987, I decided to take early retirement, having completed 40 years working, mainly on the roads, in the public service. I had been Irish representative on the OECD Steering Committee for Road Research for twenty years and at my last meeting my French colleague, Jean Coste, head of the French Road Research Laboratory, on hearing about my research, gave me a copy of *Les Ponts Monuments Historiques* and put me in touch with its author, Marcel Prade. This was an invaluable aid and contact, as will be evident. More importantly, Prade's book provided Tom and myself with an ideal model for layout and presentation.

Latterly the main centre for the research was the library of the Royal Irish Academy, and a fruitful source it was. Here I wish to identify a few who made very significant contributions, namely, my wife Terry, who apart from forfeiting the sitting room to books, maps, journals, bits of paper for a year or so, patiently endured the role of "bridge widow" for the duration but at the same time shared in the excitement when new ancient bridges and early mentions were discovered; and former colleagues in An Foras Forbartha—Maura Ryan, Gerry O'Flaherty, Paddy McGuinness and Bill McCumiskey—who gave unceasing help, advice and encouragement.

PETER O'KEEFFE
May 1991

Because professional historians have reservations about unqualified authors writing about old forgotten far-off events, I hasten to disclaim expertise in their discipline. But I belong to an equally exclusive brotherhood. Like my co-author, I am a pontist, that being the accepted term to describe an enthusiast who makes a devoted study of bridges, ancient and modern, and of their builders. My uncle, R.C. Simington, DLitt, worked for many years with the Irish Manuscripts Commission and gave me access to his researches. My own active involvement in bridge engineering began in 1927, when, having obtained a degree in civil engineering, I worked under a Great Southern Railway bridge specialist dealing with the design and maintenance of steel structures. Subsequently I became a contractor's site engineer with a succession of British and Irish firms, always seeking experience in bridge and other marine constructions, including Butt Bridge in Dublin, and the well-known Kenmare Bridge in Kerry. The latter contract included the demolition of one of Ireland's few large suspension bridges.

During the war period, because contract work in Ireland was scarce, I took refuge in local authority employment, which culminated in my appointment as county engineer of Clare. In that capacity I could regard myself as the custodian of some very handsome old masonry arches, a pleasant responsibility for a pontist. But I missed the thrills and spills of the construction industry and to that I returned when the war was over, as director in a newly-formed company. There my first major responsibility was the reconstruction of Fenit harbour in Kerry, which involved the replacement in reinforced concrete of the very long timber approach viaduct. Over the years, until I retired in 1972, I continued to deal mainly with bridges and harbour works.

My retirement has been a happy experience, giving me the opportunity to carry out a forestry project in Co. Wicklow, and to expand a lifetime collection of books, engravings, photographs and maps, some of which provided useful material for this publication. My initial contribution to it was my presidential address to the Irish Institution of Civil Engineers in 1961, which traced the history of early Irish bridges, and which urged members of the profession to preserve them wherever possible.

Since I am now an extremely senior citizen, I have relied heavily on Peter O'Keeffe's more robust energy and enthusiasm to provide a considerable volume of carefully researched information, and finally to write-up and assemble our joint contributions.

TOM SIMINGTON
May 1991

Acknowledgments

The writers wish to thank all of the many people who contributed information, photos, measurements about bridges and those who assisted in the research or helped in the preparation, editing and publication of this book. Given the large number and geographical distribution of the bridges for which pre-1830 mentions were found, it would have been an impossible task without this help. In many cases the bridges had been replaced and the originals no longer existed but this information alone saved much time and effort. Specific contributions in respect of particular bridges are acknowledged throughout the text. Here we single out a number of people who were closely identified with the overall effort.

As already stated in the preface, Bill McCumiskey, Maura Ryan, Gerry O'Flaherty, Adrian Slattery, Paddy McGuinness and Jim Sheedy gave enormous assistance and encouragement throughout the whole of the work. This covered the whole spectrum of the many activities involved in bringing the book from outline to final draft.

Significant assistance was provided by the following colleagues, associations, institutions or authorities.

Arthur Curran, Kay Doyle, Bertie Foy, Tom Holland, Aideen Joyce, Bill Keogh, Bill O'Dowd, Alicia O'Keeffe, Renee O'Sullivan, Nick Ryan and Shay Stone.

The City and County Engineers' Association, in particular John O'Flynn, Andy O'Connell, Oliver Perkins, John Carrick and Peter Kellaghan. The Association gave wholehearted encouragement to the work from beginning to end.

The Libraries of the Environmental Research Unit, the Royal Irish Academy and the Catholic Central Library were particularly helpful. Our thanks to Librarians Noel Hughes and Dorothy Corr, ERU; Bridget Dolan and Íde Ní Thuama, RIA; and Maurice Curtis, CCL.

The sponsorship of the Department of the Environment has been acknowledged in the frontpiece. Special thanks is given to Brendan O'Donoghue, Paddy O'Duffy, Sean Walsh, Eugene O'Connor, Michael Tobin and Declan O'Driscoll.

Local Authority engineers were always ready to provide information on bridges in their areas and, as mentioned above, particular contributions are given in the text. We give special thanks to Brendan Devlin, Frank Burke, John Cunningham, Brian Madden, John Lahart, Harry Lynch, Tim O'Leary and Canice O'Mahony, who provided vital information on many old bridges for which they have responsibilities.

The archive of the Institution of Engineers of Ireland was another very fruitful source of information and thanks are due to the Director, IEI, Finbar Callanan, for access to it. Matt O'Donovan, formerly Secretary, IEI, was always helpful in tracking down sources but most particularly we thank him for the loan of his personal original copy of Bartlett's illustrations.

Colm Martin and Aighleann O'Shaughnessy of the Office of Public Works were most helpful in providing bridge sections and historical data.

Michael Adams and Martin Healy of Irish Academic Press painstakingly edited the book and were responsible for its production. Jarlath Hayes was the designer.

Photographs: Many of the photographs collected or taken by the writer for research purposes were not suitable for reproduction in the book. The problem was overcome by asking the county engineers of the local authorities responsible for the upkeep of the selected bridges to provide photos of particular aspects; the response was excellent. We wish to thank:

Carlow Co. Council for the photos of Leighlinbridge taken by Seamus O'Connor; Cork Corporation for the photos of Clarkes and South Gate, taken by Tony Fleming;

Dublin Corporation for the photos of Sarah's Bridge and Milltown Bridge, taken by William Mooney;

Dublin Co. Council for the photos of King Johns, Lucan, Crooked, Gormanstown, Lissenhall and Roganstown taken by William Mooney;

Kildare Co. Council for the photos of Carragh, Harristown and Athy taken by Pat Foley;

Meath Co. Council for the photos of Mabe's, Babes, St Mary Magdalen, Scariff, Trim, Newtown, Slane, Kilcarn and Bective taken by Paul Tierney;

Waterford Co. Council for the photos of Lismore, Cappoquin and Crook taken by Billy Smith;

Waterford Corporation for the early print of Cox's bridge and for photos of St John's taken by Michael Cronin;

Wicklow Co. Council for the photos of Derrybawn, Muclagh, Bookeys and Clara taken by Con Hogan.

The photos of Feale and Gouldbourne were taken by Finbarr O'Connell some years ago. Phoenix Maps, 26 Ashington Avenue, Navan Road, Dublin prepared the clear copy from the discoloured original of Moll's Map from which Appendix 10 was prepared. The permission of the Royal Society of Antiquaries of Ireland to reproduce some illustrations from their journals is gratefully acknowledged.

Abbreviations

AFM	Annals of the Four Masters
Andrews, "Road Planning"	Andrews, J.H., "Road Planning in Ireland before the Railway Age" in *Irish Geography* V, 1 (1964), pp. 17–41
Archdall	Archdall, M, *Monasticon Hibernicum*, Dublin, 1786
Boyer	Boyer, M. Nice, *Medieval French Bridges: A History*, Cambridge, Mass., 1976
Bridge Collapse	*Bridge Collapse: Causes, Consequences and Remedial Measures*, proceedings of An Foras Forbartha seminar, Dublin, 1987
British Bridges	*British Bridges: An Illustrated Technical and Historical Record*, ed. Johnson S.M. and Scott-Giles, C.W., London, 1933
Cal. doc. Ire., 1171–1251	*Calendar of documents relating to Ireland, 1171–1251* (5 vols, London, 1875–86)
Cal. pat. rolls Ire., Eliz.	*Calendar of patent and close rolls of chancery in Ireland, Elizabeth, 19 year to end of reign*, ed. James Morrin (Dublin, 1862)
Cal. S.P. Ire., 1509–73	*Calendar of the state papers relating to Ireland, 1509–73 etc.* (24 vols, London 1860–1911)
CDI	See *Cal. doc. Ire.* above.
Chartul. St Mary's, Dublin	*Chartularies of St Mary's Abbey, Dublin, . . . and annals of Ireland, 1162–1370*, ed. J.T. Gilbert (2 vols, 1884–6)
Commons' jn.	*Journals of the House of Commons* (of England, Great Britain, or United Kingdom)
Council Book Cork	*The Council Book of the Corporation of Cork from 1609 to 1643 and 1690 to 1800*, ed. R. Caulfield, Guildford, 1870
Council Book Youghal	*The Council Book of the Corporation of Youghal from 1610 to 1659, 1666 to 1687, and 1690 to 1800*, ed. R. Caulfield, Guildford, 1878
Delaney	Delaney, R., *A Celebration of 250 Years of Ireland's Inland Waterways*, Belfast, 1988
Edwards	Edwards, R.D., *An Atlas of Irish History*, 2nd ed., London, 1981
Gwynn & Hadcock	Gwynn, A. and Hadcock, R.N., *Medieval Religious Houses, Ireland*, London, 1970, rep. Dublin, 1988
Harbison	Harbison, P., *Guide to the National Monuments in the Republic of Ireland*, Dublin, 1970
ICEI	Institution of Civil Engineers of Ireland
IEI	Institution of Engineers of Ireland
JCHAS	*Journal of the Cork Historical and Archaeological Society*
JKAS	*Journal of the Kilkenny Archaeological Society*
JKEAS	*Journal of the Kilkenny and South East Archaeological Society*
JGAHS	*Journal of the Galway Archaeological and Historical Society*
JNMAS	*Journal of the North Munster Archaeological Society*
Joyce	Joyce, P.W., *The Origin and History of Irish Names of Places*, 3 vols, Dublin, 1902

JRSAI	*Journal of the Royal Society of Antiquaries of Ireland*
Leask, *Castles*	Leask, H., *Irish Castles and Castellated Houses*, Dundalk, 1964
Leask, *Churches*	Leask, H., *Irish Churches and Monastic Buildings*, 3 vols, Dundalk, 1955
Lenihan	Lenihan, M., *Limerick, its History and Antiquities*, Dublin, 1866
Lewis	Lewis, S., *Topographical Dictionary of Ireland*, 2 vols, London, 1837
McCutcheon	McCutcheon, W.A., *The Industrial Archaeology of Ireland*, Belfast, 1980
Murrough	Murrough, M. McCarthy, "The English Presence in Early 17th Century Munster" in *Natives and Newcomers*, ed. C. Brady and R. Gillespie, Dublin 1986
OS	Ordnance Survey
Pacata Hibernia	[Thomas Stafford], *Pacata Hibernia: Ireland appeased and reduced, or an historie of the later warres in Ireland, especially within the province of Munster under the government of Sir George* Carew (London, 1633; 2 vols, Dublin, 1810; ed. S.H. O'Grady, 2 vols, London, 1896)
Prade	Prade, M., *Les Ponts Monuments Historiques*, Poitiers, 1987
RIA Proc.	*Proceedings of the Royal Irish Academy* (Dublin, 1836–)
RIA Trans.	*Transactions of the Royal Irish Academy*, 33 vols, Dublin, 1786–1907
Rot. pat. Hib.	*Rotulorum patentium et clausorum cancellariae Hiberniae calendarium*, Dublin, 1828
RSAI	Royal Society of Antiquaries of Ireland
Ruddock	Ruddock, T., *Arch Bridges and their Builders, 1735–1835*, London, 1982
Semple	Semple, G., *A Treatise on Building in Water*, Dublin, 1776
Shell Guide	Killanin, Lord and Duignan, M.V., *The Shell Guide to Ireland* (revised and updated by P. Harbison), Dublin, 1989
Sherlock	Sherlock, Archdeacon, "Some Notes on the Fords and Bridges over the River Liffey" in *JKAS* 6, pp. 293–305
Sidney	Sidney, Sir Henry, "Memoir of his government of Ireland, addressed to Sir Francis Walsingham 1582–3", reproduced in *UJA* 1–8 (1853–60)
Stalley	Stalley, R., *The Cistercian Monasteries of Ireland*, London 1987
Stat. Ire.	*The Statues at large passed in the parliaments held in Ireland . . .* (1310–1761, 8 vols, Dublin, 1765; 1310–1800, 20 vols, Dublin, 1786–1801)
Stat. Ire., John-Hen. V	*Statutes and ordinances, and acts of the parliament of Ireland, King John to Henry V*, ed. H.F. Berry (Dublin, 1907)
Stat. Ire., Hen. VI	*Statute rolls of the parliament of Ireland, reign of King Henry VI*, ed. H.F. Berry (Dublin, 1910)
Stat. Ire., 1–12 Edw. IV	*Statute rolls of the parliament of Ireland, 1st to the 12th years of the reign of King Edward IV*, ed. H.F. Berry (Dublin, 1914)
UJA	*Ulster Journal of Archaeology* (Belfast, 3 series: 1853–62, 9 vols; 1895–1911, 17 vols; 1938–)
Wilkinson	Wilkinson, G. *Practical Geology and Ancient Architecture of Ireland*, London, 1845
Young	Young, A., *A Tour in Ireland 1776–79*, 2 vols, London 1778, rep. Shannon, 1969.

Introduction

This book on road bridges of Ireland from AD 1000 to 1830 is in two parts. Part I presents the general history of the origin and development of road bridges in Ireland in a west European context over a period of eight centuries commencing at the year 1000. In Part II 74 bridges and groups of bridges are described separately in approximate chronological order. These are the examples which emerged from an extensive search over many years. It was mainly a paper search of national, diocesan and local histories, of State papers, archaeological journals, annals, maps, surviving grand jury records and many other sources. It was a pioneering task, because there was no precedent to follow. A search and identification methodology evolved as the work progressed. Important early mentions were often found in the most unlikely sources, more often than not incidental and seldom indexed. Hundreds of bridges with early literature mentions had vanished from the landscape and there were no records of their arrival or departure.

We should stress that we are writing primarily as civil engineers but we hope to provide a technical framework which will help and encourage professional and local historians and archaeologists to research the role of bridges in Ireland's development—and, indeed, help everyone to appreciate the heritage that lies beneath our roads.

There are thousands of post-1750 survivors; however, due to the destruction of grand jury records in 1922 in the Four Courts fire during the Irish Civil War, very few can be ascribed to particular decades. A difference of twenty years in this period can be of great importance as shown by the graphs of growth of arch spans at the end of Chapter 11. The neglect of the subject is perhaps best exemplified by Milltown Old Bridge (Dublin) across the Dodder, which succeeded in sleeping through the scrutinies of a millennium year. It still conceals its birthday, but was, like Cardiff Bridge over the Tolka in Dublin, registered in the 17th-century Petty Survey at least a century ahead of Vallancy's "Queen's Bridge", now known as Liam Mellows Bridge, heretofore believed to be the oldest survivor under the streets of the capital.

Practically all of the literature sources (annals, bridge laws, maps, plans, papers, drawings etc.) were in imperial units (some ancient, such as volumetric perches); that system, therefore, is used throughout the book; metric equivalents are given in the Glossary.

Where a bridge name carries an asterisk it indicates that the bridge is featured in Part II—the gazetteer section.

PART I

CHAPTER 1

The Number of Bridges

There are 57,350 miles of public road in the Republic of Ireland.[1] These figures were compiled in 1977 based on the local authority road schedules for that year; each road authority is obliged under section 86(1) of the Public Bodies Order, 1956[2] to keep an up-to-date schedule of roads in its charge, in a prescribed format; however, the form does not distinguish bridges. The word "road" (as defined in section 1 of the Local Government Act, 1925) includes any bridge, pipe or arch. Bridges can, for the purposes of this book, be divided into culverts and underbridges (called "under" because the bridge supports the road). The distinction is more a matter of convention than precise definition, but a culvert is commonly a large pipe or long enclosed channel for carrying water below road level. Traditionally in Ireland, and many other countries, structures with at least one span of over 6ft have been categorised as bridges (spanning 6ft or more was quite a problem in ancient times, so it is important in a book on the history of bridges to adhere to the tradition).

In 1918 Waterford Co. Council carried out one of the most comprehensive surveys[3] of road bridges ever undertaken in Ireland, recording each bridge (name, type, span, condition) and giving a short description and estimated cost of repairs. An analysis of the survey shows that there were 450 bridges greater than 6ft span and 140 of less than 6ft in the county's public road network at the time. The public road mileage in Waterford County in 1977 was 1585 miles compared with 1,180 miles in 1886. Most of the additional mileage was taken-in-charge under the Local Government Act, 1953.[4] Assuming the length in 1918 to have been about 1,400 miles, this gives one bridge over 6ft span for every three miles of public road.

Another source of accurate information is the road inventory[5] carried out by An Foras Forbartha on national routes in the early 1970s. Data extracted is summarised in Fig. 1.

Some small bridges without parapets may have been missed in the field survey, so the figures are not overestimates. They show that there is one non-rail underbridge for every 2.32 miles of road. The range is one per 2.51 miles on national primary routes to 1 per 2.16 miles on national secondary routes.

A survey carried out by Offaly Co. Council in 1985 showed 350 masonry arch bridges on 1,193 miles of public road—one per 3.4 miles. A survey in Co. Laois in 1986 gave 350 underbridges of all types on 1,401 miles of road—one per 4.0 miles. Partial data on larger span bridges (20ft) are available for most local authorities, but such information is insufficient for present purposes.

Route system	Length (miles)	Underbridges (non-railway)			Overbridges
		6ft to 20ft	over 20ft	Total	
National Primary	1600	321	315	636	42
National Secondary	1586	444	290	734	24
Total National	3186	765	605	1370	66

Fig. 1: *Number of Bridges, National Route System, 1971*

Dr W.H.C. Stevenson of the Department of the Environment, Northern Ireland, estimated that there are about 4,500 bridges over 6ft 6in. span, of which 3,200 are stone arches, on 14,650 miles of public road in Northern Ireland (one bridge of all types per 3.25 miles).[6] Some international data are given in an 1981 OECD report[7] but the lengths of the networks are omitted, apart from the UK which has approximately 130,000 road bridges on 215,625 miles of public road—one per 1.66 miles.

One would expect in Ireland that the density of bridges should diminish with road class because it was cheaper to detour when most of the less important county roads were being made in the 18th and 19th centuries; however, this argument might not be true for the smaller bridges. The data in fig. 1 suggest increasing density with diminishing road class.

Because an accurate estimate of the number of bridges was needed for EEC submission, An Foras Forbartha carried out a statistical exercise in 1988 based on counts of the number of road crossings of rivers/streams in randomly selected areas of the Ordnance Survey half-inch maps. It showed that the number lay between 23,320 and 39,280 with 95% confidence.[8] The Ordnance Survey 1/50,000 scale maps will provide a better basis for this type of exercise when they become available.

For the purposes of this book it can be confidently assumed that there are about 25,000 masonry arch bridges over 6ft span in all Ireland. The majority probably are post-1775. A good estimate of the number in 1830 may be obtained by sampling from the 1839 Ordnance Survey six-inch sheets—an interesting exercise for a student of historical geography. An analysis of Moll's map 1714 (Appendix 10) to determine the minimum number of bridges on the principal roads at that time shows there were 584 bridges marked on 6826 statute miles, that is, about one every 12 miles. However, many smaller rivers are not marked on Moll, so the number is an underestimate.

Some information on survival rates for bridges is given in the 1981 OECD report but none that would provide estimate of the percentage of the existing stock likely to be over even 300 years old. Current replacement rates range from 0.2 to 0.6 per cent per annum on principal roads in other European countries.

In Part II of this book 25 medieval bridges are described; of these, 20 survive in whole or in part. Most of them were identified from early mentions in historical literature. Their characteristics are summarised in chapter 11 and should enable others, especially antiquaries and local authority engineers, to discover more which are not mentioned in the literature.

CHAPTER 2

Áthanna and Clochans

Our search for early mentions of fords (*áthanna*) began with a perusal of the indexes to the various annals of Ireland. The results were disappointing: incidental references to approximately 100 *áthanna* and 40 *bel-áthanna*. The more important ones, such as Áth Cliath, Áth Luan etc., were referred to dozens of times. The annals cover the period from earliest times to 1614.

In his *Irish Names of Places*[1], Joyce gives an excellent summary of the derivation and meaning of place names embodying the word *áth* and classifies them with bridges and weirs as artificial structures, pointing out that practically all natural fords had been upgraded at some stage. Commonsense tells us that that the

earliest inhabitants sought out the shallowest places to cross the rivers and availed of fallen trees and hanging branches. It must be borne in mind that the physical features of the landscape were vastly different then and much more difficult for travellers—dense forest, bog, swamp (*criathar*). The rivers were wider and deeper because of obstructions to the channels. Knowledge of floods and their frequency had to be accumulated in the traditions of successive generations, a fact attested to in the names given to them such as *aigne* meaning treacherous, which is the Irish name of the Nanny in Meath.

The most common Irish word for a ford according to Joyce is *áth*. Variations included

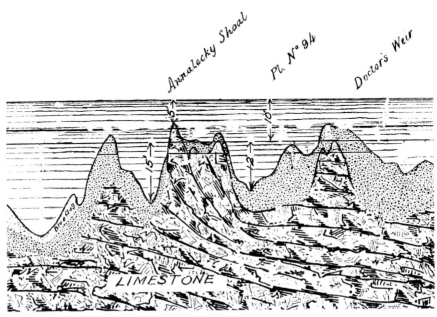

Fig. 2: *Longitudinal section of Shannon at Annalecky*

ah, augh, agh and a. These form part of thousands of place names in Ireland.(The word aith denotes a kiln as expressed in Aith na hAithe, the ford of the kiln.) They are often combined with baile, meaning a town, or bel, the entry to a habitation that grew up in the vicinity. Sometimes they are qualified by an adjective giving information on a characteristic of the ford, or of the terrain in the vicinity. The ancient name of Lanesborough was Ath Liagh, which is still retained for the townland on the western bank of the Shannon—Baile Átha Liag, the town of the ford of the stones. Further up the Shannon there is Annalecky (Ath Leacha), the flaggy ford. The longitudinal section of the Shannon at its location, taken from the Shannon survey of the 1840s, is in fig. 2. The flaggy limestone outcrops at the highest bed level and was obviously sounded out when the ford was first established. The top of the shoal in most parts formed a wide flaggy "pavement" across the river for most of the way during the summer but was submerged by about 5ft of water in winter. The longitudinal scale is very compressed relative to the vertical; hence the river-bed peaks are actually much wider than they appear on the drawing.

A rough, stoney, shallow ford is called scarbh; the one formerly across the Glencullen river in Enniskerry gave that village its name, Áth na Scairbhe. The Dublin/Wexford road crosses the Slaney at Scarawalsh or Scairbh an Solas, which some say expressed the fact that the rocky river bed reflected the light of the sun. However, Sherlock[2] maintains that the old ford across the Liffey downriver of Millicent Bridge in Co. Kildare at Castlesize (Casam Soilse) derives its name from an old Irish law by which a light had to be shown when a belated traveller shouted on a dark and stormy night in times of flood. There is a different explanation for Assolas in Cork. According to White,[3] when McDonagh, prince of Duhallow, was stopped from building a castle by the Lord Justice in Dublin, his servants dropped the glass intended for the castle and it broke, hence Áth Solus na Gloinne. The inscription on the Assolas Bridge is informative: "This Bridge was erected by Henry Wrixon of Assolas in the year 1781. Executed by Rich Staret mason."

A crossing over sandbanks in an estuary was called fearsad, the best known example being Bel Féiriste (Belfast) on the Lagan.

DEVELOPMENT OF FORDS

The simplest method of improving a ford where the river banks were shallow was to widen the river below it. This tended to happen in most places where cattle crossed frequently. Joyce gives Ballylahan, (Baile Átha Leathain), known as Broadford, in Co. Mayo as an example. Another method was to haul gravel and stones and dump them in the river; this method seems to have been applied even on large rivers such as the Boyne according to the drainage reports of the 1840s.[4] The report on the Little Maine, a small flashy river in Kerry, mentions that the principal obstruction to the free discharge was the ford of Ahnascralla, which had been raised by stones and gravel thrown in to improve the passage across and which was then 3ft above the normal bed.

Lowry[5] records that Francis Ritchie, the contractor who built Queen's Bridge in Belfast in 1842, said that when building a quay wall he had come across an artificial kind of causeway, made of very large stones, about 25ft broad at the top; during the same period, when building a dock opposite, he discovered another causeway exactly similar, and both ran towards each other. When the Long Bridge was removed and the water lowered, a large mass of stones was exposed to view at low water. This may have been a proper causeway.

There is a townland in Cork called Annakisha (Áth na Cise), near Mallow which Joyce translates as "the ford of the wickerwork causeway." It may simply have been sheets of wickerwork pegged to the bed and weighted down, or a ford with causeway approaches. Clarke[6] has offered one of the best explanations for Áth Cliath: "the word cliath refers presumably to rafts of hurdle work staked to the river bed weighted down by massive stones and designed to provide a footway for people and domestic animals across the mud flat at low tide." He appropriately adds that "when crossing a ford one gets one's feet wet".

One frequently finds stepping stones at old surviving fords. I knew several such locations in south Wicklow in the late 1940s and I was resident engineer on the construction of a bridge at one of them across the flashy Dereen river at Tourboy in 1949. The Irish name for stepping stones is clochán and the Brehon law stipulated that the honour price of building a *clochán* was two cows. There are numerous places of this name throughout the country, such as Cloghan in Offaly. Joyce states that Cloghaun is more common in the south and also draws attention to the fact that the word is also applied to a stone castle, stone house and beehive hut. Power [7] states that the word *sac*, or *bag*, occurs a few times in combination with *áth* and presumes that it designated a ford made with hides or sacks of some kind filled with gravel or sand. This would be easier than hauling large stones some distance, but such a ford would not not be as durable.

Some parts of the major rivers, such as the upper reaches of the Shannon, were too deep for fords or stepping stones, so a different type of commonsense ford was made—a porous causeway of large stones. A note published in 1906[8] mentions a causeway across the Shannon in Leitrim composed of huge boulders heaved in until they came above the water; but no source reference was given. The causeway may have been a perforated fishing weir, easy to construct where stones were plentiful.

A glance at some of the 1833–46 OS six-inch maps is sufficient to show that there were a large number of fords on county roads and farms all over the country at the time. Very few fords are shown in Taylor and Skinner's 1778 maps, which cover eight thousand miles of principal roads. The mass production of concrete pipes from the 1950s onwards, coupled with various grant-aided land improvement schemes, the Local Authorities (Works) Acts and arterial drainage schemes, brought about the end of the *áthanna* on public and private roads.

CHAPTER 3

Bridge Laws

The Senchus Mór (literally "the great tradition") maintained its authority among the Irish until the beginning of the 17th century and, as the Statutes of Kilkenny (1366) show, the Anglo-Irish also adopted these laws. From the Norman conquest in the last quarter of the 12th century to the first quarter of the 17th, the fluctuating boundary of the Pale gives a good indication of the territories where the king's writ was effective at various points in time. Ruth Dudley Edwards' *Atlas of Irish History*[1] provides an excellent summary and maps showing this boundary and the cities and boroughs outside it which were subject to English law.

Fergus O'Kelly[2] explains that the Senchus Mór, complied at a law school in the north midlands, is the most important collection of old Irish legal texts. These laws contained several provisions in relation to road and bridge building; e.g.: "The rump-steak . . . is what the head of the village is entitled to from the houses around the stone bridge which he erected with his own hands." Provision was also made for restitution for going into the wood for timber to build the common bridge of the tribe.

O'Kelly also mentions that cattle were the most common form of currency, despite the fact that coinage was introduced by the Norse in the early 10th century and reintroduced by the Anglo-Normans in the early 13th. The population of an average *tuath* ruled by a king was about 3000 men, women and children. The king was expected to ensure that his subjects carried out their public duties, such as preparing the site of an assembly for road-making. The "honour price" of the *ollamh saor* or chief builder was in proportion to his abilities. Skill in the construction of bridges, chariots and wicker houses ranked equally and commanded a fee of two cows per item.

The Brehon laws, as they were known, were studied and updated by schools of lawyers known as brehons, who also acted as judges. "March law" was a mixture of feudal and Brehon prohibited by the Statutes of Kilkenny. McCurtain[3] states that outside what in 1494 was defined as the "Pale", the country was governed by March law and Brehon law and, more often, by the law that "might is right".

One of the best descriptions of how a local king organised the building of a new road and bridge in the Early Christian period is given by Canon O'Hanlon in his *Life of St Brigid* and is taken from Cogitosus' *Life of St Brigid*, written in the 8th century; it reads:

> The king ruling over that part of the country in which St Brigid lived had ordered the construction of a road which should be able to bear the driving of chariots, wagons and other vehicles with a large array of horse and foot for purposes of a social, civil or military nature. He commanded the inhabitants of all districts and territories under his sway to be assembled and to take part in the labour. The road he intended to construct in a permanent manner. . . . When various subjects tribes and families had assembled the road was marked out in different sections to be severally constructed by the clans or people to whom these portions were respectively assigned.

The extract then goes on to describe how St Brigid performed a miracle when the largest clan unjustly tried to offload the difficult bridge section to St Brigid's weaker clan.

Confirmation of the system described by Cogitosus is contained in the entry in the Annals of Innisfallen (see Appendix 1) under the year 1071 when a muster of the Munstermen under their king built two bridges, one over the Shannon, in a fortnight. The entries for the years 1001 and 994 show that the convention in regard to bridging large rivers which formed the boundary between two kingdoms (Meath and Connaught in the example cited) was for each to build the bridge to one half of the river. The convention was absorbed into English law when the first effective bridge act was enacted in 1634 and the inhabitants of both counties were made chargeable for their respective parts and portions. In the 19th century the question of apportionment of costs commensurate with predicted benefits became so difficult that a special act (4 & 5 Will. IV c. 61) had to be passed to resolve the question with particular reference to Portumna Bridge.

St Adamnan, abbot of Iona in the 7th century is patron of Ballindrait in Donegal, the correct Irish name being Droicit Adhamhnain. The 14th abbot (726–52) was Cilline surnamed Droichteach, i.e. bridge-maker. Joyce ventures the opinion that his bridges were of timber, but the Iona building tradition was of stone, the most relevant example being the corbelled roof of St Colmcille's cell in Kells.

ANGLO–NORMAN STATUTES

The Normans brought with them the Roman policy whereby the repair of roads was considered one of the *trinoda necessitatis* to which every man's estate was subjected, namely contributions for the maintenance and repair of bridges and highways, for the maintenance of fortresses, and for the military forces. Under King John, who was made lord of Ireland by his father in AD 1195 and became king of the Angevin empire in 1199, the building and repair of bridges became such an intolerable burden on the Norman lords that it was one of the main grievances leading to the rebellion against him in England in 1215.

King John's reign (1199–1216) was of enormous importance from the aspect of bridge construction in Ireland. John has often been labelled as the bridge-minded monarch, a description fully merited in France, Wales, England and Ireland, as will be seen later in this book. When he ordered or even suggested that a bridge be erected, the baron responsible built it; otherwise he was very likely to be distrained and he and his family ruined. John's approach is clear from the last sentence of the letter he sent the mayor and citizens of London during

the construction of the famous Old London Bridge in 1201 (see Appendix 2). There must have been widespread grievance among the barons in England over bridges, for the following clause was included in Magna Carta (1215): "No community or individual [nec villa nec homo] shall be compelled to make bridges at river banks, except those who from of old are legally bound to do so."

In 1216, first year of the reign of John's son, Henry III, a modified magna carta was extended to Ireland, which contained the statute: "No town nor individual shall be distrained to make bridges over rivers except those who of old and of right ought to make them"[4]. This, the first Anglo-Norman bridge law in Ireland, let the barons off the hook, so to state, because "of old and of right" could scarcely have applied to those who had acquired fiefs between 1169 and 1216.

During the research for this book the remnants of two "King John" bridges were identified—one a tiny single arch remnant of a three-span masonry bridge in Esker*, Co. Dublin, and a single span of a once massive 11-span bridge (Babes*) across the historic Boyne about one mile downstream of Navan. Others long since gone, such as Thomond (old) Bridge*, Limerick, are also described with the object of establishing the characteristics of Norman bridges in Ireland in the early medieval period.

An act of Henry I (1100–35), prior to the Norman invasion of Ireland, defined the king's highway or *via regia* as "that which is always open and which no man may shut by any threat, as leading to a city, port or town"[5].

The act of 1216 referred to above was slightly modified by Henry III (Statute of Mailbridge) in 1268 to read that "neither a town nor particular person shall be distrained or compelled to build a bridge, or embankments to rivers, except those which are of old time and by right of special contract tenure prescription obliged to it and that none be compelled to make new bridges where none ever were before otherwise than by act of parliament."[6]

Numerous charters of King John and his successors gave rights and privileges to cities and towns to erect bridges and sometimes to charge tolls (pontage). Other taxes or services due to the king were forgiven for specific periods as aids and incentives to building and repairing bridge. One of the earliest charters is the Dublin Bridge charter of 1214 granted by King John which reads (in translation): "Royal Lord Henry Archbishop of Dublin. Let it be known that we concede to our citizens of Dublin that they may build one bridge over the waters of the Avenlith where it would be seen to the better use of our city—and that another bridge, other than that they have first made, may be erected where it may be expedient towards their indemnity. We order that this be permitted." Incorrect translations are frequently quoted which end stating that permission was given "to make a bridge beyond the Liffey water and to destroy the bridge formerly erected if deemed expedient".[7]

The next general statute relating to bridges was the act of 1297,[8] 25 Edw. I c.10, which prescribed that "bridges also and causeways be repaired in their places as they ought and used to be and where either bridges or causeways shall be broken and demolished, and he who is bound to repair them is not sufficient for such great expense, that the districts for whose benefit they shall be raised shall find means in common to rebuild them, and that nevertheless when ability shall serve him he shall restore to every person what he has paid. And that the Chief Justiciar heavily punish those whom he shall find adverse or rebellious to this ordinance."

The phrase "as they used to be" would suggest that for a decade or more prior to 1297 bridges had been neglected within the Pale. According to a map in Edwards' *Atlas*, the limit of the English marches in 1300 extended from Waterford along the Barrow on to Kildare and thence to Athlone and Carrick-on-Shannon and east to Dundalk. In addition, there were about 20 walled cities and towns in the remainder of the country. One of the few first mentions of bridges in the latter half of the 13th century is Bennetsbridge*, then called Tredingstown. Edward I made a grant of customs (tolls) to be taken at the new bridge here in 1285. In 1286 according to Boyer[9] the same king authorised the collection of a *barragium* or *barra* of "one denier bordelais on each cavalier and one obole on each pedestrian" to build a stone bridge at Agen in France. This in fact proved insufficient, so the king ordered his seneschal to convoke a general court of the whole Agenais consisting of clergy, barons, knights, consuls of all the towns and other inhabitants of the region to approve a hearth tax of six deniers arnaudins to complete the bridge. This stone bridge, which cost 30,000 sous arnandins, was washed away in 1320. This reference is one of the very few in which the full cost of a medieval bridge is given, but it would be very difficult to convert it into meaningful units such as, say, cows.

14TH CENTURY

The 14th century is barren as regards recorded bridge statutes, although there are quite a few references to new bridges built in the first quarter, e.g. Leighlin*, Kilcullen and New Bridge*. A charter was granted in 1346 "in aid of the repair and construction of the bridge of Thomastown". The impact of the Bruce invasion (1316–18) and the consequent famines together with the Black Death (1348–9) had a devastating effect on the country. Russell[10] estimates that the total population of Ireland was between 675,000 and 800,000 before the Black Death and that it was almost halved by it. Leask[11] states that the 14th century was a period of little building activity on the part of churchmen or laymen in Ireland; castles were repaired and altered but no major work in its entirety can be assigned to the years from 1320 to the end of the century. We find one significant record in relation to bridges in the Annals of the Four Masters under 1361: "A bridge of stone and lime [*droichet clochaelta*] was built by Cathal Óg O Connor [d. 1362] across the river of Eas Dara [Ballysadare]." This is the first reference in any annal to the erection of such a bridge in Gaelic Ireland.

During the 14th century the Irish parliament was so preoccupied with preventing the Norman and English colonists from becoming totally Irish that there was little time for road or bridge legislation. This is exemplified by the Statutes of Kilkenny (1366), among which one finds only one bridge reference and that an obscure one to Limerick City. The Statutes were a failure, so much so that when King Richard came to Ireland in 1394/5 he needed interpreters to converse with his lords. Richard made a second expedition in 1399, but this also failed to revive the colony.

15TH CENTURY

In the 15th century Ireland was for the most

part, in time and space, ruled by three powerful earls—Ormond based in Kilkenny, Desmond in Tralee and Kildare in Maynooth. By the end of the century the Pale was reduced to the area encompassed by the Boyne and the Liffey. It is not surprising therefore to find no new statutes enacted dealing with roads or bridges. Leask states that there was a great building revival from the middle of the 15th century and that laymen (as distinct from monks) seem to have started building for themselves and for the next 150 years or more "kept the masons busy". This activity is not reflected in bridge mentions or in survivors. More may emerge in future studies of the surviving records of these powerful medieval families. The various annals are remarkably silent on bridges in the later medieval period but do record a great plague in 1489 and the construction of a temporary military wicker bridge on the Ulster Blackwater by O'Donnell in 1483.

A search of the statute rolls yields no information on any 15th-century general laws relating to bridges—possibly a reflection of the political situation. There is a reference in the statute rolls for 1463 to the effect that "divers grants" were made by Henry VI (1422–61) "of divers customs to be levied on the towne of Trim, Naas, Navan, Athboy, Kells and Fore and in the franchises of the said towns for murage, pavage and repair of the bridges of the said towns by which the said towns are greatly strengthened." The statement is too general to identify which bridges (if any) are referred to in Naas, Kells and Fore; otherwise this would be an important early mention. The Naas bridge could be Carragh.*

The last decade of the 15th century saw the enactment of Poynings' Law at the Drogheda parliament meeting in 1495 which prevented the Irish parliament from assembling without authority from the king and from presenting any legislation until approved by the king and the English privy council. It also passed the backdated Act of Resumption. This and other repressive measures indirectly affected road- and bridge-building activities for more than three centuries.

16TH CENTURY

The first third of the 16th century saw a continuation of the political system of the 15th and there are no events of significance in rela-

tion to roads and bridges mentioned in the records. The "Reformation" parliament held in Dublin in 1536–7 initiated what might be described as a long period of reconquest which extended to 1691. Road communications, especially bridges, became vital from a military point of view, as evidenced in the wars that followed. The suppression and confiscation of the monasteries in England in the 1530s brought about a critical situation there in relation to bridges, as evidenced by the Bridges and Highways Act of 1534[12] (25 Hen. VIII c. 5). This major act was to remain the principal basis for bridge repair and construction in England until 1801. It referred to "all manner of annoyance of bridges broken in the highways" and to the fact that in many parts of the realm "it cannot be known or proved what hundred, riding, wapentake, city, borough town or parish nor what person certain, or body politic, ought of right to rule such bridges decayed." To remedy this the act prescribed that the inhabitants of the riding etc. within which the bridge was located be charged with the cost of making and repairing.

The justices were empowered with the consent of the constables to tax the inhabitants for this purpose, to appoint tax collectors and to appoint two surveyors to plan and arrange for the carrying out of the work, being accountable to the justice. The act also empowered the justices to include the bridge approaches for a distance of 300 ft each side in the works. The five ports were excluded. A similar act was passed in the Irish parliament a hundred years later but with one major difference detailed below.

There is no record of any new general statute relating to bridges in Ireland during the 16th century. There are many references to bridges being ruinous and in decay. There is a record in the Calendar of State Papers for 4 March 1585 which indicates that a circular was sent out by the lord deputy to all bishops, sheriffs and justices seeking information for a commission for inquiry into "the decay and ruin of churches, chancels and bridges and the neglect of free schools". Obviously the information was not forthcoming, because the reminder demanded returns by the first of Trinity term "under heavy penalty".

The commission's report, if still in existence and ever found, could provide a wealth of information on bridges in the 16th century.

SIDNEY, THE BRIDGE BUILDER

In the second half of the century the whole system for the construction, repair and maintenance of bridges that had evolved over the previous two centuries within and without the Pale was undermined by the suppression of the monasteries, the plantation of Leix/Offaly and Munster, and the various wars and rebellions, especially the nine years' war. This is confirmed by a memoir[13] by Sir Henry Sidney (lord deputy for three or four periods between 1558 and 1581), addressed to the secretary of state, Sir Francis Walsingham, and written in 1582/3. In it Sidney refers to bridges built at his direction in Athlone*, Ballinasloe*, Carlow and Islandbridge—all major military bridges financed by the war treasury. His memoirs also give evidence of the lack of bridges: "I passed without boat or bridge the dangerous river of Omagh, Dorg and Fynn . . . last I came to the great water of sea arm Loughfoyle when I found boats as appointed, to convey me and my army over . . . passing the great water of Assuroo." In all this we must also remember the ruthless methods he applied; e.g., it was Sidney who masterminded the horrible massacre of Mullaghmast (1577), condemned by all the annalists and still spoken of in Co. Laois. His memoir concludes: "I am now 54 years of age, toothless and trembling, being £5,000 in debt yea and £30,000 worse off than I was at the death of my deare King and master Edward VI."

Concern about bridges is evident in a fiant of Elizabeth dated 3 February 1563[14]; in a large land grant to Henry Crowley (surveyor general) containing the castle of Edenderry, a condition is prescribed that "he shall keep open or closed on all his lands as the constable shall appoint, shall not destroy any castle, bridge, pavement or togher except fords adjoining on Irish country. . . ."

A report of Lord Deputy Perrot to the privy council in England dated 25 October 1584[15] gives a deep insight into "Castle" thinking at the time and also provides invaluable information on the absence of bridges at important crossing points.

But for the more stable settling and continuance of the good of this state, let me, I humbly pray your Lordships, crave pardon to make a motion which in mine opinion,

being well advised on, will be the best purchase that ever England made. I suppose if all be true that I have heard Her Majesty hath commonly been charged with between 30,000*l.* and 40,000*l.* a year, and if a medium of her Highness's whole expenses were cast, I think not so little, one year with another, as 50,000*l.* or 60,000*l.* a year. If your Lordships can procure Her Majesty to let me have, or such as shall be thought fit to succeed me, for three years together the sum of 50,000*l.* yearly out of England, over and above the revenue of this land, I do trust with God's good favour, at the three years' end, excepting only that there be no impeachment by the descent of Spaniards, and such like foreign enemies, to leave Her Highness such a trained garrison of 2,000 footmen and 400 horsemen as herebefore I writ of, and both they and the whole government to be discharged with a small charge out of England. And besides leave Her Highness more than already she hath in this realm, 7 towns walled, every town a mile about, 7 bridges and 7 castles, viz.: Towns—Athlone, Coleraine, Sligo, Mayo, Dingle, Lifford and the Newry; Bridges—Coleraine, Lifford, Ballyshannon, Dundalk, the Broad Water in Munster, the river Veale under Sliebh Lougher, Kells in Claneboy; Castles—The Blackwater to be better fortified, Ballyshannon, Meelick to be erected, the Broadwater in Munster, Castle Martin upon the Rowte, Galin in the Queen's County, and Kilcoman in Feagh McHugh's country. By these the whole realm shall be environed and strengthened with fortifications, and all great waters made passable.

The Broad Water location is Mallow; Rowte is Shannonbridge; the Veale obviously means the Feale at Abbeyfeale or Listowel; Kells refers to a location on the Kells River, a tributary of the Maine in Antrim. Most of the bridges mentioned in the report are described individually in Part II of this book. None was erected until long after 1603, except the Mallow bridge, discussed later in chapter 9.

There is a record in the Calendar of the patent and close rolls of chancery[16] for 1601 which gives an indication of one of the methods used by Queen Elizabeth to procure the erection of bridges following the confiscation: "Demise from her Majesty to Patrick Cullen in consideration of his having built the Bridge of the Blackwater—of a messuage, a garden, 7 acres of arable of great measure, containing 21 acres standard measure and 4 acres of pasture in Carne in the County Kildare parcel of the possession of James Eustace attainted; a castle [plus a long list of lands in Naas, Athy and Dunboyne] to hold for 60 years."

The bridge referred to which spanned the Blackwater at Johnstown Bridge was a small but important one replaced under the drainage schemes in the 1840s.

17TH CENTURY

The commencement of the 17th century in relation to laws is encapsulated by Moody & Martin[17] in a single sentence "1603–9. English common law begins to be enforced throughout the country." However, there were few existing highway or bridge laws that could be enforced. Before new laws could be enacted the Irish parliament had to be packed. This was accomplished swiftly after the battle of Kinsale and the flight of the earls by the creation of 41 new boroughs. The new parliament had two sessions (in 1613–15) and ten statutes were enacted. One of these was an act "for repairing and amending of high-ways and cashes and cutting and clearing of paces" (11–13 Jas. I c. 7). The preamble to this act of 1615 gives a good idea of the condition of the roads and presumably the bridges, though bridges are not mentioned specifically: "Forasmuch as the high-ways and cashes and paces and passages throughout the woods of this Kingdom are in many places both very noisome and tedious to travel in and dangerous to all passengers and carriages." The act then went on to prescribe what was known as the statute labour system, a legacy from roman times, known in France as the hated *corvée*, introduced in England in 1555. The marginal notes in the printed statute explain it well: "Constables and church wardens of every parish, every Tuesday and Wednesday in Easter, shall choose two honest parishioners as surveyors. . . . These shall take on them the office, on pain of £10, and fix six days before the feast of St John the Baptist for repair of the highways. . . . Every parishioner owning, within the parish, one plow land or keeping a draft or plow shall send every day one wayne or cart and also two able men on pain of 20s. and two men furnished with tools

on pain of 10s. . . . Every householder and every cottier (hired servants excepted) shall each day go or send a labourer on pain of 2s. per day for default." All necessary tools and instruments had to be brought; the work-day was eight hours.

The remainder of the act deals with powers to dig for materials, drainage, fencing, gathering stones lying upon lands, etc. The justices of the peace, of the assizes, etc., were all empowered to hear and determine offences and impose fines.

The word "bridge" is not mentioned in the act; nevertheless the work would have involved the repair and construction of small stone bridges and gullets. The reason for the exclusion of bridges emerged in the record of the House of Commons debate on 5 May 1615. Evidently the original proposal was for an "Act for repairing of Bridges and Highways," considered "very necessary" on its first reading on 22 April 1615. On 3 May two bills were presented, one for a first reading entitled a "Bill for Amending of Highways and Cashes" and another for "Amending of Highways and Toghers", which was the second time read. A Mr Luttrell opposed the Bridges Bill and proposed that "it be suspended not so many hudlings upon the country together." This led to it being committed. The committee evidently recombined the bills and they were given a third reading as a "Bill for Bridges and repairing and amending of Highways" but it "was dashed". On 6 May the Highways Bill passed all stages and became law.

George O'Brien[18] gives a useful summary of the economic situation in Ireland in this century, all of which affected bridge construction. Ireland, he states, had to commence a new economic life at the beginning of the century. He then selects four periods: 1603–41, which he describes as a period of construction; 1641–61, a period of destruction; 1661–90, construction; and the last decade, destruction. In the first period efforts were made to settle the ownership and tenure of land and rebuild foreign trade; the second period was one of wholesale destruction of the population as well as commerce; during the third period a resolute effort was made to encourage industry and build up foreign trade; in the final period the foundation of the penal code was laid with the object of depriving the majority of the Irish people of all wealth and ambition and the elimination of ancient rights and the destruction of country's industry.

The information on bridges reflects this division—in particular the third period, when many roads and bridges were built, though it is difficult to find evidence and mentions. The most telling confirmation of this is to be found in a report by Lord Dartmouth and Thomas Phillips on fortifications in Ireland, presented to James II in 1685:[19]

> I have taken exact surveys of the most considerable places amongst all of which I do find not above four or five that are capable of being fortified so as to be made to resist a considerable army by reason that most of the inland towns were thought strong by being encompassed with bogs and rivers and as great passes.

> All of which I do now find to be quite contrary, for the improvement of the country hath drained the bogs, and the passes that were most considerable are now of no use; neither is it worth while to fortify them as passes by reason there are several bridges made and new ways across the bogs, and more are daily building, and making for the benefit of the several counties bordering one upon the other. . . .

This evidence is supported by the findings of our research, particularly in chapter 5.

THE 1634 BRIDGE ACT

There is a comprehensive list of bridge acts, commencing with the act 10 Chas. I c. 26 (1634), in the index to Irish Statutes covering the period up to 1799 (see Appendix 3).[20] No acts are listed for the period 1301–1633, nor for 1635–1704. The act of 1634 is of great importance not just for bridges, but generally, because it is the origin of the fiscal functions of the grand juries. It is largely based on the English act of 1534 with two major differences: first, the English act relates to "bridges and highways", the Irish one to "bridges, causeys and toghers in the highways"; secondly, the English act empowered the justices of the peace within the city, shire etc. "to tax and set every inhabitant to such reasonable aid and sum of money as they think reasonable for repairing, re-edifying

and amendment of such bridges." The Irish act (Appendix 4) states that "the said justices of assize in their circuits, and the said justices of the peace in the quarter sessions respectively, with the assent of the grand-jury, shall have power and authority to tax and set every inhabitant in any such county, barony, citty, borrough, towne or parish, within the limits of their commissions and authorities, to such reasonable ayde and summs of money, as they shall think by their discretions convenient and sufficient for the new building, repayring, reedifying and amendment of such bridges, causeyes and toghers . . ." The basic fiscal power given to the grand juries in Ireland by this act lasted, with modification, for a quarter of a millennium. (The "presentment" system and the role of grand juries are discussed in greater detail in Chapter 4.)

Because we have very few surviving records of county grand jury sessions from 1634 to 1765, it is very difficult to trace the history of bridge building and repairing. Some information based on research of estate papers etc. is given by McCarthy[21]. He makes one remarkable statement: "internal communications were reliable and the post not much worse than today. Five days was the usual Lismore to Dublin time, and seven called for a complaint." The cost, of course, was great—11s. from Cork to Dublin. He states that bridge improvements in the early 17th century tended to come from the private purse, which in post-plantation Munster usually meant the capacious pockets of the earls of Cork (the cost of stone could be immense). He also mentions that the county tax (presumably under the 1634 act) for bridge repairs was being applied in Waterford in 1641 at a rate of between 4s. and 5s. a ploughland, an imposition considered excessive. He mentions a bridge built at Bandon in 1600, and a few others financed by Boyle, who "patronised English masons and builders as a matter of plantation policy".

There is an unusual record in the Commons Journal for 1661 which states that the House resolved that a recommendation be sent to the lords justices of Meath and Westmeath to erect a substantial bridge (at grand jury expense) over the Kinnegad river. Part of this bridge* survives. In 1678 an act (17 & 18 Chas. II c. 16) was passed for the building of a bridge over the river Blackwater at Cappoquin*.

The last decade of the 17th century is

marked by mentions of five bridges described in some detail in Part II—the Old Long Bridge across the Lagan, where five arches collapsed in 1690 following the passage of Schomberg's artillery train; Slane Bridge, where two arches were broken by the Jacobites prior to the battle of the Boyne; St Mary Magdalen Bridge in Duleek, across which King James II fled and where the Irish and French almost came to blows because of the convergence of retreating batallions; Athlone Bridge, where the heroic defence by the Irish of two broken arches is remembered in ballad and tradition; and lastly Limerick, where a young French officer raised the drawbridge too soon and left several hundred retreating Irish to be drowned or cut to pieces.

The Council Book of the Corporation of Youghal[22] records under 22 November (1695) that it had received legal opinion concerning the contribution to the public charges of Co. Cork: "That by the opinion of the judges we are to join with the said county in defraying the charges of bridges and toghers only." The mayor was instructed to write to the treasurer of Co. Cork informing him about this and stating that the corporation was willing to pay when the same charges were abstracted from other charges.

THE PERIOD 1700–1836

The operation of the 1612 and 1634 acts was obviously reviewed at the commencement of the 18th century and not found very satisfactory for reasons that are obvious from the long title of 4 Anne c. 4 (1705)—"An act to prevent the illegal raising of money by grand juries and the misapplying of money legally raised and for the better execution of an act for the mending of highways by six-days labour, and for the appointment of overseers of the highways by the justices at their sessions in default of naming them by the respective parishes." The act set a limit of £20 on the amount that could be raised for public works at any one quarter session—except for repairing or supporting bridges already built and erected. Dublin county and city were excepted. The act stated that the six-day labour was a good law but ineffectual because the "pains" (fines) were too small and it was easy to escape prosecution; it increased the powers and allowed goods of offenders to be seized for default.

The act of 1710, 9 Anne c. 9, for amending highways and roads and for the application of the six-day labour states in the preamble that the word "plow-land" was not a common name throughout the country and as a result persons inhabiting counties where the lands were known by another name were refusing to pay the ploughland taxes prescribed, and the roads and keshes were remaining out of repair. To remedy this, the grand jury of each county was empowered to decide over a period of three years how the word was to be interpreted and which lands were to be so designated, and were to have this confirmed by the judge(s) at the assizes. The act also empowered the parishes to raise 40s. to buy tools for road work and the grand jury to present for designated sections of road that could not be amended in a reasonable time by a parish, but no such "causeway pavement or other reparation" could be less than 9ft wide.

There is an example of the operation of this act in the Council Book of the Corporation of Kinsale[23] under the year 1712, when a presentment by John Wrixon and John Foulke, gents, overseers for making 2,500 yards of causeway on the high road leading from Mallow to Kerry, was granted for paving, "the earth being thrown up already by the days labour".

An act of 1719 (6 Geo. I c. 10) stated that presentments had been sometimes made, at assizes, for raising money for the repairing of highways and buildings and for repairing bridges that were unnecessary and also that money had been used for other purposes. Accordingly it provided that no money should be raised by presentment for bridges or highways without affidavits of "two credible neighbours who live nearby and have viewed the place". The overseer was required to account on oath at the following assizes; if the money was misspent, he was committed to jail until repaid.

Another act passed in 1727, 1 Geo. II c. 13, contained 27 sections, mainly amendments to previous highway and roads acts. Its main object was to close loopholes in the six-day labour system. It provided for the appointment of a skilful person, to be the surveyor or director of work presented to be done, at a salary not to exceed 2s. 6d. per day. The preamble stated that experience had proved that work done under skilled persons was "much better and more lasting". The act noted that "carts and wains are very rarely used in this Kingdom" and authorised the use of three slide-cars and two men, or three horses with creels or cleeves with two men" in place of one cart and two men under the six-day labour law. The act does not appear to have applied to bridges, as it contains no mention of the 1634 act. Section 9 directed that roads be "paved or well and sufficiently covered with gravel twelve foot in breadth at least". Section 19 prescribed that "all highways or roads, hereafter to be set out, shall be at least 30 feet broad in the clear exclusive of the ditches; and all roads already enclosed which are not of the breadth of 21 feet in the clear . . . may be enlarged on presentment to that width." The foregoing probably affected the width to which bridges were built; certainly the 12ft provision would have applied. The final section stated that drawing millstones from one place to another was found "to be very destructive of causeways and bridges" and prescribed that from 1729 such be "supported and kept from touching the ground". Section 18 stated that in some countries it had not been ascertained how the word "plow-land" was to be construed, and provided for a fine of £100 on counties failing to ascertain the said plow-lands, the money to be applied to the roads.

TURNPIKE ROADS

The first turnpike road act, for the upgrading of the Dublin/Kilcullen road, was passed in 1729; the second, for the Dublin/Navan road, in the same year. None was enacted in 1730, but in 1731 at least a dozen were passed, including one entitled "an act for repairing the road leading from the city of Dublin to the town of Kinnegad in the county of Westmeath". The wording of most of the acts was similar— a long preamble on the "ruinous and bad" condition of the road; a statement that it could not by the ordinary course appointed by the laws and statutes of the realm be effectively mended; an authorisation to a long list of "right honourable gentlemen" (about 234 in case of the Kinnegad road) to improve the road and take up duties and tolls, the profits to be applied to the repair. The period was usually 21 years but could be renewed by another simple act before the expiry date. Andrews produced a map in 1964 showing the location of the sections of road turnpiked under about

80 acts passed between 1729 and 1800.[24] There were amending or extension acts in respect of many originals.

At first sight one would expect these acts to be a very fruitful source of specific information on bridges, but that is not the case. The surveyors were empowered by order of five or more of the trustees to make causeways, cut drains through or contiguous to the road, erect arches of brick, timber or stone, and widen parts including orchards and house gardens. Periodically one, finds a large bridge mentioned such as in the Dublin/Kinnegad act:

The road leading from the bridge at Lucan by the causeway of St Katherine's to the town of Leixlip . . . over the said causeway is dangerous to passengers; several persons having lost their lives and many cattle having been drowned; and it is almost impractical to raise and make the same safe and commodious, and by the building of a bridge over the river in a convenient place and turning the road another and shorter way the like accidents will for the time to come be prevented. Be it enacted by the authority aforesaid that the trustees being appointed may and shall build a bridge of stone and lime in some convenient place over the said river and make a new road through the town of Lucan and lands of Coldstream leading to such bridge. [See Lucan Bridge.]

Many of the older surviving bridges on the turnpikes were widened under the turnpikes acts, such as Kilcarn Bridge* across the Boyne at Navan. However, one finds no mention of this in the act and cannot be certain of the date. The dating error can be appreciable when an act was renewed three or four times; moreover, one is left uncertain whether or not the widening took place before the original act. Many of the acts were private bills and are not recorded in the statute books.

In 1855 an act (18 & 19 Vict. c. 69) was passed known as the Dublin and Other Roads Turnpike Abolition Act, 1855. This act prescribed that "On and after the 5th January next after the passing of this act the several acts set forth in Schedule A to this act annexed are hereby repealed and from thenceforth the trustees appointed by the said acts shall be discharged from the execution of the trusts and powers thereby vested in them and the collection and taking of tolls upon the roads in the said acts comprised shall absolutely cease; and upon and from 5th January the said roads shall be and become the same as, and are hereby declared to be, public roads of the counties in which such roads are respectively situate and shall be maintained and kept in repair in like manner and shall be subject to the like provisions as other public roads within the said counties."

The act provided for appointment of a commission to execute the act, to apportion charges, award compensation, payment and pay expenses. It also gave power to grand juries to borrow money to pay mortgages and loans, produce documents and sell the property of trusts.

The report by Edward Clements which accompanied the act of 1855 stated that: "The averment in the preamble of the original turnpike acts in Ireland and adopted in spirit in all subsequent acts of a like nature, namely that the ordinary course appointed by the laws and statutes of the realm was inefficient for the purpose of maintaining a particular line of road, has in no instance been sustained but on the contrary has been wholly disproved by the evidence taken before me during the inquiry."

He then went on to record that it was his duty to recommend that all the surviving turnpikes be abolished and these roads put in charge of the county surveyor to be repaired by a tax on the baronies in which they were located. This meant that the many bridges on these roads reverted to the "charge" of the grand juries in the respective counties.

EXPANSION IN ROAD BUILDING

The second half of the 18th century witnessed an enormous expansion in the total mileage and the condition of Irish roads. The principal factor was an expansion in trade and commerce, in imports and exports, which had to be carried on the roads and with increasing speed and efficiency. Another factor was the surplus in revenue that accrued to the Irish treasury from 1753. The disposal of this was the object of a sustained dispute with the British treasury; by tradition surpluses had gone to the monarch, but the parliament from 1753 onwards decided to give increased grants for various classes of public works, especially inland navigation, and leave no surpluses. The background is

explained in Chapter 6, which also includes a table showing the schemes aided with grants totalling £660,000 between 1753 and 1767. The magnitude of this sum can be gauged from the fact that a substantial rural six-arch bridge such as Kanturk*, could be erected for £400.

The multiplier effect of this expenditure led to increasing traffic and a demand for improved "great roads", as they were called. The parish labour system could not respond; moreover, there was increasing discontent with it, as jobs become plentiful. The parliament of 1759 brought in an act, 33 Geo. II, c. 8, to alter and amend the laws for highway repair, stating that the requirement of the 1613 act obliging everyday labourers to work six days per year without hire or wages was "generally considered to be so far bothersome to the poor and for that reason has not been in many places put into execution". The act of 1759 prescribed that "no day-labour staff be compellable to work without hire at any highroad whatsoever". The remainder of the act was devoted to the correction of abuses. One clause, for example, stated the section of the act 1 Geo. II c. 13 (1727), which empowered the grand jury to present upon the county-at-large, had provided an inlet to perjury, had been evaded, and was improperly applied. This was replaced by a section giving the grand jury power to present upon any barony for roads within its boundaries.

An act of 1763 (3 Geo. III c. 1), providing for the continuation of "an additional duty on beer, ale . . . tobacco" etc., seems from the title to have little relevance to roads or bridges, but one section providing for "payments out of the said additional duties" contained a large list of grants. Among them was "£8,000 voted to the Corporation for promoting and carrying on an inland navigation in Ireland and to enable them to rebuild John's Bridge, and Green's Bridge in the city of Kilkenny and Bennetsbridge, Thomastown Bridge and Castlecomer Bridge and to repair the bridge of Ennisteague in the said county of Kilkenny and to be by them accounted for to Parliament". Here we are interested in the fact that it was the navigation board that was directed to carry out the work and account for it, without any mention of the grand jury.

A further act of 1763 (3 Geo. III c. 8) tightened up the grand jury procedures for presenting for the levying of money, requiring in particular adequate public notice in advance. This brought to eleven the number of acts in force governing road and bridge maintenance and construction, the earliest of which was a century and a half in operation. The demand for works outpaced the powers and it was decided to introduce a consolidating act, the chief promoter of which was Arthur French of Monivea, Co. Galway.

This consolidation act (5 Geo. III c. 14) of 1765, though amended nine years later, set the foundation for road and bridge works for the following 70 years. It had a simple title—"An act for more effectually amending the public roads"—and contained 34 sections. The preamble stated that "Whereas difficulties arise from the multiplicity of the laws heretofore made for the amending or repairing the highways or roads in this Kingdom, and it is found expedient to repeal the same and to make a new act containing all the parts of such laws, as have proved effectual and are proper to be continued, with such additions and amendments as are herein contained, be it enacted. . . ." Among the eleven acts repealed was the 1634 bridge act which was replaced by section 12: "And it shall be lawful for the grand jury of any county at the assizes, . . . by presentment to raise such sums of money as they shall think fit, upon such county at large for the building, rebuilding or repairing any bridge or part of a bridge, or any wall or part of a wall necessary to the support of any road in such county"; all simple and straightforward, but subject to some constraints—no money to be presented except on the affidavit of two "credible masons" and according to a submitted plan and estimate. In an equally simple paragraph grand juries were empowered to present on baronies for repairing old roads or making new roads.

The act prescribed a set of four standard forms to be used for road presentments, but none for bridges. The plan and estimate affixed to the masons' affidavits evidently sufficed. Arthur Young[25], who toured Ireland in 1776–9, was unbounded in his praise of the act: "the effect of it in all parts . . . is so great that I found it practicable to travel upon wheels by a map . . . I will go here, I will go there . . . everywhere beautiful roads." Despite this assertion, problems began to accumulate to such an extent that virtually all the sections were repealed in 1774 by 13 & 14 Geo. III c. 32.

The changes were largely matters of procedure and detail. Section 15 dealt with bridges and stated that

it shall be lawful for the grand jury of any county at the assizes to present that such sum or sums of money as they shall think necessary shall be raised upon such county-at-large to be expended in building, rebuilding, enlarging, or repairing the sessions house, gaol, work house or house of correction, or any bridge or part of a bridge, or any gullet or pipe under any road, or any wall or part of a wall, necessary to the support of any road in such county, or for the gravelling or filling over any such bridge, gullet or pipe, and also for the wages of the overseer of any such work not exceeding 12 pence for each pound to be by him expended agreeable to such presentment.

The only changes to what we saw in the consolidation act are the reference to the road filling or surfacing over arches as part of a bridge and the provision of 8.5 per cent for overseeing. Another section of the act prescribed that an affidavit as to the necessity of the work be sworn by "two credible persons who can read and write" instead of the "two credible masons" of the previous act (see Chapter 9).

The act also enabled persons having a ferry, except in cities and corporations, to erect a bridge at their own expense and to charge a toll, and it fixed a maximum of £5 to be spent in hiring an interpreter for the assizes, which indicates that many native Irish speakers appeared before the grand jury. The grand jury was required to appoint a high constable for each barony or half barony, but constables had to be "aggreable to the act to prevent the further growth of popery".

Overall, the act contained 42 sub-chapters and ran to over ten thousand words. Based on the sanction of sworn oaths, it remained in force, with modification, for 60 years and was the legal instrument by which perhaps thousands of surviving stone arch bridges were erected. It gave rise to massive volumes of papers, records and drawings, few of which have survived.

One finds many general comments on the operation of the "presentment system" of building roads and bridges under the 1766 and 1774 acts in papers, histories and other publications.

Some are complimentary, other scathing in their criticisms. Arthur Young, a discerning commentator, was fulsome in his praise, but Townsend[26] writing in 1813 stated that "When a law of convenience and regulation is found incompetent to fulfill the purpose intended by the legislature, revision becomes necessary and alteration expedient—the security of faithful expenditure, as the law now stands, rests upon the sanction of oaths, which when they happen to militate against self interest, are found to be what they were in the days of Hudibras—'too feeble implements to bind' persons of higher order than our common roadbuilders."

The effects of the act, however, were far too widespread to permit any generalised judgments on its operation. The simple fact is that thousands of durable bridges were built in the quarter of a century up to the Act of Union and many survive unaltered to the present day. The preamble to the next major act, the Grand Jury Act of 1836, quoted later, provides the best comment on its shortcomings.

Arthur Young indicates that the consolidation act promoted road building and repair all over the country, but his evidence is not by any means conclusive. The Query Books for Co. Meath (1761–75) show that the mean number of individual presentments, including repeats, for the five years ended 1765 was 327 as compared to 506 for the period 1766–70. The number in 1775 was 520; after that the presentments for roads were listed by the barony in accordance with the act of 1774. The measure is crude but sufficient to justify Young's statement. The vast majority of presentments were for road repairs—mainly "gravelling" 14ft wide at 2s. 4d. a perch. The names of the 23 grand jurors for each assizes throughout the period are listed: half the members listed in 1762 were still there in 1775. Not an "O" nor a "Mac" appears but a man named Reilly held his place continuously.

Unlike the wars of the 1640s and 1690s, the rebellion of 1798 did not have any significant direct effect on bridges. It did lead to the construction of the military road from Rathfarnham to Aughavanna, carried out by order of the Government in the years 1800–9, and of which there is a good description in a report[27] of 1814.

The local famine of 1820–21 in the inaccessible mountainous areas of north-west Cork and in the Keeper mountains in Tipperary led to the Whiteboy rebellion in 1822. It was centred in Pobal O'Caoimh, where 5,000 acres had been attainted by Cromwell but had never been subjected and where even the Old Gaelic system of land tenure had survived. The lord lieutenant, Lord Wellesley, feared that it might become another '98 and garrisons were sent to all the peripheral towns—Newcastle West, Killarney, Kanturk, Macroom, Mallow etc.—but were unable to get into the central area. Richard Griffith* was then sent down to survey this area and construct new roads. In the succeeding 17 years he built 243 miles of new road at a cost of £148,975, which included many fine masonry arch bridges.[28]

Between 1804 and 1836 twelve amending acts were passed, modifying various aspects of the 1774 act. Some were enacted one year and repealed the following year—a testament to the influence over central affairs exerted by the elitist grand juries. In addition to these there was the Mail Coach Road Act of 1805, a most progressive act from the technical aspect of road and bridge building but not very effective because the construction work was subjected to the grand juries who often refused to present the money required.

The act of 1836 which consolidated and amended the laws relating to the presentment of public money by grand juries in Ireland, commences with the following preamble:

> Whereas the laws heretofore made and in force in Ireland for the purpose of regulating the fiscal powers of grand juries have become obscure and complicated from their multiplicity and their provisions have been found in many aspects insufficient and it is expedient, with a view to secure the better execution of public works and facilitate the transaction of local business, that the said laws should be consolidated and amended and that a uniform system of raising money by presentment of grand juries should be established in all counties in Ireland whether counties at large, counties of cities, or counties of towns: be it therefore enacted etc.

The new act contained 186 sub-chapters and ran to 73 pages and 50 thousand words. It closed most of the loopholes in the presentment system and gave the lord lieutenant power to direct the commission of public works (established in 1831) to make or repair roads and bridges if the grand jury refused to do so and have the cost levied on the county at large. It provided for the establishment of county surveyor posts and modified all the forms of application for presentments. A new standard form was prescribed for making an application to erect, enlarge or repair any building whatsoever:

SCHEDULE (X)—FORM (H)

Form of Application for erecting, enlarging, or repairing any Building whatsoever.

County of } We, ... of . . . .
　　　　　 } and . . . . of . . . .
do certify, that we have lately viewed and examined . . . . and that it will be useful to [here set out the Work], at . . . . in this County;

and we propose that the Expense of the aforesaid Work shall not exceed . . . . Pounds, and shall be defrayed by the County at large [or Barony or Half Barony of . . . .] and that Presentment for such Purpose may be made under and by virtue of the . . . . Section of the . . . . Chapter of [here set out the Reign], being an Act for [here set out the Title of this Act].

(signed) . . . . A.B.
　　　　　 . . . . C.D.

The period covered by this book strictly ends with the passing this act, so further discussion of it would be superfluous.[29] The act remained in force until 1898 when grand juries were abolished by the Local Government (Ireland) Act 1898.

CHAPTER 4

Grand Juries & the Presentment System

The counties of Ireland were formed first and foremost as areas for the administration of justice. Dublin, Cork and Waterford were delineated first, by King John in 1210. By the end of the 13th century Kildare, Kerry, Limerick, Louth, Meath, Tipperary, Roscommon and what was known as Connaught had emerged. In the following century palatinates emerged in north Kerry, Desmond and Tipperary and a few other areas. In these the baron had considerable power, ruling like a petty king.[1] Most of Ulster was shired after the battle of Kinsale and the last county to be formed was Wicklow in 1606. In 1543 Westmeath was severed from Meath. The cities of Dublin, Waterford, Cork and Limerick had separate county status from the time of King John.

The administrative system in municipal areas[2] had its origin in the early Norman charters. These are practically unanimous in declaring that the chief office should be held by one citizen, the "provost", later called mayor, who was elected for one year but could be re-elected (other titles were "portreeve" and "sovereign", borrowed from the constitutions of French communes). The holder of this office was the chief magistrate of the civic courts. In the counties he was the sheriff. He was appointed by the king or the Irish treasurer who was called "justiciar". Under the mayor and the sheriff a number of offices gradually grew up such as deputy mayor, subsheriff, bailiff, escheator, clerk etc. The king's judges visited each county, county city, and town twice yearly and held assizes (a trial in which sworn assessors decided questions of fact) with the assistance of grand juries, that is 23 property owners chosen by the high sheriff. The origin of the system was a provision in Magna Carta.

Under an act of 1615, 11–13 Jas. I c. 7, select vestries were responsible for roads and bridges.

In 1634 bridges were made a responsibility of the justices in each county but expenditure was subject to the approval of the grand jury. However, the roads remained under the authority of the parish select vestry until 1765.

The word "presentment" is used in the act of 1634 to signify the laying before the justices at the assizes of specific proposals for making and amending bridges, causeways and toghers. The 1774 act required presentments to be made on a simple standard form depending on the nature of the work (a typical presentment for a new bridge is given in Appendix 9). There was no special form for bridges as such, but a plan and estimate had to be annexed for each bridge.

The grand jury itself was empowered to present that sums be raised for such work. Seven types of form for road and bridge works were prescribed in 1763 by 3 Geo. III c. 8, but the number of forms or "schedules" prescribed in the act of 1836, was 16.

PRESENTMENT SYSTEM

The deputy keeper of public records attempted to explain the whole presentment process in an appendix to his report published in 1900. According to this explanation, an application for public works, such as making or repairing a bridge, was made first to the magistrate and cess payers assembled at the presentment sessions. The maps and specifications were examined and if the application was approved tenders were invited and subsequently considered at an adjourned session. Schedules of the application and contracts were placed before the grand jury at the next assizes and those approved were fiated by the judge. Presentments objected to were "traversed" and heard before the judge at the assizes.

All approved presentments were placed before the succeeding assizes as a "query" and if the work or a given portion of it had been carried out in the meantime and certified by the county surveyor, it was marked "allowed" by the foreman of the grand jury and payment made by the county treasurer. Those unapproved were marked "undischarged query" in the grand warrant for that assizes and succeeding assizes until such time as the work was certified as completed.

The great bulk of grand jury books and papers consisted of the documents connected with the above procedures, but there were others recording maintenance on county buildings etc. The deputy keeper lists the following as the most important documents classed as "presentment papers": "Applications for construction of public works and for payments to county surveyor certificates; specifications and maps, cess payer lists and returns; coroners' returns and certs; contractors' bonds, expenses of constables."

He also mentions "presentments rolls", which contain entries on parchment of the financial presentments made by the grand jury at the assizes, and gives an example from Kerry for the period 1789–1805. He describes presentment abstracts as lists of presentments approved at assizes together with any outstanding queries. These were printed by the county treasurer after the assizes and entitled "abstracts of presentments, grand jury warrants and list of presentment and undischarged queries"—in which form they constituted the query book for the following assizes.

Prior to 59 Geo III c. 84 (1819) presentments were made by way of affidavit stating the need for the work, the amount, and the name of the overseer. After that act presentments were granted on application to the magistrate and cess-payers at presentment sessions following which schedules were prepared for the use of the grand jury at the ensuing assizes.

The system became very complicated, as can be gleaned from Arthur Young's description of its operation in 1769[3]:

Any person wishing to make or mend a road has it measured by two persons, who swear to the measurements before a justice of the peace. It is described as leading from one market town to another . . . , that it will be a public good, and that it will

require such a sum, per perch of 21 feet, to make or repair the same; a certificate to this purpose (of which printed forms are sold) with the blanks filled up, is signed by the measurer and also by two persons called overseers, one of whom is usually the person applying for the road; the other, the labourer he intends to employ as an overseer of the work, which overseer swears also before the justice the truth of the valuation.

He then explains that approval by the grand jury meant that the applicant could go ahead with the work at his own expense and when finished he completed a certificate signed by the foreman stating he had expended the amount and submitted it to the county treasurer to receive payment. This may have been the case following the act of 1763 but from the passing of the 1774 act the process became more difficult. The following comment by McCutcheon[4] probably provides the best overall evaluation of the system: "it may well be that it [the presentment system] left room for manoeuvre and encouraged manipulation in its implementation and had a much greater chance of success than one depending on rigid interpretation within a strict legal framework."

No research paper has been found that deals with the development of the presentment system especially in the period from 1763 to 1836. It is a very important topic because, as will be seen later, the surviving records, however sparse, are a vital source of specific information on the development of roads and bridges throughout the country.

Only a small number of the grand jury records survived the fire in the Four Courts in 1922, and of these very few are pre-1836. Co. Meath is an exception because most of the query books from 1761 to 1844 had been retained in the county registrar's office in Trim. The Meath manuscript ledgers contain very valuable information on bridges as well as roads and other public works within the county—including new bridges and the widening and repair of pre-1750 bridges. This information had to be painstakingly identified and extracted from literally thousands of records of ordinary road contracts.

I examined the Meath records first because quite a few Meath bridges had already been identified as ancient. When the circuit court indexes were examined for the other 31 counties and five county boroughs the real extent of the loss became apparent: virtually no pre-1850 records had survived. This single finding explains the general lack of knowledge on bridge dates and the paucity of papers or books on the subject. Fig. 3 has been prepared giving the information extracted from the index books to the records of the circuit courts, under the headings "presentments" and "query books", including sub-headings such as books, maps, abstracts, schedules and papers. Mainly a table of relevant documents destroyed in the 1922 fire, it is not presented as being completely accurate, because it is difficult to distinguish in some cases which documents were "salved" and "not salved" in 1922. The surviving records are easy to access by extracting the bay, shelf and sub-number for the appropriate year or years from the circuit court index book for the particular county.

In the course of this search several other items of information were discovered which throw light on the subject. A volume[5] published in 1853 states that Mr Pollok, clerk of the crown in the year 1810, reported to the "commission of the records" as follows:

Grand Jury	Destroyed by fire in 1922			Salvaged or acquired after 1922
	Query Books	Presentment Books	Schedules Abstracts, etc.	
Antrim	1787–8; 1790–1; 1807; '08; '17			
Belfast			1784–95; 1808; '12; '17;' 24	
Armagh	1790–1809; '24; '47–87	1832–87;	1811–16; 1832–87	
Carlow	1758–1824; 1826–70	1836–51; Abstracts 1780–1879; 1819–71	1807–1880	Pr. Schedules 1852–59
Cavan		1809–68; 1877–81; 83–86; Abstracts 1852–64; 1870, '72, '77, '79	1842–70; 1871, '72, '76	
Clare		1809–36; 1860–81; 1885–91; 1806–65 (various yrs)	1819–28	
Cork Co.	1779–1850	1768–1880 Account Books 1773–9	1771–1886 inc.	
Cork City				
Derry	1763–1870	1763–1870 (1st series); 1800–70 (2nd series); 1869–95 (3rd series)	1821–42; 1843–93	
Donegal	1767–1892; Query Payment Bks. 1774–94	1768–1891; 1893–9	1777–80, '88; 1827–89	Pr. Bk. 1805–6; Query Bk. 1807–20, 1834, '53, '99
Down	1796–1841; '46–70; '69–72; '91	1802–54	Road Plans 1807–61	
Dublin Co.		1845–96; Pr. Papers		

Fig. 3 *Grand Jury Presentment Documents in the National Archives (1988)*

| Grand Jury | Destroyed by fire in 1922 | | | Salvaged or acquired after 1922 |
	Query Books	Presentment Books	Schedules Abstracts, etc.	
Dublin City				Some records given to National Archive in 1939 by Dublin Co. Council
Fermanagh	1800–08; 1864–70; 1881–2; 1883–6	Same as Query Bks. also 1872–5; 1880; Abstracts 1871–2; Abstracts 1873–87	1871–72; '75/6; '33–86;	
Galway		1827–75; Papers 1766–1874		Pr. Papers 1895
Kerry	No record of any books destroyed	No record of any books destroyed		Pr. Papers 1886–9 Pr. Bk. 1893–98
Kildare	1788–1882 1877–98	1879; Abstracts 1863–83 1844–60; Pr.	1782–1862; Salt Barony	Pr. Bk. North Papers 1883–99
Kilkenny				
Laois	1782–1888 '98;	1783–1803; 1789–1897		"Presentments" 1881–97; Pr. Bk. 1865, '72, '88 in Co. Lib.: Payments 1834, '73–8, '94
Leitrim		1826–87; Abstracts 1821–87	Pr. Papers 1771–1887	
Limerick	1734–1887	1756–1879; 1773–1899		Pr. Bk. 1846
Limerick City	1738–1887	1791–1887		Pr. Bk. 1885–99
Longford	1787–1887; Sec's copies: 1850–77	1787–1887; 1860–77; Presentments 1840–1849		
Louth	1779–1851	1768–1880; 1771–1886; Abstracts 1872–86	Pr. Maps 1795–1863; Acc. Bk. 1773–9	Query Bk. 1851–92; Pr. Papers 1877–9
Mayo	1779–1851 '71, '72, '88	1798–1880; 1827–70	1892–1899	Pr. Schedule Query Bk. 1866
Meath				1761/76; 1785/90; 1800–1835; '35/44; '78/99

| Grand Jury | Destroyed by fire in 1922 | | | Salvaged or acquired after 1922 |
	Query Books	Presentment Books	Schedules Abstracts, etc.	
Monaghan	1772–1884; 1730–8	1771–1886; Abstracts 1837–84; Presentments 1731–1887	Tres. Acc. 1785–1869	
Offaly	1813–87; 1757–98	1757–98; 1805–17; '19 to '87	Pr. Papers 1746–1887	Pr. Bk. 1892, '95, '96–97
Roscommon	1821–54; 1867–77; Spring 1878; Summer 1874, '82	1872; '81; '82; '83		Pr. Bk: a few between 1880 and 1898
Sligo	1806–87; 1886–7	1820–99; 1796–1878	Abst. 1872–77	
Tipperary N. Riding		Pr. Papers 1832–70; 1809/38 Co. - at-large 1839–70		
Tipperary S. Riding	1803–99	1843–54; 1860–64; 1876–84; Pr. Papers 1839–70; 1871–1887		Pr. Papers 1888–91
Tyrone	1848–86	1874–87	Pr. Papers 1846–1885	
Waterford	1760–1892	City 1859–96; Co. 1810–82	Pr. Papers 1760–1886 P. Rolls 1760–1892	Pr. 1880–82 1895–97
Westmeath	1794–1897	1767–1891; Prs. 1801–99	Pr. Maps 1815–63	
Wexford	1799–1898	1800–44; Abs. 1858–69; 1787–1890	Pr. Papers (various baronies) 1805–70 1854–5 & '69; Maps 1814–40	
Wicklow	1712–1782; 1817–82	1813–87		Pr. Abs 1859–89; Pr. Bk. 1888–98

I have a considerable body of such returns and municipal documents as would, I think, greatly aid your enquiry; . . . they began at a period previous to the year 1794, from which they were perfect down. I have little doubt that with the exception of the Queen's County and Drogheda the records of my office, throughout the province, are complete, without any chasm or deficiency for the past half-century. These records are in perfect preservation, and arranged according to their respective assizes.

The book itself, in two volumes, contains little else apart from the curricula vitae of grand jurors, judges etc. for Westmeath from 1727 to 1853.

Another book on the subject has a very long and informative title—"Tipperary County Book of South Riding, Summer Assizes 1839, held at Clonmel, July 12, 1839. Abstracts of the contracts or presentments ordered for payment, those disallowed (re-printed) and suffered to remain over. Abstracts of the presentments granted by the Grand Jury and fiated by the R.H. Justice Perm and the Hon. Baron Foster Judge . . .". The title also includes a list of grand jury members and the names of the clerk of the crown and county surveyor. It records that at the assizes new forms for the presentation of the county book had been adopted (presumably arising from the 1836 act).

The 32nd report of the deputy keeper of public records referred to previously includes some interesting facts on the records of grand juries transferred from the offices of the clerks of the crown in various counties to the Public Record Office prior to 1900. Nineteen counties had made no transfers—Armagh, Carlow, Down, Fermanagh, Kerry, Offaly, Derry, Longford, Louth, Mayo, Meath, Monaghan, Laois, Roscommon, Sligo, Tipperary, Westmeath, Wexford, Wicklow. It also recorded the following local destructions: most records in Armagh, burned in a fire there c.1855; all Co. Cork records, burned on 27 March 1891; Donegal, destroyed by soldiers in 1798; Down, many burned in 1856; Drogheda County records to 1793, destroyed in rebellion 1798; and Fermanagh in a fire in 1780; Kerry, burned in a courthouse fire; Laois, burned in 1782; Roscommon, burned 1882; Tyrone, burned 1830; and Wexford, destroyed in the 1798 rebellion. This information, coupled with that in the table, gives a good idea of the overall situation and the unlikelihood of finding many pre-19th century grand jury records.

Here and there in the deputy keeper's reports one finds records of receipts of late 19th-century records acknowledged; e.g., in 1926–36 he received the query book and schedules of applications for 1887–88 for Mayo and the presentment books (schedules of applications etc.) for 1888–98 for Meath.

The act 5 Geo. III c. 14 (1765) required the treasurer of each county to demand from the clerk of the crown a copy or copies of all road presentments made at each assizes under pain of a fine of ten pounds or gaol.

The 1774 act (13 & 14 Geo. III c. 32) laid down that the clerks of the crown respectively throughout the kingdom "shall file and keep amongst the records of each county within his province all affidavits, maps, plans and estimates pursuant to the act and shall deliver free and without charge copies of all presentments made at each assizes and of queries discharged at same to the county treasurer with four days." It also required him to deliver to the grand jury a true and faithful return of all queries and presentments not accounted for and discharged.

In 1827 a House of Commons select committee was appointed to consider what provisions might be established to regulate grand jury presentments in Ireland. The preamble of the committee's report[6] states that the subject had been discussed by many previous ones in 1815, 1816, 1822, and by parliament on many occasions. The findings are reflected in the 1836 Grand Juries Act outlined below. The report gives much useful information and comment on the system and includes, the abstracts of the accounts of presentments made in several counties in the years 1823–6. These abstracts show total expenditure per annum by county under ten headings, the first being "new road bridges" and the second "repairs to road bridges", the latter in some cases amounting to 40 per cent of total expenditure.

The act of 1836 authorised the grand jury, by presentment, to prescribe the number of copies of the schedules of applications made at such sessions to be printed and distributed by the secretary. For example, the abstract of presentments granted at the summer assizes, 1842, and fiated by the court for Co. Wicklow, include a presentment, no. 30 County-at-Large, which provided £30 for Francis MacPhail, to print 200 schedules of applications and 300 abstracts of presentments. Section 142 of the act required that a number of copies of such presentment and queries, and also a detailed abstract of his (treasurer's) account be printed and distributed, as the grand jury directed. Section 144 required that the county treasurer should each year forward a copy of all presentments made by the grand jury and fiated by the court to the secretary of the lord lieutenant to be by him laid before parliament. Neglect by a county treasurer to make his return involved forfeiture of his office.

The foregoing paragraphs indicate that an enormous number of presentment papers etc. were distributed in each county and county borough between 1836 and 1898. There must be many still lying around in private collections with owners unaware of their scarcity or of their historical value.

White[7], nearing the close of the grand jury era in 1885, wrote: "Grand juries, as at present constituted, are selected by each high sheriff very much in the order he pleases and they are for fiscal business non-representative bodies. . . . There is reason to fear if the future elected boards to replace them are taken from an inferior class, the results as regards carrying out of public business may be disastrous unless due precautions are taken." As the century drew towards a close, local administration was still in a chaotic condition. The Local Government Act of 1898 put county government on a representative basis, transferring to elected councils that business of the grand juries unconnected with administrative justice.

The simple act for repairing and amending the bridges had grown and grown for 264 years and become an undemocratic monster that was tamed in 1898 and finally buried in 1925, when a new act of the Irish Free State ushered in a decade of bridge building and repair unprecedented in the history of our island.

CHAPTER 5

Maps Showing Bridges

Most of the literature on maps of Ireland deals with a variety of cultural-landscape features including roads, but there is nothing which deals in any detail with bridges. The importance of maps as a source of information on bridge history grew as the sparsity of other records, in particular grand jury presentments, become apparent. For the purpose of this study, it was not possible to follow any systematic research procedure initially because of the huge number of bridges involved—estimated at 30,000 in all Ireland. Gradually a methodology was evolved.

The first source consulted when a bridge mention was found was the OS half-inch map; promising mentions were then checked out on the current OS six-inch maps and later on the original OS six-inch map published in the period 1829–42. Most of the survey work for the latter maps was carried out in the 1830s, but the maps were not published until the period 1933–46. The choice of terminal date for the period covered in this book was partly influenced by the fact that these maps provided a comprehensive baseline, subsequent to which it was easy to trace the history of practically all bridges. Comparison of the plot of a bridge on the first editon and its plot on later editions sometimes gives a clue to widening or replacement; however, it is difficult to scale the widths for this purpose particularly in cases where the widening is less than 10ft. Many map plots show cutwaters; by counting these the number of spans can be ascertained. There is a full set of the original six-inch maps in the library of the Royal Irish Academy, accessible to researchers, from which it is possible to take tracings for comparison with subsequent editions; this facility was used extensively in tracing the histories of nearly all the bridges described in Part II.

Taylor & Skinner's *Maps of the Roads of Ireland*[1] is very helpful in identifying whether or not a bridge existed at any point on the 8,000 miles of principal roads shown in it (in strip map format). The book was published in 1778, so 1770 is taken as the reference point. About 3,000 bridges are shown and a few dozen fords—indicative of the advanced stage of road bridging reached by that time. However, not all of the smaller rivers are shown so one must be cautious in drawing overall conclusions.

ROCQUE'S MAPS

John Rocque (1705–62) surveyed in Ireland in 1754; his "Map of the Kingdom of Ireland divided into Provinces, Counties and Baronies" and his "Actual Survey of County Dublin[2] are drawn to scales of 10.5 and 1.83 statute miles to one inch respectively. The standard convention is followed in relation to bridge delineation, though no glossary of symbols is provided. Roque's Dublin maps, in particular, provided leads to many bridges described in detail in Part II, including King John's (see Map 5). Many roads in Co. Dublin, such as the Drogheda road, were substantially relocated in the period 1733–1839; Rocque's maps are invaluable in identifying the original roads.

MOLL'S MAP

Henry Pratt's "Map of the Kingdom of Ireland" is dated by Andrews[3] at 1702. The map's title states that it is "Newly corrected and improved by actual observations divided into provinces, counties, baronies and supplied with many market towns and other places of note omitted in former maps with all the principle roads . . . wherein the Citys and Chief Towns . . . are respectively distinguished by different characters and the lakes, bogs, mountains, rivers, bridges, ferreys are described . . .". However, the map's index to symbols gives no characteristic for bridges and they are not distinguishable at the river crossings. Nor does the "explanation" of Moll's "New Map of Ireland" (1714) provide bridge symbols, but a perusal of the map shows that they are all distinguished in the conventional manner of the time.

Moll's map is reproduced in sections in Appendix 10. It is the landmarker map for anyone attempting to date a bridge located on any of the 6826 miles of "principal roads" shown on it. A copy of the original was made up for the purpose of analysis. The bridges shown were ringed and numbered sequentially by county starting with Antrim, boundary bridges being distributed between the adjoining counties. The mileage of roads in each county was also measured. The results, set out in fig. 4, show a total of 574 bridges on 6826 statute miles of principal roads, a density of one per 12 miles. However, it must be remembered that many smaller rivers are not shown. It would be interesting to know how many of these bridges have survived in whole or in part.

Moll's map is the earliest one to record a significant number of bridge names. It has been shown, however, that bridge names can be very misleading.[4] In the case of Mabe's Bridge, Kells,* it was found that the first appearance of the name was on the 1839 OS six-inch map, whereas the grand jury of about 50 years earlier recorded the name "Mapes", thus linking the bridge with an Anglo-Norman family who owned two townlands nearby for centuries but who were disposessed in the 1650s. The next bridge upriver on the Blackwater is named Clevans on the map, apparently a family name but in reality Droichet an Cleibhín, that is, the "kish" bridge, which immediately indicates that there was a *cesdroichet* (wicker bridge) there in the past.

The number of named bridges found on Moll's map is given in fig. 4. Overall only 16 per cent were named on the map and among these 6 per cent were named in Connaught, 12 per cent in Leinster, 17 per cent in Cork and 25 per cent in Ulster. Only 12 bridges or two per cent were named after persons, e.g. Dawson, Young, Poe, Maguire, Butler. Three gave their name to the towns that grew up about them. The number with names on the map is obviously not a true sample because often there was insufficient space to print the names;

County & Province	Down Survey	Moll's Map (1714)		
	No. of Bridges	No. of Bridges	Miles Statute of Road	No. of Bridges with printed names
Antrim	10	33	278	3
Down	3	25	369	9
Armagh	1	11	138	3
Derry	1	9	202	4
Tyrone	5	19	227	1
Fermanagh	3	17	171	4
Donegal	4	11	220	3
Cavan	6	8	220	7
Monaghan	3	6	113	3
Ulster	36	139	1938	37
Louth	10	13	126	4
Meath	27	27	236	3
Westmeath	7	17	123	0
Longford	5	6	112	0
Offaly	8	17	182	3
Laois	5	20	213	3
Kildare	9	12	178	5
Dublin	16	16	133	1
Wicklow	1	27	211	3
Carlow	3	11	107	1
Wexford	0	24	219	1
Kilkenny	15	18	217	1
Leinster	106	208	2057	25
Leitrim	5	9	96	0
Sligo	6	10	115	2
Mayo	1	25	207	0
Roscommon	10	14	240	2
Galway	3	24	403	1
Connaught	25	82	1061	5
Clare	3	11	135	4
Limerick	8	23	264	4
Tipperary	7	30	418	4
Waterford	2	8	156	1
Cork	19	59	533	9
Kerry	1	24	264	3
Munster	40	155	1770	25
Ireland	207	584	6826	92

Fig 4: *Number of Bridges shown on the Down Survey and Moll's Maps*

47

however, this should not affect the findings in regard to the percentage of those named that are called after families. The practice in relation to canal and railway bridges is much different, as a glance at the 20th-century OS one-inch maps will show.

In France many towns embody the word *pons* in their names, thus preserving a vital clue to their history. Boyer[5] states that "very many Gallic towns took their names from bridges", evidencing an interest in bridges which carried over into the middle ages. The Celtic equivalent of *pons* was *briva*, and there is a long list of place names in Gaul with *briva*, e.g. Briva Isare, the bridge over the Ouse, and Samarobriva (Amiens), "the bridge over the Somme". Similarly, in Ireland many place-names incorporate *droichead*, the Irish word for bridge. From a historical aspect the practice of naming bridges after politicians is to be deplored, symptomatic of a decline in Celtic imagination which so often identified a local topographical characteristic in the naming of *athanna* as well as townlands.

Another feature of Moll's map is the designation of ferries by a coracle-shaped symbol. Some 25 appear, among which the following suggest the absence of a possible bridge in the vicinity: Meelick, Lanesborough, Portumna, Killaloe, and O'Brien's Bridge on the Shannon; Wexford and Scarawelsh on the Slaney; Derry and Strabane on the Foyle; New Ferry and Toome on the Bann. An interesting reference to Meelick occurs in Cooke's *History of Birr*; to the effect[6] that by letters patent dated 20 July 1671 a grant was made to John Blysse and his heirs of "a ferry over the river Shannon to pass from the town of Banagher in the King's County to the townland of Meelick in the County of Galway, and, within a quarter of a mile each side of the said river, to receive and transport whatsoever men and other things are to be transported for such and the like fees and rewards as heretofore were received; to keep on the said ferry one or more boats within the limits aforesaid and also the whole and entire Shannon aforesaid from the town of Banagher to the said town of Meelick and within the space of one quarter of a mile each side of the river"; the grant also included two ruinous castles and land. This grant and the mention on Moll raises the question of whether there was a bridge at Banagher between 1671 and 1714, and, if there was not, of how

Sarsfield crossed during the war. The purchase of the ferry right at Portumna in 1795 required an act of parliament and £8,000 compensation.

THE DOWN SURVEY

The Down Survey, carried out under a 1654 contract by Sir William Petty, was completed by March 1656. It covered 22 of the 32 counties and was supplemented by the 1639 Strafford Survey of Connaught, Clare and parts of Limerick and Tipperary. It was so called "from having been laid down by chain and scale" to distinguish it from the Civil Survey which it supplemented.

These maps, entitled *Hiberniae Delineatio*[7], were not published until 1683. The scale of the county maps is two Irish miles to one inch, the provincial maps six to an inch and the general map of Ireland 12 to an inch. Andrews in a recent introduction to these maps, mentions that one of its principal defects was the failure to show the road system and that Petty in fact went beyond his official terms of reference when he instructed his surveyors to note highways. Very few roads are indicated on the county or provincial map; however, some bridges are delineated by short parallel strokes with the river line broken in between. Some fords are shown by short dumbbells.

Despite their limitations, Petty's maps are invaluable and in many cases provide the earliest record of a bridge. An analysis of the maps reveals 207 bridges and 127 fords. The number identified in each county is shown in fig. 4, the boundary bridges being apportioned between the contiguous counties. It is evident from the distribution by county that the bridge-noting instructions were ignored in many areas, such as the south-east. The numbers obviously bear no relation to the actual situation. The principal question is whether a marked bridge can be assigned to the date of the field survey (1655–6), given that the maps were not printed until the 1680s. The answer is yes, because several bridges built in Dublin city and county in the period 1657–83 are not shown. It is most unlikely therefore that post-survey additions were made in remoter areas. The place names recorded in the survey are a source of relevant information in some cases. A part of the Down Survey map of Co. Dublin is reproduced in Map 1.

The civil surveys of 1654–6 often contain

Map 1: *Portion of Down Survey Map of Co. Dublin*

information on bridges. A good example is Carrigadrohid* on the Lee, where the survey records that "on the premises is a castle valued at £100 on a rock in the midst of the river Lee, where there is a timber bridge which is a common passage over said river which is now out of repair yet passable on foot . . .". The bridge is clearly marked on the Down Survey map and one would naturally assume that the surviving *stone* north arches are pre-1655; however, this description precludes such an assumption. Not all of the bridges in Part II were checked for civil survey mentions, as this would have been very time-consuming relative to the information likely to be unearthed.

Speed's[8] "General Map of Ireland" of 1610 shows no bridges, but his maps of Limerick, Cork, Dublin and Galway cities show the bridges existing at the time and are used in Part II, particularly in relation to Thomond Old Bridge. The atlas of "Ulster Maps 1609"[9] in the Royal Irish Academy contains about 20 beautifully drawn and coloured maps, but only one bridge is shown—at Newry. Another promising map was the 20 x 14 inch map of Leix and Offaly (1565)[10] reproduced in O'Hanlon[11]; but it shows few bridges. Nevertheless, Watercastle Bridge* on the Nore was identified from it; a new bridge has been erected on a river diversion, but the old 16th-century one, widened on the upriver side, high and dry, is still there. The Monks Bridge* two miles upriver is not shown on the map.

Dunlop[12] mentions a map of Ireland, believed to be *c.* 1538, which shows three main roads from Dublin—the road to Drogheda through Swords and Balbriggan, the road to the west crossing the Boyne at Trim and thence to Athboy and Delvin, and a road through Naas crossing the Liffey at Kilcullen and proceeding through Castledermot and Carlow to Leighlinbridge, where it crossed the Barrow. Each of these routes is shown as continuous on Moll's map.

A bibliography of Irish maps and cartography can be found in the package "Ireland from Maps" issued by the National Library in 1980[13]. It contains a copy of Petty's general map which shows 90 of the bridges marked on the Down Survey.

CHAPTER 6

Drainage and Inland Navigation

River navigation works, the construction of canals, and drainage schemes had a considerable impact on road bridges in Ireland in the period 1700–1850. The navigation works necessitated the construction of many large new river bridges, particularly on the Shannon, and also the underpinning, alteration and repair of many others—all major undertakings. Hundreds of public road and accommodation bridges (about three for every two miles) were built across approximately 400 miles of new canals. The arterial drainage works resulted in the removal and replacement of hundreds of ancient bridges and the underpinning and alteration of thousands of others. A massive volume of literature on these topics exists ranging from pages detailing items of expenditure on wages and materials etc. on the Nore navigation, in the Irish House of Commons Journals for 1757–9, to modern books on inland waterways. From all this it is only possible to give a summary of the most relevant information relating to road bridges, bearing in mind that this book does not cover canal bridges, except insofar as their construction enhanced the state of the bridge-building art.

Prior to 1700, river transport, where feasible, was far more economic than road transport. However, from earliest times man-made obstructions to boats began to multiply on the river channels, the principal ones being weirs, mills, fords and bridges. The Irish word for a weir, *cora* or *coradh*, is part of many townland names, such as the headquarters of Brian Boru called Kincora and various anglicisations of Baile na Coradh. The Cistercians were good harvesters of eels and there are many references to ownership of such weirs in their charters. Geraldine Carville[1] describes one on the rocky bed of the Suir at Holycross Abbey, built of stone 5ft wide at the bottom, 4ft at the top, 3ft

high and sloped at 40 degrees to the bank and strengthened on the downstream side with boulders. It is still there. Fr Colmcille[2] quoting Archdall[3] records how in 1358 the abbot of Mellifont was indicted at Trim for erecting a weir on the Boyne at Oldbridge and "the jury found that from the time of the arrival of the English the king had a certain free passage in that river from the town of Drogheda to the bridge of Trim, usually called a watersarde, twenty-four feet in breadth from the bank on each side according to the discretion of twelve honest men, six of the neighbourhood of one side and six of the other; and that through that aperture boats called corraghs, with timber for building, and flotes had liberty to pass constantly free. . . ". The weir was removed and the abbot sent to goal, but he was later released on payment of a £10 fine. This reference is of special interest as it indicated that stone for building bridges, e.g. Babes*, could have been transported cheaply up and down the Boyne.

In 1537 a statute (28 Hen. VIII c. 22) was enacted aimed at the removal of obstructive weirs. McCarthy Murrogh[4] mentions that weirs were a principal obstacle to navigation on the Munster Blackwater in the first quarter of the 17th century and the cause of a tremendous struggle between those who wanted to remove and those who wanted to retain them. He also states that at that time large boats could reach Lixnaw on the Feale and Adare on the Maigue and that sawn timber was floated down the Blackwater to Cappoquin, where it was loaded on lighters for transport to Youghal. It is evident from the Ormonde papers mentioned previously that drainage works were carried out in many parts of the country in the 17th century, but these were on a small scale. The first major effort came in 1715 when the Irish parliament passed an act (2 Geo. I c. 12) "to encourage the draining and improving of bogs and unprofitable low ground and for easing and dispatching the inland carriage and conveyance of goods from one point to another within the Kingdom". This act gave a mandate for all kinds of public and private works, but there was evidently little money to implement it and the conditions were too restrictive to attract undertakers.

In 1729, the year of the first turnpike road act, another new act was passed appointing the lord lieutenant, the four Protestant archbishops and eight others to be commissioners for the purposes of implementing the act of 1715. The numbers and composition, apart from the lord lieutenant, are remarkably similar to the body of trustees in each turnpike act. A duty was also introduced on coaches, berlins and other road vehicles of £1 for every four-wheeled vehicle and 5s. for two-wheelers. Duties were also imposed on such items as gold and silver plate etc. (known as "tillage duties" because the principal object was to encourage tillage). O'Brien[5] gives a table showing total net revenue and total expenditure for each year from 1700 to 1780 and it is evident that substantial surpluses began to accrue from 1749 onwards. He also explains how parliament circumvented the payment of large amounts from the surplus to the king (a hereditary prerogative from the time of the restoration) by making substantial annual grants for public works in Ireland. The table in fig. 5 taken from O'Brien gives a good idea of the nature and extent of the grants.

These were massive amounts of money for the period, but how effective was the expenditure? O'Brien comments that: "If these large sums had been spent on the purposes for which they had been voted, they would, no doubt, have greatly benefited the country, but, as a matter of fact, they largely went to the aggrandisement of private individuals or members of parliament and their friends." A harsh verdict—too severe, if one thinks of the multiplier effect in job numbers on public works throughout the country as compared to granting the money to the king in London.

O'Brien's verdict, however, is substantiated by Watters in a paper[6] on the £20,000 spent on the Kilkenny canal: "A bridge appeared to have been built at Inistioge out of the funds granted by parliament, still the canal never reached . . . Thomastown; and whether from the failure of

	£
Newry River	9,000
Drumglass Colliery	118,200
Lagan River	40,304
Shannon Riiver	31,500
Grand Canal	73,000
Blackwater River	11,000
Lee River	2,000
Barrow River	10,500
Suir River	4,500
Nore River	25,000
Borne [?Burren,? Barrow] River	36,998
Skerries Pier	3,500
Enver Pier	1,870
Dunleary	18,500
Balbriggan Pier	5,250
Bangor Pier	500
Killyleigh Pier	1,200
Sligo Pier	1,300
Antrim River	1,359
Ballast Office	43,000
Widening Dublin Streets	42,000
Trinity College	31,000
Limerick Quay	7,773
Cork Harbour	6,500
Cork Workhouse	1,500
Londonderry Quay	2,900
Shandon St, Cork	1,500
Wicklow Harbour	6,850
St Patrick's Hospital	6,000
Public Roads	5,000
Dungarvan Aqueduct	1,300
Hospital for Soldiers' Children	7,000
Lying-in Hospital	19,300
Mercer's Hospital	500
Shannon Bridge	2,000
Kilkelly Bridge	9,150
Cork Bridge	4,000
Kildare Bridge	600
St Mark's Church	2,000
St Thomas' Church	5,440
St Catherine's Church	3,990
St John's Church	2,000
Building churches	12,000
Roofing Athlone Church	476
Cashel Church	800
Dingle Quay	1,000
Mounterkenny Colliery	2,000
Marine Nursery	1,000
Road round Dublin	1,500
Dundalk	2,000
Whale Fisheries	1,000
Dry Dock	2,000
Mills at Naul	3,498
Ballycastle	3,000
Lord Longford	3,300

Fig. 5: *Sums Granted by the Irish Parliament 1753–67 (Source: O'Brien)*

funds, or disagreements among the Board . . . the project was finally abandoned. . . . Had they begun at Inistioge, and advanced towards Kilkenny, then every mile completed would have been of use, and had it even come to Thomastown and no further, it might have been better for Kilkenny . . . but in that case we would never have had our far-famed 'Canal Walk'." The bridge at Inistioge, damaged in the great Nore flood in 1763, cost £921 to repair (good value indeed), part of the £8,000 granted to the corporation for promoting and carrying on an inland navigation in Ireland to enable it to rebuild John's and Green's bridges in the city of Kilkenny and Bennets, Thomastown and Castlecomer in the county (see Kilkenny Bridges*). There is an excellent table in the appendix to Delany's *Inland Waterways*[7] which gives full details of the year of construction, length, terminal points, expenditure etc. on all lakes and river navigation and canals over the period 1748–1929.

CANAL BRIDGES

In the archives of the IEI there is a copy of the Killaly's "Specification of the public road and private or accommodation bridges, proposed to be built on the Royal Canal Extension" dated 1810. Killaly was involved in completing the very difficult section of the Royal across the Bog of Allen and in 1814 was engineer to the director general of inland navigation. The bridge specification and drawings are reproduced in Appendix 7. There are several interesting aspects to the specification and plans. For example, there is no mention of the type of stone, whether limestone, sandstone or granite (perhaps the choice depended on the particular location). The sheeting, that is, the stones in the barrel of the arch between the facing rings, varied from 21 in. in depth at the springings to 18 in. at crown—an expensive taper considering the extrados was to be packed with spauls. There is no mention of hydraulic lime (see Chapter 8); evidently the lime was burnt locally in kilns erected near the job. The arch of the bridge was covered with 15 in. of puddle, which seems excessive. The grades on the approach road were steep, (although the Mail Coach Road Act of 1805 had already identified this as a problem). However, these are minor points in a specification which has proved its worth by actual performance. The most puzzling aspect

is that the arch is specified as a semi-ellipsis whereas the drawing shows an arc of a circle of 10ft 3 in. radius. Overall it is an interesting document because few detailed specifications and drawings for river bridges built during the canal period have survived. One thing we can be certain of—the general quality of stone masonry construction must have improved, especially in rural areas. This is apparent in the masonry and finish of small bridges erected in the last quarter of the 18th century. (When comparing the survival rates and durability etc. of river and canal bridges, it is important to remember that the latter are not subjected to the ravages of scour to the same extent as river bridges).

Delaney gives a good technical description of work on the final section of the Royal Canal between Coolnaher and the Shannon constructed by Mullins and McMahon in 1813–17. "It was a big operation. £10,000 was spent in laying down oak, pitch, pine and other timber, horse, wagons, drays, machinery etc.; and lime kilns, stone cutters' sheds and forges were built along the 25-mile length. . . . Twenty-one locks, thirty-eight bridges, one large aqueduct and several harbours and quays were constructed. The cost worked out about £8,000 per mile." The length of the whole Royal Canal is 90½ miles; it was built in 1789–1817 at a cost of £1,312,573.

DRAINAGE ACTS

In 1821 Westminister directed Mr J. Rennie to have a survey made of the river Shannon. The survey, carried out by R.B. Grantham, was a very accurate one. Dimensions and elevations of older bridges based on it are given in Appendix 8. A commission consisting of Col. John Burgoyne, Capt. Mudge and Thomas Rhodes had been appointed in 1831 to prepare the navigation and drainage scheme, which was presented in the first report of the commission published in 1834 (the detailed plans and estimates appear in the second report, 1837). Much of the information on Drumheriff Bridge, Skeagh, Athlone (old) Bridge, Thomond Bridge, among others dealt with in Part II of this book, was extracted from these reports. The Rhodes survey report in particular is invaluable from the aspect of the history of roads and bridges because it records in great detail what was there in the 1830s.

The Drainage (Ireland) Act (5 & 6 Vic. c. 89) 1842, the Drainage (Ireland) Act (8 & 9 Vic. c. 69) 1845 and a similar act of 1847 (10 & 11 Vic. c. 79) formed the basis for the great drainage schemes of the 1840s which had a large effect on road bridges throughout the country. These and some subsequent acts are collectively known as the "Drainage and Navigation (Ireland) Acts 1842–57" or the "1842 Code", where "code" means a grouping rather than a reduction to a single act. A second code, containing a group of acts from 1863, collectively known as the "Drainage & Improvement of Land (Ireland) Acts 1863–92", had an effect on many of surviving ancient bridges.

Under the 1842 Code 193 drainage districts were formed, covering about one quarter of million acres of land. The 120 districts in which work was carried out in the decade 1842–52 are outlined on Map 2.

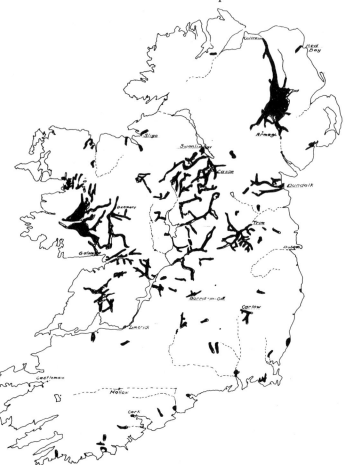

Map 2: *Location of 1842-52 Drainage Schemes*

The survey, design and implementation of drainage works on such a scale was a formidable task. William Mulvaney, appointed commissioner for drainage, gathered around him a small group of very competent engineers whose investigations and work made a notable contribution to hydraulics in the 19th century.[8]

The drainage engineers produced reports describing the existing conditions in the rivers, the works required to alleviate flooding, and estimates of the cost. There is a set of these reports in the archives of the IEI. In 50 districts for which reports were examined the total expenditure on bridge works was £41,265, equivalent to 11.6% of the total drainage costs; the bridge costs were recouped from the respective grand juries under the acts, the average costs chargeable to "county works" being £800 per district.

A typical report is the one prepared by John Kelly, civil engineer[9] for 56 sq. miles of lands along the river Nore from Curraguneen ford to Castletown, a length of 15 miles. It included a "diagram plan and section" and was dated 1845. The valuator identified 3282 acres of lands subject to flooding. The report then identified the principal causes: "it proceeds from fords or crossings made in different parts of the river for the purpose of enabling cattle etc. to pass from one side to the other, and from the extremely tortuous course of the river and its want of breadth and depth." In regard to the bridges, the report states: "The bridges in this district, except the old one near Borris-in-Ossory, though, as far as width of waterway is concerned, sufficiently capacious for discharging the floods, are totally inadequate as regards depth and will require to be underpinned. The old bridge must be taken down and a new one erected in its stead." The estimate of £6,896 included underpinning Curraguneen Bridge, Quaker's Bridge, New Bridge and Shanagoo Bridge and taking down and rebuilding Old Bridge near Borris, all for £335. 15s. 0d. The puzzle for the pontist resulting from this work in fact is that the Old Bridge became younger than the "New Bridge", which was about half a mile upriver. The position was rectified in 1982 when Laois Co. Council modernised the latter under a major road improvement scheme. No details of the "Old Bridge" were given, but it is recorded[10] that an old oak bridge and bronze sword were found 12ft below the channel nearby when the work was carried out in 1848. This was an ancient crossing point of the Slighe Dála, near Ballaghmore.

The following items of bridge information are taken from the other district reports, all relating to the 1840s:

Dunmore district (Co. Galway), River Dalgin: "A shoal exists at Fertamore (6m. NW Tuam) and is crossed by a bridge consisting of 26 arches and 650 ft in length. At this bridge also a mill dam is constructed which keeps, even in summer, the water close to the surface of the low land." The recommendation was that the rock be excavated to 11ft 6 ins below the soffit of the highest arch.

Castlemaine district (Co. Kerry), Maine River: "Within a mile of the old salmon weir the Maine (average width 70ft) is crossed by Scarravanena Bridge on the old road from Tralee to Killarney. This bridge is founded upon a shoal of apparently artificial construction and consists of three arches of 20ft span each. It is an old structure of uncoursed rubble and quite inadequate to discharge the flood water."

Lough Neagh district, Lower Bann River: "The shoal on which Kilrea Bridge stands is a quarter of a mile long and the depth of present summer water but 4ft The bridge consists of seven semi-circular arches of 28ft span each with piers 7ft in thickness. The piers and arch quoins are of ashlar stone and all the rest is rubble masonry; it is in tolerably good repair.'

Portglenone Bridge "consists of seven arches of the same size, or very nearly so, as those of Kilrea Bridge; the aggregate waterway between the piers and abutments is 193ft 9in., but it is much obstructed by sterlings and rubble stones put in to defend the foundations which occupy more than 30ft of the space below the summer level. The entire structure is in a very ruinous condition; the piers have been founded on or near the compressible bed of the channel, and from unskilfulness in construction have yielded to an alarming extent, as numerous settlements and fissures in this dislocated structure attest. The materials and workmanship are of the most inferior description and no warranty short of reconstruction can be offered for its security. It appears that a portion fell in1798 but was soon after restored; the ruins however were left in the river. The public officers in charge of the repairs, the expense of which is borne by two counties, had to resort to wrought-iron ties to

try and bind it together, but destruction has got it so firmly grasped that no mechanical expedient will long procrastinate its doom."

Verners Bridge "which crosses this river [Blackwater] may be said to be of recent construction; it has two masonry abutments, with a wooden carriageway resting on piles driven into the river bed. The distance from abutment to abutment is 110ft. The bridge is private property, for the use of which the public pays a toll".

Parsons-Green district (Cos. Fermanagh and Monaghan: Parsons Green River): "I propose that the steps between Killycaman and Clonkee be removed and a proper foot bridge substituted; likewise the treble gullet in Leitrim to be removed and a bridge of masonry substituted having an arch of 10ft span; an occupation bridge to be built in Agharoosky West; the abutment, masonry and the roadway timber. The foundations of the other bridges, named above, to be underset to correspond with the bottom of the proposed improved channel." The estimate for two occupation bridges and four footbridges was £62 and for undersetting nine bridges £195.

Swanlinbar district (Co. Cavan): "Stragowna bridge was built about 50 years ago, is rent in several places and inconveniently high. The shoal on which it is built is composed of soft yellow clay. A flooring of alder and ash trees has been laid transversely to the channel on which the abutments and pier rest." Thompson's Bridge "was built in 1801; has three arches of 20ft span each and piers 5ft thick. The foundations are of similar construction to those of Stragowna bridge . . . ; it is in good repair". Drumcannon [Blackwater] Bridge "is an old structure but in good repair. It has two arches of 14ft span, placed at a considerable distance from each other; the waterway would have been much more efficient if this injudicious arrangement had not been followed." Long Bridge [Blackwater] "is an old structure of inferior workmanship. Above the bridge the river divides, or has been divided artificially, into two branches; the eastern branch is spanned by two arches of 14ft each and the western by an arch of 15ft. The manner of dividing is very prejudicial to the effective discharge of floods."

Upper Main district (Co. Antrim): River Maine: "First, that on the sunk road 1½ miles from the source of the river. I am informed a bridge once existed here, but both road and bridge are now sunk in the soft bog and are impassable during a greater portion of the year . . . ; it is proposed to erect a gullet 4 ft wide.' The third bridge is that called Bridge End. This is an old structure consisting of five arches having a total width of waterway of 50ft. . . . It is proposed to deepen the bed of the river underneath for the two of the arches and underpin three of the piers and by these means obtain a sufficient waterway." The estimate provided £555 for rebuilding and underpinning public bridges including above and three others.

Lough Mask and River Robe district (Cos. Galway and Mayo): "An eel weir, at the Ballindine road bridge, which is raised to within 1ft of the level of the lands causes the covering of nearly the entire tract along the banks of the river, three miles above the bridge, with more than 1 ft in depth of water during nine months in the year. Another weir, used as a foot passage, crosses the river three quarters of a mile above the bridge; short shoals occur at the upper end of the reach, on the last of which is placed a weir as a foot passage, which draws back the water to Kilknock Bridge, 1½ miles." Clonbar River: "The old bridge of Lahinch must be taken down and one arch of 30 ft in span substitute for the former five opes."

Lavally district (Co. Galway), AbbertRiver: This report gives short descriptions for 12 bridges and the spans and number of arches are of interest: Ardske, five arches; Ballyglooneen good workmanship, five arches averaging 9ft span; Pallas, 10 arches with a span of 10ft 6in. each, piers 6ft thick; Abbey, five arches of 4ft to 7ft span; Chapelfield nine arches of 5ft to 9ft span; Newtown four arches of 10ft span; Abbert, seven arches from 7ft to 9ft span; Esker (new), five arches, 7ft span each; Killaclogher, seven arches of 8ft span; Clogh, apparently very old, in very bad repair; a new arch of 14ft span to be built at Ballyglass at which place cars pass at present through the river; at Glennamucka, a new arch of 12ft span instead of a totally inadequate gullet. The cost of rebuilding these usually with a single arch between 12 and 20ft span together with eleven other small bridges on tributaries was estimated at £1,226.

Argideen district (Co. Cork), Argideen River: "It is proposed to construct foot bridges across the several passes or stepping-stones which present themselves along the river-course, so as to prevent the banks being degraded in future and the nucleus of shoals formed again at these points."

The foregoing extracts give a good overall picture of the obstruction to flow caused by the many small bridges, public and private, on the smaller rivers up to the 1840s. They also give an insight into the typical size, condition and type of construction of the small bridges built before then, some obviously centuries-old. The extracts may also be of interest locally as a source of early information, though much of it can be gleaned from the 1829–42 OS six-inch sheets.

The story of the drainage works and the Great Famine has been told many times elsewhere; only 5 per cent of the cost of employment schemes was spent on drainage and less than one in 40 labourers employed were engaged on these works.[11] This, of course, was not insignificant, especially in the period October 1846 to June 1847 when the average number relieved daily by labour was 356,314 and the local expenditure £4,462,154. The amendment of the 1842 Drainage Act in 1846, by which the number of affected land-owners assenting before a scheme could be started was reduced from two thirds to one half and the detail required in surveys minimised, was actively promoted by W. Mulvaney. When the amendment was passed the survey work went ahead with such speed that between May and October 1846 operations were commenced or about to commence in no less than 101 districts—a tremendous achievement given the travel, mapping, levelling and other difficulties of the time.

NEW DESIGNS

Mulvaney and his small group of dedicated engineers were very active in the Institution of Engineers of Ireland, which had been founded in 1834 mainly to promote the acquisition and dissemination of engineering knowledge. From 1845 to 1851 they contributed no less than 24 papers, including five by Mulvaney himself, on all aspects of drainage. Surprisingly none of these papers describes their thinking on the structural design of arch bridges; yet these engineers developed a style of their own and a standardisation of design (with span ranges from 20 to 60ft) which was most economical. Like the Romans, they were well aware of the disadvantages, from the aspect of durability and flood capacity, of river piers.

Several bridges in the Upper Boyne district at Scariff, Stoneyford, Clonard—constructed between 1846 and 1849—are typical; some are described in Part II. They with others ushered in the half century in which the stone arch reached its pinnacle in Ireland before yielding completely to the new materials—steel and concrete—at the turn of the 20th century.

RIVER NAMES

Some rivers have lived up to their names in their treatment of bridges over the centuries. There is the Dinan, the strong river in Kilkenny which with its sudden big floods undermined strong bridges in 1763 and 1986. The Nanny in Meath, An Aigne, meaning "treacherous", which with its rapid rise of flood water caused many drownings as far back in 1487; a similar meaning is given to the Maine (Mang) in Kerry. An Bearba (Barrow), the "dumb water", is silent, deep and sluggish, difficult to bridge in olden times. An Abha Buidhe, the Yellow River, in Leitrim, as recently as 1986 brought down a deluge of yellow clay and sandy silts from a landship and caused a pulse of extraordinary flow which destroyed two bridges and severely damaged three others. The beer-coloured water of the Nore, An Bheoir or Feoir, which rises in the Devil's Bit and sends its waters into the sea between Hook and Crook, has perhaps swept away more bridges per mile than most.

Timber Bridges

The first bridges were formed accidentally by fallen trees. Gradually, early settlers began to make for themselves crude timber bridges across small rivers and streams. Archaeological evidence from early Ireland shows that there was no scarcity of timber and that the inhabitants were proficient in building crannogs (literally, "young trees" but used to denote a lake dwelling). Many crannogs were exposed by the drainage schemes carried out in the 1840s. In the present century several have been systematically excavated under expert archaeological direction, notably by Dr Raftery at Knocknalappa, Co. Clare[1] and by Hencken at Ballinderry, Co. Offaly[2]. Since then a replica crannog has been erected at Craggaunowen near Quinn, Co. Clare. This is 300 ft in circumference and was made of 15ft 6in. high larch poles from a nearby forest and 8,000 wattles[3].

The Ardakillen crannog, discovered during drainage operations in Roscommon in the last century, is of the most interest from a bridge-construction aspect, and its cross section is reproduced in fig. 6 from Wood-Martin's *Lake Dwellings of Ireland*.[4] Wood-Martin records that "under a slight earthy deposit there was a deep layer of loose stones bounded by an enclosing wall." The subgrade consisted of clay and peat and the raked piles formed an unbroken circle around the island. He also records that there were many finds, including a wooden mallet,

and states that the crannog is probably the one mentioned in the Annals of the Four Masters under 1368. The cross-section shows clearly that the driving of timber piles or the construction of starlings for the foundation of stone bridges would not have presented any problem on most sites in Ireland in the early Christian period.

Among the objects from the Ballinderry 7th-century site were an oak pile-driver, a mallet-head and an iron chain (fig. 7). Hencken records that the piles were 3in. to 6in. in diameter, though many were larger and smaller, and some still had the bark on. Some of the larger one had been roughly squared, and all had been sharply pointed. The timber was mainly oak, but the piles included much ash and elder. Hencken concludes that there was a high development of carpentry craft and tools in Ireland by the time of the Vikings. The Vikings were highly proficient in timber construction as evidenced by their longships and by numerous archaeological finds in Dublin. Expertise in carpentry must have spread from the Viking cities to most parts of the country by the year 1000 (Cosgrave[5] argues that Máel Sechnaill, an effective high king of Ireland, captured Dublin on three occasions, the last being in 995, not to expel the Norse but to exploit their resources).

The starting date for this study record was selected as AD 1000 because in the following year we find the first record of the construction of bridges as distinct from a reference to a bridge, in the Annals of Clonmacnoise (Appendix 1): "King Máel Sechnaill and Cathal O'Connor of Connaught made a bridge at Athlone over Synan. King Máel Sechnaill made a bridge at Athlyog [Lanesborough] to the one-half of the river." The corresponding entry in the *Annals of the Four Masters* describes the crossings as tochars. An examination of the

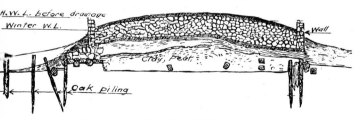

Fig. 6: *Section through Ardkillen Crannog*

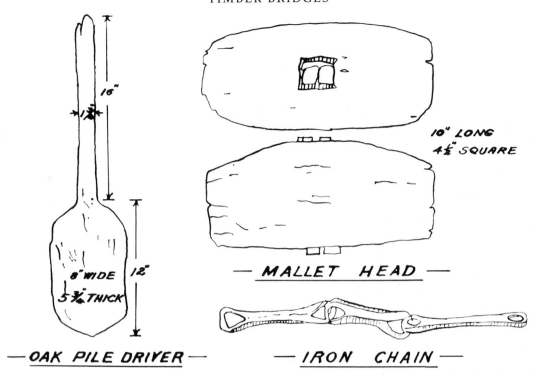

16"

8" WIDE

5 ¾" THICK

12"

— **MALLET HEAD** —

10" LONG
4 ⅛" SQUARE

—**OAK PILE DRIVER**—

— **IRON CHAIN** —

Fig. 7: *Some Objects from Ballinderry Crannog*

longitudinal and cross-sections of the bed of the Shannon in the navigation reports suggests that some form of timber bridge was built at Athlone, where the bed is a sandy clay, and that a *cesdroichet* was built on the rocky bed at Lanesborough. An entry for the year 1071 in the Annals of Innisfallen states that, in a forthnight, a muster of Munstermen built a bridge at Woodford and another at Killaloe, the latter presumably across the Shannon. Keating[6] states that Brian Boru built many bridges, causeways and highways throughout the country and in particular gives the following mention: "now when Brian heard that the king of Leinster left the longfort [at Kincora] without bidding him farewell, he sent a page of his household to detain him that he might give him wages and gifts. The place at which the page overtook him was at the end of the plank bridge of Cill Dalua (Clair Cille Dalua) on the east side of the Shannon. . ." . Brian was killed in 1014, so there was a timber bridge across the Shannon some time during the period 1000–14. The entry probably refers to a reconstruction of this.

We find other references to a *droichet* at Athlone in the Annals of the Four Masters for 1126 and 1129, but the next highly significant reference is under 1154. "The wicker bridge [*cliathdroicit*] of Athlone was destroyed by Maelseachlainn and its fortress was demolished. The wicker bridge at Ath-liag was made by Toirdhealbach Ua Conchobhair." Under 1155 the same Annals mention that "A fleet was brought by Toirdealbach O'Conchabair to Athlone and the wicker bridge of Ath Luain was made by him for the purpose of making incursions into Meath. The bridge of Ath Luain was destroyed and its fortress was burned by Donnchadh son of Domhnall Ua Maelseachlainn." These mentions are significant because they refer to a new type of bridge, a *cliath droichet*, probably constructed beside the ancient ford where the river was then about 100 yards wide.

The Annals of Boyle record that in 1159 Rory O'Connor erected a *cliath droichet* at Athlone for the purpose of making incursions into Meath. We also have an 1158 record in the Annals of Clonmacnoise of a joyste or wooden bridge over the Shannon at Clonmacnoise — the only mention of a bridge there.

Contributions towards a Dictionary of the Irish Language[7], on the evidence of these and other early references, gives six types of droichet: a *cesaigh droichet* or wicker bridge; *cliath droichet* or hurdle-bridge; *clar droichet* or woodbridge; a *cloch droichet* or stone bridge; a *droichet clochaeltra* or bridge of stone and mortar; and a *droichet long* or bridge of boats. Here we are interested in the timber and, given the evidence for the three types, the question is—what kinds of bridges structures they were? It would appear that the *ces droichet* was made primarily of wickerwork. An entry in the Annals of Boyle under 1146 states that Turlough O'Connor made a cattle raid into Meath but on his return "the multitude of beasts in passing the bridge broke the wattles with which it was covered and the bridge was destroyed by the cattle falling into the river." The *cliath droichet* would appear to have been a stronger form, with the wickerwork made of hurdles. The *clar droichet* was undoubtedly made of planks and beams, roughly worked in ancient times with an adze, and in later times sawn and wrought.

The piers of ces droichets were probably large baskets (*cessa*), woven from hazel, rowan or sally rods. Evans[8] describes how these were constructed by sticking stout rods in the ground and bending them over, when the sides were finished, to form the bottom. They could be made single or double and loosely or tightly woven according to requirements. These *cessa* or "kishes" would then be floated into position and filled with stones to form piers in groups and layers. In deeper water they were probably kept in position by large stones ("rip raps") and/or where possible by stakes. The decks, probably in the range of 6ft to 10ft long, were composed of young trees laid longitudinally, tied horizontally and secured to the kishes. The decking consisted of wickerwork sheets covered with twigs and scraggy sods (see Drumheriff Bridge).

The *cliath droichet* was a stronger version of the *ces droichet*. It is likely that sections of river within kingdoms were spanned by more durable bridges. The annals imply that the great rivers forming boundaries between the provinces were rarely bridged for fear of invasion and cattle raids.

CLAR DROICHET

An Slighe Mhór (great highway) in ancient Ireland ran along the Eiscer Riada from either Tara or Áth Cliath to Clarinbridge, Co. Galway, which was then called Áth Cliath Meadhraige. It would appear that the name was changed when the ford was upgraded by the erection of a small timber bridge. *Clairín* is the diminutive of *clar* and both should be distinguished from *clara*, a plain. Joyce[9] explains that *clar* means literally a board and is applied to flat pieces of land in many counties, e.g. Ballyclare, Claragh, Clara; however, in some places it signifies the ford of the plank, e.g. Clare, which takes its name from the village where the original stemmed from planks across the Fergus, likewise Claregalway, Belclare, Abington (Droichead a Chlair).

In early Christian Ireland it is probable that some monastic scholars were acquainted with Caesar's *De Bello Gallico*, in which there is a short technical description of the timber bridge he built across the Rhine near Cologne in 55 BC (fig. 8). The supporting piles (20in. square) were raked and braced. The bridge had fenders, that is, piles upstream, to protect the supports from tree trunks floated down by the enemy. The transoms were 30in. square, on which rested longitudinal beams supporting a deck surfaced with fascines. (The passage, considered one of the most difficult to translate in all Caesar's writings was, at one time, a favourite of examiners.)

Most bridges throughout Europe in the early medieval period were constructed of timber. They were short-lived and vulnerable to rot, fire and manual destruction but most of all to floods and ice-packs. The pre-Norman bridges across the Liffey referred to in annals and charters are most probably timber ones; these bridges are not described and most of the mentions were incidental; more often than not the word *droichet* is used with no qualifying adjective as to type. The assumption is often made that a bridge was timber in the absence of clear-cut evidence that it was of stone, especially in the period antecedent to the 14th century; this is a mistaken approach, because it discourages searches for archaelogically far more important early stone bridges. Secondary sources often omit crucial phrases when quoting from originals; e.g., James Grace[10] refers to the great flood in the Boyne in 1330 "by which all the bridges on that river except Babes were carried away"; the original Laud manuscript version[11] reads "per quam inundationem omnes pontes tam lapidei quam lignei super dictam

Fig. 8: *Caesar's Bridge over the Rhine, 55 BC*

aquam existentes funditus diruti sunt preter-
quam pontem Babe", indicating that there
were timber bridges across the Boyne in 1330,
which cautions against making assumptions
that Trim* and Slane* Bridges were of stone at
the time.

We find an interesting paragraph in Semple
(1776)[12]: "There have been several methods practised by illiterate country masons who have
built good rough stone bridges over shallow
rivers (under 6ft deep) and some of them in
much deeper water . . . ; first, kesh-work, that
is, a kind of large baskets made of boughs and
branches of trees, about the size of four or five
feet square; these they sink in rows by throwing stones promiscuously into them till they
ground, and then filling them up till the water
is about knee deep, whereon they lay timber
across and so begin to build their piers banking
the kishes all around with other stones and
hard stuff thrown in, in like manner." This
shows that the 11th-century native method of
building timber bridges continued to develop
into the stone bridge era. It also evolved in
Europe and the Orient where the word itself,
kesja, and the Latin *cista* had its origin.

TYPES OF TIMBER

There was no shortage of timber in most
parts of Ireland, especially along the river
basins, up to the 17th century. In bog areas there
were ample supplies of fallen timber such as
bog oak. By the 16th century,[13] the country
was being denuded rapidly for conquest, ship-

building, tanneries, iron works etc. The most
common native species were oak, ash, hazel,
birch, holly, mountain ash, elder (elm had disappeared since the 7th century; beech and lime
were 17th-century importations). The presence
of most of the native species is reflected in
townland names with pre-10th-century first
mentions. For kishes there were abundant
supplies of hazel and birch; for hurdles, ash;
for piles and stakes, oak and elder; for beams,
oak and holly. Holly was used for the fixed-
wheel axles of cars and carts. (Some 2,000 tons
of oak were required to build a ship of war, a
'74-foot', the equivalent of cutting down 40
acres of 100-year-old oak forest.)[14]

Boyer[15], from her research into medieval
bridges in France, came to the conclusion that
timber was by far the most important material
for the building of all kinds of bridges. In
masonry bridges the scaffolding and centering
required enormous quantities; e.g., at Albi 18
cartloads of timber were insufficient for the
repair of one cutwater, and at Romans 33 fir
trees were required for the reconstruction of a
single arch. Gautier in his famous *Traité des Ponts*
(1714) reviewed the history of bridge construction in France in detail, recommending the use
of chestnut for bridges because of its resistence
to rotting and its high compressive strength;
he also advised that trees should be felled in
late autumn or winter. There were extensive
chestnut woods in southern Europe in the
middle ages. The horse chestnut was introduced into Britain around the 16th century,
but no other European tree matches the oak

for strength, durability and hardness. Given the availability of oak in Ireland in early times, there was no shortage of materials for bridge builders and on the larger rivers no timber transport problems.

From the 3rd century BC up to the 7th century AD ogham writing was common in Ireland, as evidenced by many surviving ogham stones. Little[16] refers to a treatise on ogham in the Book of Ballymote in which there is a reference to wicker bridges. Atkinson[17] states that in the "scheme" of McMain in the Ballymote MS: "the 'AE' is formed thus ⊞ i.e. rods wrought in a hurdle as a shield or laid on beams for a bridge." This suggests that the model for the letters was a *ces droichet*, which means that these were common in the pre-Viking period. Many kinds of trees are mentioned in the ancient treatise in explaining the symbols for other letters: "royal trees are the elm, oak, hazel, vine, ivy, blackthorn, broom, spine. . ." .

DESTRUCTION OF TIMBER BRIDGES

It is noteworthy that most of the late medieval coast roads shown on the earliest maps crossed the estuaries at some miles upriver. The location of some bridges, such as those at Limerick and Waterford, was obviously the lowest at which it would have been feasible to cross; however, the choice of location on some smaller bridges is puzzling. From Home[18] we know that timber bridges erected across the Thames estuary in London in the 12th century lasted only a few decades.

In the 1930s some new timber piles in the Shannon estuary were attacked by "the gribble," a marine borer. A recent US road research report[19] on the underwater inspection and repair of bridge substructures devoted a whole section to the problem of the destruction of wood members by marine borers, namely the *Toredo navalis* (shipworm) and the *Limnoria lignorum* (gribble). The former is a mollusk whose larvae tunnel from the outside and, once inside, grow rapidly, whereas the latter eat away the timber from the surface. Both operate between the bed level and maximum high tide. A 1936 paper[20] on research into the deterioration of marine structures showed that both borers existed in all temperate and hot climates but do not live in muddy or fresh water and do not flourish in brackish water. In Arklow, however, piles on the river side of a harbour-wall were not infested, whereas the adjacent piles on the sea-side was riddled. This indicates that fresh water containing sulphate of copper and of iron prevented the growth of the borers. Arklow is one of the few estuaries where an early bridge crossing is close to the sea. (The present 13-arch bridge built in 1746 replaced an earlier one. Wickerwork mats were found under some piers during underpinning work in the 1970s. No information was found concerning the old bridge shown on Moll's 1714 map; it may have been a timber bridge like that at Enniscorthy*, as there is a fortification pier in the centre of the present bridge.)

Semple tells us that oak piles driven in Dublin harbour in 1725 rotted and decayed in a very short period as a result of worm-infestation. He also mentions that the Venetians scorched their piles and timber until they had a hard black crust and that the Dutch coated theirs with a mixture of pitch and tar covered with powdered shells and sea sand. He describes the worms as breeding like "mites in cheese" and growing to a quarter of a inch long and one tenth of an inch thick; he also believed that "sappy timber" was the cause of worm infestation.

The question remains as to whether these borers were active in Irish estuaries in the medieval period remains. Halliday's *Scandinavian Kingdom of Dublin*[21] quotes the city assembly rolls for 17 October 1729 as recording that pile frames in the harbour wall extension were "very much decayed by worms"; A paper dating from 1847[22] stated that *Toredo* and *Limnoria* "infested our shores" at that time and had been causing great damage to piers and jetties. It referred to a tract published in 1733 by Sellius on the history of the *Toredo*, following the destruction of piles in Holland and quoted from a paper read before the Royal Society, in 1834 to the effect that the *Toredo navalis* (mostly small specimens) was obtained from the bough of a tree found embedded in blue clay, 12ft beneath the surface, during recent excavations of Dunbar dock in Belfast. He concluded that it was deposited in the place of its discovery at a very remote period. We have to be careful in interpreting finds of this nature without evidence of sediment deposition and sea levels but it would appear that the Toredo was active in Irish estuaries for the past millenium.

The Romans sheeted their ships with copper for protection against marine borers; and the problem has not gone away: the US report referred to above states that no wood is immune to marine-borer attack; not even modern creosote, the most effective of all preservatives, is resistant to *Limnoria* into the wood unless components toxic to it and the *Toredo* are impregnated. Since the 1930s most marine structures in Ireland have been constructed of reinforced concrete or steel sheet piling; hence there have been few investigations of borers. It is a topic worthy of historical research because it would appear that it has had a very significant effect, not alone on bridges but on the location of towns on tidal estuaries. The salinity (35 grams/litre for sea water) reduces considerably as one moves inland along estuaries of large rivers; and because the borers have body fluids which are isotonic with seawater they are unable to adjust to changes at the saline inter-face. They are, of course, powerful scavengers, as one can see by picking up and examining fragments of driftwood along our shores.

In Part II a number of timber bridges for which reliable information has been found are described. Some may never have been built, e.g. Enniscorthy*; some were destroyed in battle, O'Brien's; others required acts of parliament, Cappoquin*; one was the subject of a superb archaelogical paper, Cashen*; most had short lives and brief historical mentions. In connection with stone bridges, mentions of timber are also found because it was used for temporary repair of a collapsed stone arch, sometimes with disastrous effects, as in 1282 at Thomond (old) Bridge, Limerick*. In the middle ages it was a convention of war that damaged masonry arches could not be repaired with stone without the agreement of the enemy.

CHAPTER 8

Mortar

Mortar is defined as the matrix used in the beds and joints of masonry to adhere and bind, fill the voids and distribute pressure. The principal binder in the matrix is commonly described as cement, but nowadays this word has become synonymous with Portland cement, invented in 1824 by Joseph Aspdin and so called because of its resemblance, when set, to the building limestone from Portland Island. The binding agent we are concerned with here is lime, obtained by calcining carbonate of lime ($CaCO_3$) to expel carbon dioxide (CO_2) and obtain quicklime (CaO). Quicklime from the kiln is slaked with water to obtain $Ca(OH)_2$, hydroxide of lime, generally described as hydrated lime. The principal source of $CaCO_3$ is and has been limestone, chalk and oyster shells (which produce limes that are almost 99 per cent pure and are called "fat," "rich" etc.). Impure limes derive from limestones, but these may also contain silica and alumina, which can combine with lime when hydrated giving it properties like those of Portland cement. Such limes are known as "hydraulic" because they set under water.

There is little doubt among archaeologists and historians of the early Christian period in Ireland that all of the many stone churches and monastic buildings up to AD 800 were unmortared. The date of the introduction of lime mortar is still a matter of contention. Leask [1] our foremost authority, concluded that "building in mortar for Ireland may be hypothecated for perhaps the 7th century but certainly in the succeeding 100 years." Champneys [2] expressed the view that few Irish buildings in stone and mortar could be earlier than the 10th or 11th centuries. Petrie placed the date between the 5th and 7th centuries. No scientific paper on the history of lime mortar in Ireland has been located.

Throughout continental Europe, Britain and the Middle East there are numerous remains of stone buildings erected by the Romans with lime mortar and with Roman cement. Literature on the composition of these binders is mainly derived from one famous source, Vitruvius' *Ten Books on Architecture*.[3] Vitruvius, writing probably in the first century BC, devotes seven short chapters to brick, sand, lime, pozzolana, stone, methods of building walls, and timber. He states that lime should be burned from a stone that is white and, after slaking, the mortar should be made of three parts pit-sand and one part lime, or two parts river or sea sand to one of lime; he suggests the addition of a third part, of burnt brick, pounded up and sifted, as a way of improving the latter mix. Pozzolana he describes as a powder found in the neighbourhood of Mount Vesuvius, which when mixed with lime and rubble not only lends strength to buildings but also sets under water. He advances some fanciful hypotheses about the origin of the volcanic ash and how it makes the substances recombine and cohere when water is added, but as we now know the basic constituents were alumina, silica from volcanic ash, and calcined lime; these are the basic ingredients of modern cement.

Casey[4] states that Vitruvius was "a standard classic of Irish eighteenth century architectural literature". Sterpos states that after the beginning of the second century AD the vaults of small Roman bridges tended to be of (pozzolanic) concrete with facings of stone. In the major earlier Roman bridges, the stone voussoirs were cut so accurately that only very thin films of mortar was needed in the joints. The great Roman road network (some 50,000 miles in length) built between 312 BC and AD 476 contained thousands of bridges, including several famous ones, such as Rimini, which have survived in whole or in part to the present day. Analyses of the mortars from such bridges have shown that they were more or less similar to those used in the 18th century and that the constituents were largely in accordance with Vitruvius. Many books on the Roman roads give the impression that they had massively thick pavements with four layers—the *statumen*, a layer of large flat stones 10 to 24in. thick; the *rudus*, a 9in. course of small stones mixed with lime; a *nucleus*, composed of fine gravel and sand mixed with hot lime about 12in. thick; and a *summa crusta*, or topping, of the well-known polygonal flags. Recent recent research in Italy has shown that this construction was used only in the centre of Rome and that most of the rural network was built with local broken stone paved on top with flags.

The mortar used in the pyramids of Egypt was calcined gypsum ($CaSO_4$). The temperature required to calcine it was much lower than for lime (160^0C v. 900^0C) and needed far less fuel, which was scarce in Egypt.

CLAY MORTAR

Reverting to the the early Christian period in Ireland, Stokes [6] states that Irish Romanesque "is marked by the introduction of cement [i.e. lime mortar] and embraces those churches in which there are but slight traces of mortar down to those of a later period in which the stones were regularly bedded."

There is an ancient church at Raholp in Co. Down known as "An Teampal Maol", described by Bigger [7], who states that its construction and features are most unusual for Ulster because "no mortar was in the masonry but there was clay." This is the only reference to clay mortar found in an extensive search of literature on early Irish ecclesiastical buildings. As might be expected, there is no shortage of mentions of its use in dwelling houses. O'Donachair [8] gives a good description of the traditional methods employed in the construction of mud-walled cabins with *daib* in the 18th and 19th centuries: the top soil was removed and the yellow clay dug up, the lumps broken and stones picked out. Water was added and the mixture kneaded to the consistency of dough, sometimes by bare feet, sometimes by animals. Binding material was added, usually

straw or rushes, sometimes hay, twigs or furze. In many places lime was mixed into the clay and added, sometimes animal blood, cow dung, ashes, or milk. The mixture was left to temper for several days with periodic rekneading. Walls or joints in stone work built of clay mortar needed frequent coats of limewash to keep them dry.

Stokes states that the mortar used by early builders near the sea coast often contained shells and sea sand, whilst inland a compound of mud and gravel was used. In many cases the wall appeared to have been built dry and the mortar poured in a liquid state to filter through from the top. Later the walls were well built with a rubble core which was grouted in a similar manner. By 950 the stones were being "well bedded in good mortar".

LIME BURNING

The earliest inhabitants of Ireland and Britain lived near the sea and consumed a lot of fish as evidenced by middens. Because the sand itself contained a high percentage of calcareous fragments, when fires were lit on it repetitiously some would be calcined and tend to bind the sand thereby providing evidence of it potential as a mortar. Lime from oyster shells is almost 99 per cent pure $CaCO_3$ (the huge oyster beds on the gulf coast of the USA are still the principal source of lime in that area). Alberti [9] mentions that near Vannes in France on the sea shore "for want of stone they make their lime of oyster and cockle shells."

The earliest reference to a limekiln in the Irish annals is in the Annals of the Four Masters under 1163 (see Appendix 1); it measured 70 ft, in "every direction", presumably in plan. Such a large kiln would suggest that the state of the art of lime burning was well advanced in 11th-century Ireland, but the fact of mention in the annals indicates that this was a rare and important structure. The round towers provide incontrovertible evidence as to the early use of lime mortar throughout the island. Harbison [10] states that all of the 65 surviving towers were most probably erected in the period AD 900 –1200. Barrow [11] suggests that the first one, which became a model, probably dates from sometime in the 7th century.

Stokes provides a very helpful table [12] showing a broad visual classification of 51 round towers into four styles by shape and texture

First Style	Second style	Third Style	Fourth Style
Rough field stones untouched by hammers or chisel, not rounded, but fitted by their length to the curve of the wall, roughly coursed, wide-jointed, with spalds or small stones fitted into the interstices. Mortar, of course, unsifted sand or squared courses.	Stones roughly hammer-dressed, rounded to the curve of the wall, decidedly though somewhat irregularly coursed. Spalds, but often badly bonded together. Mortar freely used.	Stones laid in horizontal courses well-dressed and carefully worked to the round and batter, the whole cemented in strong plain mortar of lime and sand.	Strong, rough but excellent ashlar masonry, rather open-jointed, and therefore closely analogous to the English-Norman masonry of the 12th century; or, in some instances, finest possible examples of well-dressed ashlar. Sandstone in gravel.

Fig. 9: *Visual Classification of 51 Round Towers by Masonry Style (Source: Stokes)*

of stones, by apertures and by nature of the mortar. Fig 9. is reproduced because it gives a good idea of the types of masonry to be expected in the piers and spandrel walls of bridges of the period.

The classification reflects the appearance and condition of ruins before the repairs of the last 100 years were carried out. One of the conclusions drawn by Stokes was that the towers were built after the Irish became acquainted with the use of "cement" (i.e. lime mortar). The same towers may ultimately provide the answers to when and how the Irish made mortar for building purposes during the four centuries preceding the Norman invasion. In this connection, the National Monuments Section of the Office of Public Works are to be commended for co-operating in a major USA university research project aimed at the development of a computerised carbon-style dating process for establishing the age of lime mortar. Samples from the interiors of early towers and churches of authenticated decade of construction, such as Cormac's Chapel, have been provided for model calibration purposes. This work may yield an inexpensive, reliable method for dating bridges and other artifacts. Fig. 10 shows the masonry in Donaghmore round tower, ascribed to the 11th century.

Dating individual round towers by a broad classification of masonry style is fraught with risk because a monastery raided by natives of Vikings would be impoverished and yet have the greatest need of a tower; consequently a late tower might be built in a more primitive style. There is evidence of this in Drumlane,

Co. Cavan, where the first 27ft are composed of fine ashlar-faced sandstone, whereas the upper 16ft it is in roughly coursed but well bonded limestone, a reversal of the expected order. The same happened sometimes with bridges.

The location of early lime-kilns or burning sites can sometimes be determined from townland names. Joyce [13] explains that the Irish word *teine-aoil* is derived from *teine* (fire) and *ael* (lime) signifying "fire of lime". In the anglicised form, the ending is usually "eel". Quicklime is *aol beo* (beo = alive), a sensible compound to anyone who had experience in handling quicklime. The word *sorn*, which means furnace or oven, is also used. In the past 50 years many sites of limekilns have been filled in the course of road-widening schemes. Under 13 & 14 Geo. III c.32 (1774), any person who built a limekiln within 50 yards of any road could be fined a sum not exceeding *10s*. (Grand juries were also empowered to present at the assizes for the pulling down of any kiln erected within this distance after 1774.)

Mentions of lime-burning occur here and there in the literature down through the centuries. In an Irish pipe roll of King John [14] payments are recorded of "2s. to a lyme-burner of Athboy" and "6s. 8d. to a lyme-burner between Castleknock and Clonee." No quantities or days are given but the mention indicates that it was a specialist craft and that locals were recruited for repair work to castles following a destructive military campaign. Some idea of the value of the payment can be had from another item in the same roll recording the payment of £45

6s. 8d. for 272 cows, that is 3s. 4d. each. The Dublin man obviously got two cows for his work.

There can be little doubt that during the 13th and 15th centuries there was a widespread demand for lime for town walls and for the thousands of castles erected throughout the country. Given the plentiful supply of timber and the prevalence of carboniferous limestone deposits in almost every county, there would have been little difficulty in procuring supplies. In such circumstances references to kilns or lime would be incidental.

Archaeological excavations by Drogheda Corporation along the route of a proposed new road in the 1970s revealed a 40ft length of the old town wall, which was excavated under the direction of K. Campbell. The findings mention that a limekiln associated with the construction of the wall was found nearby and cut into 13th-century deposits.[15]

Alberti devotes a chapter to lime and plaster of Paris. It begins with a discussion of the different sorts of stone used in making lime in Italy, the best being judged to be "that which loses a third part of its weight by burning". He mentions that he had observed architects in France using only river stone as the source of lime because "it has preserved an extraordinary strength to a very great age". Based on his own experience he recommends that lime be carried immediately out of the kiln into a shady, dry place and watered; he cautions against leaving it exposed, especially in summer, as "it would soon crumble to powder." He mentions that the stone is not burnt enough till the kiln, which had been swelled and cracked, settles and closes. Remarkably, he makes no reference to lime or mortar in the chapter on bridges both of wood and stone.

Palladio (1508–80) also discusses [16] lime and the method of working it into mortar, repeating the principal points made by Alberti but mentioning that it took 60 hours to calcine most types of stone. One sentence, however, is innovative and important: "There is also a spongy sort of stone, the lime of which is very good for covering and rough-casting of walls; a scaly rugged stone taken out of the hills of Padua [his native town] that makes an excellent lime for such buildings as are most exposed to the weather, or stand under water, because it immediately sets, grows hard and is very lasting." This was obviously an eminently hydraulic lime. Palladio make no mention of lime or mortar in his twelve chapters on bridges.

From the foregoing it is quite evident why George Semple said he received no help from these books when designing the foundations for Essex Bridge in 1752. In any case it is doubtful if stonemasons in Ireland were conversant with either Alberti or Palladio in the 17th century. Hydraulic mortar must have been used in the foundations and piers of such bridges as Babes*, Thomond old*, Slane*, Adare*, Leighlin*

Fig. 10: *Masonry Donaghmore Round Tower (pre-11th Century)*

Athlone*; otherwise they would not have survived for long.

Sir Peter Lewys, the builder of the 1567 bridge at Athlone*, recorded in his meticulously kept diary that £12. 7s. 2d. was spent on the wages of lime-burners. Three were employed—one at 12d. for 405 days, one at 9d. per day for 30 days, and one at 4d. for 188 days. Four 'collyers' were employed for 327 days at 4d. per day, presumably to keep the fuel supplied for the kilns, for the forges and other fires. There would have been no difficulty in procuring good limestone in the area, but it may have had to be hauled by boat or cart to a bridge-site kiln. Wilkinson, in his classic work (1845)[17] reports that the "lime of good quality is abundant at Athlone; costs 1s. to 1s. 6d. per barrel, depending on the season of the year . . .The Rathcondra stone produces the best lime which is sold in the town (Mullingar) at about 1s. 3d. per barrel. The Donore lime is also very good, and possesses hydraulic properties." He also records that at Boyle in Roscommon "excellent lime is abundant"—all of which suggests that the calp limestones were a source of good lime even though the quality might vary somewhat; and also that in some places it had hydraulic properties—a rare mention of this characteristic, which was not so important for buildings on dry land but vital for bridge piers and foundations.

Practically no information on lime or mortar was found in the 17th-century literature. This is surprising, because there was very considerable building activity in the first and third quarters. The 1685 report of Thomas Philips (see Chapter 3) contains detailed estimates for fortification works amounting to a million pounds; neither lime nor mortar is referred to; they seem to have been taken for granted in the many descriptions of proposed stone masonry work. An entry in the Council Book of the Corporation of Youghal[18] in 1613 refers to an agreement that William Greatrackes shall, for 15 years, supply the mayor with "well burnt lime at 20d. for every Bristol band barrel upheaped, and two gallons over said measure to every barrel of unslacked lime and 12d. for every barrel of slacked lime". There was a provision that for any lime required for the town walls, or other public work, the mayor would be supplied with unslaked lime at 16d. and slaked at 8d. per barrel. In consideration of this the supplier was given a monopoly within

the town and was freed from paying custom on the lime and given permission to "set up a lime kiln and burn lime with said Corporation". Sir Richard Boyle and "other statesmen" were excepted from the requirement to buy from Greatrackes and were also free to burn lime themselves. The entry gives a good idea of how lime supplies were provided in some corporate towns in the 17th century.

A record in the Council Book of Cork Corporation[19] a century later (1713) contains a very vital piece of information from the aspect of mortar. In relation to the arrangement for building the new stone South Bridge, it states that the corporation shall give the contractors, Thomas Chatterton, mason and John Coltsman, stone cutter, "all the tarras left of the North Bridge" (erected in 1711/12). This is the earliest mention of tarras in the literature. Sometimes called tarass or terres, it is a tufa volcanic stone found in the fragmented state in Andernach near Coblenz on the Rhine, where it was ground and exported as a hydraulic cement. Like pozzolana, it contained about 50 per cent silica, 20 per cent alumina and some iron and lime. Andernach was a flourishing town in Roman times and in medieval periods.

Ormond Bridge on the Liffey, built in timber in 1682, was rebuilt in stone in 1684. It had five arches and lasted until 1802 when it collapsed in a flood. A replacement, Richmond Bridge, was built in 1816 on a new location 150ft upriver at a cost of £25,800 (renamed in 1923 O'Donovan Rossa Bridge). There is a woodcut of the 1684 bridge showing it in a collapsed state, from which it is evident that scour of the foundations was the most probable cause. George Semple, asked to inspect the bridge in 1752, gives a detailed description of his investigation in his book *Building in Water*.[20] He found that the south pier had greatly failed: "The bed of the river on which it stood was washed away and the first course of the stone work also for about 7ft under the pier, and part of the second course, that part of the pier had no support but the strength of the mortar and the bond of the work." Elsewhere he states that the mortar had "exceeding great strength". This finding is important in the present context because it indicates that the mortar used in 1684 must have had good hydraulic qualities to retain its strength in salty water.

The year 1750 is a significant one in Irish

public works because from that year onwards until the Act of Union annual surpluses in the exchequer began to accrue and to be applied to building projects both public and private as described in Chapter 6. We are fortunate in having a first-class account of the local state of the art in relation to lime, mortar and grout in Semple's book. The chapter on these materials is reproduced in Appendix 5. Before his dissertation is analysed, it is necessary to dispose of some myths which were prevalent at the time and which were only established as such in the following hundred years culminating with the invention of the prototype of modern cement by I.C. Johnson in 1845.

The state of the art in relation to mortar was thoroughly analysed by an American engineer in a book published in 1845 in Edinburgh, Dublin and London.[21] The book was popular in Ireland at the time, as evidenced by the fact that many copies have survived (see Appendix 5). Mahon incorporated the principal findings of French research on roads and bridges (including those of Szanzin and Vicat). Vicat had developed a controlled method of manufacturing hydraulic limes between 1812 and 1818. The proportion of SiO_2, Al_2O_3 and CaO were predetermined in the process.

De Courcy[22] has traced the development and use of concrete in Ireland, stating that he found no mention of the use of Portland cement concrete here before 1850. One can safely assume therefore that with a few exceptions Portland cement concrete had not displaced mortar for bridge-building purposes here until after the 1850s.

The following summary of the Mahon extracts shows that the state of knowledge in the 1840s and helps in the interpretation of practices and properties mentioned by Semple but not understood in the 1750s: Lime is divided by engineers into two classes: "common lime" and hydraulic or water lime. Mortar of common lime will never harden under water or in very moist places and is only suitable for dry positions and thin walls, whereas hydraulic lime yields a mortar which sets readily and soon becomes nearly as hard as stone in all moist situations. The simplest method of testing consists of calcining a small of the stone over a common fire on a plate of iron, slaking it and kneading it into a thick paste, which is then placed in a glass and covered with water. If within a few days it has not set, it is common lime; if it hardens, it is hydraulic and its quality will be indicated by the quickness with which it hardens. Artificial hydraulic lime can be made equal in quality to the best natural varieties. Previously, great importance was attached to the methods of slaking the lime, but the inefficacy of any of these methods for the improvement of mortar, according to Mahon, had long been established and engineers no longer paid regard to them. There was no subject with which more ingenuity had been uselessly expended than upon that of mortar. Misled by erroneous interpretations of Vitruvius, various hypotheses were formed to explain the superior properties of the mortar found in ancient edifices but these had never been subjected to rational analysis. It was now beyond doubt that the methods of slaking, mixing the ingredients, and age are not the causes of great strength. No perfectly satisfactory explanation had yet been given for the hardening of either common or hydraulic mortar.

On the basis of the foregoing it is possible to dismiss much of the subjective from Semple's dissertation and reach to the core of his findings which, in the light of Mahon, go a long way to explain the durability of the mortar in Essex and other bridges described in Part II. Semple explained that he has long experience of making mortar and had carried out many experiments. He asserted that, if prepared properly, mortar will almost turn to "the consistence of stone". In support of this he states:

In pulling down [1689] Essex Bridge and repairing Ormond Bridge [1684] we found the mortar of the lower courses of the piers better cemented to the stones, than it was in the upper works.

There are several sorts of limestone; some, indeed, set much sooner and harder under water than others; but any good lime properly mixed and tempered with clean sharp sand, will bind and cement as effectually under water as above it.

Chalk will make lime, it will neither polish nor make good lime for any purpose. . . . Rich mortar will not stand the weather so well nor grow so hard as poor mortar will do.

It is not within my province to account for the petrifying qualities of limestone, lime or lime water . . . . It is sufficient for my present purpose that they may have these petrifying qualities, to great degrees, but all sorts of limestones do not have in the same proportion, yet I believe no limestone whatever can have more excellent qualities than such as we have, in perhaps, every county in the Kingdom: and indeed, it has some useful qualities not much known—for instance, our limestone will make exceeding good tarass for water works.

Semple makes no mention of the source of the lime used in Essex Bridge, foundations or elsewhere, nor of the source of the limestone from which it was burned. However, he indicates that he got the roach (unslaked) lime hot from the kiln, so it can be safely assumed that it was Dublin calp limestone.

There is a list of quarries in Dublin county in an essay[23] written by John Rutty in 1771. Among his comments on limestone I found the following: " v.g. that from Sutton, approaching to Marble, and makes a stronger Cement, like Terras, and enduring under water as Gypsum . . .". In a footnote he states that a Dr Short "remarks that the dark brown, the grey, blackish and jet-black limestone, though difficult and expensive to burn, is seldom used but for building bridges or churches, because it presently turns hard after burning and is of perpetual duration, even more lasting than the stone itself, neither air, time nor weather weakening its cement."

Semple's conclusions and recommendations, coupled with the statements of Mahon, indicate that most of the limes burned from native limestone, particularly the calps, had moderately hydraulic properties, and that these sources were well known, having been established empirically over the centuries, perhaps from early Christian times.

The durability of the mortar used in Semple's bridge was endorsed by a decision of the Dublin Port & Docks Board to retain the "thorough foundations" when the superstructure was taken down and replaced for functional reasons.[24] Unequal settlement, found to have occurred in some of the piers, was rectified by a tapering course of masonry below the springing of the new and flatter semi-elliptical arches. The new arches up to high water level were built with Portland cement and above that a 1 (Portland cement) 3 (lime) 12 (sand) mix was used; this being more plastic, it

adhered to the almost vertical sides of the arches near the crown. The joints on the intrados were pointed with Medina quick-setting cement to prevent from being washed out at high tides during construction.

Wilkinson includes a description of the geology and lists of sources of stone masonry, flagging, bricks, lime and sand in each county in Ireland. His book is also an excellent source of information on the quality, availability and price of lime for the period. Wilkinson, an architect, geologist and antiquary, was involved in the design and construction of the massive workhouses all over the country in the 1840s, so he had detailed and accurate local knowledge. His general comment is:

Much variety occurs in the limestone throughout Ireland, some producing a very meagre lime requiring two or three measures or bushels of lime to one of sand and this is particularly the case with some of the primary limestone in which the silex (S_1O_2) appears mechanically united and on burning runs to sand while others of a fat rich quality will make equally good mortar with three or four parts of sand to one part of lime. Hydraulic limes, or limes which will make a mortar to set under water, are also met with but no extensive formation is known whence hydraulic lime can be obtained. Beds of the calp limestone have been extensively used on the Shannon in the works under the Shannon Commissioners which have produced good hydraulic mortar but the quality of the lime varies within limited areas and even in the same bed.

An analysis of Wilkinson's county reports shows that Wicklow, the only county without limestone, imported it from Howth (Co. Dublin) and neighbouring countries. On the west promontory of Howth, he records, there are two varieties of limestone, one darkish blue and the other a grey magnesian limestone which makes good cement of hydraulic property. Based on his subjective description 10 counties had very good or excellent sources and 14 had good ones, leaving 8 with fair or no local supplies.

A few years after Semple had finished Essex Bridge, John Smeaton conducted many experiments for the purpose of finding a durable mortar for Eddystone lighthouse, which he had been commissioned to design. He investigated the mortar used in the construction of early Norman building in England, including Salisbury cathedral. Eventually he selected the well-known hydraulic lime from Aberthaw and pozzolana from Italy, and designed a mixture containing all the ingredients of modern cement. In 1796 J. Parker patented a Roman cement which he made a calcining concretions of clay and calcareous matter found in the south of England. He ground the resultant product of reddish colour and believed he had discovered the cement used by the Romans. It was in fact an eminently hydraulic lime.

Mention must be made of lime for agricultural purposes which was extensively used in Ireland for many centuries. Arthur Young reported that in the 1770s it was made at sites along bogs close to cheap fuel sources. The statistical surveys carried out in most counties in the first quarter of the 19th century contain many references to lime-burning for agricultural purposes.

In the 1860s, when parts of the retaining walls of Ringsend causeway, erected in 1748, began to collapse, the chief engineer of Dublin Port and Docks, Bindon Stoney, investigated the causes and noticed that the mortar in the walls below high-water mark was like soft putty which became friable when dried and without any bonding property. He consulted an experienced colleague who confirmed his own conclusion that purer limes when in contact with sea water for a lengthy period are liable to alteration in their chemical constituents. Not satisfied with generalized causes, he mentioned the problem of Professor Apjon, at Trinity College, who offered to analyse specimens.

Stoney presented the finding of the investigation in an 1862 paper.[25] It showed that the hydraulic property of a lime was very dependent on "the amount of soluble silicic acid because the induration depends on the presence of silicate of lime which it must of necessity form". The comparison between samples of mortar from above and below high water showed that chloride of magnesium in the sea water gradually converted the silicate of lime into soluble calcium chloride. Professor Apjon's analyses also showed that lime calcined from Dublin calp limestone was only moderately hydraulic and in such situations eminently, hydraulic lime was needed. Stoney recommended the use of Portland cement in mortars for marine work.

The findings of Stoney's investigation cause one to wonder what is the present condition of the mortar in Semple's through foundation and in other underwater pre-1875 stonework in Dublin and other estuaries round the country.

Over the past quarter-century much research has been carried out in the USA and elsewhere on the use of lime and lime-pozzolana for the stabilisation of soils for road and airport runway bases and sub-bases. The literature shows that the pozzolanic reaction is still not fully understood, that the strength continues to increase albeit slowly until all the free lime is used up, and this more rapid in hot climates. Pozzolans, with the exception of some volcanic dusts, must be ground very fine, to a surface area of 3,000 sq. in. per gram, to enable it to react properly with calcium hydroxide at ordinary temperatures.[26] This explains the benefit of the pounding of the calp quicklime recommended by George Semple in 1753.

CHAPTER 9

Stone Bridges

In early medieval Ireland stone bridges were commonly referred to by the terms *cloch droichet* (stone bridge) and *droichet cloch aeltra*, the (stone-and-lime bridge)[1]. However, *cloch droichet* often embraces both types, the annalists' main object being to stress that a bridge was made of stone. (We have the boast of Aed Allán king of Ireland 734–43), that he would build "marvellously a bridge across the Boyne at Clonard in such a manner that his name would live forever"[2]. We do not know if his ambition was fulfilled.)

"IRISH BRIDGES"

Before discussing the development of stone bridges it might be useful at this point to explain the term "Irish bridge" which has caused confusion over the years (the writers have had queries about it from places as far apart as Israel and India). The "Irish bridge" is defined[3] as: "A paved ford incorporating pipes to take the dry weather flow." Appendix 6 shows one conforming to this definition constructed in recent years by our Forestry Department in Co. Wicklow. In simple terms, the water flows over the bridge when river levels exceed those of normal dry weather periods. The specific term seems to have originated in an Indian military engineering manual in the 19th century, but the concept is much older; in fact it is one of fundamental importance from the aspect of engineering economy.

In the Annals of the Four Masters it is recorded that in 1253 "a great *leat* or drought prevailed in this summer so that the people crossed the principal rivers of Ireland with dry feet." If we go to the other extreme, we have the example of the "Hurricane Charlie" offshoot on 25/26 August 1986, when some modern bridges in the Dublin-Wicklow area became "Irish bridges" for 24 hours or so, the best example being Ballsbridge over the Dodder, in Dublin; excluding the effect of damaged bridges, flooding at bridges caused considerable disruption of traffic with resultant economic loss on the morning of 26 August, but such loss would have been negligible given the same bridges and floods in medieval times. It is obvious therefore that in building a bridge both the medieval stonemason and the 20th-century engineer faced an important question: how often can disruption of traffic by water flowing over the bridge be tolerated? The answer in either case is dictated by the funds available.

In the early medieval period in Ireland most bridges had no parapets and were described in English as "unbattlemented" and in Irish as *maol* (terms are borrowed from descriptions of castles). A later example was the Ormond Bridge* over the Liffey erected in 1684, which lasted until 1812. The omission of parapets was due not to lack of funds but, to the knowledge that a narrow bridge with parapet walls was more likely to be washed away in severe floods. In the grand jury records (Meath) for the period 1750–1850 several entries provided for the erection of an "additional arch" at various bridge-locations such as at Dardistown on the Nanny River. Clearly, people's toleration of travel disruption decreased as time passed. A river crossing could be impassible for weeks in early times and cause little inconvenience. As journey-time expectations diminished, especially from the 17th century onwards, bridges with greater water discharge capacities, i.e. additional or larger arches, became necessary

McEvoy, writing in 1802, gives a good description of this "bridge philosophy"[4]. "I have introduced, in the neighbourhood I live

[Tyrone], a species of bridge some years ago which I find to answer extremely well for a small mountainy brook. When the water is low, the whole of it passed under; and in times of flood, part goes under, and part over the bridge. The passenger, notwithstanding, is seldom stopped, as mountainy floods soon subside; they seldom last longer than an hour or two; and in roads not very public, it seldom happens that any person may go that way during the flood; and, in case a person should pass during that time, if on horseback he may ford it; if on foot, there are stepping stones convenient." The cost of such a bridge was one third that of an arch; and if well executed, these bridges seldom called for repair (a detailed sketch of the structure is reproduced from McEvoy in Appendix 6). McEvoy does not the use the term "Irish bridge" and refers to the stone gullet as a "pipe"; moreover, the stepping stones would seldom have been as high as he implies.

CLAPPERS

Most people are familiar with the famous clapper bridges in the south of England; "clapper" comes from the Latin *claperium*, a pile of stones. The most notable example is the much-photographed Post Bridge in Dartmoor composed of cyclopean stone piers and monolithic slabs of granite of up to 12ft x 6ft. A detailed description of the Irish equivalent, a clochan, across the Camoge river at ancient Knockainey* in Co. Limerick, has survived. This clochan was bypassed by a small reinforced concrete bridge in 1924 and removed under drainage works in 1931. It may have been rebuilt and improved over the centuries, but it is typical of what must have been the first type of stone bridge built in Ireland.

What may be an early Norman equivalent of Knockainey survives in Ballybeg*, Buttevant, Co. Cork. Four spans remain. The longest limestone flags measure 112in. x 48in. x 7 in. The adjoining friary of St Thomas was founded in 1229 and the bridge is believed to date from the same century, though no specific early mentions of it have been found.

EVOLUTION OF STONE ARCHES IN IRELAND

We come now to the question: were there stone arch bridges in Ireland before the coming of the Normans in 1169? Petrie[5] says that "the origin of stone bridges in Ireland is not very accurately determined, but this much at least appears certain—that none of any importance were erected previous to the 12th century"(the 12th century presumably because the Cistercians came in 1148 and the Normans in 1169).

Joyce[6] seems to support him: "*Droichet* as it is given in Cormac's Glossary or, in modern Irish *droichead*, is the word universally employed to denote a bridge and under this name bridges are mentioned in our oldest authorities. It is almost certain however that these structures were of wood and that bridges with stone arches were not built till after the arrival of the Anglo Norman."

Although these are opinions of eminent archaelogical and literary authorities, to the writers, as engineers, it seemed presumptuous to state that an ancient nation with a tradition of building in stone going back to 3000 BC would not have evolved the stone arch form of construction following the discovery or introduction of lime mortar (see Chapter 8). Moreover, given how widely Irish monks travelled throughout the continent of Europe there can be little doubt that information on stone arches found its way to Ireland particularly between AD 500 and 800. The Vikings, originating in Scandinavia, caused interruptions in communications between 800 and 1000 but they also must have accumulated information on stone building in Normandy and in other parts of Gaul, although their traditional building material was timber. It has been said that Ireland and Britain in the medieval and earlier periods were in a climatic zone where the timber tradition of the colder northern European countries met the stone tradition of the warmer north Mediterranean regions and that this was reflected in the native architecture.

Lugli's authoritative work on bridges (1957) shows that "the voissoir arch originated independently in various parts of the ancient world, earlier in some places than in others, and always in modest buildings."[7] There is no reason why Lugli's findings should not apply to Ireland, which had never been occupied by the Romans. Most writers on bridges in Britain agree that the Romans did not build stone arch bridges there during the occupation from 55 BC to AD 411. The *pontes lapidei* were timber spans on stone piers.

The statute rolls (1459) mention "the bridge of the Maudelynes" at Duleek, "by which bridge the people have used to pass from time whereof no memory is, and by the default of repairs the said bridge is so ruinous and ill repaired that divers people have fallen from the bridge when the water was high and some of them were engulfed and died and some others in great peril of their lives."[8] The three-arch bridge is still there but is now known as the "De Bath-Dowdall" Bridge from a plaque on it stating that the bridge and causeway were "repaired and builded" in 1587. A close inspection suggests that the upriver section is the original, and most importantly that the arch rings were corbelled for approximately one third of the span from each springing, and that the crowns were closed with radial jointed stones—reminiscent of the supporting arches of the 9th-century stone-roofed churches in Kells and Glendalough, so ably documented by Stokes and Leask. Further research and analysis of photographs indicates that the arches are in the style that Leask christened Irish Romanesque.

The bridge's true name, "St Mary Magdalen", suggested that it was erected c.1200 when Norman land grants to support leper hospitals and bridges were made in many parts of Ireland, evidenced by the Maudlin townlands. This was in the tradition of the "Peace of God" movement which began in Aquitaine in the 10th century. Under it, as Boyer[9] explains, the erection or repair of a bridge was a charitable work. This idea had spread to most of the territories in the south west of France, mainly along the catchments of the Rhone and the Loire. It was the same zeal as produced the great cathedrals of Paris, Charters, Lyons etc. that financed and built the great bridges at Avignon, Lyons, Rouen, Blois etc. The church and clergy were actively involved in these works. Sometime in the 12th century, sites on the banks of rivers beside bridges were favoured for hospitals, presumably for sanitary and alms-collecting reasons. The fabric of the bridge or as it was named, the opus pontis, sometimes included a hospital and a chapel. The chapel on the great 20-arch bridge over the Loire at Blois, for example, was dedicated to the Irish saint Fiacre.

Purdon[10] states that the first mention of leprosy in Ireland is in the Annals of Innisfallen under AD 546 and the first of a leper hospital under 869. He concludes that the term leprosy included all chronic diseases of the skin such as lupus etc. Most of the hospitals, or spitals, were in the Norse cities and were often called after saints, commonly Brigid, Nicholas, Stephen, Mary Magdalen. There is a comprehensive list in Gwynn and Hadcock[11] who tell us that in every parish in the parts of Ireland where the Norman and English influence did not reach, some of the parish lands were set aside for the poor and to maintain a teach aeidheadh. One of the examples quoted is in Timoleague, Co. Cork, where there was a leper hospital in the townland of Spital by Spital Bridge. There are several Maudelins, which almost invariably indicate a medieval hospital of St Mary Magdalen. The entry for Duleek states that there was a leper house of St Mary Magdalen there c.1202; and there is a mention of a hospital erected at Kells in a charter of 1117–22, probably the hospital of St Brigid mentioned elsewhere. Logan[12] suggests that the Kells hospital may have been renamed Maudlin.

All of this suggests that the bridge and hospital at Duleek may have been renamed and that the phrase "from time whereof no memory is" could be greater than 257 years before 1459. Given the uncertainty, it was necessary to try to find another bridge with arch rings in Irish Romanesque style. The find was made in Kells, less than a mile north of St Columcille's stone-roofed church. Now called Mabe's Bridge*, it carries the Kells to Moynalty road over the (Lough Ramor) Blackwater. The bridge has been widened twice on the upriver side, but the original 12ft wide section is intact and has two arch rings partially corbelled like Duleek, two with non-radial ring stones and other two with a mixture of both.[13] Though the earliest mention found of this bridge was in Down Survey (1656), the circumstantial evidence is that the downriver section is probably 13th-century.

Another bridge with the same construction is the Abbeytown Bridge* beside the Cistercian abbey in Boyle. In his work on Irish Cistercian abbeys Stalley mentions that the abbey was built over the period 1161–1220 and that it contains a barrel-vaulted presbytery with Burgundian imprint together with some Romanesque pier forms.

Taking all the evidence together, it seems likely that the original sections of the bridges, although dated to the post-Norman period, were constructed in the Irish Romanesque style. Such a style seems to have evolved here for stone arch bridges, as well as for ecclesiastical buildings, from the 8th to the 13th century.

Cogan[14] tells us that a poem by Flann, professor in Monasterboice (d. 1056), mentions three stone masons who accompanied St Patrick: "His three stone masons,/ good was their intelligence,/ Creman, Cruithneach, Luchraid strong;/ they made *damliags* first in Erin;/ eminent their history". Their successors were kept busy for many centuries building impressive monasteries, round towers, clochans and other buildings, as were the stone carvers, cutting high crosses and stones for entrance doorways.

NORMAN ARCHES

Assuming that there was a distinctive Irish bridge style, the question remains as to which style the early Norman settlers used. The fact that they were masters of the art of building in stone is evidenced by the numerous great cathedrals that survive in France and Britain, by the ruins of their great stone castles, and by the detailed documentary records of great bridges such as Old London Bridge, and the major bridges across the Loire and the Rhone which survived until they became functionally obsolescent in the 19th century. At home we have numerous surviving ruins of the Cistercian abbeys in the Burgundian style brought here in 1148 by Robert the architect and other monks who came from Clairvaux. We have good records but disputed dates for King John's Bridge, Limerick,* demolished in 1842; as also for the surviving ruins of 13th-century Norman stone castles. All of this evidence is to a large extent circumstantial and the problem was to find a surviving part of a Norman bridge dating from c.1200 until Mrs E. Hickey of Skryne Castle, Meath, a member of the Meath Archaeological Society, drew our attention to early mentions of Babes Bridge in the Register of St Thomas' Abbey, Dublin.

The existence of the surviving arch of Babes Bridge on the Boyne, around two miles downriver from Navan, and the knowledge that it had survived the great flood of AD 1330, has been well known for a century and a half or more. The important facts emerging from the aspect of date and style are that it was a major bridge, 17ft wide, of eleven arches, across a large river, of superb construction. The surviving arch is a pointed segmental one having unique tapered rings of 17ft span. The surviving pier is slim and the springing stone (skewback) of the next missing arch shows it was of similar construction to the surviving one, which indicates the latter is an original. Most importantly there are five mentions of it—e.g. "juxta pontem Johanne le Babe"—as a landmark in separate charters, all pre-1223.

There were several other bridges, such as King John's across the Shannon in Limerick, the records of which indicate that they were early Norman, but the dates of erection are less certain; and they were all of a very different style to Duleek and Mabe's*.

Leask[15] points out that the corbel vault is "a natural and obvious expedient for the covering in of spaces of moderate dimensions and one which would suggest itself to, and be adopted by, primitive builders". He states that the classic example is a tomb in Greece built c.1500 BC and that the principle was used at Newgrange and Dowth. Most of the early Irish examples are circular, e.g. Gallarus, but "the use of mortar made it possible to construct, on a small scale, corbel vaults of the straight -sided form".

All the typology marker bridges mentioned above are within a day's walk of Mellifont, where the first Cistercian monastery was erected in 1148. In the succeeding 32 years a dozen houses were founded throughout the four provinces, notably at Bective, Baltinglass, Boyle and Jerpoint, most of them daughter houses of Mellifont. Stalley's exhaustive study of Cistercian buildings in Ireland[16] finds no evidence that the monks had ever built a public road bridge not even Monks Bridge* across the Nore, traditionally attributed to the Cistercian abbey that flourished there in the 13th and 14th centuries. He draws attention to the rule which forbade members working on projects external to the order. However, Boyer records that at Romans (Drome) on the Isere river in France, the 11th-century bridge, its hospital and its chapel, all belonged to the chapter of St Bernard in the 13th and 14th centuries. At many of the monasteries located on the banks of large rivers, e.g. Bective, Boyle, Baltinglass, access to the monastery from half the hinterland would have been frequently disrupted without a bridge. In a few instances there are records of ferries operated by the monks. However, many of the monasteries were impoverished and in debt for long periods from about 1250 up to the time of suppression, and it is unlikely they would have assumed responsibility for bridge construction and maintenance. One of the most important findings by Stalley is that "by the middle of the 13th century there is plenty of evidence to show that most [Cistercian] building was being carried out by teams of professional masons."

MASONS' MARKS

The arrival of the Cistercians undoubtedly brought a new status and improved finesse to the trades. Perhaps this is best exemplified by the masons' marks which began to appear on some of the worked stones in 13th-century masonry at Mellifont. Stalley reports 18 different marks, many occurring often, and suggests that this number of masons was involved in the work. At present we have no record of a mason's mark from a stone in a road bridge in Ireland, though we did observe one on the soffit of the old bridge across the Fergus at Clarecastle erected in 1826 before it was demolished in the 1960s. The twin of this bridge still spans the Barrow at Graiguenamanagh, but Carlow Co. Council engineers failed to find any mason's mark on the surface during an inspection of the bridge in 1988. (John Greenhalg, who made a study of masons' marks on bridges in the UK over many years, supplied the writers with much information on the topic and said he would expect to find masons' marks on 17th century bridges which is the period when they were used on bridges in England.) A 19th century paper[17] on ancient masons' marks found on the interior of St Mary's church, Youghal, states that the marks, "are confined to the wrought stones of piers, quoins and arches, exclusively to 13th century work". No marks were found on earlier or later work there. This is an important finding because we have no surviving bridge with stones of that quality that can be dated to before c.1750. The French for masons' marks is *les signes de techerons* (marks of piece-workers); Okey[18] explains that they were used during the construction of the walls of Avignon in the 12th century or earlier to measure the quantity and quality of the work of stonemasons. We had hoped that mason marks would turn out to be a valuable aid in dating Irish masonry bridges, but now

conclude that, apart from curiosity, they are of little help and not likely to be found on pre-1750 bridges.

CRAFTSMEN

There is an increasing number of references to craftsmen in the literature from 1200 onwards. Orpen[19] states that King John had carpenters, quarrymen, ditchers and miners in his 1210 expedition to Ireland. Warren[20] mentions that in the following year John assembled an army for an expedition to Poitou in France Wales, but redirected it to bring Wales under English rule. Castles were built as the army advanced and for this purpose instructions were sent out to the sheriffs in 30 shires for recruitment of "2,230 skilled ditchers and carpenters and 6100 labourers with axes".

The Irish pipe rolls for 1211–12 have survived[21] and there are also some details for 1210 in CDI 1171-1251. It is difficult to make much of the majority of the payment records because diverse items are lumped together; however, the following are of interest in the general context of construction work at the time: 14 July 1210—"to Nicholas Carpenter 10s.; Master Osbert Quarrier, Albert Ditcher 1s. 6d.; Master Pinnel and Ernulf miners, 1 mark August 3rd, at Downpatrick, Nicholas the carpenter 20s.; Osbert Quarryman and Albert Ditcher 10s."

In 1211–12 the following are recorded at various times: "12s. to the smiths who were at Clones". . .12s. to Randolph the carpenter at Clones . . .; 48s. 3d. for 193 horses and as many men for one day at the fortifications of the castle of Trim—for each horse and man 3d. per day. . ..; 30s. for a new bridge at Moycove (Co. Down) and for repair of the pailing and for a new pallisade . . .; wages of a smith for one year 20s." The most interesting entry is the Trim one as it shows that supplies of, presumably, stone and gravel etc. were brought in by a virtual army of packhorses. Many of the larger payments—some up to £1,000, for soldier's pay—are recorded as "prests" which means that the men were required to work for the king for good pay but under pain of imprisonment if they refused.

It is very difficult to find information from which unit costs, etc. can be calculated; nevertheless, given the sparsity of bridge mentions let alone details, any construction information is helpful. The pipe roll of 1280 (8 Ed. I) gives

BEALTAINE 2015

Marino Library
The Art of Biodiversity

In this introduction to biodiversity in Dublin City, learn more about the natural world where you can observe, engage and be inspired by your surroundings.

United Nations Decade on Biodiversity

At the end of the talk, (weather permitting) join the biodiversity officer for a guided walk in nearby green or urban spaces to appreciate all the wonderful natural diversity in our city.

Wednesday 6th May at 2pm

Admission free. Booking essential.

Marino Library, Marino Mart, Dublin 3
T. 8336297. E. marinolibrary@dublincity.ie

DUBLIN
UNESCO
City of Literature

1-31 may
bealtainefestival
celebrating creativity as we age
Brought to you by Age & Opportunity

Comhairle Cathrach
Bhaile Átha Cliath
Dublin City Council

an indication of the scale of some of the work. In that year £3,200 was expended "on strengthening the castle of Roscommon and the ditch round the town there, on repairing the castle houses and bridges of Roundoon and repairs to the castle houses and construction of a new chamber in Athlone". More meaningful is an entry for 1298: "£16.1s. 9½d. in payment to workmen and masons engaged in making a new well at Kildare castle." (The reader who is interested in such information will find more in the 35th & 43rd reports of the deputy keeper of public records.)

The great stone castle building period in Ireland extended from about 1180 to 1310.[22] These were truly military castles which dominated the country for 200 years or more. Leask estimates the numbers of all types of castles and tower houses etc. (over 2900, listed up to 1964) as ranging from 10 in Wicklow to 405 in Limerick. The vast majority were built before the end of the 16th century. When one allows for repair, maintenance and reconstruction it is apparent that the demand for masons and carpenters was large and fairly continuous.

When the Normans had built the great military castles, many towns began to grow up around them and establish markets which led to increased traffic and a need for more durable and permanent bridges. It is not surprising, therefore, that we have several surviving stone bridges that can be confidently dated from the 14th century. The pointed segmental arch is almost invariably the hallmark of such bridges. They include Trim*, Slane* and Adare.* Surprisingly, most were built in the first half of the century, which the historical chronology shows to be literally plagued by disasters, including the great flood in the Boyne in 1330 which swept away all bridges except Babes.*

Adare Bridge*, attributed to Gerald, 5th earl of Kildare, marks the end of the 14th century and the start of the 15th. Two new-style bridges also appear—Newtown* and Glanworth.* Leask tells us that in this century there was a boom in private building. The question of who was responsible for the construction of bridges outside the Norman towns is unclear, and it would appear that the Gaelic resurgence resulted in a negative attitude to bridge construction for fear of facilitating access to the king's armies from the Pale. The fifty years ending in 1534 were dominated by the earls of Kildare; the period is sparse in records of road and bridge works.

The second half of the 16th century was one of conquest and colonisation by the Tudors in the wake of the Reformation and the suppression of the monasteries. One of the principal instruments of conquest was the erection of bridges at strategic locations on the major rivers. The traditional Celtic view that stone bridges were instruments of conquest was fully vindicated, as the royal's armies bridged the defences and cut roads through the dense woods year after year until the plantations of Leix, Offaly and Munster were accomplished and the earls of Ulster defeated at Kinsale in 1603. The chief architect of the campaign was Sir Henry Sidney, who came as lord justice in 1557 and served three periods as lord deputy over the succeeding 22 years. It is clear from his memoir written in 1582/3 that he attached great importance to bridges and was instrumental in erecting about a dozen including Ballinasloe*, which still survives with its distinctive Tudor arches. Others at Islandbridge, Athlone*, Belfast, Dungannon and Enniscorthy,* were replaced in the 18th and 19th centuries. A Tudor arch also survives at Askeaton.* Many bridges were also broken down, such as the one at Mapastown, north or Ardee, which was rebuilt in 1577 in stone and lime by Laurence Clinton. The pre-vious bridge, broken down by Shane O'Neill, was described as the "common passage" from most of the Pale to Dundalk.

A report to the privy council in England in 1584, by Lord Deputy Perrot, Sidney's successor, shows that he held similar views to Sidney, as it recommended the erection of bridges at Coleraine, Lifford, Ballyshannon, Dundalk, Mallow, Abbeyfeale and Kells in Antrim. In the case of the Mallow crossing, Berry found some very interesting information in a document among the Carew Papers which he included in an article[23] published in 1893. It made suggestions as to how the province of Munster might "be kept from any revolution heretofore" and suggested that the bridges and passages be kept in the main at Mallow, Cassan and the fords on the Shannon. In relation to Mallow, on the highway between Kilmallock and Cork, it stated that there was a faire ford in summer on the "broadwater" but in winter and in moist weather, there was no passage but in troughs or cotts and even horses had to swim. Armies had to halt for three or four days or hazard attack or retreat. This was the

Fig. 11: *Surviving Plaque from 1635, Quinspoole Bridge*

only impediment for the passage of an army in any place between Limerick and Cork or between Cork and the uttermost south west of Munster. The erection of a bridge at Mallow was not considered a difficult undertaking because "stone and tymber were very plentiful upon the shore" and on the south end some "little pile would be made for which Lyme was burned".

From a letter from the earl of Ormond to Burghley dated 24 April 1583 complaining greatly on the need for the bridge, Berry concluded that a bridge was built there soon afterwards. In 1666 Lord Orrery in a letter to Ormond stated that there was "but one bridge over the Blackwater which is 40 miles navigable for boats—at Mallow; it is one of the greatest passes and thoroughfares in the province and if seized by the enemy would divide the country into two parts." The reference to Cassan in the 1580 document suggests that there was no bridge across the Cashen River in Kerry at that time, but that it was a priority site. The importance of the Boyne crossing at the time is mentioned in connection with Slane Bridge.*

The 17th century saw the emergence of a landlord class in the planted areas, which owned vast tracts of land which it was anxious to capitalise on as quickly as possible. The sale of timber and the smelting of iron were two ways of making money fast but both timber and iron had to be exported, which necessitated roads and bridges. The earls of Cork were very active in this regard in the first quarter of the 17th century.

The period from 1634 to 1765 is scarce in detailed bridge mentions, yet by 1714, as shown on Moll's map, most of the principal rivers had been spanned in many places. Four new stone bridges were erected across the Liffey— Bloody 1670, Essex, Ormond 1684 and Arran 1684, all since rebuilt and renamed. There is plenty of evidence that the act of 1634 was availed of, but surprisingly few authenticated survivors were identified. The Latin plaque from Quinnspole Bridge (fig.11) is preserved in the parapet of the present 19th-century bridge. It reads, "Peter Creagh, Son of Andrew, Mayor of Limerick, had this bridge and street made at the expense of the city of Limerick, the year of the Lord 1635." A new style of multispan masonry arch bridge emerged which had its origins in Buttevant*, Glanworth* and Kilcarn.*

Several bridges described in Part II, tentatively assigned to the 1670–1770 period, are of uncertain date, in particular Leighlinbridge and Bective. From 1750 to the end of the century there is ample evidence of a strong Palladian influence, especially in the Kilkenny* bridges of the period.

TRADESMEN, BUILDERS, ARCHITECTS & ENGINEERS

Carpentry and stonemasonry have been identified previously as the main trades involved in the construction of bridges in Ireland up to the mid-16th century. One early mention of an engineer was found in a pipe roll of Edward III (c. 1470): "£3.13s. paid to Master Robert the engineer (injenitor) for two mill stones bought for the king's mill at Leixlip."

Bridge-construction under the Tudors was a more rigorous affair, involving more pre-planning, as shown by the preparation of a model of the proposed Enniscorthy timber bridge* and the appointment of Sir Peter Lewys as "surveyor and overseer" of Athlone Bridge.* The stonemasons in Dublin were obviously a well-organised body at that time, as evidenced by a Dublin City assembly record of 1569: "the free masons of the city being few in number not permitting other masons that be good craftsmen to occupy or labour in this city without extracting and paying . . . half their daily wages to the said free masons; for avoidage of which abuse it is agreed by this assembly that such forren masons being good craftsmen, as will come to the Mayor and Mr. Recorder shall be by them licensed and permitted to work in this city . . . till the next assembly for proof of their workmanship . . .".

The act of 1615 required parishes to "elect and choose two honest persons of the parish to be surveyors and orderers of the works"; these were obliged to take on the job or forfeit ten pounds. The act also mentions supervisors and orderers of works. The surveyors were required to collect monies and were allowed eight pence in the pound for themselves.

The act of 1634 enabled the justices of the assizes to appoint two tax collectors who would name and appoint two surveyors "which shall see every bridge . . . builded, repaired and amended from time to time as often as need shall require."

On 9 April 1711 the corporation of Cork ordered "that the person who built the Newry Bridge be sent for by the Mayor to come down

to be treated with about building a Stone Bridge". The bridge was the one over the north channel of the Lee. At the meeting a month later it over agreed that the stone bridge be built. The entry suggests a lack of expertise in the city at the time.

The problem of the planning and design of roads was highlighted in the act of 1727 (1 Geo. II c. 13): "and forasmuch as it has been found by experience, that the roads made or amended by and under the direction of persons skilled and practised therein are much better and more lasting than such as are made by the ordinary workmen and labourers . . . be it enacted . . . that it may be lawful . . . for the grand jury in every presentment to nominate and appoint some able, knowing and skilful person to be the surveyor or director of the said work . . . salary not to exceed two shillings and six pence per day . . .". The act related only to highways but it also authorised the parishioners in every parish in their vestry to appoint a director with the same upset limit on his wages.

The consolidation act of 1765 (5 Geo. III c. 14), as we have seen, repealed all the previous highways and bridges acts, including the act of 1634 and vested the parish powers for roads in the grand juries. It prescribed that no money shall be presented by the grand jury for bridges "unless it shall appear by the affidavit of two credible masons, sworn . . . that the sum therein set forth is a reasonable charge to the best of their judgment and that the work is necessary and cannot be effectually done for a smaller sum according to the plan and estimate annexed to such affidavit . . .". This is the first mention of a specific trade or profession in any road or bridge act. However, it did not long remain on the statute books because the whole act was repealed in 1774 and replaced another act, 13 &14 Geo. III c. 32, which was very similar in most respects. The act of 1774 provided that no money be presented for bridges "unless it shall appear by the affidavit of two credible persons, who can read and write, sworn before one of the judges of assize that the sum therein required is a reasonable charge, that the works is necessary and cannot be effectually executed for a smaller sum . . .". Apart from the replacement of masons, the clause also dropped the requirement that a plan and estimate be annexed in the case of repairs of existing or new bridges presented instead of old ones. For bridges at new locations, the requirement remained. For sudden damage, the justices were empowered to appoint "proper overseers" for repairs. The wages of the overseers for all building works, including bridges, as distinct from road works, was set at a maximum of 12*d*. pence for each pound expended.

It is quite clear that this act, which remained in force until 1836, set the framework for the appointment of consultants to design, supervise and account for all major bridge works. However, Nimmo in evidence to the select committee on grand jury presentments in 1827 stated that: "In Connacht the gentlemen have pressed me very much to take commissions of the work: I could only do this by being appointed the overseer by the grand jury." County surveyors were appointed under an act of 1817 and were allowed to present for direct labour work in 1836 in respect of works for which no tender was received. Under the latter act, the justices and grand jury could direct the county surveyor to prepare plans, specifications and conditions of contract.

From the foregoing and from surviving grand jury presentment records for Co. Meath, it would appear that the vast majority of stone bridges up to the end of the middle of the 18th century were planned and built by stonemasons but from 1750 onwards most large bridges were designated and supervised by engineers and sometimes by architects. From 1750 to the end of the century there is evidence of a strong Palladian influence on the design of some bridges in Ireland, particularly the Kilkenny Group.* Palladio's book[24] was first published in Italian in 1570. The first English translation was published in London in 1715. Albertis's book[25] was first published in Florence in 1485 and translated in 1726. The distribution of both books in early 18th-century Ireland has been researched by Casey[26] and her findings show that Palladio's book was second in preference only to Vitruvius. The principal bridge recommendations in Alberti and Palladio are given in Appendix 5.

CHAPTER 10

Bridge Fortifications & Mills

On 3 June 1208 King John granted a licence to Walter de Lacey to "erect a mill at the bridge of Drogheda"[1]. This is the first Irish record we have been able to find of what Boyer aptly describes as "parasitic" construction on bridges. Fifty-four years earlier, the Annals of the Four Masters say, Máel Seachlainn, king of Meath, destroyed the *cliat droichet* of Athlone and its fortress. We therefore have two early records of two types of buildings that had adverse effects on the capacity and life-cycles of bridges throughout the middle ages, in Ireland as well as the rest of Europe. Although they were not part of the *opus pontis*, like the chapel and the hospital, they were, nevertheless, essential for food and for defence, especially in towns.

In 9th-century France, Boyer explains, a new concept emerged of the role of bridges in warfare—that of fortifying and garrisoning bridges to prevent the enemy crossing over or passing under them. Charles the Bald constructed bridges on the Seine to prevent the Norsemen from rowing upriver. In 886 a battle, as famous if not as effective as Clontarf, took place at the Grand Pont of Paris in which the defenders held off a fleet of 700 Viking ships and 40,000 warriors. However, the invaders by-passed the city, dragging their boats overland (a similar successful defence was made at London's wooden bridge in 1016).

The early Normans in Ireland built castles at or near the fords and crossing points on the major rivers such as Athlone, Trim and Limerick etc. as bridgeheads for further expansion. King John's castle in Limerick was built primarily to protect the entrance to the city from the Thomond (old) Bridge. When the Normans initially colonised Meath, the points at which the major rivers of the area, the Boyne and Blackwater, could be forded or bridged, were

selected as sites for initial mottes because of their strategic value, and later became focal points of settlement. By controlling navigation and crossing-points they regulated communications in the area. Graham has found significantly positive correlations between the distribution of settlements and the distribution of crossings on navigable rivers.[2]

FORTIFICATIONS

We have many records and surviving examples of castles erected near bridges, but here we are concerned not with these but with fortifications built into, on or at the ends of bridges. By far the most interesting example from a historic aspect is Thomond (old) Bridge* in Limerick. The bridge and castle were erected *c*.1210. The first mention we have of a tower at the bridge is in 1325 when Edward II declared "whereas our progenitors kings of England and lords of Ireland from the time of the building of the bridge at Limerick and the tower thereto adjacent have been used to repair, maintain and keep the same at their own expenses, we command you [the barons of the exchequer] that you cause the said bridge and tower to be repaired and sustained and kept out of the issues of your bailiwick."[3] The progenitors of Edward II were, in reverse order, Edward I (1307–1272); Henry III (1272–1216); John (1216–1199). Immediately we know from the use of the plural "progenitors", that the bridge and tower go back at least to 1272, to the time of Edward's grandfather, and most probably to John.

That the city was under frequent attack from the "Irish enemies" is clear from a grant of murage by Edward II in 1307 to enclose the suburbs with a stone wall. A charter was granted in 1340 for the building of a bridge which is generally accepted to be Baals Bridge, that is, An Droichet Maol, the bridge without battlements.

Local tradition has always held that Thomond (old) Bridge, demolished in 1840, was the one erected by King John; however the documentary evidence was far from conclusive. Given an accurate plan and elevation drawn by an architect experienced in bridges dated 1814 it was possible to determine how much of the bridge was original. Our investigation is detailed step by step in Part II. It shows that 11 piers and 4 arches were most probably surviving originals.

There is one long gap in information between the 1325 mention and Greenville's map[4] of 1590. This is most likely to be filled by research into the nature and extent of the fortifications and their similarity with French ones. For example in a letter of 1201 (Appendix 2) King John refers to the bridges at Saintes and Rochelle which Isenbert had reconstructed in a short time and to how he was sending him to London to advise on the building of London (old) stone bridge. Given the strong links between both Limerick and Dublin (the king's cities) and these French cities, and the common language (Norman French was spoken in Limerick at the time), one would expect some cross-fertilisation of ideas especially on matters of defence. No records were found to confirm this; however, an 1839 sketch of the old bridge of Saintes[5] shows a striking similarity of towers, battlements and other characteristics. The Saintes bridge was built on the remnants of an old Roman bridge, including its triumphal arch. Two barbicans in stone were added at the entrance to the bridge in 1244. The bridge was demolished in the 19th century, but the Roman arch was re-erected in the town.

Gwynn[6] records that in 1651 "the Clare end of Thomond Bridge was held by a fort for the possession of which there was sharp fighting, till the garrison contrived to evacuate it (after the walls had been breached) and regain the city, blowing up the bridge behind them." Westropp[7] recalls that during the siege of 1691 a French major panicked during an attack on the bridge and ordered the drawbridge at the castellated tower at the seventh arch to be raised, thereby cutting off the retreat of 600 of the defenders who were then slaughtered by the assailants or drowned. The towers and fortified gateways were all removed in1760.

WESTBRIDGE GALWAY

The ancient bridge across the Corrib in Galway City, demolished in 1880 and replaced by the present two-span William O'Brien Bridge, deserves special mention from the aspect of both fortifications and mills because of the number of sketches and mentions that are available. It was erected in 1342 by Edmund Lynch Fitzstephen who was called "Ed of the Tuns" because of his successful wine trade with France and other countries. The bridge connected the city with "the island" and was described as the "Westbridge" in a Galway Council mention of 1688[8].

The bridge is shown on the 1838 OS six-inch map and on a drawing (fig. 12), by William Bartlett made about the same time. The drawing, from a viewpoint on one of the Claddagh boat piers, indicates five arches which could be either pointed segmentals or Tudor four-centred. It is not clear from the drawing whether or not the whole bridge is included due to peripheral sight restrictions by foreground buildings. A correlation of the drawing and the map shows that the span plus pier module was approximately 24ft, the same as found in the surviving mid-14th century pointed segmental arches in Trim and Slane Bridges described in Part II and summarised in fig. 68. This suggests that the arches, many of which may have been rebuilt over the centuries, were pointed segmentals.

There is a mention dated 1558[9] which states that Thomas Martin was granted a place for a watermill "at the further end of the bridge of Galway and backwards from it on the side nearest the sea provided that within two years he built a gate at the west end of the bridge and a tower of stone and lime to guard the gate". The bridge is shown with five arches on B. Gooche's 1583 sketch map of Galway. It is shown fully fortified with gates and towers at both ends and in the centre and with five semi-circular arches on Speed's map of 1611. It is also sketched in the 1652 *Pictorial Map of Galway*, as shown in Fig. 246, Appendix 8; this shows six, possibly seven, upriver cutwaters and a drawbridge span west of the central tower. The bridge is marked on the Down Survey map compiled in 1656. The most informative sketch of all is the elevation shown in Thomas Phillip's drawing of 1685[10] which shows nine

Fig. 12: *Westbridge, Galway; Bartlett's Downriver Elevation, c.1840*

spans, eight being arches and the third from the east end a timber span. At the meeting of the Galway Common Council held in February 1688[11] it was ordered that "a drawbridge on the Westbridge before the wall be forthwith made up and that the blindegate at the key during the present troubles be shutt up". The bridge is also shown on Moll's map (1714). Hardiman writing c.1820 states that all the bulwarks had been demolished long before his time.

The foregoing short summary of information readily available on the Galway bridge shows that there is great scope for further research, particularly on the construction of extra arches at the bridge ends and their removal as in Thomond (old) Bridge. The first step in such a search is to find a scaled drawing showing the bridge as it was at the time of its demolition a mere century ago and examine in detail the information in M.D. O'Sullivan's lengthy paper of 1834.[12]

There were several other fortified bridges in Ireland including O'Brien's Bridge on the Shannon, Fethard, Askeaton*, Castlemaine, Carrigadrohid* and Athy. There is also the entry in the statute rolls for 1456 (34 Hen. VI c. 28) of an ordinance of the Irish parliament "that two towers with two gates be made, one upon the bridge of Kilmainham another upon the bridge of Lucan, and a tower with a wall of 20 perches in length and 6ft in height be made by the wall of St Mary's Abbey". The object was to prevent "Sundry Irish enemies and English rebels" entering into Fingal by night. After the Cromwellian wars it became evident that medieval castle and bridge fortifications were becoming more and more redundant with the advent of new developments in artillery. However, many remained in service until the mid-18th century, having survived the Williamite Wars in the 1690s. In 1812 Martello-type artillery towers were erected at Shannonbridge and Banagher bridges as a defence against a possible Napoleonic invasion.

MILLS

There is no shortage of records of mills at bridges in Ireland. Many mills were erected on the banks in the immediate vicinity of bridges, primarily to allow people to have easy access from either side of the river; others, erected on the bridge approaches, had a separate arch specially constructed for the head or tail race. The "parasitic" mill was the one built on a bridge arch extension upstream or downstream, invariably with a head weir. The worst example was at the bridge erected by direction of the lord deputy, Sir Henry Sidney, over the Shannon in Athlone* in 1567. This fine bridge of seven arches was built in a different location in one year under the supervision of Sir Peter Lewis. Sidney in his memoirs later described it as "a piece found servicable; I am sure durable it is and I think memorable." However, a government lease[13] to Edmund O'Fallone (1568) includes "two water mills upon the bridge of Athlone and a castle on the east side of the bridge with a parcel of land adjoining in Co. Westmeath. To hold for 21 years, rent 12*d*. In consideration of having himself built the mills and castle, which mills grind only for a quarter of the year and his undertaking to grind toll free the corn required in her Majesty's house of Athlone"; but for those considerations the rent would have been £3.10s. A third mill was added subsequently. The bridge with all its additions is shown in Rhodes' downstream elevation (Appendix 8). The mill buildings were used as fortifications by General Grace in the famous defence of the bridge in 1691. Story[14] related that on 23 June of that year "a prisoner [Irish] was brought in, who was the only man out of sixty-four who escaped with life from a mill on the bridge which had been fired by our grenades." One of the plaques on the bridge records that four arches in the centre were rebuilt in 1730. They were rebuilt from the top of the foundations upwards, so it would appear that they were undermined or overturned in a flood which the free arches were incapable of discharging. When the old

bridge was removed in 1844 under the Shannon navigation the compensation paid to mill-owners was some £10,000.

The plans and maps of the Shannon navigation show several mills under bridges elsewhere along the river. The drainage reports of the 1840s record that many had to be altered or removed at great expense even though they had been closed for decades before.

A few bridges in Ireland, such as Baals Bridge, Limerick, had houses on them; these also proved costly to remove, as evidenced by a record in the House of Commons Journal for 1759 that £2290 had been paid already for purchasing houses and for repairs and that £619 was still to be paid for houses pulled down.

The topic of military, commercial and other constructions on, in, under or on the entrance, to road bridges in Ireland has received little attention heretofore. Boyer's comments on French bridges, however, provide us with insights into the nature of parasitic constructions on bridges: "At various times and places in the middle ages it was possible to be born on a French bridge, to attend scholarly lectures on a bridge, to earn one's living and to purchase one's supplies on the bridge, to attend services and receive the sacraments there, and to spend one's old age in a hospital for the aged". Only saints, such as Benezet at Avignon, were buried on them. Ireland can add a dimension to this because in Kanturk*, after 1760, a town then owned by the earl of Egmont, it was possible to be incarcerated in a "black hole or secure prison" built into the abutment of the newly constructed bridge.

CHAPTER 11

Bridge Characteristics

With few exceptions, the grand jury records have been irretrievably lost, leaving a void in information on bridges built in the period 1700–1898 and, more importantly, on alterations and extensions of older bridges. The identification and documentation of the physical characteristics of bridges can assist in dating when historical records fail to provide essential information.

However, the number of authenticated survivors and well documented casualties identified in the course of our research was insufficient to develop local dating criteria and had to be supplemented by relevant information from western Europe. A skeleton methodology then emerged which was applied in the evaluation of the examples in Part II. It had been hoped that several hundred survivors would be identified and that these could be grouped by century to give a typology, but that did not prove to be the case.

The evolution of radial arched vaults from corbelling in the middle east c.3000 BC is well illustrated in an article by Van Beek[1] which describes various kinds of mud brick vaults found in archaeological excavations. At Tell Tazuk in Iraq there is an example of a vaulted roof in which successive courses of bricks are corbelled and canted inwards. Barrel vaults of rectangular bricks laid radially were common down to the first millennium BC. The oldest vault with wedge-shaped brick voussoirs dates from 675 BC. Sun-dried mud bricks and clay mortar occasionally strengthened with chopped straw or dung were the raw materials; always available locally, they were easy to work, shape and use.

ARCH SHAPES IN IRISH BUILDINGS

Banister Fletcher[2] describes the development of arch shapes in ecclesiastical and other buildings in Europe and provides a diagram showing the various types and shapes of arches, many of which are found only in churches. No general study has been made of the evolution of arch forms in Irish churches, though many publications deal with specific periods; the reason may be that many forms persisted in some regions for centuries after they had been discarded elsewhere and, in many cases, such as chancel arches, they are deceptive later additions. Leask includes helpful little diagrams in his book on Irish castles[3], showing the shapes of arches to doorways, windows and other openings. Semi-circular arches, he points out, are usually associated with the Romanesque of the 12th or earlier centuries and when built in wrought sandstone and boldly moulded are a sure indication that a castle can be dated at c.1200. Rough barrel vaulting he found to be no criterion of date whatsoever. Most interestingly he mentions an arch consisting of a segment of a circle in Trim dating from the end of the 12th century. The blunt pointed segmental dating from "somewhat later" persists in doorways up to the 17th century. The pointed segmental consisting of two segments of a circle, however, "indicates a date in the 13th or 14th centuries". The semi-elliptical or three-centred and the four-centred Tudor "belong to the 16th and 17th centuries in Ireland".

It was evident from the historical records relating to bridges that one should expect to find a considerable French as well as British influence on bridge typology in Ireland in the medieval period from 1169 to 1550 or thereabouts. Several good books and many articles provide descriptions of British bridges—notably Jervoise[4] and the Public Works Congress production *British Bridges*.[5] Many famous French bridges, such as Pont-du-Gard, Avignon, Cahors etc. are well documented; detailed descriptions of smaller ones are to be found in Prade.[6] This invaluable book gives technical descriptions of 500 surviving pre-1750 bridges in France which are classified as national monuments, with a superb summary of principal characteristics by period.

Very few medieval British bridges were found which had similar characteristics to contemporary bridges in Ireland. The basic reason for this is that most early British bridges are of ribbed construction; that is, three or more separate narrow single rings are built first with wrought stone, like curved beams, and the intervening spaces are filled in with flags laid across them. This type of construction was first carried out in the cathedrals. In England hundreds of churches with ribbed vaulting were built in the century following 1066. It became part of a native style called "Early English", later perfected in the great cathedrals such as York Minster. Quality masonry on such a scale was inevitably reflected in local stone bridges.

Durham Cathedral, commenced in 1093, is one of the noblest examples of Norman architecture in Britain. Old Elvret Bridge over the river Weare was begun c.1160 by the bishop of Durham and took 65 years to complete; indulgences were granted in 1225 and 1495 to these who contributed towards its cost and repair. Two chapels were built on it in the 13th century and space for shops and houses was later rented out. The bridge had ten arches of between 23 and 32ft span. The intrados are pointed segmental composed of five ribs with rectangular cross sections. The facing rings are double, in two orders, both chamfered. The original bridge, 15ft wide, was extended in the 19th century.

Ribbed arch construction had many advantages, though the overall economics have been questioned. The volume of stone to be wrought accurately was about one-third of that needed if the full width were to be constructed in such stone; the dead weight and hence the lateral thrust on piers was reduced; less centering was needed when the ribs were constructed in sequence. In Ireland very few medieval bridges had wrought stone or proper voussoirs even on the vulnerable upriver-facing rings, so it is evident that master masons with such skills were rare. In such circumstances the less durable, but adequate, rough-cut facing ring

stones and rubble barrels of the arches would be much cheaper. Many medieval bridges in England appear, at first sight, to be prototypes for some of the survivors in Ireland, such as Babes* and Adare,* but on closer examination are found to be ribbed. While ribbed construction is found in many surviving abbeys in Ireland, such as Holy Cross, we came across only one masonry ribbed arch road bridge—at Carrigrohane in Cork. Built in the 1840s it is described by its designer, Benson,[7] as follows:

The bridge measured on the square is 20ft in clear of abutments, and 30ft in the span of ribs. It consists of six ribs, each 30 ft span, with 8ft rise—2ft 4 in. thick by 2ft in depth of sheeting. Two ribs form the outer face of the bridge, the other four are placed between them at equal distances. The width from outside of parapet to outside of parapet is 29ft; 26ft road-way; and 1ft 6in. each parapet.

The material used is limestone, the description of work rock-ashlar. The inner ribs are left rough as they came from the quarry, no part being dressed except the radiating joints, and the soffit roughly.

The ribs are connected by large flags, 10in. thick, which form the platform to carry the road; under the road-metal, concrete 10in. thick is placed on the covering flags. The actual quantity of sheeting on the six ribs, each of which, as stated before, is 2ft 4in. thick, is only 14ft, whereas if thoroughly sheeted there should be 29ft making in the item of sheeting alone a saving of one half. No heading joints were necessary, as each rib is independent of the other; no regularity of coursing was required, by which all thicknesses of stone came from the quarry were used. All skew or twisted jointing on beds or headings is avoided, an item which forms fully four-fifths of the labour.

The centres consisted of two frames, on which the ribs were built. These were removed, as each rib was keyed, to the next, and so on to the completing of the last rib; thus saving all the timber required for the centres of a thoroughly sheeted arch.

The first generation of Normans who came to Ireland, mainly from Wales, were of recent French origin and spoke and wrote in Norman French. They had strong connections with Aquitaine and the north west of France, particularly during the reign of Henry II, and with Henry's Plantagenet successors, who spent most of their time in France and continued to give large land grants in Ireland to barons of French origin (such as de Briouse). All of this suggests the possibility of a strong French influence on bridge construction here in the 13th and 14th centuries; as this is indeed the case, many of the characteristics of the French bridges derived by Prade can be used with confidence in the dating of Irish bridges.

In determining what characteristics are useful for bridge assessment one must be conscious of the fact that most survivors are still in service with traffic flowing over them and water flowing under them. This limits the scope and extent of ordinary investigations. The elements that can normally be measured and photographed are piers, cutwaters, soffits and faces of arch rings, spandrels, parapet walls and copings and widths and type of masonry. Sometimes, of course, these are obscured by trees, bushes and ivy, especially near the bank where one can get close in for detailed photographs. Unfortunately when water levels are low the vegetation is at its thickest.

Prade's stone bridge characterisation includes the 1st and 2nd centuries AD because France has a small but rich heritage of Roman bridges. It omits the dark ages for obvious reasons and resumes from the 11th century onwards to the 19th. For Irish purposes the period from the 11th to the 19th century is sufficient. The principal relevant criteria are given in fig. 13.

It must be emphasised that these are general guides but they are quite useful when a combination of characteristics points to the same century. For example, there are nine pointed segmental arches described in Part II and all but one of them fit the 13th to 15th century dating criterion.

The characteristic which seems most useful in the dating of Irish bridge arches is the shape of the intrados curve. In view of this fig. 14 has been prepared based on information in Prade but taking account of the broad findings from the bridges described in Part II. It must be emphasised that it is very difficult to get accurate measurements or close-up head-on photos of most bridges; also in many instances the intrados curves have been distorted due to initial or later settlement or flattening of the haunches.

Most pre-19th-century Irish segmental arcs

BRIDGE ELEMENT	CENTURIES
Arch Intrados	
Semi-circle	10 to 19
Pointed segmental	13 to 15
Arc of circle	13 to 19
False ellipse	Mid-16 to mid-19
Pier Thickness	
greater than ⅓ span	Roman
c. ⅓ span	11 to 16
⅛ to ⅒ span	Mid-17 to 19
Upriver Cutwaters	
Triangular	10 to 19
Almond	13, 14, 18
Rectangular	14 (rare)
Circular curve	19
Downriver Cutwaters	
Triangular	13 to 18
Almond	18
Rectangular	11 to 16; 17 & 18 (rare)
Trapezoidal	17 & 18; 16 (rare)
Circular curve	19

Fig. 13: *Characteristics of Bridge Elements by Century (based on Prade)*

have rises close to half the span—almost semicircular. Bridges of this type began to be constructed in France in the 13th century, the classic span being the 177 ft. one over the Allier river at Vielle Broude built in 1340 which remained the longest single span in the world for 400 years. The earliest in Ireland is the tiny King John's Bridge* at Esker, Co. Dublin. The problem with low-rise circular arc segments is the high component of lateral thrust

Shape of Intrados	Comment
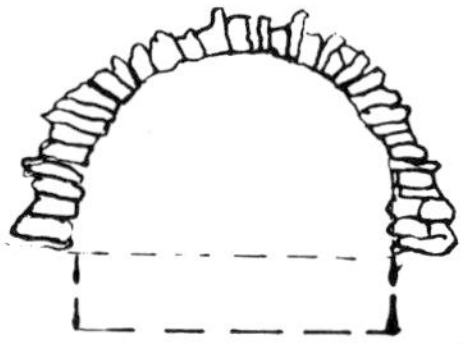	Semi-corbelled arch with the projecting stones tilted progressively until they become radial about half-way up on the curve; found in Irish Romanesque stone-roofed churches, such as St Columba's (Kells) and in several bridges including St Mary Magdalen's,* Mabe's,* Monks.*
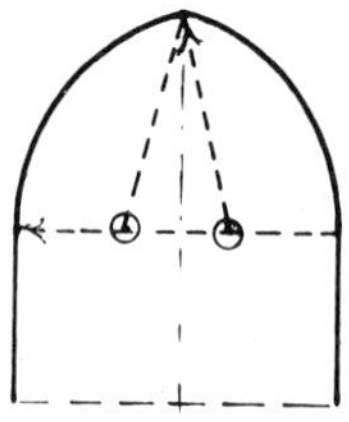	Pointed segmental arches with the centres of the segments located on the intrados base line or span are common in church architecture and are sometimes described as ogives. When r = span, it is called equilateral; r = ⅘ span, a five point; r = ⅔ span, three point or drop arch. They are often found in old bridges in France. The only example found here so far is the central arch in Buttevant Old Bridge.
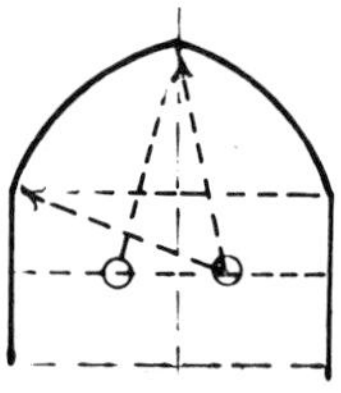	Ordinary pointed segmental arches have the centres, sometimes called striking points, located below the intrados base line commonly on the river bed. The curves spring from "skewbacks", that is sloped stones at the pier tops. Common in Ireland before 1450. Many examples are described in Part II, e.g. Slane, Askeaton, Adare, Trim, Babes.
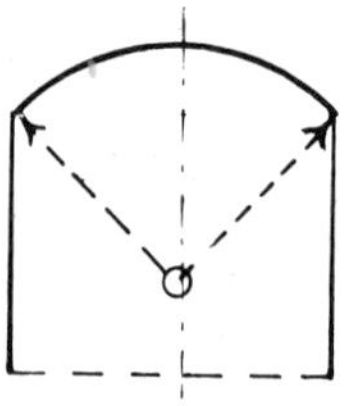	Segmental arcs less than a semi-circle were rare in medieval bridges. Several early examples were found, e.g. King John's, Newtown, Athassel and are described in Part II. All have span-to-pier ratios less than about 1.5. There are numerous examples from the 16th and 17th centuries which have arcs that are almost semicircular. Flat arcs and thin piers are common after 1750 when the theory of balancing the horizontal thrust came to be understood.
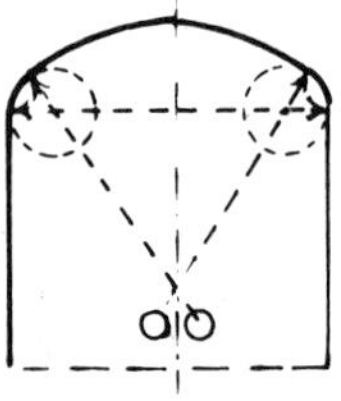	The Tudor or four-centred arch originated in the reign of Henry VII (1485–1509). Good examples, described in Part II, are found in Ballinasloe Bridge (erected *c.* 1570) and Askeaton. It would appear that the Tudor gradually evolved into the three-centred by merging the radii of the larger arcs on the vertical axis through the crown.
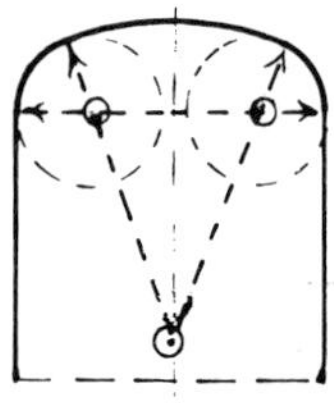	The three-centred arch is said to have originated in Italy *c.*1575. The earliest example found in Ireland was the first Essex Bridge erected in 1676. Known as Anse-de-Panier, or basket handle, in France. Variations include the oval composed of a number of arcs of circles of an odd number with radii increasing from the springing to the keystone. A few bridges were found with true semi-elliptical curves, e.g. Avoca*. Became very common in the 18th and 19th centuries mainly to reduce the road gradients as spans increased. South Gate Bridge* (Cork) and Quoile* (Northern Ireland) are early surviving examples.

Fig. 14: *Common Shapes of Intrados Curves (based on Prade and our research)*

on masonry piers or abutments. Usually all the arches had to be built together in multi-span bridges; otherwise the pier, if high, could overturn when the centering is removed. Such construction was costly. Newtown* Bridge, Trim, erected before 1476, is the oldest surviving example of a multi-span segmental arc bridge in Ireland, but it has abutment-type piers. Other early examples are Grace Dieu* and Gormanstown*. The twin-arched bridge at Milltown*, Dublin, is a fine example from the 17th century.

Alberti[8] says that the strongest of all arches is the semi-circle: "but if by the disposition of the piers the semi-circle should rise so high as to be inconvenient we may make use of the scheme arch only taking care to make the last piers on the shore the stronger and thicker". In book 1, c. 8 the "scheme arch" is called *arco scemo*; the imperfect arch "that whose chord is less than a diameter".

Another arch curve not included in the table is what the French call "pseudo-corbelled". These have horizontal joints and are formed by corbelling successive courses. For identical elements in strict equilibrium, taking a brick lengthwise as unity the half span should follow the regression

$$\frac{\text{Span}}{2} = 1 + \frac{1}{2} + \frac{1}{3} + \frac{1}{4} + \ldots \ldots$$

There is a good example (fig. 232) of a pseudo-corbelled arch over a doorway in the ruins of the 12th-century Corcomroe abbey in Clare. The semi-corbelled 12th- or 13th-century arches in St Mary Magdalen's*, Abbeytown*, Mabe's* and Monks* bridges differ from the "pseudo". They have projecting stones in each course, purposely tilted with accumulating declivity until approximately half-way up the haunches and then become radial.

POINTED SEGMENTAL

The early Normans adopted pointed segmental arch on the principal element of their style; examples include Babes, Thomond Old Bridge*, Trim*, Slane* and Adare*. There were good reasons for adopting this shape: bridges of this type were easy to set out; settlement (inevitable when inadequate centering was used or when it was withdrawn) did not unduly distort the visual appearance or risk causing collapse to the same extent as it would for a semicircular arch; these arches provided greater headroom for boats and, sometimes, greater cross-sectional area for flood discharge. The ogival-type pointed arches were common in Cistercian and other churches built in Ireland from the 12th to the 14th centuries so that the stone-masons were familiar with them and naturally sought to adapt them for bridges. Such bridges are often described as Gothic, especially in the 19th-century drainage reports. Alexander Nimmo erected a lofty 65ft span pointed segmental Gothic arch across the waterfall at Pollaphuca* in the 1820s —a very unusual design for the period, particularly since the abutments were solid rock. The inspiration for it seems to have come from the 15th-century *pont romain* at Lauzet-Ubage in the province of Alpes-de-haute in France.

TUDOR

The four-centred Tudor arch emerged in England during the reign of Henry VII. Diagrams in fig. 14 show that it was a small modification of the pointed segmental, involving the rounding of the intrados above the springing by the insertion of two small radii curves, one each side, with their centres located on the span and on radii of the segmental section. Some 18th and 19th century sketches of the 1567 Athlone* bridge showed pointed segmental arches like Babes* and Trim*. However it seemed odd that a shape then almost two centuries out of date would have been erected by an expert like Sir Peter Lewys for the Lord Deputy. The problem was solved when Phillips's 1685 sketch was found and showed the rounding at the springings. The surviving arches of the 1570 Ballinasloe Bridge* confirm this evidence. A close examination of the Tudor arch at Ballinasloe (fig. 109) shows that the rounding effect was achieved by cutting a curve on the intrados of the skewback, a remarkable example of how local masons gradually changed style. One other example of a surviving Tudor arch was found in Askeaton Bridge*.

THREE–CENTRED ARCHES

A new form of arch emerged in the 16th century called the basket-handle arch. The first major example was the Ponte Santa Trinità in Florence. The intrados consisted of two half-parabolas like two tilted camber boards. The slight kink at the crown was camouflaged by a decorative escutcheon. From it the false ellipse was developed which later became the standard curve for canal and railway over-bridges where headroom at the sides was critical. It was very difficult to cut the wedge-shaped voussoirs for a true semi-elliptical arch ring— the number of stones of different shape being equal to the total less one divided by two. In the false ellipse the number was limited to the number of different radii (normally three). Full-scale templates were easily constructed with the required accuracy. As late as 1837 we find William Bald[9] describing a practical method he had developed for forming the stones for four elliptic arches in the bridge he erected over the Owenmore river in Co. Mayo.

Samuel Ware in a report on a proposed bridge at Dungarvan dated 1813 states that "the arches of the proposed bridge are false ellipses composed of segments of circles drawn from three centres. I am of opinion that they ought to be true ellipses and the voussoirs should be at right angles to the intrados, requiring a mould for each voussoir in the semi-arch." His advice was not adopted. When the arches of the truly elliptical arches of Avoca Bridge (1869), damaged in the Hurricane Charlie offshoot floods of August 1986, were being repaired, great difficulty was experienced in eliminating the saw-tooth surface from the intrados of one half arch which had been rebuilt with accurately sawn granite voussoirs.

There are two examples of what is called a depressed three-centre arch in the wall of the 15th-century cloister garth in the ruins of Bective abbey. The rise is so small that one wonders how they continue to stand. Scotchstone Bridge over the Ward river in Swords, Co. Dublin, has two spans with extraordinarily depressed three-centred arches, though it was built after 1756. The arches are consequently very weak and now subject to load restriction. Other examples of three-centred arches can be found at Derrybawn*, Clara*, Cork City*.

FOUNDATIONS; PIERS & CUTWATERS

The most frequent single cause of failure of masonry bridges is scouring of the foundations. This has been the case ever since the Romans built their first stone bridges. Scour is a complex phenomenon involving diving vortex flows of high velocity generated where flood waters meet obstructions such as piers and abutments. These flows cut holes in the river bed at the upstream and downstream ends of the foundations, the depth during the flood peak sometimes being more than the width of the pier. The holes usually fill up rapidly as the flood recedes making them difficult to detect afterwards.

The nature and extent of the scour problem in Ireland was clearly summarised in the conclusions of the Bridge Collapse Seminar[10] organised by An Foras Forbartha in 1987:

1. Scouring of the subsoil under the foundations of piers and abutments was the cause of collapse, partial and total, of the vast majority of the twenty bridges described at the Seminar. Scour occurred upstream and downstream, under both masonry and concrete piers and abutments. The predominant type was scour under the upstream ends and cutwaters of masonry piers.
2. The piers and abutments of most masonry bridges in Ireland consist of a coursed masonry facing with rubble infill and are therefore very vulnerable once cracks or dislodgement of stones occurs. The foundations are usually shallow and highly susceptible to scour. Most bridges do not have paved beds.

One early collapse stands out in the history of bridges in Ireland—that of Essex Bridge*, erected in 1676. On December 1687 an exceedingly high flood scoured the foundation of one of the piers, causing a collapse. Repairs were carried out but the pier settled again in 1751. George Semple, a Dublin builder, was commissioned by Dublin Corporation to carry out repairs, eventually building a new bridge and writing a classic textbook *A Treatise on Building in Water*.[11] Semple reviews the various methods used up to that time at home and abroad for building bridge foundations, such as kishes mentioned previously. The main point to note here is that from the earliest times scour was a destroyer of thousands of arch bridges in Ireland and is the principal reason why we have so few survivors from medieval times. Most of the notable survivors, including those like Thomond (old) Bridge* (replaced in 1840s for functional reasons) were founded on rock and or very stiff boulder clay such as at Mabes.*

From a hydraulic aspect the gradual reduction in pier thicknesses, the addition of downriver cutwaters and the paving of river beds reduced the risk considerably.

Pedestrian refuges were often incorporated in the parapet walls of bridges from about the 13th century to the 18th. The obvious purpose was to afford some protection to pedestrians (especially on long bridges) from onrushing herds of cattle and later coaches and carriages. The usual method of construction was to carry up the cutwater to the parapet so the shape of the former dictated the latter—usually a vee. There are some unusual ones such as Milltown* (corbelled), Reddenagh (rect), Thomond (old) (semi-circular), Adare* (massive). Sometimes they have been added as traffic increased, e.g. on the 12ft wide Athlone Bridge (1567), graphically described by Weld in 1815 as being "the only passage between the two divisions of the town, which are nearly of equal size and very populous, . . . the mere crossing of the inhabitants of the place occasions a constant throng upon it; but on market days and when there are fairs in the vicinity, more particularly during the great cattle fair of Ballinasloe, human beings, cattle, cars, carriages are so closely wedged, that the passage becomes an affair of absolute danger."

Overall, we have not found the shape, size, frequency or location of pedestrian refuges of much assistance in dating bridges; indeed sometimes, as in the case of Duleek, they can be deceptive in the absence of close scrutiny of the masonry.

PARAPET COPINGS

The parapet copings are one of the most obvious characteristics. The masonry in the copings of Carragh Bridge*, for example, resembles a shelf of tilted books with the tilt reversed every 10ft or so. Somewhat similar copings are to be found in Mabes*, Craughwell* and Clara Vale*. The tilt was less pronounced at Clara and the stones far less secure due to deterioration of the mortar. The technique, which goes back to the Middle East brick walls of 3000 BC is more difficult to use in stone. The parapets of the Thomond Old Bridge were battlemented in the 16th-century drawing in *Pacata Hibernia*[12], but the bridge had continuous large limestone slab copings in 1810. In towns the large slab copings were often

removed for use as washboards at the clothes washing inlets found near bridges (before the advent of cement mortar they were often easily dislodged or stolen). Many bridges originally had no parapets. Given all the uncertain factors copings are seldom a reliable indicator of age.

ROAD WIDTH

The first characteristic of a masonry bridge the layman notices is the width between the parapet walls; when it is insufficient for two cars to pass, an early date of construction is often assumed. This is a commonsense approach, given the knowledge that most traffic consisted of horse-drawn vehicles up to the present century and that, prior to about 1750, the volume of such traffic was so small that two carts or coaches seldom met on a bridge and, if they did, there was negligible risk of accident.

In order to see if there was any overall pattern in the growth of bridge roadway widths, fig. 15 was prepared, giving the widths of all the pre-1775 bridges described in Part II which have reasonably well established periods of construction.

The average bridge width up to the end of the 15th century is 13ft 6in. It increases to almost 14ft during the 16th century, to 16ft during the 17th, and 18ft in the first seven decades of the 18th. However, in many cases, bridge width was estimated by adding 3ft to road width to allow for parapet walls, and overall the measurements are too crude to draw conclusions. Nevertheless the table gives some idea of the trend.

I was puzzled about the factors that influenced the choice of bridge widths in Ireland outside the few larger urban areas, apart from the obvious economics, but then I recollected that in the decades after World War II there were still many narrow bridges having widths equal to or less than the paved widths of the approach roads. These became very hazardous as the volume and speed of traffic increased, and had to be widened. This suggested that the criterion in preceding centuries may have been to make the bridges the same width as the approach carriageways excluding margins. An examination of the various acts of parliament, outlined in Chapter 3, showed that no road or bridge widths were prescribed under the 1615 act (11–13 Jas I c. 7), the 1634 act (10 Chas. I c. 26), or the 1705 act (4 Anne c. 4). The

Bridge Name	Period/ Century	Overall Width (ft)
St Mary Magdalen	13th	12.5
Esker	1210	9.0
Babes	1210	17.0
Thomond (Old)	1210	13.5
Mabes	13th	12.5
Boyle	13th	19.0
New Bridge	1308	12.0
Gormanstown	14th	6.0
Trim	14th	21.0
Adare	14th	14.5
Grace Dieu	14th	11.0
Slane	14th	16.0
Craughwell	14th	10.5
Newtown	15th	14.0
Glanworth	15th	12.0
Kilcrea	15th	12.0
Kilcarn	16th	12.0
Athlone	1567	15.0
Ballinasloe	1570	14.0
Carlow	1569	15.0
Enniscorthy	1581	14.0
Caragh	16th	13.0
Carrigadrohid	17th	15.0
Kinnegad	1661	18.5
Belfast (Long)	1686	22.0
Sir Thomas'	1690	15.0
Milltown	17th	13.0
Clara	17th	13.0
Bective	17th	21.0
Callan (NI)	17th	15.0
Shannonbridge	1700	15.0
Kanturk	1761	18.0
Scariff		18.0

Fig. 15: *Widths of Bridges up to 1775*

1710 act (9 Anne c. 9), however, prescribed that "in all cases where presentments are made for roads, no causeway, pavement or other reparation shall be less than nine foot wide ... and to be well gravelled or paved according to the breadth aforesaid at least". This explained the 9ft width between parapets which seemed to have been the mode in previous centuries.

The act of 1727, 1 Geo. II c.13, prescribed that all highways, causeways, toghers, or roads to be repaired and amended under it or any former act, should be paved or well and sufficiently covered with gravel 12ft in breadth at least.

The 1765 consolidation act, 5 Geo. III c. 14, required a sworn affidavit before payment that every part of an existing road which had been repaired under the particular presentment had been made 14ft wide in the clear with stones or gravel and that it was 21ft wide in the clear between ditches, drains or fences. In the case of new roads, the respective widths were 14ft and 30ft. The same widths were repeated in the 1774 act, 13 & 14 Geo. III c. 32.

No widths were specified in the first series of turnpike road acts in the 1730s. This changed over the succeeding decades; e.g., in 1765 the Cork/Kanturk Road Act specified that it should be 30ft broad within trenches and 16ft to be sufficiently gravelled end to end. The Mail Coach Road Act 1805 specified an overall width of not less than 42ft. Most of the bridges on the turnpike and mail coach roads (the forerunners of the present National Route System) were rebuilt or widened in the period 1729–1856, with the result that few surviving ancient bridges are now found on these routes. The 1836 consolidation act simplified all the legislation by prescribing that the overall road width should not be less than 16ft nor more than 50ft in the clear.

The 9th-century guideline in Cormac's Glossary for the width of a *bothar* was "two cows fit upon it, one lengthwise, the other across". Perhaps the practical criterion for the 9ft was two truckle cars passing. In Britain, Thomas states, the widths between parapets remained narrow until the 19th century and that "the minimum width of 9ft specified in the Statute of Bridges [1531], was rarely exceeded"[13]. However, no mention of bridge width appears in that act but a marginal note states that the 1 Anne c.18 (Britain) "enforced" it, so the provision may be in the latter. Ruddock reports that a survey carried out in the West Riding of Yorkshire in 1752 showed that out of 115 bridges one small one was 8ft 6in. wide, eleven exceeded 15ft inclusive of parapets, but the majority were between 10ft and 14ft wide. He also mentions that a contract by General Wade for a large bridge over the Dumble river in Scotland (two 42ft spans), specified a width of 12ft including parapets. The old Carr Bridge erected in 1717 had a width of only 7ft between parapets.

All this suggests is that bridge width is a useful criterion for dating bridges and one that could become more accurate as further information becomes available.

ARCH SPANS

There are many surviving Roman arches in

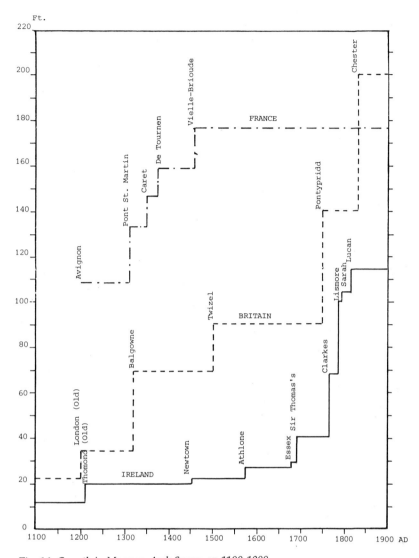

Fig. 16: *Growth in Masonry Arch Spans, AD 1100-1900*

Italy with spans of less than 10ft which are constructed with large, perfectly shaped radial voussoirs. Others, such as the Augustan bridge at Narni, have spans of almost 100ft. Here we are concerned with the evolution of the masonry arch in the period after AD 1000, mindful of what Giuseppe Lugli stated[14]—that the arch originated independently in various parts of the ancient world. The question is: how useful a criterion is length of span as a criterion for dating stone bridges? Obviously single spans of up to 10ft were adequate for many small streams and in such cases no choice had to be made; however, when the river width was greater, the builder would seek to construct a larger span to avoid building piers in the river with consequent risk of scour. It is logical therefore to assume that, in general, multi-arched bridges are a good indicator to the maximum spans that could be constructed locally at the particular period.

It would be easy to give a list of bridges of various spans in various countries by century including the *greatest* spans but such a table would be of little assistance to the reader. Various ways of presenting the information were considered and it was decided that the most meaningful would be a set of graphs enveloping the maximum spans of bridges, by date, over the period 1000–1900. The plots are given in fig. 16. The data were taken from Prade for France, from *British Bridges*, and from Part II of this book. No statistical analysis was carried out because span information was not available in many instances. Despite their limitations the envelope lines give a useful picture of arch development and, more importantly, in the case of Ireland give cause for second thoughts when the span of a particular bridge of uncertain date lies appreciably above the line for its assumed period, particularly in the middle ages.

The rapidly increasing spans of arches during the 18th century reduced the risk of scour and the cost of construction; however, it also created a new problem that of excessive grades on the approaches to the central arch(s). The outstanding example is Pontypridd, which as shown in fig. 16 was the longest span arch in Britain from 1756 to 1832. The story of Pontypridd is detailed by Ruddock; briefly, William Edwards, a stonemason and part-time farmer, built a bridge across the Taff at Pontypridd for £500 in 1746. Two years later it was washed away due to pier scour. He was obliged under the seven-year maintenance clauses to replace it. The second bridge was a long single span with no river piers, but this collapsed when almost finished due to centering failure. He reduced the ring thickness and built a third which stood for six weeks but collapsed before the parapets were erected due to uplift of the arch crown. The haunches were too heavy and the crown too thin and light. He solved this problem by building hollow cylindrical voids in the haunches in his fourth 145ft span bridge, which still stands and which he completed in 1756. Ruddock states that the hollow spandrel design was copied particularly in south Wales, but his bridge was a failure because it was so steep that wagons had to use drag chains to descend it. I believe that the jump in spans of bridges in Ireland from 1760 to the close of the century was probably inspired by Pontypridd (see Cork Bridges*). However, in most cases, the gradient problem was avoided.

The seriousness of the gradient problem on bridges in towns was highlighted by Charles Forth in a paper to the Institution of Civil Engineers (*Proc. ICE*, II, p.165) in 1842, on the bridge over the Slaney at Tullow, Co. Carlow. Before outlining his description it is appropriate to mention that Tullow was a very ancient crossing place, part of the Slighe Cualann. Shirley [15] quotes an extract from Dineley, who visited the town in 1680, which refers to the tenant of the castle, William Crutchley, J.P., who "repaired the Town Bridge which is of stone with arches". In a footnote, written in 1862, she states that the bridge had been twice rebuilt since Crutchley's time, and that the first bore an inscription "This bridge was built by Mr Thomas Nowlan of Rathvaran, farmer, in the year 1747; Sir Richard Butler, Bart; Thomas Bunbury, Robert Eustace, Esq.; Messrs Robert Lecky and John Brewster overseers." This was the bridge which Forth states was "very dangerous from its steepness, its narrow roadway (only 18 feet wide) and the awkward approaches to it". Forth states that he designed a new superstructure for the bridge using very flat segmental arches which reduced the grades from 1 in 7 to 1 in 40 while at the same time adding to the abutments on the upstream side; the road width was increased to 28ft. He mentions that the floods "forbade any diminution of the waterway". One of the three new arch rings had a radius of 60ft, a span of 17ft and a versed sine (rise) of 7in. This is extremely flat—a rise to span ratio of 1 in 29. He states that the completed bridge was tested with loaded carts of 35 cwt. and that the cost of the alterations was £485. The bridge failed to carry the flood of 1963 when the nearby houses and hotel were flooded to a depth of 6ft. Carlow Co. Council strengthened the bridge in the 1980s. The present bridge has three uniform piers and four spans and it would appear that the whole superstructure from the foundation up was replaced in the 1840s.

STONES

It was very expensive to haul stone any distance by road in the middle ages and right up to the 19th century. Fieldstones were plentiful and for small bridges enough could usually be found in the locality; however, they were difficult to work and shape even crudely. Stones were re-used of course but as stone houses, out-offices and boundary walls became more common the supply diminished. The number of historic monuments, such as passage graves, churches, castles etc. that were literally swept from the landscape during the 17th and 18th and early 19th centuries and used for the construction of roads and bridges may have been enormous. I did not find a single sentence in all the road and bridge acts for the period 1611–1836 prohibiting this vandalism, whereas confirmatory evidence emerged in the case of the first Essex Bridge* and Derrybawn Bridge* Newgrange almost vanished under a road presentment in the 1840s. For the larger bridges it was usually necessary to quarry stone, as evidence by early mentions of "quarries". On navigable rivers the stone could be transported cheaply enough. The predominant factor was the geology of the area and the type of rock. Sandstones, shales and schists came away easily enough in well shaped slabs, provided of course that there were suitable outcrops in the vicinity. Limestone was more difficult to quarry and to work. Leask states that "free working" stones were mainly used up to and including the 13th century, but from 1260 on-

wards abundant native limestone came into use for castles. The word freestone is used very frequently in literature on masonry; it is stone without appreciable lamination or bedding planes and which can split in any direction when sledged.

It is quite difficult for anyone other than a geologist to determine the type of rock in old bridges because the exposed faces are usually covered with moss and lichens and also becomes discoloured. Even where they are not obscured, it is difficult to get close up and clean off the surface of a ring stone. Samples adequate for geological examination cannot be taken. Often one finds a wide variety of rock types in the same arch or pier. In Mabe's Bridge* the arch rings are sandstone and some of the spandrel wall, limestone. These difficulties explain the lack of identification of rock type for many bridges described in Part II.

CHAPTER 12

Masonry Arch Design

The word "design" is not used in the hundreds of pre-1830 grand jury presentments for road bridges examined in the course of the research for this book. What the jurors normally agreed was that a specified sum "be raised and paid" to a number of named individuals "to build a bridge" at a specified location. Semple[1] mentions the bridge at Blois (France) as having been "designed" by Jacques Gabriel, and also that he (Semple) "designed" Essex Bridge as well as building it. The word is of French origin and usually means to draw, to form a plan or to contrive.

From 1774 onwards, as explained in Chapter 9, the practice of appointing an architect or engineer to prepare the designs and oversee public works began to obtain in Ireland, mainly in relation to canals. In England, in the period 1735–7, we find many "designs" for Westminster Bridge being prepared by architects, tradesmen and others and submitted as pamphlets to the men who were promoting the petition for an act to authorise construction of the bridge. Bart Langley, e.g. entitled his pamphlet *Design for the Bridge at Westminister* (1736).

The state of the art in bridge design at this period in England and Ireland was obviously lagging behind France, where the central board of Ingenieurs Ponts et Chaussées had been established in 1716 (the first head of the Board was Gabriel). Ruddock[2] records that Hawksmoore, who summarised the reports and pamphlets on Westminster Bridge for the committees of the houses of parliament[3], stated that all the books on bridge design and construction he found came from the continent—Palladio, Scamozzi, Serlio etc. The man appointed to design and oversee the erection of the bridge as "engineer" was Charles Labelye, a Frenchman living in Westminster, who was competent in mathematics and mechanics. Ruddock gives a very thorough and penetrating analysis of the design and construction of Westminister Bridge in his book and shows that it was a turning-point marking the introduction of a scientific approach to the subject.

Labelye wrote a description, *A Short Account and Description of Westminister Bridge*, a copy of which Semple found printed in Dublin by Ewing at the Angel and Bible bookshop in Dame Street (see Essex Bridge*). Semple met Labelye several times in London, and he also purchased £40 worth of books on bridges, which would have included all the classical ones from the continent mentioned above, because Semple devotes ten pages of his own book to summaries of their principal recommendations concerning bridges.

The section on Kilkenny Bridges* in Part II shows that this knowledge was disseminated by Semple even before publication of his own book in 1778. Progress in the analysis of the engineering problems relating to arch bridges made rapid strides in France following the foundation of the École des Ponts et Chaussées (School of Roads and Bridges) in 1745 and the appointment of Jean Perronet as its first director. Perronet, in the words of a recent French publication[4] "developed new theories and initiated the first great technical developments. He built several bridges with diminished [flat] arches and very narrow piers, using the equilibrium of the thrust from successive arches". This is endorsed by the German Leonhardt in his recent book on bridges[5], in which he states that during the 16th to 18th centuries France remained the country of ingenious bridge builders, who contributed most to the development of stone bridges and who were the first "to date to build flat segmental arches".

The development of the theory of arches is summarised objectively by Ruddock in Chapter 5 of his book. Heymans in his book[21] published in 1982 devotes Chapter 3 to the same subject and concludes by stating that with the publication of Gauthey's *Traité de la construction des ponts* in 1809 "the engineering problems of the masonry arch had been effectively solved." There are two copies of Gauthey in the archives of the Institution of Engineers of Ireland, one of which was donated by Bernard Mullins and had obviously been acquired by him in the 1830s.

From the foregoing it is evident that by the turn of the 19th century it was possible for engineers to design arches in the accepted sense of the word, that is, from an understanding of the forces involved and the properties of materials used; however, is there evidence that such an approach was used in Ireland at the time? It would appear that until the 1820s the designs were largely based on empirical rules (e.g., St Patrick's Bridge, Cork; Carlisle Bridge, Dublin, the notable exception being 110ft span Lucan Bridge* designed and built by George Knowles which had a low rise-to-span ratio by contemporary Franch standards).

The Mail Coach Roads Act of 1805 (45 Geo. III. c. 43) amended the laws for improving and keeping in repair the post roads in Ireland and brought a new radical and rational approach to road planning. Under the act the postmaster general in Ireland was required to survey and make maps for the several lines of road on which the mails were carried and of the alterations required. For this work he was empowered to engage competent surveyors who were required to swear to carry out the surveys and the plans without "fear, favour or partiality to the true intent of the Act". Stringent standards were laid down for realignments, which became in effect the first geometric design standards. Andrews[6] estimates that in the 11 years following the act 2068 miles were surveyed and planned. Most of the plans have survived and are preserved in the National Library. The principal surveyors employed on the post office surveys were young engineers including Larkin, Coote, Cook, Bald and Nimmo. Soon afterwards the bog surveys[7] commenced and here again we find districts being assigned to Nimmo and Bald, and to Richard Griffith, who had returned to Ireland from Scotland in 1809. The bog survey work finished in 1814.

Nimmo, a fluent linguist, spent about two of the next six years in France, Germany and Holland increasing his engineering knowledge. He must have spent a considerable time in Paris because he designed Wellesley Bridge (now Sarsfield*) as an exact half-scale model, longitudinally, of Perronet's famous Pont Neuilly in Paris. Early in his career he had worked with Telford in Scotland and contributed articles on hollow spandrels with Telford to the *Edinburgh Encyclopaedia*[8] in 1812. When Ballyward Bridge over the Liffey collapsed in 1986 in the wake of Hurricane Charlie, the cross section showed it had hollow spandrels of the type advocated by Nimmo. This bridge was erected before the 1830s as evidenced by the 1840 six-inch OS map; however, a bridge is also shown at Ballyward on Griffith's bog survey map of Co. Wicklow of 1813 so if it was the same one it is unlikely that it was designed by Nimmo (see Pollaphuca Bridge*).

William Bald's career is well documented by Storrie.[10] He came to Ireland from his native Scotland in 1809 as a trained surveyor and spent most of the following 30 years working on public works and other projects in Ireland. His work and writings establish him as a competent and even original surveyor, cartographer and civil engineer. He designed and supervised the coast road in Antrim and hundreds of miles of new roads in other parts of Ireland. He lived for sometime in Paris in the 1820s, where he had engraved his famous map of Co. Mayo. His 1832 timber bridge over the Bann is described in the Northern Ireland entry in Part II. In 1837 he presented a paper[11] describing a practical method he had developed for forming the stones for four elliptic arches in a bridge he had erected over the Owenmore river in Co. Mayo. He was obviously responsible for the design of hundreds of bridges on the roads he built in Ireland. The key to Bald's thinking on bridge design is found in his evidence to the all-important select committee on public works in Ireland, 1835, [12] when he submitted that "it would be a most desirable object to have a school of roads and bridges established in Dublin, for the purpose of imparting theoretically and practically knowledge to young men." The type of school he had in mind was one like the École des Ponts et Chaussées in Paris, for which Storrie states he had great enthusiasm.

Unlike Bald and Nimmo we have no information on where Richard Griffith acquired the experience that enabled him to build 128 bridges in north Munster in the period 1822–31 (see Griffith Bridges). It is quite possible that he acquired his knowledge of bridge design from a study of reports, drawing and documents his father had accumulated as a director of the Grand Canal Company in the 1790s.[13] In 1812 Griffith was appointed part-time mining engineer to the Dublin Society, which gave him access to its reports and other literature (including works on road building). The most remarkable fact about Griffith's roads and bridges is that they were built by direct labour under his personal supervision, and relatively cheaply.

There were other engineers and architects in Ireland in the period who had a good knowledge of bridge building but not many who had the innovative zeal of Nimmo, Bald and Griffith. It must be remembered that in this period there were few facilities for the training of engineers or for the exchange of information by papers of discussion. All this was to change in the decade or so after 1830 with the establishment of the Board of Public Works (1831), the foundation of the Institution of Civil Engineers of Ireland (1835), and the School of Engineering in Trinity College (1841).

Given the contacts that Nimmo and Bald and perhaps others had with the École des Ponts et Chaussées in Paris, one would expect to find some evidence giving French recommendations on roads and bridges in the relevant engineering literature in Ireland dating from the period 1800 to 1835. Mention has been made above of the copies of Gauthey's treatise published in 1809 which are in the IEI archives. The archive also holds a small book entitled *An Elementary Course of Civil Engineering: translated from the French of M.I. Sganzin*[14] printed in Boston in 1827. Sganzin was inspector general of bridges and roads in professor in the Royal Polytechnic in Paris. The translation stated in the preface that the book "has long had a high reputation in France and has been used as a textbook in the Department of Civil Engineering in the Royal Polytechnic School in Paris. . . ". In 1823 it was adopted by the US Military Academy at Westpoint. The author's preface states that it was intended for students destined for the Corps des Ponts et Chaussées and for those in other branches of the public service.

Sganzin's book was by far the best and most comprehensive on road and bridge design in the early 19th century. Chapter 16 deals with the *appareil*, that is the art which determines the forms which materials should have for a stone bridge; Chapter 17 with pressure of arches and earth and principles of design; Chapters 18 to 20 with construction. There was a rapid advance in the quality of bridge design and construction in Ireland in the period 1820–50; much of this may be attributed to French influences pioneered by Nimmo and Bald and disseminated by Sganzin's book. The following is a summary of the statements and recommendations from it considered most relevant in the Irish context. The semicircle, or the full centre as it was sometimes called, is the most beautiful and simple but it sometimes raises the bridge too high; also the flood discharge diminishes rapidly as it rises through the arch. Flat arches satisfy the flood problem but cannot often be employed because of difficulty of construction and the great expense of abutments. The arc of a circle suffers from the same problems. Architects generally have preferred the eccentric semi-ellipsis, as the curve best suited for arches of bridges, being a mean between a semi-circle and arc. The rise of the semi-ellipsis varies from ¼ to ¾ the span. The difficulty of drawing an ellipsis on a large scale (on the site) causes the oval to be preferred, as it is constructed with arcs of circles and approaches very near the former. All ovals (*anse de paniers*) have an uneven number of centres (generally three but Pont Neuilly had eleven). Various methods of drawing ovals, including those used by stone cutters on the site, are described and illustrated in the book. Where a sufficiently large building was not available at the site, it is suggested that a masonry wall with a thick coat of plaster be erected; where the centre of a curve fell outside the template surface, offsets from chords were used.

Several pages are devoted to a discussion of "pressures of arches" and the determination of points of rupture. In order for rupture not to occur, Sganzin says, the abutments must withstand "overthrow" and sliding and the mortars must be sufficiently adhesive. On the analysis of forces he says that while "several engineers and geometricians of the first reputation have occupied themselves on the investigation . . . their results do not agree." He mentions

Perronet's experiments and then says that Chezy calculated tables from La Hire's formula and determined the point of rupture for a full centre and an ellipse: "these tables have been used with success for determining the dimensions of the abutments of all the large bridges which have been constructed of late years in France." The tables also give the thickness of the piers for arches of full centres and for those lowered by one third for all spans and divers heights of piers and for different weights of earth and pavement and of the keystone. Sganzin also refers to Prony's *Memoire* and *Mecanique* as a basis for calculating earth pressures.

Bridges, he says, should be usually narrower than the roads leading into them. Piers should be as thin as possible, and the axis of the bridge should be perpendicular to the course of the river as far as is possible; if the bed is composed of substances capable of being raised by the current, the width of the "debouche" should be nearly equal to the stream. A practical rule is given for determining the thickness of the keystone of large arches: "To $1/24$ of the span, add the constant quantity of one foot, from which sum subtract one hundred and forty fourth of the span, the remainder is the thickness of the arch at the keystone." On the thickness of piers Sganzin refers to the differences of opinion among celebrated engineers: "some think that the opposite thrusts should be regarded as nothing for equal arches." Other theories suggest that the piers should be twice the thickness of the keystone. Attention is drawn to the extra cost of centering for their piers and the risk of sequential collapse if one pier is undermined. On architectural character: "bridges should correspond with the locality— simple and plain upon roads; bold rich and varied in cities."

Chapters 18 to 20 deal with foundations, piling, grillage, coffer dams, caissons, centres, decentering and wooden bridges. Several features of Griffith's Bridges*, in particular the method of joining the voussoirs with the horizontal courses of the piers called "elbow appareil" (fig. 205), seem to have their source in Sganzin's book. These bridges were an inspiration and a decade or so later the Board of Public Works were designing and building fine large span arches on the Shannon and in the late 1840s across many other major rivers such as Scariff* on the Boyne. From 1839 onwards most

new masonry arch bridges in Ireland were connected with the railways. The monumental bridge erected at Avoca* gives a real insight in to construction methods; Bowen's paper[15] on the rebuilding of the central arch of Ballyvoyle viaduct which was blown up in 1922 is also relevant.

From the 1870s onwards interest in the design of masonry arches waned as engineers and researchers turned their attention to new materials. But new problems presented themselves in the form of locomotives, steam rollers and other heavy loads crossing the existing masonry arch road bridges. In 1862 Rankin[16] stated that the stability of an arch would be satisfactory if a linear arch balanced under the forces acting on the arch could be drawn within so as to lie within the middle third of the ring section between the intrados and extrados. This became known as the middle third rule. Castigliano[17], an Italian, used the newly developed theorems of strain/energy to develop a method of calculating how an arch ring would deform under load. Research at Trinity College, Dublin in the 1890s further developed Rankin's methods and produced semi-graphical methods for arch design. The findings published in 1900[18] made a notable contribution to the subject by demonstrating the importance of horizontal forces generated by fast heavy locomotives on railway arches and the resistance provided by backfill over the haunches. Today this aspect has become equally important for road bridges with the advent of fast-travelling juggernauts. The research at TCD was continued into the 1920s by Dr Lilly, who published many papers[19] on the topic. Pippard's[20] experiments in the late 1930s led to the Military Engineering Experimental Establishments (MEXE) system for assessing the strength of existing arches which was of vital importance during World War II and which had since been updated and modified several times, the most recent being 1984. Heyman's research and the plastic methods and mechanism procedures described in his excellent book[21] for practising engineers, published in 1982, has contributed much to our understanding of the behaviour and the assessment of arches.

Since 1982 the Transport and Road Laboratory has had an ongoing research programme to re-examine the methods of assessing the carrying capacity of brick and masonry arches which includes full scale tests and the development of computer programmes for arch analysis. Already this research is making a very important contribution to understanding of arch behaviour.[22] All of this is important not alone from an economic aspect, but also in the preservation of the small and diminishing number of medieval arches that have survived here and in other countries.

PART II

Location of Selected Bridges

Selected Bridges and Bridge Groups

An italicised bridge name indicates that the bridge does not survive.

No	Bridge or bridge group name	City or county	Probable year/century of erection	Grid Reference number
1	*Skeagh* (Shannon R.)	Leitrim/Roscommon	Early type	12N 013 936
2	*Knockainey* (Camoge R.)	Limerick	Early type	18R 655 360
3	*Drumheriff* (Shannon R.)	Leitrim/Roscommon	Early type	7G 941 086
4	Garfinny (Garfinny R.)	Kerry	Early type	20Q 475 020
5	St Mary Magdalen (Nanny R.)	Meath	12th or 13th	13O 050 685
6	Babes (Boyne R.)	Meath	13th	13N 892 700
7	Mabe's (Blackwater R.)	Meath	13th	13N 736 744
8	Monks (Nore R.)	Laois	13th	15S 412 832
9	*Thomond (old)* (Shannon R.)	Limerick	1210	17R 577 578
10	Abbeytown (Boyle Water)	Roscommon	13th	7G 806 028
11	King John's (Griffeen R.)	Dublin	13th	16O 040 343
12	*Castlemang* (Maine R.)	Kerry	13th	20Q 835 031
13	St John's (John's R.)	Waterford	13th	23S 608 115
14	Athassel (mill race)	Tipperary S.R.	13th	18S 018 364
15	Ballybeg (Awbeg R.)	Cork	13th or 14th	21R 543 094
16	Gormanstown (Devlin R.)	Dublin/Meath	13th or 14th	13O 170 658
17	*New Bridge* (Liffey R.)	Dublin/Kildare	1309	16N 993 344
18	Baal's (Shannon R.)	Limerick	14th	17R 578 573
19	Trim (Boyne R.)	Meath	14th	13N 800 570
20	Slane (Boyne R.)	Meath	14th	13N 963 735
21	Carrick-on-Suir (Suir R.)	Tipperary/Waterford	1350s	22S 401 217
22	Clonmel (Suir R.)	Tipperary/Waterford	1350s	22S 202 222
23	Adare (Maigue R.)	Limerick	1410	17R 470 466
24	Askeaton (Deel R.)	Limerick	14th or 15th	17R 342 503
25	Newtown (Boyne R.)	Meath	c.1450	13N 815 568
26	Glanworth (Funsion R.)	Cork	1446 ?	22R 758 041
27	Grace Dieu (stream)	Dublin	15th	13O 178 523
28	*Bennetsbridge* (Nore R.)	Kilkenny	13th	19S 552 492
29	Watercastle (Nore R.)	Laois	15th or 16th	18S 425 805
30	Holycross (Suir R.)	Tipperary	15th	18S 089 541
31	*Enniscorthy* (Slaney R.)	Wexford	1581	19S 972 398
32	Kilcarn (Boyne R.)	Meath	16th	13N 884 655

33	Carragh (Liffey R.)	Kildare	16th	16N 853 208
34	Lissenhall (Broadmeadow R.)	Dublin	16th	13O 186 482
35	*Drogheda* (Boyne R.)	Louth/Meath	–	13O 090 751
36	*Athlone* (Shannon R.)	Westmeath/Roscommon	1567	15N 042 415
37	Ballinasloe (Suck R.)	Galway	1570	15M 855 312
38	Roganstown (Broadmeadow R.)	Dublin	16th or 17th	13O 150 502
39	*Abington* (Mulcair R.)	Limerick	1620	18R 710 535
40	*Ballyshannon* (Erne R.)	Donegal	17th	3G 876 614
41	Carrigadrohid (Lee R.)	Cork	16th or 17th	21W 413 724
42	Sir Thomas's (Suir R.)	Tipperary/Waterford	17th	22S 238 228
43	Leighlin (Barrow R.)	Carlow	16th or 17th	19S 691 655
44	Milltown (Dodder R.)	Dublin	17th	16O 168 302
45	Craughwell (Dunkellin R.)	Galway	17th	14M 511 199
46	*Cappoquin* (Blackwater R.)	Waterford	1665	22X 100 992
47	Bective (Boyne R.)	Meath	17th	13N 860 598
48	Kinnegad (Kinnegad R.)	Meath	1670	13N 601 452
49	Leabeg (stream)	Wicklow	17th	16O 295 063
50	*Old Long* (Lagan R.)	Antrim	1682	5N 35 76
51	Cork City Group (Lee R.)	Cork City	17th & 18th	Several
52	Crooked (Camac R.)	Dublin	17th	16O 036 248
53	Group N.I. (several)	N. Ireland	17th & 18th	Several
54	Kilbeg (stream)	Meath	1750	13N 777 818
55	*Essex* (Liffey R.)	Dublin	1753	13O 090 752
56	Kilkenny Group (several)	Kilkenny	1760s	Several
57	Killaloe and	Clare/Tipperary	1770	18R 705 730
	O'Briens (Shannon R.)			18R 668 665
58	Avoca (Avoca R.)	Wicklow	1770s	19T 203 799
59	Scariff (Boyne R.)	Meath	1762	13N 733 527
60	Kanturk (Dalua R.)	Cork	1760s	21R 382 032
61	Clara (Avonmore R.)	Wicklow	17th	16T 146 921
62	*Cashen* (Cashen R.)	Kerry	?	17Q 860 382
63	Lismore (Blackwater R.)	Waterford	1775	22X 048 988
64	Laragh (Glenmacnass R.)	Wicklow	18th	16T 168 967
65	*Lemuel Cox's* (several R.)	several	1790s	Several
66	Sarah's (Liffey R.)	Dublin	1793	16O 128 344
67	Lucan (Liffey R.)	Dublin	1814	16O 035 355
68	Pollaphuca (Liffey R.)	Wicklow	1820s	16N 945 082
69	Newrath (Vartry R.)	Wicklow	1839	16T 285 967
70	Causeway Bridge (Colligan R.)	Waterford	1813	22X 261 933
71	Cromaboo (Barrow R.)	Kildare	1796	16S 682 938
72	Griffith's Group (several)	Cork/Kerry	1820s	Several
73	Goleen (stream)	Cork	1824	24V 810 282
74	*Kenmare* (Roughty R.)	Kerry	1841	20V 910 699

Fig. 17: *Selected Bridges and Bridge Groups*

Skeagh Causeway

A note in a learned journal (1906)[1] refers to the construction of primitive causeways: "On larger rivers a 'tochar' or causeway was made of huge boulders heaved one after the other till eventually they came above the surface." Such a causeway exists across the Shannon at Skeagh between Co. Roscommon and Co. Leitrim placed there by a giant race of earlier inhabitants of the country and afterwards utilised by the monks of Kilmore and Mohill Abbeys. It is still known as The Friars' Walk." This form of construction would be the most obvious and the simplest primitive method that would suggest itself in an area with plenty of loose field stones. The name Skeagh suggests an eel weir of particular construction. There is a townland in Upper Ossory called Aharney, shown on the Down Survey, which Joyce states is At Carna or the heaped ford—a similar type of structure—and another in Co. Meath. A skeagh or skea is described in the Drainage Report for Lough Neagh District *c.* 1847 located between Toomebridge and the lough:

These weirs are very substantial structures consisting of a double line of piles, from 5 to 8 inches in diameter, driven into the bed of the river, and bound together by horizontal pieces treenailed on to them; between these two rows of piles, the 'skeas', that is, strong wattle or hurdle work was placed; and to enable the weir thus constructed to resist the force of the current, which, from the closeness of the work lies heavily against it, it is supported by numerous sloping strut piles firmly driven and well secured.

Gwynn and Hadcock[2] record several references in the Annals to monasteries dating back to the 5th century at both Mohill and Kilmore. The Shannon Commission Reports[3] contain a plan and section of the river dated 1838 with Skeagh Point clearly marked (fig. 18). It also shows a shoal there with a depth of water of 5ft 3in. (determined by the upper cill of Roosky lock). The shoal was marked for removal under the proposed improvements. There was no indication of an eel weir at Skeagh, but down-river at Cloonfad one is clearly marked and indicated by a triangle of rock jutting up from the bed level. The bed at Skeagh is composed of gravel and clay about 30ft deep overlying rock. It is evident from the long section that the shallowest part of the river was the narrow neck linking Lough Tap and famed Boderg.

The townland of Skeagh in Leitrim has a two-mile frontage along the neck of the Shannon between the two lakes and probably served a large hinterland for eel fishing purposes; this may explain the origin of the name.

In 1987 I asked Michael McD. Fleming, retired county engineer of Leitrim, to investigate the feasibility of constructing such a causeway and the local historical aspects; this he did, with characteristic enthusiasm, and reported back as follows:

I know the area well as I shoot snipe and duck there. I have spoken to a few people as to usage of the "Friars' Walk" and J.J. Murphy who lives there vaguely remembers his uncle's use of the phrase. I do not think it is in general use today. Starting at Kilmore Church, where local tradition suggests there was an ancient 'Monks House', a narrow, black-topped road runs down to J.J. Murphy's house near the river. A short distance away across a field there is a navigation channel marked on the Roscommon bank. From the marker to the Leitrim bank the river bed is shallow and firm; nearby is a primitive stone jetty which, I am told, was used for crossing by boat up to recently.

There are many loose stones in this general area of a size of about one quarter of a cubic metre down including a wall containing about 250m³. There are many boulders nearby at Skeagh Point. There would be no difficulty, given enough men, in filling in the narrow channel which formerly existed. A primitive raft and a few timber levers would obviate the need of "giants". About 300m³ of boulders would make a causeway to normal river levels and not cause any significant back-up of water apart from some flooding out on to the callows on the east bank.

On the Leitrim side the ground is firm and rises quickly. I walked dry shod from the jetty to the public road a few hundred meters away. From thence there is a pathway shown on the 1837 OS six-inch map which leads directly to the road to Mohill about four miles from the river and five from Kilmore.

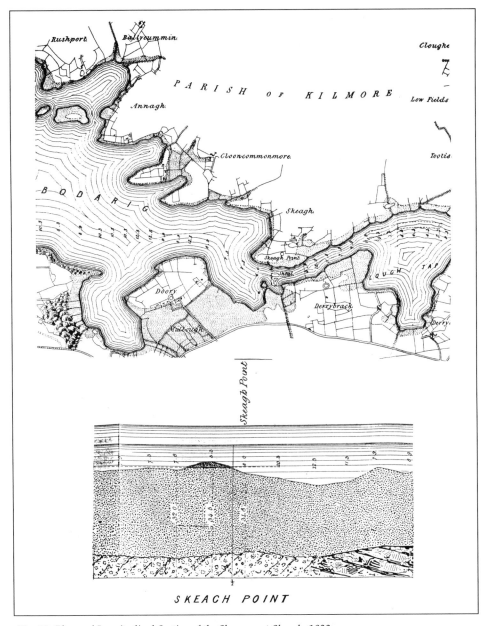

Fig. 18: *Plan and Longitudinal Section of the Shannon at Skeagh, 1833*

It is surprising that there is no definitive term in Irish for such a type of construction. A togher is generally understood to mean a timber causeway across bog or soft ground as evidenced in many townland names. No specific names were found for similar types of improved ford abroad.

For construction in areas without a suffi-

cient local supply of stone it would have been easy to gather stones from a wider area. Michael Murphy, the present county engineer of South Tipperary, recalls that when he worked in North Kenya in the early 1960s an old winding trail was being realigned at the time and many new river crossings were involved. One of the overseers in charge of the bridge building had a very simple method of building temporary causeways in remote areas in the bush. He contacted the local chief and offered to pay the local people one penny for every stone of a specified minimum size brought to the site. The response was always more than adequate. A modified version this method was employed in the erection of Clones Castle by King John's agent in 1211. A pipe roll record of 1211 mentions: "48s. and 3d. for 193 horses and as many men for one day, at the fortification of the Castle of Trim, for each horse and man 3d. per day"[4]— which suggests that King John's agent used an improved method to procure stones for Trim Castle.

Knockainey Clochan

The Camoge river flows through an ancient and historic area in Co. Limerick to join the Maigue near Croom. It derives its name from *cam* and *óg*, meaning the small winding river. Lough Gur, the centre of an area with numerous prehistoric and Early Christian sites, is within its catchment. Many of its remains are Stone Age dwellings, stone circles and forts with archaeologically authenticated dates of 1000 BC or older. Knockainey, a village situated on the river, derives its name from Cnoc Aine, in Irish mythology the seat of Aine, a daughter of an early king of Munster or, as some say, a pagan sun-goddess.

In a note published in 1911[1] Henry Crawford provided a scaled plan and elevation of a "primitive bridge or causeway" in Knockainey, reproduced in fig. 20. In his short description he states that the flagstones were 12 to 14in. thick and the largest 8ft 3in. in length by 6ft 3in. broad and that there was a ford about 120 yards lower down the river for vehicles. Three large stones were set upright at the ford to indicate its location in times of flood. The clochan is marked "stepping stones" on the 1844 OS six-inch map.

In response to our request the county engineer of Limerick, Andy O'Connell, asked the area engineer, Michael Hayes, to enquire about this rare example of a well constructed cloghan. He reported(1987) that "the site is about half a mile from Knockainey village on County Road No. 873. Mr Thomas Walsh, a local man, who is now almost ninety years old, remembers the structure described by Crawford and recalls that when the present bridge [iron girders and a reinforced concrete slab] was built in 1930

Fig. 19: *Knockainey Clochan in 1924*

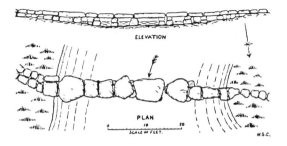

Fig. 20: *Knockainey Clochan: Plan and Section, 1911 (Crawford)*

the stones from the clochan were broken up and used as pitching in the road." Michael Hayes also obtained from Mrs Roche, Post Office, Knockainey, a photograph (fig. 19) showing the clochan in 1924. These enquiries stimulated considerable interest in the old bridge in the village. The photo shows that the clochan was a pedestrian bridge and a sure-footed one at that. It may not even have been built in the Early Christian or the medieval period (we shall never know), but the importance of the record is that it is a first-class example of an early clochan from an ancient historic area.

Drumheriff

A footnote in Lenihan's *History of Limerick* [1] records a communication by Mr John Long, an "eminent civil engineer", who surveyed most of the upper reaches of the Shannon under

Rhodes in the 1830s. He stated that there was "until recently one of these wicker bridges stood over the Shannon above Carrick-on-Shannon and it was built of loose stone piers, such as a common labourer would build, placed close to each other; some rough black oak logs thrown across from pier to pier, and these covered with wicker work in several layers, and gravel, etc. strewn on these. It was very frail, and the horse was unyoked from the cart, and the latter pulled across by men." This note is a vital piece of information for the history of bridges in Ireland; Long stated that he had crossed the bridge many times, so his is first-hand evidence. The Shannon Navigation Survey of the 1830s shows that the longitudinal and traverse sections for Plan 59, Vol. 4, Jamestown section were prepared in 1838 by William Mulvaney, civil engineer and John Long, surveyor; the bridge referred to was the one designated on the survey plan as "wooden bridge" linking Drumheriff and Dereenasoo townlands in Leitrim and Roscommon. Most importantly an elevation of the bridge is contained in Rhodes' 1833 report[2], and is reproduced here in Appendix 8, fig. 217. The bridge was replaced by a five-span stone-arch bridge in the 1890s.

Given the historical importance of the wicker bridge I sent the basic information to Michael McD. Fleming, former county engineer of Leitrim, with a request for his views and any local information. This he did with an antiquary's delight replying (1987):

The wooden bridge was sited approx. 120m upstream of the present bridge. Part of the right bank approach road to it still remains, about 20m back from the river bank where it is approximately 3m wide at the top, 2m high with 2 to 1 side slopes. It is composed of local "danbig" boulder clay. I spoke to a local man, Mr Crawford, who is 82 years old and has a very lucid memory. His house is located a few hundred metres down the road from the site in Dereenasoo. His uncle had used the bridge to bring home turf and had told him that on reaching it he would lift the cart at the rear by the "heels" and with the shafts on the donkey they crossed over. It was also used extensively for bringing corn to a mill, the ruins of which are still standing (shown on 1837 six-inch OS). Major improvements were carried out to the river channel in 1896 evidenced by large volumes of rock and boulders piled on the river banks upstream of the present bridge. A man fell from the old bridge and was drowned some years before it was replaced and this had hastened the decision to replace it.

Michael adds that the gorge spanned by the old bridge was narrow and carried torrents after heavy rain but that three of the five arches of the 1896 bridge are dry during normal flows. The present bridge is still called the "wooden bridge".

The deck of the old Drumheriff Bridge as described by Long conforms very closely with the construction one would expect to find on one of the 12th century Shannon cesdroichets, mentioned so frequently in the Annals and discussed in Chapter 9, Part 1. Given the plentiful supply of oak, both bog and fallen trees, it would not have been difficult to gather about fifty 12ft long, roughly hewn timbers for the main beams. Once these were in position the decking would present little problem given the native skill in wickerwork. With several layers, the effective mesh would be small enough to hold a layer of coarse gravel sufficient to prevent an animal's hoove bursting through. This would give extra dead weight and help to offset the buoyancy of the timber. There is no information on how the deck was built into the piers and fastened down to resist winds and floods. Presumably tie ropes made from roots were used originally. Molyneux[3] records that ropes made from the roots of fir trees were still used in many parts in 1709, for example, for drying linen. Ropes and cables of any description were an expensive item in the medieval period as illustrated by an entry in the Pipe Roll of 14 John (1212): "22s. for a large cable which is for work at Trim, that is to say, for demolishing the tower, and 16s. for 6 ropes sent to Clones." For comparison, the wage of a smith for one year was 20s.

Long's remarks on the quality of the masonry in the piers must be read in the context of the very high quality ashlar work specified for the Shannon Navigation Works. The piers look well shaped and evenly spaced on the drawing. They were 4ft 6in. wide at the top and about 9ft at the bottom, a good bulk of dry masonry and one which could accommodate large stones. The subsoil in the river bed would not have been very susceptible to scour, given the nature of the boulders excavated in

1896 and spread on the banks. There was no need for kishes as the river here was shallow in dry summers.

Overall, therefore, the evidence from the records of this bridge is important because of the insight it gives into the traditional early form of Irish bridge on large rivers in the late Christian period.

Garfinny

There is an unmortared stone-arch bridge, a cloch droichet in the fullest sense, located on the old road from Dingle to Annascaul about two miles east of Dingle, in the townland of Garfinny. It spans a river of the same name which rises on the slopes of the 2000ft Shevanca mountain and falls to the sea in the space of five miles and is "flashy". Harbison[1] mentions no less than 37 ancient stone monuments in the western half of the peninsula. A glance at the 1846 OS six-inch map shows the area to be festooned with every possible kind of ancient stone monument from stepping stones to ancient churches. Barrington[2] states that many, such as Kelmalkedar Church and Gallarus Oratory, display perfection in the art of dry stone walling and roofing.

The bridge was taken into State care after investigation by the National Parks and Monuments Branch of the OPW in 1982–4. A notice to this effect is displayed on the site. A new reinforced concrete bridge was built just upstream of the old one in the 1970s (fig. 21). Some repairs were carried out by the OPW in 1984, but nothing that altered the shape or character of the original.

In 1987, Jim Penny prepared a sketch (fig. 22) giving the key measurements. The width between the abutments is 12ft 6in., whereas the chord of the segmental arch ring is 9ft 2in. The reduction was accomplished by corbelling slightly from abutment base to riverbank level and then significantly, with three or four massive stones, to springing level. The "skewback" is formed with two very large stones and some packing with smalled ones; all are loaded with a large heavy counter-balancing rock. Stability here is of vital importance, as any slippage of the skewback would lead to the formation of hinges and eventual collapse. The importance of this seems to have been well understood by the artificer. The arch ring is 20in. thick and, as evident from the photo (fig. 21), built with weathered flat slabs of old red sandstone.

The first indicator that the present arch is not old is the fact that it is a segment of a circle (90⁰ of arc); also, unlike the Meath bridges, the springings of the radial arc are not formed by successive cumulative tilting of the corbelled stones. They are horizontal as in the inside of the entrances to the "guard room" at nearby Dunbeg Fort, which are topped with flat lintel stones. Perhaps the construction is in the tradition of Kilmalkedar, which is oblong and the fallen roof of which, according to Leask,[3] seems to have been formed internally of "a curious ogee, reversed-curve form". However, we need not dwell on these technicalities, important as they are, because the literary dating evidence seems to have answered the question. The Down Survey map shows a bridge at Milltown across the river of the same name, just west of Dingle, one of two shown for the whole of Kerry. Moll's map (1714) shows the road from Castlemain to Dingle and Ventry. It crosses the

Fig. 21: *Garfinny Bridge: Old and New Bridges, 1988*

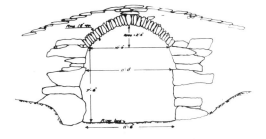

Fig. 22: *Garfinny Bridge: Downriver Elevation, 1988*

Owenalondrig directly north of Minard (Kinard on map) and obviously follows the old high road via Gowlin and Garfinny to Dingle, though no rivers or placenames are indicated. Rocque's map (1794) is obviously a copy of Moll's for this area. The Taylor and Skinner map (1778) shows the new line (the former T68), dead straight from Lispole to Dingle. Andrews[4] mentions the turnpike made in 1748 from Millstreet to Listowel and then states that at the same time "other new roads, most of them equally straight, were cut by the local gentry from Castleisland to Abbeyfeale, Tralee and Killarney and from Castlemain to Tralee and Dingle". From this we can deduce that the old Garfinny Bridge, which local tradition holds was crossed by Lord Deputy Grey and 800 troops in October 1580 on his way to perpetrate the ruthless massacre of Smerwick where 600 men, women and children who had surrendered were executed, had greatly diminished in importance by 1750.

The next map with detail is the 1846 six-inch OS which gives no indication of a bridge at Garfinny, but closer scrutiny reveals a solid line stretching three-quarters way across the road on what should be the north-east abutment of the bridge. It looks like a barrier wall for vehicular traffic with perhaps sufficient bridge left for pedestrians. On the 1912 edition we find "Garfinny Bridge" written on the map; however, about 50ft upriver a "ford" is indicated, which indicates that the arch of the present bridge is post-1846. Further local study, using the 25in. scale map, may establish the date more accurately; however, without the grand jury records for Kerry which, as stated in Part I, were burned in a courthouse fire, it may be difficult. Presumably the grand juries never agreed to a presentment for the proper reconstruction of the bridge because there was an alternative road down through Flemingston townland to the main road, so the inconvenience was minimal in a time when there would always be higher priority works to be done. The rebuilding may have been a local repair without using lime mortar, which was costly. In 1845 Wilkinson[5] recorded that Dingle was chiefly supplied with lime from kilns situated five miles from Tralee on the Killarney road and it cost a shilling per barrel (42 gallons) at the kiln. It would have taken a lot of mortar to fill the voids as evidenced from the photos.

The foregoing findings do not diminish the importance of the Garfinny Bridge from a historical, as distinct from an archaeological, point of view. It is constructed in the ancient tradition of the area. However, there is evidence nearby of the use of mortar at an early date. Barrington mentions the walls of the ruins of the early Christian 'Temple Martin' in Lispole: "The large stones, inside and out, were set without mortar and the interior filled with rubble grouted with mortar. The west door is of well dressed stone, with the usual slanting jambs, but trabeated, the first setting back of doorway within doorway that was to receive such development in Irish Romanesque but here, of course, the lintel is still flat in traditional style. No doubt this church dates from the 8th century." The fact that the fluid lime mortar was poured would not be a good dating criterion as it was still a practice in bridge building in Ireland in later medieval times (see Mabe's Bridge); however, the other dating evidence is convincing. The important question that emerges is: where did the lime come from? Oyster shells are mentioned as a probable source in Chapter 8, Part I and this theory is advanced by the many references in Barrington to middens along the coast on the Dingle peninsula. One reference is of special interest: "at Inch strand, in the middle of the sandhills of Moghaglass, is a valley between high sandhills with, in places, stretches of water. High above one, to the south, is a raised beach with shell middens of primitive shore dwellers. Charcoal and other traces of fire are visible. There are 'hammer stones' and 'grain rubbers' broken and whole, sandstone knives and axes, bones, traces of iron smelting." There would have been no problem in burning oyster shells for lime in such a settlement.

Finally, in relation to this most interesting bridge, there was the question of how it behaves structurally under its own weight, how stable is it. An analysis (see Chapter 12) was carried out by Tom Holland to ascertain the line of thrust, the reactions and, most importantly, the magnitude of the mean stress. It showed that thrust line lay along the axis of the ring and the mean stress at the springings is 12 lbs per square inch (very low); this does not mean that it is safe for modern traffic loads because vibrations and punching could cause stones in the arch barrel to drop out. This has happened in a few bridges around the country in recent years where the mortar had been

Fig. 23: *St Mary Magdalen Bridge: Upriver Elevation*

leached out. Generally, however, the friction force between the rough textured unmortared stones under dead load thrust is more than adequate when the stones have contact with the adjoining ones.

St Mary Magdalen's

"By which bridge people have used to pass from time whereof no memory is" (Stat. Rolls Ir. 1459).
I came across the above phrase in the course of a search for all too rare early mentions of bridges. It was an exciting find but the chances of the bridge being still there seemed remote. Soon afterwards I visited the site and found it in the middle of a causeway containing three separate bridges, high and dry, but intact. There was a plaque on the parapet, difficult to decipher on the spot, but the date, 1587, and the word "Builded" were clearly discernible. A first glance at the arch rings on the upriver side (fig. 23) showed that the stones were corbelled from the springings with accumulating declination to about half way up the haunches each side and the crown filled in with truly radial jointed stones; this brought to mind the supporting vaults of the 9th-century stone-roofed churches in nearby Kells and in Glendalough (see Glossary), and convinced me that the bridge was ancient.

The text of the statute referred to (37 Henry VI c. 22) gives a rare insight into the mal-practices of the king's officials in Dublin Castle and some clues as to the age of the bridge:

Also, at the request of the Commons: That forasmuch as there is a bridge at Duleek which is called the bridge of the Maudelynes, by which bridge people have used to pass from time whereof no memory is, and by the default of repairs the said bridge is so ruinous and ill-repaired that divers people have fallen from the bridge when the water was high, and some of them were engulfed and died, and some others in great peril of their lives. And heretofore fourteen acres of land and meadow with the appurtenances were given to the Chapel of the Maudelynes of the said town, to the support and sustenance of the lepers there from ancient time remaining; and notwithstanding that the said fourteen acres with the appurtenances were from ancient times given so charitably, yet for these forty years past and more the said land has been taken and seized into the hands of the King, and the rents and issues thereof by the King's ministers assigned and received in divers manners and converted or distributed to no alms. Whereupon the premises considered: It is ordained and agreed by the authority of the said Parliament, that the proctors of Lanthony for the time being or in time to come in Duleek may have and enjoy the said fourteen acres with the appurtenances

Fig. 24: *St Mary Magdalen Bridge and 1774 Overflow Arches, Upriver*

arched multispan bridge that collapsed in the flood of 8 December 1953. The latter bridge had been erected in 1884 when the new river channel was cut under a drainage scheme that cost £7,629 and stretched from Kilsharva Weir to Balrath Mill Weir. There is a concrete plaque in the field with the following inscription: "Nanny Drainage 1884, J.H. Moore CE, Engineer; N. Hatch CE, Contractor". Mr Moore was county surveyor and a prominent antiquary.

2. The three-arch Maudlin Bridge is now an overflow channel. Its overall width is 21ft consisting of a 10ft 6in. original on the upstream side and a 10ft 6in. extension. The butt joints, clearly visible on the arch soffits, are from one to three inches wide; in places the intrados has lips of up to 2in. There are no cutwaters on the extension.

3. One of the cutwaters has been extended up to form a recess in the parapet in which there is a roadside plaque with the following inscription, in bas relief: "This bridge with/the cavsies/were repaired/and bvilded bi/William Bathe/of Athcarne Justice and/Iennet Do/wdall his wife/ in the yeare of/ovr Lord God 1587/whose sovles God/take to his mercie, Amen". The inscription is surmounted by the Bathe Dowdall coat of arms. The last line has been broken off but was recorded in an antiquarian journal.[1] It is also illustrated in a Du Noyer sketch.

4. There are two overflow arches in the causeway, located about 60ft east of Maudlin's bridge forming in effect a third separate bridge (fig. 24). It is 25ft wide, consisting of an original upstream section 16ft wide and a 9ft downstream extension. The butt joint is clearly visible. The soffits of the better-shaped ring stones which formed the original downriver face are clearly distinguishable, whereas those on the butt edge of the extension are in rubble stones indistinguishable from the barrel. The present facing rings at both ends are composed of uniform well shaped stones.

from henceforward, for the repair and building of the said bridge for ever, without any impediment or impeachment of the King, his officers or his ministers; rendering account of the expenses to the portreeves of the said town of Duleek for the time being, and not to the King's Exchequer in Ireland; without paying any fine or fee for the same into the King's Hanaper in Ireland for the King's great seal. And that all manner of seizures of the said fourteen acres with the appurtenances and of every parcel thereof into the hands of the King that now is, or into the hands of any of his noble progenitors or predecessors made or to be made, be void and null in law, and that the said proctors and their servants be no more henceforth vexed, molested or aggrieved, of all impeachments towards our lord the King. Provided always that the lepers be sustained and that the residue be expended upon the repair of the said bridge. To continue for the term of twenty years, and that the seizure into the King's hands remain in its force.

Given the importance of this bridge in a national context, an in-depth search of relevant literature was carried out. The findings together with data on its physical characteristics are summarised and presented in reverse chronological order below:

1. The 40ft single-span reinforced concrete bridge over the present main channel of the Nanny was erected in 1954. It replaced a stone-

A search of the Meath grand jury query books in the National Archive for 1761–1837 (excluding the years 1777–84, and 1811–15, which are missing) discovered the following records of expenditure on the causeway bridges:

1827: That £47.15s.5d. be raised and paid to G. Smith and M. Reiths to repair and rebuild the battlements of a bridge at

Duleek on the road from Drogheda to Dublin via Duleek.

1802: That £27.7s.6d. and £1.7s.4d. be raised to cope the bridge of Duleek on the road from Duleek to Dublin and £26.16s.10d. and £1.6s.10d. to cope the battlements of the Bridge of Duleek on the Road from Drogheda to Dublin.

1801: That £100.6s.4d. and £5.0s.4d. be raised to build a bridge on the lands of Duleek on the road from Trim to Drogheda.

1774: That £69 be raised and paid to Mr Trotter, Mr Dillon and Mr Codlis to build three additional arches to the bridge of Duleek on the road from Duleek to Dublin, 280 perches of mason work at 4s. with £3.9s.6d. for the overseer.

1774: That £12.3s.0d. be raised to repair an arch of the Bridge of Duleek (the £5 presented for the above use at the Summer Assizes 1773 not being sufficient) 25 perches of mason work at 3s.6d with 17s. to the overseer.

1775: New Query Co.-at-large, Whether £10.16s.0d. be raised as before and paid to Thos. Trotter and Robert Castles to complete and finish the Bridge of Duleek, road from Duleek to Dublin, 54 perches at 4s. and 10s. 9d. wages.

1761: That £79.12s.6d. be raised, as before presented, and paid to Stephen Trotter [et al.] for enlarging and widening the bridge of Duleek on the great route leading from Kilcock and Dunshaughlin to Drogheda, which said bridge is in a ruinous condition and too narrow for carriages and passengers to pass which will require 170 perches of mason work at 3s. 6d. a perch and 261 perches for side walls 9ft high, and 4 perches in a corner of a side wall 6ft high amounting in the whole to 435 perches of mason work, pursuant to an affidavit.

The first three items, with the exception of the £27. 7s. 6d and £1. 7s. 4d. under 1802, apply to the next bridge downstream, on the Duleek by-pass road built in 1801-2. That bridge collapsed in the 1953 floods and was replaced with treble span "Armco" culvert. The parapet

copings on Maudlin are of a type common in Meath c. 1800 and were probably erected in 1802. The 1774 item of £69 must refer to the twin additional overflow or flood arches described in paragraph 4 above, as the other item seems to refer to the repairs of an arch in the existing bridge. The 1775 item is for the completion; however, the £69 was re-presented at the Spring Assizes in 1775, so it must have been refused in 1774: there is no way of knowing this except from the records of the immediately succeeding years and these are lost. Perhaps the query was modified and the number of arches reduced to two as that was all that was built.

The 1761 item clearly refers to Maudlin because it specifies "enlarging and widening". Boulge in his book on the battle of the Boyne mentions that "About four miles south of the Boyne was a place called Duleek where the road to Dublin was so narrow that two cars could not pass each other and where on both sides of the road lay a morass which afforded no firm footing." The Irish infantry retreating from Oldbridge and the French from Rosnaree reached the narrow pass at Duleek at the same time and confusion resulted; however, William of Orange failed to force the pass. The road boundary and retaining wall on the widened side, downriver, runs the whole length of the field and is about 600ft long, excluding Maudlin's Bridge. The height in the vicinity of the bridge is 9ft over ground level. Assuming an average thickness of 2ft and allowing for a reduced height on the east end, the volume of masonry, 261 perches, would be about right. The volume given for the bridge extension, 170 perches, is on the high side, but if the foundations were deep and wide it would account for the extra volume; alter-natively some repairs may have been needed on the upriver side, seeing that the bridge was then "in a ruinous condition". It is reasonable to conclude that the widening was carried out in the 1770s. The bridge is shown on the Down Survey map so it was in service in 1656.

The next reference is the plaque; my conclusion, based on a careful consideration of the wording in the context of the phraseology of the period as expressed in bridge acts and other bridge mentions, is that the bridge was repaired and the causeway built up in 1587. Without careful archaeological excavation and detailed examination of the masonry in the upriver retaining walls, it is impossible to be precise as to the extent of the work. However, it would appear that prior to the work Maudlin Bridge was humpbacked and had low level approaches on each side over which the river flowed in high floods. This was common problem pre-17th-century bridges as evidenced by the special causeway clause in the English act of 1534 referred to in Part I. The wording of the prayer could indicate that William Bathe and Janet Dowdall were deceased at the time of its erection. (The wayside Dowdall Cross in Duleek shows he died in 1599; his wife died in 1599. William Bathe was created Justice of Her Majesty's Court of Common Pleas in 1581.)

Fig. 25: *St Mary Magdalen Bridge W. Arch and Raised Cutwater*

Fig. 26: *St Mary Magdalen Bridge: E. Arch Upriver*

The bridge is known locally as the "de Bathe Bridge" because of the plaque, but this is wrong because it implies that the bridge is not as old as it actually is.

The key mention of the bridge is the 1459 statute. We know from it that the original bridge was then ruinous and that provision was made for its repair. We also know that it was then called Maudelin, a name which Dr Logan[2] states "almost invariably indicates a medieval hospital of St Mary Magdalen, often for lepers". Gwynn & Hadcock[3] state that the Irish chartularies of Leanthony record that there was a leper-house at Duleek *c*. 1202, which in a record of 1419 is mentioned as "Le magdelyns". The 1459 statute assigned the 14 acres to the proctor of Leanthony in Duleek for "repair and building of the said bridge" provided the lepers were sustained, "the residue to be expended on the repair of the bridge". It should be noted that an acre in 1459 was probably of greater area than the modern equivalent or indeed than the Petty Plantation or Irish acre. Andrews[4] discusses this problem in detail and points out that it largely depended on the length of a perch which in Ireland in the 16th century varied from 16ft 6in. in Finglas to 29ft in Munster.

Some references to lepers and leper hospitals found in Gwynn and Hadcock are relevant. Hugh de Lacey erected a hospital called "the leper-house of St Brigid in Kilbixy, Co. Westmeath in 1192. He gave permission for the internment of lepers in his territory in 1215. He founded a richly endowed St Michael's Priory in Duleek in 1180. There was a leper hospital of St Brigid in Kells in 1117, the name of which was changed to St Mary Magdalen's and where there is an 18th-century replacement bridge across the Blackwater in the townland of Maudlins. All of the foregoing strongly suggests that the Duleek Maudlins dates at the latest from the last quarter of the 12th century. There is the possibility that there was a spital of St Brigid in Duleek in pre-Norman or "ancient times" and that it was regranted and renamed by de Lacey. Perhaps there was an early Irish equivalent of the continental *opus pontis* combining a bridge, a hospital and sometimes a chapel as suggested by the townland name of Spittal Bridge in Co. Cork (see Buttevant Old Bridge).

Finally the archaeological evidence that is visible on the facade of the original section and under its arches must be appraised. Much of it is self-evident from figs 25 and 26 and need only be summarised here. The cutwaters are triangular upstream; we do not know if there were any downstream. There are no pedestrian refuges but one cutwater was extended up in 1587 to accommodate the plaque (clearly evident from the masonry); the intrados are semi-circular though a bit irregular; the ring stones are broken slabby field stones and vary considerably in shape and thickness; the spans and piers are 10ft wide, the average depth of the facing ring is 21in. In the left hand arch looking downstream there are 12 stones on the left and 16 on the right; the first eight of the 12 are corbelled from an almost level springing with each successive stone cantilevered about 4in. and dipping progressively until the eighth which is almost radial. The barrel stones as evidenced by their soffits follow the same pattern.

No other bridge including Mabe's and Boyle exhibits the evolution of the radial arch in Ireland as clearly as Duleek; moreover, the documentary evidence of age is much stronger. It is located in a town that is recorded as being the site of the first stone church in Ireland, founded by St Cinian in the 5th century and from which it took its name, Daimh-liac.

The death of St Cinian is reported in the Annals of the Four Masters under the year 488. The following is recorded by Cuffe[5]: "It is said in the office of St Kenan which is still extant in the public library at Cambridge that St Kenan built a church of stone in this place (Argetbor) and that from thence it took its name Dam-leagh for that before this time the churches of Ireland were built of wattles and boards."

Babes

The existence of the single surviving arch of this bridge has been well documented for exactly one and a half centuries since William Wilde wrote his classic *The Beauties of the Boyne and Blackwater*. Ellison included a reminder in his book[1] published in 1978: "Strangely, the [Civil] Survey does not mention one of the most ancient Boyne bridges, known as Babe's or Mabe's and later as the Rogues or Robbers' Bridge, near the Round Tower of Donaghmore."

I came across a most important early mention of the bridge in the autumn of 1986 when searching for such information in the statute rolls of Ireland. The statute, 3 Edw. IV c. 82 (1463),[2] prescribed:

> LXXXII. Also, at the request of the Commons of the county of Meath. Whereas there is a bridge in the said county called Babesbridge, which is great ease to all the Commons of the said county, and through default of repair, the said bridge is ruinous and like to fall speedily, unless it be now remedied; and one Babe left for the repair of the bridge yearly six acres of land with the appurtenances, which six acres of land with the appurtenances were taken and seized without reasonable causes into the hands of the King our sovereign lord, and so still remain, so that no profits accrue there from to our said sovereign lord the King, nor to the said bridge. By reason whereof the said bridge yearly suffers great injury. Whereupon the premises considered: It is ordained and agreed by authority of the said Parliament, that the hands of our said sovereign lord the King be removed from the said six acres of land with the appurtenances; and that the custody thereof be committed to the parson of Dunmoe and the vicar of Donaghmore for the time being, for the repair of said bridge, without interruption or hindrance of our said sovereign lord or his officers; and the said parson and vicar for the time being to render an account yearly of the issues and profits of the said six acres of land, with the appurtenances, to the Abbot of Navan for the time being.

This exciting find showed that the bridge was an *opus pontis* owning land for its maintenance, the fruits of which, to its ruination, were being corruptly misappropriated by the king's own men in Dublin Castle. Bob Fenlon, a former county engineer of Meath who lives in the vicinity, verified that the single surviving stone arch (fig. 27) was still there and also pinpointed its location on an OS 25in. map. I also traced the reference given by Ellison to a mention in James Grace's *Annales Hiberniae*[3] under the year 1330: "There was a great flood, especially of the Boyne, by which all the bridges on that river, except Babes, were carried away, and other mischief done at Trim and Drogheda . . .". I later discovered that Grace had omitted a key phrase after bridge, namely "stone and timber" (see Chapter 7

Fig. 27: *Babes Bridge: Surviving Arch, Downriver Elevation*

under clardroichet). In the spring of 1987 I had an opportunity to inspect the arch and concluded in, the light of the overall research, that the arch was part of the original. I set out the findings in the course of a paper to a seminar[4] on Bridge Collapse (June 1987) which dealt with the great damage to bridges, caused by the "Hurricane Charlie" offshoot on 25 August 1986. The Babes arch was in imminent danger of collapse due to severe scouring of the abutment pier. The arch seemed to be no one's responsibility. Thanks to the combined efforts of Frank O'Brien, Meath County Manager and Oliver Parkins, county engineer, and the Office of Public Works a way was found by which it was underpinned by the OPW in 1988—a nationally important salvage job as it turned out in the light of subsequent finding described below.

When the arch was cleared of parasitic growth and the underpinning was in operation it became possible to obtain some photographs and to inspect the outer face of the surviving first pier. The latter was important in order to establish if the arch was an original or a later reconstruction. The following are the principal characteristics of the bridge.

The river pier is 15ft long and 6ft 6in. thick of solid masonry (fig 28). The height above bed level and depth of foundation are not known as yet. There are cutwaters fore and aft bonded into the piers. The upstream one has disintegrated but sufficient is left of it and the aft one to indicate that they were short, triangular rising to the springing point with low semi-

pyramidal caps. The masonry in the piers is composed of coursed rubble masonry with a good percentage of larger (quarter cubic foot) stones. The land abutment is constructed of similar type masonry and about 6ft thick.

The arch ring is the most significant feature of the bridge. The intrados curve is a pointed segmental of 17ft span. The radii are approximately 14ft with the centres on a plane 3ft below the springing and 3ft 2in. to the left and right of midspan. The ring tapers from a thickness of 2ft 4in. at the keystone to 4ft 6in. at the springings. Many of the thin flat sandstone flags comprising the ring extend for the full thickness, but others are shorter and above these flags of similar thickness are used to fill in. One gets the impression that the arch is double-ringed but this is not the case. The additional stones are more in the form of supplementary, in-filling saddles over the haunches though they have small perched skewbacks. The stones in the barrels of the arches are generally small in length and rounded at the base, though this may be due to almost eight centuries of erosion by wind and water. The upriver keystone is a heart-shaped field stone and not a good fit; the downstream one is missing. The skewback (fig 29) on the downriver abutment is 28in. at base and 18in. high and 12ins. wide with a thickness of 3in. at the intrados edge. There is a remarkable resemblance between the skewback and keystones in Babes and those in the surviving buildings on the grounds of St Michael's Church Duleek erected by Walter de Lacy in 1285, shown in fig 30. The springing angles are approximately 35°. There is a single propping stone between the skewbacks in the pier. It is a massively strong arch that would contain the thrust line of a locomotive within its middle third. In fact Alexander[5] recommended tapering arches for trains in his classic analytical paper at the peak of the railway era; however, his main object was to counteract the lateral thrust generated by a train braking on the opposing half arch.

I found only one arch with a similar profile among hundreds of photos of medieval arches in the UK and France. Le Pont Bohardy over the river Evre at Montrevrault in the Department of Marne et Loire described by Prade.[6] I sent photographs and other particulars of Babes to Marcel Prade who replied that, based on photographs, there can be no doubt that Babes and Bohardy have many similarities—

Fig. 28: top left: *Babes Bridge: N. Face of surviving Pier*
Fig. 29: below: *Babes Bridge: Skewback, Springing and Haunch Upriver*
Fig. 30: bottom left: *St Michael's Church, Duleek: Arch dating from AD 1182*

same shape of intrados, same ring and same use of materials. He thought there was a common denominator so to state in the fact that the Thouarsais region in which Bohardy is located has other non-classified ancient bridges of the same type whereas there are only two in the rest of France. The lord of this region was loyal to the Plantagenet kings from the 12th to the 14th centuries. Dating Babes from the beginning of the 13th century, he thought, not unreasonable. Prade also mentioned that many bridges in England between the 11th and 14th centuries had arches reinforced with transverse ribs and double-ringed arches with the upper protruding beyond the lower. I had already reached the same conclusion independently from a search of many books on old English bridges; very few from the medieval period were similar to Irish bridges.

The 1837 OS six-inch map shows the sur-

viving arch and also some remnants of piers across the river. Two are still visible above the water and the others are indicated by the ripple effect on the surface (fig 31). The width of the river scaled from the 1837 map is 264ft. The arch plus pier module is 23ft 6in.; hence there were 11 spans in the water and 10 piers, assuming all were similar to the survivor. No investigation was made of these piers nor of the opposite bank where the 1837 map indicates the remnant of an abutment no longer visible above the ground. It is not possible to determine from the remnants whether or not the bridge had parapet walls, or if it was approached by causeways on the wide flood planes on each side. The line of the roadway leading to Donaghmore Church can be identified from the map, but the south approach has been severed by the canal built in 1760. All of these aspects merit detailed local investigation.

Fig. 31: *Babes Bridge: Remnants of Other Piers*

The volume of masonry in the whole bridge was estimated on the basis of the measurements given above including parapets and the volume came to 36,500 cubic feet. There would have been no great difficulty in transporting stone in boats to the site. The stone in the bridge is composed of limestone and sandstone, the latter mainly in the arches. Both are found along the river as the silurian and carboniferous deposits meet in the deep valley of the Boyne in this area.

There are notable differences between Babes and Thomond (Old) Bridge. The Babes piers are half the thickness, but the spans and pointed segmental intrados are similar. The tapering arch rings are not evident on any of the drawings or sketches of Thomond, but these features are often sketched in purely diagrammatically. The pier thicknesses in Thomond were almost double those of Babes. This was necessary to obviate overturning during removal of the centering arch by arch because the former is a much higher bridge. The Shannon is tidal at Limerick, whereas the Boyne at Babes is not. No sandstone slabs were available in Limerick, and much more effort was involved in working the local limestone; moreover, there is plenty evidence from ecclesiastical work that the early Normans disliked it. Apart from these considerations there were undoubted links between Meath and Limerick, as explained by Warren:[7] "William de Briouze . . . went over to Limerick as soon as John granted it to him in January 1201, and in getting it under control no doubt used that ruthlessness that had made

him the terror of the Welsh March. He had to rejoin [King] John in France in 1202, but his brother-in-law, Walter Lacy, was on hand to watch his interests in Ireland . . .". Eight years later King John invaded Ireland with the primary objective of breaking the power of these two barons, which he did. Were the two bridges built between 1200 and 1210? Perhaps they were not finished until 1216, as such bridges could take years to build at the time. However, both barons were rich and powerful.

The problem of dating Babes was solved by Elizabeth Hickey of Skreen Castle, Co. Meath, member of the Meath Archeological Society, who, following a note about the bridge in the Co. Council Information News (Vol. 3, No. I, Oct. 1988), sent a letter to the county engineer drawing attention to early mentions in the Register of the Abbey of St Thomas, Dublin.[8] I followed this lead and found five separate references, mainly land grants, or episcopal correspondence witnessed or signed by Simon de Rochfort, bishop of Meath from 1194 to 1224, the year he died. The bridge was used as a marker for land grants and as a distinguishing indicator between two Donaghmores (the second being in Navan) e.g. "prope pontem Johannis le Baub", "juxta pontem Balbi". Most documents of this nature were undated at that period and have to be timed by deaths of witnesses etc. The bridge was in existence at the mention dates, so it can certainly be assigned as a "King John", that is, pre-1216. No information is available about John le Baube, but he obviously was a Norman who owned land since he left some for the maintenance of this bridge. I believe that he financed this bridge and that it was built by a master mason sent over from Thouarsais by King John (perhaps after 1210 because John crossed the Boyne at Trim in that year).

The final problem regarding Babes is that of a late mention: it is not shown on Moll's map nor on the Down Survey, nor is it mentioned in Hugh O'Neill's invasion plan of 1599 (see Newtown Bridge). My view is that it became impassable between 1500 and 1550 and that the Navan burghers and local landowners realised it was cheaper to build a new bridge at Kilcarn upriver of the confluence of the Blackwater than to repair and maintain Babes, there being a bridge across the Blackwater at Poulboy, Navan at the time (see Kilcarn Bridge). It is mentioned as a landmark in a deed of settlement executed in 1549.

Cromwell's troops never crossed the bridge, for they slighted Dunmoe Castle from the south bank. In 1468 a "John Babe son and heir to Thomas Babe of Darver esquire" *et al.* were ordered to surrender at Dublin Castle in answer to a charge of kidnapping and stealing "in a manner of war" from Dowdalls of Castlelumney, Louth;[2] perhaps the name "Robbers' Bridge" came from that. More likely it was a good place for highwaymen to operate. Ferganstown and Donaghmore, adjacent townlands, have also lent their names to the bridge. Marcel Prade has included it and St Mary Magdalen's Bridge Duleek in his latest book[9] published in 1990. Hopefully the outline of the cooperative effort that led to its dating and repair given above will be an encouragement to others seeking to solve similar problems concerning other bridges.

The underpinned arch of Babes Bridge is now the oldest surviving authenticated bridge arch in Ireland.

Mabe's

This six-arch masonry arch bridge (fig. 33) across the river Blackwater is located about three-quarters of a mile north west of Ceanannas, Co. Meath. The discovery of the fact that it was a very old bridge was rather fortuitous when Frank Burke and I stopped to look at it, more in hope than expectation, in the course of other work in February 1989.[1] Its north-west arch on the downriver face (fig. 32) brought to mind George Wilkinson's sketch[2] of an pre-Norman non-radial arch; another arch is partly corbelled like St Mary Magdalen's Bridge in Duleek, which I had earlier linked with the

Fig. 32: *Mabe's Bridge: N.W. Semicircular Arch Non-radial Joints*

Fig. 33: below: *Mabe's Bridge: Downriver Elevation 1987*

propping arch supporting the stone roof of the 10th-century St Colmcille's House. Mabe's was almost within the proverbial stone's throw of it.

The bridge had been widened on the upriver side by what appeared to be a 19th-century extension. References in the query books of the Meath Grand Jury in the National Archive reveal discrepancies in the name: 1808 called Mapes, 1803 Mapon, 1771 Malpasses, also Malpas. The 1803 grand jury query reads: "Item 634 Whether £110. 5*s.* and £5. 10*s.* 3*d.* (overseer's wages) be raised to repair the bridge called Mapon Bridge on the road from Kells to Cootehill" (probably

a reference to the upriver extension). There is also a middle section in the bridge, increasing the probability that it is ancient.

Meath Co. Council kept the bridge under observation because the upriver extension had been classified as defective in 1986. In April 1988 movement was detected above the second arch on the upriver side and the road was closed. A partial collapse occurred which led to a decision to rehabilitate the whole bridge. This provided a rare opportunity to get extra information, measurements and photos. It also provided a stimulus to search deeper for early mentions. This effort identified new sources, in particular an excellent papers on "Kells, Early and Medieval" by Philip O'Connell,[3] which clearly established that the townland of Maprath, one mile north west of the Bridge, had belonged to an Anglo-Norman family called Mape or Mapas, dispossessed in the Cromwellian plantation. He also referred to a 1503 entry in the Annals of Ulster which recorded that "The Mape was slain in his own castle" by the O'Reilly of Breffni in 1503.

The bridge was in existence at the time of the Down Survey in 1656 and is clearly marked on that map. Further searches failed to produce a specific earlier mention. It was thought that the bridge might have been located at Ath-da-Laarg (the ford of the two forks), referred to as the scene of a battle in 937 and in the *Vita Tripartita* as the location of a church founded by St Patrick. That avenue of search proved fruitful in establishing the nature of that ford and confirming local opinion that it was a short distance downstream of Maudlins Bridge, north of Kells (see Abbeytown Bridge). Another reference checked out was from the seven charters[4] contained in the Book of Kells where an "Ath Catan" is mentioned as a land marker, but this proved inconclusive. The conclusion drawn from the literature search is that the Norman family of Mapes probably financed the bridge or repaired it soon after they settled in the area in the 13th century.

During the rehabilitation work it was possible to examine the arches and piers from the river bed as each pair of arches was dammed off for repair. A detailed elevation was prepared, reproduced in Appendix 8. The following principal characteristics were identified. The bridge is founded partly on rock and glacial till containing large boulders. It is in three abutting sections—a 12ft 6in. wide original

(downriver) followed by 3ft 6in. and 7ft 6in. upriver extensions. The piers vary in width from 7ft 6in. to 13ft 2in., the latter possibly an abutment pier. The piers below the springings are built of roughly coursed field stone masonry. There are no cutwaters on the downriver face. The first upriver extension appears to have been built on the upriver cutwaters of the original partly evidenced by continuity of masonry in the bottom courses. The joints between sections were open, the gap in some arches being up to 4in. wide. The intrados are semi-circular, though some arches have a slightly pointed appearance due to the ragged edges of the stones when viewed from the river banks. The ring stones on the upstream face are proper voussoirs—evidence of late 18th- or early 19th-century work.

The most important characteristics of the bridge are the orientations of the thin, field-stone, sandstone slabs forming the arch rings of the original as evidenced on the downriver faces. The first two arches, Nos. 1 and 2 in the elevation on the Moynalty end, have ring stones at the springings with joints sloped at 45° to 55° to the horizontal—like a makeshift springing for an 80° segmental arch. The joint slopes remain more or less parallel through the haunches; however, the top third through the crown is composed of radial jointed and oriented stones. There is no identifiable keystone as such. It would appear that the masons commenced building the ring as they would for a pointed segmental arch. Arch 6 on the Kells end (fig. 34) commences on both sides as

Fig. 34: *Mabe's Bridge: S.E. Partially Corbelled Arch Ring*

a corbelled arch with the notable difference that each successive stone is given an inward slope as in St Mary Magdalen's Bridge in Duleek. Halfway up each side the top corbels have an accumulated slope of 30° to 40°. The remainder of the ring along the upper part of the haunches and through the crown is radial. This is exactly the form of construction used in the propping arch of St Columcille's House. Arches 3, 4 and 5 vary having one side corbelled like arch 6 and the opposite half sloped like Nos. 1 and 2. The variations are evident in the photograph. The upriver soffits of the original section have a similar type of orientation and were obviously facing rings originally. The sheeting stones while smaller also show uniformity with the facing stones as far as could be judged from underneath.

Healy[5] gives a superb description of the interior of the arch support the stone roof of St Columcille's Cell: "It has in the interior a 'barrel roof' which exhibits in an interesting way the transition from the primitive arch formed by overlapping stone, to the true arch built with a keystone. For half the way up it is constructed in the primitive manner and then it is finished by stones built on the radiating principle." This is what one saw underneath some of the arches in Mabe's before the guniting. I am not aware of any description of an actual cross-section of the arches in the stone-roofed churches either in Kells or Glendalough though restoration was done on the latter at some stage in the past century. Perhaps it is in the bridges such as St Mary Madgalens*, Mabe's, Abbeytown* and Monks* that one finds the best evidence of the evolution of the arch in Ireland.

On of the very interesting features of the bridge was the soffits of the arches. The middle section seemed to contain more mortar than the original allowing for the fact that joints had been eroded over a considerably longer period and that the mortar in the centre seems to have been poured in as mentioned in Part I. There were no signs of wattle marks. It suggests that the centring was lined with an impermeable lining such as animal skins.

Meath Co. Council evaluated the strength of the bridge using the MEXE System.[6] The safe load rating for arch 5 was 4.0 tonnes and for the others it ranged between 6.0 and 8.0 tonnes. The rehabilitation work was carefully planned to maintain the downriver elevation.

Fig. 35: *Mabe's Bridge: N.W. Arch after Rehabilitation*

Fig. 36: *Mabe's Bridge: Downriver Elevation after Rehabiliation*

The works carried out included the re-erection of the collapsed part of the arch reusing the original stones, the provision of a concrete apron extending 6ft upstream and 3ft downstream, the construction of a 6in. thick reinforced concrete curtain-wall on all faces, except the head of the downriver original, the grouting of foundations, piers, abutments and arch barrels; the provision of a 3in. thick reinforced gunited shell on the arch soffits (fig. 35). The joints in the old masonry were cleaned out and the recesses were pointed. The all-in cost of the work was £82,300. The road was reopened to traffic on 3 June 1989. This was a fine job and the fabric of the original has been carefully preserved even if some of it has to be wrapped in a protective concrete shield. The finished bridge is shown in fig. 36.

Monks

For a long time this eight-arch bridge (fig. 37) over the Nore in the De Vesci Estate in Abbeyleix has been referred to as one of the oldest, if not the oldest, surviving masonry arch bridge in Ireland. However, there was negligible information apart from the name and general appearance to substantiate the assumption, so it was the subject of an in-depth search for this book.

Abbeyleix takes its name from the Cistercian monastery founded there in 1183 by Cochegerius O'Moore in honour of the Blessed Virgin Mary. The history of Laois was exhaustively researched by Canon O'Hanlon over many years and published in two large volumes in 1907, the second volume being completed after his death by E. O'Leary.[1] They mention that the origin of the name Looighie, Latinised Logisio, goes back beyond the Christian era. There is a chapter on Abbeyleix parish and its antiquities, but there is no mention of the bridge. The old town of Abbeyleix grew up around the monastery. Tradition, according to O'Hanlon, had left the belief that the monastery was sited in the exact position now occupied by the mansion built in 1774. The abbey and lands were seized in 1551. No trace of the abbey could be found at the close of the 18th century according to Archdall. The old village of Abbeyleix was demolished by the De Vescis in the 18th century and the present planned town, "New Abbeyleix", built three miles away. Stalley[2] states that "there is no

architectural certainty that the ancient stone bridge over the Nore, the so-called Monks bridge, was in fact built by the Cistercians, as commonly supposed."

Stalley gives many insights into the Cistercian order in Ireland that are relevant to bridges. For example, many monasteries in the 13th century began to acquire feudal rights such as tithes and pontage, though this was forbidden by the order's statutes. During the 13th and 14th centuries many changed from direct farming to renting of their lands. He also points out that from the mid-13th century most building done by the order was carried out by masons outside the order as evidenced by masons' marks at Boyle, Inch etc. However, a monk called the *costos operis* decided on the nature and extent of the works. Many of the surviving ruins show a Burgundian influence, that is, pointed arches and pointed barrels, vaults etc., well into the 15th century.

I carried out an analysis to find out how many Cistercian abbeys were located on rivers as distinct from streams and how many of these had bridges indicated nearby on either Petty's 1680 map or Moll's 1714 map. Nineteen were on rivers and among these 10 had bridges nearby. The sites with old bridges extant are Boyle, Holycross, Abbeyleix and possibly Bective; in each case the bridge is called after the abbey. The key question Did the monks build the bridges? is discussed briefly in Part I and the conclusion reached that while the monastery was the *raison d'etre* and the form of construction was influenced by the monks, they did not finance them. In the case of Abbeyleix, therefore, we must not read too much into the name, but what we can say is that the very

Fig. 37: *Monks Bridge: Upriver Elevation*

existence of the monastery, normally a place of pilgrimage, created a need and demand for a safe, durable bridge—a pious work—and there was every reason why a Gaelic chief or Norman baron should arrange for its construction just as they sometimes funded abbeys and churches.

There is an ancient map of the "Irish district" in the Queen's County and County Kildare dated 1563 in the British Museum. It was the subject of a paper[3] by Hore in 1863; a facsimile included with the paper shows very few bridges. On the Nore it shows one bridge at "Water Coote", now Watercastle*, which is downriver from Abbeyleix, but none upriver. There can be two explanations. The bridge had become private because the abbey lands, on which Monks Bridge was located, had been granted to Ormond in 1662, or the bridge was broken and out of service. No bridge is shown across the Barrow at Carlow (this information is correct because Henry Sidney built a bridge there in 1669).

A small booklet on "Abbey Leix"[4] states that the Monks Bridge was "part of the main road from Dublin to Waterford" in the 13th century. It was always known as "The Wooden Bridge". Another useful bit of information is that there was a family house on part of the site of the present 1774 house, but no remains of it were left. The De Vesci Estate has no records which throw any light on the history of the bridge.

There are 14 public road bridges across the Nore in Co. Laois. The next bridge, one mile upriver of Monks, is named Waterloo and the next downriver (two miles) is Watercastle. The latter bridge is discussed under a separate heading. The mention of an early main road from Dublin to Waterford running through Abbeyleix can hardly have any substance. The Slighe Culann of ancient origin ran from Dublin to Tallaght, Baltinglass, Tullow, Leighlinbridge and thence to New Ross and Waterford. All of the Plantagenet kings and other Normans who landed at Waterford followed this or the Leighlin to Naas route to Dublin. However, the Slighe Dala went through Abbeyleix.

Given all the foregoing literary information it is evident that the problem of dating the bridge depends on the analysis of its characteristics. When I inspected it in the 1970s it was much obscured by trees and foilage. In recent years it has been cleaned and when Paddy McGuinness, an engineering colleague,

called there in 1988 he was able to take fine photos from the river banks showing many details previously obscured. The carriageway is 11ft wide flanked by stone parapet walls, each side coped with rough-cut stones laid transversely on edge and rounded at the top. The piers are approx. 7ft thick and the spans 10ft clear. There is one larger pier in the centre flanked by a wider arch c.12ft, perhaps a navigation arch for small boats at the deeper part of the river. There are triangular cut-waters capped with semi-pyramidal copings on the upriver ends and no cutwaters down-stream. The cutwaters are built with tell-tale hammer-dressed ashlar-coursed stone which also extends into the piers. As far as can be determined from photos all of the cutwaters with the notable exception of the first one from the left hand bank facing downriver are ashlar. The semi-pyramidal coping on the latter pier is steeper than the rest and rises 1ft higher well above the extrados of the adjoining arch crowns. The cutting edges on the cutwaters are of well wrought stones.

The arch rings on the upstream side are relatively flat segments of circles with a few slightly pointed. The stones in the facing rings are radial, fairly well cut and of fairly uniform thickness, about 18in. long on the face, with the notable exception of the first and possibly the second arch.

The downstream ring faces of the four arches on the right (fig. 38) are similar to the upstream (the remainder cannot be seen pro-perly on the photos). The sixth arch is more pointed as on the upriver face. There can be

Fig. 38: *Monks Bridge: Downriver Elevation*

Fig. 39: *Monks Bridge: Upriver Elevation of Bank Arch and Cutwater*

little doubt that at least five or six arches and cutwaters with parts of the piers between them were rebuilt between about 1670 and 1800—a judgment based on other limestone bridges of known date such as Kinnegad.*

The first arch from the left hand bank (fig. 39) has been left to last for the obvious reason that it holds the clue to the date. It is a partly corbelled arch of rubble stone; few joints are radial; it has two heart-shaped keystones separated by an inverted third. The masonry in the first pier and cutwaters alongside it are also of random rubble with many small stones. Monks is in the mould of Duleek and some of the arches in Mabe's, except that it is segmental rather than semi-circular. It was obviously intended as a pointed segmental that probably settled into the form of an arc when the crude centring was loaded and later removed.

From all the foregoing I conclude that the original stone bridge was built in the traditional Irish style depicted in the surviving original arch and first pier, that it was built early in the 13th century and that the originals of all the replaced arch rings were slightly pointed but otherwise the geometry of the bridge was similar to the present bridge. In regard to its history, it was probably well maintained up to the end of the 15th century. The 16th century was one of turmoil in Laois with constant attacks on the inhabitants, suppression of the monasteries, confiscations and plantation, so it is easy to see how the bridge could have succumbed to successive floods for want of repair, so that by 1563 it was impassable. It was probably repaired from time to time in timber

and by 1675 or thereabouts most of the broken arches were probably bridged over in timber such that it became known as "the wooden bridge".

Most medieval bridges, here and abroad, have been repaired many times. Once they retain their overall characteristics and have one or two original arches they are entitled to be listed as medieval. The Monks Bridge still has at least one 13th-century arch and pier.

Thomond (old) Bridge

This bridge was a focus throughout all of the research for this book because it was a major bridge, spanning the longest river at the saline interface, had survived up to 1840, and was well documented, but there was no definitive evidence that it was a "King John" dating from pre-1216 as local tradition has always held. A decade ago Roger Stalley reawakened the issue as to whether the original was timber or stone in the course of a well researched paper[1] on William of Prene, the 13th-century king's carpenter. He marshalled good evidence in favour of timber. It was a very important question from the aspect of the history of road bridges in Ireland until I established that the surviving arch of Babes on the Boyne was erected before 1220.

The military history of Limerick is interwoven with its ancient walls, castle and bridges and much of the evidence about the bridge comes from that source. There was no city of Limerick until the Norsemen settled on Inish Sibhton, later King's Island, in 922, according to Gwynn and Hadcock.[2] The Vikings, experts in carpentry, have no bridge (timber or stone) accredited to them in Ireland except the incidental reference to a Liffey bridge in the story of the battle of Clontarf (1014). The Norse held Limerick until King Donal Mor O'Brien took the island in 1176. On the death of Strongbow, Raymond le Gros abandoned Limerick and entrusted it to Donal O'Brien, who broke down the bridge and set fire to the town as the (Norman) garrison marched away. Here we find the first dilemma: why did he not burn the bridge if it was timber? King John burned bridges in Aquitaine when retreating before the French, and Rochester Bridge over the Medway in England in 1215. The Annals of Clonmacnoise record the burning of Sligo Bridge in 1188.

Lenihan[3] states that the introduction of English government did not occur until after the death of Donal Mor and that John (then Earl of Morton and Lord of Ireland, a title given by Henry II in 1177) showed great zeal in establishing the English writ in Limerick. He granted a charter on 19 December 1197 which was confirmed by Richard I who extended to the city the privileges already granted to Dublin. In 1198 McCarthy of Desmond drove-out the English, but soon after they recovered the city. The Dublin Charter (see Part I, Chapter 3) included the right to build a bridge so, whatever about previous bridges, it would appear that from 1199 the Limerick burghers had regal authority to build a permanent stone bridge. Some histories state that John visited Limerick during his failed expedition to Ireland in 1185 when he was nineteen years of age and known in France as "Lackland". He became king of England on the death of his brother Richard I in 1199. He has been described as the "bridge-minded monarch", a title well merited and discussed in Part I, Chapter 3, where it is shown that if he wished a bridge to be built, it was built or else the Norman baron might lose his fief. For this reason it is most likely that the old Thomond Bridge was built during his reign and before the extension of the Magna Carta exemption to Ireland in the first year of the reign of his successor Henry III in 1216. The dating problem is addressed below by starting in 1840, when the bridge was demolished, by describing it, and then tracing its history back century by century. The Norman objective in building a permanent bridge was the conquest of Thomond.

James Grene Barry presented a paper[4] on "Old Limerick Bridges" to the North Munster Archeological Society in 1909. It is accompanied by a note by P.J. Lynch, architect. These are a fruitful source of information. They review the main historical facts contained in Lenihan's and other histories of Limerick but also give some other details from unpublished information then available. Most important are a plan and elevation by the architectural firm of J. & G.R. Pain (fig. 40), who were consultants to the Limerick grand jury and who designed the new Baals and Thomond Bridges in the 1820s and 1830s. The Pains were a branch of the famous London firm which had an extensive practice in London and was responsible for several large bridges at Chertsey, Kew, etc., all outlined by Ruddock.[5] Lynch records "From Pain's notes of the condition of the old bridge in 1816, 'arches cracked', 'piers undermined', etc., it is surprising how it was preserved in a condition of safety until its removal in 1838."

In the report of the Commission of Public Work Ireland, 1837 there is a drawing dated February 1837 by William N. Owen, resident engineer, to a scale of 20ft to one inch, entitled "Plan and Elevation of the Thomond Bridge now erecting in the City of Limerick, showing the Old Bridge in Dotted Lines." There is also an elevation of the bridge on the drawing of all the bridges on the Shannon prepared by Thomas Rhodes published in the House of Commons Journal, 1833 (see fig. 219 in Appendix 8). All of these records have been used in the analysis that follows. Pain's 1814 plan and elevation are reproduced in fig. 40; the rock levels and scaled dimensions have been added by me. Several 18th- and 19th-century prints are also available, but they are not very helpful because, as Barry states, most are inaccurate in important details. From an examination of the foregoing I have identified the basic characteristics of the old bridge as it was in 1814.

There were triangular cutwaters fore and aft. They rose to the level of the arch spring-

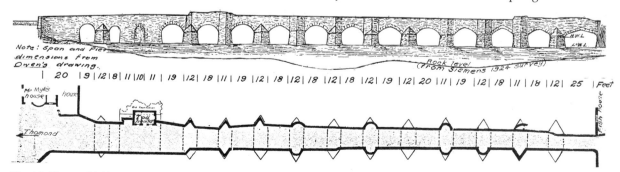

Fig. 40: *Thomond (old) Bridge: Plan and Elevation by J. Pain, 1814*

ings and above that they were capped with semi-pyramidal masonry copings reaching to arch crown level. Some cutwaters were brought up to form both circular and triangular pedestrian refuges, but many of these were added long after the bridge was built. Rhodes' elevation shows 10 of the 14 arches as having pointed segmental intrados; the other four arches are in positions where superstructures were added and removed at various periods. Pain's elevation shows seven of the ten as pointed segmental, and Owen shows six. There can be little doubt that all the originals had pointed segmental arches like Babes Bridge. The spans of these characteristic arches varied a little, from 17ft 6in. and 19ft, as determined by scaling from Owen's drawing. There is no evidence of double or tapering rings. The piers were massive, a typical one being 12ft thick and 17ft long (excluding cutwaters). We have no descriptions of the stone masonry, and it is important not to draw any conclusions from sketches or etchings because more often than not they show random rubble as ashlar. Barry mentions specifically that the engraving in Lenihan's history is "idealistic and inaccurate". This is not to state that general overall information from sketches is not useful. Pain and Owen show the piers as slightly battered and this was probably the case as it was a feature of the bases of many 13th-century castles in Ireland. Barry also states that the arches were turned on wicker work and that this is indicative of great age but here, as Leask advises, it is necessary to be cautious unless one has first hand detailed evidence. I found wicker indents on the soffits of several bridges but they were of limited use in establishing construction periods.

Due to the destruction of the Limerick City and County grand jury records in 1922, there is a paucity of information on alterations and repairs to the bridge over the period from 1700 to 1814 when Pain's drawing was prepared. Lewis[6] records that in 1760 Limerick was declared to be no longer a fortified city and that the dismantling of its walls was commenced and completed by "slow degrees". It is highly probable that any remaining obstructions on the bridge were removed at that time and extra pedestrian refuges etc. provided. There was a storm accompanied by high tides in 1751 which overflowed into the streets and did great damage. The tidal range at Limerick Docks is from 18.75 OD HWST to 13.5 HWNT;

however, the highest high and the lowest low are 22.0 OD, plus and minus 3.4ft respectively.[7] In all probability the bridge was obstructed "at the ends" by the fortification remnants which caused a backwater upriver. Owen's drawing of 1837 records that the seven arches of the new bridge provided a waterway (aggregate of the spans) of 350ft compared with 277ft in the old bridge of fifteen arches. The 1751 bridge was probably less than 277ft.

There is a small map of Limerick at the bottom of Moll's 1714 map, reproduced in fig. 41a. The gross length of the bridge scaled from this map is in the range 420 to 500 feet. Lewis records that in 1698 the city also suffered severe damage from a storm and flood. There is a map (fig. 41b), of the city showing the fortifications etc. in Story's *Impartial History* of the siege of 1691. The scale is small but sufficient to show that the space occupied by the first three or four arches shown at the Thomond end on Pain's drawing was part of the bank. Story records that in the siege the defenders were driven from the outworks on to the bridge, but a French major who was in command of Thomond Gate raised the drawbridge prematurely and over 600 were slaughtered or drowned. The Thomond gate was at the castle end of the bridge.

The Ormond Manuscripts[8] contain a very detailed report on fortifications in Ireland prepared by direction of Charles II and carried out by Lord Dartmouth, and Thomas Phillips in 1685. The report gives detailed quantitative estimates for masonry work of all descriptions and is a useful source provided one knows that the "perch of masonry" is 44 cubic ft compared with the then conventional 31.5 cubic ft. It does not mention the bridge but from its description of the castle and walls we can picture the overall state of the city: "Limerick having been reported to be the strongest place in all this kingdom, it is quite contrary, the walls having gone much to decay by the neglect of the Corporation, the improvements made upon the bogs hath made approach to it more easy, it being two towns of an indifferent circuit, and neither of them any great strength, especially the Irish town . . .". He then goes on to state that the Irish town had the high ground and "commands" the English town. He recommended the erection of a citadel at a cost of £78,310 and that the corporation be questioned for not keeping the walls in better repair etc. There is one item "For draw bridge and guard houses £2,000", but it is not made clear where it was intended to be erected. There was a "ground plan of Limerick", which evidently accompanied the original report but to which I did not have access.

Shirley brought together extracts from Thomas Dineley's *Journal* with notes by Maurice Lenihan in a useful article[9] published in 1864. It contains two sketches of the bridge. Dineley stated in 1681 that "The Thomond Bridge is said to have been built by King John, it crosseth the river Shannon, it consists of 14 stone arches, at the time of whose foundacon, that of London was but of Timber." The sketch (fig. 41c) shows 13 arches and it seems that the 14th was the drawbridge at the Thomond Gate. The guard house seems to be located on the third pier from the Thomond end. The third arch is shown filled in on Pain's elevation. The second sketch, fig. 42a, confirms this. More importantly, it shows a timber section spanning one of the arches. It is left to the reader to correlate this sketch with Pain's elevation. It would appear that the sketch was made after 1685.

There is a record of 1673 which states that the bridge was then in such a bad state of repair that the freemen of the city were deprived of their exemption from paying a toll to cross the bridge: "The Freemans libertys without tax or rate, repaired this place—the Thomond Bridge and Gate." The toll house, partly cantilevered, is shown on Pain's plan, also on a sketch in Lenihan's *History*.

The bridge is shown on the Down Survey map surveyed in 1656, but the scale is so small that no other inferences can be deduced other than it was in service at the time. Gwynn[10] records that during the 1651 siege "the Clare end of Thomond Bridge was held by a fort for the possession of which there was sharp fighting, till the garrison contrived to evacuate it (after the walls had been breached) and regain the city, blowing-up the bridge behind them." The arch destroyed may have been the one spanned in timber in the sketch in Shirley's paper. Limerick had been taken by the confederates in 1642 and surrendered to Ireton in 1651. There is a footnote on p. 208 of Lenihan's *History* which records that the inscription recording the freemen's deprivation of 1673 had been placed in cut stone over Thomond Gate

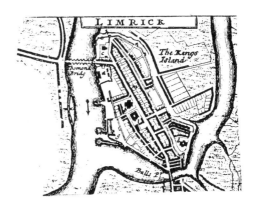

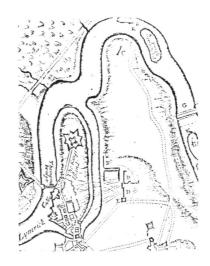

Fig. 41: *Thomond (old) Bridge: depicted by (a) Moll (b) Story (c) Dinely*

42a

42b

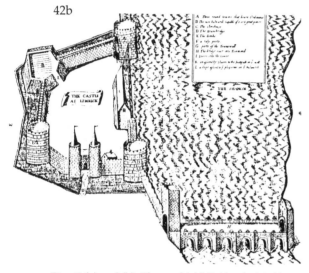

Fig. 42 (a) and (b): *Thomond (old) Bridge depicted by Dineley and Pacata*

"which was a castellated solid stone building at the Thomond side of the Bridge, and the drawbridge was placed between it and the stone or ancient bridge, as appears by a map of the city taken in 1641". That map may help to clarify the question of the location of the drawbridge at the time.

Strafford's *Pacata Hibernia*[11] contains two plans relating to Limerick, one of the castle, the other of the city, both drawn in "relief". The parts of each map showing the bridge are reproduced in figs. 42b and c. In each the bridge is shown as having six arches with castellated gate towers at each end. The gate at the castle (city) end is marked "Thomond Gate" and the drawbridge is indicated at the Thomond side of the other gate. Each has a portcullis. These plans are probably as late as the 1630s. If they

are a true representation the original bridge may indeed have had only six arches (perhaps seven if one allows for the drawbridge).

Speed's map of 1611 (fig. 42d) shows the bridge with the gate towers at each end but also a delta-shaped bastion on the Clare end beyond the gate and with a moat fed by the river outside its walls. The *Pacata* plan of the castle shows a four-sided bastion at the southeast corner which is not shown on Speed (suggesting that the *Pacata* plan is of a later date). To complete the jigsaw there is the map of Limerick by Sir R. Greenville (Map MS 57 TCD 1209), ascribed by Westropp[12] to the year 1590. The bridge part, reproduced in fig. 42e, clearly indicates by eddies and cutwaters that the bridge then had 13 arches with gate towers at each end. A scale of paces is given (each pace being 5ft) and the bridge length scales 365ft bank to bank. The overall scale errors are less than five per cent when checked against the current OS six-inch map.

The explanation for the differences between Greenville and Speed's plans of the bridge is provided by Lieut. Col. A. Crowe, a keen military historian, who explained to me that the bastion-type fortification was introduced here by the Spanish, who constructed one at Kinsale in 1603. Sweetman[13] records that in 1585 Limerick Castle needed considerable repairs and that these were carried out between 1608 and 1625. The chief function of the castle was to protect the Thomond access to the city. Clearly many changes were made to the bridge fortifications over this period and these must have affected the first four or five arches on the Clare end and the terminal arches at the city end.

Accepting Greenville's map as an accurate 1590 baseline and Pain's elevation of 1814 as an accurate picture of the arches before they were demolished, the question remains as to whether any of these arches were 13th century. We can be confident that an architect of Pain's stature in bridge design gave a reasonably accurate representation of the shapes of the intrados in his drawing because this was an important factor in deciding what to do about the bridge (as it is today). The first three arches, from the Clare end, were built after the bastion was removed in the 17th century. Arches 4, 5 and 6 are segments of circles and were obviously replacements, though the piers may be original. Arch 7 is a pointed segmental and therefore pre-16th century. Arches 8 and 9 and 11 are segments of circles and replacements. Arches 10, 12 and 13 are, like 7, pointed segmental and pre-16th century. Arch 15 is a Tudor four-centred and No. 14 appears to have the same rounding at the right hand springing, so they were constructed in the 16th or 17th century. It would appear that Arch 11 is the one shown with a timber deck by Dineley, probably the one blown up in 1651. From all this we can conclude that about eleven of the piers and cutwaters and four arches of the original survived till the whole bridge was demolished.

I found no relevant mentions of the bridge in the 15th century, the next one being the order of Edward II of 18 December 1325[14] which is of major importance in establishing the date of the old bridge: "Whereas our progenitors Kings of England and Lords of Ireland from the time of the building of the bridge at Limerick and the tower thereto adjacent have been used to repair, maintain and keep the same at their own expense, We command you [the barons of the exchequer] that you cause the said bridge and tower to be repaired, sustained and kept out of the issue of your bailiwick." McGregor and Fitzgerald's *History of Limerick* states (p. 400) that "In 1359 Edward II granted an aid towards (probably repairing) a bridge in the City of Limerick in a direction towards the Irish enemies of Thomond and erecting a tower at the end of same for repelling said enemies." The note clearly states Edward II but he had died in 1327. No mention was found under Edward III for 1359. The note may well have been the cause of much of the confusion about Thomond Bridge evident in the histories. The order of 1325 uses the word "progenitors" (*p(ro)genitores* in the original Latin). The plural would not have been used if the stones bridge was built by his father Edward I (1272–1307)— so it has to refer to either Henry III who reigned (1216–72) or John (1199–1216).

William of Prene, the king's master carpenter in Ireland, appointed in 1284 to supervise royal works, such as repairs to the royal castles, e.g. Rindown, was charged with cutting and taking away oaks in the king's woods and with other offences in 1286–88. Prene was fined £20 but as Stalley[1] explains "corruption was rife in the Dublin administration" at those times so William was not deterred by the penalty and was possibly living beyond the means afforded by his official salary of 12

Fig. 42 (c), (d) and (e): *Pacata, Speed and Greenville*

pence per day. In 1292 he was back in court again for stealing a cart load of iron spikings, for attending to his own work in official time, for taking a salmon from the Liffey and a charge that "the aforesaid William took twenty pounds of the lord King's money to build Limerick Bridge and by reason of the faultiness of his work on the aforesaid bridge eighty men were drowned, and in this way he defrauded the lord King of his money." Stalley states that he was fined £200 on some of the charges and dismissed from the king's service but the charge relating to the bridge was deferred to be held before the chief justice in that area. Stalley found no further records of the Limerick charge, but concluded:

> One of the most severe charges levelled against William of Prene was the accusation of faulty workmanship on the bridge at Limerick. Assuming the figure of eighty deaths is not an exaggeration, the heavy loss of life indicates that this must have been the main bridge across the Shannon, known as Thomond Bridge. The history of this bridge is far from clear. The existing structure was erected between 1838 and 1840 and it replaced a medieval bridge, which had fourteen arches and a tower and gateway towards the north end. This bridge has been traditionally ascribed to the period of King John, since the first reference to a bridge at Limerick occurs in 1199. But several facts indicate that the stone bridge demolished in 1840 was constructed in the fourteenth century and that it had more than one predecessor of wood.

The number of deaths resulting from William's error was so great that it is hard to imagine how it could have occurred on a stone bridge. It is true that the construction of masonry piers by piling had its dangers, but disasters on the scale of Limerick do not seem likely. Another possibility is that William was engaged on centring for masonry arches, but again the numbers drowned seem too large. The fact that master carpenter was in charge strongly implies that the whole structure was made of wood. Twenty-two years before William's appointment as King's master carpenter it seems certain that Limerick bridge was a timber construction, for in 1262 the sheriff of Limerick accounted for ten shillings spent on joists to repair it. There are thus strong indications that William was repairing or rebuilding a bridge made of timber and not of stone.

It has to be admitted that Stalley's deductions in the light of the sparse information then available about Thomond (old) bridge are not unreasonable. In fact he diligently searched for more and commented on the lack of any survey or study of the styles and characteristics of bridges in Ireland. His paper stimulated me to search deep for the truth, given the importance of the question in the national context.

The directive of Edward II mentioned above establishes that there was a stone bridge at the site in 1272 before Prene's time. Could 80 people have been drowned as a result of faulty work by a carpenter who spent £20 on building work on a large 14-arch stone bridge? The answer is yes, because a history of Toulouse[15] records that in May 1281, when a large crowd had gathered on the Old Bridge over the Garone at Toulouse to attend the ceremony of the bathing of the cross, the bridge collapsed and 200 persons were drowned. The bridge was built in the second half of the 12th century and evidently was a stone bridge. Boyer[16] investigated the surviving (1402–10), very detailed accounts of wages and materials for the repair of the ancient stone bridge at Albi over the Tarn in France. From her analysis she concluded that frequent repairs were necessary, that even for rebuilding one stone arch carpenters, not masons, did most of the work—cutting down trees, sawing them, erecting centering and scaffolding etc., and that altogether 285 man days were involved and the cost was equivalent to £41. A few early pipe rolls have survived for Ireland, but in most cases the descriptions of the work done are far too inadequate to enable conclusions to be drawn. The closest found was an expenditure in 1298 of £16. 1s. 9½d in payments to workmen and masons engaged on making a new well at Kildare Castle (Pipe Roll 8. Edw. I).

Another possibility is that Prene was engaged in building one of the drawbridges. These were made of timber and often collapsed. This would explain the phrases "build Limerick Bridge" in the charge. The word "build" was often used in place of "repair" (see St Mary Magdalen's Bridge). Perhaps the most likely of all explanations is that the masonry in a pier collapsed, bringing down two arches, and these were replaced temporarily by wooden spans. This was common practice here and abroad right up to the 19th century and there are many engravings etc. showing it—e.g. Islandbridge in 18th century. The spans at Thomond were long, 18ft in the clear, and the construction of a centre support would have been very difficult because of the rock in the bed. The sketch in fig. 42a confirms these facts in respect of Thomond.

There is a sketch in Viollet-le-Duc[17] of the ancient bridge over the Charente river at Saintes in the west of France reproduced in fig. 43. It was drawn in 1837 shortly before the bridge was demolished. It was an old Roman bridge reconstructed in 1202 by Isenbert at King John's direction (see Appendix 2). The Roman triumphal arch was relocated in the town after the demolition. The remainder of the Saintes bridge, which had pointed segmental arches, bears a resemblance to Old Thomond Bridge as depicted in the *Pacata* plans. Perhaps the inspiration for the Thomond Bridge came from Isenbert. There are many records of contacts between the cities of Dublin and Limerick on one hand and the town of La Rochelle and Saintes in the west of France during the 12th and 13th centuries, evidenced by the directive of 1221 by Henry III[18] "to the good men and maire of La Rochelle: We command you not to levy from the goods brought to your ports by our good men and merchants of Dublin, other customs than those usual in the time of our father, king John, and to admit them to all the liberties they had in our town of La Rochelle in his days . . .". Whatever about Dublin, there was no problem in regard to language in Limerick, where Norman French was commonly spoken at the time.

Reverting to the general question: was the bridge built in the reign of King John a "stone and lime" one? The answer depends largely on the material in the river bed: is there rock at the site? There are no surviving records of the present bridge which was built on the very same line as the old, nor was information available in the Corporation records or those of the Harbour Authority. I contacted Michael Quinn, regional engineer, ESB, Ardnacrusha who kindly supplied copies of four abstracts from the station archive giving the level sections and borehole drawings from the 1924 Siemens and Schuckertwerke survey. From these it was possible to plot the bed profile

Fig. 43: *The Ancient Bridge at Saintes, France (source: Viollet-le-Duc*

inserted in fig. 40. Fortunately a bore had been taken beside the bridge site which showed solid rock surmounted by 18ins. of "broken rock". From an analysis of this information, it is clear that while there are shallower points 0.3 and 1.5 miles upriver, the bridge site, though a little deeper, was on a shelf and more suitable. The cross-section showed that on the day of the survey in 1924 the deepest water was not more than 6ft over the bed for about one third of the river width. Working at low tide the medieval masons would have been able to build the piers without much difficulty. It would however have been very difficult to erect secure durable trestles for a timber bridge.

Finally in regard to cost, I have estimated that the volume of masonry in the old 13-arch bridge was about 40,000 cubic feet. At the prices prevailing in 1684 when Phillips prepared his fortification estimates, it would have cost 3*d*. per cubic foot, a total of £450. In King John's time carpenters were paid 10*d*., quarriers 7*d*., ditchers 5*d*. per day. Based on these rates using 20th-century output data the bridge would have cost about £200 or half the annual income of a barony lord of the period.

Wilkinson[19] writing in 1845 records that the limestone at Limerick and other towns in the vicinity afforded excellent lime and that good limestone for building was available at Bridge Quarry and Thomond Gate Quarry.

Given all the foregoing information there can no longer be any doubt that the old Thomond stone bridge can properly be called a "King John" and like Babes, be used as a marker, in evaluating other bridges.

Abbeytown

This five-span masonry arch bridge (fig. 44) spans the Boyle Water at the entrance to the former Cistercian abbey. It is a very important bridge from a historical point of view because it seems never to have been widened or reconstructed. It is built in the Irish Romanesque style like Mabe's Bridge in Kells, though there are a few notable differences. It is a public road bridge in charge of the Co. Council. There are two other bridges in the town, New Bridge bridge and Town Bridge, both 19th-century.

Fig. 44: *Abbeytown Bridge: Downriver Elevation*

The Down Survey (1656) map of "The Province of Connaught" shows four bridges across the Boyle Water—one at Boyle, one at the outlet from Lough Key and two others at the third points between Boyle and the outlet from Lough Gara. Moll's map shows one bridge, part of the road from Coollooney crossing the river to "Abbey Boyle". It branches into three roads south of the bridge—one to Carrick, one to Elphin and the third to Ballintubber. This suggests that Abbeytown, south of the Abbey Bridge, was the focal point of the town in 1714. There are numerous references to Boyle and its Cistercian abbey from the time of the latter's foundation in 1161 to its suppression in 1569, all well documented in Gwynn & Hadcock[1] and Stalley[2], but there is no mention of the bridge. The former state that there was an early Irish monastery in Boyle called Ath-da-Larc and that this was colonised by monks from Mellifont in 1161, and that the abbey was known by this name in 1197 and was "sometimes confused with Ath-da-Larc north of Kells". Stalley states that building work continued till 1220 and that by 1231 the abbey had become a place of pilgrimage. In the absence of any specific early mentions of a bridge and taking account of Stalley's general assertion that there is no record of any Cistercian monastery in Ireland ever having built or financed one, the question of the ford and its location becomes of paramount importance because the bridge was most likely to have been erected at or near the ford.

The only two locations mentioned in the literature at which there were Ath-da-Larcs are Boyle and north of Kells, Co. Meath. At both locations churches were established by St Patrick. Some of the Kells references are in original Latin—*vadum duarum furcarum*, the ford of the two forks. But what type of ford was this? I solved this problem when preparing a paper on Mabe's Bridge[3] by comparing the physical characteristics of the Blackwater north of Kells and the river in Boyle when I noticed on the Boyle 25in. OS map that there were two eccentric, slightly overlapping, islands at the bend in the river just upstream of the abbey. A ford at such a location would be shallow and the person crossing would see two forks, one to the left and one to the right. The test was to find a similar set of islands on the Blackwater north of Kells. There was none on the current maps, nor on the river, but the 1838 OS six-inch map shows that one of the islands had

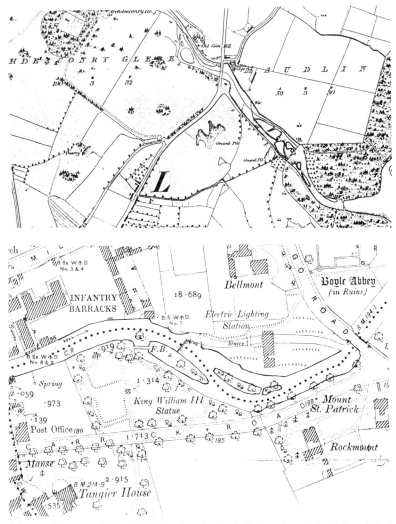

Map 4: *Abbeytown Bridge OS Maps showing Probable Locations of the Kells and Boyle "Two-forked Fords"*

then been split by a third river channel giving an identical topography to Boyle. The respective map sections are reproduced in Map 4. The islands at Boyle can no longer be identified on the site because one has been incorporated in a car park in recent decades. This is a great pity, because the existence of the ford, a very important one geographically, obviously influenced St Patrick in the choice of a site for the first monastery as at Kells, and the proper Irish version of Boyle ought to be Ath-da-larc—a name which would place its origins in the 5th century.

Richard McGee of Boyle drew my attention to a sketch in Grosse's *Antiquity of Ireland*[4] dated 1791 which shows toll gate piers extending up 10ft or more above the parapet on each side of the second pier, which he states were removed between 1830 and 1860; also the abbey was used as a garrison station early in the 17th century and remained so until the 1790s. The Grosse sketch shows that there has been no significant alteration in the downstream facade since then—an important fact in view of the loss of grand jury records.

From all the foregoing I conclude that the most likely period for the construction of the bridge was between 1190 and 1220. The next step was to examine the characteristics of the bridge relative to the various criteria set out in

Fig. 45: *Abbeytown Bridge: Pointed Segmental Arch, Downriver*

Fig. 46: *Abbeytown Bridge: Upriver Elevation of Three Arches*

Part I and see if they corroborated the hypothesis. These were examined from a set of ten objective photos taken by P. McGuinness. The most notable feature is the massive, triangular upriver cutwaters which extend upwards to road level and are coped with stone slabs laid flat (fig 45). There are none on the downriver face. The piers and spans are each approximately 10ft wide, a ratio of 1 to 1. There are no pedestrian refuges for the good reason that the roadway between the parapet is 16ft wide and there is no evidence whatsoever to suggest the bridge was ever widened. Finally and most important are the intrados of the arch rings and there we find a fascinating combination:

four are arcs of circles, almost semi-circles; the 5th, on the east end, is a pointed segmental (fig. 46). The remarkable fact about the arch shapes are that they reflect, albeit in a cruder way, the heterogeneity of shape in the arch forms in the nave of the nearby abbey described by Stalley: "For some years the nave of Boyle Abbey terminated at the fourth bay and it was not until *c.* 1202–20 that the final phase of construction was undertaken. Both north and south arcades were built together this time, though in selecting his arch forms the new master mason faced an embarrassing choice. He decided to compromise by continuing with round arches on the south side and pointed arches on the north."

The arches in the abbey are true semi-circles and true pointed segmentals in ashlar masonry, whereas those in the bridge are a random selection of flat stones but considerably better shaped than in Mabe's. The bridge marks a transition from the traditional Irish to Anglo-Norman forms of construction. Most importantly it is one of the very few early survivors with some (circular) segmental arches.

The stone in the bridge appears to be mainly sandstone with some limestone. Both occur in the area, the sandstone beds being capped with limestone, according to Wilkinson[5].

King John's

This abandoned bridge was identified from Rocque's map[1]. It spans the Griffeen river at Esker, Co. Dublin and is marked clearly, Map 5, as "King John's Bridge". A visit to the site left one perplexed for a moment and wondering if like so many others it had been replaced, but it quickly became apparent that the road from Newcastle had been realigned many years ago and a glance upriver revealed a gem of a little arch (fig. 47), half broken with trees growing out of it, but quite sufficient to see it was most probably the original, that is, pre-1216. A closer inspection revealed that formerly it had three spans and that the orientation matched the lines on the 1756 map.

The new bridge consists of a small segmental stone arch of 18th-century vintage, widened on the upstream side with a reinforced concrete slab, dating, at the earliest, from the 1930s and now festooned with service pipes. There is no possibility of checking the date of the realignment because of the destruction of the grand

Map 5: *Part of Rocque's Co. Dublin Map, c.1760, showing King John's, Bridges Lucan, New Bridge, and Leixlip*

jury records for Co. Dublin, but it has to be post-1773, the date of publication of Rocque's map. It is shown on the 1844 OS six-inch map and designated "Esker Br" so it must have been constructed in between. The old bridge is marked but not named on the 1844 map, but no approach roads are shown.

The following are the principal characteristics of the old bridge (fig. 48). Span of central arch 8ft clear; the two other spans appear to have been the same. Width of pier and of arch 9ft; thickness of pier 5ft; cutwaters: triangular upstream, none downstream; the arch ring is a segment of a circle springing from roughly shaped but solid skewbacks; the ring stones are solid blocks of roughly shaped calp limestone from the locality; the joints in the arch ring stones are, with some exceptions, radial; the pier is of good quality, coursed stone masonry, and the apex stones in the cutwaters have sharp points. The bridge obviously had adequate flow capacity seeing that one arch is now sufficient to carry the normal flows; the river has been realigned upstream of the bridge. The mortar in the interior and exterior is of good quality; the latter may have been repointed over the centuries. The keystone (fig. 49) is wedge-shaped and was obviously

Fig. 47: *King John's Bridge: Downriver Elevation of Surviving Piers and Remnants of Central Arch*

Fig. 48: *King John's Bridge: Upriver Elevation*

Fig. 49: *King John's Bridge: Arch Crown Upriver*

Fig. 50: *King John's Bridge: Tree Roots in Action*

hammered in but was slightly too large to fit exactly. The masonry is of excellent quality for the period and was probably built by a master mason attached to the manor who had plenty experience in building door and window arches. The destructive power of trees is illustrated in fig. 50.

The literature search yielded no mentions pre-1756. Two papers on Esker were traced.[2] These show that Esker was part of the demesne in the Liffey valley which Henry II annexed to the crown and which under King John was organised as a royal manor. It was farmed by the sheriff (seneschal) and governed by royal bailiff; the office continued into the 19th century. There is no mention of a bridge in either

reference; given its proximity to the city, this is surprising. I am convinced that the bridge is, true to its name, a "King John", that is, was built between 1199 and 1216.

The bridge is an obvious choice for restoration, being located on a Co. Council park. The boundary between the surviving original work and restorative masonry should of course be carefully demarcated.

Castlemaine

The Annals of Innisfallen record that in 1215 "Maurice son of Thomas Fitzgerald built a castle in Duloath and the castles of Killforglas and Magne were also built by him." This is generally accepted as the foundation of the famous castellated bridge across the Maine river which flows into Dingle Bay. The history of the castle is given in a paper[1] written in 1908. Few facts are available about its early history, but there are some mentions. In 1357 McOge, second son of Desmond, died in the castle; Gerald, earl of Kildare, took it in 1510; it withstood a siege by Sir J. Perrot in 1571. In 1598 all the castles in Munster were taken by the earl of Desmond except Mang which later succumbed. In 1601 it was again in royal hands. The confederates held it from 1641 to 1647. It was taken finally by the Cromwellians in 1649 who, according to local tradition, dismantled the castle. There is an idealistic but informative sketch of the castle in *Pacata Hibernia*[2] (fig. 51), which illustrates the castle and the bridge *c.* 1600. The 1846 Drainage Report for the Maine[3] says that "Across the tidal part of the river there is one bridge at the village of Castlemaine. It consists of four arches of about 15ft span each, with piers from 13 to 15ft each in thickness. This is the lowest bridge across the Maine, and is said to be one of the oldest bridges in Ireland being, I believe, coeval with the old Thomond Bridge at Limerick. Upon an extension upstream of the two most northern piers was erected a tower or castle for defending the passage. Of this tower there are still some vestiges remaining." The report then goes on to mention that the bridge was entirely inadequate to discharge the accumulated fresh and tidal water for the proper drainage of the lands up to Scarravaneena bridge. Among the works proposed for the catchment was the undersetting or rebuilding of no less than fifteen bridges including Castlemaine Bridge and the construction of numerous gullets, all of which work was chargeable to the county and estimated to cost £3,314. The overall estimate was £49,686.

The loss of the grand jury records makes it difficult to check other than by actual observation how much of the work, if any, was carried out. There are two photos of the bridge, from each elevation, in Fr Carmody's article, but they are obscure and merely indicate that the castle remnants were gone, that the bridge then had four arches and that the piers and spans were about equal—which indicates that deepening the eyes and underpinning the piers and abutments was the solution, if any, adopted in the 1840s.

Mang is supposed to resemble the ancient Ponte Nomentano castellated bridge, over the Arno about three miles upriver from Rome. Perhaps the idea for it came from there, but the two are of very different construction. Nomentano is built over a large single-span arch springing from two abutment-type piers with no extensions beyond the bridge up or downriver.

No bridge was found in books on surviving British or French bridges of fortifications resembling the Mange castle. It is clear from the Drainage Report descriptions that in the *Pacata* sketch the supporting piers are much too narrow relative to the spans; the ratio was one to one. The arches are also sketched as semicircular; one would expect them to be pointed segmental if they were erected at the time the Old Thomond Bridge was built. However, as pointed out above, the *Pacata* sketch is idealistic, perhaps based on second-hand evidence.

The OPW surveyed the river in the 1970s and subsequently carried out a drainage scheme which involved the removal of the old bridge,

Fig. 51: *Castlemang Bridge and Castle: Elevation from Pacata Hibernia c.1630*

by then stripped of all remnants of the castle. The drawing in fig. 220 in Appendix 8 is reproduced from an OPW cross-section and shows the actual measurements. The word "rock" is clearly written under the bridge on a longitudinal section of the river which is also shown on the OPW drawing. This, of course, explains how it lasted over the centuries and the choice of location when built originally.

The arches are semi-circular on the drawing; those of the Old Thomond Bridge were pointed segmental. The typical arch span in the latter was 18ft and the average pier width 12ft. The Ponte Nomentano was built on a circular arch of much greater span. Overall, given the rock foundation just below the river bed, there is no reason to doubt that the bridge and castle were built early in the 13th century. There is a need of a local article which would bring together the surviving information and photographs.

St John's

There is one of the few bridges for which we have good information from the second half of the 17th century in the surviving Council Books of the Corporation of Waterford 1662–1700.[1] The earliest mention is 1674:

Item 958, 1674 AD "Concluded that twenty pounds sterling shall be forthwith raised, collected, and levied upon the inhabitants for this year's fire and candles for the guards and the repairs of the arches under John's bridge; and that Alderman Seager do apportion it according to the last books for the deficiency of the years value.

This is followed by six other items as follows:

Item 1664 of 1685 AD, "Concluded, upon reading the presentiments of the grand jury last quarter sessions referred to this board, that twenty seven shillings eight pence be paid to Nicholas Green according to presentiment aforesaid, No. 4, for mending of St John's bridge . . .".

Item 1803 of 1687 AD "Also that Mr Mayor, Alderman Denis Barker, and two sheriffs, and Mr Nath Marriott are to agree with carpenters to build St John's bridge."

Item 1819, Feb. 1687 AD "Concluded that the agreement made by Mr Mayor and others with John Petford and Richard Graves, carpenters, that they be paid six pounds sterling out of the city revenue for repairing of St John's bridge and twenty shillings *per annum* for keeping the said bridge in repair at their own proper charge for the term of one and twenty years."

Item 1944, May, 1693 "Ordered, that Mr Richard Graves, carpenter, be paid his bill for John's bridge repairs and for the carriages etc. when examined by Mr Mayor and the auditors and St John's Bridge be sufficiently repaired."

Item 2127, 1698 AD "Concluded that Mr Richard Graves do by Michelmas next build a new drawbridge at John's Gate, or strike the top of the present bridge and pave it over at his own charge or be sued on his contract."

Item 2165, June 1700 "ordered that [the] causeway on St John's bridge be forthwith repaired."

Item 2127 may not relate to the bridge but it is an informative entry as to how the corporation dealt with defective work at the time. It would appear that the word "build" in Item 1803 in the light of the next entry for the same years means repair. The main conclusion is that the bridge needed frequent maintenance and that most of this work was done by carpenters. We learn little about the physical characteristics not even the number of arches.

There is a perspective map reproduced in Ryland's *History of Waterford*[2] showing Waterford City in 1673. The bridge is shown very clearly (albeit not to scale) and from the sketch (Map 6) it is possible to discern that the bridge had four arches and that there was a mill on a small stream that joined John's river immediately upriver of the bridge. The bridge had high parapet walls which were doubled in height over the central pier on the approach to the mill. The perspective gives the impression of a severe grade, but part of the effect is caused by a curve in the approach road from the east. Ryland, writing in 1824, mentions in the text that John's river was navigable at high

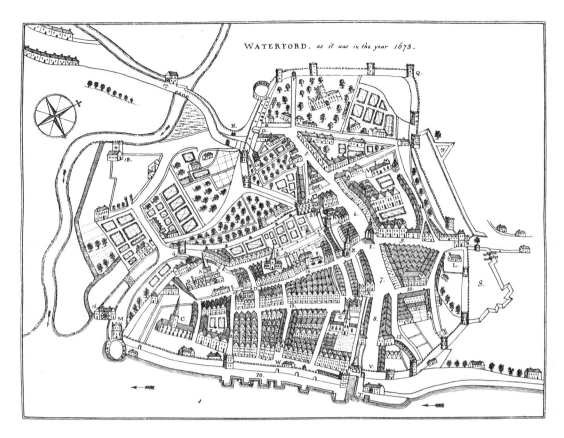

Map 6: *Waterford City in 1673 (source: Ryland)*

water and that it was traversed by three bridges within the city—two of ancient date namely, John's and William Street. The third, St Catherine's, had been recently erected near the old abbey of St Catherine. He also states that Waterford did not have a bridge across the Suir till 1794 (see Lemuel Cox's Bridges), but that is not strictly correct because Cromwell made a temporary bridge of boats in 1649.

From the foregoing information collected several years ago I had concluded that the bridge had been replaced until in August 1989 Paddy McGuinness heard about the bridge, incidentally, from a corporation engineer and, spotting the pointed segmental arches, took some photos and a few key measurements which he communicated to me. This information coupled with the mentions established its antiquity.

The bridge now has two arches and has been widened twice on the downriver side.

The original is 11ft wide, the first extension 14ft wide and the second 7ft. The northwest arch has a 15ft span and the other of a 17ft span with a 10ft wide pier between. There is a plaque in the upriver parapet recording that "This bridge was enlarged in the Year 1765 John Lyon Esq. Mayor, William Bates (and) William Barker Esq. Sheriffs."

A check on the 1843 OS six-inch map showed that the mill had been removed before then and that the distance between the banks upriver was approx. 80ft and downriver 60ft. The width of the bridge scales about 20ft on the 1843 map; however, as the thickness of a line can represent up to 5ft it is impossible to be anyway precise. Without the plaque one would deduce that the second extension was added after 1843 as the present overall width is 33ft. If that were the case it would mean that the plaque referred to the first extension, that is, the 14ft wide mid-section. However, the ring stones in the downriver face are not voussoirs and the widths of the stones vary considerably—not the type of facing ring one would expect in the 19th century. The ring had to be matched to an existing one that had already been adjusted to a pointed segmental, so one would expect some contortions in the centering.

The upriver arches are shown in (fig. 52) and it is these that help most of all in dating the bridge. First the cutwaters and parapet copings must be disregarded because they are relatively recent additions. Unfortunately the cutwater obscures the springing of the arches, while the later road retaining wall makes it difficult to discern those at the banks. The intrados are pointed segmental. The facing ring stones are thin, irregular-shaped limestone and sandstone flags, and there are about 40 in each semi-ring, making it easy to turn the arch to a reasonably regular curve. The semi-arch on the left bank has deformed such that it is almost a straight line, and a propping wall has been built to give it extra support. The radii of the intrados curves are about 7ft; their centres are located on the river bed about 2ft left and right of the mid-span respectively—like some of the arches in Slane Bridge.*

There can be little doubt that the upriver arches date from the 13th or 14th centuries. The 17th-century records establish clearly that its name is St John's Bridge, called after the Evangelist like the hospital founded in Waterford in 1191. Gwynn and Hadcock[3] mention a leper hospital founded after 1185 and confirmed by King John (Leper's town in the parish of Killea). A chapel called after St Mary Magdalen was located outside the town walls and it probably had accommodation for lepers. Further local research would probably establish a link between the bridge, hospital and chapel in which event the bridge might be dated from the early 13th century.

Several months after reaching the conclusion that this was a 13th-century bridge, I came across a sketch of the surviving gable wall of the old church of Crook, in Passage, Co. Waterford in volume IV of the copies of the early 19th century Du Noyer sketches in the RIA. The drawing (No. 71) caught my eye because of the manner in which the crowns of the arches over the three windows are drawn and how the problem of the keystone was solved. They had an arrangement of stones which immediately suggested arch evolution (fig. 248). A check of dates in Gwynn and Hadcock revealed that a manor at Crook was granted to the Knights Templar by Henry II before 1180 and that the church was mentioned in 1278. This information, with a tracing of the Du Noyer sketch, was sent to John O'Flynn, who soon afterwards forwarded a photo (fig. 53). The reader is left to draw his own conclusion about the correspondence of the style and composition of the arches and to compare both with Gormanstown Bridge.*

Athassel

This four-arch bridge is part of the extensive remains of the medieval Augustinian priory on the west bank of the river Suir one and a half miles south of Golden, Co. Tipperary. The priory was founded c.1200 by the Norman baron William de Burgo and confirmed by King John in 1205[1]. Harbison[2] states that it was the largest medieval priory in Ireland, and its prior was a peer of Parliament. De Breffny and Mott[3] give an aerial view of a four acre site containing the ruins showing the bridge and the gate house located about 150 yds from the main buildings which are located on the bank of the Suir. He states that the church was built in stages from 1230 to 1280.

The Irish version of the placename is Áth Asail or Asal's ford which was on the Suir. The bridge evidently spanned a mill race which took its water from the Suir about half a mile upriver of the abbey. It is now closed in

Fig. 52: *St John's Bridge: Upriver Elevation*

and the bridge merely crosses a shallow pond. It never formed part of a public road.

Michael Murphy provided a dimensioned drawing (fig. 221, Appendix 8) and the photograph (fig. 54). It was evident from these that this is a marker bridge if the date could be established with reasonable accuracy. It is in perfect condition.

The bridge was an integral part of the monastery as it provided access to the gate house. It can reasonably be assumed therefore that it was built as part of the priory and erected in the first half of the 13th century. The *Shell Guide*[4] states that a town grew up in the vicinity but that it was burned in 1319 and in 1330 so no remains are visible. The priory was burned in 1447.

The stone work in the bridge is similar to the remaining priory walls, well-built random rubble, roughly coursed. There are no parapet walls and it is evident from the top layer of stones on the spandrels that they were intended as a capping layer, indicating that the bridge was unbattlemented. There are no cutwaters fore or aft. The arch spans are 10ft clear and the piers 8ft thick with minor variations. The ring stones are well shaped of fairly uniform thickness. Overall the quality of the masonry is excellent for the period. Finally, the most significant characteristic from the aspect of bridge history, the curves of the intrados are true an and accurate segments of circles of 6ft 6in. radius subtending an angle of 90° at the centre. The skewbacks are solid triangular blocks of stone with springing faces at 45° to the horizontal as required for a true 90° segment. This is the earliest example of a true segmental circular arch found in a road bridge in Ireland. Strangely, the portcullis entrance gateway at the end of the bridge is semicircular and the gateway beyond it pointed segmental. The date can only be firmly established by detailed comparison with all the arches in the ruins. However, segmental arches that spring at 45° or less require strong abutments and this was easily provided in the bridge by thick piers and in castles by thick walls, but not always feasible in relatively thin walls of churches and their ancillary buildings.

Buttevant Old Bridge

Joyce devotes a page of his *Irish Names of Places*[1] to the town of Buttevant, stating that it

Fig. 53: *Crook Church: Central Arch in Surviving Gable*

Fig. 54: *Athassel Bridge: Downstream Elevation*

was called Cill-na-Mullach by the Four Masters in their record of the foundation of the Franciscan monastery there in 1251. The Latin version of is "ecclesia tumulorum"—the church of the hillocks or summits. The *Shell Guide*[2] attributes the name to "botovant", the Norman French for a defensive work, but Joyce derives it from "Boutez-en-avant", meaning to push forward. This was the motto of the Barrymores (de Barrys), the Anglo-Norman family who founded the town.

There are two public road bridges over the Awbeg in the vicinity. The north bridge is called Rathclare after the townland in which it is located. It was built in the late 18th or early 19th century and was reconstructed by Cork Co. Council in 1969 when it was in danger of collapse. The bridge to the east of the town is called Buttevant Old Bridge (fig. 55), and is designated by this name on the 1841 OS six-inch map. It would appear that the "Old" was added to distinguish it from Rathclare. It is located at the junction of three townlands—Creggane to the west, Lockaroe to the north east and Waterhouse south east, which suggests that the crossing formed a boundary in ancient times. Creggane indicates rock and Lockaroe a place full of stones or flags.[1]

Three hundred yards upriver, the south west boundary of the ancient townland of Spital containing 500 acres fronts on the Awbeg for a distance of about 200 yards in a manner which suggests that it was given an extra field specifically for that purpose. In Chapter 9, Part I, the early Irish and Norman tradition of setting aside lands for lepers is outlined. The early Irish name for such lands was "spital", whereas the Norman one was usually "Maudlin". The townland included a hospital as the Irish name implies and often a small church and a bridge collectively called an *opus pontis*. Gwynn and Hadcock devote a chapter of their book[3] to medieval hospitals and hospices. They include two mentions of Buttevant: "Spital, Co. Cork (1.5 miles north-east of Buttevant)" and "Spitle-Bridge, Co. Cork (1 mile east of Buttevant). There were ruins of an isolated chapel here c.1749: Smith i.315. This, with the name, seems to indicate a hospital, perhaps under Ballybeg Priory." They point out that all the information for the chapter was provided by Logan whose paper is discussed here in the bridge context in Chapter 9, Part I. No in-depth study of the Cork "Spital" was found; however, the site of the hospital ruins is clearly marked on the six-inch map close to the field abutting the Awbeg. The townland is marked "Spittle" and the hospital indicated by a symbol on the Down Survey map (1656). The small river Lougheragh forms the east boundary to Spittal townland and is crossed by one road, but the bridge is not named. I am of the opinion that Spittle Bridge was located on the site of Buttevant Old Bridge in pre-Norman times, as this would conform with other sites, such as Maudlins in Duleek and on the Blackwater in Kells—that is an *opus pontis* consisting of land, hospital, chapel, river (as distinct from stream) and bridge. It is a topic needing further research, local and national.

Buttevant was the scene of much building

activity in the first half of the 13th century. The Augustinian canons founded Ballybeg Abbey at the south end of the town in 1229 and the Franciscans erected a friary in the town in 1251. Both were endowed by the de Barrys. The former was suppressed in 1540 and the friary in 1575. Full details are given in Gwynn and Hadcock.

The first historical mention that I came across of bridges in Buttevant was a note and an illustration relating to a clapper bridge (Walter Jones, 1906)[4]. The second source was a mention of the Old Bridge in Grove White's *Notes on Buttevant*[5] which quotes Windle's comment on the bridge: "The old bridge over the Awbeg river at Buttevant is a curiosity. Many years ago it was widened, but not much. It now presents two different faces. The arches at the south side are pointed; those on the north side, being the more modern additions, are rounded. The original breadth was about one third of the present." This excellent note (MSS 12 I. 10 p.169.RIA) compiled c.1850—in particular the mention of pointed arches—caused me to list it for checking to see if the original is still there. The check was done by Brendan Devlin in September 1990 and finding it still there he provided some photographs and measurements. A glance at the overall photo (fig. 55) was sufficient, in the light of the information on other surviving pointed segmental arched bridges, such as Trim, to indicate that it was 14th- and possibly 13th-century and worth researching in detail.

The bridge is 21ft 6in. wide face to face consisting of a 14ft 9in. original and a 6ft 9in. extension. Windle obviously confused the sections but not the proportions. The arches in the extension (fig. 56) are segmental arcs with well cut radial voussoirs. The upriver cutwaters on the extension are fairly massive for work carried out c.1800, but the builder had no choice as he had to extend the original piers. They may be replicas of the originals. The masonry in the vicinity of the butt joint in the piers appears to be continuous in the bottom courses, suggesting that the extension was partly erected on the foundations of the original cutwaters as in Mabe's Bridge*. There are no cutwaters on the downriver (original) face—an indicator of early construction. The pier bottoms and foundations are protected by concrete aprons; this work was probably carried out under a Board of Public Works Awbeg

Drainage Scheme in the 1930s. The bridge is founded on rock—further evidence that it could have survived many a flood without damage. The gradient of the river bed is also relatively flat along the Buttevant section.

The bridge has four arches. The downriver elevation is shown in fig. 223, Appendix 8. The spans and pier widths are as follows starting from the west abutment: 11'-2"/8'-6"/10'-2"/9'-10"/8'-10"/9'-10"/8'-6". It will be noted that the variations are random, an indicator of the difficulty experienced by masons or carpenters when setting out in water especially on a rock river bed. The span-to-pier ratios are almost unity like Mabe's, St Mary Magdalen's* and other early bridges. The ratios for the Thomond (old) Bridge averaged 1.5 to 1 whereas those in Trim, Slane and Babes are closer to 2.0 to 1. The inspiration for the bridge may well have come from Thomond because Buttevant Old Bridge formed part of the ancient road linking Cork and Limerick, mentioned below.

Among the photos there was one (fig. 57) showing the second arch from the west exactly head on. Given that the span is 10ft 2in. it was possible to analyse it in detail. The following is a summary of the findings: the arch intrados curve, allowing for construction irregularities, is a drop arch, that is, a pointed segmental with radii equal to two-thirds of the span, the centres being located on the line joining the imposts (horizontal stones on the piers from which the arch springs: see Glossary). This is the only such arch found by us among the many examined in this book. In Slane and Trim bridges the centres are located on the river bed. Drop arches are common over the window opes of medieval churches. It will be noted that the right hand half of the arch is distorted, a fault found in many other pointed segmental arches such as Adare*, Trim* and St John's*, attributable to yielding of the centering during construction. Other characteristics that suggest an early date are the non-radial joints and the heart-shaped keystone. The ring stones are well cut. It would appear that the six stones on the left hand of the crown slipped a few inches, probably when the shuttering was withdrawn or when the keystone was being hammered in. It is possible that it was intended as an ordinary pointed segmental and the left half was set out in error tangential at the springing.

Fig. 55: *Buttevant Old Bridge: Downriver Elevation*

Fig. 56: *Buttevant Old Bridge: Upriver Extension*

Fig. 57: *Buttevant Old Bridge: Drop Arch Downriver*

The other arches shown in fig. 55 are ordinary pointed segmentals. The springing points are more or less level with each other and it would appear that the rises were deliberately reduced in order to achieve falling gradients on the roadway and parapet walls, outwards from the crown of the drop arch. The reductions in the spans of the two arches on the east end helped to reduce the crown rises slightly; however, the span of the west arch was increased and the crown lowered by using a flatter arch. The drop arch may have been given a greater rise for the purpose of providing headroom for boats. The mason probably planned to achieve this overall profile (it would have been simpler to build a conventional level deck bridge at the site, given the downgrades on the approach roads on either side). Perhaps this was the origin of the "Glanworth profile" (see Glanworth Bridge).

The bridge is shown on the 1841 OS six-inch map having a width which is similar to that shown on the 1932 revision. The earliest literary mention is on the Down Survey map compiled in 1656 on which it and Doneraile Bridge are clearly marked. It is also shown on Petty's General Map of Ireland (1685). The latter is a very significant indication because it is shown as part of the Cork to Limerick road which ran through Newcastle townland, Mallow, Copestown, Buttevant and Kilmallock. The section from Buttevant Old Bridge ran northwards along the west boundary of Spittal townland to Ballyhoura. Less than two decades later we find the main road running from Mallow to Two-pot-House crossing the Awbeg at Cahirmee, three miles east of Buttevant and thence to Ballyhoura, Charleville and Kilmallock. The Cork-Limerick main road was turnpiked in 1731, and by 1778 we find it back on the old line from old Two-pot-House to Ballybeg, thence across the old Buttevant Bridge and on to Ballyhoura. The present line across the Awbeg at Rathclare had not been built at the time but it is shown on the 1841 six-inch map. From all of this we can deduce that the upriver extension of Buttevant Old Bridge was most probably built by the turnpike trust in the period between 1731 and 1800. The extension arch characteristics are compatible with this period.

It was mentioned at the outset that the abbey and a friary were erected in Buttevant west of the Awbeg between 1229 and 1251.

These would have generated considerable traffic from the east side of the river and the need for a durable stone bridge. The construction of the monasteries must have generated a continuous demand for stones and for stonemasons during the period. The friary remnants indicate good quality stonework and according to Harbison[6] contain some lancet windows, a type quite similar to the drop arch found in the bridge (see Glossary). The bridge has four arches like most of the early bridges describes below, e.g. Trim,* New Bridge,* Baals,* and the Dublin (old) Bridge. Given all the evidence, Buttevant (old) Bridge can confidently be assigned to the 13th century, in which case it becomes a landmark bridge in the national context.

Ballybeg Clapper

One mile downriver from the Old Bridge there are the remarkable and substantial remains of a clapper bridge that once spanned the Awbeg. W. Jones of Doneraile has described[4] it as "an unusually perfect and well finished bridge . . . erected in the early part of the 13th century by the Augustinian friars of Ballybeg Abbey for convenience in crossing the Awbeg to their mill and lands beyond." He also mentioned that the slabs were limestone of which there was an abundance in an adjacent quarry.

The mention was investigated by Brendan Devlin in 1988. He found substantial remnants high and dry on the north bank and supplied measurements on which the longitudinal section shown in fig. 222, Appendix 8 is based. The spans are now covered in moss, briars and scrub, such that it is not possible to obtain a reproducible photo. The surviving span slabs are 4ft wide by 7in. thick in wrought limestone. The lengths vary from 4ft to 9ft.

Jones's illustration shows the river flowing under the five surviving clapper spans. The 1932 revised editions of the OS six-inch map (Cork sheet 17) shows the remnants marked "Clapper Bridge" extending from the small building on the north side to the river edge for a length of 50ft as they are at present. The north bank of the river is hatched on the map for a distance of 10 yards or so upriver and downriver indicating that a bank had been built up. The 1841 OS map shows the river extending right up to the little building on the north bank; moreover, its overall length scales

110ft compared to 70ft on the 1932 revision. All this evidence establishes that the river was deepened and embanked in the period between Jones's 1906 note and 1932. One might assume therefore that the south half of the clapper had been removed under the drainage works but this would be erroneous because the bridge is not shown or designated on the 1841 map. Two closely spaced lines are shown extending 60ft back on the south bank to a small building at the rear of Springfield House, also shown on the 1932 map. It is most unlikely that the clapper was missed by the Ordnance surveyors in the 1840s, as they would have crossed it many times during the field work.

Further research and investigation by local antiquaries are needed to solve these problems and to find an early mention that would confirm Jones's statement that it was erected in the 13th century. The most remarkable feature of the surviving spans is not the quality of the slabs because they could easily have been wrought by 13th-century grave slab sculptors; rather it is the overall profile which shows increasing spans from the ends towards the centre. This aesthetically pleasing and functional layout is found in few early Irish bridges.

Gormanstown

The road from Dublin to the north serving as a connector between all the seaboard towns right up to Dundalk and on to Belfast has been a busy one right down through the ages. Its alignment has been changed many times. In our time it is being built along another new line as a motorway, part of Euro Route 01. One of the results of the shifting lines has been the construction of new bridges and the relegation of others where successive routes crossed the many rivers that run east into the sea—the Tolka, Broadmeadow, Delvin, Nanny, Boyne, Dee and Glyde, Fane, Castletown, Newry, Upper Bann and the Lagan. Many of the bridges were rebuilt, others widened, often twice, then relegated as a new road line was cut elsewhere. We are fortunate that a considerable number have survived. One of the most interesting, and possibly the oldest, is located where the old coach road from Balrothery to The Cock crossed the Nanny at Gormanstown. This route was replaced by the present road when the bridge at Knocknagin, close to the sea, was built in the last quarter of

Fig. 58: *Gormanstown Bridge: High Parapet on Original Upriver Section*

Fig. 59: *Gormanstown Bridge: Upriver Elevation*

the 18th century. It incidentally was replaced by a reinforced concrete bridge in 1936.

I came across Gormanstown Bridge in 1980 when the unusually high upriver parparet wall caught my attention (fig. 58). A quick inspection showed that it had been twice widened, had two small arches, and that the original upstream section was obviously ancient (fig. 59), a view confirmed by a glance at the arch ring and spandrel wall masonry, which looked more like an ancient tapestry than the fabrication of a mason.

The 1844 OS six-inch map designated it as "Gormanstown Bridge", a boundary bridge between Meath and Dublin linking Gormanstown and Tobersool townlands. Taylor and Skinner's atlas show a very interesting change: the main road follows the present line through Balbriggan on to and across Knockagin Bridge and then turns left up what is now the county road leading to Gormanstown, where it joins the old Balrothery-Drogheda road. The Knocknagin-The Cock section of the turnpike had not been built in 1771. Moll's map (1714) shows the principal north road running from Balrothery to the bridge and on thence to Julianstown. The bridge is also shown on the Down Survey completed in 1656.

The next part of the search was to find out when the widenings had taken place. The Dublin grand jury records were destroyed in the 1922 fire; however, any major work on boundary bridges such as extensions was required by law to be presented to the contiguous grand juries so the Meath records had to include all improvements. The following items were found:

1809: "£25 and 11s. 11d. to Lord Gormanstown and Fran Flanagan and Mr Caffrey to repair and rebuilt a bridge called Gormanstown on the road from Trim to Balbriggan."

1800: "Whether £10. 10s. be raised and paid to . . . to build battlements to half the bridge over the river Gormanstown dividing the Counties Meath and at Oatlands on the Dublin to Drogheda Road—the county of Dublin granting the like."

1775: "Whether £9. 15s. 9d. be raised to rebuild half an arch of the bridge of Gormanstown on the road from Dublin to Drogheda as which divides the counties of Meath and Dublin and 9s. 9d. wages as approved as before."

1769: "Whether £6. 10s. 1d. be raised to build half the bridge over the river Delvin between counties Meath and Dublin."

The 1800 entry may not refer to the present bridge and the 1769 item could apply to several other bridges on the Delvin. However, the 1775 query, though ambiguously worded, relates to the bridge. A single arch of 8ft span cost £10 at the time on average, so Meath built

the arch on its half and Dublin the one on its side of the centre of the river. The item obviously covered the downriver second extension. This is evident from the quality of the masonry and the finish of the large coping stones. The 1769 query may have been a first presentment which could have been refused and been re-presented again in 1775 as that often happened (as indeed it does today when local authorities apply to the Government for road grants).

A close examination of Rocque's Map (1756) shows two rivers flowing under the road. The second is on the Meath side about 150ft north of the bridge; however, an examination of the site showed that it was in fact a mill race long since filled in.

Searches of historical literature yield no earlier mentions of the bridge but some related facts. Sir Robert Preston, the first Lord Gormanstown, was knighted in the field in 1361 and purchased from Almeric de St Amand the manor of Gormanstown in the counties of Dublin and Meath. He filled the office of lord high chancellor of Ireland. The Statute Rolls (XX Edw. IV c. 8) 1482 record that 'to build a castle at Gormanstown at the prayer of Robert Preston, Viscount of Gormanstown, it is ordered, granted and enacted by authority of the Parliament that the said Robert have a cart from every ploughland within three miles of Ballymadun as for once such be servicible whom he will severally on such days appoint to come to help him draw stone and sand for one day and he who will make default on the day appointed to him be amerced in 8 pence." Given that the manor existed in the 14th century and that the Prestons were an influential family, it is probable that a search of the Gormanstown Register[1] would yield further information on the bridge.

The photographs of the bridge, taken after it was defoliated and cleaned up by Meath Co. Council in 1986, clearly indicate that the original upriver section is ancient. The south arch (Dublin) (fig. 60) has a span of 8ft, the pier is 7ft thick and the other arch is 8ft 6in. Each of the three sections section of the bridge is 7ft wide. The joints are butt type. The upriver parapet is 7ft high above road level and the downstream 3ft. The parapet on the upriver side of Dineley's 1680 sketch of Abington Bridge,* Limerick, shows something similar; it was probably for defensive purposes. There may have been a similar one on the down-stream side of the original Gormanstown Bridge before it was widened. A rider on horse-back would have been very vulnerable to distant arrow shot when crossing a bridge with low parapets.

It is difficult to determine what kind of arch the masons had in mind because some settlement of the rings obviously occurred when the centering was removed. In fact, the bridge is a good illustration of one of the advantages of pointed segmental arches set out in Part I, namely, that when settlement occurred due to frail centering or too early removal the distortion was not very noticeable relative to a semi-circular arch. It would appear that all the well shaped stones available in the vicinity were used up in the left-hand (Meath) arch which was probably built first. The cut-water is triangular but we do not know whether or not there was one downstream due to the extension.

Given all the evidence and noting the importance of the road, it would appear to be a 13th-century bridge. There is a wall across the river just above the bridge containing two tiny ancient arches which must have been equipped with sluices to regulate the flow to the mill race.

New Bridge

St Wolstan's Abbey of Augustinian canons at Leixlip was founded by the Anglo-Normans c.1205. It was well endowed and when suppressed in 1536 had over 1200 acres. The four-arch bridge across the Liffey in the vicinity, financed by the mayor of Dublin, John Le Decer, was erected in 1308. It was taken down in 1949 under the Leixlip Hydro-Electric Development and a replacement bridge was built with a roadway of similar width and plan as the original. Apart from the road layout, the replacement is of interest to the bridge historian or antiquarian. Rather than destroy the bridge, it would have been far better to have let it rest beneath the waters like Horsepass Bridge, had that been possible.

Apart from the informative Lawrence photo (515 5WL, National Library Collection) of the upriver face (fig. 61), very little detailed information is available about the old bridge. Sherlock[1] writing in 1896 mentions the ruins of St Wolstan's Abbey close to which he states

Fig. 60: *Gormanstown Bridge: Detail of S. Arch Upriver*

Fig. 61: *New Bridge: Upriver Elevation c.1800 (5155 W.L., NLI)*

"is a bridge said to be the earliest bridge in Ireland though it bears the inappropriate name of Newbridge. John Decer, a worthy citizen and mayor of Dublin built it in 1308 . . . . Better far than building castles or taking them by storm." He then states that the roadway is 9ft wide, that the underside of the arches bear wattle marks, that there was a large deserted mill nearby and than an ancient ford was somewhat below the bridge. He also, states, that in the early part of the 18th century "some barbarian proposed to take it down but this was strongly opposed by Mr Richard Cane, who deserves the thanks of posterity for his successful resistance, particularly as he offered to build another bridge lower down at his own expense."

Useful information can be distilled from the late 19th-century Lawrence photo given the foreknowledge that the bridge was built in 1309. A look at the intrados of the arches shows, from the left, a false ellipse, two pointed segmental and a semi-circle—almost an anthology. The pointed segmental were obviously originals, from 1309, the false ellipse most likely a late 17th or early 18th century replacement. The semi-circle is a bit puzzling but the masonry suggests it could be 15th or 16th century. There is a photo in Craig's book[2] taken in 1946 which shows that one of the pointed segmental arches had a segmental arc, almost semicircular, intrados on the downriver face. It may have been partly rebuilt at some stage. The springing points of the outer arches are at different levels, but these were obviously dictated by the level roadway above and the desire to keep the crown of all arches more or less in line. The spans are about 15ft and the piers half of that. The cutwaters are triangular, have sharp apexes and are built of good quality masonry. The centre pier cutwater is capped with a semi-pyramid. A rectangular pedestrian refuge is brought up from the capping of the cutwater on the first pier from the left-hand bank. There would appear to be no downriver cutwaters and none were reproduced on the pseudo-replica. The bridge does not appear to have had more than four arches. The elongated appearance of the left bank arch is due to it being more oblique to the camera. Moreover, more of the soffit is exposed to view by the semi-elliptical arch.

The evidence from the photo substantiates the conclusions drawn later for Trim and Baal's Bridge regarding four-arch bridges and raises the question: were four arch bridges common in the 14th century? The ancient tradition was to have odd numbers and avoid a pier in the centre of a river where it caused the most obstruction and was most difficult to build (and unsightly). A detailed study of the three bridges, including any information on New Bridge available in the ESB Archives, would make a fruitful contribution to knowledge of 14th-century bridge construction in Ireland given the firm dating evidence for New Bridge. In an article on Leighlin Bridge the *Irish Penny Journal*[3] states: "The present name of the town

however is derived from the bridge, which was erected in 1320 to facilitate the intercourse between the religious houses of old and new Leighlin, by Maurice Jakis, a canon of the cathedral of Kildare, whose memory as a bridge-builder is deservedly preserved, having also erected the bridges of Kilcullen and St Woolstan's over the Liffey, both of which still exist." Kilcullen Bridge was demolished in or before the 1640s but apart from this, the most remarkable piece of information is the attribution of, presumably, the construction of "St Woolstans" to Canon Jakis. This is the only mention I have found of New Bridge as "St Woolstans" bridge.

There are interestiong mentions of Jakis in the Calendar of Christ Church Deeds[4]. One dated 19 July 1317 refers to the prior of the monastery of St Mary of Conall and Maurice Jacke, precentor; the second records "Maurice Jacke precentor of the Church of Kildare 13 Jan. 1318". The cathedral of Kildare was built in the 1220s and it had an Anglo-Norman type of secular chapter which Gwynn and Hadcock explain consisted of four major dignitaries, a dean, precentor, chancellor and treasurer; a definitive source of income was assigned to each canon. The precentor was normally in charge of the choir but must have had other duties. In 1564 Sir Peter Lewys, who had been precentor, was made proctor of Christ Church Cathedral and in that post had responsibility for major building works (see Athlone Bridge). Other records indicate that there were many contacts between Leighlin and other dioceses and Avignon during the period 1309 to 1377.

De Burgo[5] records that John le Decer was a great benefactor of the large stone church erected by the Dominican friars of St Saviour's Priory on the north bank of the Liffey near the present Four Courts in 1308. It was rebuilt at the end of the 14th century having been partly demolished during the Bruce invasion in 1315. It is recorded[6] that in 1428 "The Dominican Friars erected with the assistance of their benefactors the Old Bridge, and to repay them, a lay brother of the Order (*sodalis laicus Dominicanus*), one of the common Council of the City, received at the bridge a penny (*denarius*) for every carriage, horse and beast of burthen passing over it." This bridge was located on the site of the present Father Mathew Bridge. It replaced King John's Bridge built in 1214. Mallagh[7] records that King John's Bridge,

"Ostman's", was broken down by the citizens during the Bruce invasion, rebuilt, then swept away by flood in 1385 and restored in 1394. He states that the Dominican bridge was known by various names: Old Bridge, The Bridge, Old Stone Bridge, Dublin Bridge. It was replaced in 1816 and named Whitworth Bridge. Gilbert[8] records the full text of the grant from Richard II to the city in 1385–6 for the repair of King John's Bridge. It indicates that the previous bridge was "broken down beyond repair" and that the mayor, and Philip de Courtenoy and others, were granted permission to erect a bridge.

The history of all the Dublin city bridges across the Liffey was outlined by de Courcy, who researched the topic in depth, in a paper[9] and in a book, *Anna Liffey*[10], both published in Dublin's Millennium Year (1988). These include several incidental mentions of the 1428 bridge, but few quantitative details were found by him, which is surprising, given that it was removed as recently as 1815. The Malton sketch of the Four Courts and the collapsed Ormond Bridge (1802) shows the 1428 bridge in the background. It resembles Newbridge. Two of the four arches and possibly three are shown from a head-on position looking upriver as pointed segmental arches. There is also a resemblance to the four-arch bridge of Trim and to the old Baals Bridge, Limerick. Further research may yield more definitive information on the characteristics of the Old Dublin Bridge, for which there is a specific date, but a dearth of reliable information on shapes and measurements.

Baals

Bridges without battlements, that is, parapet walls, were quite common in the Middle Ages; the same applied to castles. In Irish they were described respectively as *droichet maol* and *caisleán maol*, that is, a bald bridge, bald castle. The water could flow over the bridges in heavy floods and there was less risk of overturning in the case of high narrow bridges or of flooding upstream in the case of low bridges. In the early 19th century there was much uninformed speculation that such bridges and indeed the round towers were called after Baal, a pagan God. Balls seems to be the most frequently used name for the Limerick Bridge. Speed's 1610 map describes it as "The thye bridge", a most appropriate name at the time

because it linked the Irish and English towns. From this literature the following data on (the non-extant) Baals Bridge is relevant.

Barry[1] gives the inscription on the present bridge: "This bridge was erected in virtue of an Act of XI George IV. The Right Hon. Thomas Spring-Rice MP for the city of Limerick. Commenced taking down the old bridge Nov. 1830. The new bridge finished Nov., 1831." He also states that five houses on the west side of the old bridge were taken down in 1830. This is evidenced by a water colour *c*.1810.[2] The Journal of the House of Commons, 1759 states that one of the House committees enquired into "the application of the sum of £3,000 granted for the purchase of the East side of Balls Bridge in the City of Limerick and for repairing the said Bridge." The accounts had been laid before the committee with an affidavit stating that £2,900 had been received from the Treasury; £2,910 had been spent on purchasing houses and repairing and pulling down; and the Bridge had been completely repaired. Barry states that in Lenihan's *History* it is assumed that the houses were erected before the 1690 sieges, but the siege maps show no houses; moreover, Viscount Shannon obtained a grant of Baals Bridge from the king and, after the surrender, let both sides for building. "Two rows of brick houses were erected on the bridge leaving just enough room for a horseman to pass" (Viscount Shannon got his parasitic idea obviously from London Old Bridge, which had double rows of houses at the time: see Appendix 2). This shows that the bridge was at least as wide as Trim Bridge and probably wider, allowing that the houses were cantilevered out beyond the parapet lines.

Finn's *Leinster Journal* of 15 February 1775 carried a news item from Limerick that "Last Sunday night [6 Feb.] the high flood now in the river made a chasm inside one of the arches of Baals Bridge and yesterday at noon as Mr Betty (tinman) was sitting in his house on said bridge, the floor suddenly giving way he suddenly fell into the river, and floated to the slip at the New Bridge where he was fortunately taken up alive." The note went on to state that the occupants of the other houses moved out and quit possession "of those tottering mansions which a few minutes after tumbled into ruin."

A drawing in *Pacata Hibernia* shows four arches and a drawbridge plus three house

Fig. 62: *Old Baal's Bridge: Bartlett's "Vieu Pont De Baal" c.1830*

together with a tower at each end. According to Lenihan, Sir Henry Sidney is said to have recommended the building of a bridge when he visited Limerick for the second time in 1569.

There is a tradition that John de Burgo (John of Galway) gallantly defended Baals Bridge in attacks by the O'Briens in 1361 and 1364, for which service Lionel, duke of Clarence, knighted him and granted him and his descendants "the figure of the bridge as an augmentation of their arms".[3] The successors of de Burgo, the Galweys, erected tombs in memory of their relatives in Kinsale Church in 1627 and in St Mary's Cathedral, Limerick in 1636 and the armorial tablets on these depict the bridge—readily identifiable by comparison with the *Pacata* drawing, though one tablet shows six arches and the other five.

King Edward II made a grant of murage to the city in 1310: "you may take for five years in the said city the usual tolls and customs for that purpose." The purpose was to enclose with a stone wall the suburb on the south bank, the Irish town or, as delineated on the *Pacata Hibernia* drawing, "the base town". The only connection between the main "island city" and the suburb was a ford at the site of Baals Bridge. It is logical to conclude that a bridge would not be erected here until the walling of the Irish town was at an advanced stage. This

appears to have been the case because the charter for the erection of Baals Bridge is stated by Barry to have been granted in 1340.

At the Parliament held in Kilkenny in 1340 a charter was granted in aid of building a bridge at Limerick.[4]

Fleming[5] states that defence walls began to appear in the Irish town in the 14th century but that it was not completed until the end of the 15th. He states that early in the development of King's Island two focal points emerged and these were the safest crossing points to the mainland and were located near Thomond Bridge on the northwest and at Baals on the south.

The Limerick grand jury books 1738–1887 and the presentment books for 1791–1887 were destroyed in the Four Courts fire in 1922, which explains why we have so little detailed information on the bridge. The architects for the demolition of the old bridge and the design of the replacement for both Baals and Thomond were J. and G. R. Pain. Lynch[6] indicated clearly that he had access to Pain's notes and drawings on the condition etc. of Thomond Bridge, made in 1814, but these do not appear to have survived.

The characteristics of the bridge are discussed under Trim Bridge* insofar as key ones such as cutwaters, pointed segmental arch shape and cutwater cappings can be discerned from the Brocas watercolour and from Bartlett's drawing (fig. 62). The latter shows the four arches and a single row of houses.

Bartlett died in 1854 at the age of 45 so the drawing was probably executed shortly before the bridge was demolished in 1830.

Trim Bridge

The town takes its name from the ford Áth-Truim, the ford of the boor trees or elders which Joyce[1] states grew in the area. It is called Vadum Truimm in the Book of Armagh. Conwell[2] writing in 1878 states: "Immediately above the town bridge, over the Boyne are still very discernible both the ford or shallow and the low hill stretching along its northern bank, the river being deep both above and below this point. Ath truin, so-called from *Ath*, a ford, and *Truim* the genitive case of Drom or Druim, signifies a long low hill." St Patrick appointed St Loman bishop there in the 5th century. The earliest reference to a bridge is in the Annals of the Four Masters under the year 1203: "Cinandus Ath Truim agus an droichitt nua do loscad" which Donovan translates as "Kells, Trim and Newbridge were burned." However, in the Gaelic script, presumably copied accurately from the original, the *droichitt nua* has lower case initial letters and possibly meant the new bridge. A researcher in this field confirmed that the latter part of the sentence means the new bridge was burned; also Kells was usually written Cenannas Mor, so an alternative translation is "The entrance to Trim and the new bridge were burned." This implies that there was a timber bridge across the Boyne in 1203. The ford is reputed to have been upriver from the present bridge. One would expect a timber bridge to be elsewhere because the bed of the river at the present bridge is solid rock. Alternatively the piers might have been in stone and the deck timber.

The next early mention is in the Laud Manuscript which states that with the exception of Babes* no Boyne bridge survived the exceptional flood of 1330 and that much damage was done to Trim monastery. Next we have a mention[3] (20 June 1425): "The King orders payment to be made to John Swayne, archbishop of Armagh . . .of £4. 8s. 3¾d. being one half year's rent due to him for the site of the castle, town and bridge of Trim belonging to the archbishop in right of his church at Armagh; the said sum to be paid half yearly as long as said site is in the King's hands" (Rot. Pat. 3. Hen. VI). This is the only example of the rent of a bridge site found in all the literature searches for this book. It does not tell us anything about the bridge itself.

The Down Survey maps clearly indicates a bridge at Trim. It is recorded[4] that Petty wrote the following comment on the Down Survey map of Trim (1657): "There is a fair stone bridge consisting of three or four large stone arches by which commege is communicated between the Barony (indecipherable on map) distinguished half of the Town."

No mention of the bridge was found in an examination of the surviving records of the corporation of Trim in the National Archive. The only mention in the Meath grand jury records was under 1777: "£12 to be raised, as before, by J. Bolger (et al.) to repair the Bridge of Trim over the Boyne." One would expect more minor references as the bridge was a county-at-large responsibility. The Blackbull-Trim-Athboy Turnpike Act passed in 1731 and led to many improvements, mainly along the then existing roads, and it is possible that the parapet walls were recoped while the act was in operation. One would expect it to have lasted for 21 years to 1752 and perhaps to have been extended for a further 21 to 1773. During that period the trustees would have been responsible for all expenditure on maintenance and improvement and few such records survive. The road is not designated as a turnpike on Taylor's 1802 map of Co. Meath, whereas the Dublin-Navan road is. The act is not listed under the Turnpike Abolition Act 1855. A note appeared in the *Irish Times* some years ago to the effect that "the bridge in Trim was altered in the 18th century around the time Swift's friend, Mr Beaumont, built his business and residence on the corner there now demolished for a car park and supermarket."

In 1976 I prepared a short note[5] for the then county engineer of Meath, Bob Fenlon, on the history of the arch bridges over the Boyne in the vicinity of Trim, mainly as a background information for his report to Meath Co. Council which recommended the retention of Newtown Bridge in its present state. The note was a summary of the historical information available from maps and a few other sources: meagre as the information was, it proved helpful in resolving a problem that would never have arisen had accurate historical information on bridges been available. All ended well in the circumstances with a decision by the council to erect a new bridge and retain Newtown intact. In my note, I expressed the opinion that the Bridge Street Bridge was probably older and of greater historical interest than Newtown. At the time I obtained an elevation of it from the OPW (reproduced in fig. 224, Appendix 8).

The bridge (fig. 63) is founded on rock. The bed under the arches was lowered by an average of 4ft as part of the 1970's Boyne Drainage Scheme. The piers were left intact perched on solid rock but with the footings protected by reinforced concrete "pontoons". An admirable piece of work; a credit to the Arterial Drainage Section of OPW and Gerry Algar, the engineer in charge, and his staff. There are triangular cutwaters fore and aft. One downstream cutwater extends up to the level of the pavement and may have been a pedestrian refuge. The remaining two reach a level just above the arch springings and are continued in the form of long tapering, semi-pyramidal, masonry cappings, 5ft 6ins. high, reaching to the level of the soffit of the keystone. This type of capping is found on many old bridges in Co. Meath and sometimes elsewhere. The intrados of the arches are pointed segmental, of identical shape to the surviving arch of Babes Bridge.* The arch rings are formed of roughly trimmed, rectangular stones of varying thick-

ness (3in. to 6in.) (fig. 64). There is a second ring, faintly visible on all the upstream and downstream arches except the east arch on the castle side (fig. 65). It is evident that this arch was rebuilt at some stage—not very well, for it is still distorted and rounded at the keystone in a manner suggestive of shuttering yield. The thickness of the arch ring is uniform, unlike Babes. The arch spans are 16ft and the piers are 8ft, the same ratio as in Babes. The springings are obscured by the cutwaters which are built into the piers up to that level indicating that they were constructed as a unit. The spandrel masonry is random rubble roughly coursed. The stonework in the sheeting of the arches is also good. The ribbon pointing, probably 19th-century, gives a false impression of regularity and adds nothing to durability. The keystones are no different from the ring stones. The width of the bridge including the parapets is 21ft and there is no evidence whatsoever of widening in any arch or pier. The coping stones on the parapets are well shaped 18in. x 15in. x 4in. limestone flags.

What date is the bridge? It is a landmark survivor in excellent condition, in an historic town over an historic river, yet the literature failed to yield a date. Eventually after a careful re-examination of the collection of photos of the bridge which I had taken I recalled a postcard that bore a close resemblance to one of the photos. It was a reproduction of Brocas' (1790–1846) painting of the old Baals Bridge, across the Abbey River, Limerick. The elevations were quite similar, but the painting shows only three arches.

The charter for Baals was dated 1340. The Laud Manuscripts record that Trim Bridge was washed away in the flood of 1330. Barry[6] states that Baals had "four arches c.1810". Bartlett's drawing (fig. 62) shows the bridge precisely and matches a photo of Trim. Baals was rebuilt in 1831. They are obviously contemporaries and may even have been erected by the same master masons in the period 1330–50. We have a certain reference to the existence of Baals in 1361 and even in a period that had suffered from the devastation of the Bruce invasion and the Black Death, it is difficult to envisage the royal outpost town of Trim being without a bridge for very long.

The foregoing assumes that there were good communications between the king's cities and boroughs in the 14th century, a period when the

Fig. 63: *Trim Bridge: Downriver Elevation*

Gaelic resurgence was gathering momentum, so it is valid to ask; was this so in practice? The answer is found in an order of Edward I in 1285: "The mayor and citizens of Waterford covenant with the mayor and citizens of Dublin, Cork, Limerick and the mayor and burghers of Drogheda towards Meath, mutually to maintain their liberties to hold counsel together and to bear proportionately the expenses thus incurred." The fine for failure to observe this order was a massive £20. Certainly Drogheda and Trim must have been in frequent contact (see Slane Bridge).

Slane

The history of Slane village and townland in encapsulated by French in an excellent booklet[1] published by An Taisce in 1975. Most of the early buildings, he states, have disappeared and what is now left dates from the medieval period. There is a record in the Annals for *c.*948 which states that the Danes burned a round tower in which many people had taken refuge at the site of a monastery founded by St Earc, who had been made bishop by St Patrick. Nothing remains of these buildings.

Slane is not shown as an ancient crossing place on the Boyne on Colm O Lochlainn's map (1941) of the Ancient Roads of Ireland. If there was an important ford here one would expect it to be reflected in a townland name, but that is not so; the townland on the south bank is called Fennor. The Flemings, originally from Flanders, took the land here in 1169 and erected a timber tower and later a stone fortress which finally became Slane Castle. The castle was rebuilt in 1785 by the Conynghams, who were granted the estate in 1641.

The bridge (fig. 66) crosses the river at right angles and is over 500ft long. The roadways descend along steep grades more or less parallel to the river and turn sharply right on to the bridge. The thirteen arches are visible from a distance on both approaches and are very scenic. A number of serious accidents occurred at the bends in the mid 1980s and interim traffic engineering improvements were carried out by Meath Co. Council to alleviate the situation pending the construction of a new bridge downriver, scheduled for 1992–3.

Mervyn Archdall, the famous antiquary and author of *Monasticon Hibernicum* frequently quoted in this book was rector of Slane, where

Fig. 64: *Trim Bridge: W. Arch Upriver*

Fig. 65: *Trim Bridge: E. Arch and Pier Downriver*

Fig. 66: *Slane Bridge: Downriver Elevation of Original*

he died in 1792. Therefore, one would expect many early references to the bridge, but that is not the case. In fact, late mentions are almost as scarce as early ones. I found no reference to the bridge in any of the surviving Meath grand jury books which, with a few gaps, cover the period 1760–1890. The bridge was widened on the upriver side by 8ft sometime in the last 200 years (apparent from the masonry) and lack of mention of this is very surprising as it was a major job. The reason may be that the road was a turnpike. In 1849 an act (12 & 13 Vic. c.68) was passed "to continue and amend the powers of an Act for repairing the road from Dublin by Ashbourne to Slane and Drogheda". This was repealed in 1855 under the General Turnpike Abolition Act but the wording indicates it was a renewal so there must have been a previous act or acts, possibly in 1828 and 1807, as they usually ran for 21 years. Trench states that the Slane tradition is that the improvements were completed in 1812; however, advances were made in 1816–17 amounting to £7022. The Dublin-Ashbourne road was turnpiked in 1819 (56 Geo. III c.86). It is clear from Andrews[2] that there was no act for these roads in the 18th century. The Slane road is not included on Larkin's map of Mail Coach and Post Roads (1803)[3] but the Navan-Slane-Drogheda road is shown, as a post road. The Slane road became important from a commercial aspect in 1773 with the passage of the law giving a good bounty on the carriage of corn by road. The act was sponsored by J. Foster, who lived at Collon. Further research on these acts might yield information on the date of the bridge extension. The bridge is not shown on Taylor's

map[4] (1802) but it is shown on Moll's 1714 map. It would appear that the two arches broken down by King James 's army to prevent the Williamites crossing there before or during the battle of the Boyne were repaired soon afterwards. The bridge is shown on the Down Survey of 1656. There is a mention of 1599 (see Kilcarn Bridge) when Hugh O'Neill planned to send some of his army across it into the Pale during the intended invasion that did not materialise. Edward Bruce's army crossed the Boyne at Slane on the way south in 1317 but returned north via Trim.[5] Whether there was a bridge there in 1317 or not we do not know, but, if there was, we know from the Laud Manuscripts that it did not survive the flood of 1330 (see Babes Bridge*). Apart from the latter, there is no mention in any of the Annals of a bridge at Slane, but this may be due to it being within the Pale from about 1200 onwards.

From the foregoing it seems that the bridge was built sometime between 1330 and 1599. There was no bridge at Drogheda between 1472 and 1506. Babes Bridge seems to have collapsed sometime after 1500 and was out of service in 1463. Slane would therefore have been an important crossing place in the second half of the 15th century and must have had a stone bridge. The river is tidal here; consequently timber bridges would have been subject to attack by the teredo and have life spans of less than a decade or two.

Seven of the 13 arches on the downriver section have pointed segmental intrados in the style of Trim Bridge. Five of these arches are in the river and two are flood arches (fig. 67) at the south-west edge of the flood plane. Trim is dated in this book by analogy with the original Baals Bridge, Limerick, at c. 1340. Was Slane also built by the same master mason or lodge of stonemasons? Ordinarily it would be impossible to answer this, but in the case of Slane the OPW took accurate measurements of the pointed arches during the planning of the Boyne Drainage in the 1960s for the purposes of calculating flood discharge capacity. I obtained a copy of the elevations (courtesy of the OPW) which is reproduced to reduced scale in Appendix 8, and was able to carry out a detailed analysis of the arches and, more importantly, gain a good insight into how the master mason went about his task. It is possible that having completed Trim Bridge successfully, albeit on a rock foundation, the master

Fig. 67: Slane Bridge: Downriver Elevation of Flood Arches

mason was commissioned by the Flemings to build a bridge at Slane that would have a total waterway equivalent to Babes and be adequate for a 1330-type flood. If this were so, then we would expect to find a close similarity in the eyes of the arches but not necessarily in the pattern of the stone work—the thickness of the rings and certain other characteristics that would have changed between 1215 and the mid-14th century and be more dependent on the properties of the local stone.

Bridge	Intrados	Radius	Span	Pier	Rise	Bridge Width
Babes	Pointed segmental	14'	17'	6.5	8'	17'
Trim	Pointed segmental	13'	16'	8.0	6'	20'
Slane	Pointed segmental	15.5'	17'	7.5	7.5	16'

Fig. 68: *Comparison of Characteristics: Babes, Trim and Slane Bridges*

The north-east bank of the river in the vicinity of the bridge was altered in 1776 when the weir and mill races were built but from an examination of the OS six-inch maps it is evident that the line of the original bank would have included one of the two mill-race arches. The aggregate waterway was therefore approx. 180ft compared with an estimated 187ft for Babes Bridge. The foregoing hypothesis seems correct. Next, one must consider how a master mason in an impoverished country without much knowledge of geometry and with relatively crude measuring equipment would plan and set out the eight arches and seven piers over the river, excluding the flood arches, which could be built as separate small bridges on normally dry land. He would have to select a soffit level sufficiently high to enable small boats to pass through during normal flows. His inclination would be to select what is now called a module similar to Babes and Trim. Fig. 68 indicates that this was the case.

The dimensions vary between the arches by plus or minus ten per cent within Slane and within Trim. There is only one arch of Babes left.

There is a very close resemblance between the downriver cutwaters of Trim and Slane. The fore and aft cutwaters on the surviving pier of Babes are damaged, and the fore ones

Fig. 69: *Slane Bridge: Downriver Elevation of Two-Pointed Segmental River Arches*

Fig. 70: *Slane Bridge: Semicircular Upriver Extension Arch*

on Slane have been incorporated in or removed by the 8ft extension. The variation in the overall, face to face, width of the bridges (Slane original) is surprising at first sight but military considerations were probably dominant in the case of Babes and Trim, whereas Slane was mainly economic; however, information on width criteria for pre-1450 bridges is sparse. The choice of a pointed segmental arch intrados (fig. 69) instead of the alternative semi-circular (fig. 70) was probably dictated by other factors as well as boat headroom. A semi-circular arch with the same crown level would have involved ten per cent extra masonry for the same width and ring thickness; settlement

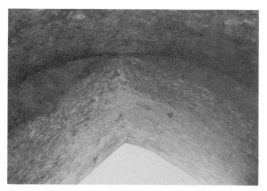

Fig. 71: *Slane Bridge: Arch Soffit at Joint*

the ring stones were placed on a bed of mortar on the shuttering and the rest poured on from the top. The butt joint between the semi-circular extension and the pointed segmental is illustrated in fig. 71.

No information is available on the soil under the foundations of Slane. It is most probably a hard glacial till like Mabes Bridge; otherwise it would have been scoured away centuries ago. If it were founded on rock the bed paving would not have been needed. Overall one can have little doubt that the downriver original section of this picturesque bridge dates from the mid-14th century.

Carrick-on-Suir Old Bridge

The town takes its name from the rock outcrop in the middle of the river Suir. A castle was erected here c.1309 on the north bank. The Butlers acquired the territory some-time in the 14th century and probably founded the town. The mansion on the north side of the castle was added by Thomas, earl of Carrick and Ormond, in Elizabethan times. Bradley[1] states that pontage grants were made in 1343 and 1356. Part of the present "Old Bridge" may date from this period.

The bridge is shown on the Down Survey of 1656, together with a postage stamp size, neat sketch of the then walled town. The present bridge is 300ft long and stretches from Abbey Street on the south to Bridge Street on the north (fig. 72). Bradley states that the latter is mentioned in a deed of 1470 and takes its name from the bridge.

There are eight arches in the present bridge. The spans and pier widths starting from the north (Tipperary) bank, viewed from upriver, are: 20'/11'/20'/15'/20'/16'/20'/27'/ fortifica-tion pier/21'/12'6"/20'/12'6"/50'/ 12'6". It is evident that the 50ft span replaced two 20ft span arches separated by an 11ft wide pier at some stage. There are massive triangular cut-waters, brought up to parapet level to form pedestrian refuges, on the upriver side (fig. 73). The pier ends on the downriver side are rectangular and brought up to form similar-shaped refuges in the parapet wall. The fortifi-cation pier surmounted by the "Nailers House" is extended fore and aft, with a cutwater on the upriver end. The carriageway is about 15ft wide.

The arches are all segments of circles, the rise being between a third and a quarter the

of the rings after removal of shuttering might have led to unsightly distortion at the crowns; perhaps some of the centering from Trim was floated down the river and reused as Slane. However, it would have been much easier to strike out a semi-circular intrados, given the timber and tools available.

In the medieval period the usual practice was to mark out the arch ope on a flat surface before erecting the centering. One of the diffi-culties with a pointed segmental was to trans-late the curved shuttering for the rings to the vertical plane *in situ*—an easy task for a land building but a difficult one in a river. It would have been vital to fix two points each side of the arch from which a rope or long lath could be radiated. Other methods, simple today, would probably have been too complex for rural medieval carpenters. I surmised that the curve centres would have to be located on or above the bed of the river and to test this I checked the centres for the Slane arches from the OPW drawings (fig. 225, Appendix 8), allowing for the fact that the original bed was below the present paved cills which were prob-ably added when the extension was built. The centres are shown on drawing. It would appear that the spans were divided into six sections at river bed level and, in the case of some arches, the two points nearest the piers used, whereas in others the points each side of mid-span were preferred.

The stones comprising the arch rings in Trim and Slane are similar but very different from Babes. The stones are rectangular on the face and well shaped though the thickness varies. The soffits of the barrels of the original arches at Slane are smooth with a high per-centage of mortar visible, which suggests that

Fig. 72: *Carrick-on-Suir Bridge: Upriver Elevation of Six Arches*

span with the exception of the later large arch, which is very flat (rise to span ratio is 1 to 7). None of the seven surviving older arches has any semblance of a point at the crown so they were built as segmental (circular) arcs. There are no signs of a joint in the intrados or piers so the bridge was not widened at any period. From the accompanying photographs, taken in 1937, it will be seen that the ring stones are composed of roughly shaped flags (sandstone) 15in. to 18in. long and 3in. to 9in. thick, on the head. The joints are non-radial in many places. In a few arches they are almost corbelled as in Mabe's Bridge*. There are no skewbacks and the springings are formed by tilted stones. If the arch curves were pointed segmental or semi-circles one would have little hesitation in dating them from the 14th century, from the period of the pontage grants (1343–56), but they are not, so they could be a century or two later.

The 1843 OS six-inch map shows seven cut-waters on the upriver side, this suggests that the 50ft span replacement was built before the 1830s. This is also evident from the ring stones which are well cut, about 18ft high and between 4in. and 9in. thick; however, none are true voussoirs. One might assume that this was a navigation arch erected under the same scheme as the 55ft arch of Sir Thomas's Bridge in 1755–7, but the date is uncertain in both cases. The original central span in the latter bridge, dated 1690, is 40ft and this indicates the segmental arches of this span presented no problems to local builders in the last quarter of the 17th century. McCarthy Morrogh[2] states

that most of Munster's trade in the 16th century was conducted through Waterford, but that in the 17th trade moved further west, with Youghal handling many exports and Cork many imports. Disagreement between corporations, he states, forced Clonmel to direct some of its trade over the mountains to Dungarvan and later to Youghal. The fact that the Irish parliament passed a special act for Cappoquin Bridge* in 1668 corroborates this.

A reference to Carrick-on-Suir in Loeber[3] states: "As far as is known, from the late 17th century civilian engineering was largely in the hands of military engineers. James Archer built a bridge and cleared part of the Suir." Describing Archer's works he mentions Carrick-on-Suir Bridge and states that "near the Ormond residence Archer in November 1668 finished one half of the bridge in ten weeks, and cleared

Fig. 73: *Carrick-on-Suir Bridge: Upriver Detail of Two Arches and Cutwaters*

the river Suir at this place from rocks in order to make it navigable for ships and stimulate commerce at Carrick. He was offered £3 for his work but found this too little." The source quoted is the *Ormonde MSS.*, n.s., iii, 288–90. Elsewhere he mentions that Archer in 1688 "oversaw repairs on the residences (and a bridge) of the duke of Ormond" and cautions that Archer should not be confused with a person of the same name who was a surveyor in the Strafford and Civil Surveys. Archer left Carrick in 1669.

There is a note in the *Dublin Builder* of 1 January 1880 stating that a new bridge was to be erected at Carrick-on-Suir: "It will consist of three spans of 92ft, lattice-girder top and masonry piers and arches and abutments and cost about £13,000." The consulting engineer was the famous Robert Manning, Board of Works; the contractor, William J. Doherty, "whose name in connection with bridge building in this city [Dublin] is well known." The wrought-iron lattice girder bridge came into usage in Ireland following the construction of the famous one over the three river spans of the Boyne railway viaduct in 1855. Conceived by Sir John MacNeill and designed by James Barton, the centre span was 267ft and the side ones 141ft each. The principle of multiple-lattice construction was first applied on a large scale in this bridge. It is described in a paper by Howden[4] presented to the ICEI in 1934.

The girder bridge at Carrick-on-Suir was named Dillon Bridge in commemoration of John Dillon MP, who was imprisoned under the Coercion Act in 1888.

Clonmel Old Bridge

The town of Clonmel is believed to have been founded by the de Burgos in the 13th century. From 1338 to 1583 the lands were owned by the earls of Desmond. Bradley[1] states that Bridge Street is mentioned as early as 1388 and the laneway east of it in 1424. A grant of murage and pontage was given in 1356. The bridge is depicted on the town's coat of arms which is similar to that of New Ross.

The selection of this site for the town in the 13th century was probably influenced by the fact that the river was divided into two channels by Suir Island. The walled town was located on the north bank apposite this island. There is a satellite island, called Stretches,

immediately upriver of Suir. The Old Bridge now connects the town proper with Suir. Formerly the bridges linking Suir and Stretches and the latter with the south bank of the river were part of it, but these have been replaced.

The bridge is shown on Moll's map (1714) as part of the principal road leading to Dungarvan and to Cappoquin. The Dungarvan branch is omitted on Petty's General Map of 1683. The Down Survey map, compiled in 1656, clearly indicates the bridge together with a miniature perspective sketch of the walled town located at its northern extremity. Mentions of the bridge are scarce, given its importance as a crossing point in the late medieval period on the route leading from Dublin via Leighlinbridge and Kilkenny to the Norman towns of south Munster. Chetwood[2] gives an informative mention in 1748: "there is a very spacious bridge over the Suir just out of the gate to the right, of twenty arches." This suggests that all three parts were considered one bridge at the time.

The Norman antiquities of Clonmel were discussed in a paper by Lyons[3] in 1936. He states that the three remaining arches are all that was left of "a bridge series of thirteen arches in all". He indicates that the bridge was widened by one third of its present width about the middle of the eighteenth century and that it is "in the ancient state" on the west [upriver] side. He gives the width of that part as 18ft and mentions that the arches are comparatively modern and that the old piers were lowered to accommodate the roadway to the arches.

The present upriver elevation of the bridge is shown in fig. 227, Appendix 8 with the cutwaters omitted. The spans and piers, from north, and 18'/12'/18'/11'6'/19'. The arch rings are almost semi-circular. None of the arches contains irregular shaped ring stones which would suggest a date earlier than c.1750, so Lynch's information on the rebuilding and extension seems correct. The 12ft thick piers (fig. 74) and the span to pier ratio of 1.5 to 1 are compatible with an early date and strong indicators that they are originals apart from the top courses immediately below the springings. The most remarkable feature of the bridge is the cutwaters. The downriver cutwaters on the extension are trapezoidal in plan, 10ft long and 8ft 6in. thick at the pier face (scaled from a recent edition of the 1/1000 OS map). The upriver cutwaters are also 10ft long and trape-zoidal, but are almost as thick as the pier faces. It is evident from the masonry that the blunted tips of the cutwaters were constructed originally to this shape very like those on the downriver side of Carragh Bridge*.

The angle of the cutwaters is about 75°—quite sharp. They are built of rubble masonry with small stones, and if they had spear points they would have been vulnerable to damage by tree trunks washed down in floods; in fact there is evidence of damage to one downriver cutwater shown in fig. 74. The blunt tips were obviously an attempt to prevent such damage. It would appear that when the extension was built, every effort was made to replicate the original upriver cutwaters on the downriver side. Further evidence of the later date of the downriver extension is provided by the parapet wall copings which are larger and better hewn on the downriver side.

Lynch states that about 1830 a Mr Hughes, miller, obtained a reduction in rent from Clonmel Corporation on condition that he remove portion of a building projecting on to the roadway on the downriver side at the south end of the bridge. This provides further evidence of the downriver widening. He was also of the opinion that the south abutment of the bridge was the base of a former barbican tower. He mentions a culvert on the north end which carried the flow from the former Manor Mill. The Civil Survey states that there were two grist mills "on the bridge", which Lynch doubts because he interpreted the phrase literally. It is quite likely that, as at Athlone in 1570, the mill frontage projected on to the roadway. The original width of the Clonmel Bridge was 18ft, not unusual for a 14th-century bridge as shown in fig. 13.

This bridge merits more detailed analysis as it is quite possible that the sections of the mill race culverts under the public road on the north and south approaches may not have been rebuilt and are original arches. If so, one would expect them to be pointed segmentals like those at Holycross* or Adare.*

Adare

The substantial ruins of the Desmonds' castle in Adare are located on the north bank of the Maigue, a few hundred yards upriver of Adare Bridge. The town takes its name from the ancient ford Ath-Dara, the oak ford. Like the

Fig. 74: Clonmel Bridge: Downriver Cutwater & Rebuilt Arches

elder trees in Trim, there must have been many oaks growing here in ancient times. Leask[1] states that there is no mention of a castle here prior to 1226, though some parts of it are of an earlier date. The *Shell Guide*[2] states that nothing is known about the history of the area prior to the erection of a manor south of the river by Geoffrey de Marisco in the early 13th century.

The difficulty of establishing the dates of early bridges in Ireland is very apparent here because the third earl of Dunraven (1812–71), whose ancestors acquired the castle and lands of Adare in the 17th century and who was an expert in early Irish architecture, did not solve the problem of the bridge. In his historical notes[3] he states that according to Lewis's *Dictionary* the bridge of Adare was built by Gerald, fifth earl of Kildare, between 1390 and 1410, but this statement he had unfortunately been unable to verify. Writing in 1865 his description of the bridge surpasses any photo: "The Bridge has all the appearance of considerable age; and was originally scarcely wide enough for one cart to pass over; many years ago its width was nearly doubled. The arches are very irregular in size, and in distance from each other. Richly mantled with ivy, this ancient Bridge is very picturesque, blending as it were with the ivy-clad walls of the castle; and at full tide the river assumes the character of a calm lake reflecting the ancient towers and varied arches on the clear surface of its tranquil waters, forming a scene of considerable beauty and peculiar interest." He then goes on to state that a large pile was found some years before under one of the piers while it was being repaired and that there was a tradition that there was a timber bridge prior to the stone one. However, his qualitative description includes no dimensions and leaves it to the reader to find out which side was widened and when.

In 1837 the Maigue River was surveyed as part of the Survey of the Shannon referred to in Chapter 6. A section of the plan shows the bridge, but none of the "proposed improvements" relates to the bridge although many major ones, including a section of new canal, are indicated nearby. A brochure published by An Taisce[4] in 1976 states that when the bridge was being widened in the last century, the earl saw to it that the large pedestrian refuges on the south side were retained and that the widening was done on the north side. The road runs from north to south so this statement is a bit confusing. The 1844 OS six-inch map shows 10 arches, six on the north end of the island and four on the south. Cutwaters are indicated for all the piers upriver and downriver. The 1912 edition shows only three cutwaters upriver on the north end adjoining the island. There are three large cutwaters on the upstream side at present, between arches 4, 5, 6 and 7 (counted from north to south), and none on the downstream side. Two of the cutwaters are brought up to parapet coping level to form truly massive "V"-shaped pedestrian refuges. The present overall width of the bridge is 28ft 2in. It is evident from the foregoing that the widening was carried out on the downstream side sometime between 1844 and 1865.

In 1987 the county engineer, Andy O'Connell, on behalf of Limerick Co. Council, commissioned Michael Punch and Partners to carry out a structural appraisal of the bridge in connection with an application by the ESB to move a heavy abnormal indivisible load across it. As a result of this investigation I was able to obtain, courtesy of the county engineer, accurate details on many characteristics that would not normally be available for such a bridge. There are 16 arches including three small normally dry overflows at the south end. The total length of the bridge is 400 ft. It is divided into two parts by a small 90ft wide island near the centre of the river. The spans range from 6ft to 15ft and the piers from 10ft to 16ft. The consultants who examined all the arches reported that when the piers were

underpinned the arch barrels on the downstream portion were rebuilt in concrete, to the shape of the old profile, but the outer ring stones, spandrel walls and parapets were re-erected. It appears that the bridge was widened on the downstream side by 12ft (average), by building partly on the old cutwaters and partly on new foundations. The masonry in the extended arch barrels was matched in shape (excluding local deformations) to the original. No cutwaters were erected at the ends of the extended piers. In 1976–7 the OPW, under an arterial drainage scheme, underpinned the whole bridge, strengthened the piers, removed the masonry sheeting in the arch barrels of the 19th-century widening and replaced them with reinforced concrete to the same shape; all without disturbing the 19th-century downriver masonry facade.

Here we are interested in the original bridge which, given all the essential functional and structural additions, has been ingeniously preserved and unobtrusively underpinned in a most creditable manner. Arches 5 to 10, numbered from the north bank, are most relevant as they are obviously originals. The span of arch 5 is 11ft, arches 6 and 7 are 12ft 6in., arch 9 is 13ft 6in. and arch 10, the largest in the whole bridge, is 15ft. Detailed photos of arch 5 were available and from them the characteristics of the original were deduced. It is a pointed segmental arch of 11ft span. The right-hand half became deformed a little over the centuries so that the intrados has lost its curvature to become almost a chord. The ring is composed of limestone slabs, roughly shaped, generally 13in. x 6in. on the face; however, the thickness varies by plus or minus 3in. There has been some slippage of the stones adjoining the keystone, which is heart-shaped and displaced upward (perhaps it was not wedged in fully at the time of construction). The stones in the barrel are much the same but more rounded at the corners. The joints are now very raw, the mortar having been partly leached out. The river is tidal for a mile upriver of the bridge, and the saline content, though small, would cause deterioration in times of high wind and high tide.

The varying widths of the piers and spans suggest that there was difficulty in building the foundations. The large pile under a pier referred to by the earl of Dunraven suggests that some of the piers may be built on piles.

The OPW drawing indicates that the river bed is composed of gravel and boulders. A note in the consultant's report states that the underpinning was well done and the foundations are now in good condition. Bideford Bridge in Devon erected in 1315 across the tidal estuary of the river Torridge had 25 segmental arches with spans from 10 to 20ft. It was built on piled foundations and no two arches are of the same span. The masonry in the bridge is much superior to Adare and though it had large triangular cutwaters and is not likely to have been the model. Bideford Bridge was widened and improved in 1923 at a cost of £40,000. It was a successful toll bridge and always well maintained.

The three surviving upstream cutwaters of Adare are massive and two were brought up to form refuges big enough for a truckle car. They were important because of the long length of the bridge and may have been part of the original. Large cutwaters were also found on Boyle and a few other early Irish bridges.

The Augustinian friary known as the Black Abbey in Adare founded by John FitzThomas Fitzgerald who was created earl of Kildare in 1316 and died soon afterwards. The cloisters of the abbey contain pointed segmental arches shown in Plate 17 of the *Memorials*.[3] It is evident therefore that the bridge builders did not even have to go to Thomond* or Baals Bridge* in Limerick to find a model for the arch shapes. Adare has all the characteristics of a 14th-century bridge, so there is no reason to dispute the date range 1390–1410 given in Lewis, which may have originated from records of the earls of Kildare.

Askeaton

The ancient history of Askeaton is given by Westropp[1] in his *Antiquities of Limerick and its Neighbourhood*. The town is called after the Gebtini, a pre-Celtic tribe who settled in the area in the vicinity of the waterfall. It is mentioned in the list of royal forts belonging to the king of Cashel given in the 9th-century Book of Rights. A castle which was built on the heart-shaped limestone island in the river Deel, Inish Eeibthine, in 1199 in the time of King John became the focal point of the town and its medieval history.

Spellissy[2] states that the earls of Desmond made the castle their principal residence from 1348. Westropp attributes the foundation of the Franciscan friary to Gerald, "the Poet Earl", c.1389, and its restoration to the seventh earl in the mid-15th century. Both writers show that there was a tremendous amount of building activity in the area between 1440 and 1460, including the erection of the great hall (72ft x 30ft) and the 90ft high castle keep. Substantial parts of these buildings still remain. Spellissy also mentions that the earls of Desmond had close connections with another branch of the family, the Di Gheradini in Florence, and that a member of the family stayed in Askeaton in the 1440s; such a connection could have had a significant bearing on building work because the architect of the great church of St Maria Novella in Florence was Leon Battista Alberti (1404–76), who completed his great work, *The Ten Books of Architecture*,[3] in 1452.

No early mentions of a bridge were found, which is surprising because the sole land entrance to the castle is from it. One would expect the bridge to be of stone because timber would have a short life in the tidal estuary and a timber bridge would have been difficult to construct due to the rock in the river bed, as explained in Chapter 7. Given that the original castle was Norman, one would also expect bridge arches constructed before the mid-15th century to be pointed segmental with wide abutment-type piers and low span-to-pier ratios like Thomond (old) Bridge*. The castle and presumably its entrance was besieged many times over the centuries, so that arch destruction and rebuilding was inevitable.

Fig. 75 shows a perspective sketch of the bridge and castle taken from the original Latin version of *Pacata Hibernia*[4] (1633). Copies of the sketch produced in some of the 19th century translations contain alterations which can lead one to misinterpret some significant characteristics of the bridge. There would appear to be six spans in the *Pacata* sketch evidenced by the pier-end eddies. The piers and spandrels are shown as stone masonry. The width of the bridge, to judge from other elements in the photo, is about 9ft. The parapet walls are low. The third arch from the west bank runs under the castle barbican. The most remarkable characteristic is the set of trap doors, one at each end of the bridge. They appear to have strap hinges so that when opened up they could be removed. These were obviously for defensive

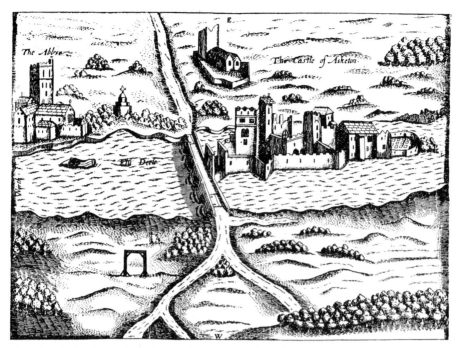

Fig. 75: *Askeaton Bridge: Drawing from Pacata Hibernia c.1630*

purposes and one must assume that there were no arches underneath, otherwise they would be like shallow pits in the roadway and easily filled in. The road width was 9ft; therefore each door, to judge from the sketch, would have been about 9ft x 4ft 6in., giving a pit of say 8ft x 8ft. This would fit within a pier but the shell walls would be weak relative to the thrust of a pointed segmental arch. It will be noted that all the buildings and the bridge shown in the sketch are in perfect repair apart from the church tower in the background.

Before comparing the findings from the sketch with the present bridge, it is necessary to examine some mentions of Askeaton in the Carew MSS. On 29 January 1580, the earl of Ormond reported that he found Adare in a very good state and that he broke far into Conneloughe towards the gates of Askeaton but then returned to Waterford. On 1 April, Pelham, then acting lord deputy of Ireland, reported to the privy council that he was ready to march towards Askeaton and "may be doubtful how it may hold out for the seat is strong upon a rock in the midst of a deep river". He again reported on 5 April: "The terror of taking Carrigofoill has given us two other castles namely those of Askeaton and

Ballegellohan . . . . I hope to chase Desmond beyond the mountains into Kerry." McCurtain[5] states that "coercion, military regimes and martial law" became the pattern of the Tudor conquest. Earlier in the campaign Askeaton Castle had withstood a siege by Sir Nicholas Malby, who built the bridge of Ballinasloe* in the early 1570s. Edward Berkeley remained as constable of the castle from its capture into the 1590s. Spellissy states that it withstood a siege of 247 days by the earl of Desmond until Essex relieved it in June 1599. It was then granted to Sir Anthony St Leger, who held it until 1610. The town was incorporated by charter in 1612. Berkeley had offered to erect town walls and make the castle a safe refuge for the English in the area. From all of this, it is evident that the *Pacata* drawing, often dated 1599, must be of later date, as mentioned above.

No bridge is shown at Askeaton on the Down Survey map; however, the Civil Survey contains the following description: "Askeaton town and lands, being a manor with the Priviledge of a Courte Lette and Court Barron, five plowlands and a halfe with a Castle and a great stone buildings, an Abbie and Church; a corporate town; two mills, whereof one belongs to Mrs Crofton with a great Bridge, a fishing leape, Three Eele wears, Three Salmon Weares, Two ffaires in the yeer and a markett one in the weeke."

The bridge is not mentioned in the long and detailed memorandum submitted by the earl of Orrery to Queen Anne in 1712, when he tried to persuade her to restore the castle then in a ruinous condition. His memorandum, quoted in Spellissy, states that the castle commanded the best passes for carriages etc. leading to the confines of Kerry and suggested that the Government give him £500 for its repair, following which he would maintain it at his own expense. The request was not granted and the castle remained thenceforth as a ruin. The bridge is shown on Moll's 1714 map but not in Taylor and Skinner's 1778 atlas nor on Rocque's map of Ireland. Askeaton ceased to be a borough following the Act of Union. Spellissy quotes the vice-provost as stating, in 1811, that "he had never heard of there being any public record, roll, manuscript book or paper belonging to the borough".

Westropp[1] shows two engravings of Askeaton which include the bridge, one by Sandby dated 1779 and the other by G. Holmes, 1799. The Sandby sketch is interesting because it shows the downriver elevation of the bridge, in the background, containing about 10 arches and also triangular cutwaters on each of the nine piers having semi-pyramidal cappings reaching up to road level. The Holmes sketch, also downriver, is more obscure but seems to indicate six arches and no cutwaters.

The 1844 OS six-inch map would appear to show the bridge as it is today. The roadway scales about 20ft to 23ft wide, so it is evident that the upriver widening took place before the 1830s. On the basis of the foregoing information and a photograph taken in 1980, we came to the conclusion that this bridge was an important one from a national point of view. Andy O'Connell, county engineer, provided some more details including dimensions and close-up photos of most arches.

The present bridge has six spans consisting of a five stone arches and one reinforced concrete slab, the latter an early 20th-century replacement. It was widened on the upriver side. The layout is unusual and best explained by reference to Map 7 on which the arches are numbered 1 to 6 from east to west. There are three arches (Nos. 1 to 3) carrying the flow in the main river channel and three (Nos. 4 to 6)

the flow from the mill race on the west side of the island. Arch 6 turns east after passing under the road and emerges through the quay wall. The entrance to arch 4 is through the side wall of the building at the castle entrance; it runs west for 20ft and then north under the castle entrance road and the main road to emerge on the downriver face. This may have also been the layout in *Pacata* drawing. Fig. 76 shows the downriver face.

The overall width of the bridge ranges from 21ft to 25ft. The average width of the piers is 10ft and the spans 12ft with minor variations. There are no cutwaters downriver. The joint between the extension and the original is clearly visible under some arches. The bridge is founded on rock, a major factor in its survival. There are three pointed arches on the downriver face (Nos. 1, 3, 5); the shape of the obscured sixth arch is not known.

Three of the arches (Nos. 1, 3 and 5), all in the downriver older section, have a pre-1600 appearance. The outlet from arch 6 is obscured. Arches 1 & 3 are a pointed segmentals with their point slightly rounded (fig. 77a). Arch 5, however, is a depressed Tudor. The difference if of great significance from an age aspect, so it is necessary to outline the characteristics separately (all determined from photographs including additional ones taken by B. Foy). Taking arch 5 first, it will be noted from fig. 77b that the skewback is curved in a similar manner to

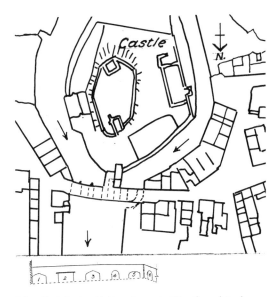

Map 7: *Askeaton Bridge: Layout of Castle and Arches*

Fig. 76: *Askeaton Bridge: Downriver Elevation*

Fig. 77: *Askeaton Bridge: Skewback of (a) Pointed Segmental Arch and (b) Tudor Arch*

arch 3 of the Ballinasloe Bridge.* The joints are radial. From this it is deduced that this arch was built in the last quarter of the 16th century, probably reconstructed after one of the many sieges. Arch 1 shows no trace of curving at the springing; in fact there is a skewback forming a springing slope of about 30°, but this is dissipated through the first and second ring stones, such that the joints become almost vertical. The intrados along both haunches are almost straight. Arch 3 has more or less similar characteristics.

The voussoirs on the upriver extension all have a late 18th-century or early 19th-century appearance, with one unusual characteristic—the chamfer on the intrados. In the 19th-century chamfering was introduced in France with the object of improving the hydraulic discharge; the best example in Ireland being Ringsend Bridge in Dublin, erected in 1802. It would seem that the surviving old arches in Askeaton were chamfered *in situ* when the widening was carried out, probably to improve the appearance. It demonstrates how a small modification can make it difficult to date a bridge.

From the foregoing we conclude that Arches 1 and 3 are pointed segmental arches dating from the 14th or 15th centuries, most likely from the mid-15th century period of reconstruction of the castle and Arch 5 is a rare example of a depressed Tudor from the later quarter of the 16th. Overall, the bridge while not very pleasing aesthetically contains a greater variety of arches from different centuries than any other ancient survivor known to us. It merits detailed archeological investigation.

Newtown

The necessity for this bridge (fig. 78) obviously arose from the traffic generated to, from or between the cathedral of St Peter and Paul on the north bank immediately upriver from the bridge and the friary/hospital of St John the Baptist downriver on the south bank. The cathedral was founded by the Norman bishop of Meath, Simon Rochfort in 1206, and the friary shortly afterwards. He had transferred his see from Clonard to here in 1202. Both houses were suppressed 1536–9 and had considerable lands both sides of the Boyne at the time.

In 1975 Meath Co. Council considered a number of proposals for reducing the high accident rate at this narrow bridge, one of which involved widening the present bridge. This led to a controversy in which a key question was the age of the bridge. Mr McDonald Scott tracked down a 1475 incidental reference which made a major contribution to the Council's decision to erect a new bridge further upriver.

There are surprisingly few historical or other references to the bridge. The reason may be that Castle Street Bridge one mile upriver was the main crossing from about 1350 onwards. During the widening discussions the late Tom McAterian, who had been district engineer in the area for almost 40 years, stated that the bridge had only once needed repairs, of a minor nature, in all that time. The OPW lowered the bed of the river under the Boyne Drainage Scheme in the 1970s. Like Trim, the piers are founded on rock and the only work required was to put in a concrete apron round the pier foundations and the foundation masonry. The arches were grouted by the Co. Council in 1977.

I found no reference to expenditure on the bridge in the Meath grand jury records which cover almost the whole period 1750–1840. This is remarkable and must be interpreted as a testimony to the durability of the masonry. The fact that the bridge is founded on rock is of course a major factor in its performance.

The bridge is named as "St Peter's" or "Newtown" on OS maps. It is shown in Taylor and Skinner's atlas of 1778, on Moll's Map (1714), and on the Down Survey compiled in 1656. There is another bridge shown across the Boyne on the latter, one mile or so downriver at Grange. Richard Haworth[1] found a most interesting reference to the latter bridge in the Calendar of State Papers, namely a sworn spy report of 14 October 1599 which stated that Hugh O'Neill "would shortly invade the Pale with what forces he could every way, and that their resolution was that their forces of foot should pass over these bridges of Slane and Kilcarn and that O'Donnell with his forces would come over the bridge of the Grange and that all of their horses should for more expediency pass over the fords, if they were passable." The bridge at Grange is shown on the Down Survey but not on subsequent maps. No other reference to it was found in the literature. Presumably Newtown Bridge was too close to the fortified town of Trim to be included as a crossing point.

The earliest reference to Newtown is the 1475[2] "At the prayer of William Grete, late prior of the house of St John the Baptist, near the bridge of the Newtown very close to Trim, and Richard Bellewe of the same, gentleman, by whatsoever names they or either of them be called . . .". If there was a bridge here in 1330 we know from the Laud Manuscripts (see Trim Bridge) that it was swept away in the great flood of 1330, so the date is within the period 1330 to 1475. With the devastation of the Bruce Wars and the Black Death this can be narrowed down to say 1375–1475.

Fig. 78: *Newtown Bridge: Downriver Elevation*

Fig. 79: *Newtown Bridge: Chamfered Triangular Cutwater Upriver*

The geometric characteristics of the bridge are remarkable especially for one founded on solid rock. The coursed masonry and well-shaped stones in the piers and spandrel walls are far more superior to that found in Trim Bridge and most others of the 14th century. There are no cutwaters downriver and the upriver ones are massive triangles of solid masonry (fig. 79). The capping is a new type for the period, an inverted triangle. One cutwater is brought up to form a pedestrian refuge. The intrados curves are proper segments of circles with well-cut trapezoidal voussoirs and proper keystones (fig. 80). The arch spans are, from the north bank, 19', 19', 18', 15' 6" and 13' 6". The piers are 8', 14', and 8'; massive in the centre of the river. The bridge was never widened. There are corbels projecting from under the skewbacks for supporting the arch centering during construction and to facilitate reconstruction in the event of the collapse of an arch or part thereof. Projecting corbels under the springings are a feature of stone bridges from Roman times until the 19th century and are of no use for dating purposes. The roadway is 14ft between parapets (min. 13ft). The aggregate waterway is 86ft net. The bridge is slightly curved towards the current in plan. The roadway is humpbacked. The present bridge shows five arches (fig. 228, Appendix 8) but there is evidence of cutwaters at each bank so it possibly had seven or more originally.

This a much more substantial bridge than Trim and shows a radical departure from conventional Irish practice as evidenced in the bridges described with earlier dates or first mentions. The pointed segmental arch has been discarded and a genuine segment of a circle adopted (fig. 81); however, the piers are massive so there would have been no problem in regard to unbalanced lateral thrust had the centering been reused arch by arch; but given that only two of the five arches have similar spans, it appears that all were constructed together.

The final question is: who financed the bridge? The best answer is given in McDonald Scott's letter[3]: who more likely to have built the bridge than William Sherwood as bishop of Meath, from 1460 to 1482; and then, as lord deputy, to have rented it for the Crown. This implies that it was built between 1460 and 1475.

Glanworth

There is a bridge of limestone work
That contains twelve arches.
'Twas never stirred by mountain floods,
It dreads neither wind nor waters.

The above verse composed by a local bard in the 19th century was quoted in a note by Fr M. O'Sullivan (1913)[1] in response to an article on Glanworth by J. Byrne, published in 1912.[2] More importantly the note stated:

Being a native of Glanworth, I read the article very closely, and feel a pardonable conceit in being able to enlighten Mr Byrne on one historical matter of detail, viz. the date or period of the building of the bridge over the Funcheon at Glanworth. This bridge was completed in 1446, and its narrow dimensions would probably account for Vavasour's preference for Manning Ford as his route to Fermoy.

This categorical statement about the date of erection led me to believe that the superb bridge would become a landmarker and indeed be of great assistance in dating many other similar type bridges. The opposite was the case because extensive searches of the literature and other sources failed to find the source of Fr O'Sullivan's dating or any corroborative mention. Nevertheless it was decided to assign the bridge to the 15th century and present the reader with all the relevant information from the search because the bridge could be pre-17th century and, if so, a very important one in the national context.

The paper by Byrne states that the village derived its name from Gleann Lubhar, the glen of the yew trees. He had made enquiries about the age of the bridge but got no reliable information. He surmised that it was very old and had been built by the Roches, who had displaced the O'Keeffes from the territory after the Norman conquest.

Gwynn and Hadcock[3] state that the priory of the Holy Cross in Glanworth was founded by the Roche family and that while Smith gives the date 1227, it is not listed in the Dominican catalogue of 1300, but is given by Fr Flanagan OP as 1475. It was held by the viscount of Fermoy in 1588. The friary is in Early English architectural style. The castle is one of a half dozen or more along the banks of the Funcheon within a radius of five miles. It is 13th-century and was slighted by Ireton's artillery in 1649. At the south end of the village there are the remnants of a small Teampall Lobhair or leper's church. Perhaps this was a "spital"type settlement with church, hospital and bridge in the early medieval period; however, none of the

Fig. 80: *Newtown Bridge: Second Arch from S. Bank Upriver*

adjoining townlands reflects the name. Glanworth is listed among the principal towns and manors in Ireland *c.*1300 in the *New History of Ireland.*[4]

My attention was drawn to Glanworth Bridge in 1983 by Niall Brunicardi, a local antiquary, who believed that it dated from 1446. Neither the bridge nor the town is delineated on the Down Survey map compiled in 1656 but the district is given as "Glanor".

Fig. 81: *Newtown Bridge: Three Arches Upriver*

Fig. 82: *Glanworth Bridge: Downriver Elevation*

Manning townland is shown a few miles downriver but the ford is not. A ford is shown at Carrig about the same distance upriver. Glanworth is shown on Moll's 1714 map. However the road (Mitchelstown-Ballyhooly) crosses the river about one mile northwest of the town, near "Carroghoo More", where a ford and castle are depicted on the OS six-inch map. This road was the principal one from Cork to Mitchelstown in the latter half of the 17th century. While one cannot be confident about precision in relative locations on a map such as Moll's, the crossing is north of the loop in the river, and this raises further doubts about the existence of Glanworth Bridge at the time. The mention of Vavasour's preference for Manning Ford refers to the military movements of Sir Charles Vavasour, who had landed in Youghal in 1642 with a thousand men, part of Cromwell's army. One must discount the suggestion by Fr O'Sullivan that a 9ft 6in. wide bridge would be too narrow for military purposes, given the fact that this was the minimum prescribed in acts of Parliament at the beginning of the following century, both in Britain and Ireland.

Information on the characteristics of the bridge was supplied to the writer by Brendan Devlin, divisional engineer, and Flan Groarke, area engineer, in 1989. Given the importance of the bridge in the national context, a short questionnaire was prepared focussing on data which might help to identify the century of its construction. The replies showed that it is founded on rock, which outcrops in the river bed. It has 13 semi-circular arches, one of which is buried in the west bank and not discernible in photos. The span and pier widths, starting from the west bank, are as follows: 14'/5'/14'/ 5'/14'/ 5' 7"/14' 5"/5' 11"/14' 1"/7' 6"/17' 5"/ 7'/17' 5"/6' 6"/17' 5"/6' 9"/14' 3"/6' 6"/16' 1"/ 7' 4"/13' 5"/8' 2"/13' 5".

Examining fig. 82 with the aid of these data, it will be seen that there are three larger arches in the centre and, excluding the buried arch, the bridge is almost symmetrical about the centre. There are minor variations in spans and piers, but these can be attributed to inaccuracies in setting out. The span to pier ratios are between two and three to one. There are triangular cutwaters upriver with the cappings slightly above the springings and none downriver. The rings are composed of unhewn limestone slabs, the stones ranging from 3in. to 6in. in thickness and 15in. to 18in. in height. The spandrels, parapets and piers are in random rubble. The roadway is 9ft 6in. wide between parapet walls. There are no pedestrian refuges. The outstanding characteristic of the bridge is the overall arched appearance in elevation. The three larger-span central arches lift the roadway above the approach roads and generate a longitudinal profile best reflected in the parapet copings, consisting of two grades connected by a vertical curve—aesthetically very pleasing. This profile was not found in any pre-17th century multi-span arch bridges in Ireland. There are several surviving examples in France dating from the 15th and 16th centuries, particularly in the department of Haute-Loire. Some good examples, such as the Pont Vieux over the river Senouire and Pont Quezac over the Tarn, are given in Prade. None were found in *British Bridges*.[5] There are many commonsense reasons why this style should evolve or be adopted. The larger spans at the centre meant less piers in midriver; the approach causeways could be kept lower albeit with risk of periodic flooding; the style provided more space for boats in the deeper part of the river etc. as outlined for pointed segmental arches in Chapter 11, Part I.

From the bridge characteristic aspect there is no good reason why such a bridge could not have been built in Co. Cork in the 15th, 16th or 17th centuries. However, in the national context all of the well authenticated multi-span bridges with pre-15th century dates, such as Slane*, Adare*, Trim*, have pointed segmental arches and level roadways. The 15th-century Newtown Bridge has some similar features. The 16th-century examples— Ballinasloe* and its vanished contemporaries such as Athlone*, Carlow and Kilmainham—had level roadways and Tudor arches. The post-Cromwellian bridges, however, such as Sir Thomas's*, have Glanworth profiles. Two bridges (Kilcarn* with a 1590 mention and Bective* with no pre-1714 mention) broadly resemble it in arch configuration. It was evident from the foregoing that Glanworth itself could not be dated by analogy with other bridges in Part II. In these circumstances, given the importance of the problem, a solution was sought by reference to other bridges in Co. Cork and their histories.

Bridgetown

There is an entry in the Close Rolls of Henry II (1225) which states "The King wrote to Richard de la Rochelle, Vice Justiciar of Ireland to the effect that the Priory of St Mary of the Bridge of Fermoy founded for the soul of King John should be restored two acres of land in Finnon."[6] This entry relates to Bridgetown in the barony of Fermoy, not to the present town which was founded in 1791. This priory, founded between 1206 and 1216, was colonised from Newtown, Trim; however, no information was found about the bridge over the Blackwater other than one was indicated on Moll's map (1714). Nevertheless it establishes a link with Meath.

Fermoy Town Bridge

Among very useful information supplied to me some years ago by Niall Brunicardi was a copy of a coloured sketch of the bridge erected at Fermoy by the earl of Cork in the 1680s, reproduced in outline in fig. 237, Appendix 8. The resemblance to Glanworth is remarkable. In 1985 Brunicardi wrote a booklet[7] on the history of Fermoy bridges. Stalley states that the Fermoy monastery (Castrum Dei) was impoverished in 1467 due to the wars and was dissolved in 1539-41. Evidently the monks operated a ferry because there is a record that Boyle, who acquired their property, estimated that the bridge he built there in 1625 cost him £500, as well as the loss of £23 per annum income from the ferry formerly operated by the Cistercians. This information supplied by Brunicardi is important because it is the only record of a ferry operated by the order which had monasteries on the banks of many large rivers through Ireland, such as the Nore and the Slaney.

The bridge built by Boyle in 1625 was washed away in a flood of 1628. Boyle in his will dated 1642 provided:

> I desire the ease and safety of the neighbours and travellers, and to have a strong and substantial bridge of lime and stone built in the place thereof as it is at Moyalla. I do hereby signify that it is my will and desire that my brother-in-law William Fenton, Knight, Richard Fishers, Esq., His Majesty's Attorney of Munster, and Joshua Boyle, Esq., with the assistance of my tenant George Hartwell should cause a very graceful and substantial bridge to be built of lime and stone over the river of Fermoy and for the defraying of the charge thereof I do hereby give £200 sterling . . . and upon security given by such masons and workmen as they make choice to build

the said bridge in such a manner and form as the bridge of Moyalla is now built or better, to pay and distribute these monies as the work shall go forward until it be strongly and substantially in all respects finished and that my arms may be cut in a table of stone and set upon a side wall thereof.

No bridge is shown at Fermoy on the Down Survey compiled in 1656. Confirmation that the bridge was built in the 1670s was found in the Council Book of the Corporation of Youghal[8] under 7 March 1674 when the mayor was delegated "to go the next Assizes at Cork, and the normal allowance of 3li be given him towards his charges. It. That if the additional charge of 7li ordered by the former Judges of Assize to be paid by this Corporation towards building Fermoy Bridge cannot be avoided, Mr Mayor take course for the payment, and a rate levied." Brunicardi mentions a letter of 1687 stating in relation to Fermoy, "Here is a stately new bridge lately built over the Blackwater which cost about £1,500." There are many mentions from the Williamite wars in the early 1690s. The bridge is shown on Moll's map (1714). it was widened by J. Anderson in 1797, such that it had six arches on the widened upriver side. The expedient of extending every second pier and spanning between them with low rise oval arches was probably adopted. Brunicardi's booklet includes a photo, taken about 1860 shortly before the bridge was demolished and replaced by the present one of seven low-rise segmental arches which was designed by A.O. Lyons, county surveyor and built by J. Hargrove and opened in 1865. The photo shows six of the thirteen arches all with segmental arc (almost semi-circular) arch rings like Glanworth. From the foregoing it can be deduced that the 1670s stone bridge at Fermoy outlined in fig. 237, Appendix 8 was like the one that spanned the Blackwater in Mallow in 1642. The date of erection of the Mallow stone bridge was discussed in Chapter 9 and the best evidence is Barry's that it was built in stone and lime shortly after 1588. It was destroyed by the Williamites in 1690. The Kinsale Council Books[9] record an item under 1712: "Towards erection of a stone bridge at Mallow to replace existing structure, Law Clayton £200."

The foregoing information provides strong evidence that the Glanworth profile was not a post-Cromwellian importation.

Kilcrea Bridge

There are two other surviving bridges in Cork and probably several others, built in the same style as Glanworth. One is now submerged in the Lee Hydro-electric Scheme reservoir at Bealahaglashin near the confluence of the Sullane river which, according to Milner[10], was located about 50 yds east of the replacement bridge and formed part of the old Cork-Macroom road. The sketch of the old bridge in Milner's book shows that its profile is very similar to Glanworth. It had seven arches, is clearly marked on Moll's map, but not shown on the Down Survey.

The other, at Kilcrea, spans the river Bride, a tributary of the Lee. It now has six arches, one of which is a post-1865 drainage scheme replacement for three of the original arches. It is 9ft wide between parapets. The bridge is mentioned in a paper[11] by Johnson Westropp in 1908, which also includes a contemporary photograph (fig. 83). He states that the local tradition attributed it to Cromwellian times and local people said there was a date cut on it but he searched and failed to find it. There is a sketch of the upriver face in Hall's book[12] published in 1865 which shows eight arches and the ruins of the Franciscan abbey founded by Cormac Laider McCarthy in 1465 in the background (fig. 84). The sketch shows triangular cutwaters with semi-pyramidal cappings. Lewis's *Dictionary* states that the bridge was

Fig. 83: *Kilcrea Bridge: Downriver Elevation (Westropp 1908)*

Fig. 84: *Kilcrea Bridge:*
Upriver Elevation
(Halls 1865)

built by order of Cromwell but gives no source for the information. The OS 25-inch map shows cutwaters on the two central piers of the original, and Westropp states that one of these was brought up to form a pedestrian refuge in the parapet—the only refuge. This characteristic links the bridge with Kilcarn.* The river Bride is not shown on either the Down Survey or Moll's map.

The fact that a bridge similar to Glanworth was erected across the Blackwater in Fermoy downriver of Mallow in the 1670s suggests that there was considerable confidence in its ability to withstand floods. Its model, the Mallow Bridge of the last decade of the 16th century, lasted a century and succumbed to war rather than floods. Was Mallow modelled on Glanworth or the reverse? Further research is required to give a definitive answer. Perhaps Kilcrea and Glanworth are both by products of the building of the friaries in the mid 15th century. The superb masonry of the ruins of these abbeys leaves one in no doubt about the ability of the masons to build fine bridges at the time.

Grace Dieu

There is a townland in north Co. Dublin, off the Blakes' Cross to Ballyboghill road, which takes its name from the priory for Arroasian nuns who translated there from Lusk *c.* 1195. Gwynn & Hadcock[1], who devote almost half a page to its history, with many records up to its confiscation in 1541, state that it had many possessions at that time including 203 acres with a water mill, a horse mill and another 632

acres elsewhere. The priory was granted to Patrick Barnwell who, according to McCurtain,[2] had been spokesman for the opposition in the passing of the Supremacy Bill in the Irish parliament but when tempted with monastic spoils gave way. He then became lessee of well endowed religious property including Grace Dieu. He built Turvey House, Donabate, in 1565 and dismantled the Grace Dieu buildings to get stone for it. Fortunately he left behind a fine stone bridge which is still there, though the roadway on which it is located has long been abandoned and is now totally overgrown.

I first noticed this bridge on Rocque's 1756 Map of County Dublin clearly marked "Grace Dieu Bridge", and Paddy Healy, archaeologist, confirmed that it was worth a visit. It is located on the lands of Joseph Byrne and has not been used even for farm or pedestrian access for a long time. The roadway and arch width is 11ft. The single arch (fig. 85) has a span of 15ft and is a segment of a circle, almost semi-circular. The ring stones are well-squared stones 18in. deep of varying thickness, generally 3in. to 6in. It is mainly limestone with some slate. The sheeting in the arch barrel is random rubble, one quadrant of the soffit being coated with mortar that is wattle marked. The abutments are shallow as the springing is just above normal water level. There are holes, about 9in. x 4in., at more or less regular intervals in the abutments just below the springing each side which look like weep holes but most probably were used for the centering. There are no skewbacks of any kind and the segment

Fig. 85: *Grace Dieu Bridge: Upriver Elevation*

Fig. 86: *Grace Dieu Bridge: Arch Crown, Downriver*

was commenced by tilting the first ringstones slightly .

There are approximately 20 ring stones in each half arch; the keystone on the downstream side (fig. 86) is heart-shaped; the upstream one is missing. The joints between the ring stones are for the most part non-radial, and it is obvious that the mason did not know how to "turn an arch", to use a phrase that was a hallmark of capability up to the 1960s when voussoir bricks became available. The arches are not corbelled in the ancient Irish tradition. Unfortunately, Barnwell removed all the walls of the church and other buildings so there is nothing left in Grace Dieu to compare with.

The characteristics of this bridge suggest that it is medieval, possibly 14th-century, and complement the evidence based on the history

of the townland. Hinges have formed at the springings and each side of the buckle in the intrados in the top half of the haunch of the left-hand ring, visible in the photo, a danger signal that collapse is on its way unless it is repaired soon under some heritage conservation programme.

Bennets Bridge

The present five-arch bridge (fig. 87) across the Nore at Bennetsbridge was erected in the late 1760s in place of the one washed away in 1763. The flood in the Nore is graphically described by Tighe:[1] "On 2 October 1763 both Kilkenny bridges were destroyed and the damage done by the flood was estimated at £11,381. 14*s*. 4*d*.; several lives were lost, as it rose in the night, Bennet's Bridge and that of Thomastown were thrown down, and two arches of Inistioge bridge were split. Parliament granted £5,417 for the rebuilding of Johns & Greens bridges. The rest of the damage was repaired at the expense of Co. Kilkenny." The rebuilding of these bridges with greatly increased waterway and new styles of architecture is discussed by Ruddock[2], who concluded that it "established a local style". Two of the bridges are described under the heading "Kilkenny Bridges", below, with an extract from 3 Geo. III c.1 (1763) which provided £8,000 for the work (not the figure quoted above).

In the case of Bennetsbridge we are more concerned with the vanished ancient bridges at this historic crossing-point on the Nore. Canon Carrigan has recorded the early mentions in his superb *History of the Diocese of Ossory* (1905). He states:[3] "Bennetsbridge is called by Irish speakers Drehidh-Binny-addh (accent on last syllable), i.e. Droiced Beinead, St Bennet or Benedict's Bridge. Why the bridge was called after St Bennet does not appear; it was, however, so called as early as 1384. On the bridge there was formerly a chapel dedicated to the blessed Virgin." The next earliest (unreferenced) mention he gives states that a writer in 1743 remarked: "After it leaves the city [Kilkenny] it [Nore] runs southeast throu' a beautiful country to Bennetts Bridge, where there is a stone bridge over it, and a few yards below ye present (bridge) the Ruins of an old bridge which had a small castle at ye end of it to defend the passage." From this it is apparent that sometime, probably in the previous century, an earlier fortified bridge had been washed away and that it was located just downriver of the 18th-century bridge.

On Moll's map (1714) two roads lead into the bridge, from east and west—from Gowran and Thomastown; and from Ennisnag and Kilkenny city. The bridge is described as "Bennets Br" on the map. The Down Survey map clearly delineates the bridge and records the name as Bennets Bridge on the East as well as the West; it also includes symbols for a chapel or church on the north-east end, fortifications on south-east and some other building on the north-west end. Whether these are related to the bridge is not clear, but they appear to be. All the mentions in the journals of the Kilkenny Antiquarian Society states that Cromwell passed over the bridge, having come from Gowran, on his way to Kilkenny.

The next mention is 1419: (Nov. 22). The king (Henry V) granted John Lydington, chaplain the free chapel of the Blessed Mary on Benetsbrige, Ossory diocese, vacant and in the king's gift, with all appurtenances (Irish Council Roll XVI, Rich. II).

There are three mentions between 1384–93 (quoted from Carrigan):

1393 (Jan. 29). John de Midiltoun, clerk, and guardian of the chapel of Bene[ts]bridge, was granted leave to be absent in England for five years; receiving in the meantime all the profits of the said chapel. (Irish Council Roll XVI, Rich.II).

1393 (April 29). John Middultown, guardian of "the chapel of Our Lady on the Bridge of St Benet, in the County of Kilkenny in Ireland", petitions the lord justice and council of the king in Ireland, "forasmuch as before now, the Irish enemies, as well as the English malefactors, have passed and returned by the said bridge, and inflicted many evils and injuries on the King's lieges of these parts, as is well known to you, until lately that there was commenced there by the said John Middultoun and his predecessor, a tower within the said bridge adjoining the said chapel, to the hindrance of the passage of the said enemies and malefactors, to the great benefit and succouring of the said lieges; that it may please you to take this into consideration, and to grant him license to perfect the said tower and all the fortifications which it is possible for him to make upon the said bridge saving a reasonable passage there and a road for the King's

Fig. 87: *Bennetsbridge, 1990, erected in 1760s*

lieges by the same, and the said tower and fortress so perfected to hold to him and his successors, guardians there, without impeachment on that account of our said Lord the King, his heirs or ministers" (Pat. Rolls). De Madiltoun or Middultoun was outlawed some years later. He received pardon in May 1407. In 1417 he was rector of Callan.

1384 (Nov. 5). The King (Richard II) ratifies the status of John Horley, parson of the free chapel of Benetbrygge, Ossory diocese, in the aforesaid chapel (Pat. Rolls).

From these references it is clear that the chapel was located on the bridge and that a fortified tower was under construction beside the chapel in 1393 and other fortifications were intended. It seems likely that my interpretation of Petty's map symbols, outlined above, is correct and that the buildings were still there in 1653-4. Another word of great interest in the 1393 record is "aid" qualifying "chapel". This implies that the bridge users gave donations which helped to support the chaplain and perhaps to maintain the chapel and the bridge. It is notable though that in the 1384 record it is called "a free chapel"; whether or not this implies that no donation was expected or that the chapel and its parson were independent of the jurisdiction of the diocesan bishop is not clear. There was also obviously some problem in regard to Middultown's activities.

One record dated 1653, not recorded by Carrigan, states that "In this year Sir Edmund Blanchvilla forfeited Bennetsbridge whereon there were a small castle in repair, and one good stone house built by Colonel Daniel Axtell." The keyword here is "whereon", showing it was the bridge that was forefeited not the town. In fact, that is confirmed by the statement that follows the quotation that at the same time Tradingstowne was found to belong to the earl of Ormond and was not forfeited. There is no mention of the chapel, so it appears that it was suppressed, probably in the 1550s, and granted to a conformist who converted it into a house. There are several examples of this in Britain, for example, Chantry Bridge, Rotherham, where after Elizabeth's accession the chapel became an almshouse and in 1779 was converted into a dwelling house for the deputy constable and secure gaol and was used until 1826.

The next mention of Bennetsbridge and the oldest is 1285: "Edward I made a grant of customs to be taken at the new bridge of Trenedinestone . . . in aid of the bridge and for the benefit of the parts adjacent."[4] Like many such records in the rolls and statutes of the period it does not indicate whether the new bridge was of stone, but the granting of pontage implies an expensive bridge, so we can assume that it was and that it had the chapel dedicated to the Blessed Virgin.

In a recent article on the civil parish of Treadingstown[5] Mary Breen explains that Treadingstown derived its name from an Anglo-Norman family and that there is a reference of a land grant in 1284 with a mention of "Villa Trenedyn". Her conclusions are that, when the bridge was dedicated to St Benet and the chapel on it to our Lady, that part of the parish subsequently came to be known as "Bennetbrygge". She also states that

in 1594 the earls of Ormond set aside the sum of £200 to be spent "upon the reparation of the bridges of Bennetsbridge and Deynyn" (Dinan) and that the ancient Irish name of the district recorded in manuscripts was Ath Noo or Ath Noa meaning Oa's ford, which formed part of the ancient Bealach n-Gabhrain.

My interest in the problem of Bennetsbridge dates back to the 1970s when after an OECD Steering Committee for Road Research meeting I had a discussion with the US delegate, a structural engineer, a Dr. Scheffy who had recently inspected the remnants of Pont d'Avignon, the most famous bridge in the world. The discussion prompted the idea that Bennetsbridge might also be called after Little Benedict. While the difference in scale of the bridges was enormous, there was the similarity of the chapel and the bridge, the period (13th-century) and above all the name. The life of St Benezet is summarised in the *New Catholic Encyclopedia*: "Patron of bridge builders, initiator and prompter of the bridge across the Rhone at Avignon; born *c.* 1165, died *c.*1184. Arriving as a young man in Avignon in 1177, Benezet convinced the Avignonais that God willed them to build the first bridge across the turbulent Rhone. For seven years he collected funds and organised a group of laymen as the *fratres pontis* to carry on his work. The bridge was completed in 1188. Documents in 1202 refer to him as blessed, in 1237 as a "saint". The surviving four arches and chapel of the bridge which originally had 23 arches are shown in fig. 88.

An enquiry to Mrs Breen, chairperson of the local "Duchais", revealed that there was no local knowledge about the St Benet from which the bridge across the Nore and the town

Fig.88: *St Benezet's Bridge, Avignon: Surviving Chapel and Arches*

takes its name and that the hypothesis about St Benezet could be correct. There is no Irish St Benet listed. The significance of Dr Carrigan's statement that the name was pronounced Binnyaddh in the last century could imply that Little Benedict was the traditional name. The main basis for the hypothesis is the fact that Edward I, in 1252, was given the government of Gascony and in 1254 he married Eleanor, sister of Alfonso of Castile. He went on the crusades in 1270; became king of England and large parts of south-west France in 1272; granted the men of Condom (on a tributary of the Garonne) the right to collect a barra to repair the town bridge in 1281. St Benezet's work was famous throughout France and England during the 13th century and it seems a much more likely explanation than that put forward to the Kilkenny Archeological Society by Hogan[6] in 1860 when he wrote, "Bennet's-bridge . . . being an English proper name, it requires no other evidence to prove that the bridge was originally an English construction."

There is also some oral evidence that the bridge is called after an abbé de Saint Benet who founded a monastery in the area, but no records of this were found. The legend of St Benezet has been thoroughly researched by Boyer,[7] who states that it "affirms that as a 12-year-old boy, keeping his mother's sheep, he had a vision which required him to proceed to Avignon and to build a bridge across the Rhone. Arriving at the town on the day of an eclipse of the sun he harangued the people to persuade them to carry out the divine mission. After meeting with jeers from the populace and threats of physical violence from the bishop of Avignon, he performed the miracle of raising and throwing into the Rhone, to found the first pier, a stone which would required thirty men to move it. This triumph assured an enthusiastic response to his requests for donations." Witnesses later attested at Benezet's beatification process that they had seen the miracle. Boyer's findings also establish that the crucial function of the *fratres pontis* was the collection of funds (the building being done by the town authorities), and that the society was formed for the express purpose of promoting construction and subsequent maintenance. Similar societies were founded for the famous bridges in the valley of the Rhone at Lyons, and Pont-St-Esprit but the romantic notion of a religious order sending out flying squadrons to construct bridges, elsewhere has no foundation. Boyer's findings do not preclude the possibility that the inspiration for the first bridge at Bennetsbridge came from the valley of the Rhone or that it was called after St Benezet, who was canonised in 1237.

Watercastle Old Bridge

In the search for early mentions of Monks Bridge* this bridge was discovered by chance. It was marked as "Castle Coote" and clearly designated on the 1563 Map of Irish Districts in the Queen's County and County Kildare. The original map is in the British Museum but a facsimile appears in a paper by Hore.[1] A check with Laois Co. Council confirmed that there was a Watercastle Bridge across the Nore at the location. Sometime afterwards a colleague engineer, P. McGuinness, was passing and checked out the bridge. He found that the Nore had been diverted and a new bridge built, but on the west bank he found the old bridge. The bridge has four arches, a pair in the centre and two others one at each side some distance away. It was high and dry and overgrown with scrub and bushes on each side; nevertheless he succeeded in getting photographs of some arches upstream and downstream. The difference in the arch rings indicated that the bridge had been widened on the downriver side. One of the visible arches on the upriver side appeared to be an original.

The 1841 OS six-inch map shows that the bridge was located on the Durrow-Abbeyleix section of the old Mail Coach Road; however, the river widened appreciably at each side of the bridge, which was very narrow and difficult to scale with any accuracy. There were three cutwaters, fore and aft, indicating four spans, the same as found on the ground. These are not visible in the photos because the arches have been filled up with spoil from the new cut.

The new arch rings on the widened section (fig. 89), obviously constructed after 1841, are intended to be circular segments; not all of the joints are radial, though the ring stones were voussoirs in the true sense of the word. The stones were obviously cut to match a template and fitted in tightly, despite the edge slopes which are matched but non-radial. There are

Fig. 89: *Watercastle Bridge: Two Downriver post-1841 Arches*

Fig. 90: *Watercastle Bridge: pre-1563 Arch Upriver*

no properly-cut skewbacks for the springings and the mason obviously did not know his trade properly.

Fig. 90 shows half of what must be an original pre-1563 arch. It is also a circular arc segment. A skewback has been roughly cut to give a springing at approximately the right slope. The first two ring stones have slipped down a few inches, collapse being prevented by a lug on the first. Underneath the arch barrel there is evidence of punching of some stones. The mortar has obviously been leached out over the centuries making it a *cloch droichet* rather than a *droichet cloch aeltra*.

In ancient times there was a church of importance here and St Fintan was abbot for a period. There was also an old castle converted into a dwelling house in the 18th-century Watercastle House.[2] Because of the early map

mention the bridge merits further detailed on site investigation.

Holy Cross

This masonry arch bridge spans the Suir four miles south of Thurles at the famous Cistercian abbey of Holy Cross, founded by Donal Mor O'Brien, king of Thomond, in 1180. The history of the abbey has been well documented by Hayes[1], Carville[2] and Stalley[3]; however, the bridge has received scant attention. The reason may be that there is a plaque on it with an unusual inscription in Latin in which the bridge addresses the traveller which reads, "To the traveller, Nicholas Cowli constructed me. James Butler, baron of Dunboyne, and the Lady Margaret O'Brien, his wife, rebuilt this bridge which had fallen, and .ornamented it with their arms in the year of our Lord 1626. Say, I pray you, before you go away, this short prayer: May the two who built it escape the pit of hell." A humble prayer indeed were it not for the fact that Nicholas Cowli who did the work seems to have been forgotten, or was he? Notice the subtle use of words "constructed me" (*me fabrikavit*); rebuilt this bridge which had fallen" (*hunc pontem collapsum erexerunt*). Perhaps Hayes's translation, the same as the one used by Bord Failte, is unintentionally misleading. One could interpret the inscription to mean that the original bridge was fabricated by Nicholas Cowli, that *part* of it had collapsed in the 1620s and that the Butlers financed its repair in 1626. This is my interpretation, hopefully substantiated in what follows.

The abbey flourished in its early years and became famous after it obtained a relic of the True Cross, according to one theory a part of a larger portion of the Cross brought to England by Richard de Lion. In 1567 Lord Deputy Sidney complained to the queen that "there is no small confluence of people still resorting to the Holy Cross". In 1414 James Butler, earl of Ormond, extended special protection to the abbey and a major rebuilding took place. After its surpression monks remained in or near the abbey. Hayes states that in September 1601 a good strong watch was kept on the abbey as O'Neill was expected to penetrate Munster on his way to Kinsale via the ford near the abbey. In the the event it was O'Donnell who did so, "the river being in high spate so he used the ford nearby and halted at the monastery for a blessing". The sources for this information are not given. The Civil Survey states that there was at Holy Cross "an old abbey church and two stone houses out of repair, a stone bridge on the River Suir . . .". The bridge is not shown on the Down Survey map (1656)—surprising, seeing it was repaired in 1625 and mentioned in the Civil Survey. These are the basic facts relevant to the bridge. Before drawing any conclusions from them it is necessary to describe the bridge.

The present bridge has eight spans (fig. 229a, Appendix 8). It consists of two sections, an original and a downriver extension. The overall length, bank to bank, is 150ft. It appears to be founded on rock which is close to the bed of the river and from which limestone was quarried further downriver, to build the abbey.

The average width of the piers is 8ft with only minor variations. These are triangular cutwaters on the upriver side and none downriver. The one non-ivy-clad pier capping that is visible appears to have an inverted triangular capping with the base at the level of the arch crown. Some of the others rise to road pavement level and may have been pedestrian refuges originally. The arch spans are 13ft 4in. with little variation. The intrados of the original are pointed segmental with rises ranging from 17in. to 19in. The downriver extension has circular segmental arches with rises that are 12in. greater. The springing points are more or

less at the same level; there is a lip of 12in. at the butt joint.

The key characteristic is the pointed segmental arches almost identical in span, rise and overall shape to Adare Bridge* which has been dated at 1410. The stones in the facing rings are thin, irregular-edged limestone flags, like Adare. The roadway over the arches is level from bank to bank. No information was found which would give a clue to the period in which the extension was built, but it would appear to be post-1700. A sketch of the abbey by the earl of Portarlington is represented in Carville's book. It shows the downriver face of the bridge in the foreground and from this the outline shown in fig. 229b, Appendix 8 has been prepared. The sketch is undated but it must be post-1700 because the earldom did not exist before then. It shows nine arches and, more importantly, an entrance gate to the abbey across the road just beyond the end of the bridge. However, the parapet wall bends left on the bank suggesting that the road also ran past the gate as well as up to it. The road from Thurles to Cashel crossing the Suir at Holycross is clearly marked on Moll's 1714 map. The only road to the west between Roscrea and Cashel is shown on Moll (map of principal roads) as running from Holycross to Nenagh. The west road from Thurles was one of the "Anglesea" roads built in the 1830s. The earl's sketch shows the downriver arches as

Fig. 91: *Holy Cross Bridge: Bartlett's Upriver Elevation c.1830*

pointed, whereas a current photo from the near the same sketch point gives no semblance of this. Perhaps the original downriver face was visible *c.* 1750 which suggests that the widening was later. The small arch over the doorway of the 15th-century mill at Blakestown (where the abbey bakery was located) is a pointed segmental in the same style. The approximate bridge width in 1843 as scaled from the OS six-inch map was 25ft. The Bartlett drawing of Holycross abbey (fig. 91) shows five of the upriver arches *c.* 1820; they appear to be Tudor four-centred rather than pointed segmentals.

The plaque is located on the downriver parapet which suggests that it was relocated or else that the widening took place in 1626. The inscription is in bas relief of an identical style to the 1644 plaque commemorating Fr O'Duffy and Fr Keating on the ruined mortuary chapel at Tubbrid, five miles southwest of Cahir. It too is in Latin.

There is a bridge at Abingdon over the river Thames linking Berkshire and Oxfordshire which according to Medcalfe[4] was built in 1416 by the Guild or Fraternity of the Holy Cross of Abington, a charitable mutual aid society. A few of the original arches survived and are shown in *British Bridges*[5]. They are identical in shape size and appearance (pointed segmental) to Holycross; moreover, the cut-waters are chamfered on the top. The main difference is that the Abingdon Bridge had ribs. The Society was suppressed before 1553 when the abbey from which the town takes its name was also dissolved (see Abington Br). Perhaps there was contact between the Society and Holy Cross Abbey.

From all the foregoing I conclude that the upriver section of Holycross Bridge dates from the first quarter of the 15th century, the period when the abbey was largely rebuilt. The expense was probably borne by the earl of Ormond, who would be aware of the fact that his fellow Norman, the fifth earl of Kildare, had erected Adare Bridge in 1410.

Enniscorthy Bridge

Apart from New Ross, where William Marshall spanned the Barrow with a timber bridge before 1210, one of the few early mentions of bridges in Wexford is a contract drawn up by the Lord Deputy Grey for the construction of a timber bridge across the Slaney, at Enniscorthy, in 1581. The contract is described in a paper by Graves[1] in 1868. It is an extremely important document from the aspect of the history of bridges in Ireland, even though there is no evidence as yet that the bridge was built. In the description of the Old Long Bridge at Belfast, it was mentioned that Sir Henry Sidney arranged a contract for a bridge to be built there in October 1568 but there are no other details. Graves, in a foot-note, states that the source of the Enniscorthy contract was an MS. "lately purchased from private hands for the Government", being an extract from a volume of the proceedings of the Irish privy council then (1868) preserved in the Record Tower, Dublin Castle.

It read as follows:

Articles of Covenant and Agreement between the Right Honourable the L. Arthur Grey [obliterated] and Lorde Deputy of Ireland, with the consent of her Ma[ts] Counsell of the said Realme of Ireland, of the one partie, and Paule Finglas, carpenter of the other partie, for and concerning the erecting of a Bridge of Tymber over the River of Slane att Enescorthy, in the County of Wexford, with a Castell of Lyme and Stone in the middle thereof, to be perfected by the said Paul Finglas according to the contents of the Articles followinge, set down and agreed the 18th of September, 1581.

First, the said Paule Finglas doth covenante and promise to and with the Lorde Deputie & Counsell that he will erect and set up a bridge at Enescorthie afforesaid of good, sound and substantial tymber, to be in length ccxl fote, or thereabout, and in bredeth, within the rails, xi foot. The said bridge to stand upon xiiii arches, every arch to conteine three pillars, and every pillar to be in square xviii ynches, and in height, the shortest of them, xxiiii fote, and some of them xxviii, and some xxx fote, according the depth of the water, and shodde with yron, and every shoe to containe ii stone of yron; upon every three pillars of the said arches a pece of tymber of xviii ynches broad and xii ynches thick the pece, and foretene fote in length, with mortesses and tenors, and two crosse lats upon every of the arches as appereth by the modill.

Also fyve beames, every beame of xii

ynches square, and xii fote in length, to be laid betwene every of the said arches and plancks, [and], to [be] laide upon those, beames of iii ynches thick all along the bridge, and the same to be fased over with stone. Also three railes to be sett on either side of the said bridge, with a standing pillar of fyve fote in height, and ix ynches square, placed upon every arch. The lower raile to be xvi ynches broade, and iii ynches thick, the middle raile x ynches broad and ii inches thick, and the upper raile eight ynches square; the entry into the said bridge on both the ends to be made with stone and lyme.

Item. The said Paule doth covenante and promise to and with the said Lorde Deputie and Counsell to build in the middle of the said River and Bridge a Square Castell or Tower of Lyme and Stone, built upon a new foundation, with two gates to goe through the said Castell of tenne fote in breadth, and tenne fote in height; the said castell to have two storyes in it above the vault of the gate, and to conteine in breadth on the outside xxviiii fote the one way, and xxii fote the other way, with battlements, a strong roof, and Flower wyndowes, and murdering holes as many as shall be needfull; and at ech of the ii gates aforesaid to place a Drawbridge with crossebarres of yron, greate spikes, and cheines of yron to drawe the said two bridges close to the Castell, and which the said Paule Finglas doth covenante and promise to finish betweene this and Lady Day next in March come twelve months, which will be the xxvth of March, 1583.

For and in consideration of which worke so to be performed and finished by the said Paule Finglas, at his proper cost and charge of all things necessary for the same, the said Lord Deputie and Counsell doe in the behalf of Her Maestie covenante and promise to gyve and paye unto the said Paule Finglas, or his assigns, the some of three hundred't fiftie pounds ster., whereof one hundred pounds to be ymprested beforehand to the said Paule for the making of his provisions for the said buildinge, and one hundred pounds more at our Lady Day next in March, and another hundred pounds when the tymber work of the said bridge is sett up, and the Castell sett to the height of the Vault, and the rest when the whole work is perfected and ended according to the Articles or Covenant afore expressed.

And for the better furtherance of the said worke, and speedyer perfecting of the same, the said lord Deputie and Counsell are pleased that the said Paule shall have commissyons yssued for carriage and provision of victles for his workmen and other necessaries as he shall think needfull, and to be allowed by the Lord Deputie.

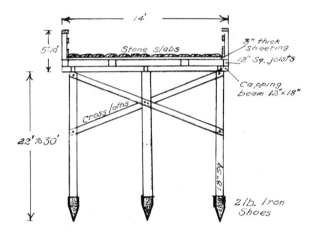

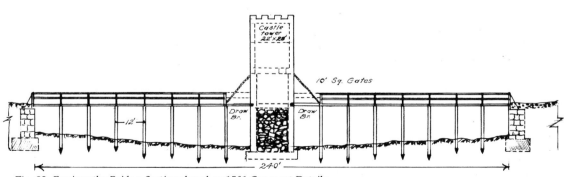

Fig. 92: *Enniscorthy Bridge: Sections based on 1581 Covenant Details*

We have prepared a drawing (fig. 92) of this bridge based on the information given above. The shape of the "Square Castell or Tower of Lime and Stone" is based on Du Noyer's sketch of the one at Fethard, Co. Tipperary. The words used for some of the items are important; for example, the spans are called "arches", so one has to be careful in drawing conclusions about isolated referenced to other bridges as arches. "Cross lats", Graves explains in a footnote, appeared "like lacs" in the original. Strong cross-bracing was essential so they were hardly laths. The specification used the phrase "as appereth by the miodill" which shows it was customary to produce a model for the carpenters to work from at the time. It is probable that the military had a number of standard models that could be easily modified and adapted to suit local conditions because rural carpenters or masons, especially following the suppression of the monasteries, would not have been able to read drawings. The plank deck was to be covered with stone. The Council Book for Cork Corporation[2] records under 1639 that the mayor and others decided that the timber North Bridge "shall be well paved over with stone, gravel, and sand, according to the best bridges of that nature and quality within the kingdom of Ireland". Rotting of the decks due to moisture accumulation and lack of proper camber was a great problem in timber bridges of that period and later. The period for the contract was 18 September 1581 to 25 March 1583, approx. 18 months. This allowed only one summer/autumn period when the flow in the river was likely to be low. The type of timber was not specified apart from "good, sound and substantial".

The "Flower" windows meant cusped stonework, an ornamental feature. The end spans were to be supported by masonry abutments, very necessary to prevent the river eroding away the approach roads at each end. The method of payment indicates an imprest of £100 to start work. The second gives a clue that there was a stone arch over the passageway in the tower. The last paragraph suggests that like many large bridges of the period and abroad the contractor was responsible for feeding the workmen and that the cost was an extra.

Graves expressed the hope that Wexford members of the Royal Society of Antiquarians would find out "if this bridge and castle" were actually built. To judge from an article published in one of the Wexford newspapers a few years ago it would seem that his hope was not realised. Clonegal is the only bridge shown across the Slaney or any other river in Wexford in the Down Survey of 1656, so no positive evidence is provided by that source. Would such a timber bridge having 12ft opes, having long survived the floods and the debris brought down by them (such as uprooted trees)? It is hard to say. The piles were 18ins. square—a large cross-section compared with the 18ins. x 14ins. used by Cox* two centuries later which lasted 100 years at Waterford and 70 years at New Ross. The first stone bridge in Enniscorthy, erected in the last quarter of the 17th century, was replaced by the present one in 1715. One would expect to find some reference to the stone fortification in the middle of the river in the previous 100 years if Grey's Bridge had been built. Perhaps, like New Ross, it was demolished in the wars of the 1640s. The mention of a "new foundation" for the tower in paragraph four of the covenant could imply the existence of a previous tower and bridge.

Kilcarn

There are two parts in this bridge, an original 12ft wide and a 9ft extension on the upriver side. Here we are interested in the original (fig. 93) because the extension, as in most widened as distinct from lengthened bridges, is constructed to butt in with similar span arches and is therefore not representative of its period. The whole bridge was retired from service in May 1977 when the new precast concrete beam and slab bridge, having three central spans and two end spans, was opened to traffic. The old bridge which crossed the river at right angles was an accident black spot due to the sharp bends at each end. The scars of many accidents are still evident in the parapet walls.

The bridge is located two miles upriver from Navan; nevertheless its history is bound up with that of Navan itself. Navan, An Uaimh, was called Nuachongbhail in the early Christian era when St Fechin came there according to Cogan.[1] The town was walled and fortified by Hugh de Lacey after the motte had been erected by the early Normans. There was an

Augustinian abbey in the town, located in the quadrant formed upriver of the confluence of the Blackwater and the Boyne, before the Normans according to Gwynn & Hadcock.[2] Cogan states that the town was bestowed on Jocelin de Angelo, or Nangle, a Norman knight, and became a flourishing town, one of the first boroughs in the palatinate of Meath. It was granted a charter by Edward IV. The Nangle family restored the abbey towards the end of the 12th century. The Boyne crossing was via a ford from which the townland, opposite, on the south bank takes its name, Athlumney (ford of the bare place), site of a 15th-century castle. The Blackwater was spanned by a bridge which, according to Ellison,[3] is mentioned as Swynes Bridge in the Civil Survey and gave access to the Watergate. It is clearly marked but not named on the Down Survey map of 1656. The present bridge is called Pollboy (Yellow Hole) reflecting a characteristic of the river bed. There was a church at Kilcarn in the 13th century.

The main north-south crossing of the Boyne in the vicinity of Navan must have been via the 1210 Babes Bridge opposite Donaghmore round tower and church, 2 miles downriver from the town. The bridge (see Babes*) was ruinous in 1463 when the land left by John le Baube for its maintenance was given into the "custody of the parson of Dunmoe and the vicar of Donaghmore for the repair of said bridge". Both however were required to render an account yearly to the abbot of Navan. This certainly implies that it was of concern to the abbey and the town. At that time there was probably no bridge at Kilcarn. Navan Abbey was suppressed and confiscated in 1538 at which time Donaghmore was a local church. Assuming that the responsibility for the maintenance of Babes continued into the 16th century, it certainly came to an end in 1538. From that date it is most likely that no one had responsibility for Babes Bridge, as had happened in many instances in England after the suppression in the previous decades. Navan was plundered by Con O'Neill in 1539 and a great quantity of spoils carried off. It was so impoverished, according to Cogan, that Henry VIII decreed that every plough-land in Meath and Westmeath was to be charged with payment of 3s. 4d. for four years for the purpose of repairing the walls of the town.

Reverting to Kilcarn, the bridge is shown on the Down Survey maps so it was there in the 1656. The earliest mention of the bridge was found by Richard Haworth.[4] It is worth quoting because it indicates the diversity of sources in which early bridge mentions are found, in this case a spy's report recorded in the Calendar of State Papers Ireland, Vol. 8, p. 191:

A declaration of Captain Gerrott Fleming: 'Upon Saturday last, being the 12th of October, one Patrick McGuy came up unto me from Charles Halpenny, my Constable of Ballylagan, and told me that he and the said Charles being the Tuesday before at Con McCollo's (MacMahon's) house in Clancarroll (Donaghmoyne in Farney), where Ever McCooley (MacMahon of Farney), Tirlogh McHenry (O'Neill), and Art Bradagh, Hagan's son, were drinking, they began to use some speeches of my Lord Lieutenant's departure, saying that his going with that expedition was not for their good, but to land forces beneath in Ulster upon them, because he saw that he could do no good by going one way into Ulster, and that O'Neill would take his opportunity, and that he would be no longer cosened by the State. And further, Art Bradagh's son said unto the rest, "You have warning already to provide a month's victual, and let it be done in haste, to meet O'Neill at the end of the truce".

Fig. 93: *Kilcarn Bridge: Downriver Elevation*

Fig. 94: *Kilcarn Bridge: Downriver Cutwater*

'Further, he said that one Richard Halpenny, one of the said Gerrott's followers, who is most commonly with Tirlogh McHenry and Con McCollo, the next day after the said (Mc)Guy and Charles Halpenny returned to Ballylagan, followed them home, and willed them to be put on their guard, and to send me, the said Gerrott, word, that O'Neill would very shortly invade the Pale with what forces he could every way, and that their resolution was, that their forces of foot should pass over these bridges of Slane and Kilcarn, and that O'Donnell with his forces would come over the bridge of the Grange, and that all their horse should for more expedition pass over the fords, if they were passable. All which speeches the said Richard Halpenny heard spoken by Tirlogh McHenry, . . . and this I do declare upon my oath', 14th October, 1599.

The invasion of the Pale did not occur because O'Neill went south with an army in 1601 to defeat at Kinsale.

This is an invaluable mention not just in relation to Kilcarn but for all the other bridges and crossings on the Boyne between Trim and Drogheda. From all the foregoing we can be certain that there was a bridge at Kilcarn in 1590 and that Babes was impassable. I suggest that in the period between 1550 and the commencement of the nine years war in 1594 Kilcarn Bridge was built—a period when there was a preoccupation with building bridges as part of the Tudor conquest. The original part of Kilcarn Bridge is, from an engineering aspect, well designed, so it is logical to assume that an equal amount of thought went into its planning. Looking at the situation from the aspect of Navan town, the money from the cess may have been applicable to pontage as well as murage; therefore, careful consideration would have been given as to whether the money should be spent on repairing Babes, building a new bridge across the Boyne in Navan, or at Kilcarn. The latter solution was by far the best for the simple reason that it is above the entry of the Blackwater and rock was not far below the bed. Hence the number of arches to carry the floods would be less, and the foundations easier to build and far less susceptible to scour.

The bridge, shown in fig. 230, Appendix 8, has 11 arches. The four central arches have spans of 20 to 22ft, and are flanked (looking upriver) by three of 11ft to 12ft on the left and four of 10ft to 12ft on the right. Some of the peripheral arches may be subsequent additions especially on the right where the outside pair is separated by a 20ft pier. The original may have consisted of four central arches with two on each side. The piers are from 6.5ft to 8.4ft wide (excluding the 20ft). The cutwaters on the downriver side are triangular, one being brought up to form a pedestrian refuge. We do not know about the upriver cutwaters due to the extension. The capping of the cutwaters is in the form of an inverted isosceles triangle (chamfered) with the top level with the crown of the intrados (fig. 94). The curves of the intrados are segments of circles, having a rise equal to one third the span. The ring stones are rectangular, about 15in. x 6in. on average, well-shaped; in fact some arches appear to have proper voussoirs (it is difficult to see them from the bank, or to get head-on photos without a boat; moreover, some are plastered over). The span to pier ratio is 3 to 1 for the larger central arches and 3 to 2 for the outer ones. There is a butt joint 1in. to 2in. wide between the original and the extension. The sheeting is random rubble in both, but the stones in the extension are larger, as might be expected. Studying the characteristics from photographs I noticed that the inverted triangular cutwater cappings were similar to Milltown (Dublin)* and the 17th-century Ardstraw Bridge in Tyrone and somewhat like Newtown.* A check through the photos of hundreds of old bridges in Britain showed only two similar, the ancient (undated) Auld Bridge of Ayr and Stirling Bridge (c.1400), both in Scotland. There are probably others here and abroad, but they are obviously rare; moreover, the photos usually only show one face of each bridge. There is no borehole evidence to show that the bridge is founded on rock, but it was found 6ft under the bed upriver when the new bridge was being built, so it cannot be far below the surface.

The question of the preservation of Kilcarn Bridge has been discussed by Meath Co. Council at the behest of the "Save Kilcarn Bridge Committee" on many occasions in the past decade. Hopefully, this summary (which has drawn on the findings of the committee, especially the 1599 mention) will add to the facts. The upriver extension is of little historical interest: it is the original that matters. The basic question now remaining is whether the present downriver section is the actual bridge O'Neill planned to cross in 1599 or a post-Cromwellian replacement. It is a vital question, as explained under Glanworth Bridge.*

Carragh Bridge (Liffey)

This six-arch bridge (fig. 95) spans the Liffey on a Regional Road, 2.5 miles north west of Naas. It is named after the townland on the north bank of the river. Joyce[1] gives the meaning as "rock land" and cautions against confusing it with *coradh*, which means a weir. Most of the Liffey through Co. Kildare has a deep channel, and consequently the bridges, such as Carragh, are high with level roadways.

There are now 16 road bridges across the Liffey in Co. Kildare, the first at Poulaphuca and the last at Leixlip. When Major Taylor carried out his survey and published his map[2] in 1783 there were eight—Harristown (Old), Kilcullen, Newbridge, Carragh, Clane, Celbridge, New Bridge (St Wolstan's), Leixlip. At that time Ballymore Eustace was in the barony of Upper Cross which was an "island" part of Co. Dublin. Moll's map of 1714 shows all of the foregoing save Harristown. The Down Survey map of Co. Kildare, compiled in 1656, shows Kilcullen, Carragh, Clane and New Bridge (St Wolstan's).

The first question concerning Carragh is whether or not the present bridge is the one recorded in 1656. No earlier mentions were found in the literature so the estimation of its age rests on its engineering characteristics and

Fig. 95: *Carragh Bridge: Upriver Elevation*

Fig. 96: *Carragh Bridge: Central Cutwater Uprivei*

Fig. 97: *Carragh Bridge: Downriver Elevation*

Fig. 98: *Carragh Bridge: Largest original Arch*

historical factors. A section of the bridge is given in fig. 231, Appendix 8. The spans range from 14ft 6in. to 18ft 9in. and the pier thickness from 8ft to 11ft. The upriver cutwaters are triangular (fig. 96) with semi-domed cappings—an unusual characteristic. The downriver cutwaters (fig. 97) are trapezoidal in cross-section tapering from normal water level to road level. The tops have been concreted to carry a watermain. They actually form buttresses, somewhat like those on the 1567 Athlone Bridge*. Three arches, numbers 1,2 and 6 on section, have wedge-shaped voussoirs and were obviously rebuilt in the 18th and 19th centuries. The

roadway is 10ft 6in. wide between parapets. All the arches are segments of circles.

A head on view of the larger of the three surviving and undoubtedly original arches is shown in fig. 98. Its span is 18ft 9in. compared with 14ft 6in. for each of the other two originals. The intrados curves of all three are true segments of circles. An analysis of the smaller arches showed that they have radii of 7ft 6in. and a rise to span ratio of 0.41. The larger arch has a radius of 10ft and a rise to span ratio of 0.34. The springing levels and crowns of all the arches including the rebuilt ones are all level with each other. The variation in spans would appear to have arisen from pier foundation problems. There is no rock near the surface in the river bed, so some juggling may have been needed during the construction. The crowns of the arches were kept level by the simple expedient of adjusting the rise of the larger arches and using a larger radius intrados curve.

The ring stones in the older arches are between 18in. and 24in. deep and 3in. to 6in. thick all rough hewn. The joints are more or less radial. The stonework throughout, apart from the rebuilt rings, is in random rubble of high quality. None of the piers show signs of rebuilding so it would appear that ring deformation, slightly evident in the surviving large arch, was the cause of arch failure; they may have been broken down as a defensive measure.

The parapet walls, 4ft high by 18ins. thick, of this bridge are an attractive feature apart from a few rebuilt sections. The copings consist of tilted stone slabs with the tilt reversed about every 10ft by the insertion of a triangle of horizontal stones. There are three road drainage outlets each fitted with an anti-dribble cill. None of the cutwaters was extended to form a pedestrian refuge.

From the foregoing there can be little doubt that this bridge could fit into any period between about 1450 and 1650. An earlier bridge would probably have some surviving pointed segmental arches like New Bridge* (St Wolstan's) further downriver. If the bridge was erected in the time of Sir Henry Sidney one would expect it to have some Tudor characteristics like Athlone and Ballinasloe. Sherlock[3] states that there was an old bridge at Clane, of great antiquity, with six arches. Clane was an important crossing in the 15th and 16th centuries and a terminal of the pale rampart from Kilcock. The replacement bridge, called

Alexandra, was erected in 1864. Newbridge, upriver on the road from Kildare to Naas, was mentioned by Dunton in 1698; it does not appear on any of the Down Survey maps. The bridge is shown on Moll's map (1714). It collapsed in a flood in the 1780s. The present reinforced concrete bridge was erected in 1936.

The ancient and historic town of Kildare remained a Norman outpost during the Gaelic resurgence in the 14th and 15th centuries. Communication between it and the diminished Pale east of the Liffey was obviously through Kilcullen, evidenced by the fact that Maurice Jakis, canon of the cathedral in Kildare, erected a stone bridge there in 1319 (see Leighlin Bridge). Given this evidence it would appear that Carragh Bridge led to nowhere of importance, as the ways to the west and northwest were stopped by the Bog of Allen. However, a closer examination of Taylor's, Moll's and Petty's maps shows that it was the principal road to Carbery via Graig, or Killmeague. Carbery, like Naas, was an important medieval town and was linked with Phillipstown, Clonard and Cloncurry, all of which were key junction locations on roads to the west and south west of Ireland. The importance of the Cloncurry, for example, was shown in Chapter 3, Part I, by the munificent land grant given to Patrick Cullen in 1600 for erecting Johnstown Bridge (replaced in 1840s). The Down Survey map shows that the Naas barony boundary encompassed Carragh Bridge. This could imply that the statement in the Statute Rolls for 1463 (see Chapter 3, Part I) that grants made by Henry VI (1422–61) for murage, pavage and repair of the bridges of Trim, Naas, Navan, Athboy, Kells and Fore had greatly strengthened these towns. It is difficult to envisage the commerce of Naas being improved by a bridge other than Carragh.

Local historians and antiquaries will, it is hoped, pursue the dating problem because apart from Carragh being the oldest survivor on the Liffey, it seems to be a rare example of the transition from the pointed segmental to the segmental arc form in bridge construction in Ireland.

Harristown Bridge

There is a tall stately seven-arch bridge across the Liffey in Harristown estate near Brannockstown between Kilcullen and Ballymore

Eustace. The bridge is shown as part of the public road from Harristown to Brannockstown on Taylor's map (1783). The present public road is carried across the Liffey by the four-span Carnalway bridge which carries a plaque "Ino La Touche Esq/Built this Bridge/AD 1788." A journal note explains: "The enclosing with a wall of the Harristown Estate c.1783 necessitated the changing of the road from Naas to Dunlavin and when this was changed a bridge called to this day New bridge was built by John La Touche. The right to make these changes was secured by act of Parliament. The bridge bears the date 1788 having been built about two years after the Harristown property passed into the hands of the La Touche family".[4]

I was unable to track down the authorisation act; however under 5 Geo. IIc. 1 (1765), an act for granting to his majesty an additional duty on beer, etc . . ." I found the following provision: "The sum of six hundred pounds to Sir Dixon Burrowes baronet and Arthur Pomeroy Esq., knights of the shire of the county of Kildare, to be by them, or either of them, applied in aid of the said county to repair and finish the two bridges of Harristown and Kilcullen over the Liffey in said county, in such proportion as the necessities of each bridge may appear to them, or either of them, to require, to be accountable to Parliament." It would appear from this that Kilcullen Bridge was substantially reconstructed or rebuilt in the last quarter of the 18th century. This in fact explains the well-cut voussoirs in it. The new

Fig. 99: *Harristown Bridge: Central Arches Upriver*

Harristown bridge was strengthened by Kildare Co. Council in 1981.

The old bridge in the estate has seven semicircular arches. The central arch (fig. 99) has a span of approximately 26ft flanked by three with spans of 22ft, 21ft and 20ft approximately, on each side. The piers are about 7ft 6in. thick. The arch rings, 24in. deep, are constructed of thin slabs of unhewn stone, the joints being radial. The masonry in the whole bridge is random rubble of excellent quality. There are triangular cutwaters fore and aft. The height of the bridge from parapet coping to river bed is 24ft.

The width of the road between parapets is 17ft. The parapet walls are 2ft 6in. high and have piers over the central arch and the second arches from each end. The piers are supported by corbels on the river side an unusual feature. There are no pedestrian refuges. The parapet copings have a slightly curved overall profile accomplished by increasing the spans towards the centre while keeping the springings level—somewhat like Leighlin Bridge* but less pronounced; nevertheless sufficient to

distinguish it from Carragh and other pre-17th century Liffey bridges.

The bridge probably dates from the second half of the 17th century. If it were pre-1660 one would expect it to be marked on some of Petty's maps. It is located at the point where the 16th-century rampart of the Pale from Naas to the south met the Liffey and within the barony of Naas.

Lissenhall

This five-arched bridge (fig. 100) is located on National Route 1 one mile north of Swords. It was retired from service in the 1970s when traffic was diverted on to a new dual carriageway which crosses the Broadmeadow sixty yards downriver. The old bridge has been retained as part of a neat, tidy and well kept Dublin Co. Council roadside rest area to which it provides pedestrian access.

St Colmcille founded a monastery in Swords as far back as the 6th century. The original, Irish, version is Sord Columcille, that is, the pure well of Colmcille. There are numerous

Fig. 100: *Lissenhall Bridge: Upriver Elevation*

references to the area in the Annals up to the 13th century.[1] It became an important Norman town *c.*1200 when John Comyn, the first Norman archbishop of Dublin, came to reside there and built a castle on an episcopal manor. After the Bruce invasion in 1326 the residence was transferred to Tallaght. Among all these mentions no reference was found to a bridge over the Broadmeadow. It would appear that the principal route to the north from Swords was through Rathbeale and from there via Roganstown, the Naul and Dardistown to Drogheda and the north.

The Down Survey for the area compiled in 1656 is shown in Map 1, Part I. Lissenhall Bridge is clearly marked in its present location. The Lissen, that is, fort later castle, is also shown just north of the bridge. The bridge is also shown on Moll's map (1714), Rocque's (1756) and all later maps. It can be assumed therefore that there was a bridge here since the first half of the seventeenth century. In the absence of earlier literature mentions the question of dating depends on the characteristics.

The bridge has three abutting sections evident in fig. 101, which shows part of the intrados of the second arch and second pier counted from the south bank, looking downriver. The Armco culvert under the by-pass road is visible in the background. The middle section, indicated by the larger pier stones and continuous higher level shutter corbels, has been rebuilt. However, the first arch is intact and it is evident from the masonry in it that the central part, 15ft wide, is the oldest. There are slight lips at the extension joints. The central section has much more mortar adhering to the surface of the sheeting and some traces of wattle marks; it is slightly pointed at the crown. The mortar was obviously poured into the joints. The spans of the arches are between 8ft and 10ft and the piers 7ft wide.

The upriver extension is 16ft wide and the downriver 12ft. The spans of the extensions were kept the same as the original. The face ring stones on the upriver extension (fig. 102) are composed of thin stone slabs averaging about 18in. deep and 4in. thick, whereas those on the downriver face (fig. 103) are wider and better shaped but not true voussoirs. There are about 25 per cent more ring stones in each arch upriver for the same length of intrados curve. The joints are radial in both extensions

Fig. 101: *Lissenhall Bridge: Pier and Intrados of Repaired Central Section, and Upriver Extension*

Fig. 102: *Lissenhall Bridge: Central Arch Upriver*

Fig. 103: *Lissenhall Bridge: First Arch S. Bank, Downriver*

Fig. 104: *Lispopple Bridge: Downriver Elevation*

apart from a few erratics. The arches are segmental arcs, almost semi-circular.

The upriver cutwaters are triangular and bulky due to the need to adhere to the thicknesses of the original piers. The semi-pyramidal cutwater cappings are a feature of the bridge because they are faced on the arises with tailor-made-cut-stone slabs which have a banded support plinth. There are no cutwaters on the downriver side. It is not possible to determine whether the original arch had cutwaters because all the piers are securely underpinned with concrete. This work was probably carried out in the early 1950s under the Local Authority Works Act. I recollect seeing this bridge flow full and the water on to the road in the great flood of 1955 when Rolestown Bridge four miles upriver was washed away. The two-span bridge at Lispopple (fig. 104), three miles upriver, has ring stones somewhat similar to the upriver extension of Lissenhall, but its date of construction is after 1760.

The evidence from the characteristics of the original middle section of Lissenhall bridge— that is, spans of 10ft or less, span to pier ratios of between 1.0 and 1.5, overall width of 15ft, poured mortar joints, wattle marks, slightly pointed crowns—suggest that it is pre-1600. If it were earlier than 1450, one would expect to find some evidence of pointed segmental arches at the butt joints such as in Slane Bridge*, but there is none. The most likely period is between 1450 and 1550, which would

make it the oldest surviving road bridge within a 10-mile radius of Dublin city centre. Further research in the context of the history of Swords and the adjoining would probably define the date more precisely.

Drogheda

All the present bridges across the Boyne at Drogheda are relatively modern, but they had many predecessors with frequent mentions in historical documents. The first recorded mention of the word *droichet* refers to a bridge across the tidal estuary of the Boyne: " . . . and the cave of Gobhann at Droichead ata were broken into and plundered by the foreigner" (AFM 861). That bridge was obviously located at a ford— the first clue to its location on the river. Was it at Oldbridge, within the present town, or in between? Hamilton[1] produces evidence indicating that the northern road from Tara in ancient times, the Slighe Miodhluchra, crossed the Boyne in the neighbourhood of Drogheda and then ran on to Dundalk and the north. He quotes Caithrein Conghail Clairinghnigh:[2] "Conghal marched northwards from Tara reached Benna Anann which is called Benna Briog and thence saw the host of the King of Ireland's son whom he met at Ath fuar, alias Ath in Oighe on the Boyne where the fresh water and the salt water rush together and it is thereby the colder." Benna Briog is between the baronies of Upper and Lower Slane; Ath Oighe means the deer ford. This would suggest a ford upriver from the present town, near the saline interface, in the pre-Christian era when Tara flourished. D'Alton[3] states that Drogheda has been described as Pons Vadi, Pontana Civitas, Droheda, Drocheda, Drohed, and sometimes Treaid and Tredagh.

The problem of the location of the original bridge was discussed in depth by Fr Colmcille, the historian of Mellifont, in an appendix to his book[4] in 1958. In his research he drew upon the information in the charters of Mellifont and established that it was known as the Monastery of the Bridge of the Ford in the 12th century. The monastery is located on the Mattoc river which enters the Boyne near Oldbridge. The latter derived its name from the fact that the early bridge erected on the site of the present town of Drogheda was then known as Novus Pons. Gradually the original site became known as Vetere Ponte (Old Bridge). He concluded "that by the year 1214 or thereabouts the original bridge of Droichead Atha was already being called the old bridge and that name became stereotyped afterwards".

There is the record, mentioned in Part I, of Walter de Lacey being granted a licence by King John in 1208 to erect a mill at the bridge of Drogheda; also, evidence that a town was built before that by Hugh de Lacey on the south bank of the Boyne in Drogheda. Bradley[5] reviewed all the relevant literature recently and came to the conclusion that Fr Colmcille has gone a long way in explaining the problem. He also states that the Anglo-Norman town lay at a narrow bridging point on the tidal estuary, five miles from the open sea.

In 1213 King John granted the law of the bridge toll to the burgesses of Drogheda.[6] In 1228 Henry III authorised his good men of Drogheda to levy tolls in aid of making the bridge of Drogheda. These bridges were most probably timber bridges which had short lives, particularly in saline estuaries, as explained in Chapter 7, Part I. Drogheda Castle was taken over by the king as a royal stronghold of the Pale in the 13th century. In 1330 the Annals record[7] (see Babes Bridge) that all the bridges on the Boyne, timber and stone, save Babes, were washed away and much damage done at Drogheda. We have independent evidence of the damage in the history of the Franciscan abbey,[8] St Mary's de Urso, but also mention of the fact that it was shortly afterwards restored.

There is an early record in *Analecta Hibernica*[9] on Duleek barony which states that "This city (Drogheda) is built of stone houses very decent part whereof is situated on the north side of the river in the Co. Louth and part on the south side of the river over which there is a very fair stone bridge." The date is not given but it is certainly medieval.

D'Alton's *History of Drogheda*[3] states that in 1472, on the feast of St Jerome, the bridge of Drogheda is recorded to have fallen down in consequence of a flood. The replacement bridge was a timber structure on low stone piers and was not completed until 1506. This record (source not given) suggests that the arches of a stone bridge were washed away and a timber deck was then put on the piers. It was a period when the Pale was on the defensive and funds may have been very scarce in the town.

There is a map of Drogheda by Robert Newcomen dated 1657 which shows the bridge very clearly between the two walled towns with a gate and fortification on the north bank. The small map diagram of the bridge outlined in fig. 247, Appendix 8 shows four circular arches and clearly indicates that there was a masonry arch here at the time shortly after Cromwell's slaughter of the defenders and people alike in 1649.

Boulge[10] gives interesting information on the Boyne in 1691 stating that it was easily fordable when the tide was out and even when it was high several fords remained passable. He refers to several fords at Oldbridge which were "quite easy at half flood" but that lower down at Donore was only crossable at low water. It was forded by the Williamites during the battle.

Moll's map shows a bridge at Oldbridge in 1714 but the town symbol obliterates the crossing at Drogheda so it is impossible to identify. Ellison[11] states that a stone bridge was erected by Stephen Price of Clones and J. Bencher in 1722 at Drogheda at a cost of £3,000 and that the old bridge was demolished in 1723, which suggests a different site. Parts of the 1722 bridge collapsed in 1814.

The *Dublin Builder*[12] gives a very interesting report on St Mary's Bridge in 1866: "The contractors Messrs (Brennan & Costello) are pushing on the works in a spirited manner. The northern abutment is already up as far as the springing and the cofferdam for the south side will be complete for this bridge in a few days. The preparations for building centre pier are also in an advanced state. From what we have seen of the structure so far we may say that the *modus operandi* of the present contractors will bear favourable contrast with that adopted by former one, whose failure in carrying out the work we noticed in our pages some months ago."

The news from upriver in the following year was not so good: "within the past fortnight . . . an occurrence has taken place to the wooden bridge, which was erected about fourteen years ago, over the River Boyne at Oldbridge. It would appear that the ice in February last had so completely shaken the bearing timbers of the bridge that its fall was daily anticipated."[13] It then goes on to report that warning notices had been put up and that the entire north side had fallen. It was proposed to erect a substantial stone bridge in its place a few hundred yards eastwards at a place where the water was shallower. The 1837 map shows a ford about a quarter of a mile downstream of the bridge that was there at the time. The bridge eventually erected in 1867 was the present iron lattice one.[14]

The Drogheda Bridge of 1867 was demolished in 1981 and during the construction of the present bridge the contractor's engineer, Mr Doyle of Irish ENCO, told me that his firm were having great difficulty in excavating within the sheet pile cofferdam for the centre piers, due to ancient structures. Drogheda Harbour Commissioners have a record showing that the pre-1867 bridge was a three-span masonry arch.

A 250ft long, two-span, pre-stressed concrete bridge erected in 1975–6 downriver is described by McMahon and Faherty in a paper[15] presented to the IEI in 1976.

Athlone

This survey of the history of the most historic river crossing in Ireland focuses on the bridge erected in 1567 but excludes the present bridge opened in 1842. The early mentions in the Annals are given verbatim in Appendix 1 and fully discussed in Part I, so it is sufficient to list them briefly: AD 994 bridge made, 1120 and 1132 bridges made; 1135 and 1154 destroyed; 1155 *cliath droichet* made by O'Connor and destroyed by Maelseachlainn; 1159 battle over the erection of a *cliath droichet*.

In 1210 the king's justice, de Grey, advanced on Athlone to build a stone castle and a wooden bridge. In the same year King John commanded the archbishop of Dublin (then justiciar) to cause the Cluniac monks of Athlone to have a tenth part of the expense of the castle in the town, in exchange for their land on which the castle was situated.[1] In 1233 the Annals of Ulster record that "the masonry work of the castle of Rinndun was ordered to be suspended so as to enable the bridge of Athlone to be completed out of money from the King's treasure." It was estimated that the completion of the bridge would cost 80 marks, 30 marks to be employed on carriage and 50 marks on the works. This is also recorded in *CDI* 1171–1251. (A mark was worth 13s. 4d.) In 1233–4 there are entries in the Pipe Roll of 13 Henry III for expenses for work and wages at the bridge of

Athlone and the castle and receipts for pontage. The Annals of Lough Ce record that Hugh O'Connor burned the mill of Athlone and broke down its bridge in 1270–72. The bridge must have been repaired quickly because in 1279 Edward I granted to the Cluniac monks the weirs, fisheries of Athlone, the toll of the bridge and eight acres at the rent of £12.[2]

Early in the 14th century, between 1302 and 1306, payments were made "for making a bridge at Athlone" according to a pipe roll reviewed in the *38th Report* of the Deputy Keeper of Public Records. No information was found about this bridge as to whether it was stone or timber or both, it must have been lasted a long time because the next mention is by Sir Henry Sidney, the lord deputy in his "Miscellany of Irish Affairs" addressed to the Secretary of State in England in 1583, preserved in London and reproduced in successive volumes of the *Ulster Journal of Archaeology*, 1853–60. Sidney records that "Sept. 1566, I passed without boat or bridge the dangerous river of Omagh, Derg, Finn; at last I came to the great water of sea arm Lough Foyle when I found boats as appointed to convey me and my army over . . . Passing the great water of Assuroe . . .From there I went to Athlone . . . I gave order then for the making of the bridge of Athlone which I finished, a piece found servicible. I am sure durable it is and I think memorable." The commemorative tablets on Sidney's bridge were taken down by the Commissioners of Public Works before it was demolished with the intention of re-erecting them on the new bridge, but "Athlone declined the honour" and the Commissioners brought them to Dublin. They were later presented to the Royal Irish Academy and eventually found their way to the National Museum. The tablets are important from another aspect. Dr John Jackson, former director of the Natural History Museum, told me some years ago that as a rough rule inscriptions such as these before 1700 are in bas-relief; and after 1700 they are incised. The plaques comply with this guide. Joly[3] states work on the bridge commenced in the summer of 1566 and ended July 1567 (Mills[4] gives November as the finishing date).

When Sidney got back to Dublin he evidently recruited Sir Peter Lewys to organise and supervise the bridge's construction. Berry[5] states that a commission was issued to Lewys at the residence of the lord deputy in Kilmain-

A transcript of portion of the general account of Lewys for the works (in the Public Record Office of Ireland), which is for one year ending 20th October, 1567, will be of interest.

The Declaraçon of Thaccompt of Sr Peter Lewez, clerke, s^{r}veior or overseer of the works there, that is to saie, as well of all and singler such somes of money as he hath hadd and received of Sr Willm ffitzWillm, knight, Treasorer at Warres, and of others victualls and muniçons to and for the building of the said bridge. As also of Thissewing emploing and defrainge of the same for wagies pviçons cariages and other chardges whatsoever defrayed expended and laid owte and about the foresaid bridge, beyng thereunto assigned and auothorised by thonorable Sr Henry Sydney, knight of the most noble order, president of the counsaile established in the m^{r}ches of Wales and L. Deputie Gen^{r}all of the said realme of Ireland by commission to the said accomptant in that behalf directed, the tenor whereof ensewith.

Wagies of sundrie artificers and laborers, viz. :

Carpenters. ffirst, paid wthin the tyme aforesaid for the wages of lviij carpenters, viz. : one at ij^s ster p diem st lxxij^d xvi. at xij^d str le pece p diem st xxviij^{li} xviij^s xl at ix^d le pece p diem s. lxj^{li} xviij^s iiij^d and one at x^d p diem s. liij^s iiij^d In all as in the saide pticuler books is at lardge contained s——

iiij^{xx}xvij^{li} xx^d

Shipp Wryghts. Also paid for the waiges of ij shipp wryghts thone at xviij^d ster p diem and thother at xij^d p diem amounting to wthin the said tyme as by the pticuler book may appere.

lxvij^s vj^d

Masons. Also paid for the wagies of cxxxiij masons, viz. : lxxiij at xij^d ster le pece p diem s. vij^c iiij^{xx} viij^{li} xix^s l^{tie} at x^d the pece p diem cccciiij^{xx} x^{li} iij^s iij^d and x at ix^d the pece p diem s. x^{li} xvij^s vi^d In all as in the two pticuler booke is at lardge contained may appere.

m^{l}ccciiij^{xx}ix^{li} xix^s ix^d

Lyme Burners. Also paid for the wagies of iij lyme burners wthin the tyme aforesaid, viz. : one at xij^d p diem s. viij^{li} ij^s the second at ix^d p diem s. xxij^s vj^d and the third at iiij^d p diem s lxij^s viij^d In all as in the said pticuler booke may apperes.

xij^{li} vij^s ij^d

Collyers. Also paid to iiij^{or} colliers making of charcoole wthin the said tyme for there wagies at iiij^d le pece p diem amount to in all as in the said pticuler booke yt may appere. s.

cix^s j^d

Smythes. Also for the wagies of two smythes making and reparing thartificers Tooles wthin the tyme aforesaid at xviij^d le pece p diem amounting to as by the said pticuler booke maye appere. s.

xlv^{li} xiiij^s x^d

Laborers. Also paid wthin the tyme aforsad for the wagies of ix laborers at vj^d le pece p diem, amounting to as by the said pticuler Bookes doth appere.

viij^{li} xiij^s ix^d

Fees and wagies of officers :

Sr Peter Lewes. Also paid and allowed unto the said Sr Peter Lewez accomptaunt for one hole yeres fee or wagies, ended the xxth of Octobre, 1567, as by his pticuler bookes apperithe. xl^{li}

Prest Money.

First, paid to cxiiij masons of Gallway for there prest money at xij^d sterling the pece, as by the pticuler bookes aforesaid apperithe. s.

cxiiij^s sterling.

	£	s.	d.
	97	1	8
	3	7	6
	1289	13	9
	12	7	2
	5	9	1
	45	14	10
	8	13	9
	40	0	0
	5	14	0
Total	1508	1	9

Fig. 105: *Athlone Bridge: Lewys's Account for the 1567 Bridge*

Fig. 106: *Athlone Bridge: T. Phillips's Sketch c.1680*

ham on 10 November 1566 "which after reciting the necessity for a new bridge of stone, and declaring Sidney's confidence in his fidelity, experience and circumspection in that kind of building, authorised him to act as surveyor and overseer of the works in connection with the building and repairing the said bridge at Athlone". Lewys was required to repair thither immediately to make provisions, at reasonable prices, in the matter of timber, boards, planks, lathes, stone, lime, iron, rails etc. and to engage all manner of artificers, as carpenters, masons, hand hewers, quarriers, and labourers together with means of carriage by land or by water.

At this stage it is necessary to point out that the main sources of our information on Lewys, apart from plaques placed on the bridge when it was completed which have survived, are James Mills, deputy keeper of Public Records, and Henry Berry, assistant keeper, both writing at the turn of the century. Their basic source of information was a meticulously detailed diary kept by Lewys as proctor of Christ Church Dublin, 1564–5, and his general account for the Athlone Bridge for the year ending 20 October 1567 when the bridge was finished. Mills[6] stated that Lewys's Journal for the year 1564/5, was kept in Trinity College Library and Berry stated that the general account was a transcript of a portion in the Public Record Office. It appears that the latter perished in the fire of 1922.

Mills states that Lewys was an English regular, appointed rector of Kilteel (Reformed Church) by the Crown, c.1540, and that he afterwards held some small benefices in Dublin and Kildare before his appointment to Christ Church as precentor and from October 1564 as proctor. In the latter capacity he was in charge of major building work including the underpinning of foundations and construction of walls and arches in the crypt—a major work and an intricate one, all described in Lewys's 1564/5 diary and recounted in Mills' paper. The extraordinary Athlone tradition about the beginning and the end of Lewys's career, as outlined on one of the bridge plaques, will be adverted to later.

The general account for the bridge is an invaluable record in the context of bridge building in Ireland in the last half of the 16th century and is reproduced in fig. 105 in full with an additional column giving the Arabic equivalents of the Roman numerals in which Lewys recorded the accounts for the bridge.

The total cost for wages was £1,508 1s. 9d. An engineer might be inclined to add the same amount for materials and for plant etc. and say the overall cost was about £5,000, but that would be wrong, because the cost of producing and transporting much of the material (stone and lime) is included in the wages. From the first paragraph of the account, we see there were other accounts for "victuals and municians" etc. and note that the money came from the treasurer for war. This was a military operation with civilians employed as well. The O'Connors on the west bank of the Shannon would not have allowed work to proceed for long if there had not been a small army of troops guarding the works. In these circum-stances it is useless to speculate about the total cost of the bridge, which was certainly very high. The Tudor lord deputies thought little of the expense as evidenced by Perrot's report of 25 October 1584 reproduced in Chapter 3, Part I. There was almost a province to be annexed once the bridge was built, or so it seemed in Dublin Castle. Joly states that "the Rev." Sir Peter Lewys was architect and "Robert Damport" overseer, who was later appointed provost marshall of Connaught.

The times and prices are not very meaningful without information on the original bridge and its characteristics. It was altered extensively between 1568 and 1833, when it was measured and an accurate plan and elevation prepared by Thomas Rhodes. The elevation is shown in fig. 232, Appendix 8. There are sketches prepared by Lover and Petrie dating from the mid-19th century. This is later than a partial rebuilding in 1731. Fortunately Joly discovered a copy of a print described as "Athlone in 1625 from Phillip's ordnance maps made for Charles II and now amongst the Ormond papers in Kilkenny Castle", reproduced in fig. 106. The date must be wrong because Charles II reigned from 1660 to 1695. In fact it must be from the same report[7] referred to in Part I, prepared by Thomas Phillips presented to James II on 24 March 1685/6, though I found no reference to it when I examined the published version of that report. The difference is not significant because the mills were added in 1568 and the arches were not rebuilt until 1731.

I first thought that the four arches were pointed segmentals in the style of Babes*, Adare*, Trim* and the old Limerick Baals* bridges, and was puzzled why Lewys should choose such an arch style, then obsolete in Ireland as elsewhere, for such an important bridge. However, on re-examining the print in the knowledge that it was made by such a competent engineer as Thomas Phillips, it became apparent that the intrados of the first and second arches on the right of the sketch have a sharper curvature at the springings. The arches are therefore "four centred, Tudor".

Leask[8] confirms that the four-centred Tudor belonged to the 16th and 17th centuries in Ireland (see Ballinasloe Bridge).

The next remarkable feature of the bridge is the downriver cutwaters; they are really buttresses and they extend to the top of what must have been low parapet walls. The sketch gives the impression that the piers and buttresses are thin; however, the arch ring was at least 18in. and, using that as an indicator, the sketch suggests 2ft-thick buttresses; therefore the piers were at least 5ft and probably more. The corresponding pier on Rhodes's drawing is 9ft, but it may have been rebuilt in 1731. It is tempting to read more into the sketch, but the range of possible estimates would be too great. The remaining four arches are incorporated in the mills erected in 1568 described in Chapter 10. There are notches in the parapet coping probably a defensive rather than an aesthetic characteristic.

The bed of the river in Athlone is described by Mullins[9] as having "a porous sandy bottom, extending to great depth". In fact, it is worse than that, as evidenced by the borings and the expensive measures that have had to be adopted in recent years in building the new by-pass approach roads to the new bridge now under construction. What kind of foundations did Lewys adopt for the 1567 bridge? Mullins (who incidentally was contractor on the massive drainage and navigation works carried out in Athlone in the 1840s) thought up the brilliant plan, albeit used by Queen Nicore of the Assyrians BC., whereby the river was drained off just above the bridge and the water diverted into the old canal having previously allowed the level in Lough Rea to drop such that it could gradually rise 2ft 6ins. and store water, leaving 30 days to excavate and lower the river bed in the town below the new bridge. In his description of the works he notes: "There having been a large quantity of excavation to be removed from the bed of the river, consisting in a great part of the foundations and sterlings of the old bridge and of old walls and mill dams not removable by dredging . . ."—which shows that the piers were built on sterlings, that is, small *crannoga* made with timber piles and bigger than the piers, with the centre filled with gravel and stones. This was not a great problem, as explained under Timber Bridges in Part I. Pile-driving rigs operated by men or animals would have been available. In fact Lewys's diary records that on 17 May 1564 work was in progress under the steeple of Christchurch: "I did build a pile with oak timber. I filled in the foundation with rock lime and then piled upon the same stakes of spires ten feet long, set down in the ground with great violence and strength of foundation by great sledges, beaten by men. And upon that, pieces of oak ten inches square, laid upon that again and set with rock lime upon the same that the mortar to fill all the work and to fill betwixt all the timber." Another layer, the same was set before he set the foundation stone. He probably built a similar type of grillage inside the bridge starlings for the foundations for the piers of the Athlone Bridge.

There is a much-quoted comment from a letter by the dean of Armagh, dated 1567, that "all Connaught was tamed by the building of the new bridge". However, a paper on Sts Peter & Paul's Church, Athlone[10] states that in 1570 the Elizabethan government converted the priory into a store but O'Conor Don with Irish and Scottish allies angered by this desecration burnt down all the buildings on the site in 1572.

There is a record[11] of 16 May 1654: "It is Ordered, that the Commissioners of the Revenue at Athlone do Issue out their Warrants to the Treasurer of the Publick Revenue there to pay out of the Receipts of Excise coming into his hands the Sum of fifty pounds upon Account, unto such person as they shall think fit to receive the same, for and towards the finishing of the Reparation of the Bridge of Athlone; and the said Commissioners of the Revenue are to take a particular Account upon Oath of the person abovesaid how the said Money shall be so by him disbursed for the Use aforesaid."

The repair work must have been on an arch or arches broken down by Viscount Dillon as part of the unsuccessful defence of the town by the confederates against the Cromwellians in 1650. The work must not have been carried out satisfactorily because on 11 August 1654 another order of the same kind was made, this time "to pay such person . . . for management of that work" such sums as from time to time were needed. The bridge is shown on the Down Survey map, so there probably was a temporary plank bridge across the broken span (s).

The bridge became part of Irish and European history in 1690–1 when it was the focal

point of the Williamite siege. The Jacobites, commanded by Colonel Richard Grace, threw down "two arches" as part of the defenses of the crossing as De Ginkle attacked. Story[12] records that on 26 June 1691 "Thirty wagons laden with powder came to us; and that night we got possession of all the bridges [i.e. arches] except one arch on the Connaught side which had been broken down. We repair another broken arch in our possession; all night our guns and mortars play most furiously. For the design of passing the river at the ford (Lanesborough) being frustrated . . . we labour hard to gain the bridge; but what we got there was inch by inch . . . . June 28, Sunday. By the morning, our beams were laid over the broken arch and partly planked." The remainder is immortalised in Aubrey de Vere's stirring but poignant ballad[13]:

Break down the bridge six warriors rushed
Through storm of shot and storm of shell"
. . . .
Again at the rocking planks they dashed;
And four dropped dead; and two remained:
The huge beams groaned, and the arch
    down crashed,
Two stalwart swimmers the margin gained.

The passage was forced by a party who crossed at the old ford a little downstream of the bridge and by another over a bridge of boats upriver on 30 June 1691 and the town was taken by the Williamites. No mention was found about the repair of the bridge.

In Phillips' sketch there is a pedimented niche in the upriver parapet on the pier between the 4th and 5th arch. This housed a collection of tablets relating to the bridge. They are fully documented by Weld in his Statistical Survey of Co. Roscommon[14] and have been the subject of many papers and discussions. The main tablet recorded the date and praised the "good industry and diligence" of Peter Lewys and recorded some of the important events in the reign of "our most dere Soveraign Ladie Elizabeth". The arms of the queen, with those of the earl of Essex and of Sir Henry Sidney were each carved on a separate stone. It records that the head of Shane O'Neill had been set on the gate of Dublin Castle and the whole realm brought into obedience. Another tablet records that "in 1730 this part of the bridge being four arches in ye center was undertaken and built by Benjamin

Price at the expense of the Right Hon. Lady Katherine Jones and the Corporation of Athlone, the Hon. Col. St. George, Sovereign" and that the work was completed in the following year, William Handcock being surveyor and Gustavus Handcock supervisor; John Plume and Edwin Thomas were overseers. This is a very important plaque because it indicates that four of the visible arches were rebuilt and hence sketches made after 130 years do not illustrate the originals, nor does Rhodes' plan and elevation. Tighe states that tolls and pontage (that is, a distinct toll for cattle passing the bridge) was vested one half in the corporation and the other in a society for promoting charter schools, the latter being represented by Lady Hamilton. He also had caustic comment on the charging of tolls in 1815 for passage over a totally inadequate bridge and said that 90 years of accumulation of such ought to have been enough to improve it if applied to the bridge. The grand juries of adjoining counties had refused to contribute for this reason.

Reverting to the plaques and the local tradition about Sir Peter Lewys, one of the tablets (fig. 107) carried the inscription "Petro Lewys Clerico demus nostrae despensatori: hujus operis Praesidi." The raised figure in flowing Geneva gown extends the right arm. The hand holds an unknown object on which is poised a rat in the act of biting the hand. The traditional explanation of this curious sculpture is hotly rejected by all sober historians. It is given here in the words of Caesar Otway who published his *Tour in Connaught*[15] first in the *Dublin Penny Journal* and later in book form a century ago.

Peter Levis is said to have been an English monk who turned Protestant, and coming over to Ireland, was made a dignitary of Christ Church; being a man of great scientific and mechanical knowledge Sir Henry Sidney sent him to superintend the erection of this important bridge; but being a turncoat, a righteous rat, vexed with such tergiversation, followed and haunted him—by day and by night, at bed and board—on horseback or in boat, the disgusting vermin pursued him, slept on his pillow and dipped and dabbled its tail or whisker in all he ate or drank—the church itself could not save him from the persecution. One day in the church of St Mary's, Athlone, he ventured

Fig. 107: *Athlone Bridge: Tablet from the 1567 Bridge Depicting Sir P. Lewys and Rat*

to preach, and lo, this unclean beast kept peering at him with its bitter, taunting eye, all the time he was holding forth; and when he descended from the pulpit after having dismissed the congregation, the cursed creature still remained mocking his reverence. This was too much. Master Lewys presented a pistol, which he had always about him, to shoot it—the sagacious and unaccountable animal, to avert the shot, leapt up on the pistol, as represented on the monument, and seizing the parson's thumb, inflicted such a wound as to bring on a locked jaw, which terminated in his death.

Two very painstaking authors may be consulted by those who wish to read how this tradition can be refuted. Both base their theories on the existence of an older sculptured stone which is now in the National Museum, but which formerly figured on one of the old buildings of the town of Athlone. it is similar to the stone illustrated here, except that the animal on the older stone has no tail. Revd John Joly says it is a lamb, representative of Lewys's spiritual charge. Berry assures us that it is a porcupine, in compliment to the lord deputy on whose crest the latter animal figured!

The reader is free to take his choice among these speculations as to the species of the animal which perches on the hand of Peter Lewys. Caesar Otway was convinced of the veracity of the more picturesque tradition. So much so that he asserted that the origin of the phrase "to rat" as applied to a turncoat is to be found in the story of Peter Lewys's perversion!

Hopefully, the history of the road bridges of Athlone will be suitably depicted, somewhere that is accessible to pedestrians and passing tourists as part of any artwork commissioned to mark the building of the new motorway bridge and approach causies. More importantly, if the new bridge is given a name, let it be a meaningful one reflecting the best traditions of the Celtic imagination as expressed in so many townlands and other names of places and river crossings in Ireland.

Ballinasloe

"I caused a bridge to be begun at that time [c.1570] over the great river Sowke, hard by the castle of Balislogh which since was perfected by the worthy soldier, counsellor and colonel, Sir Nicholas Malby, who finished my work, and a good work for, after I had settled him in that province, I had no cause to care for that province as it well proved by valiant overthrows of the rebels."[1] So wrote Sir Henry Sidney, lord deputy, in 1582. Four centuries later we can confirm that it was indeed "a good work" because it is still there, albeit perforated by a sewer, but now carrying juggernauts in place of slide or truckle cars. Egan[2] summarises from Faulkner's *Dublin Journal*, 1754: "We hear from Ballinasloe that the additional bridge of 912ft and 15ft wide in the Co. Roscommon side of town was begun on 18 May by Wm. Brennan and is now finished, so that the business of the great fair will be carried on with more ease and less confusion than formerly." The report was dated 10 September 1754. The contractor must have had an army of men on the job to complete it in less than four months (that is, before the October fair).

There is confirmation of the first mention of the bridge in the Rolls of Chancery[3] in 1579: "Orders to be observed by Sir Nicholas Maltby for the better government of the province of Connaught . . . And as at our charge a bridge hath been lately built at Ballenslowe upon the River of Sucke and as there is great

likelihood that the same should be shortly overthrown, if the castle there were in the keeping of the Irish or any doubtful or undutiful subject, we have thought meet, in respect of our service, that the said castle be continued in our hands and possession, being the common passage to Galloway . . . and therefore we will you to keep it in our use, with a ward theirin . . .".

On 1 May 1568 Sidney was instructed to "return into Ireland" to his former charge as lord deputy (C.S.I. 1500–73).

Sidney was lord deputy from 1565 to 1567. Another term ran from 1575 to 1578, when Pelham, the lord justice, took over the duties. It is recorded that he was made lord deputy on four occasions between 1558 and 1578. He died in 1586 in Ludlow Castle at the age of 56. The memoir does not give the year of construction of Ballinasloe Bridge. Athlone was erected in 1567 and the question of which came first is relevant. The 1579 Roll uses the word "lately", so it would be prudent to refer to the original Ballinasloe Bridge as the 1570 bridge.

Leask[4] states that the Annals record that in 1124 a castle was erected at Ballinasloe but it was "burned by casual fire" in 1131; hence he concludes it was not of mortared stone. The ford was obviously a most important crossing point on the Suck from early times. The Down Survey map shows the bridge, the castle and small groups of houses on or near each bank. The bridge is shown on Moll's map (1714). The two bridges are shown on Taylor and Skinner's map (1778) and most interestingly the river is shown as having two channels, one at the west end of Bridge Street and the second where the present 1878 main channel is located. The single surviving tower of that keep of the medieval castle is shown and immediately east of it the Ballinasloe (East) Bridge is indicated by black dashes, north and south, but without extension of the channel in either direction.

The grand jury records of Co. Galway or Roscommon have not survived (apart from any that may be in private collections) and as a result we have little information on the bridges until 1878 when the sluice gate bridge was built over a new channel under a drainage scheme. This became the main channel of the river. Sometime in the early 20th century a sewer was laid along Sraid an Droichid, presumably to serve the mental hospital erected in 1838. The sewer is carried on a composite beam of tramrails and concrete which cuts through all but one of the crowns of the Tudor arches of the 1570 bridge.

I had an opportunity to inspect and take photographs of this bridge, for the first time, in August 1989. I expected to find none of the Sidney arches remaining and did not have a map of larger scale than the OS half-inch with which to figure out the river channels. The surviving bawn tower on the right travelling west was a signal to stop and park. No river channel was visible on either side; however, a closer look there was a bridge underneath obscured by undergrowth. The first glimpse of an arch with ashlar voussoirs, scrambling down the sloped bank of the filled-in downriver channel, suggested a mid-18th century structure. The bed was dry so it was possible to walk in under the arch; half way along it the intrados curve changed from a segment of a circle to a pointed segmental which sprang from the pier and abutment 18in. higher up. This had to be the 1570 bridge because the intrados was similar to the Phillips 1665 sketch of the 1567 old bridge of Athlone. Closer inspection in the dim light showed that there were small radii curves at the springings, making it a Tudor arch of lower stature than Athlone.

The old arch had been perforated by the sewer beam mentioned above but was otherwise intact. A 7ft 6in. wide reinforced concrete slab supported on concrete pier extensions had been added upriver. There are, therefore, three generations of bridge here. The original is 14ft wide and the 1745 downriver extension 13ft 6in. The span is 12ft and the height of the crown 7ft over the bed. There are two other similar arches in this bridge with 20ft wide piers in between. There is a detectable difference in the sheeting stonework: the original has more mortar exposed and, surprisingly, the stones in it are more angular than in the 1745 extension.

Most of the field stones in the vicinity had been probably used up in building the castle, so quarried stone may have had to be used for the bridge in 1570, whereas Brennan in 1745 may have pilfered the stone from the castle walls and ruins to build the extension. The lip between the segmental and Tudor arches is about 9in. at the springing point of the latter. The crowns and the lower courses of the abutments are in line at bed level. There are no cutwaters downriver. The concrete extension destroyed any evidence of upriver cutwaters.

Having completed the inspection I proceeded across the 1878 bridge between its dour, massive, parapets and just at the end of Sraid an Droichid there appeared the second bridge, later identified from the OS six-inch map as Ballinasloe Bridge, the former being designated "Ballinasloe Bridge East". Here there is a multiplicity of river and mill race channels, all now dry. Entry to the river bed was easy through an open gateway in the downriver parapet. Again the first glimpse confirmed that Brennan had extended this bridge also in 1745. The weeds and vegetation had all been cleared and the whole presented a very neat appearance. Halfway through the first arch the Tudor intrados appeared, but the abutments and pier supporting it were constructed in ashlar masonry so that one could mistakenly assume the downriver section to be older. Emerging on the other side all doubts were dispelled when the upriver elevation came into comprehensive view because each arch had its own unique intrados curve.

The upriver elevation of the four arches of the former main channel, based on an OPW drawing, is given in fig. 233, Appendix 8. Each arch is numbered, 1 to 4, to correspond with the photographs below. The facing ring of arch 1, has a segmental intrados with a rise of one-third the span. It is half-covered with ivy. The sheeting behind it has the appearance of a Tudor arch.

Arch 2 shown in fig. 108 has a three-centred intrados curve with a rise of approximately one third of the span. The ring stones were obviously cut from templates, but many joints are not radial. I believe that this arch was one of the last to be built in Sidney's bridge and that it was deliberately made into a three-centred by extending the curvature at the crown.

Arch 3 (fig. 109) has clear-cut Tudor four-centred characteristics. The crown, which should be pointed, is slightly rounded. The curvature at the springings, particularly on the right, is obviously an attempt, probably by two different masons, to imitate a Tudor depressed arch. It was easier to round off the crown rather than cut a proper keystone. Fig. 110 shows the downstream face of arch 4 and the radial jointed arch form erected by William Brennan's masons in 1745 when attempting to

Fig. 108: *Ballinasloe Bridge: Three-centred Arch 2, Upriver*

Fig. 109: *Ballinasloe Bridge: Four-centred Arch 3, Upriver*

Fig. 110: *Ballinasloe Bridge: Downriver Extension to Arch 4*

Fig. 111: *Ballinasloe Bridge: Four-centred Arch 4, Upriver*

marry the sheeting with the older arch. Fig. 111 shows the upriver face of the same arch.

There are massive cutwaters on the east bridge upriver between the arches. They are filled with gravel and faced with 12in. x 18in. x 6in. stone slabs, probably erected when the bridge was underpinned as part of a 19th-century drainage scheme.

From the foregoing description and the photographs it is easy to see how the four-centred Tudor arch evolved into a three-centred and the latter, in some cases, to a segmental arc. The local masons had their own intuitive way of adapting to improved forms.

One question remained: did the central "sluice gate" bridge in 1887 replace an earlier bridge? The answer was found in a copy of a rough drawing and advertisement sent to me

some years ago by John Cunningham, senior executive engineer, Roscommon Co. Council. The advertisement (paper unknown) inserted by James Lynam, CE, Ballinasloe, on 2 April 1884 stated: "The River Suck Drainage Board require to get a Temporary Wooden Bridge built across the Suck River beside the present old Stone East Bridge near the Castle to carry the traffic while build a New Stone Bridge . . . ." The drawing showed the existing bridge in plan. There were three piers 26ft to 30ft long, 19ft thick with substantial cutwaters upriver only. This indicates that it had at least four spans, though the end abutments were not shown. The word "arch" is written on the east side of the east pier next to the bank. "Piers to be removed" is written on one pier. The two piers and two abutments of the new bridge are shown (8ft thick 34ft spacing). The new bridge had the same bank-to-bank width but was shifted 30ft to the west. The most remarkable finding was that the spans between the three piers of the then-existing bridge marked "present stone bridge" on the drawing, were 19ft clear. The spans of the arches in the other two bridges ("Ballinasloe Bridge" and Ballinasloe East Bridge), described above, are all in the 10ft to 13ft range. From this I conclude that the former middle bridge did not contain any part of the original 1570 bridge. It must have been rebuilt in the 1750s or earlier. Local records should provide an answer.

The 1841 OS six-inch map shows four river channels, narrow ones *c.* 20ft each side of the castle, obviously moates, but flowing through the East Bridge. The centre channel has a bridge with four piers and cutwaters fore and aft. The west is the main channel, spanned by the main bridge. It would appear that the construction of the castle and its keep interrupted river erosion and the formation of an oxbow lake. Further research at local level could add considerably to the foregoing summary of the history of this remarkable set of bridges.

Roganstown

This bridge carries Route L6 across the Broadmeadow in north Co. Dublin. This was part of the old road to Drogheda, one of the principal roads shown on Moll's 1714 map, on which the bridge is also clearly indicated. It takes its name from the townland. The bridge is not delineated on the Down Survey map, but it shows a major north/south territorial boundary crossing the river on the line of the L6 and the site is marked "lege Rogans". The townland is marked "Rogan". No mention of the bridge was found in historical literature. Newtown Bridge, two miles downriver, is also indicated between the latter and Lissenhall Bridge.

Roganstown Bridge (fig. 112) has four small segmental, almost semi-circular, river arches with a fifth dry arch 20ft back from the south abutment. The piers were underpinned and the river bed paved with concrete probably under the Local Authority (Works) Act in the 1950s. The concrete was extended upriver and downriver by about 10ft to form anti-scour aprons. There is a separate stream shown passing through the dry arch on the 1844 OS six-inch map; it joins the Broadmeadow. The

Fig. 112: *Roganstown Bridge: Downriver Elevation*

Fig. 113: *Roganstown Bridge: Arch Ring and Parapet Coping*

spans are 8ft and the piers 4ft wide. The bridge is 18ft wide including the parapets, with no sign of widening. There are no cutwaters on the downstream face. The triangular upstream cutwaters are constructed of ashlar masonry blocks and are clearly a later addition, evidenced by a bottom course in random rubble and lack of bonding into the pier. They carry a watermain across the arches, all of which ruin the upriver elevation.

The arch rings are composed of rough cut stones with about 12in. x 4in. faces (fig. 113). The spandrel walls and piers are in random rubble stone. A notable feature of the bridge is the massive 3ft- to 4ft-long 15in.-wide and 6in.-thick coping stones with circular stones at the terminals. These look like later additions or replacements. The original cutwater copings were obviously semi-pyramidal, reaching to the level of the crown of the intrados, but they were removed when the watermain was laid.

This is probably a 17th century bridge and could be 16th century.

Abington

The present bridge across the Mulkear river at Abington, Co. Limerick, has six arches with the piers almost equal to the spans. The arches are nearly semi-circular and the roadway overhead is level. The spans are about 15ft. It is a substantial bridge, probably dating from the first half of the 18th century. There is a plaque set in the parapet. It is about 2ft 6in. long by 2ft high and the letters are almost illegible. It does not belong to this bridge but to an earlier one which previously spanned the river about a quarter of a mile downstream. The letters are in bas relief and about 1.5in. high. It reads: "The arms of Sir Edward Walsh and his wife Ellyce Walsh, also Grace Knight who erected this bridge after the death of her husband for devotione and Charitie prayinge passangers to praye for the rest of their Soules in Heaven AD 1621." The plaque came from the six-arch bridge which spanned the river at the former Cistercian abbey of Abington. The abbey was changed into a secular establishment in 1557 following the suppression, but "In the fifth year of the reign of Elizabeth the Abbey and lands of Abbeyowney were granted in capita to Peter Walsh, Rent £57. 2s. 3d. His son, Sir Edmund Walsh, was Vice-Lieutenant of the County and was drowned crossing the Mulchair at the ford under the Abbey, AD 1618. His wife built the present bridge in 1621." This

note from the Limerick Field Club[1] was sent to me by Paddy Lysaght, a keen local antiquarian, who confessed to being a bit confused. The confusion arises from the word "present" which should have read former, as explained below.

The inscription would be only a matter of local interest but for the fact that Dineley[2] made a sketch, reproduced below (fig. 114) of the 1621 bridge and the ruins of the abbey in 1681. The sketch gives the erroneous impression that the river flows from left to right. Stalley[3] states that Abington, founded in 1205, was known also as Mainister Uaithne, Woney or Owney; that the exact position of the buildings, somewhere near the present graveyard, is unclear; that it was colonised from Furness in Lancashire; and that the extensive ruins were swept away by Joseph Stepney, who built a manor house on the site shortly after Dineley's visit.

Joyce[4] states that Abington was formerly known as Droichead a'-chláir; however he may have mistaken it for Clare Bridge which spans the Clare river on the same ancient road three miles northwards and which may have been on abbey lands. Dineley wrote: "Four or five miles from Limerick, worth the sight of ye curious are the ruins of Abby ony anciently Abbey of the Order of St Bernard (in going to it is crossed a stone bridge of six arches over ye river)." It is stated in the Dineley extracts[2] that the present bridge is not the one shown on his sketch and that the ancient bridge probably stood higher upriver, but below the weir, and that the inscription stone was removed from the old bridge and built into the new one.

The bridge is shown on the Down Survey map compiled in 1656. It is evidenced in 1714 by Moll's map which shows it located on the principal north-south road west of the Holy Cross-Thurles road. The next mention is Taylor and Skinner's atlas, which shows two bridges in 1778. From this it can be inferred that sometime between 1714 and 1778 the present bridge was erected. Subsequently the 1621 bridge and link road of which it formed part vanished. The 1844 OS six-inch map shows several section of fence in the fields with double ditches between Abington and Millbank Lodge, but there is no trace of a bridge on what was obviously the old road line. There should be no problem in identifying it.

The most interesting feature of Dineley's sketch of the bridge is the raised battlement

Fig. 114: *Abbey Owny Bridge: T. Dineley's 1681 Sketch*

on the centre pier on the upriver parapet. It appears to be perforated. It resembles the high section of parapet on Gormanstown Bridge previously described and could have been a raised battlement. The most likely explanation is that it was the plaque housed in a niche.

There is a surviving multi-span bridge with pointed arches across the Thames in Abingdon on the Berkshire-Oxfordshire border. It dates from 1416 and was maintained by the Fraternity of the Holy Cross prior to the dissolution. The abbey in Abingdon owned lands in Limerick in the early medieval period. Metcalf[5] recalls a legend about the former which says that the bridge was once haunted and that "the Patron Saint of Bridges, St John of Nepomucen, was called upon by the Abbot of Abingdon Abbey in order to exorcise the spirit." St John Nepomucen[6], whose feast day is 16 May, was martyred in 1393 by being thrown bound and gagged by order of Emperor Wenceslaus into the Moldau river and drowned. He is invoked against floods.

Ballyshannon

The name derives from Ath Seanaigh, the ford of Senna, who was the grandson of Ceenal Gulban, the progenitor of St Columcille.[1] There was no bridge there in 1584 because this was one of seven locations where Lord Deputy Perrot recommended that one be built.[2] There was no bridge there at the time of the Down Survey, compiled in 1653–4. Sometime after that a 14-arch bridge was built; it is shown on Moll's map. That bridge remained until 1946 when five arches on the northern end had to be removed to accommodate the tailrace of the Hydro Electricity Scheme. The tailrace was spanned by a 71ft reinforced concrete arch faced with stone masonry.

The ESB kept an excellent record of the work and, more importantly, one of their engineers, P.A. Jackson, presented a paper[3] on the new bridge to the ICEI in 1947. The resident engineer on the Scheme, Vernon Harty, proposed the vote of thanks at the meeting in the course of which he gave a synopsis of the history of the old bridge. In 1988 a booklet, *Ballyshannon: The Rare Old Times*,[4] was produced in which some of the many excellent photos taken by the ESB during the scheme are presented with explanatory notes.

Vernon Harty stated that Chichester reported to the earl of Salisbury in 1606, proposing two places on the Erne for bridges—one at Ballyshannon, the other at Liscoole in Fermanagh, but the former was not built until *c.*1700. He referred to a "1739 manuscript" which described the bridge as having 14 arches and a tower gate in the middle of the bridge and a toll house at the northern end. Seanach's Ford was some hundreds of yards upriver from the bridge and could then (1946) be seen; there was another at the Falls of Assaroe called "Hero Pass". He mentioned that the original part of the bridge was about 12ft wide and that it had been widened to 20ft around 1850.

In his paper Jackson stated that the old bridge had 11 arches and the greatest span was 21ft. The tailrace was 48ft wide and was excavated through the rock and was much deeper. The new bridge is a three-centred arch with masonry facings to match the old bridge. Few of the stones from the demolished five arches suitable for re-use, and none of the local quarries had stones large enough for the voussoirs. It was not possible to obtain stones large enough for the voussoirs specified so they were reduced to 2ft 6in. x 2ft x 1ft 3in. minimum cube envelope, and stones from demolished buildings in the town were acquired. The stone cutting was unexpectedly slow: it took three stone cutters to supply one mason. Full-size plywood templates were made of each new voussoir for use by the stone cutters. The remaining arches of the old bridge were filled in after the Hydro Scheme was completed and the road widened to 40ft.

There is a good long-distance picture of the old bridge in the booklet. The large v-shaped cutwaters were all brought up to parapet level. The arches all appear to be semi-circular or almost so. The spans varied a little, the average being about 20ft and the pier thickness 4ft 6ins. The elevation in the photos bears a remarkable resemblance to bridges such as Maudlin in Kells and other locations for which no dates were found but which are thought to be from the period 1680 to 1710. For this reason the dating of the old section of Ballyshannon is important. Among the photos there is also one of the roadway looking down and along the bridge northwards; it shows a British Army checkpoint in operation in the "early part of the century", and, more interestingly, that the cutwaters were filled solid to the top of the parapet and did not form pedestrian refuges. Another photo shows the five arches of the old bridge stripped to the extrados, and the caption states that "experienced men on the job say that their predecessors were excellent tradesmen". The six remaining, high and dry, stone arches now filled in are, like Scariff and Kinnegad, structures for investigation in the distant future.

Assaroe Bridge

One mile north west of Ballyshannon there was a Cistercian abbey at Assaroe founded in 1178 and suppressed in 1586. Access to the Abbey Island is via a small two-span arched bridge over a little river that flows into Abbey Bay. The booklet states that Allingham described it as one of the oldest in Ireland. A colleague examined the bridge in 1989 and took two photographs, one of which is reproduced below. He concluded, like Allingham, that the bridge had been substantially rebuilt at some stage. From the photo (fig. 115) it will be seen that the bridge is covered with ivy and weeds so that it is difficult to see it properly. The upriver photo, more obscured, gives the impression that the left-hand arch facing downstream is pointed because the haunch on the land side is almost straight. However, the photo below shows that the pier half of the arch is flattened on the downstream end, whereas the crown is an arc. From this I conclude that the flattened parts are bulges that could snap through unless repaired. The ring stones are reasonably well shaped and the joints radial apart from the bulges. The cutwaters fore and aft are rounded at the nose, which is unusual on medieval bridges. Overall there are no obvious characteristics that suggest it is medieval.

Fig. 115: *Assaroe Bridge: Upriver Elevation*

Carrigadrohid

The word *carrig* according to Joyce[1] is part of the name of over fifty townlands in Ireland, such as Ballinacarriga, the town of the rocks. However, there seems to be only one Carrigadrohid or rock of the bridge. The name suggests that there was a bridge here in ancient times, but the earliest mention of one found so far is in the Down Survey carried out in 1656. Certainly the location, with the rock island splitting the river into two channels and perhaps other rocks in between, was an obvious one for a bridge.

Windle[2] states that the castle was erected in the 14th century by the McCarthys and subsequently transferred to their liege men, the O'Learys. The imaginative origin of the bridge is recounted by "J.C."[3]: briefly, an O'Sullivan saw a leprechaun in the forest nearby, but the latter suddenly shouted "Look, McCarthy Mor's lovely daughter is coming down the path" and vanished during the distraction. A few days later Sullivan, wise to the ruses, captured the leprechaun at Leamh-a-thawney, extorted his crock of gold and built the bridge with the money. The first printed record of the castle states that in 1580 Sir James Sussex Fitzgerald was detained there overnight. From that date onwards, there are many mentions, particularly in the Cromwellian wars when it was taken and retaken many times. The most infamous event was the hanging and beheading of Bishop Boethius MacEgan, chaplain to the confederate forces, by order of Lord Broghill, commander of the parliamentary forces, in 1648.[4] The castle was lived in up to 1758. Leask[5] states that this is "a late castle", meaning a 16th-century one.

The present bridge, whilst continuous from bank to bank, consists of two parts, one spanning the north channel and the other the south. The island castle abuts but is not part of the bridge. The roadway across the island edge linking the two parts is built up and supported by retaining walls; it also provides access to the castle. Photos of this bridge, taken by Tom Murphy, executive engineer, who supervised repairs and strengthening work on the south arches in 1988, were supplied to me by Fred Lynch, divisional engineer, Cork Co. Council, early in 1990. They are reproduced below and to the reader they will cause quite a surprise because the two arches on the south section

Fig. 116: *Carrigadrohid Bridge: Downriver Elevation of 19th-century Pointed Segmental Arches*

Fig. 117: *Carrigadrohid Bridge: Downriver Elevation of Original Semicircular Arches and the Castle*

are pointed segmentals (fig. 116)—an arch form that would normally date the bridge as 15th-century at the latest. Closer scrutiny, however, shows that the masonry is of 19th-century quality, whereas that of the two semi-circular arches and pier of the north channel has a much older appearance. This anomaly prompted a further search for information, primarily to establish when and why the two pointed segmental arches, were built. The answer was found by Aighleann O'Shaughnessy, senior architect, in the Ancient Monuments Section of the OPW, who discovered an incidental note in their Carrigadrohid Castle file which states that the (south) bridge was erected after 1860 to replace the earlier one which had been "carried away by a great flood", together with a reference to mentions in the 1864–66 proceedings of the RIA.[6] The latter mention led to a Du Noyer sketch which showed four semi-circular arches on the south channel and the (existing) two on the north channel. I had gone through the 700-odd Du Noyer sketches many years earlier and found that less than five had illustrations of bridges, but I failed to note down that three were of Carrigadrohid because this bridge was not on my short list at the time.

While the search outlined above was in progress, Ms P. McCarthy, Librarian, Cork Co. Council, found the evidence about the great flood in a *Cork Examiner* report of 11 November 1853. It was the same flood of 3 November 1853 that had brought down two arches of the 1793 St Patrick's Bridge in Cork. The *Examiner* summarised the discussion at the Cork Co. grand jury meeting a few days before, at which

the county surveyor provided details of bridge damage in the catchments of the Lee and the Blackwater. In relation to Carrigadrohid he stated: "The bridge of Carrigadrohid . . . had shared the same fate as the others and out of seven arches the two central have been demolished and communications suspended. At six o'clock on Wednesday morning the flood was at its height at Carrigadrohid and the bridge successfully resisted it for some hours. In the latter part of day an opening was perceived in the foot-way and shortly after two o'clock next morning the central arches fell with a crash that terrified and alarmed those who lived in its neighbourhood." Other bridges that are mentioned are the one at the castle in Macroom, which contained 11 arches, "two of which were completely destroyed and the others are supposed to have received such an amount of injury and will involve the renewal of the whole structure". Another bridge totally swept away was the "new bridge" over the Lee one mile east of Macroom built after a previous one had been demolished in a flood of 1788. The collapse was caused when 36 stacks of oats were carried down the river to it and presumably blocked the arches. (The collapse of the picturesque bridge at Castlehoward in Avoca in 1986 resulted from large hay rolls being carried down in the Hurricane Charlie floods.) The foregoing description is indicative of the invaluable information about the destruction or damage to older bridges that can be gleaned from 19th-century local newspaper reports. While information from such sources was tapped for several bridges in this book, no systematic examination was carried out for obvious reasons. However, local historians prepared to spend time scanning hundreds of microfiches of a local paper could find the search a fruitful source.

The present Carrigadrohid Bridge was surveyed and a plan and elevation prepared by Cork Co. Council in connection with the strengthening and remedial works carried out in 1988. The span of the semi-circular land arch on the north end (fig. 117) is 20ft and the second 17ft. The pier between is 6ft thick. There are triangular cutwaters fore and aft. The arch rings are composed of thin slabs of local sandstone about 18ins. x 3ins. on the face, the thickness being variable. The joints in the arch rings are radial. If these arches were pre-17th century, one would expect the pier to be thicker, to have no cutwater on the downstream end, and to have more irregular joints in the rings. The photo shows a general uniformity in the masonry compatible with the castle walls, apart from a few sections. This suggests that both were erected by the same masons. However, the most convincing evidence of contemporaeity is to be found in the tapering semi-circular buttress in the retaining wall opposite the centre of the castle which seems to have had a machiocoulis at road level, perhaps for defence against scaling of the bridge from the river. The masonry in the buttress is bonded into the retaining wall and of identical pattern.

The Du Noyer sketch indicates that the pre-1853 four arches on the south section of the bridge were similar to the northern pair except for the land arch, which was of small span and built upon the river bank. The sketch also confirms that the northern pair were similar to those still existing.

The roadway width is almost 12ft between parapets. The parapet coping is composed of irregular stone slabs slightly tilted with a reverse in tilt every 20ft or thereabouts. The piers, abutments and the retaining walls are all founded on solid rock.

The two arches on the south channel are pointed segmentals. The spans are unequal, the one at the castle and being 47ft and the bank arch 41ft with a 6ft pier in between. The reason for the unequal spans is evident in a 1913 photo[7] and from the Du Noyer sketch, both of which show rock above the water surface in the vicinity of the pier base. This is also

evident in the photo. The water levels are now controlled by the Inniscarragh dam erected in 1949. The rise of the larger arch is slightly less than one quarter the span and the second about one third. The versed sines of the arch soffits are about 18in. Given the flatness of the curves, a special survey of the profiles would be needed to determine the radii and the location of the curve centres. They appear to lie below the surface of the rock in the bed of the river, so the centering probably had to be profiled by offsets and preassembled. Both arches would need to have been built simultaneously given the high springing level on a thin pier. The masonry in the arch rings while rough cut is of superior quality than that in the northern arches. The OS six-inch map shows some quarries beside the river bank, three quarters of a mile upriver, so there was no problem in securing and transporting stone for the bridge and the castle. Given the large spans, flat intrados, curves and the thin rings, it is not surprising that the bridge needed strengthening for modern axle loads.

The bridge is shown on the 1845 OS six-inch map, on Moll's 1714 map and the Down Survey. The Civil Survey of 1654–6[8] states that the castle was valued at £100 and mentions "a timber bridge which is a common passage over said river (Lee) which is now out of repair yet passable on foot". This raises the question: was the pre-1853 bridge of six arches (including two survivors on the north end) erected after 1656? Some characteristics (the road width almost 12ft and the radial joints in the north arches) suggest it was; however, the availability of the stone, rock foundations and the difficulty of erecting a timber bridge would suggest that the Civil Survey implies temporary timber spans over arches that had been broken down in the Cromwellian war.

The Cork County grand jury records were destroyed in a fire in Cork in 1891 and in the Four Courts fire of 1922. As a result, it will be difficult to establish the date of erection of the pointed segmental arches, which are rare specimens of medieval arches built in the latter half of the 19th century. The inspiration for the arches would appear to be a similar pair in the principal room in Ballinacarrig Castle which were of sufficient interest to merit a Du Noyer sketch in the 1840s, or else the fine examples in the ruins of Kilcrea Abbey. Local investigations may provide answers in due course.

Sir Thomas's

A few miles downriver from Clonmel the Suir is spanned by an asymmetrical bridge of six arches located on a county road linking the townlands of Twomilebridge in Co. Tipperary and Tikincor Lower in Co. Waterford. The local tradition is that the bridge was built by Sir Thomas Osborne, the fourth baronet, who died in 1713. Lyons[1] calls it Sir Thomas Osborne's Bridge at Kincur and states that it was built on the site of a weir formerly held by the Franciscans. The bridge is not shown on the Down Survey map compiled in 1656, and it is unlikely that it was an omission because those at Carrick and Clonmel are clearly indicated. This confirms to some extent that it does not predate the last quarter of the 17th century. The bridge is not shown on Moll's 1714 map but this omission is explainable by the fact that he recorded only principal roads. More surprising is its omission on Taylor and Skinner's map of the Clonmel to Carrick road, which shows the short county road branching south from "Two Mile Bridge" but stopping short of the river. "Newtown", the house of "Rt. Hon. Sir W. Osborne, Bar" is clearly marked at the end of an avenue close to the county road junction north of the river. Tikincor is marked as "Kincur" on the south bank. The bridge is not shown on Rocque's map of Ireland (c.1774). It may have been a private bridge on the Osborne estate at that time.

The present bridge has a most unusual array of arches (see fig. 235, Appendix 8). Starting from the north (Tipperary) end (fig. 118) there is a small 10ft span semi-circular arch (not shown), like a supplementary flood arch but within the overall normal flood channel of the river. This is followed by a large 55ft-span segmental arch with a rise of 15ft. The normal channel of the river commences 10ft out from the abutment type pier beyond the towpath. The river channel under the remainder of this arch is four feet deeper than the rest of the river. The succeeding four arches are all segmental consisting of a 40ft span, a 36ft, a 23ft and an 18ft 6in. at the Waterford bank. The bridge is 15ft wide inclusive of parapet walls.

From an examination of the profile it was evident that the original bridge had seven arches and was symmetrical about the 40ft span; that is, it had a 36ft, 23ft and 18ft 6in. spans to each side. The three arches on the Tipperary end were obviously replaced to form a navigation channel and towpath. The Waterford Co. Council 1918 *Report on Bridges* confirming that the spans were then the same as now and that the condition was then "fair", repairs estimated at £10 being needed "to the outer ring and paving". Barry[2] states that "the central arch was blown up in 1922". Presumably, it is the large arch that is referred to as there is no central one, and the photo in his book shows a concrete soffit to the south half

Fig. 118: *Sir Thomas's Bridge: Downriver Elevation (Lawrence Postcard)*

of this arch. Precise information on the latter is probably available in contemporary local newspapers and in the Waterford or Tipperary South Riding Road Works Schemes records for the 1920s.

Delaney[3] records that the Irish parliament issued a grant for navigation work on the Suir between Clonmel and Carrick in the 1755–7 session but also states that "when the three contractors were questioned by a parliamentary committee two years later, there seems to have been very little accomplished". She adds that one contractor, Joseph Grubb, said he had be obstructed from completing his contract; the second, Richard Shaw, could not appear as he had fallen from his horse; and the third, William Markham, begged to be excused on the grounds of age and infirmity. The money involved was £3,000. Delaney also records that in 1816–18 a sum of £16,490 was expended mainly on dredging the channel between Waterford and Clonmel. From all this it would appear that the bridge was altered either in the 1750s or in the second decade of the 19th century.

Like Scarriff Bridge* in Co. Meath, the characteristics of the original bridge are fully represented by the four surviving original arches. They are important in a national sense because dated survivors from the second half of the 17th century are rare. The piers (fig. 119) are all less than four feet high above the bed of the river and their thickness ranges from 10ft to 13ft. The designer was obviously very careful to ensure that the lateral thrust from the segmental arches fell well within the bases. It is very unlikely that the bridge was built arch by arch because of the span difference. Four arches were probably built first and the centering for the outer three taken down and reused at the other side. The skewbacks are obscured by the cutwater cappings which rise to a point about half the height of the arches. The gradient on the approach roads over the three flanking arches is 6 per cent. The central arch has a rise to span ratio of one third and the land arches one half. It is apparent that the designer gave a good deal of consideration to aesthetic factors and chose the design parameters so as to give the overall bridge an arched silhouette bank to bank—the same style as Glanworth* and Leighlinbridge*. The spans are larger than Leighlin—a 40ft central arch compared with 35ft.

The bridge is now load-restricted mainly because of defects in the 18th-century arch.

There is a similarity in style between the four-span Gashouse Bridge in Clonmel, the navigation arch in Carrick-on-Suir* and the navigation arch in Sir Thomas's. However, the intrados of the three river arches of the Gashouse Bridge which had a central span of 60ft, are three-centred or ovals.

The deduction from the map evidence outlined above is confirmed by a note in Power's *Place Names of the Decies*[4] stating that Tikincor (Tig Cinn Coradh), the house at the head of the weir, refers to Osborne's mansion and that Sir Thomas erected the bridge, also known as Two-Mile-Bridge, in 1690. He adds that it was a private bridge with a gate in the middle until the mid 19th century.

Leighlin Bridge

This has been one of the most important river crossings in Ireland for more than a thousand years. The reason is obvious from the physical geography of the south of Ireland. First, the river Barrow itself is what geologists call rejuvenated, that is, it has cut a deep valley in its lower region from Muine Beg to the sea, whereas upriver of this "knick point" it flows through relatively flat country. The emergence of the crossing point at Leighlin was dictated more by the east-west valley between the Slieve Margy hills and Blackstairs mountains and by the distant barrier bogs extending in ancient times from Cashel to Roscrea than by the river characteristics. The ancient Sligh

Fig. 119: *Sir Thomas's Bridge Cutwater and Springing*

Chulann from Dublin to Waterford joined the Barrow at Leighlinbridge but continued south along the east bank before crossing it at New Ross. It was joined at Leighlinn by the Bealach Gabhrain which linked Ossory with Idrone and Hy-Kinsella. Gowran was the focal point for the roads to south Munster and Limerick.

The Synod of Rath Breasail in AD 1111 established five dioceses in Leinster including Leighlin and Kildare. The see of Leighlin was located in Leighlin town, two miles west of the Barrow crossing, the site of an abbey founded in 1600. The cathedral church was rebuilt in the middle of the 12th century.

Following the Norman invasion the territory was granted to Hugh de Lacey, who built a castle at the river crossing known as the Black Castle. Between 1260 and 1270 the first Carmelite friars' foundation in Ireland was built on the east side near the castle.

Hogan[1] states that after the Norman invasion Bealach Gabhrain continued to be the great highway between the south east and the south west of Ireland and that the road from Gowran through Bennetsbridge*, Ballymeck, Mullinahone was opened as the link with the colonial settlements of south Munster. From 1202 onwards the see of Leighlin was held mainly by Norman bishops. Gwynn & Hadcock[2] record that in February 1248 Pope Innocent IV stated in a letter to the archbishop of Dublin that Bishop William of Leighlin had proposed that the see be moved to some more convenient and accessible site because the cathedral was situated "in the midst of a wicked and perverse nation, at the far boundaries of the diocese, in a mountainous, inconvenient and barren place". The western limit of the English marches in 1300 ran along the Barrow, from Waterford to Ross to Athy and from thence to Kildare and Athlone.

There is no record of a bridge of any kind across the Barrow in the vicinity of Leighlin prior to the end of the 13th century. In 1320 we have an abrupt, simple and remarkable first mention recorded in Ware:[3] "the bridge of Leighlin was built by Maurice Jakis, a canon of the Cathedral of Kildare who also built the bridge of Kilcullen." Sherlock[4] draws attention to a more detailed mention in the 1577 Hollingshed *Chronicle* of Ireland[5] which states that in 1318 "there hath been a worthie prelate, Canon of the Cathedrall Church of Kildare named Maurice Jake (Jakis) who among the

rest of his charitable deedes built the bridge of Kilcoollenne and the next year followyng he builded in lyke manner the bridge of Leighlinn, to the great and daily commoditie of all as are occasioned to travaile in those quarters." Neither of these secondary mentions tells whether the bridges were built of timber or stone. An original mention in respect of Kilcullen in the Laud manuscript Annals of Ireland 1162 to 1370 preserved in the Bodleian Library, reproduced in Gilbert[6], records: "1319, item pons lapideus de Kilcolyn construitur per Magistrum Mauritium Jak, Canonicum ecclesie cathedralis Kildarie" (likewise the stone bridge of Kilcullen is constructed by master Maurice Jak, canon of the cathedral church of Kildare). This confirms that Kilcullen was in stone and we can confidently assume that Leighlin was also. The title "master" is very significant because, according to Harvey,[7] in the 13th and 14th centuries stone masons were divided into three categories—apprentice, journeyman and master. In Germany the aspirant had to attend a monastic school where instruction was given, chiefly in Latin, until the age of 14, when apprenticeship began. The canons of a cathedral chapter in 14th century Ireland and elsewhere were often secular clergy and more men of the world as distinct from true churchmen.

Kilcullen was an important crossing point of the Liffey from earliest times, and it is understandable that a canon from the nearby cathedral of Kildare, who was obviously well versed in stone building, would be selected to plan and supervise the erection of a bridge. Gwynn and Hadcock[2] record a mention of 1494 in which a new house of the Observant Franciscans is described as "juxta pontem de Kilculyne". Sherlock states that the bridge at Kilcullen was destroyed in the Cromwellian wars, evidenced by the fact that in 1644, when Ormonde quartered his troops at Ballymore and Sir Frederick Willoughby's detachment crossed the Liffey, they had to go by Athgarvan ford. Crofton Croker[8] records that a French traveller on a journey to Limerick in 1644 wrote: "The second day we dined at Kilcolin Bridge where ends the English ground. We swam over a little river with much trouble, carrying our clothes upon our heads; the Irish having broken the bridge during the religious wars. All the country was laid waste and we found none but poor unfortunates on the roads who sold buttermilk and a little oaten bread."

Map 8: *Leighlin Bridge; Sketch in 1571 Barony Map*

That bridge, which may have been the one erected by Jakis, was obviously broken down by the confederates. It must have been repaired or rebuilt after the Cromwellian campaign because it is shown on the Down Survey map compiled in 1656 and on Moll's 1714 map. Chetwood[9] writing in 1748 mentions "Killcullen Bridge of six handsome arches over the Liffey" and a very good inn (the Globe) beside it. These may be the downriver arches part of the present bridge which has excellent masonry which is obviously post-1700 and contains no visible evidence of early work. However 5 Geo. III c. 1 (1765) contains a provision of £600 to repair and finish the two bridges of Harristown and Kilcullen over the Liffey. Harristown new bridge was erected in 1788 and the Killcullen arches may have been rebuilt at the time (see Carragh Bridge).

Confirmation of the 1318 Leighlin bridge is found in a 1378 record when Richard II granted the prior of the Carmelite monastery an annual pension of 20 marks in consideration of the great labour, burden and expense they had "in supporting their house and the bridge contiguous thereto against the King's enemies". According to Ryan,[10] this grant was confirmed in 1394 and ratified by Henry IV and Henry V in the first years of their reigns, 1399 and 1412 respectively. The *Irish Penny Journal* for 1844[11] contains an article on the bridge which states that "the present name of the town, however, is derived from the bridge, which was erected in 1320 to facilitate the intercourse between the religious houses of old and new Leighlin, by Maurice Jakis, a canon of the cathedral of Kildare, whose memory as a bridge-builder is deservedly preserved, having also erected the bridges of St Wolstan's over the Liffey, both of which still exist." It would be reasonable to assume from the foregoing that the bridge was financed by the bishop of Leighlin and the Carmelite friars, which would explain how Jakis became involved. However, the accuracy of the latter quotation must be questioned given the error in relation to the existence of Jakis's Kilcullen Bridge in 1844. The attribution of St Wolstan's Bridge (see New Bridge) to Jakis is surprising but could be correct as it was built in 1309; moreover half of it was in the diocese of Kildare; it was financed by le Decer, a benevolent lord mayor of Dublin.

In 1408 Gerald, fifth earl of Kildare, erected the White Castle, the site of which is unknown. Comerford[12] states that from the time of Edward III (1327) to the end of the reign of Henry VIII (1547) the Kavanaghs and MacMurroughs from their position in the surrounding hills commanded the passage at Leighlin Bridge and that during this period MacMurrough was paid a yearly stipend of 80 marks from the king's exchequer for liberty to pass. Richard II, who landed in Waterford with a huge army in 1399, obtained the submissions of the Irish chieftains on his way to Dublin via Leighlin, but these were short-lived as he was deposed in the same year on his return to England.

There are no further mentions relating to the bridge until 1547, when the friary, following its suppression in 1541, was converted into a fort and surrounded with a high wall by Sir Edward Bellingham, lord deputy. This mention, from Hooke's notes on Giraldus Cambrensis's *Conquest of Ireland*, is contained in the OS Letters on Co. Carlow[13]. An entry in the State Papers (CSP 1509–1573) under 1549 records a requisition for six pickaxes, 20 shovels, some ordnance, powder and money for the commencement of work at "a very good quarry of slate near Leighlin Bridge".

There is a remarkable sketch of the town, in Map 8 part of the Carlow Barony[14] which is said to date from 1571. The sketch clearly indicates an arched stone bridge and a wall extending from the end of the downstream parapet eastwards and around the town. Only two arches are indicated but the numbers are of no significance as the object was to indicate the existence of a multi-span masonry arched bridge. No bridge is shown across the Barrow at Carlow, but one is indicated on the Burren river just upriver of its confluence.

Sir Henry Sidney records in his memoirs[15] that "In the wars with Rory Oge [O'Moore of Laois] I lay for the most part of Monastr-Evan confront with the rebel . . . During my abode I began the bridge at Carlo, over the great river of Barrow which shortly afterwards was finished to very good purpose." Connel Og O'Moore was sentenced to death as a stubborn rebel in 1557 and executed at Leighlin Bridge. Rory Og, the rebel leader, was killed in 1578. Sidney left Dublin on 19 July 1569 with an army to quell the Desmond rebellion in Munster; he travelled through Naas, Cloughgrennan and Gowran to Kilkenny which he reached on 27 July. On 1 August he resumed his march via Callan, Sleevenamon, Clonmel and Cahir to Cork, which he reached on 17 August. This record shows he crossed the Barrow at Leighlin and is also indicative of the principal routes at

the time. A sketch of the bridge he caused to be built at Carlow has survived and is shown in fig. 120. This print was incorporated in Vol. X of the *Journal of the Royal Society of Antiquaries of Ireland* with a note from the society's honorary secretary for Carlow which stated that the drawing for the wood engraving from which it was printed was "drawn upon the block by the late lamented G.V. Du Noyer and was undoubtedly the only pictorial representation of the ancient bridge of Catherlough ever presented to the public". He deduced it represented the bridge and castle c.1810. The bridge was replaced in 1814 by the present Graigue Bridge, then called Waterloo. The sketch shows the upriver face and contains a few detectable characteristics that suggest it was like the 1567 Athlone Bridge shown in fig. 106 and that the arch rings are Tudor.

There are many mentions of Leighlinbridge town as distinct from the bridge in the wars of the 1690s and in the Cromwellian war of the 1640s. For example, Col. Walter Bagnall, confederate, in charge of the fort at the bridge, allowed Lord Ormond passage over the bridge in August 1646. No mention of damage or repairs to the bridge was found. The Down Survey map shows that it was in service in

Fig. 120: *Carlow 1570 Bridge: Upriver Sketch*

Fig. 121: *Leighlin Bridge: Downriver Elevation*

1656. It is shown on the 1683 Benny edition of Petty's General Map of Ireland, which shows few roads but Leighlin Bridge is clearly indicated as the crossing of the Barrow on the road leading from Dublin through Ballymore Eustace, Baltinglass, Carlow, Goran to Carrick-on-Suir, Dungarvan and Youghal with a branch from Gowran to Kilkenny, Clonmel, Cappoquin and Cork. The bridge is shown on Moll's 1714 map.

Delaney[16] gives a good outline of the history of the Barrow Navigation. She concluded that the 1537 act prohibiting the construction of fishing weirs on the river without leaving a "King's Gap" or watersarde for boats confirms that it was used by shallow draft boats in the 16th century. She refers to a 1703 committee of parliament set up to draft a bill for the Barrow Navigation and to the authorisation of a scheme for making the river navigable under

Fig. 122: *Leighlin Bridge: Downriver Elevation of Boat Arch*

the 1715 act. Little, if any, action followed until 1759, when grants were made available. The works were under the direction of Thomas Omer and John Semple (see Kilkenny Bridges and Chapter 6, Part I). Drainage and navigation works on the Barrow continued intermittently for 100 years afterwards. No information was found among the general reports on these bridge works along the river south of Athy; however, one important point emerges, namely, that prior to the construction of navigation weirs in the 18th century, the normal flow in the river was considerably less deep than it is at present. The construction of the foundations and piers of Leighlin Bridge was therefore a far less formidable task than it appears today.

An examination of the 1840 OS six-inch map suggests that the upriver widening of the bridge was in existence at that time. The Kilcullen, Carlow, Leighlinbridge, Kilkenny, Turnpike Acts were passed in 1731 and it is most probable that the widening was carried out by the trustees in the succeeding 21 years. I have not searched for records of these turnpike trusts because few, if any, seem to have survived. Here we are primarily concerned with the older downriver section of the bridge. Comparisons between the 1840 map and subsequent revised editions show no significant changes nor has the Co. Council any records of any up to the 1970s. In 1976 a cantilevered reinforced concrete pathway was constructed on the upriver face and the whole bridge was pressure-grouted and gunited. The downstream face was kept intact, as shown by the illustrations below. I examined the bridge some years prior to the improvements and noted the butt joint between the original and the upriver extension which was clearly visible on the arch soffits, about 10ft in from the upriver face. The improvements have been carried out in an excellent and tasteful manner and, most importantly, preserve the bridge for a long time into the future. The Leighlinbridge by-pass including the new three-span reinforced concrete bridge (Cardinal Moran Bridge) was opened to traffic in June 1986. This has relieved the old bridge from the loads and vibrations of a large volume of heavy commercial traffic.

The findings of the literature search outlined above failed to answer the key question about Leighlin Bridge, namely, is the present downriver section the original bridge built by Jakis in 1319? No evidence was found in the relatively large number of mentions down through each century, which would suggest that it is not. The answer rests therefore on the assessment of the geometrical and engineering characteristics, and for that reason, given the importance of the bridge in a national historical context, the description and assessment of its characteristics was kept last, not only here but in writing this book as a whole.

The downstream elevation of the bridge is shown in fig. 236, Appendix 8, and in fig. 121. It has nine arches. There are three spans of 30ft, flanked by 21ft and 18ft spans east and west, with two of 15ft and 10ft on the east end only. This configuration raises the question as to whether there were originally two matching arches on the west, making 11 in all and symmetrical about the central 30ft span. Alternatively the 15ft and 10ft could be later additions, given an original of seven spans. The increasing arch radii with all rings springing from the same datum give the bridge its very pleasing overall profile. Chetwood records that the bridge had nine arches when he passed over it in 1748. The piers range in thickness from 5ft 3in. to 6ft 6in. and may be considered uniform at 6ft. The downriver cutwaters are triangular and capped with semi-pyramids. The upriver cutwaters on the extension are of similar shape, which suggests that they replicated the originals. The width face to face of the original was about 13ft. The road width before the 1976 addition was 22ft and the thickness of the parapets 18ins., making 25ft overall.

Fig. 122 shows a head-on view of the downriver face of the 30ft span arch used by boats. The intrados is a true segment of a circle of 17ft radius. The rise-to-span ratio is 0.3. The span-to-pier thickness is five to one. Apart from span length there is little variation in the geometric characteristics or the nature of the masonry in the arch rings. The ring stones are between 18in. and 24 in. in height on the face, and the thicknesses vary. The joints are irregular and over 60 per cent are non-radial to some extent. No information is available on the bridge foundations.

From the foregoing I conclude that the bridge is not the original one built by Jakis in 1319 because it would have had pointed segmental arches, thicker piers, smaller spans, like New Bridge.* The bridge that most closely resembles it is Kilcarn, which is also of uncertain date but pre-1600. The overall profile of Leighlin is like Glanworth, which is said to date from the mid-15th century. The Ordnance Survey Letters, 1839, contributed by T. O'Connor of Leighlin Bridge concluded that "the original bridge that gave name to this town was, it is said, long ago destroyed and several other bridges erected on its site were at various previous periods carried off by the overwhelming floods of the Barrow."

From all the foregoing we can safely assume that the bridge was rebuilt sometime between the mid-15th and mid-17th centuries. The large segmental arc spans of 30ft suggest the later period, but the shape of the ring stones and their orientation leave open the possibility that it was rebuilt c.1547 by Bellingham. It is unlikely to have been erected in the last half of the 16th century because, like Carlow, the arch intrados would be four-centred Tudor.

Milltown Old Bridge

This two-arch bridge (fig. 123) spans the Dodder at Milltown, Dublin. It is located 100 yards upriver of Milltown Bridge (Dundrum Road) where the boundary between the city and the county runs down the centre of the river. It is often referred to as "packhorse bridge", but this is incorrect because it is 10ft wide between parapets and well able to carry the biggest and widest horse wagons at any period in its history (fig. 124).

This bridge was among the last to be investigated for this book, in the firm belief that its history was well known and that information would be readily available on it from the many Dublin Millennium publica-

Fig. 123: *Milltown Bridge: Upriver Elevation*

Fig. 124: *Milltown Bridge: Roadway and Traffic Barrier*

tions. This was not the case. Further enquiries revealed that a colleague, Jack Walsh, former senior engineer, Dublin Corporation, had dealt with repairs to the parapet wall of the bridge in the early 1970s. Jack knew all that was available as he had endeavoured to establish its history at the time; moreover, he has an antiquary's interest in its preservation and a firm conviction that it is one of the oldest survivors in the city. He said that the present ownership of the bridge was not yet established; it was not in charge of either of the local authorities, and repairs to the parapets in 1973 were carried out within the meaning of s. 1 of the Local Government (Sanitary Services) Act 1964 in the interests of public safety. His search had established that the half-width wall at the Milltown Road entrance was erected between 1882 and 1908, because it is shown on the latter OS sheet (XXIII 18) but not on the former. This wall restricted access to pedestrians and cyclists. Representations regarding the repair of the bridge had been made by the Old Dublin Society and other bodies in 1973 but none had been able to furnish information on its origin or early history. Ball[1] and other historians of the city had little to add other than a mention of drownings of horseback riders at the nearby ford now spanned by Milltown Bridge.

My search began with the 1844 OS six-inch map which showed the two bridges spanning the Dodder and a "Blue mill" on the north-east approach. An article in the *Irish Penny*

Journal, 1841[2] featuring a sketch of the bridge was found to contain only one relevant sentence: "Amongst the many picturesque objects which this little mountain river presents, the Old Bridge of Milltown has always been with those children of genius [painters] an especial favourite and many an elaborate study has been made of its stained and timeworn walls." The sketch showed the bridge as it is today, so it was not altered in the past century and a half.

The bridge is shown on Rocque's 1756 map and more importantly on the Down Survey map compiled in 1656. Rocque's map is quite informative, showing bridges across the Dodder at Ringsend and Ballsbridge with other bridges on several channels of the river in between. It shows Donnybrook, Clonskea, Milltown (old) bridge, Classons and Rathfarnham Bridge. The road from Kilgobbin, Churchtown and Dundrum terminates at a ford on the site of the present Milltown Bridge, but the laneway over the old bridge links through to Milltown Road. The lord chief justice's estate is shown nearby on the west bank on the far side of the road. The scale of the map is small, but one can discern that the old bridge is about 12ft wide. No buildings are shown abutting the south-east wing wall. The continuity of the laneway would suggest it was a public road at the time. Classons Bridge, next upriver, did not connect with any road on the west bank and may have served only the river quarries at the time.

Ball[1] writing in 1903 states that Milltown

"still exhibits traces of antiquity in an old bridge now disused except for foot traffic". He also notes a 14th-century mention of a mill and states that 'Milton' was included within the manor of St Sepulchre held under the archbishop by a family called Brigg. Classons Bridge, he states, was built by John Classon, mill owner, in the latter part of the 18th century and up to then the old (Milltown) bridge was the only local means of crossing the river. He states that the ascent from the ford was dangerous. The photo of the bridge in his book shows a cavity in the bottom of the central pier on the downstream face.

At that stage of the search it was clear that the bridge could be pre-1656. Moll's map showed that it was operational in 1714. It showed the bridge as part of the "principal road" which passed through the following towns and villages: Dundrum, Kilgobbin, Kilternan, Powerscourt, thence via the Old Long Hill road to Roundwood to C. Cain (Castle Kevin), Ballinderry, Ballymanus, Hacketstown, terminating at Carlow. The only other principal road south was from Donnybrook to Bray, Greystones and thence by the coast road or "low road" through Newcastle, Rathnew to Wicklow and on to Arklow. The present Wicklow road through Newtownmountkennedy did not exist at the time.

A check up of an earlier reference to a bridge on the Dodder which I had come across in Sir Henry Sidney's memoirs[3] held promise of a 16th-century mention. It relates to the escape of Sir Edmund Butler from Dublin Castle in 1575: "but he went on in the dark of the night till he came to the bridge of the water of Dodder, a mile and a half distant from the Castle of Dublin and there what mad joy soever took him in the head I cannot tell, he went into the river and there stood (as he constantly after affirmed) the most part of that cold and long night in the water up to the chin. From thence he crept away . . . and was conducted into the county of Kilkenny . . . and was secure." It is probable that the bridge was Rathfarnham rather than Milltown, but both would fit the distance criterion—about one and a half miles from the castle. There was a bridge at Rathfarnham—evidenced by a bequest of one mark in a 15th-century will. It also is shown on the Down Survey. Some writers have attributed Milltown (old) bridge to Sir Peter Lewys, who built the bridge in

Fig. 125: *Milltown Bridge: Arch Soffit and Pier*

Athlone in 1567 and who quarried stone for Christ Church repairs in the Dodder at Milltown in 1565. There is no evidence whatsoever for this in any of the papers on Lewys (see Athlone Bridge).

From an engineering aspect Milltown (old) Bridge is a first-class job. It is founded on rock—both the central pier and the two abutments. The limestone rock outcrops all along the bed of this section of the Dodder and was quarried extensively over the centuries and in recent times. The central pier (fig. 125) is six feet thick, founded on a pedestal of rock. It looks as if the rock in the river channel has been quarried out after the construction of the bridge. The bottom course of masonry and the

Fig. 126: *Milltown Bridge: Downriver Elevation*

top of the rocks has a concrete band which suggests that the masonry became loose sometime in the present century. The abutments have concrete aprons with one underpinned on the upstream face, to a height of three feet. The concrete was obviously placed inside sandbags. This work highlights the principal danger to the bridge—the risk of masonry being dislodged especially at the rock interface. The quoins are well-cut ashlar, but the rest of the pier and abutments are in rubble masonry roughly coursed. There is no cutwater on the downstream end (fig. 126). The upriver cutwater is triangular, composed of well-bonded cut stones. The capping of the cutwater, an inverted isosceles triangle with its base at the level of the top of the keystones, is a significant characteristic. I have found similar types on only two other surviving bridges so far—the downriver old section of Kilcarn Bridge* dating from perhaps the 16th century and the 17th-century Ardstraw Bridge over the Claudy in Tyrone. However, reading through Conlan and de Courcy's recent book on the Liffey[4], I noticed a small sketch of the unbattlemented Ormond Bridge built in 1684 and destroyed in a flood in 1802, and was struck by the similarity of the arches and cutwater coping to Milltown. Regrettably Semple left no elevation—only a plan of that bridge (see Essex Bridge).

The span of the Milltown arches is 23ft 9in. The intrados are segments of circles with a rise of about 4ft 6in. The facing ring stones are ashlar and, viewed from the bank, appear to be proper voussoirs. The barrel is in random rubble. Both arches were obviously erected at the same time; otherwise there would have been a risk of overturning the high, thin pier due to unbalanced lateral component of the thrust when the centering was removed. The machiocoulis-type pedestrian refuge above the cutwater coping but independent of it is unusual. It gives a refuge space of 36in. long by 19in. deep. It may be a later addition. The cutwater, if carried up, would have been too small when allowance is made for the 18in. thick walls. Its main purpose was probably refuge from a herd of cattle. The parapets appear to have been rebuilt; they were most likely washed away in floods many times over the centuries; however, it is hard to see them properly from the bank.

If this bridge was ever in the charge of Dublin Corporation or the County Council or both, one would expect some mention of expenditure on it to have emerged from the records. Given the nature of 16th- and 17th-century activity in the area of milling and quarrying, it was most likely a private bridge, which would explain the lack of early mentions. The physical characteristics suggest that it was erected in the second half of the 17th century. However, the fact that a bridge is shown at the location on the Down Survey map surveyed in 1656 leaves open the possibility that evidence of an earlier data will be found.

Craughwell

There used to be a sharp bend in the arterial road from Dublin to Galway as one entered the village of Craughwell travelling west. It was the scene of frequent accidents but the remedy was costly because it involved the construction of a new bridge. The scheme was completed in the 1960s. The old bridge was retained as a feature. When I investigated it during the fine summer of 1976, the river was shallow and it was possible to get under the dry arches and examine it in detail.

The bridge has a central core section 10ft wide and was extended on both the upstream and downstream sides. The upriver extension is 11ft 6in. and the downriver 3ft 6in. The overall present width of the bridge is 24ft 6in. There are wattle marks on the soffits of the original central section which, though not a good indicator of age, are found in the ruins of the vaults of many pre-1500 castles in the area. The bridge has seven spans of 8ft. The piers are 4ft 9in. thick. There are no cutwaters

Fig. 127: *Craughwell Bridge: Upriver Elevation W. Arch*

downriver but it is likely that the 3ft 6in. widening was built on the cutwater foundations.

The arch rings on the upriver extension are circular arc segments and have properly cut voussoirs. The masonry in the cutwaters and piers is ashlar. It has all the appearance of mid19th century work. The rings on the downstream face (fig. 127) are also circular arc segments, but the stones are rectangular on the face and not wrought. The most interesting characteristic is the lack of a skewback. A large, partly-corbelled stone serves as an impost and on this another stone with sloped edge is placed to form a pseudo skewback. The mason was obviously learning how to spring a segmental arch. There are small corbel stones projecting from the piers just under the springing on this extension to support the arch centering during construction. The whole bridge is built in local limestone.

A large drainage scheme was carried out on the Dunkellin River in the 1840s, but Craughwell bridge was apparently left unaltered. The 1844 OS six-inch map shows quite a different alignment for the river on the upstream side. There were ornamental lakes in the grounds of the estate that was there at that time. Many of the rivers in this area are called "strounds": they disappear underground into caverns in the limestone. About one mile north of Craughwell on the Kiltullagh road, a substantial bridge of five arches (three 10ft flanked by two 8ft spans) with 6ft-wide piers has been left high and dry due to the river entering a swallow hole about 100 yards upriver.

No early mention of these bridges was found in the literature but Craughwell Bridge is shown and named on Moll's 1714 map and the Down Survey map compiled in 1654. Further searches and more detailed investigation of both bridges could establish the periods in which they were constructed.

Cappoquin

In the 16th century the road from Clonmel to Youghal assumed increased importance as an avenue for trade and commerce. One of the physical obstacles was the crossing of the Blackwater. McCarthy Morrogh[1] mentions that Richard Boyle, earl of Cork, financed the construction of bridges at Cappoquin and on the Nier in the first quarter of the 17th century. The Nier bridge was washed away in

Fig. 128: *Cappoquin Bridge: the 1665 Timber Bridge* (Dublin Penny Journal, *1834*)

1657. The Blackwater becomes tidal at Cappoquin, but it is unlikely that the saline content would be sufficient to sustain the *Toredo navalis* (referred to in Chapter 7). The Down Survey shows a bridge at Cappoquin in 1656. This bridge must have been washed away because in 1665 the Irish parliament passed a special act for building a bridge here. The upper limit on the cost was £600. In 1834 the *Dublin Penny Journal*[2] published a good sketch of the bridge (fig. 128) and stated that "The bridge existed prior to the time of Charles the Second, as an act was passed during his reign for its repair. It is now exceedingly crazy; the passage of a single individual caused it to tremble from one end to the other." The old bridge was taken down in 1850 when the present five-span masonry arch bridge was built.

The act referred to above (17 Chas. II *c*.16) gives a very good idea of how the 1634 Bridge Act was applied and the costs apportioned in situations where several counties benefited by the construction, so it is reproduced in full below.

The uniformity of the substantial and well braced trestles supporting the Cappoquin Bridge indicates that this part was newly built in 1666, so the repair work probably referred to the abutments and approach roads. There is an entry in the Council Books of the Corporation[3] under 1672 (item 668): "Warrants shall issue for applotting and collecting the twenty pounds four shillings laid on this county towards building Cappoqueen bridge."

An Act for the Building a Bridge over the River of Blackwater at Cappoquin in the County of Waterford.

The bridge over the Blackwater at Cappoquin to be new built before 23rd of October, 1666, at charge of certain counties

Whereas the repairing and new building of the bridge over the river of Black-water at Cappoquin, in the county of Waterford, will be of great use and convenience not only to the inhabitants of the said county of Waterford, but also to the several inhabitants of the county of the city of Waterford, the county of the city of Cork, the counties of Cork, Kerry, and Tipperary: be it therefore enacted by the King's most excellent majesty, by and with the advice and consent of the lords spiritual and temporal, and the commons in this present parliament assembled, That the said bridge over the river of Black-water, formerly at Cappoquin aforesaid, be new built and repaired before the twenty third day of October, which shall be in the year of our Lord God one thousand six hundred sixty and six; and that the same shall be built and repaired at the charge of the said several counties of Waterford, and county of the city of Waterford, Cork, and the county of the city of Cork, Kerry and Tipperary.

Sum not exceeding 600 l. to be raised, and apportioned as chief governors and council think fit

II. And be it further enacted by the authority aforesaid, That for and towards the repair and new building thereof, such a sum of money shall be raised out of the said several counties of Waterford, and of the county of the city of Waterford, Cork, and the county of the city of Cork, Kerry and Tipperary, as to the lord lieutenant or other chief governor or governors of this kingdom of Ireland, and the council for the time being, shall be thought fit and necessary for the new building and repairing thereof, not exceeding six hundred pounds; the same to be raised within such time, and to be divided and apportioned upon the said counties in such manner, as to the said lord lieutenant, or other chief governor or governors of this kingdom, and the council for the time being,

by distress and sale etc.

shall be also thought fit: and the said several sums to be apportioned upon the said several and respective counties, to be levied by distress and sale of the goods of the parties refusing or neglecting to pay the same respectively, or otherwise in such manner, and by such other lawful ways and means and persons, as to the said lord lieutenant or other chief governor or governors of this Kingdom of Ireland, and the council for the time being shall be thought fit.

Fig. 129: *Cappoquin Bridge: Downriver Elevation*

The present bridge, (figs. 129 and 130) was erected in 1845–6 with the aid of a loan (No. 296) of £4,000 to Waterford Co. by the Office of Public Works. There was a great flood in the Blackwater in November 1853 which caused the destruction of about 40 bridges in Co. Cork. A contemporary newspaper report states that "The new and handsome stone bridge of Cappoquin erected within the last few years

Fig. 130: *Cappoquin Bridge: Arch Detail*

and which replaced the old dilapidated wooden one which stood there before escaped most providentially, without any injury, the water having formed a passage for itself at a low point of land on the south side of the bridge by which means the bridge escaped the full weight and fury of the flood."

In the same report it is stated that the wooden bridge which crossed the Blackwater at Ballyduff, four miles upriver, the only one between Lismore and Fermoy, was completely carried away. This may be the bridge clearly marked "B. duff" on Moll's 1714 map. No approach roads are indicated.

Bective

This bridge (fig. 131) links the townland of Bective on the north-west bank of the Boyne with "Bective or Ballina" townland on the south-east bank. Bective has been the dominant name for the area. Ballina, Beal an Atha, means the mouth of the ford, so there must have been a well frequented ford here in early times long before the Cistercians came to build their monastery on the opposite side in 1147. Two miles downriver there is the townland of Assey, that is, Aith na Sidhe, or the ford of the fairies, which the imaginative railway engineer chose as the most suitable site to span the river in the 19th century. Physical evidence of the fords disappeared with the removal of shoals under the 19th- and 20th-century drainage schemes.

No record of the building of Bective Bridge has been found so far and it is a puzzling problem. Perhaps the solution rests in the history of the abbey founded by Murchad O'Meloghlin, king of Meath, descendant of the master builder of cesdroichets across the Shannon. Gwynn & Hadcock[1] record that Richard II made an order in 1380 that no mere Irishman or king's enemy should be admitted to it; its abbots sat as peers in parliament but in 1536 it was suppressed and seized; by 1540 the church had been partly demolished. Was the bridge built before 1536? It is very unlikely that a bridge of this size was financed by the Cistercians. Stalley found no evidence to suggest they have ever done so in Ireland. They did build at least one major bridge in Britain known as Stare Bridge. It crossed the Avon near Stoneleigh Abbey on the Leamington-Coventry Road[2]. It has nine arches with spans of 11ft to 13ft 6ins.,

Fig. 131: *Bective Bridge: Upriver Elevation*

is 11ft wide and 219ft long overall. It was by-passed in 1929 and is believed to be a 13th-century construction. It is classified as a national monument.

Garret Mor Fitzgerald, known as the Great Earl of Kildare, who virtually ruled Ireland from 1477 to 1513 and was viceroy on many occasions, was a benefactor of Bective Abbey and might have arranged for the building of the bridge as his predecessor had done in 1410 at Adare*. He had his arms "Si Dieu Plet Crom ABO" embellished on the church, as did his successor on the plaque on the 1791 Cromaboo Bridge* in Athy.

John Alen, lord chancellor, held the abbey and its extensive lands in 1544; it was granted to Andrew Wise for £1,380 at a rent of £4. 5s. 4d. c.1552. The abbey then became a mansion and passed through a succession of owners. It is most unlikely that it was built in the period from 1550 to 1608 because, as mentioned in Part I, there were far greater priorities from a military aspect in the areas outside the Pale. No mention is made of it in O'Neill's plan to invade the Pale in 1599 (see Babes Bridge). The bridge is not shown on the Down Survey map (1656) whereas those at Trim*, Newtown*, Grange and Kilcarn* are—strong evidence against the bridge having been built before then. The Trim-Navan road is shown on Moll's map (1714) with Bective marked as a town on it, but there is no branch road to the river or south of it; however, the map only showed principal roads. It is not shown on Rocque's General Map (c.1774). There is no record of expenditure on the bridge until 1821.

Fig. 132: *Bective Bridge: Downriver Elevation*

The bridge has 10 arches over the river and one small flood arch set well back on the north east bank. The four central arches are 14ft span, flanked each side by two 12ft spans. The land arches at each bank are 10ft. The river bed is composed of hard gravel and boulders on rock. The piers vary in thickness between 4ft and 7ft 6in. There are exceptionally long, 6ft triangular cutwaters on the upriver face and none downriver (fig. 132). The intrados curves are segments of circles, almost semi-circular in some arches. The ring stones are 20in. high, varying in thickness from about 3in. to 9in. Some are wedge-shaped like proper voussoirs. They are well shaped but not ashlar quality (fig. 133). The joints are radial. The keystones are heart-shaped in a few arches but generally wedge-shaped. The masonry is good-quality random rubble. The cutwaters' cappings are semi-pyramidal, stretching from the springings to the level of the crown of the extrados (fig. 134). The third cutwater, from each bank, is brought up to the top of the parapet to form pedestrian refuges. The roadway is 18ft wide between the 12in. thick parapet walls. These are battlement-type cappings which were "reset and doweled" under a presentiment approved by the grand jury in 1821.

There are no joints in the piers or arches so the bridge was never widened. It was underpinned by the OPW in the 1970s under the Boyne Arterial Drainage Scheme. There are no signs of any arches having been rebuilt as far as can be seen from the banks or from the parapets; however, it would require detailed examination of the arch barrels to be certain. Any such evidence could explain its absence from the Down Survey maps, assuming it was in existence at the time.

It may be possible to date the bridge on a topology basis in the future when sufficient information is available for a large number of bridges. The second half of the 17th century is the most likely period.

Kinnegad

The Irish version is Ceann Atha Gad, which it translates the ford-head of the gad or withes. There may have been a developed kind of ford here with twisted or woven willow rods of some sort on the river bed to improve the foothold. The river takes its name from the ford. Though none of the ancient *sligheanna* passed through it, the crossing must have been an important one because of the proximity of many early Christian monasteries such as Clonard.

Fig. 133: *Bective Bridge: Arch Ring Downriver*

Fig. 134: *Bective Bridge: Arch and Cutwater, Upriver*

A bridge is shown here on the Down Survey map (1656) and on Moll's map (1714). An act was passed in 1731 for repairing the road leading from the City of Dublin, to the town of Kinnegad. The preamble refers to the road being "so ruinous and bad, that in the winter many parts are impassable for wagons, carts, cars and carriages and very dangerous for travellers, and cannot by the ordinary course appointed by laws and statutes be effectually mended and kept in good repair" and then goes on to designate the turnpike trust. It is one of the few acts that mentions a particular bridge—over the Liffey at Leixlip—and direct the trustees to make a new one. It contains no mention of Kinnegad Bridge.

There is a brief mention of the bridge in the Statute Rolls under 1661. It is also on the "Map of the Mullingar Turnpike" (1829), preserved by Dublin Co. Council. The appearance from the roadway to a car driver is that the bridge had been replaced by a concrete one except for two remnants of pedestrian refuges in the field boundary wall on the eastern approach road to the new bridge.

Three arches of the 1660s' bridge and three upstream cutwaters have survived. The river has been diverted into a new and deeper cut immediately north west of the surviving arches of the old bridge. This work was obviously carried out under the Upper Boyne District Drainage Scheme in the 1840s. The Kinnegad river changes its name to the Kilwarden and then to the Clonard on its way to the Boyne at Ballynakill. The bridge erected across the new channel in the 1840s was replaced by the present reinforced concrete bridge in 1936—discernible from a date plaque on the bridge. It appears that the old bridge in the field is the one shown on the 1829 turnpike map and also the one mentioned in the House of Commons Journal under 22 March 1661:

22 March 1661. The House upon motion of one of their Members that the bridge of Kinnegad is much out of repair and that great damage and loss hath happened to travellers and cattle in their passing over same have ordered that two letters be written from the Speaker of the House, one to the Judges of Assize for the Co. of Meath and another to the Justices of Peace for the Co. of Westmeath to take care that according to Law a substantial bridge can be made over the said river Kinnegad.

Fig. 135: *Kinnegad (old) Bridge: Surviving Arch of the 1661 Bridge*

The Speaker's Letter to read: My Lord. The House of Commons having received information of the great want of a bridge over the river of Kinnegad between the counties of Meath and Westmeath so that neither carriages, horses or other passengers can safely pass that way without hazard and loss have resolved that it be recommended to the Justices of Peace for the County of Westmeath to take effectual course according to the laws that a substantial bridge be erected over the said river whereby his Majesties subjects may have a ready thorough-fare that way; which I am commanded by the House to make known unto you and the rest. H.C. Dub. 24 March 1661.

The same letter *mutatis mutandis* was sent to the justices of the peace of Co. Westmeath and directed to Sir Henry Pierce, Bt, Thomas Long, William Cancooke, William Markham Esq., to be communicated to the rest of the Justices of the Peace or any of them."

In effect the letter in a direction to implement the 1634 act, but no mention is made of a grant or funds from parliament so the funds had to come from the counties at large despite the exigencies of the situation. No further mention was found so we have to fall back on the geometric characteristics to see if the remains are of 1660s vintage.

The span of the surviving arches is 9ft with a rise of 3ft 6in., a 105⁰ degree arc segment. The piers are 10ft thick. The ring stones (fig. 135) are wedge-shaped, 7in. on extrados and 4.5in.

on the intrados averaging 18in. in depth on the head. They are well bonded into the barrel. The stones are not ashlar. The joints are not truly radial, especially in the haunches. The masonry in the cutwaters is coursed random rubble. The points of the upriver cutwaters are well cut stones and well bonded. The masonry in the cutwaters is coursed rubble, but the spandrels are of random rubble. There were probably several more arches as there is a truncated cutwater left on the west end which abuts the new bridge. The level of the field has been raised with fill from the 1840s' cut so the old channel may have been 5ft or 6ft lower. The width of the river as shown on the 1829 turnpike map is 168ft, with a module of 18ft (arch plus pier); this would give about nine arches; it probably had seven. It is a matter that could be readily established by detailed site measurements. The width of the roadway between parapets was 18ft.

Scariff (old) Bridge, located six miles away also high and dry with four of its surviving arches still carrying the road, was erected a century later. It has larger spans and radial-jointed segmental arches. It shows a considerable progression from Kinnegad. Both are built in local limestone. I conclude that Kinnegad (old) Bridge was built in response to the "directive" of parliament in the 1660s.

Leabeg

One mile south of Kilcoole on the low road to Wicklow there is a little three-span bridge (fig. 136) over a mountain stream in the townland

Fig. 136: *Leabeg Bridge: Downriver Face*

of Leabeg. It is noticeable from the road because the parapet walls stand out on each side of the 20ft-wide carriageway. It was the coping of the parapets that attracted my attention to it some years ago. The upright flags are tilted at an angle of about 60[0], with the direction reversed at the centre, somewhat similar to Mabe's* and Carragh* Bridges. An examination of the elevations of the bridge showed that the ring stones and general features matched the copings.

Fig. 137 clearly illustrates its characteristics. There are no cutwaters on the downstream side, and tiny ones, which appear to have been rebuilt, on the upstream face. The piers are 2ft 6in. wide. The centre span, approximately 7ft, is larger than the two side spans and gives a beautifully balanced and aesthetically pleasing profile. The intrados curves are segmental arcs which have been rounded at the springings to form pseudo three-centred. This is what dates the bridge more than any other characteristic as a post-1675 model. The stones in the arch rings are long, thin, well-shaped fieldstone slab, which enabled the builder to turn the sharp curves above the springings neatly without excess mortar thickness at the extrados. There are single triangular skewbacks on each pier, though the upstream ones are camouflaged by the cutwaters. There are no joints in the piers or arch barrels underneath, so the bridge was never widened. One would expect it to be narrower for the period, but it suggests that the 10ft to 15ft convention was not applied in the case of bridges as small as this one. Similar type arches are found in other small bridges in Co. Wicklow such as Glenmalure Br, (fig. 138), where roads cross shallow channel streams. The main object probably was the avoidance of hump backs in a period when carriages were badly sprung.

The bridge is shown on Moll's map (1714). Only one bridge is shown on the Down Survey maps in all of Co. Wicklow, so its absence is of no significance. Moll's map clearly indicates that this was the principal road to Arklow and Wexford in the 17th century. In fact, Orpen[1] describes it as the "great road" of the medieval period. In 1279–80 Hugh de Cruys was employed to "build the new castle of Mackinegon" and was allowed £26. 19s. 2½d. for works there[2]. In 1359 Nicholas Bathe was given permission to construct a new castle

Fig. 137: *Leabeg Bridge: Upriver Elevation*

Fig. 138: *Newcastle Footbridge: Upriver Elevation*

there (32 Ed. IV c. 4). Lewis's *Dictionary*[3] states that Newcastle was the principal military station and town of the English on the eastern side of this tract of country and it received a grant of tolls for repairing the walls in 1303.

Newcastle

Just south of Leabeg Bridge a county road forks to the right. This was the old road which ran through Newcastle village, past the Protestant church and thence south rejoining the present main road at Tiglin, two miles south of the village. Just below the church this old road crosses the Little Vartry, where a bridge is also indicated on Moll's map. Revd T.R. Jennings, the present rector of Newcastle, drew my attention to a small narrow "packhorse" bridge at this crossing, located upstream beside the modern reinforced concrete bridge (fig. 139). He said there was no vehicular bridge here in the 1920s—just a ford paved with large flat stones. The packhorse bridge (as shown in photo) is, he said, a model for artists and a feature of the locality. The current, 1912, OS six-inch map shows a ford and the footbridge. The 1839 map also shows a ford, but it is difficult to decipher whether the upriver extremity depicts a bridge or a fence. The new road line Leabeg-Tiglin is also shown. From this information I conclude that after the new line was built sometime in the early 18th century the bridge shown on Moll's map was washed away and was replaced by a paved ford and the little twin-arch 6ft-wide footbridge for pedestrians, not horses. This was a com-

Fig. 139: *Glenmalure Bridge: Upriver Elevation*

mon form of construction in Wicklow where raging mountain streams do not tolerate gullets like Goleen. The paved ford are described as "water pavements" by Major Taylor in his 1803 report on the Glencree-Aughavannagh Military Road. The grand jury records for Co. Wicklow, for which the query books extended from 1712–82 and 1817–82, were destroyed in the 1922 fire; hence the dearth of local information.

There is a considerable difference in the masonry work and in the arch curves of the bridges. Leabeg Bridge is the work of a professional stonemason who had to make the best of local materials and did so in expert manner.

Old Long Bridge

The very name of the city, Beal Feirste, the ford of the farset, is derived from the ancient crossing which formed at the mouth of the Lagan, where the opposite forces of tide and river form a sandbank. Joyce[1] states that *fearsad* is common in the west. The best example is Farsid near Aghada off Cork harbour. People could cross at low water when the sand became firm. The Irish word for the river is Lagan, meaning a shallow valley or hollow plane.

The history of the Old Long Bridge was very well described in an article in the *Belfast Telegraph* by "J.J.H.", 6 February 1931. This was kindly sent to me by Mr German, principal engineer, structures, Belfast Division Road Services, N.I., in 1981. In 1682 there was no bridge at the site now spanned by Queen's Bridge. This is confirmed by the Down Survey map which shows no less than seven bridges across the Lagan, from the source to the sea, the last one being "Shawes Bridge". Belfast itself is shown as a small town astride two streams that enter Belfast Lough just north of the Lagan entry-point, which is marked "Tide ends". The *Shell Guide* states that the Clanneboy O'Neills had a castle here commanding the ford in the 15th century and that the city owes its origin to Sir Arthur Chichester, lord deputy, who secured for himself a grant of the castle, which he rebuilt.

There is an interesting reference[2] dated 1568: "Oct. 8. five articles between the Lord Deputy Sidney and Sir Brian McFelim Bacagh and Brian Carragh for building a bridge over the ford at Belfast, to cut passes, defend wood-cutters, protect shipping and the delivery of the castle and manor of Belfast." It is unlikely that these Irish chieftains complied with this. Sidney makes no reference to a bridge at Belfast in his memoirs written in 1582, by which time one would expect the bridge to be completed if it went ahead. Negative evidence, of course, is not very reliable, but Sidney took great pride in the bridges he caused to be built e.g. Athlone*, Carlow—and mentions most of them. The source documents probably contain additional information.

J.H.H. states that in 1682 the ford consisted of stepping stones available at times of low tide but on each end there were long stretches of slobland. "So dangerous was the crossing we are told that wayfarers used to go into the Chapel of Ease—on the site now covered by St George's Church—to pray for a safe crossing of the ford." He states that in 1680 a demand was made by the town's inhabitants to the

grand jury for a bridge here and in 1682 the foundations of the long bridge were laid. The cost was borne by the grand juries of Antrim and Down, the cost being between seven and twelve thousand pounds. The bridge was probably a county-at-large charge divided between grand juries in accordance with the 1634 act. The bridge was finished in 1689 and its length was "2562ft". It had 21 arches. The cutwaters were carried up to parapet level to form pedestrian recesses as the width was 19ft between parapets. There is a stone in the New Museum Belfast (1931) taken from the Old Long Bridge which bears the name James Chad.

Schomberg's army passed over the bridge on its way to join William III who had landed at Carrickfergus in 1690. After the artillery had crossed seven arches collapsed. It was repaired in 1692, but soon afterwards a ship was blown into it during a storm, causing further damage. This led to a by-law requiring proper mooring of ships under penalty of "forty shillings a tide". At the end of the 18th century the bridge was declared dangerous to traffic but it was not until 1841 that the foundations of the replacement, Queen's Bridge, were laid. It was opened in 1843 and was built on the same site and the old bridge was demolished beforehand in 1841.

Francis Ritchie, the contractor for the Queen's Bridge, stated[3] that in 1842 Queen's was built on the exact site of the Old Long Bridge and when building the quay wall he came across "an artificial kind of causeway, made of very large stones and about 25ft broad at the top; about the same time . . . when building the wall at Mary's Dock opposite another causeway was discovered exactly similar, 25ft on top. Both ran towards each other. When the Long Bridge was removed while building Queen's Bridge, the water was lowered and exposed to view at low water a large mass of stones in the river." It is also stated that the remains of "another ford composed of large stones regularly laid which crossed the river exactly opposite the Ballast Office were lately removed by the Belfast Corporation".[3] The word "another" obviously relates to the original ford on the opposite side of the river.

There is a painting in the National Gallery of Ireland by Andrew Nicholl (1804–86) showing the Long Bridge and its 21 arches in the distant background. It shows the 21 circular segmental arches high over the river, about

10ft water level to crown, with a ramp down to bank level at the end. The most interesting detail that can be discerned from the painting is that there are abutment piers at least double the width of the others between the sixth and seventh arches from each bank, leaving nine arches in the central section.

Seven arches collapsed under Schomberg's artillery, so it must have been the centre section, perhaps a sequential collapse after one had failed. The length mentioned by J.J.H. of 2562ft must have included the approach causeways, because otherwise the span plus pier module would be about 120ft—totally at variance with the painting and with commonsense. An examination of the 1834 OS six-inch map (Antrim, Sheet 61) showed it was 760ft long and had 20 piers. Someone probably got the correct measurement, in feet, but J.J.H. may have assumed they were yards. The actual module was about 35ft, say 10ft ordinary piers and 25ft spans. A longitudinal section based on the foreoing is given in fig. 239, Appendix 8.

Cork City Bridges

The existing bridges in Cork City have been the subject of a number of articles in the *Engineers' Journal* in recent years. Walsh[1] discovered 44, including railway bridges, and among these 54 per cent were stone arches. The oldest survivor is the three-span South Gate Bridge, the upriver part of which dates from 1713. The map of the city in *Pacata Hibernia*[2] shows two fortified timber bridges, the North Gate and the South Gate, providing access to the walled island city *c*.1600. The second oldest survivor is the single 68ft-span Clarke's Bridge erected in 1766. The *Shell Guide* states that scarcely a fragment is left of medieval Cork and nothing at all of the 16th- and 17th-century town. The lack of early bridges, however, is fully compensated by the valuable bridge mentions that are contained in the Council Books of the Corporation of Cork.[3]

The first bridge mention is 12 June 1615: "That three butts of sack prize wines, now in the hands of Dominick Roch fz. James, were canted at Court, and the most preferred for said wine is 37 pounds ster. by Mr David Tyrry fz. David, Ald. Therefore, by the consent of the Mayor etc. the said David shall receive the

wines at the hands of said Dominick for 37 pounds paid him for same, to the use of the Corporation, said money to be bestowed towards the mending of the bridges of the City." This gives an insight into one of the many ways that repairs were financed before the 1634 act. In 1617 a man was made a freeman in consideration of his erecting a penthouse on the North Bridge and taxes were imposed for the repair of the walls and the two bridges which were ready to fall unless present order for their repair were taken. In 1621 the mayor "in court bestowed freely of himself two hogsheads of Gascony wynes due unto him of the Corporation towards building the north bridge now decayed." In 1630 a former mayor was acquitted in court after he had paid three score pounds sterling—money which he had received in the time of his mayoralty for the building of bridges etc.

The city corporation seems to have anticipated the passing of the 1634 act when, in April that year, "It was agreed by consent of the Mayor that whereas a Jury of select men being duly sworn for the taxing of this Corporation for the building an erecting of the bridges of this City . . . to the intent that a work of so great a consequence should not be delayed but take a speedy and hilarious effect." Three people were also appointed to be "overseers of the work" and three others to levy the money. A mention in May 1635 indicates that the North Bridge was underway.

The mention of 26 September 1638 shows the problems being encountered in building in stone on the silty deposits that formed the subsoil in Cork: "It was agreed that D. Roche FzWilliam Ald. shall continue the pinning, mending and repairing of the walls of this city in such a manner as he began; and as we hold it very dangerous for the walls of this city, through the narrow passage of the river, to build our bridges with stone, we therefore require said Domnick to surcease building said bridges with stones to provide all materials for building the castles and timber bridges only." This mention was followed by one a year later, 14 November 1639, which states that it was agreed "that the North Bridge shall be substantially built with sound and good timber and that the same shall be well paved over with stone, gravel and sand according as the best bridges of that nature and quality within this Kingdom of Ireland be or have been erected heretofore." The entry also mentions "the fall of our late castles and bridges". Permission was also granted to the inhabitants of the East Marsh to build a bridge at Kearle's Key provided it was at their own cost and that they kept it in repair without expense to the Corporation.

In 1695 there is an order that "an arch be cast over that part of the river below the County Bridge"; evidently it was financed by Alderman Rogers who was repaid from fees for making freemen. In 1697 there was approval of an account for repair of the North Bridge. In 1698 a Captain Dunscombe was given liberty to build a stone bridge "from Tuckey's Quay unto the great marsh making the arch of arches so high and broad that any lighter may pass through laden at spring tide and that the same be for ever kept in repair at the charges of said Dunscombe his heirs etc." He was also required to build a drawbridge 16ft in the clear and keep it in repair. In 1705 Christopher Tuckey was given leave "to build a stone bridge over the river between the City and said Tuckey's Quay the same to be made as high and as broad as the bridge to the Marsh, at his own charge and so keeping same during his life". Matthew Deane was given liberty to build a drawbridge at Cockpit over the Channel to the North-east Marsh.

The foregoing mentions show that private enterprise had a major role in providing bridges at the turn of the 17th century and that the corporation was making more stringent conditions in regard to navigation, repair etc. Duncombe's bridge must have been quite satisfactory as it is used as the model for ship convenience in the later mentions.

In February 1709 the members of the council were asked to meet at the North Bridge "to view battlements proposed by Alderman Crone". More importantly it was unanimously agreed, excepting the mayor and Alderman Rogers, "that it would be very convenient for the City that there should be a stoney bridge if it could with safety be done". This decision was followed up on April 1710 when the council was informed that the sheriff wished to go to Carrick, or "such other places where he shall be informed woods are to be had fit for the bridges of this City and endeavour to bargain for what quantity shall be thought necessary". A year later the mayor made an agreement with a merchant in New Ross for

"a parcel of timber from 80 to 100 tons, and the council agreed that a fit person be sent "to make choice of such timber as shall be fit for building the North Bridge".

At this stage in the records it is not clear whether the corporation intended building a stone bridge or a timber bridge; it seems that the Corkmen had lost their confidence. But in the record for 9 April 1711 the council ordered "that the person who built the Newry Bridge be sent for by the mayor to come down to be treated with about building a stone bridge." Why Newry? The minutes give no clue. Whatever happened a decision was made quickly because at the council meeting on 7 May 1711 it was agreed "that a new Stone Bridge be built over the North River where the Old Wooden Bridge is . . .". Just one year later, in April 1712, it was agreed "that 100 pounds be taken out of the iron chest and paid to Ald. Will Goddard" towards building the North Bridge. On 4 August 1712, J. Huleatt was authorised "to purchase at the wood as much oak timber for piles for the support of the North and South Bridges when wanted". The work must have proceeded satisfactorily and to completion because the next mention of the North Bridge is in May 1720 when the widow Mitchell was given leave "in rebuilding her house *on* the North Bridge near the gaol to face the bridge and open a door and windows, without window shuts or anything else standing out". This implies that like Baals Bridge* in Limerick space on the bridge was rented for houses.

The corporation did not have much respite from its bridge problems after paying £100 from the iron chest in 1712 because we find a very important entry for 12 january 1713: "Forasmuch as the South Bridge of this City is in a dangerous and tottering condition, agreed, that the same be built with stone and that Alderman Chartres, and Goddard, Mr P. French, Common speaker, Mr W. Lambley and T. Tuckey be overseers of said work but not to make any agreement for doing the same by the great without the advice of the Council." The overseers moved fast, because on 18 January 1713 they reported that they "were upon agreement with Thomas Chatterton, mason, and John Coltsman, stone-cutter, to build the same by the great, to wit, £300 and the old wooden bridge, the Corporation finding what cramps may be thought fit, and to allow them the use of what centres may be convenient,

Fig. 140: *South Gate Bridge: Upriver Elevation*

with boards for the same, also to give them all the tarass left of the North Bridge, with some other small privileges". The overseers were ordered to proceed to finish the agreement and enter into articles which shall be made good by the corporation. This mention is of great importance from the aspect of bridge history in Ireland because it gives important details on a bridge that survives, albeit widened in the 19th century. It shows that the system applied was somewhat similar to that used by the citizens of Albi in France in 1408—one of the few surviving detailed records, mentioned in Part I. Tarass was a ground basaltic rock which was mixed with lime to form an hydraulic mortar; it was imported from Holland. It is surprising that carpenters are not mentioned but they were probably employed by the masons. There is an entry for 7 February 1714 ordering that the account relating to South Bridge as audited be laid before the council.

The original part of the South Gate Bridge (fig. 140) was approx. 15ft wide. There are two relatively thin 4ft 5in. river piers. The central arch is 26ft span with a three-centred intrados. The 21ft and 23ft side arches are also three centred. The ring stones are proper wedge-shaped voussoirs. With further detailed investigation the western original section could prove to be a landmark bridge. The oldest three-centred arch found in the research for this book was the 1676 Essex Bridge* in Dublin (demolished in 1753). South Gate and Quoile Co. Down seem to be the oldest survivors in the country. Brunicardi[4] states that Alexander Deane, architect, designed the downriver extension in 1824.

Reverting to the council book, an entry of 1745 states that the South Gate Bridge was greatly endangered by throwing rubbish into the channel; the solution was a direction to the water bailiff that no boat take ballast in any other place until the rubbish was removed.

In 1760 several inhabitants "petitioned the Council for liberty to build a stone bridge over the south river from Pelican's corner to Sullivan's Quay". The council agreed provided it was at least 20ft in the clear and a convenient lifting passage included for ships and masted boats and that the corporation to be at no expense for its erection or subsequent repair. In 1761 a clause was included in the by-laws to build a stone bridge from the quay opposite Prince's Street to Lovit's Island from thence to Red Abbey Marsh with a drawbridge of wood in the centre for vessels. These bridges complemented each other. There is no mention of the fine single 68ft-span 1766 Clarke's Bridge in the minutes, nor of Winderford's Bridge, as it is named, on Beauford's 1801 map. Clarke's Bridge (fig. 141) had the longest span in Ireland from 1766 until the Lismore Bridge main arch was erected by Thomas Ivory in 1775 (see fig.14). It was the concept of a carpenter, Thomas Hobbs. The intrados curve has not been measured precisely so it is difficult to determine what shape of curve was intended. On the basis of data available and photographs, the best fit is an arc of a circle of 50ft radius subtending an angle of 90⁰ at the centre with a rise of 14ft. The ring stones are thin slabs, 38in. deep at the crown and of such a nature that there would not have been any difficulty turning the arch compared with one with voussoirs. Most of the joints are radial. The model for this bridge would appear to be the famous Pontypridd Bridge built by William Edwards over the river Taft in Wales in the 1750s, described in detail by Ruddock.[5] After 10 years and two unsuccessful attempts it was opened in 1756. It has a span of 140ft a rise of 37ft and a radius of 85ft—a segmental arc. The large rise led to a very steep approach grades and difficulties for horse-drawn traffic—a problem avoided by Hobbs. In the light of the

foregoing, it is apparent that Clarke's Bridge merits detailed investigation from a structural and historic aspect.

From 3 December 1773 onwards, there are many references to the predecessor of St Patrick's Bridge and the act of parliament (1788) (which cost £1000) obtained for its construction. That bridge collapsed in the calamitous flood of November 1853, graphically described in the *Illustrated London News* (12 November 1853): "On Tuesday evening the water commenced rising at about 4 o' clock and in the space of half an hour the whole of the city was inundated . . . . A terrific crash was heard and it was discovered that a great piece of the bridge had given away carrying down, it is believed, eleven persons. They were borne down with the tide and all were drowned with the exception of one." The contemporary artist's impression, reproduced in the *Cork Examiner* of 10 March 1934, shows a failure remarkably similar to Avoca Bridge* collapse in August 1986.

The Crooked Bridge

There is a fine abandoned bridge in the Slade of Saggart, Co. Dublin, a picturesque valley below and west of the Tallaght-Brittas Road between the Embankment and Crooksling (fig. 142). It is over a small stream which becomes the Camac after flowing through Clondalkin.

The exact location of the ancient Slighe Culainn which ran from Tara to Dublin and then south has for long been a matter of debate. In 1938 Morris[1] made a strong case, backed by many historical references, showing that the route came to Dublin via Garristown, Mullaghoo, Hollywood and Feltrim and ran southwards via Butterfield, Oldbawn and thence along the foothills to Brittas, Ballymore Eustace, Baltinglass, Tullow and the south. He states that "Bother colyn" was the name of a carucate of land in "the royal manor of Tassagard" and is defined in 13th-century documents as running through Oldbawn. From there to Brittas one of the possible routes was through the Slade of Saggart. Slade, he points out, is an old English word meaning a dell or valley or moist ground. An old road, Bothar a'Chnuic, "runs up the west side of the Slade from Craddle Bridge Saggart to Brittas, but the oldest road of all, said to have been the old coach road, ran from the bottom of the valley,

Fig. 141: *Clarke's Bridge: Downriver Elevation*

Fig. 12: *Crooked Bridge Downriver Elevation*

Fig. 143: *Crooked Bridge: Arch Detail, Upriver*

Fig. 144: *Crooked Bridge: Arch Springings, Downriver*

Fig. 145: *Crooked Bridge: Pier Face and Arch Soffit*

crossing the river on a four-arched bridge about half way up. The bridge, called the 'Crooked Bridge', which carried the road over the river still stands." This old road, he states, was open to pedestrians (1938) but had been closed at the top of the glen since about 1820. It made a wide detour to the east to avoid a swamp when it was constructed (before the river was split for mill races); it was then switched from east to west across the Crooked Bridge, hence the name.

I was amazed to find, in 1987, this fine structure standing up boldly in the middle of the field with a very small stream flowing under one span. The river is now regulated at the outflow from a storage reservoir about two miles upstream, which probably did not exist when the bridge was built. Based on stepped measurements, the arch spans are 15ft outer pair and 18ft centre pair; the piers are 5ft 6in. thick. The intrados are segments of circles (fig. 143). The rings are constructed with thin slabs of local mica schist which vary in height on the face from 18in. to 36in. The sheeting is composed of smaller slabs. It was easy to turn the arch with slabs of their shape and size, and this is reflected in the trueness of the intrados. There are triangular cutwaters on the upstream ends of the piers, but none downstream (fig. 144). The cutwater cappings have been damaged but were semi-pyramidal, rising to a point about half-way up the haunches. The first pier on the Brittas end is partly scoured out, exposing the infilling above the springing which consists of rounded spalds. The mortar is of good quality and well

Fig. 146: Craddle Bridge: Downriver Elevation

Some Northern Ireland Bridges

bonded to the stones. The keystones are roughly trimmed wedge-shaped field stones, obviously selected to fill the crown space without too much hammering. There are shuttering or drainage holes in the bases of the abutments (fig. 145). The height of the arches is about 8ft and their length (road width) 16ft. No construction joints are visible so the bridge was never widened.

There are feint traces of the old road on Rocque's map (1758). At that time the stage coach road ran from Kiltalowen by Mount Seskin to Brittas about a mile to the east of the present road. The mile posts are marked on the map.

Overall it would appear that the bridge dates from the 17th century and, if so, it is one of the rare remaining integral examples well worth preserving.

There is a smaller bridge on the same river just north of the junction of the Coolmine Road and the road that runs along the west boundary of Slade called Bothar a Chnuic by Morris, who states: "Craddle is pronounced to rhyme with 'straddle' and even tradition assigns no meaning to the name." He also mentions that O'Curry found no meaning to it when the Ordnance Survey townland names were being deciphered in the 1840s. Morris believed it is a much corrupted form of Greallach mentioned in the Annals of Ulster under AD 458 as a location near where the high king was killed. The present Craddle Bridge, a 10ft-span single arch, had a set of ashlar voussoir with curved soffits (fig. 146) that were re-erected when the bridge was widened and are uncommon.

Part I of this book relates to Northern Ireland as much as to any part of the country. In this part only two bridges have been described individually, basically because of lack of detailed information, especially early mentions. There are many historical reasons why such mentions are scarce, the fundamental one being the lordship of Ulster in the middle ages by the O'Neills and O'Donnells, who like other Gaelic chieftains, such as the O'Moores in Laois, viewed roads and stone bridges as instruments of invasion. This is borne out by the boast of Lord Deputy Sidney in his hurried march through Ulster in 1566: "I passed without boat or bridge the dangerous rivers of Omagh, Derg and Fynn; at last I came to the great sea over Lough Foyle when I found boats as appointed, to convey me and my army over . . .". Earlier during 1551 Bagenal had reported to Sidney that in his sally into Shane O'Neill's country he found "the great bridge that leadeth to Dungannon broken". The general remarks do not apply to the same extent at all to crossings of the Lagan and other rivers east of the Bann.

Fig. 4 in Part I shows that 50 per cent of the 38 bridges shown on the Down Survey maps in Ulster were in Antrim, Cavan and Down. Only one bridge, at Newry, is shown in the 1609 volume of Ulster maps in the RIA. From about 1650 onwards there is no shortage of interesting bridges. Several years ago, I acquired from colleagues in the various Road Services Divisions of the Department of the Environment in Northern Ireland, copies of lists giving the locations, names (in some cases), and a few other general details of bridges that had been statutorily listed by the Department's Historic Monuments and Buildings Branch. Over 100 are listed, indicating considerable local interest in their identification and preservation. Over 50 of the bridges were pre-1830, which means that they existed at the time of the first Ordnance Survey.

My examination of Moll's 1714 map showed 33 bridges in Antrim, 25 in Down, 11 in Armagh, 9 in Derry, 19 in Tyrone and 17 in Fermanagh—a total of 114. Many of the grand jury records for the Six Counties perished in the Four Courts fire in 1922 and none was savaged, so records are sparse.

During the past 20 years several publications have been issued in Northern Ireland which include some general information on historic bridges, such as booklets on historic buildings etc. in various towns, published by the Ulster Architectural Association. By far the most important source is McCutcheon's *Industrial Archaeology of Northern Ireland*[1] (1980). A whole section of this book is devoted to roads and bridges. Among the bridges illustrated are 24 that are pre-1830. The earliest of these with established dates are Quoile (1680), Shaw's (1709), Ardstraw (1727), Cladagh (1737), Campsie (1750). The best known is probably Shaw's Bridge.

Shaw's Bridge

Before the construction of the Old Long Bridge* at the mouth of the Lagan this was the lowest bridge crossing. On the Down Survey 1656 there are no less than seven bridges shown across the river between Belfast Lough and Magheraglin, a length of 15 miles. This concentration no doubt resulted from the funnelling of northbound traffic from a 50-mile wide band (Armagh-Downpatrick) into the neck of land between Lough Neagh and Belfast. The name "Shawe" is evidently derived from the Scottish word for a wood. A 1931 article in the *Belfast Telegraph*[2] states that the first bridge here was constructed in 1699 with stones from the ruins of an old castle called "Castle Colm" located on the hill on the north side of the river and that the bridge was carried away in a flood in 1709, when the present bridge was erected. The Down Survey map indicates that there was an earlier bridge here.

The 1709 bridge has five arches of field stone rubble masonry. The intrados are segments of circles and the ring stones consist of irregular flat stones. These are triangular cutwaters on the upriver face capped with semi-pyramids rising to about 18in. above the springing points. The spans are *c.* 15ft, the piers 4ft to 5ft thick. Given the scarcity of survivors from this period, it is hoped that all its characteristics will be measured and recorded in the near future.

Callan Bridge

This bridge of five arches spans the Callan river near its confluence with the Ulster Blackwater north of Armagh town. The bridge

is not shown on the Down Survey map but is named on Rocque's 1760 map of Co. Armagh and was obviously an important crossing place at that time because three roads converged on the north end. The carriageway is 15ft wide. The bridge has five spans of about 12ft. The triangular cutwaters on the ends of the four piers, fore and aft, are brought up to form pedestrian refuges in the parapet walls. No principal road is shown crossing the Callan river north of Armagh town on Moll's 1714 map, so the fact that the bridge is not marked is of no significance. No dates are given in the many contemporary references of this bridge, but it would appear to be pre-1700.

Ardstraw Bridge

This five-arched bridge (fig. 147) spans the river Derg in Co. Tyrone, a few miles upriver of its confluence with the Mourne. McCutcheon gives the date of erection as 1727. It is shown as a ford on the principal road from Omagh to Raphoe on Moll's map—a random confirmation of the accuracy of Moll's delineations. There is a good photo of the upriver face in McCutcheon and from it one can detect several interesting characteristics. The arches are about 12ft span and the piers 5ft thick. The triangular cutwaters are capped with inverted triangles with the base level with the soffit of the keystone. The masonry in the piers, cutwaters and spandrels is field stone random rubble. There is a buttress in place of a cutwater on one pier. This is a landmark bridge for the area.

Fig. 147: *Ardstraw Bridge: Upriver Elevation*

Quoile Bridge

This bridge, spanning the Quoile river about two miles north of Downpatrick, is shown on Moll's map but not on the Down Survey. The river is not shown on the latter, which, apart from Downpatrick, is very sparse in details of east Down. Joyce[3] states that the name derives from *cuaille* which means a pole or stake. McCutcheon gives a good photo of the downriver face of the bridge which he states was a strategic crossing place at a narrowing in an estuarine marsh. He also states that the present bridge dates from *c*.1680 and has been substantially rebuilt.

From the photo it is possible to estimate that the piers are *c*.4ft thick and the spans are *c*.12ft. The downriver cutwaters are triangular and rise to road level. It has six spans. The intrados of the arches are three-centred. The bridge has been underpinned with concrete. There is a resemblance between this bridge and the bridge at Clara*, Co. Wicklow. One wonders if the present bridge is older than the South Gate Bridge in Cork city (see Cork Group), in which case it would be the oldest known surviving three-centred arch in Ireland.

Another bridge that merits detailed investigation is the six-arch one of Newtown Stuart shown in fig. 148.

DRAINAGE REPORTS

The Drainage Report on the Lough Neagh District *c*.1848[4] contains very useful information on the bridges on the Bann and its tributaries of Lough Neagh. The description of Portglenone Bridge is a classic of bridge literature:

> The bridge consists of seven arches of the same size, or very nearly so, as those of Kilrea Bridge; the aggregate waterway between the piers and abutments, is 193ft 9in. but it is much obstructed by sterlings, and the rubble stones put in to defend the foundations, which occupy more than 30ft of the space below the summer level. The entire structure is in a very ruinous condition; the piers have been founded on or near the compressible bed of the channel, and from unskilfulness in construction have yielded to an alarming extent, as the numerous settlements and fissures in this dislocated structure attest. The materials and workmanship are of the most inferior description, and no warranty, short of reconstruction, can be offered for its security. It appears that a portion of the bridge fell in the year 1798, but was soon afterwards restored; the ruins, however, were left in the river, and add considerably to the inconvenience caused by former obstructions.
>
> The public officers in charge of the repairs of this bridge, the expense of which is borne by two counties, had to resort to wrought-iron ties to try and bind it together, but destruction has got it so firmly grasped that no mechanical expedient will long procrastinate its doom.

There is an excellent drawing of Toome Bridge with its nine arches of unequal dimensions—20ft to 41ft-span in the report. The piers were founded upon "masses of rubble stone, thrown promiscuously into a space enclosed by a single row of piles bound together by wale pieces and tied". The bridge was built in 1785. On of the piers settled alarmingly after construction and various devices were tried to lighten the load, but it was still in service in 1848, located on private property; a toll was charged to users.

Other bridges mentioned are Kilrea Bridge of seven semi-circular arches of 28ft spans with piers 7ft thick, in ashlar; Verners Bridge on the Blackwater of recent construction, is 110ft long, with two masonry abutments and a wooden carriageway resting on piles.

Any discussion of bridges in Northern Ireland would be incomplete without reference

Fig. 148: *Newtownstuart Bridge: Five of the Six Arches*

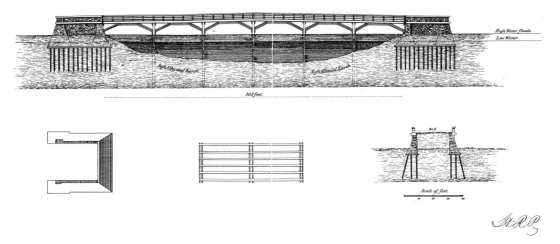

Fig. 149: *Aghivey Bridge: William Bald's Design for a Timber Strutted Bridge*

to William Bald. His work on the Antrim Coast road is well documented. Less well known is some of his work on bridges. There is a full drawing of a timber bridge he designed and supervised at Aghivey on the Lower Bann in the *Second Report* on Public Works in Ireland printed in 1834, reduced and reproduced in fig. 149. A loan of £1,250 was advanced by the Commissioners of Public Works to Co. Antrim for its construction, in 1832. In 1839 a loan of £10,900 was advanced to Co. Down towards rebuilding Long Bridge.

Kilbeg

The oldest surviving grand jury query book for Co. Meath covers the period from the summer of 1761 to the spring of 1776. When I examined it in 1987 in the National Archive, the earliest entry that I found relating to bridges was:

No. 10 Summer Assizes 1756. Whether £21.1s.6d be raised and paid to Thomas Mesclyth and Hugh Reilly to erect a bridge over the river Kilbeg on the road from Kells to Nobber. Grand Jury made no return.

This was followed by a further entry:

No. 15 Lent Assizes 1758. Whether £5 be raised and paid Thomas Mesclyth Esq., and Hugh Reilly to finish the bridge Killbeg on the road from Kells to Ardee, Grand Jury made no return.

The third entry was:

Summer Assizes 1758. Whether £5 be raised and paid Thomas Mesclyth and Hugh Reilly to finish the new bridge over the ford of Killbeg on the road from Kells to Ardee over and above the sum of £17.12s presented last Assizes for erecting said bridge and for building battlements. Grand Jury made no return.

I later discovered that these were recorded in 1761 as "undischarged queries". There was obviously some difficulty in getting the contractors to finish the bridge. However, they must have been paid, because there is no further record. It was obvious to me that the bridge had been erected. Although the river was small, given the scarcity of specific mentions of new bridges it merited investigation.

The site of the bridge was easy to find because there were masonry boundary walls on each side of the road (obviously the "battlements" referred to in the summer 1758 query). The road is 21ft wide, and the stream is a tributary of the Moynalty river. The little arch (10ft span) is shown in fig. 150 (a local landowner has installed a concrete intake pipe for a water supply beneath it). It is a segment of a circle with a 10ft chord or span. On the upstream face the skewbacks were not trimmed to the correct angle so the first voussoir was adjusted to give the necessary tilt. The keystone is a well shaped voussoir as are most of

Fig. 150: *Kilbeg Bridge: Upstream Elevation*

the other stones in the ring. Overall it is a well constructed little bridge, but it is evident that apart from the immediate approaches to the bridge, unnecessary expenditure was incurred on the long approach walls. Perhaps this is what caused the grand jury to delay so long in making payment.

Essex

The builder of second Essex Bridge, George Semple, wrote a book about it, his famous *Treatise on Building in Water*[1] (1776). The bridge, erected in 1753–5, was reconstructed in 1873–5 by the Dublin Port & Docks Board and re-named Grattan Bridge. The reconstruction was solely for traffic reasons, the new super-structure being erected on the foundations laid by Semple, the original designer and contractor.

Most of the many articles on Semple and his books focus on the 1753 bridge; however, the books also contain invaluable detailed information on the original bridge erected at this site in 1676 and on Ormond Bridge erected 300 yards upriver in 1684.

The first Essex Bridge (1676)

The Calendar of Ancient Records of Dublin[2] records that Arthur, earl of Essex, during his vice-royalty which ended in 1676, supported a proposal to erect a new bridge over the Liffey connecting the then Custom House with the lands of the dissolved St Mary's Abbey on the north bank. The proposal came from Alderman Sir Humphrey Jarvis, who with others had

bought undeveloped land on the north side. Part of the cost of construction came from the Custom of the Gates granted to the city in 1676. The earl also made a contribution.

There is a plan and elevations of this bridge in Semple's book, reproduced to reduced scale in fig. 241, Appendix 8. The bridge had seven arches and a drawbridge. The Records note that on 26 March 1685 the drawbridge was "much out of repair and may prove dangerous". The cost of repairing it was estimated at £100 and the annual charge for attendance and repairs at £50. The corporation ordered that "to prevent the said great charge and the hazard and trouble of the said draw bridge . . . it be taken down, arched over and gabbard owners ordered to make their masts to strike". It got the whole job done in exchange for the iron work and materials of the drawbridge. This explains the origin of the twin 18.5ft semi-circular arch spans at the south end. The original had five arches and a drawbridge over the 40ft-wide boat passage.

The spans of the five main arches ranged from 25ft to 28ft and the pier thicknesses from 10ft to 13ft, adequate to act as abutments. The most important characteristic is the three-centered intrados curves of the arches. This is the earliest bridge of this shape found by me in Ireland. The rise of the 28ft span arch is 9.5ft (scaled from Semple's drawing), giving a rise to span ratio of one third. The radius of the crown was 18ft and the haunches 6ft. The first major arch of this shape abroad is the Pont Santa Trinita in Florence built in 1567, which was destroyed during World War II but restored afterwards. Prade states that three-centred arches occur occasionally in 16th-century bridges in France and became common in the 17th and 18th. The advantages have been summarised in Chapter 11, Part I.

In December 1687 a pier of the bridge collapsed in a great flood, throwing a hackney coach, horses and driver into the river. The driver was drowned. In 1722 a massive equestrian statue of George I was erected on a masonry base built in front of the third pier upriver. In 1751 pier 5 collapsed and George Semple was asked to repair it temporarily, which he did in ten days at a cost of £100. Semple obviously measured the bridge accurately because he reported that considerable settlement (1ft to 3ft 6in.) had occurred in the four piers nearest the northern end, mainly on the upriver side. This he rightly attributed the deflection of the current by the statue base (see Kilkenny Bridges). The aldermen were so impressed with Semple's temporary timber repair job that they asked him to design and build a new bridge.

Before describing this second bridge it is appropriate to record some of Semple's findings recorded during the demolition of the 1767 bridge: "All the piers were originally built on frames of oak of about 9 or 10 inches square, the clear of which was just the size of the pier from out to out; the bottoms were made of 2-inch oak-boards dovetailed into the frame cross-ways, but done in very coarse rough work; these frames were laid on the bed of the river, on which they built the piers . . .". Semple mentions that from his borings for the new bridge he found the bed was composed of coarse sand, gravel and mud and other loose and fluctuative matter and that he concluded he could not have the least hope of building a substantial bridge there without removing all the loose substance and getting down to or tolerably near the rock which he found across the river, in places 27ft below high water. Semple thought that the twin semi-circular arches on the south end had been built to replace a fallen arch, but he was incorrect in that assumption as evidenced by the city record of 26 March 1685 given above.

Overall one must conclude that Jarvis's Bridge, the second stone bridge built across the Liffey in the city after 327 years, which lasted for three quarters of a century, was a remarkable bridge, a pioneering one in the fullest sense of the word. Its partial collapse was due to the parasitic statue; had Semple been asked to carry out permanent repairs as for Ormond Bridge, it too might have survived for a long time. The decision to rebuild was obviously influenced by its inadequate width—34ft out to out, composed of a carriageway 20ft 5in., footpath 9ft 5in., and two parapet walls each 2ft 6in.

Ormond Bridge

This five-span bridge was erected in 1684 and lasted until 1802 when it was carried away in a flood. Again thanks to Semple there are good records of its principal dimensions but no elevation. An engraving of 1802 shows it in the collapsed state with the arch next the

south bank the only survivor. It is depicted as a semi-circular arch, but the sketch is too crude to draw a positive conclusion. Semple gives the dimensions from the south—20ft arch/11' 3" pier/24' 3"/11' 10"/27' 8"/11'/25' 2"/10' 11"/20'. The mean span-to-pier thickness was 2.6.

Semple reports that in April 1752 it was "in utmost danger of sharing the same fate that Essex Bridge had so lately met with". He and his brother John were ordered to go and examine it. Their findings (the upriver end of the south pier had been scoured) have been outlined in Chapter 8, Part I. Semple was so convinced that it would fall ("there is no doubt but when Ormond Bridge has fallen down") that he took borings across the river and later prepared a design for a new five-span bridge described in detail in his book. However, after he completed the thorough repair job on the south pier, its life was extended for half a century. The bridge was 24ft wide. It is a great pity that no elevation of Ormond Bridge has been found so far, as it would be interesting to know the true shape of its arches and whether they were three-centred, semi-circular or segmental arcs.

The second Essex Bridge

Dublin Corporation were so impressed by the cheap and expeditious manner in which George Semple carried out the temporary repairs on Essex Bridge in 1751 that they pressed him to engage in rebuilding the whole bridge. He consented to this though "he knew it would be a very arduous task".

In 1750 a new bridge of 13 arches, each 44ft wide, across the Thames, known as Westminster Bridge, had been opened to traffic. It had been designed by Charles Labelye and constructed under his supervision. The work had taken 12 years to carry out. It had semi-circular arches with a span to pier ratio of 4.5 to 1. A detailed technical description of the bridge and its construction is given in Ruddock[3] who designated it as a "point of reference" in stone-arch bridge design and construction. Labelye, who brought a scientific approach to the work, wrote a description of the bridge[4] in 1751. Drawings of Westminster and the second Essex Bridge, are reproduced in fig. 151.

Semple obtained a copy of a version of Labelye's book which had been printed in

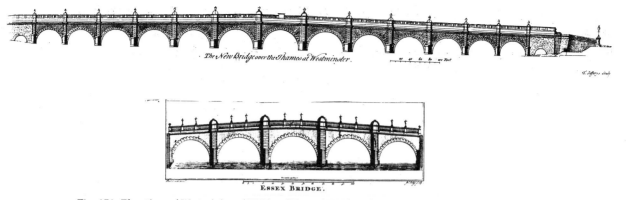

Fig. 151: *Elevations of Westminister (1750) and Essex (1753) Bridges*

Dublin by Ewing at the Angel and Bible book-shop in Dame Street. He paid several visits to London and had discussions with Labelye concerning his plans for Essex Bridge. His big problem was foundations and how to build them at a site where the spring tides rose to a height of 27ft over the river bed. Labelye thought them risky and susceptible to the scour which had undermined Jarvis's and other bridges. At that stage he had decided to make the superstructure of the bridge an exact but truncated replica of Westminster Bridge.

His boring had revealed that the greatest depth to rock was 30ft below high water. He searched his books, of which he then had "a fine and valuable collection", but, while he found many elegant designs, all the authors were silent on the laying of foundations in deep and rapid water. He went to London again and ordered £40 worth of books and plans to be sent after him and returned home full of hopes, but after attentively perusing them he found himself no further on. Ewing, the Dublin bookseller, who had a son in Paris, offered to get him to search for books and prints on the topic. Semple records: "He [Ewing] most zealously performed his part and it happened at that juncture, Colonel Belidor[5] had competed his fourth volume of Hydraulic Architecture which was sent to me together with the other three volumes, and also a perspective view of men at work in a cofferdam, at the bridge at that time building at Orleans. The language I was a stranger to, but on turning over the plates I quickly perceived his construction of cofferdams. My drooping spirits then instantly revived, and I immediately went on with my

work with vigour and entertained the most sanguine hopes of success."

Semple then set down with the assistance of his brother John and prepared as estimate for the bridge amounting to £20,500 and made a declaration to the overseers of Dublin Corporation and a committee of the Irish parliament that for this amount he would build a bridge that would last as long as the Sugarloaf Hill. He did not bind himself to the performance. He began work on 19 January 1753 by stopping up and demolishing the old bridge. He kept a diary right through the work. During one of his several visits to England in 1752 Semple purchased pumps, jacks, dredging engines and several sorts of Tarrass. He went to Leigh near Warrington to procure some Leigh-lime which he was informed would "set under water as well as Tarrass". He made many modifications and adaptations to Belidor's cofferdam system and on many occasions disaster was avoided by strokes of ingenuity, such as when within 3.5ft of rock a spring boiled up and he controlled it by driving in a 6in. hollow boring tube to relieve the pressure and then laying the foundation at that level as quickly as possible. The foundations of stone and hydraulic mortar was laid within the cofferdams which enclosed half the width of the rivers first. The width of the continuous foundation was slightly greater than the width of the piers plus cutwaters and bounded by 6in.-thick interlocking timber piles at each face. The thickness ranged from 5ft to 9ft.

A full description of the work is outside the scope of this summary; however, anyone interested will find a very objective and detailed analysis in Chapter 4 of Ruddock's excellent book. His description is by far the best because it places the work in the context of the international state-of-the-art of the construction of deep water bridge foundations in the middle of the 18th century. Ruddock concluded that while Semple's boast that the bridge would last as long as Sugar Loaf, the foundations may still do so as they are still there carrying Grattan Bridge.

Semple completed the bridge in two years and eight days at the cost of £20,661, a mere £161 more than his estimate and eight days longer than his predicted time. There were five arches, the centre one being 31ft span flanked by 28ft spans and the land arches 25ft. The two central piers were 6ft thick and the arches were segmental, the rise being one third the span. A section is given in fig. 242, Appendix 8.

There is a note in the Journal of the Irish House of Commons for 1758 (p. 229) recording a "Disbursement attending the opening of Essex Bridge £336'; also one dated 14 November 1759 by a Mr Pery: "Essex Bridge £1000 spent on works and it was finished." The superstructure of the bridge down to the piers was removed in 1873 and the bridge widened as described in a paper[6] presented to the ICEI in 1880. Some piers showed signs of settlement and were levelled up.

Semple's health broke down with a few years of the completion of his great work and he was forced to retire to the country. Nevertheless he laboured on writing his book, a difficult and tedious task at any time, but particularly so as early as the mid-18th century. His knowledge of detail was profound and obviously followed his own dictum: "in such matters as you be not furnished with precedent strike out boldly on your own initiative". It was the first Irish textbook on bridge building and was illustrated with 63 plates. The technical information is quaintly intermingled with personal narrative, e.g. "I must beg leave to acquaint you that from my earliest days I was employed to do things and not to write upon them; for in truth the whole of my scholarship, except what little I got whilst I was a mere child, was acquired within the compass of six winter weeks in the 13th year of my age. In order to shelter myself I was driven to the necessity of contriving to delineate my ideas rather than to convey them or my sentiments

by words; and this is the reason of my having gone to the expense of engraving so large a number of plates for so small a book." The cover of the book states that it was addressed principally to "young unexperienced readers". He obviously had strong feelings on what in our time is called the "West British Outlook", as he expressed the hope that "my young countrymen will now exert themselves, and use their utmost endeavours to make themselves masters of the art of bridge building and not lay the Corporation of the City under a necessity of procuring artists from other countries where they have, or may have, as fit persons for their purpose at home." This advice went unheeded. Semple himself was obliged to petition parliament for a grant for subsistence in 1761; he was awarded £500.

There are two editions of Semple's book, the first published in 1776 and the second[1] in 1780. The first is in two parts common to both editions, but in the 1780 edition he added a third part "on improving the commercial and landed interest of Ireland . . ." which is largely devoted to his conception of a grand road of 170 miles from Derry to Enniskillen to Banagher, Limerick and Cork. The road would be 120ft wide like a great linear street with houses each side, be intersected by a similar road from Dublin to Galway near Athlone and have several other branches. It was the product of a fertile imagination but far removed from reality. He estimated that the 45 Irish miles from Leixlip to Athlone would cost only £5,000. This was indeed a small sum relative to the largesse that was handed out for public works, particularly inland navigation, in the heady days of the 1760s, and his whole scheme has to be read in that context.

In his introduction to the 1780 edition he explains that in 1755 after finishing Essex Bridge the Commission of Inland Navigation informed him that they would get him nominated as controller of these works and his department would be to inspect into the works of all the canals. Whatever happened, his final observation is that after he had been at great expense "he was shamefully circumvented".

Kilkenny Bridges

On 2 October 1763 a great flood occurred in the river Nore. The two bridges in Kilkenny city, John's Bridge and Green's, were destroyed

Fig. 152: *Castlecomer Bridge: Downriver Elevation*

during the night, and as the river continued to rise the bridges at Bennetsbridge* and Thomastown were thrown down and two arches of Innistioge split. Several people lost their lives. This is a summary of the description given by Tighe.[1]

The Irish parliament responded to the appeals for funds quickly, providing relief under 3 Geo. III c.1 (1765) as follows: "the sum of eight thousand pounds to the Corporation for promoting and carrying on an inland navigation in Ireland to enable them to rebuild John's Bridge, Thomas Town Bridge, and Castlecomer Bridge [fig. 152] in the county of Kilkenny, and to repair the bridge of Ennisteague in said county of Kilkenny, and to be by then accounted for to parliament." There is a veritable mine of information in this paragraph.

The reconstruction work was entrusted to the Inland Navigation Corporation, the history which is outlined in Chapter 6, Part I. One of the schemes it had responsibility for was the construction of the Kilkenny Canal from 1755–75. These works were in progress in 1763 and the engineer in charge was William Ockenden, who had come to Ireland from the Netherlands in 1755. In the House of Commons Journal for 1759 it is recorded in Appendix 207 that his salary for the period 1 January 1757 to July 1759 was at a rate of £250 per year. He died in 1761 and was succeeded by his deputy director, George Smith, whom Ruth Delaney[2] describes as an engineer. Smith's salary as deputy is given as £80 p.a. The corporation accounted to parliament for expenditure on the Nore navigation in minute detail

(e.g. "a shovel 1s. 6d,") in 1758, all set out in Appendix 199 of HCJ, 1759.[3]

Smith is reputed to have worked with George Semple on Essex Bridge* in 1751–2. Such experience would have equipped him well for the job; more importantly it would have given him access to Semple's architectural library including the classics of Alberti and Palladio which had been translated into English sometime previously, as described in detail in Chapter 9, Part I. The results of Smith's work on the Kilkenny Bridges in 1760s is fully discussed and analysed in an international context by Ruddock,[4] who gives a description of most of them. Ruddock shows that the rebuilt downriver face of Innistioge is directly derived from Milnes' design for Blackfriars Bridge over the Thames in London, and Green's bridge is "as true a copy of Rimini Bridge as ever built in Britain or Ireland". Rimini which spans the Marecchia river on the Via Aemilia in Italy has five spans between 28ft and 35ft and a road width of 29ft; it was built between 3 BC and AD 2 and is still in use today. It is described by Palladio whose description is outlined here in Appendix 5. Ruddock also mentions that these Kilkenny bridges established a local tradition which can be traced in the spandrel decorations of other bridges on the Nore and the Barrow.

Murphy[5] states that William Colles (1702–70), who founded the Kilkenny Marble Works, built John's Bridge in Kilkenny. Colles, she states, was a man of talent with a knowledge of mathematics and mechanics who invented machines for sawing, boring and polishing marble-work which had previously been performed by hand. The works remained in the Colles family until 1920. There is an interesting item in the HCJ of 1759 mentioned above, which records expenditure on "Hewn stone raised and cut and the beds and ends wrought true to the square and chiselled six inches from the face", and also that William Colles was paid £400 for stonework. The role of Colles in the navigation and bridge building work in the 1750s and '60s in Kilkenny was vital and has been neglected in the literature.

The engineering aspects of the fine bridges erected in the broader Kilkenny area on the Nore and the Barrow and their tributaries has been overshadowed by their aesthetic properties, but they are no less significant. They had low piers to span ratios about 1 to 6, the lowest recommended in Palladio. They have segmental arches with rises of about one third of the span. These characteristics greatly increased the water-ways and minimised the risk of flooding and of scour. The bridges merit further research and technical papers individually or as a group. Here three have been selected for description—Thomastown, Graiguenamanagh and Dysart. Bennetsbridge has been described separately. The outline of Graiguenamanagh includes information on its twin which spanned the river Fergus at Clarecastle in Co. Clare.

Thomastown Bridge

Thomastown was an ancient crossing point on the Nore. Its history is summarised in a booklet by Pilsworth.[6] In 1346 a royal charter was granted for the repair and construction of the town's bridge and the right to charge a custom's toll on all merchandise coming to the town for four years. The bridge was broken down by Ormond in the Cromwellian wars. In the 1763 flood, according to the *Old Kilkenny Review*, 1952, the "ancient bridge" was swept away, many houses destroyed and 18 people drowned. The new bridge (fig. 153), erected after the floods by the Navigation Board, was again damaged in a flood in 1787. A subscription was opened for its repair, and there is a plaque which records that this work was done "under the inspection of Edward Hunt, Esq., and Anthony Sing Oxciferous, Thos. O'Bryan Mason". The first part is missing but it probably only contained the name, the date and a reference to the flood and the grand jury. The bridge was again damaged in the floods of 1947. In 1978 a parapet wall was removed and a cantilever slab constructed to give a width of 32ft. One of the most interesting characteristics of the bridge is the small segmental arches over the piers probably covering voids in the spandrels to reduce the load on the piers; this was the solution adopted by Labelye in 1748 when settlement of a pier occurred during the construction of Westminster Bridge. It is also a variant of the hollow cylinders in Pontypridd Bridge.

Graiguenamanagh Bridge

The Barrow crossing point at Graiguenamanagh has been thoroughly investigated by Hughes.[7] He posed the question: when in relation to the town was the first bridge erected?

Fig. 153: *Thomastown Bridge: before and after the 1978 Deck Widening*

The earliest positive evidence he found was the Down Survey map of 1656, but adds that when the navigation lock at Tinnahinch was in course of erection the timber remains of an earlier bridge were found, and this would appear to indicate that the road led from the Cistercian abbey through Brandondale and the Park to connect with the Coolroe-Aclare road. In regard to the 18th-century bridge, he states that it is built of local granite and has seven arches. I looked into the question of the designer of this bridge and came to the conclusion that it was John Semple.[8] Hughes puts the erection of the bridge within the period 1750–80.

There is a rough sketch (fig. 154) by Dineley[9] of *c.*1670 showing a five-span masonry arch

Fig. 154: *T. Dineley's Sketch (1680s) of the 1621 Clarecastle Bridge*

bridge across the Fergus in Clarecastle with the castle in the background. The bridge is also shown on the Down Survey map and Moll's map (1714). Whatever happened to that bridge it was evidently replaced sometime in the second half of the 18th century. The replacement bridge is shown on Plan No. 107 in the Fourth Report of the Shannon Commission 1838.[10] The elevation together with a photo of Graiguenamanagh Bridge is reproduced in fig. 155. The bridges are almost identical, the only difference being that in the Clare bridge the small arch at each extremity was omitted, leaving five as compared with seven in Graigue. A plinth is shown at the level of the road in the face of the Clare bridge. The central span is 35.5ft followed by a 30ft and 28ft on each side. The voussoirs project about 2in. from the spandrel wall. There are pedimented aediculae over two central piers and oculi over the remainder, a typical Palladian-style bridge. The bed of the river Fergus at the bridge is solid rock. The Clare bridge had a 20ft carriageway and there were sharp right-angled bends at each and so that it became a notorious "black-spot" as motor traffic increased in the late 1950s. The bridge was demolished in the 1960s as part of a major road realignment scheme.

I found no records or information on Clarecastle Bridge other than Henry Buck's drawings. The common denominator between it and Graiguenamanagh is the Navigation Board. The Fergus was considered part of the Shannon Navigation in the 1830s when the cost of a canal from Gorey Quay to Ennis was estimated at £26,000 and was considered too dear for adoption. The fact that a scheme was prepared suggests that one had been proposed in the heady days of the Corporation for Inland Navigation before it was dissolved in 1787. Perhaps some work was carried out, including the bridge. In such circumstances, John Semple was probably assigned to the work. The Inchquin MSS record a John Simple as tenant of a house in Clarecastle in the 1770s. It is an important question because Graiguenamanagh is considered by many to be one of the most aesthetically pleasing bridges in the country.

Dysart Bridge

The structure of late 17th-century Kilkenny bridges is best illustrated by a simple bridge that was erected across the Dinan river on the Kilkenny-Ballyraggart Road, N.78, in the townland of Dysart following the 1763 floods when the previous bridge was destroyed. The road crosses the Dinan just above the confluence of the Deen river, which is spanned by a similar bridge called Dysart North Bridge. Both bridges spanned the respective rivers at right angles, creating a series of sharp reverse curves which became accident black spots as traffic flows increased in the 1960s. A major realignment was commenced in 1979, and two new bridges completed in 1984. The old bridges were retired from service—fine archaeological monuments right beside the new road which has wide hard shoulders on which one can stop and park in safety.

In July 1985 there was a very heavy storm in the area accompanied by torrential rain and

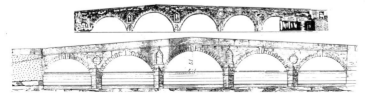

Fig. 155: *Elevations of Clarecastle and Graiguenamanagh 18th-century Bridges*

lightening. The cutwater and upriver half of one pier of the old bridge was scoured by the flood and collapsed, bringing down part of the adjoining arches. I saw the bridge some months afterwards and noticed that all its main internal components were exposed very clearly to view in a manner seldom encountered nowadays (figs. 251 and 156). The county engineer, Michael Barry, agreed that it would be a most interesting permanent roadside monument if made safe and preserved. Soon afterwards Kilkenny Co. Council decided to make it the historic focus of a roadside amenity facility. However, when the Hurricane Charlie offshoot came on 26 August 1986, it caused a further collapse, as a result the whole bridge had to be removed. A full description of the bridge and the factors that contributed to its collapse were given by Michael Barry in a paper to An Foras Forbartha's Bridge Collapse Seminar[11] in 1987. The principal factor identified was scour brought on by the deflection of the river flow by the support columns of the new bridge located just upriver of th old bridge—a significant finding from the point of view of scour prevention measures at other bridges.

Given that the composition of the barrel of the arch, the type of spandrel fill, and other geometric and material characteristics were known, it was decided to analyse its structural capacity for modern traffic loads. The findings, given in an appendix to the paper, showed that the arches were more than adequate from this aspect. Overall the investigation gave many insights into late 18th-century bridge construction. One failing revealed when the bridge was removed was the shallow depth of foundation—the Achilles heel of many masonry bridges not founded on rock.

Killaloe and O'Briens

The Down Survey maps show no bridges across the Shannon between Athlone Bridge* and Thomond (old) Bridge* in Limerick City at the time of the survey in 1656. By the time of Rhodes's survey in 1833 there were six—at Shannon Bridge, Shannon Harbour, Banagher, Portumna, Killaloe, O'Brien's Bridge and Athlunkard. Wellesley Bridge, west of Thomond, had also been opened at that time. Moll's map (1714) shows one at Banagher but none at the other intermediate locations. Ferries at

Fig. 156: *Pair of Ring Stones*

Portumna, Killaloe and O'Brien's Bridge are clearly indicated by the pontoon symbols at each bank of the river. By 1778, as evidenced by Taylor and Skinner's atlas, the bridges were in service at Killaloe and O'Briens.

The history of these bridges from 1715 onwards is bound up with that of the various navigation schemes for the Shannon. These schemes are described by Delaney.[1] Shannon Bridge was discussed in the Irish House of Commons in 1759 when a committee enquired into an application by Henry L'Estrange and William Talbot for a grant of £2,000 towards its cost. It was called Raghra Bridge. John Eyre, member, said he knew the work was completely finished and "believed that considerably more than two thousand had been expended on same".[2] Portumna Bridge was built under a special act, 35 Geo. III c. 1, in 1795, as a toll bridge; however, another act had to be passed in 1834 (4 & 5 Will. I c. 61) to rescue the Commissioners because they were £3,000 in debt and "the bridge was in such a state of dilapidation and decay as to be nearly impassable and useless". Athlunkard was built in 1830, cost £7,000 and was tolled until 1884. It has five 67ft span segmental arches.

Banagher Bridge erected *c.*1690 is discussed in Chapter 5, Part I. This leaves two—O'Briens and Killaloe, both historic crossing places. Before describing them, one must refer to the entry in the Annals of Ulster under 1510 AD (see Appendix I), which states that ' . . . the Earl of Kildare reached a very good bridge of wood that was made by O'Briain across the

Shannon . . .'. This bridge was at Portnacrusha and is mentioned here because it is often confused with the other two, especially O'Brien's Bridge.

There is a report[3] of Lord Leonard Grey's expedition into Munster in 1536 that begins the history of the present bridge: 9 August . "O'Brien's bridge being fifteen score paces in length, is broken down with bills, swords and daggers, with great labour for lack of pickaxes and crows." The difficulties were ascribed to the unwillingness of the lord deputy, the master of the rolls, and the chief justice to procure some honest aid to be levied amongst the subjects. The record ends with an interesting remark "the Master of the Rolls never speaketh as he thinketh nor thinketh as he speaketh." On 10 August Lord Deputy Grey sent the king "an account of the capture of O'Brien's Bridge with the fortification". In 1538 the same source records: "James of Desmond commanded to cast down the strong castles built on O'Brien's Bridge."

In 1914 there was a very informative correspondence in the *Limerick Chronicle* about the history of O'Brien's Bridge. It included two anonymous letters together with one by Ernest Brown and another by P.J. Lynch, the antiquary. The letters are reproduced in the *North Munster Archaeological Journal*.[4] It started with a query about the date and the following is a summary of the facts that emerged. The Co. Limerick half is of much later construction than the Clare half. There was no bridge here when Captain Draper forced the passage of the river at Killaloe on 2 June 1651. The six arches (stone) at the Clare side were built after 1691 by John Brown of Clanboy at a cost of £800 at his own expense. Donal O'Brien had agreed to build the other half but he did not do so and there was a temporary structure on that half until it was built by the county. There was a "bridge head" at the Clare end of the bridge. It may be inferred from the State papers (referred to above) that in 1537 there was a strong castle "builded all of hewen marbell" (that is, limestone) on the Limerick side and at the other end a castle not so strong "both built within the water but not much distant from the land. The O'Briens had broken four arches at the end next to the land on the Limerick side. The guns (Grey's) had no effect on the castle, "for the wall was at least 12 or 13 feet thick".

The present bridge is not the one referred to or shown on Rhodes's elevation of 1833 in fig. 245, Appendix 8. That elevation shows a bridge of 14 arches and interestingly the 11 arches on the Clare side seem to be Tudor with spans ranging from 18ft to 26ft. The draughtsman has sketched in a short radius curve at the springing joints in practically all of the arches. The model seems to have been Peter Lewys's 1567 bridge at Athlone. The three remaining arches are three-centred and therefore of later construction; they are located on the Limerick side according to the correspondence quoted above; hence Rhodes's elevation is seen looking upriver. A massive amount of money was pumped into the Limerick-Killaloe navigation works from 1757 to 1799 and the bridge was probably altered in that period because the lateral canal ended downriver of the bridge. All of the 12 arches in the present bridge are segmental arches. Overall the information that the bridge was commenced in 1691 seems to be correct.

Killaloe Bridge

This is a more historic crossing point because we know from the Annals that there was a plank bridge here between 1000 and 1014 AD as detailed under Timber Bridges in Chapter 7. No bridge is shown here on the Down Survey and none on Moll's map (1714). One is shown in Taylor and Skinner. It seems to have been erected sometime between 1715 and 1770. There are large detailed plans and sections of the bridge in the Report of the Shannon Commissioners, 1837.[5] (fig. 245, Appendix 8) It shows 15 arches of which there were six on the Clare side with 20ft span segmental arches, five in midriver of 40ft span and four at the Tipperary end with 20ft spans. All the arches had segmental (circular) intrados. The piers between the smaller arches were 10ft thick and those between the larger, 7ft 6in. The roadway was 18ft wide between the stone parapet walls. There were triangular cutwaters fore and aft coped with semi-pyramidal cappings except for eleven that were brought up to parapet level to form pedestrian refuges. Some of the latter have semi-circular niches, others triangular. The stones in all the arch rings are drawn as for ashlar voussoirs, those on the larger spans being greater; however, one cannot draw specific conclusions from this such as one could from photographs. The bed of the river shows old red sandstone at the surface at the Tipperary end, dipping uniformly across the river to a depth of 10ft below the bed of the Clare bank. The wedge-shaped stratum over it is described as "tenacious yellow clay mixed with fine sand". It is overlain with layer of "gravel mixed with stone" varying in thickness between one and two feet petering out at the fourth arch from the Clare bank. The drawing also shows three 40ft-span proposed arches to replace the four smaller ones and part of the abutment at the Tipperary end. There are "skeas" shown on the plan immediately above and below the bridge— surprisingly in the Tipperary half of the river, where it would have been difficulty to drive stakes. The grand jury query or presentment books for the 18th century for either Clare or Tipperary are not listed among those destroyed in the Four Courts 1922 fire, so there is a slim chance that they may have survived somewhere. They should contain the answers to the dating problems for Killaloe and O'Briens.

A very interesting letter[6] dated 10 February 1837 concerning the present bridge written by Professor Thomas Mulvany, director of the Royal Hibernian Academy, to his son William, then Drainage Commissioner in the Board of Public Works and resident in Limerick working on the Shannon Navigation Scheme, contains the following paragraph.

I send you the intended alteration of Killaloe bridge by which you will have perceived that I got rid of nine piers! which taken at the average of ten feet each, removes 90 feet of obstruction. —The arches you will perceive are not all of the same dimensions but that has arisen from the desire to avail myself of the piers already standing and the difference of size in some of the arches cannot disadvantageously affect even the symmetrical effect of the whole, owing to its length which exceeds the angle of vision by which all could be viewed at one glance. The arch you will have perceived is a segment of a circle and the radiating point of the cast metal work I have kept at a considerable depression in order (whether truly or not) to keep the pressure of the arch as perpendicular as possible.—My intentions were that the pressure should be thus ending in each pier at the little a . . . [Here

follows the sketch.] Whether theory would be sustained by practice is the question. The plan if intelligible will show you how I would bind and connect the cast metal work—seeing me enter so seriously into business you need not be surprised if you should hear of me offering myself for some great public work—Perhaps this is with me but the commencement of some scientific foolery; if so my security against the disgrace of defeat will be found in the cautious resistance which the world always offers to mere pretenders. I may continue to build on paper at all events without disappointment to myself or disadvantage to the public.

My next attempt shall be a landing pier at Tarbet.

Farewell, my dearest William, ever your affectionate father, Thomas J. Mulvany

The sketch was not available so it is not clear whether the professor's advice was followed. However, it clearly illustrates that the drainage engineers of the 1940s were they conscious of aesthetic factors when they prepared designs for the many bridges erected under the various schemes.

Avoca Bridges

One of the finest and most beautiful bridges in Ireland spans the Avonbeg just a stone's throw above Tom Moore's tree, where the bright waters of two, periodically savage, rivers meet. Neither the Avonmore nor the Avonbeg nor the Avoca as they are called after the Meetings, are respecters of even strong bridges. In August 1986 in the wake of Hurricane Charlie, no less than four major bridges succumbed—Sally-Gap, Annamoe, Castlehoward and Avoca Village. Two have since been repaired at substantial cost and the others, still spanned by "Baileys", are due for replacement.

The Meetings Bridge is shown on Taylor and Skinner's atlas of 1778; also the bridge in Avoca village, designated as New Bridge. On Moll's 1714 map the Arklow-Aughrim road runs north east of the river from Arklow Bridge and crosses the Avonmore at Castlehoward so it would appear that there was no road from Arklow to Woodenbridge and the Meetings. The section of the latter road from Avoca to the Meetings is shown on Taylor and Skinner. The Down Survey map shows only one bridge

Fig. 157: *Meetings Bridge: Upriver Elevation of Two Arches*

in Co. Wicklow, at Kilcommon. From all of this we can confidently say that both bridges were first built in or about the middle of the 18th century. The road is described as a Mail Coach Road on the 1840 OS six inch map.

The Meetings Bridge (fig. 157) is in two sections—an original downriver 17ft wide and an upriver extension of 27ft. It has three arches, a central span of 27ft flanked by two 19ft spans. The piers are 6ft thick. There are triangular cutwaters on the upriver extension. There are no cutwaters on the original, downstream ends, but the piers are extended 9in beyond the spandrel face and then brought up to support rectangular partly-corbelled pedestrian refuges in the parapet walls. This type of downriver pier end with or without refuges is

Fig. 158: *Meetings Bridge: Pier, Springing and Pedestrian Refuge on Downriver Section*

common in east Wicklow and occurs on stone bridges at Ballinaclash, Derrybawn, Redenagh and several others. The intrados of the arches are segments of a circle with a rise of a third of the span. The ring stones on the original are between 18in. and 30in. long and shows a uniform lip of 6in. tapering out at the springing. It would appear that the original had sagged slightly during removal of the centering and that the extension did not. The upriver granite voussoirs are 24in. deep, 11.5in. wide at the top, and 9.5in. at the soffit (fig. 158). They are well bonded into the sheeting and the lengths alternate from 12in. and 9in. The sheeting in both parts is in random rubble flat slabs. There are nine centering support corbels, projecting 9in., located just below the springing on the pier and abutments faces of the extension, but there are none on the original bridge.

Avoca Village Bridge

The first stone bridge in the village seems to have been erected in the 1750s and was called Newbridge. The bridge is shown on the 1840 OS six-inch map from which it is possible to discern that it had four cutwaters fore and aft, hence five spans. Nothing else seems to be known about the bridge except that it was carried away in the floods of 1867.

The plaque on the existing three span-bridge records: "Ovoca Bridge/H. Brett C.E. Engineer,/M. Clarke Contractor/AD1868." The 1868 bridge is described here because it marks the climax in masonry and a lot more is now known about its construction then others of the post-1830 period. The *Dublin Builder* of 1 September 1869 records: "The new bridge at Ovoca, Co. Wicklow has been opened for public traffic. It is a handsome granite structure, perfectly level, and having three spans or arches. Its length is 120ft and width 24ft, the foundation of the buttresses being 8ft below the surface of the bed of the Ovoca river. It cost £3,000, which was contributed by the Co. Wicklow. It has been built to replace the old bridge carried away by the floods consequent on the sudden thaw of the snows during the severe spring of 1867. Although it is a very creditable work and supplies an important want—namely a means of crossing the river between the extreme points of Rathdrum and Arklow . . . ". The last sentence is of considerable interest because it implies that there was no bridge at the Lion's Arch in 1869. From 1792 onwards for a century there was a lot of mining activity in the Vale and this, of course, influenced the roads and bridges in the area.

During 1986 two sets of floods caused considerable damage to bridges. The first occurred in June and washed away bridges in Co. Leitrim and in several counties in the south west of Ireland. The second came on the 25–26 August with similar consequences in Waterford, Kilkenny and Wicklow (fig. 159). In all 17 bridges were damaged or destroyed, fortunately with no loss of life or personal injury but with material loss running into millions of pounds. I thought it a very opportune time to organise a seminar to determine the factors that contributed to the collapses with the object of preventing similar losses in the future. It was most important that the evidence be collected before it was destroyed by the temporary remedial measures that commenced the next day. The engineers concerned were contacted immediately and An Foras Forbartha held the seminar nine months later. As a result there are detailed papers on record describing what happened. The paper on Avoca Bridge was prepared and presented by J. Solan, senior executive engineer, Wicklow Co. Council.[1] It gives a full description of the bridge, inside and outside.

Fig. 160 shows that this was no utilitarian bridge but one which matched the best of ancient Rome in the precision of the cutting of the massive granite voussoirs with which the bridge was constructed throughout. However, the replacement of one hundred of them lost or damaged in the collapse cost £50,000. The total cost of reinstating the bridge was £135,000—much less than the cost of a new prestressed concrete bridge—but it is easy to see why the stone arch yielded to the new materials, steel and concrete, at the end of the 19th century. The cause of the collapse was scour of the gravel foundations, which were very shallow. The *Dublin Builder* had recorded in 1869 that they were 8ft below the river bed but this was not so. Comparison of the bed levels of 1839 and 1986 showed little change. Perhaps the word buttress did not include piers.

The intrados curves of the arches on this bridge were true semi-ellipses which meant that each of the 20 voussoirs in a semi-arch

Fig. 159: *Avoca Bridge: Partial Collapse, August 1976*

Fig. 160: *Avoca Bridge: Interior of Bridge and Bailey Bridge*

had to be cut individually and precisely. In fact, when the replacement and salvaged voussoirs were built in during the restoration, an angle grinder had to be used to eliminate the saw-tooth effect that still occurred. This demonstrates the reason why the false semi-ellipse became so popular in stone bridges with ashlar masonry from 1800 onwards. Avoca Bridge was built after the great Railway Era of arch bridge construction from 1840 to 1860, so there was no shortage of skilled masons experienced in precision work.

Scariff

There is a most informative entry concerning this bridge in the query book for the Meath grand jury for 1761–76 in the National Archive:

Summer Assizes, 1760: Item 35. Whether £160. 2*s*. 6*d*, be raised and paid to George Nugent, Walter Dowdall and James O'Reilly for 915 perches of mason work at 3*s*. 6*d*. a perch towards finishing and completing a new bridge now building over a ford on the River Boyne, commonly called Scarivenaharna on the great road leading from Castlepollard to Rathmullion and the same being necessary to complete and finish said bridge over and above the sum of £200 already granted by the county for building said bridge, work doing.

The OS half-inch map showed the crossing was on the Rathmoylon Road (L4) and marked Scariff Bridge though it is not a townland. I had an opportunity to visit the bridge and was surprised to find it high and dry in a field but still carrying the L4. The Boyne had been diverted into a new channel about 15ft below the old one and a new bridge built abutting part of the original (fig. 161). There is a plaque on the new bridge: "Drainage, under the Acts 5th and 6th Vict. cap. 89, 1849." Closer examination showed that the new bridge had been underpinned as part of the Boyne Arterial Drainage Scheme in the 1970s. An historic site from an engineering aspect even if the bridge spans but a few centuries back.

Three townlands meet at the bridge—Moyfeagher, Batterstown, Ballymulmore. The derivation of the anglicised, phonetic version of the crossing place name in the query book is best left to experts, but the shortened "Scariff" does not accurately represent the terrain as it is difficult to imagine it ever having been a rough rocky crossing point like Enniskerry.

There are four arches of the 1760 bridge left. It would appear that the original had at least seven and that three were removed to make way for the 1849 bridge. The roadway is 18ft wide between parapets. The piers are 7.5ft thick with substantial triangular cutwaters fore and aft. All the cutwaters are brought up to form pedestrian refuges in the parapets. The span of what was the central arch (fig. 162) is 18ft flanked by two of 14ft and a 10ft end arch. The intrados are segments of circles. The ring stones are 15in. deep, well cut and slightly wedge-shaped of varying thickness but almost true voussoirs. There are no proper skewbacks and the springing plane is formed by a tilted stone; in some arches the springings are camouflaged by the cutwaters. The sheeting is in good quality random rubble (fig. 163). it is a difficult bridge to photograph because the south face is obscured by shrubs and the north is usually in shadow. The road is 17ft wide.

There is another bridge three miles downriver for which there is a grand jury query book record under the summer assizes 1762: "Whether £330 be raised for a new bridge over the ford of Drinadelly on the Boyne; road from Johnstown to Ratholdren." This six-arch bridge, like Scariff, was altered in the 1840s. It now has five arches, the central span being a 1840s replacement of two arches.

Particulars of the changes made in both bridges together with other relevant information are given in a report[1] by Richard Gray, district engineer for the Upper Boyne Drainage District, 1849: "The masonry executed during the season consisted in the erection of a new arch at Scariff in place of the old bridge which had been formerly underpinned for the Blackwater drainage. The arch has a clear waterway of 60ft in width; the abutments are founded 6ft below the old underpinning and the bottom of the waterway is now 4ft below the general range of the gradient line, and 2ft below that of the dishing line, falling gradually to this depth from 20 perches on either side of the bridge. The roadway was opened to the public on the 23rd of November and the temporary bridge removed and stored; on the 5th of December one parapet was nearly finished and half the string course set in the opposite side when the order to stop was received; there

Fig. 161: *Scariff Bridge: Downriver Elevation*

Fig. 162: *Scariff Bridge, 1761: Central Arch, Downriver*

Fig. 163: *Scariff Bridge: Sheeting Masonry*

was a railing put up to protect the thorough-fare on the side the parapet was not built." His report commenced by stating that during the first five months of 1849 no work had been done for want of funds. In the Scariff Division the average number employed was 187 per day with a peak of 376. Two similar style bridges were built nearby at the same time at Stoney-ford and Inchamore. The main difference between the surviving arches of the original (1760s) bridges at Scariff and Drinadelly is that the intrados are true semi-circles in the latter, whereas the former are segments (almost semi-circles).The 1837 OS six-inch map shows that the length of Scariff was 190ft between the outer abutments. Based on the measurements of the remaining four arches and piers and assuming the bridge was symmetrical, the most likely combination was three 18ft central arches flanked by two 14ft and a 10ft on each side—a total of nine arches. The references to the under-pinning of the bridge as part of a drainage scheme to relieve flooding on the Meath/Kildare Blackwater which joins the Boyne three miles upriver at Inchamore Bridge indicates that a scheme was carried out before 1830 and after the 1760s. The underpinning is not visible because the old Boyne channel was filled in to field level under the surviving arches. The Stoneyford river joins the Boyne between Scariff and Drinadelly so one would expect the number of arches (nine and six respectively) to be reversed, as they are about the same span and the criterion at the time was net waterway width.

The 1849 Scariff Bridge (fig. 164) of 60ft span has a rise of 9ft, a ratio of almost 7 to 1. It was a daring arch for the period and it is obvious that the talented team of engineers in the Office of Public Works were insistent on avoiding piers in the river and obtaining maxi-mum hydraulic capacity. The piers however had to be very substantial (as explained in Chapter 10) to withstand the high lateral thrust. The 16ft deep sheeting in the arch is com-posed of proper voussoirs as are the facing rings. An interesting feature of the bridge are the joints in the spandrel masonry which are a continuation of the voussoir joints. This type of appareil is also found in some of the 18th-century bridges on the Shannon, such as Shannonbridge. Most of the other 1840 bridges in Meath have horizontal joints. The 1840 arches in both Drinadelly and Scariff have been listed for strengthening by Meath Co. Council fol-lowing recent examination and assessment.

Kanturk Bridges

The river Dalua joins the Allow at Kanturk and the latter flows south to join the Black-

Fig. 164: *Scariff Bridge, 1849: Downriver Elevation*

water above Banteer. Like many other towns it followed from the construction of the castle which was erected by MacDonagh at the commencement of the 17th century. The Dublin Castle authorities prevented him from roofing it and so it has remained to the present day. It is now a national monument. It has many interesting features from a stone masonry aspect, including flat (arch) stone window lintels and a semi-elliptical doorway arch—mentioned by Leask.

The Down Survey map shows both rivers but no bridges. The lands of the extensive territory of Duhallow and the castle were attainted and granted to Philip Percival in 1666. The area amounted to 100,000 acres. The successors of Percival grew in wealth and power and in 1733 the fifth in line was made the first earl of Egmont. The line continued until 1939 when the title became dormant. In the period from 1750 to 1850 the Egmonts were extremely wealthy and influential.

The first mention of a bridge in Kanturk that I came across is in the Council Book of the Corporation of Youghal.[1] Under the year 1682 there is an item:

Whereas, by an order grounded on a presentment of the Grand Jury, last Assizes, held at Cork, 17 Aug. 1682, this Town is charged with £4. 5s. 7d. towards finishing the County Court House, and making the west angle uniform with what is done, by another order of the same date, with £10. 16s. 11½d. towards building a substantial stone bridge over the river Lee at Ballyglassan, Barony of Muskery, also 3d. a plowland for finishing Downe bridge, in the great road 'twist Cork and Kinsale, and 2½d. a plowland for making a causeway in the great road to Limerick, betwixt Milebush and Two-pot-house; 3d. a plowland for repairing Clanturke bridge, and 4d. a plowland for finishing the two Glanmire bridges and likewise 4d. a plowland towards the building of Ardskeagh Bridge. It is there-fore ordered, that £20 ster. be levied on the said town and liberties for payment of said sums.

This is a very valuable record from a national aspect because it refers to several bridges and demonstrates that the Cork grand jury were implementing the 1634 act vigorously. It also corroborates the evidence in

various Chapters in Part I that the period from 1660 to 1690 was one of construction in the literal sense in relation to roads and bridges. It verifies that boroughs were required to contribute to "county-at-large" presentments. The principal question raised by the mention is: where was "Clanturke bridge"? Before attempting to answer it another rare and detailed bridge mention must be considered. It is in the surviving manuscripts of the old Corporation of Kinsale:[2]

William Freeman Esqr. to erect a good stone bridge with lime and sand on the River Awndallow where the old wooden bridge formerly stood leading into the town of Kinturk, the main arches to be made with (? carved) stone and all the pillars sufficiently supported and laid on a firm foundation and the upper part of the bridge well paved filled and raised with side walls and broad stones on the top of them and a sufficient key to be made above the bridge to prevent the water from changing its course or undermining the first great arch adjoining to the river of Awnalla, the said Freeman having undertaken to complete the said work for the said money and to support and keep it up for seven years and is to enter into bonds with security . . . £250.0.0.

In 1988 I sent this information to Brendan Devlin, deputy county engineer, Cork Co. Council, and asked him if the bridges were still there. The reply brought full details of the existing bridges in Kanturk, called "Greenane" and "Kanturk", together with the photos and the wording of a most remarkable set of inscriptions on the parapet copings. It was at once evident from the photos and dimensions, in particular the pier thicknesses, that in the national context they were advanced bridges for their period. The dates on the plaques were 1745 and 1760 respectively. It was also clear that neither of the bridges in the grand jury mentions above had survived and the descriptions did not locate them precisely. Moll's map (1714) provided the answer to the 1682 mention because it shows a road from Mallow to Newmarket crossing the Allow just south of the Dalua confluence near the castle and entering the town marked "Clanturk" on the west bank. The map shows no roads or bridges leading to or crossing the Dalua or Allow upstream of their confluence.

The wording of the Freeman presentment shows that the bridge spanned the Dalua. One would be inclined to interpret the phrase "leading into the town" as suggesting that it replaced the bridge south of the confluence; however, the mention of the "first great arch next adjoining to the river of Awnalla" confirms that it spanned the Dalua. The presentment makes it quite clear that this was not the first bridge at the site and also that the grand jury was determined to build a stone bridge exceptional for the period. It also shows that the approach road to the bridge from the north was in danger of being cut through by floods. What happened to Freeman's bridge? It obviously collapsed in the 1750s or earlier because the present bridge was erected in 1760. I suspect that it was in trouble before 1745 and that this prompted the grand jury to investigate the design very thoroughly before embarking on the construction of another bridge in the vicinity.

Greenane Bridge

The next bridge erected was Greenane (fig. 165); its the plaque, in Latin, gives us some very useful historical information. The translation is:

This bridge was constructed in 1745 by Joseph Clahesy, stone mason to the inspectors Boyle Aldworth of Newmarket, Francis Gore of Assolas, Richard Purcell of Kanturk, Arthur Bastable of Castlemenager.

Fig. 165: *Greenane Bridge: Downriver Elevation*

The 1634 Act (see Appendix 4) empowered the justices at the assizes "to name and appoint two surveyors who shall see every bridge, causeway, and togher builded, amended, and repaired from time to time as often as need shall require" and to allow them reasonable costs. The concern in this case is apparent by the appointment of four, described as inspectors. Two of them, the Revd. Richard Purcell and Arthur Bastable, reappear as trustees on the plaque on Kanturk Bridge described below, erected in 1760, and as nominated and appointed trustees in the list in the 1765 Cork-Kanturk Turnpike Act (5 Geo. III c.13). Purcell was agent for the earl of Egmont's estate. Egmont, an absentee landlord, was well versed in architecture.

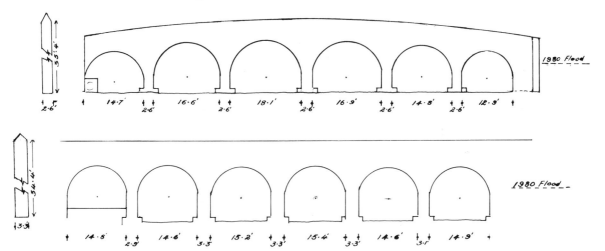

Fig. 166: *Sections of Greenane and Dalua Bridges*

Fig. 167: *Greenane Bridge: Downriver Elevation of One Arch*

The dimensions of Greenane and Kanturk bridges are given on the downstream elevation shown in the Cork Co. Council flood study report, reproduced to reduced scale in fig. 166. The remarkable characteristic of Greenane is the thin piers ranging from 3ft to 3ft 3in. thick, and 5ft 9in. high to the springings. The arch spans are small 15ft but the span-to-pier ratio is 5 to 1. The piers are in ashlar masonry with through bonders. The downstream cutwaters are curved (perhaps a Palladian influence). The bridge was widened on the upriver side so there is no information about the original upstream cutwaters. The arch rings are segmental (165°), almost semi-circular, rise-to-span ratio 0.43. The facing ringstones are well cut voussoir, but the sheeting is of random rubble. The ring is 16in. thick. The lengths of the ringstones, along the intrados (fig. 167), vary. The first ringstones are actually long skewback, the upper joint face being cut to an angle of 15° to give the springing. The soffits of the arches are all at the same level and the gradient in the road is accommodated by a uniform increase in the height of the spandrel walls, evident in the photo but not shown on the drawing.

Grove White[3] states that in 1909 there was a square stone slab in the centre of the southern parapet partly defaced but bearing the words "Grand Jury". Perhaps this referred to the widening of the upriver side. No information was found regarding the date of the widening, nor on the date of the extension of Kanturk Bridge. There is a difference in the thickness of the spaces between the lines designating the bridges on the 1845 OS 6in. sheet of a magnitude sufficient to suggest that the latter

was widened before the survey and Greenane after; however one wold expect the "Grand Jury" plaque be located on the parapet of the extension if it referred to it.

During the period from 1730 to 1750 there was considerable public interest in bridges throughout western Europe, particularly in London, in connection with the design of Westminster Bridge. English editions of the classic architectural books of Alberti and Palladio were published (see Chapter 9, Part I). Did this literature influence the design of Greenane Bridge as it did Essex Bridge* Dublin a decade later, or did the inspectors and stone mason evolve the design from local knowledge, tradition and experience. On the basis of the information in Chapter 9, and that given for other Cork bridges described in this book, I conclude that the credit is due to the locals. Some piers of Glanworth Bridge*, for example, built at least a century earlier, are only 5ft thick. The main criterion of flood capacity at the time was aggregate waterway width and to reduce them to 3ft almost gave the equivalent of an extra arch. If the design had been copied from abroad, they would have selected one with larger spans and fewer piers.

Kanturk Bridge

From an aesthetic aspect the bridge over the Dalua, fig. 168, is a much finer and more interesting bridge than Greenane. However, between 1745 and 1760 there were many developments in the state of the art of bridge building throughout the country, so that a comparison between the two bridges would be meaningless. From a functional aspect Greenane is a pioneer. Its performance over a 15-year flood period obviously satisfied all concerned that its infrastructure could be copied, more or less, for Kanturk. In fact, pier thickness was less, reduced to 2ft 7in., the minimum essential as an impost for two arches back to back.

I had completed my assessment of this bridge and its remarkable inscriptions had written it up when Christine Casey, who was completing a PhD. thesis on 18th-century architecture in Ireland, drew attention to a remarkable photographic print of an engraving of Kanturk by an anonymous author which she had discovered in the Irish Architectural Archive. The title of the engraving is "Plan and Elevation of the Bridge over the River

Dalua between the Towns of Kanturk and Littletown in the County of Cork both belonging to the Right Hon. the Earl of Egmont." Beneath the plan both inscriptions are given in full, also the six sets of poetic lines inscripted on the fronts of the coping stones with some explanatory notes.

The plan and the elevation are outlined in fig. 169. They show it in what must have been its original condition before the widening on the upstream side. The original width was 18.5ft compared with 35.5ft today. It had seven arches symmetrical about a central one of 18ft span. The most remarkable and unique features were the "black hole" or prison in the south western abutment and the sets of toilets in each abutment. The overall profile indicates that the designer was influenced by Palladio and was at pains to ensure symmetry as evidenced by the "fictitious door made for the sake of uniformity" in the north-east abutment wing wall.

The cutwaters on the original were triangular and projected 2ft 4in. from the pier head. There were six recesses in the parapet walls above the cutwaters with seats. Grove White records that "the recesses were stone roofed, the inscribed limestone being to the front, and when the bridge was widened the old stones were preserved and placed along the copings of the present north parapet." The inscriptions are still there. From an examination of the 1839 OS six inch it would appear that the black hole and the toilets and the seventh arch had been filled in and built up at that time because the two boundary walls along the river are shown and the length of the downstream parapet is equal to its present length.

There are no cutwaters on the downstream pier ends, as shown on the plan of the original. The ring stones project slightly from the

Fig. 168: *Kanturk Bridge: Downriver Elevation*

spandrel walls, as does the keystones from the ring. Two square oculi are shown in the centre of the spandrel walls each side of the central arch, but these are now gone. The central arch span is 18ft (larger than Greenane) and is flanked on each side by a 17ft, a 15ft and on, the north-east end, by a 13ft (the corresponding one having been filled in). The arches are almost semi-circular and the span to pier ratios range from 5 to 1 to 7 to 1.

The inscriptions on the bridge are incised on two separate plaques. Both are in English. The last two lines on the "prices" plaque are obscured by the concrete footpath and this caused some frustration until the engraving print was discovered. The second plaque records that: "This bridge was erected in the year one thousand seven hundred and sixty, by Richard Purcell of Kanturk and Arthur Bastable of Castlebretrige, Esq., who were appointed trustees for that purpose; as they also were two of the trustees, who erected Blackwater Bridge at Gortmore in 1757."

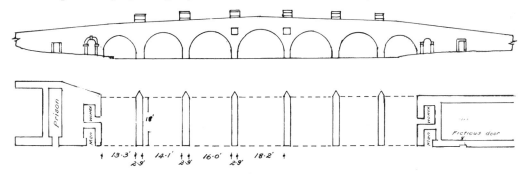

Fig. 169: *Outline of 18th-century Drawing Kanturk Bridge*

Apart from giving the date of erection this inscription contains clues to other relevant facts. First, we must ask: why the mention of Gortmore Bridge? After all, the two names were already established by the plaque on the superb Greenane Bridge erected by the grand jury. Secondly, why were they recorded as trustees. Part of the answers were found in the Kanturk-Cork Turnpike Road Act of 1763 (5 Geo. III c.13), which states that "from a late survey it appears that a much better and shortened road, by 2 miles and 23 perches plantation measure, may be made from Kanturk to the city of Cork, to wit from Kanturk to the new bridge over the Blackwater from thence to and through the lands of Gortmore . . . Kilgobnet . . . Newcastle . . . Fair Lane." Many intermediate townlands are named. A Richard William of Kanturk covered the expenses of soliciting the act and defraying the fees of the procedure. The road was to be 30ft broad within trenches and 16ft of it in breadth sufficiently gravelled; it was to be made "in short and straight lines"; the term was for 61 years from 1766. The first name on a list of about 50 trustees was the Rt. Hon. John, earl of Egmont, and among the rest were the Revd Richard Purcell, and Arthur Bastable. From this we can deduce that the bridge at Gortamore (now known as Roskeen Bridge, it joins the two townlands) was a prerequisite to the act; also that Richard Purcell was a learned man. The use of the word "trustee" implies that the bridge was financed from a trust fund and that the grand jury had no involvement. It is unlikely that either bridge was tolled. Most likely the money came from the super-affluent earl. Local historians will be able to fill the gaps. Roskeen Bridge had about 10 arches in 1839; it was reinforced in the 1960s.

The second and unusual plaque states: "The expence of erecting Westminster Bridge in 1750, amounted to three hundred and eighty nine thousand five hundred pounds. Lond. Mag for 1751. Of Essex Bridge in Dublin, built in 1758 to twenty two thousand five hundred pounds, Dublin City Accts. Of this Bridge, in 1760, to four hundred and (?) pounds six shillings & four pence—County Acct. Sic Parvis compenere Magnum Selebam. Virg." The Latin quotation—"Thus I chose to compare great things with little things"—makes it quite clear that the Earl considered Kanturk Bridge great value relative to Essex and Westminster.

Ruddock[4] recently carried out an in-depth study of the principal arch bridges built between 1735 and 1835 and included a chapter on Westminster Bridge built between 1738–1850, and several pages on Essex Bridge*. He states that Westminster cost £198,323 and quotes Semple's figure and dates for Essex viz. £20,661 and 27 January 1755 completion. Ruddock's figure for Westminster is correct because Blackfriars Bridge on the Thames cost £160,000 in the 1760s. The errors do not matter because the cost ratios per square foot of deck taking Kanturk as one are Essex 20, Westminster 40—sufficient to justify the quote from Virgil, even if Kanturk is founded on bedrock whereas the others are on tidal rivers, in deep water and on clay-gravel beds requiring piling. However, George Semple was not the kind of man who would let such a public comparison go unchallenged and in section 3 of the second edition of his famous book,[5] which is headed "Concerning the building of stone pier in a deep tide-river on a hard rough bed" he included a paragraph (p.109) which commences "Let us now compare small things with great ones" and then goes on to compare his method with that used by Apollodorus when erecting Trajan's bridge across the Danube in AD 104. It could of course be the other way round if the Kanturk plaque was erected after 1780 when the book was published. The superstructure of Essex was replaced in 1882, Westminster was found unsafe, closed and replaced in 1846–57. Kanturk like Greenane discharged the mighty flood of 1981 without submergence of their springings.

Clara

This picturesque six-arch bridge (fig.170) spans the Avonmore river in the beautiful vale of Clara in Co. Wicklow. The village name means the plane; Joyce refers to it as Clarabeg, the little plane, which matches its claim to be the smallest village in Ireland containing a church, a small schoolhouse and two houses. The flashy Avonmore river has flooded the village many times and is no respecter of bridges as evidenced by the Hurricane Charlie flood in 1886, when one bridge, Lions Arch, was swept away and another damaged severely at Avoca*. Clara has withstood many floods and only suffered minor damage to the end of the parapet wall, which was superbly restored by Wicklow Co. Council.

Fig. 170: *Clara Bridge: Upriver Elevation of Four Arches*

Fig. 171: *Clara Bridge: Downriver Elevation of Five Arches*

No early mentions of the crossing or the bridge was found in the literature, apart from maps. The next bridge two miles downriver is at Rathdrum. There was a battle at the latter crossing in 1599 when the Crown forces under Henry Harrington were defeated by the O'Byrnes and O'Tooles. A contemporary sketch of the scene of the battle has survived[1] and it shows a ford at the site of the present Rathdrum bridge. Clara is not shown on the Down Survey map. Moll's map of 1714 shows the road from Dublin (see Miltown Bridge) as a principle continuous road through Kilternan, Enniskerry, to Roundwood via the Old Long Hill, to Castlekevin and thence to Ballymanus and Hacketstown. It crossed the Avonmore at Clara, the bridge being clearly delineated, but neither it or the village is named.

The bridge is 10.5ft wide between parapets. It has six arches; the spans, from south bank are 14'/21'/21'/21'/17'/14'. The rise-to-span and the pier-to-span ratios are approx. one third for the larger arches. The piers thicknesses are 5.5ft with minor variations. There are triangular cutwaters on the upriver side but none downriver (fig. 171). The cutwaters rise to road pavement level and have shallow rounded cappings mainly of mortar. The arch ring stones are thin, about 3in. thick, slabs of mica schist. The parapet walls are coped with thin slabs, in two rows, tilted at about 70° angle. The mortar binding the rows and the slabs is very friable. There is a very neat curved capping stone on the north end of the downriver parapet. The intrados are three-centred.

There is a considerable resemblance between the style of the stone masonry in Clara and the present bridge across the Slaney at Enniscorthy* which was erected in 1790 by Oriel Brothers of Enniscorthy—particularly the cutwater slope and cappings, the arch ring stones and the parapet coping. Both have six spans, but Enniscorthy is considerably larger and its intrados are arcs of circles. Enniscorthy was widened in 1836 and partly rebuilt following flood damage the previous year.

It would appear that Clara is a late 17th- or early 18th-century bridge because a later one would have been made wider. It is unlikely that it is older than the first Essex Bridge in Dublin (1676) which I believe to have been the first with three-centered arches in Ireland.

Cashen

In 1953 when the Office of Public Works were carrying out a drainage scheme on the Cashen river, as the terminal section of the Feale is called, from below the confluence of the Galy and Brick tributaries to the Atlantic, the floating dragon dredger came across the remnants of an old timber bridge in the bed of the river, just above Island Sock in the tidal esturary. The find was brought to the attention of the National Museum who requested the late Michael J. O'Kelly to investigate it. Between 1953 and 1957 when the new channel was being excavated he was able to carry out a detailed examination of excavated timbers and some that were *in situ* and had become exposed

251

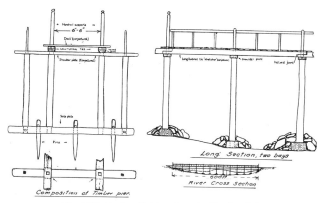

Fig. 172: *Cashen Bridge: Longitudinal and Cross Sections*

as a result of the drainage works. In 1961 he published a full description of the work[1] including scale drawings of the timbers, photographs and a perspective reconstruction of one bay; some of these are reproduced in fig. 172.

The length of the bridge was approximately 600ft. Kelly's extensive search of the literature, summarised in the end of the paper, failed to establish the date of the bridge. The structure was unusual insofar as the trestles had been preassembled on the bank and then dragged and floated out to their positions. The sole plates were pegged to the bed of the river at 10ft centres. No part of the superstructure had survived. The spacing of the piled trestles for the proposed 1581 bridge at Enniscorthy was 12ft, and 12in. square joists were specified. No cross braces were inserted in the Cashen river bridge so the lateral stiffness depended on the deck and the mortice and tenon joints to resist the current. The base plates were loaded with large rocks. The structure had to resist the ebb and flow of the tide often accompanied by high wind velocities.

Searching for early mentions of this bridge I came across a statement[2] referring to Munster in the early 17th century, to the effect that "Four main routes in Munster suffered from a lack of bridges. Military advisers said coastal roads from Limerick to Kerry needed a bridge over the mouth of the Feale", which the writer states was bridged upstream and not where originally advised. These (unreferenced) bits of information clearly indicate that the military headquarters in Thomond Castle wanted a bridge across the Cashen not far from the coast (this area came under Limerick command). In Limerick it was quite likely that

portable, prefabriced trestles were stored as a precaution against collapse or destruction of part of Thomond (old) Bridge* because the ordinary method of temporary repair by driving piles could not be used due to the rock in the bed of the river. Moreover, Prene had been charged in 1282 with shoddy work that caused a collapse and led to the death of 80 people. The type of trestle must have been given considerable thought over the intervening centuries and a system evolved for Limerick. The Cashen-type trestle was the ideal solution because the pegs could be driven into the 18in. of broken rock which the Siemens borehole revealed in 1924. The sole plate needed to be loaded with rocks. Perhaps these were used at Cashen. This hypothesis merits further investigation because Barry[3] conjectured that the bridge broken down by O'Brien as Reymond le Gras marched out in 1190s was built on timber uprights set in kishes of stones and gravel.

Rocque's map shows a continuous road connecting Ballyheigue and Farrenferris across the Cashen in the vicinity in the 1760s. One would hope that the date will be established because O'Kelly's paper gives details that are seldom found in bridge records.

Lismore

An ancient road existed before the 12th century linking Cashel, Ardfinnan, Lismore and Ardmore, called the Rian Bo Phadraigh or track of St Patrick's cow. It crossed the Blackwater at Lismore, probably by a ford. Joyce[1] states that St Carthac, the founder who died in 638, named it Liass-mor or the great enclosure. It became a great centre of learning. The first castle is attributed to Prince John, the Norman Lord of Ireland in 1185, who became the "bridge building monarch" in 1199. No reference to an early bridge at Lismore was found; perhaps there are mentions in the famous Book of Lismore compiled in the 15th century, as it is said to contain much secular information in addition to the lives of Irish saints.

The Down Survey maps show a ford about five miles upriver and a bridge at Cappoquin in the 1650s. Moll's map shows bridges at Ballyduff and Cappoquin, but no crossing in the vicinity of Lismore. The importance of the town diminished after it was burned in 1645. It revived when the fifth duke of Devonshire

Fig. 173: *Lismore Bridge: Brook's Drawing c.1824*

Fig. 174: *Lismore Bridge: Brenan's Drawing c.1833*

inherited the castle and large estates in 1753. Ryland's *History of Waterford* (1824)[2] states that he spent large sums erecting a sessions house and a gaol, an inn and offices and importantly the bridge. Ryland includes a sketch of the bridge by Brooks (reproduced in fig. 173) and states that "it was built at the sole expense of the late Duke . . . in 1775 and is 100ft in span of the arch." Various secondary sources give a range of cost, up to £9,000 and state that the bridge was designed by Thomas Ivory, the noted 18th-century Irish architect.

McParland's 1973 booklet, *Thomas Ivory, Architect*[3] gives the source as "Council Minute Book, 1770–1801, Waterford Town Hall; 13 July 1773. Austin Cooper noted on 11 June 1781 [Nat. Library of Ireland Ms. 772] that according to the Duke of Devonshire's Agent, the Lismore Bridge 'designed by Mr Ivory and executed by Messrs Darley & Stokes' had cost £7,200."

Fig. 175: *Lismore Bridge: Lawrence Postcard c.1900*

This is an invaluable mention and from it we can deduce that the six-span bridge shown in the sketch was the original designed by Thomas Ivory and erected in the 1770s.

There is another sketch of the bridge, drawn by John Brenan and printed in the *Irish Penny Magazine*[4] in 1833 (fig. 174). This sketch shows five arches, the sixth small arch being obscured by trees. The overall profiles, drawn from locations well back from right bank looking upriver, are quite similar. The main arch and the first have a deceptive pointed appearance at the crowns due to the oblique angle from which they were viewed. The article in the magazine on Lismore has one sentence about the bridge: "Here is a fine bridge, over the Blackwater, erected at very great expense, by a former duke of Devonshire, and particularly remarkable for the extent of its principal arch, which spans ninety feet." One important deduction that can be made from Ryland and the latter article is that there must have been no plaque on the bridge; otherwise one would expect specific information from it to be quorted, including a mention of Thomas Ivory.

There seems to have been no public road here before the erection of the bridge; otherwise the Waterford grand jury would have received some mention. New roads were being built all over the country at the time in accordance with the provisions of the 1774 act, outlined in Chapter 3 in Part I, but it would be difficult to envisage any grand jury spending over £7,000 on a new crossing on the estate of a wealthy, often absentee landlord. The insertion of the note in the council minute book tends to confirm this opinion.

The 1842 OS six-inch map shows the river to be about 220ft wide between the banks at the bridge. A substantial pier with cutwaters fore and aft is shown in the river, such that the main south arch had a clear span of about 100ft, the second scales about 70ft. The land arches are not distinguished, indicated by a lack of cutwaters.

I had looked at this bridge briefly in 1986, before searching out the foregoing information, and noted down the inscription on the present plaque: "1858/Lismore Bridge/Rebuilt/C.H. Hunt and E.P. McGee Contractors/Charles Tarrant Engineer. C.S." It gives the impression that the whole bridge had been rebuilt, though the plaque is not located on the main span, but on the third pier on the downriver parapet. A close examination of an old Lawrence postcard (fig. 175) in which the main arch is depicted clearly without foreground camouflage, showed that the main arch spanning the river had not been rebuilt and was obviously Thomas Ivory's original. A difference was noticeable, particularly in the appareil on the arch ring extrados. This was confirmed by the county engineer. John O'Flynn, who also drew attention to a distinct change in the masonry in the parapet walls.

Information on what had happened to Thomas Ivory's land arches emerged fortuitously in a search for information on Carrigadrohid Bridge.* Among the reports in the *Cork Examiner* of 11 November 1853 on the damaged caused to bridges in Co. Cork by the big flood of 3 November was a mention of Lismore. It stated that some dry arches have been destroyed and that a ferry had been established just below the bridge and that the county surveyor was making arrangements for the erection of a temporary wooden bridge which would not interfere with the rebuilding of the arches which were destroyed. The report also mentioned that the wooden bridge at Ballyduff, four miles upriver from Lismore, was completely carried away by the flood.

There is an entry in the records of the Co. Waterford spring assizes, 1854 providing "To the county surveyor, amount of magistrates' warrant for repairs of a sudden damage to the bridge of Lismore £20" and another in the summer assizes 1854 "To Albert Williams, of Dublin for repairing the bridge of Lismore, on the road from Waterford to Cork, pursuant to the plan and specification of the county surveyor, and that the treasurer do, out of any funds in his hands available for the purpose, make advances to the contractor during the progress of the work, on the certificate of the county surveyor, in sums not less than £250 and in the whole not exceeding £1,000 . . . (provision) £2,000". These items obviously relate to the temporary wooden bridge at the fallen land arches because the plaque states that Hunt and McGee were contractors for the 1858 rebuilding.

Robert Manning, in his presidential address to the ICEI in 1879, stated that Lismore brige "is a stone bridge with a (centre) arch of 103ft span and a rise of 23ft. It is the largest span in Ireland except that over the Liffey at Islandbridge, which has a span of 104ft and a rise of 30ft." Manning had carried out a survey of Lismore, north of the river Blackwater in 1870 (Lismore Papers Ms. 7219–7720 in N.L.I.). The Waterford Co. Council *Report on Bridges*, 1918 records that Lismore Bridge was 24ft 4in. wide overall, had seven arches with spans and piers

as follows: 101'/33'-6"/47'-3"/9'-7"/ 44'-3"/6'-9"/44'-3"/6'-9"/44'-3"/6'-8"/43'-9"/6'-8"/40'-9".

On its general condition, it stated it was good apart from partial undercutting of some floors under the land arches in high floods which was repaired for £65. Fig. 175 shows the bridge *c*.1900.

The main span of Lismore, that is, the surviving arch of Thomas Ivory's bridge (fig. 176) was measured and examined by Pat Corbett, assistant engineer, Waterford Co. Council in 1990 using electronic distance measurement. He found the span to be 100ft from abutment to the face of pier 1 at the springing points. He also measured and plotted the intrados curve and found that the springing on pier 1 was 7ft 9in. below the level of the abutment springing. This remarkable characteristic is not visible to the eye or on old or new photographs due to obscuration by trees and shrubs. This was how Ivory avoided minimising the visual effect of the change of grade in the parapet coping over pier 1, slightly evident in the Brooke sketch. The rise of the arch is 29ft, giving a rise to span ratio of 0.29. The river bed is 10.5ft below the span line and almost parallel to it. The abutment is founded on rock and most probably pier 1. The intrados curve has not been fully investigated but from the measurements it would appear to be a segment of a circle of 57ft 9in. radius with an internal angle of 120°. The ring is composed of voussoirs approx. 46in. deep at the crown and 30in. by 18in. wide on the soffit. There is a significant difference in the stone masonry in the main 1775 arch and the 1858 land arches, clearly evi-

Fig. 176: *Lismore Bridge: Surviving 1775 Main Arch*

dent in the parapet and spandrel walls. There is no significant difference in the masonry in pier 1, which is 34ft wide and obviously designed by Ivory as an abutment pier; this, together with the lowering of the main arch springing plane, saved the 100ft arch from sequential collapse in the 1853 flood. It is a landmark arch in the history of Irish masonry bridges and a monument to a courageous architect, a master of stonework who was born in Cork in the 1730s. His interest in long spans was probably stimulated by the 60ft span of Clarke's Bridge erected across the Lee by Hobbs in 1766 (see Cork Bridges).

Laragh & Derrybawn

Three bridges in the immediate vicinity of Laragh, Co. Wicklow reflect developments in bridge building in Ireland over the period 1750 to 1950 in a most striking manner. They span the cool sparkling, flashy waters of the Glenmacnass and Glendasan rivers short distances above their respective adjacent confluences with the Avonmore. Two miles upriver on the Glendasan there are the peaceful, plentiful remains of the ancient monastic sites of Glendalough. Among them lies St Kevin's Church and its steep stone roof propped by the semi-corbelled, semi-radial mortared stone arch that bears witness to the evolution of stone arches in Ireland. Into this peaceful,

Fig. 177: *Laragh (old) Bridge: Upriver Elevation, 1955, with New Reinforced Concrete Bridge Foundations in Foreground*

beautiful valley Dublin Castle in 1799 sent Taylor and his Scottish Fencibles, "to open a direct and easy line of communication between the City of Dublin and the barracks of Glen Crie, the Seven Churches, Glen Malur and Aghavanagh which were built in times of rebellion to keep the mountaineers in subjection". The quotation is from Richard Griffith's description[1] of the building of the Military Road from Rathfarnham to Aughavanna in 1800–9. Griffith himself was to propose and carry out a similar assignment in south Munster a few decades later (see Griffith Group).

Laragh Bridge is in the village. The plaque in Gaelic script bears the name of two men who were active in bridge building in Ireland for half a century after Independence, J.J. Rowan, consulting engineer, and J.T. O'Byrne, co. engineer of Wicklow. The bridge, a fine single-span reinforced concrete arch, was opened in 1956. Here we are concerned with the old bridge which it replaced. Fig. 177 records its unusual construction. It is not certain that this bridge was erected by Major Taylor because the 1840 six-inch OS map shows three cutwaters on both sides. The Wicklow grand jury records, dating back to 1712, were destroyed in the 1922 fire so it is unlikely that the problem will be solved. The extent to which the narrow, old bridge had deteriorated in 1953 is indicated by the propping pier built up to support the springing on the left side: the reinforced concrete springings for the upriver half of the new bridge are shown in the foreground. The cut granite semi-circular coping stones from the old bridged were reused in the new one. Half the new bridge was built first and then the old one was demolished to make way for the second half on the same site.

The second bridge, at Derrybawn, fig 178, is most likely the one built by Major Taylor because Griffith's map shows the Military Road crossing the Glendasan. It is now part of an avenue and not in charge of any authority. The clue to its privatisation is found on the plaque of the third bridge 150 yards downriver. The inscriptions reads: "Erected by/William Bookey Esq./at his own expense on changing the road/William Rourk Arch/1838." This puzzled me when I first read it because of the fine if narrow Derrybawn Bridge which it duplicated. Later when I had an opportunity to consult the 1840 six-inch OS map the explanation became crystal clear. The military road over Derrybawn bridge turned sharp left and ran almost through the lawn of Derrybawn House and then swung left, continuing along the present and original line about one mile south east. By building the new bridge there and constructing about a mile of new road, traffic was transferred to the other side of the river and the abandoned section converted into a private driveway. How all this was arranged with the grand jury under the 1836 act is a bit of a mystery. Presumably a deal was done, a new 40ft single-span 20ft-wide bridge for a 15ft-wide old one.

Bookey is reputed to be the yeoman mentioned in the famous ballad commemorating the 1798 Rebellion, 'Boolavogue': "Twas at the Harrow the boys of Wexford/Showed Bookey's regiment how men could fight."

Reverting to Derrybawn Bridge, it has three spans—a 20ft central span flanked by 12ft bank arches. The piers are 4ft wide with triangular cutwaters upriver; the downstream ends project 9in. from the spandrel face. The piers are in coursed wrought stone. There are projecting corbels about 1ft below the springings to support the centering during construction. The intrados of the arches are three-centered. The voussoirs are large, well-cut stones with headers and bonders into the sheeting (fig. 179). The joints are radial. The spandrel walls and parapets are in random rubble masonry, mainly rounded river stones of local mica schist. Slabs of schist laid transversely and tilted at about 70° angle were used to cope the parapet walls—same style but not as neat as Carragh Bridge*.

The ruins of many ancient ecclesiastical structures in Derrybawn and other townlands along the "Green Road" which leads down the valley to the right from the west end of the bridge were not vested in the State until 1869. One gets an impression that many of the larger wrought stones, especially in the piers of the bridge, may have come from those ruins. Leask[2] records that Piers Gaveston, the English royal favourite, made his offering at St Kevin's shrine following his defeat of the O'Byrnes and the O'Tooles in 1308. In 1398 the place was finally destroyed by the English forces. From the time of the suppression of the monasteries onwards all fell to ruin.

Kerrigan[3] reproduced the manuscript progress report, dated 10 February 1802, by Major Taylor which gave general details of expen-

Fig. 178: *Derrybawn Bridge: Downriver Elevation*

Fig. 179: *Derrybawn Bridge: Detail of Ring Sheeting and Cutwaters Upriver*

diture on the 15 miles of the road from Rathfarnham to Seven Churches to that date. £9400 had been expended; of this, £1550 was spent on "86 small bridges, sewers and water pavements". He estimated that £10,900 would be required to construct the remaining 18 miles from Seven Churches to Aughavannagh, of which sum £1,900 was for "bridges, sewers and water pavements". There was no major bridge in the first part of the road. Laragh barracks was built north of Laragh Bridge and this would seem the logical terminal point of the first 15 miles; however, Taylor states Seven Churches which implies the junction of section 1 and section 2 was south of Laragh bridge. If so, the old Laragh bridge was already there. The estimate for the second section, 18 miles, states "bridges" not "small bridges", and this implies at least one large bridge. There are

Fig. 180: *Bookeys Bridge: Downriver Elevation*

Fig. 181: *Bookeys Bridge: Skewback and Voussoirs Upriver*

only two on the section that could be called large—Derrybawn and Greenan (Avonbeg river). Hence it is possibile that the former was built by the military. Further research is needed to answer the problem. My impression about the wrought stones in Derrybawn bridge and my estimate of the period of its construction were confirmed when I came across the following statement by Thomas Davis[4] from the *Nation* newspaper of the early 1840s: "Two or three of the seven churches [Glendalough] are levelled to the ground; all the characteristic carvings described by Ledwich and which were 'quite unique to Ireland' are gone. Some were removed and used as key-stones for the arches of Derrybawn-bridge". This finding adds a new dimension to the historical importance of the bridge.

Bookey's Bridge (fig. 180) is a very fine 40ft-span segmental arch. It has cut granite

voussoirs, 18in. deep by 18in. (mean) width on the face. The skewbacks are perfectly cut and somewhat unusual in that the extrados curve meets the base to form an apex (fig. 181). The abutments and spandrels are also in ashlar granite. The photo shows a 1in. diameter hole drilled into the first voussoir and another in the spandrel stone above it; these were bored during World War II by the Irish Army so the bridge could be blown in the event of an invasion. The bridge is 20ft wide between the parapets. Whatever Bookey's motives may have been, he left a first class bridge, a beautiful and serviceable monument that matches the grandeur of the scene.

Lemuel Cox's Timber Bridges

In an 1982 paper[1] on the evolution of wooden bridge trusses James, having dealt with the remarkable timber bridges built by the Gruberman brothers in Switzerland and Germany in the mid-18th century (including the famous Schaffhausen erected in 1756/8) goes on to mention the lack of interest in timber bridges in the United Kingdom at the time (apart from the "ripple of interest" created by Frederick Harvey in the 1770s). Harvey, who was chaplain to George III, visited Schaffhausen and made measured drawings of some of the Gruberman bridges. In the year 1768 he was appointed bishop of Derry and eleven years later succeeded to the family title, the earldom of Bristol.

On his appointment to Derry he found the city greatly handicapped by the lack of a bridge across the River Foyle. He obviously stirred up the corporation because in 1769 they sent a memorial to the Irish Society, who owned the ferry rights and had leased them to the corporation at a rent of £20 per year, seeking their consent to a bridge. It took eleven years to get this consent and in 1790 the corporation obtained an act (30 Geo. III c.31) empowering them to build a bridge and to borrow the money and charge tolls. Harvey had offered £1,000 towards the cost and no doubt was influential in cutting through the red tape that seemed to make the venture impossible.

During the second half of the eighteenth century the need for and the art of constructing long timber bridges in North America was growing rapidly, particularly in the wake of migration to the west which encountered major obstacles in crossing large rivers. James records that many very long, multi-span, pile-and-beam timber bridges were constructed by Samuel Sewell (1724–1815) including one over the river Charles in Boston and one consisting of two strutted beam spans of nearly 100ft each by Hales over the Connecticut river in 1784/5. Among these pioneers Lemuel Cox sprang to fame on 17 June 1786 when the wooden bridge her erected to replace the ferry between Boston and Charlestown was opened. Caleb Snow in his *History of Boston* states that it was then "considered the greatest event that had ever been undertaken in America". The bridge was opened amidst much firing of ceremonial cannon, great festivity and congratulations for "the master workman", Mr Lemuel Cox.

Following these events, Cox's fame spread to Europe and obviously came to the attention of Derry Corporation which invited him to submit a proposal for erecting a timber bridge across the Foyle. This he did and the results are summarised in an Ordnance Survey Report:[2] "At length in 1789 the erection of a wooden bridge was begun by Lemuel Cox, of the firm of Cox and Thompson of Boston, in New England, near which city they had constructed such bridges over waters as deep and rapid as the Foyle at Derry, and of greater length. In 1790 it was opened for foot passengers, and in the spring of 1791 for vehicles." Cox then went on to build six more bridges in Ireland.

We found no single paper among the literature of historical, antiquarian societies or professional institutions dealing in depth with Cox and his work. What follows is based on incidental mentions in books, journals, acts of parliament, and in relation to Waterford, a most informative booklet prepared by Tom Ryan, senior staff officer of Waterford Corporation, entitled "A Tale of Three Bridges" which was issued in May 1983 as part of a display organised by the corporation.

One of the earliest mentions of Cox's work in Ireland is from the diary[3] of an American manufacturer named Gilpin, who visited Ireland in 1796; he recorded that "travelling on to Londonderry, he was impressed by an entrance [to the city] over a bridge built of oak and fir by an American carpenter named Cox with the aid of twenty four American workmen." This note suggests that the tradition

that Cox came in a ship fully equipped with all the necessary materials, equipment and workmen for the job is correct. The seven bridges built by Cox and his team seem to have been erected in the following order—Derry, Waterford, Wexford, Ferrycarrig, New Ross, Mountgarret and lastly Portumna, completed in 1796. His ship must have made many trips to and fro to North America over the six years because the principal material used in all of the bridges was Quebec oak in hewn lengths of up to 80ft. The fact that suitable size Irish oak could not be found shows the extent to which the country had been denuded of its large oak forests in the 17th and 18th centuries.

The literature search for information on Cox's Irish bridges left many gaps still to be filled, possibly from contemporary newspaper reports, examination of plans of the Derry & Waterford bridges that are stated to have survived, and Boston sources. In these circumstances the best that can be done here is to outline the principal facts that have been garnered concerning six of the bridges, focussing in detail on the seventh, Waterford, which is well documented by Tom Ryan and also in the *Transactions* of ICEI.

Derry (Foyle)

The drawing by William Bartlett (1809–1854) reproduced in fig. 182 is undated but, taking account of his age, it was probably executed in 1830 when he also drew the old Baals Bridge, Limerick, demolished in that year. The left half of the drawing shows a strutted beam bridge which was erected after 350ft of Cox's simple beam original was carried away by large masses of ice in February 1814. The original act, 30 Geo. III c. 31 (1790), empowered Derry Corporation to build a bridge and to charge tolls to be applied for lighting, watching and maintenance etc. The following technical details are given in the OS report. The cost of Cox's bridge was £16,594. It was 1068ft long and 40ft broad. The oak piles composing the trestles were from 14in to 18 square, the heads being tenoned into a cap-piece 17in square and 40ft long. The trestles were spaced at 16.5ft and connected by 13 stringers, equally spaced and bolted transversely, which supported the decking. An elevation of one of the trestles is shown in fig. 183. There were three sets of diagonal braces and three girth pieces, the

Fig. 182: *Derry Bridge: Bartlett's Drawing c.1830*

bottom one obviously intended to rest on the river bed after the vertical had penetrated about 5ft into the silt. A drawbridge was installed at the midpoint of the western half of the bridge for navigation purposes.

In 1800 an increase in toll charges was granted under 40 Geo. III c. 41. In 1814 a third act (54 Geo. III c. 230) empowered Derry Corporation to borrow on debenture a sum not exceeding £60,000 for various purposes including the bridge to be secured by the tolls and other estates. The lord lieutenant was empowered to order the treasury to advance £15,000 for repairing the bridge, to be refunded over 20 years. By 1831 no part of this had been repaid and the government procured from the court a sequestration against the bridge tolls, subsequently mitigated to 20 annual instalments of £816—an arrangement confirmed in another act, 2 & 3 William IV c. 107. In 1835 another act was passed setting up a new body corporate called "The Trustees of the Londonderry Bridge". This body was charged with accounting to the lord lieutenant and the grand juries of the three adjoining counties annually and with applying residue from tolls to the repairing of the timber bridge or the erection of a new one. The estimates for a new bridge designs prepared by John Rennie were: stone £126,663; cast iron, three arches £81,917; a suspension bridge having a clear opening £56,960; and for an improved wooden bridge £46,120.

The subsequent history of the crossing is outside our present scope. There are many more financial details in the OS report, all of which relate to the subsequent financial mismanagement of Cox's superb pioneering bridge.

A wrought iron bridge of eleven spans, Carlisle Bridge, replaced Cox's in 1863. It in turn was replaced in 1933 by a double deck tubular-steel truss-type bridge (Craigavon Bridge) to carry rail and road traffic. A fine additional three-span box-girder steel bridge with pre-stressed concrete box-girder approach spans was built in 1984.

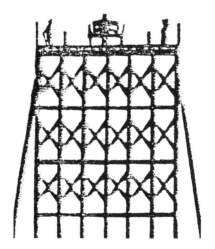

Fig. 183: *Derry Bridge: Outline of Trestle*

Wexford (Slaney)

Records of this bridge are sparse. It was erected by Cox in 1794-5 in nine months at a cost of £15,000. It was 1554ft long and 34ft wide. It had 75 trustle piers, each containing six verticals. In October 1827 portion of the bridge fell. The repairs including the replacement of portions at each end by stone causeways and the removal of the footways. In 1851 J.B. Farrell presented a paper[4] giving a proposed design for a new bridge, in the course of which he stated that it was deemed prudent, not only to remove the old bridge, then 1370ft long with its causeways of solid masonry, but to make the waterway of the new one to be sited three quarters of a mile upriver, ample. He stated that an act of parliament had been obtained in 1847 with the sanction of the grand jury for the construction of a new free bridge, it being of considerable importance for the improvement of the harbour. The remainder of the paper deals with the proposed bridge. The grand jury erected a new bridge in 1872.

Ferrycarrig (Slaney)

Little information was found on this bridge though the abutments are still to be seen upriver of the present bridge. The target sum for subscription in 1794 was £7,000. The bridge was replaced in 1912 by a 12-span reinforced-concrete bridge. It, in turn, was replaced by a new precast pre-stressed concrete bridge in 1979.[5]

New Ross (Barrow)

In June 1210 King John issued writs from "Pontem Novum",[6] also described as the Town of the New Bridge of William Earl Marshal. The bridge connected the two parts of the Liberty of Leinster, Wexford and Kilkenny which the earl had acquired through marriage with the heiress of Strongbow. The bridge was replaced in the 14th century. In 1643 it was broken down by the Irish retreating from the battle of Kilrush townland. A bridge is depicted on the town's coat of arms. No bridge is shown on Moll's 1714 map, but a ferry service is indicated both here and at Passage West. The first bridge shown on the river is at Graiguenamanagh.

In 1988 the remnants of a 12th or 13th century Norman, timber trestle bridge were found during drainage works involving excavations under the foundations of the 1272 stone arch bridge across the river Mannow in Monmouth in Wales.[7] The report on the archaeological investigations has not yet been published but from an artist's impression in the note it would appear to be not unlike Cox's bridges, apart from the trestles being founded on sole plates. The research report should throw considerable light on early timber bridges here as well as in Britain.

Lewis's *Dictionary*[8] states that Cox's bridge at New Ross was initiated by a company incorporated by act of parliament, which raised £11,200 by means of shares. The bridge constructed of American oak, in 1794, was 358ft long, 40ft broad and rested on 24 piers (trestles). It terminated in a 150ft causeway on the Kilkenny side and included a drawbridge for the passage of large vessels. The tolls, let annually, produced £800 p.a. The bridge was damaged by ice in 1814; the repairs involved removal of the footways. It was carried away by ice on 18 January 1867. In July 1867 an act (30 & 31 Vic. c. 50) was passed "to afford further facilities for the erection of certain bridges in Ireland". Section 28 throws considerable light on Cox's Bridge

And whereas a Bridge at New Ross, over the River Barrow (which River is the Boundary between the Counties of Wexford and Kilkenny), the Property of the Commissioners for building a Bridge over River of Ross, was partly carried away in the Month of January last, and great Inconvenience and Loss was resulted therefrom: And whereas the Tolls of said Bridge are the Property of the said Commissioners, and the Right of Ferry over the said River is the Property of the said Commissioners, and it is desirable that a free Bridge shall be erected in place thereof, and for such Purposes it is necessary to purchase the Property of the said Bridge Commissioners: And whereas the Grand Juries of the Counties of Wexford and Kilkenny assembled at the last Spring Assizes, by Resolutions entered on the Record of their respective Proceedings, have signified their Consent to such Purchase, and to the building of a Bridge under the Provisions of the recited Act, in place of that which was destroyed as aforesaid, and have respectively presented

Memorials to His Excellency the Lord Lieutenant of Ireland under the Provisions of the recited Act, and have stated therein, in addition to the several Matters by the recited Act required, the Nature and Particulars of the Property necessary to be purchased, and the Necessity of such Purchase: Be it therefore enacted, That the said Resolutions shall be as valid and effectual to signify the Consent herein-before required as if such Consent had been given and signified, and such Resolutions had been passed and entered, after the passing of and under the Provisions of this Act, and that the said Memorials shall also be as valid and effectual as if the same had been presented under the Provisions of the recited Act and this Act, and all the Acts and Proceedings herein-before provided shall and may be done, had, and taken thereupon accordingly; and for the Purposes of this Act the Grand Jury of the County of Wexford shall be deemed to be the Grand Jury which shall have presented the Memorial, and the Secretary of such Grand Jury shall be the Officer to do all Acts herein-before provided to be done by the Secretary of the Grand Jury presenting a Memorial under this Act; and in ascertaining the Purchase Money to be paid to the said Commissioners the Value of all the Property to be taken from them shall be included, and no further Obligation shall rest on the said Commissioners to restore the said Bridge.

The bridge was replaced by the grand juries in 1869 at a cost of £50,137 including £12,336 paid for the old bridge rights. It, in turn, was replaced by the present bridge in the 1960s. The minutes of the New Ross Bridge Committee for the years 1795–1868 are preserved in the manuscript section of the National Library in Dublin. The entries for the first year, covering the period of construction, give many interesting sidelights on the job. Under date 7 March 1796 we find an entry recording the presentation of a souvenir to Mr Cox on the conclusion of the work: "a piece of plate valued £10 with an inscription expressive of their approbation." The majority of the later entries in this minute-book are concerned with the type of weighty matters in the discussion of which local committees excel—e.g. the colour of the toll-gatherers uniform and the correct tolls to be levied for an ass loaded and the same animal unloaded. One can imagine the heated debate which preceded the passing of the resolution that "the chips made by the carpenters repairing the bridge shall in future be the property of the toll-collector".

Mountgarret Bridge (Barrow)

The bridge erected by Cox c.1794 at this location, three and a half miles upriver from New Ross, was replaced by a reinforced concrete bridge incorporating a 40ft steel lifting span, commenced in 1925 and opened in 1929. The new bridge was the subject of a detailed paper[9] presented to the Institution of Civil Engineers of Ireland in 1932 by John Maconchy of Delap & Waller, consulting engineers for the project. Like all good papers it contains a short synopsis of the history of what went before. The old structure, he said, was erected at the same time as New Ross and by the same builder, Lemuel Cox, who was described in an old record as "the inventor" of the wooden bridge which could be erected "where art had despaired of erected one in stone". Cox's bridge at Mountgarret was 209ft long, had six main spans, two short end spans and an opening span of 26ft, all in timber. The width was 18ft. The piles, extracted, were unshod hewn oak driven to depths of 3ft 6in, to 8ft 6in. below river bed level. New pieces had been spliced in to many of them and those extracted were found to be sound below bed level but much worn at that level. There was a 3.5in. iron staple in one face in each pile just above the terminal pointing. Maconchy expressed the opinion that "these may have been used for keeping foot ropes in position if the bents were launched and driven as trestles." Three bays on the Wexford side had been damaged by fire a few years earlier. Tolls had ceased in 1902. The decision to replace the old bridge had been taken in 1910 but the money available at the time £4,700 proved inadequate. An examination of the masonry abutments of Cox's bridge in 1925 showed that with some small repairs they would be safe provided they did not carry weight from the new bridge (the end spans were cantilevered for this purpose). J.H. Waller, principal of the firm, made a contribution to the discussion which provided useful information on Cox's Waterford bridge which is outlined below under that sub-head.

Portumna Bridge (Shannon)

The act for this bridge (35 Geo. III c.1) was passed in 1795. Eight thousand pounds was subscribed and Cox commenced work in 1795 and finished it the following year. Moynan, county surveyor of N. Tipperary, who presented a paper to the ICEI in 1910[10] which dealt with the replacement of Cox's bridges at Portumna and Waterford, stated that no record of Portumna Bridge was to be found. It had been repaired and strengthened in 1818 at a cost of £3,000 but in 1834 it was in a ruinous condition.

A full description of the original act is given in another act, 4 & 5 William IV c. 61 (1835). The relevant sections give a very clear description of the powers of the commissioners, how they operated and the problems that arose:

Section XI: And whereas by an Act passed in the Parliament of Ireland in the Thirty-fifth year of the Reign of His late Majesty King George the Third, intituled An Act for building a Bridge over the River Shannon at Portumna in the County of Galway, certain Persons therein named were constituted Trustees for receiving Subscriptions for building a Bridge over the River Shannon where the Ferry of Portumna then was, and the Subscribers thereto were created, united, and elected into One Company, and were thenceforth to be One Body Politic and Corporate by the Name of the Commissioners for building a bridge over the River Shannon at Portumna, with certain Powers and Duties in the said Act particularly mentioned and set forth: And whereas the said Company was by the said Act authorised to demand and receive certain Sums therein specified in the Nature of Toll for Passage over the said Bridge, and also to raise Money for the Purposes of the said Act in any Manner which they or any Eleven or more of them should judge necessary: And whereas the said Commissioners afterwards caused a Bridge to be erected and built across the said River Shannon pursuant to the Provisions of the said Act, and thereupon received and have since continued to collect the several Tolls thereby given, as well for the Purposes of maintaining and keeping in repair the said Bridge as reimbursing the several Persons subscribing

Money for the Execution of said Act vested in them, have from Time to Time borrowed considerable sums of Money on the Credit of the said Tolls, on account of which Loans the said Commissioners are now indebted to the Extent of Three thousand Pounds or thereabouts: And whereas, notwithstanding the Receipt of such Tolls, and of the Funds so produced on the Credit thereof, the said Bridge hath been neglected, and is now in such a State of Dilapidation and Decay as to be nearly impassable and useless, and it is therefore expedient that the Management of the said Bridge should be otherwise conducted, and the Revenue arising therefrom more judiciously and properly applied; be it therefore enacted, That from and after the Commencement of this Act the said Act of the Thirty-fifth Year of the Reign of His late Majesty King George the Third shall be and the same is hereby repealed, save and except as to any Matters or Things heretofore done or which have heretofore taken place under the Authority thereof.

Section XII. Provided always, and be it enacted, That nothing herein contained shall have the Effect of reviving, creating or validating any Right of Ferry or other Right or Privilege abolished or affected by the said Act.

Section XIII. And be it enacted, That the said Bridge at Portumna, and all the Right, Title, Interest, Property, Claim, and Demand, in Law or in Equity, of the said Body Politic and Corporate thereto, and in and to all Tolls, Revenues, Profits, Emoluments, Income and Benefits arising therefrom or thereout, shall be and the same are hereby transferred to and vested in the said Commissioners for the Execution of the said Act passed in the First and Second Years of the Reign of His present Majesty, and their Successors, in like Manner as any Public Work to which the said last-mentioned Act may now apply.

Subsequent sections enabled other counties deriving benefit to contribute to the cost of rebuilding; authorised the Commission of Public Works to charge tolls and the lord lieutenant to advance money from the half million pound consolidation fund towards the "substantial cost". Moynan gives a detailed description of the 1834 replacement timber bridge which cost

£24,000 and was somewhat similar to Cox's, and details of the third, plate girder, bridge which was in course of erection in 1910 and which has lasted to the present time.

Waterford Bridge

The stupendous role of Lemuel Cox in the history of Ireland's road bridges and his great technical ability, ingenuity and competence, both as designer and contractor, are best exemplified by Waterford Bridge because more technical information was discovered about it. Moreover, there is no record of anyone having succeeded in erecting a bridge or a ford across the Suir in the city nor downriver of it before it was bridged by Cox in 1792. The nearest crossing point upriver appears to have been Carrick-on-Suir, but is not clear whether or not it was fordable at any point in between.

Waterford City was founded by the Vikings c. AD 850 and according to Joyce was spelled Vadrefiord by early English writers, fiord meaning an inlet of the sea. Power[11] states that the Irish version, Port Lairge, is certainly Danish and probably means "Snug Haven", though authorities differ on this. Colm O'Lochlainn[12] shows the ancient Slighe Cualann from Tara and Dublin crossing the Barrow at New Ross and terminating in a ford at the city. There is a mention in 5 Geo. III c. 1 (1765) allocating £1,500 to the mayor of Waterford and others "towards clearing and making deeper by six feet the ford in the river of Waterford from the little island to the opposite shore on the Kilkenny side . . .". The grant was not taken up and was repeated in a 1767 act with the added prescription that sufficient security be given "to complete the said works before the next session of Parliament". The work was obviously in progress at the time. Information on the consequences of this work are given in a paper[13] by Otway in 1886 which stated that work carried out in the 1860s had deepened the Queen's Channel (the Ford Channel) to 13ft LWOST, at the shallow west end and that "before this work was executed there was only 6 feet at low water over some of the upper portion, and nearly all commerce went round the circuitous course to the south of Little Island, involving considerable danger in navigation both to steam and sailing vessels . . .". From this evidence it was quite clear that the north channel was fordable before 1767, but

very unlikely that there was any ford over the south (King's Channel). Confirmation of this is found in Power's book (p.191) which also indicated that the deep south channel separated the island from the Co. Waterford mainland and that no trace or tradition of a church or monastery on the island itself had been brought to light. It is evident therefore that O'Lochlainn was misled by early mentions of this ford into thinking it connected Kilkenny and Waterford.

There may have been some attempts to build a timber bridge across the Suir in the vicinity of Waterford during the medieval and Tudor periods, given the beneficial effect it would have had on the commerce of the city, and the charters and privileges it received from successive English monarchs. Yet one finds no record of a grant of pontage. In 1649 Cromwell had to construct a pontoon bridge to convey his army across the river. The failure to bridge the Suir here is explained technically rather than politically, namely, that it was simply not feasible because of the great depth of the river along the waterfront—ranging from 30ft to 60ft. The need of a bridge became acute in the mid-18th century and numerous ideas began to emerge as to how the problem should be solved.

George Semple was called in to advise following his successful completion of the second Essex Bridge* across the Liffey in Dublin in 1753. His recommendations are set out in Section IV, part II of the expanded second edition of his famous book[14] published in 1780. The relevant chapter is headed "concerning Bridges principally contrived for the Use of Londonderry, Waterford and Wexford and for such other large and deep Rivers". He too was baffled by the problem and the only solution he offered was the one adopted by Trajan when he wanted to convey his army across the Danube in AD 104: "You have been repeatedly informed, that in building Trajan's Bridge, Apollodurus had 'ten outward piers built on an artificial foundation, by wheeling in vast quantities of large and small stones, and other filling, after the usual manner of carrying a mole into the sea'." In earlier chapters he described Trajan's bridge and stated it was "one of the most amazing works in the world . . . composed of twenty arches, nineteen piers and two land abutments, all of solid masonry, each arch was 170 feet span. The piers, we are

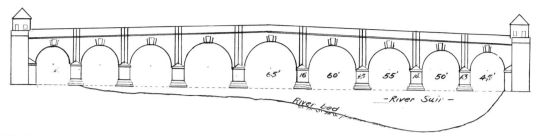

Fig. 184: *Waterford Bridge: Outline of Bridge Proposed by T. Covey in 1760*

told, were 60 feet broad, and 150 feet high; that each of the land abutments was 120 feet (which is twice the thickness of the piers) that the arches were all true semi-circles . . .". The bridge was demolished by Emperor Hadrian (117–38) to prevent barbarians making incursions. One of the massive piers on the Romanian bank at Drobeta, Turmu-Severin, has survived.

Semple's recommendations were to raise the bed "as high as you think convenient, and reduce the depth of the low water to perhaps 8ft, allowing 4ft for the banking and 4ft for the navigation. Build the bridge thereon according to the preparations most agreeable to the situation, paying due regard to the heights of banks and quays and particularly observing that the higher you raise the bed the less expensive the bridge."

The "battle", as it was latter described, as to how Waterford Bridge should be built raged throughout the 1760s and at the end of the decade a book on the topic financed by public subscription was published by one of the proponents, named Thomas Covey, entitled *A Scheme for building a Bridge over the River Suire at Waterford."*[15] There is a copy in the National Library and it is a revealing document not just in relation to Waterford but generally because it gives a good insight into the state of knowledge at the time when there was a massive programme of public works in progress (see Chapters 3 and 6, Part I). The principal elements discussed in the first half of the book are the best site for the bridge, Waterford's trade and its severed local catchment area, the limitation of the ferry services, the impracticability of building a wooden bridge, Palladio's ideas, various bridges in London, arch bridges and methods of constructing foundations. He reached the conclusion that the "only practicable method is by raising a bank to within five

feet of low water at lowest and then building the bridge thereon"—a Trajan solution.

The second part of the book is devoted to an elaboration of his scheme. The proposed arch bridge would be 44ft wide, "as broad as that at Westminster" and this would require a bank 126ft wide on the surface. He then 'discussed the choice of arch shape and opts for semi circular ones. A plan and elevation is included, outlined here in fig. 184. The book concludes with a detailed estimate amounting to £36,745. 18s. 6d.

The first thing that is apparent from a reading of the book is that the solution proposed and the bridge design were largely based on Semple's recommendations, which were presumably available to Covey though Semple's book was not published until 1778. On p. 53 Covey states that "The manner of Essex Bridge would never answer for founding a bridge over this river even in the shallowest place: and it appears to me to be the most difficult yet described. The Liffey is but a mere brook in comparison to this river for breadth and depth."

I broke down Covey's estimate into four parts and found that the bankfill accounted for 21%, the arch centering for 25%, stone masonry 44% and general items the balance. In regard to wooden bridges Covey stated that "it is in no way doubtful that a wood bridge was formerly opposite Mr Strangman's on the upper Quay to the other side of the Black Slip. It is said built by the Danes"; however, the only evidence he put forward is that some pieces of timber were taken from the bottom of the river according to reports of "many living". He states that the upright standards for a wooden bridge, assuming 10ft penetration into the bed, would have to be 73ft long, and for such a length they could not be less than 3ft square at the head. He also

Fig. 185: *Waterford Bridge: Early Photo of Cox's Bridge*

mentions that the cost of keeping up Cappoquin* timber bridge would have covered the cost of a stone one and concludes that "the attempting to build a wooden bridge over this river [Suir] at the place most convenient for it would be as idle as it is impractical."

In regard to Covey's conclusions, one can only remark that the river Suir in full spate would not have tolerated such a massive mole across its channel for very long before scouring it and any stone bridge erected on it out of its path. Ryan states that Covey's proposal fell through either on grounds of impracticality or for lack of support or because of the obstacle of ferry rights or a combination of these. He also outlines the various resolutions adopted by the corporation in a continuing effort to obtain a bridge from 1779 until an act of parliament was obtained in 1786. The act established a company, "The commissioners for building a bridge over the Suir at Waterford", and empowered it to procure subscriptions up to £30,000.

Cox's Waterford Bridge

It is easy to see why the commissioners, given the foreknowledge of progress on the Foyle

Bridge, invited Lemuel Cox to tender for a similar bridge across the Suir and to accept his quotation of £14,000. The bridge, shown in fig. 185, was completed in nine months and opened on 18 January 1794. There was a plaque on the bridge, and the inscription was recorded in a letter published in the *Irish Builder* of 15 May 1891 from the internationally famous engineer Robert Manning, who had copied it down as a boy. It read: "In 1793/A year rendered sacred to national prosperity by the extinction of Religious Division/The Foundation of this bridge was laid, at the expense of associated individuals unaided by Parliamentary grants,

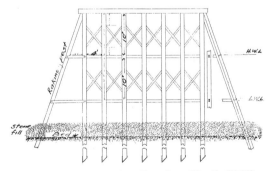

Fig. 186: *Waterford Bridge: Elevation of Trestle (1910)*

by Sir John Newpark, Bart., Chairman of the Committee/Mr Lemuel Cox/A native of Boston in America/Architect." Manning concluded his letter as follows: "The bridge is still a good one, but I well remember hearing of the apprehension of destruction by ice."

The Waterford Bridge was 832ft long, 40ft wide, consisting of a 26ft carriageway and two 7ft footpaths; it had 38 spans, cost £27,000 and was replaced in 1910 by Redmond Bridge, opened in 1913.

Moynan in his ICEI paper[10] of 1910 gave invaluable technical information on Cox's bridge. He included an elevation of one pier reproduced here in fig. 186. The trusses (trestles) he stated were built on shore, floated down the river, and up-ended in their permanent position; they were sunk in the river bed, by weighting, as far as possible and steadied by large quantities of stone ballasting tipped in round each pier. The original design provided for no opening span but one 26ft wide was provided. In 1852 a new one 40ft wide was constructed by the commissioners. The pier trusses were about 20ft apart, the decking consisting of 3in. Quebec oak planks. The cost of upkeep had been small but in recent years it had reached £1,200 p.a. It was a toll bridge till 1909 when the corporation purchased the rights for £63,000 and made it toll free. Many of the original piles were still in the bridge and found to be in "splendid condition". Moynan was a member of the 1907 viceregal commission that, for traffic reasons, recommended that a new bridge be erected. His elevation shows iron shoes on the trestle legs; this may be wrong as none were found on the salvaged pile at Mountgarret bridge.

The consulting engineer, J.H. Waller, in his contribution to the discussion on the Mountgarret Bridge paper[9] mentioned above, stated that he had been assistant engineer in connection with the construction of Redmond Bridge in 1910 and had "practical experience of the wonderful work performed by Lemuel Cox". He had been involved in the pulling down of the old bridge in 1910 to make way for the new structure. He mentioned Covey's proposal which "fortunately Lemuel Cox knocked out". He had been unable to discover how Cox weighted the trestles into the silt but it was apparent that he had not driven them as piles because he could never have fixed the bottom wailing had he done so. (This wailing is shown

in the sketch of the Derry Bridge but was obviously missed out in Moynan's elevation.) He concluded his contribution by mentioning that there were "in Waterford drawings of the Old Bridge" and stating "there was certainly no doubt that the American carpenter had constructed one of the finest bridges of his day and if an account of his works was put together it would form a gracious acknowledgement of his valuable services to Ireland and to the profession."

The best technical description of the bridge, given in Ryan's booklet, is the report of William Friel, resident engineer on the contract for its removal in 1910. It states:

The old timber bridge had a length, when first constructed, of 832 feet, but owing to quay extensions the length was reduced to 734 feet, consisting of 38 spans varying in width from 9 to 22 feet. It appears strange that the spans should vary so much in width, but I think the explanation is that the timber piles composing the supports for roadway were not driven in the ordinary sense by a pile-driver and each pile separately, but each pier or bay, which consisted of seven vertical piles, was assembled on the shore and braced together with two sets of longitudinal walers bolted to the piles, one set about the level of L.W.O.S.T. mark, and one about 8 feet above same. Above, below, and between these horizontal walers there were double diagonal braces notched into and between the piles, the lowest set being, when in position, 7 feet below L.W.O.S.T. Each bay consisted of the seven vertical oak piles, all braced together and many of the piles were made up of various lengths halved and bolted together, the average length of each piece composing the built up pile being twenty feet. When the braced structure was ready for placing in position it was run out from the shore and up-ended, and sank of its own weight to an average depth of 6 feet into the river-bed. The inclined cutwater piles, one on the up and one on the down-stream side, were then placed in position and probably driven by a pile driver, and braced in position to their respective bays. As the bays were placed in position, rubble stone from Bilberry and the Dunkitt quarries was then dumped round the pile bases to an average depth of 4 feet. This rubble sank into the soft mud about 2 feet, and left its top surface about 2 feet above the adjoining natural bed of the river. The original size of the piles varied from 13 to 13.5 inches square, and owing to the erosive action of the silt-laden water many of the piles, when removed in 1913, were found to be reduced to 9 inches square just above the bed of the river and for about 18 inches above same. The wearing surface of this bridge was oak planking 2.5 inches thick. The width of the roadway was 26 feet, with two 7-foot wide footpaths.

The former timber bridge across the Blackwater has sometimes been attributed to Lemuel Cox. That bridge was a strutted beam bridge like the 1835 reconstructed left half of Derry Bridge, as shown in Bartlett's drawing and the one shown in fig. 149. Youghal Bridge was designed in the 1830s by Alexander Nimmo, who died before it was built. The construction was supervised by J.E. Jones, who described it in detail in a paper[16] presented to the Institution of Civil Engineers in London in 1832. The bridge is shown in a Lawrence photo. It was replaced by an iron bridge in 1882 and it in turn by the present reinforced concrete bridge, on a new site upriver, in the 1950s.

Trestle bridges with simply supported spans as built by Cox particularly those without transverse bracing between trestles are very vulnerable to shock impact by blocks of ice or by ships. On the other hand, such bracing would have impeded boats and rendered the bridges vulnerable to impact by tree trunks and other flood debris. I did not search for evidence of the *Toredo navalis* or *Limnoria terebrans* in the estuaries but the shorter lives of the Wexford and New Ross Bridges suggest that they may have been a factor as described in Chapter 7, Part I.

Ryan states that in 1794 Cox was presented with the freedom of the City of Waterford in a silver box "as a testimonial of the very able, workmanlike and expeditious manner in which he executed the building of the new wooden bridge across the river Suir in this city." He also mentions that he died in poor circumstances, that the inventory of his estate came to only 20 dollars, and that eventually his executors succeeded in realising a sum of 2,555 dollars which was divided in ten shares

between his children and grandchildren. The house in which he died in Charlestown, Massachusetts, was destroyed by fire in 1855. The date of his death is not given.

Marquis's *Who's Who*[17] states that Cox was born in 1736 in Boston and married Susannah Hickling in 1763. They had two sons and he died in Charlestown on 18 February 1806.

Recalling John Waller's plea in 1910, set out above, that an account of Lemuel Cox's works be put together as a "gracious acknowledgement of his services to Ireland", one can state that Tom Ryan's booklet goes a long way towards fulfilling the debt in relation to Waterford City; this present account may go some of the way to meeting the national debt.

Sarah

The early history of the ford at Kilmainham across the Liffey in Dublin is summarised by Conlin and de Courcy,[1] who draw attention to variations in the name (Kilmehanoc, Kilmehanfach) and possible locations along the stretch of river. There are references to a ford in the Annals of the Four Masters under the year 919; to "fords" in King John's Charter, of 1200 and to free fishing from the bridge of Kilmainham to the sea in the 13th century.

The precise location of the boundary between the city and the county and where it crossed the river grew in importance from the 17th century onwards because of statutory obligations regarding the financing of bridges. In this context the mention of fords in the charter could imply one inside and the other outside the boundary.

There is a very clear-cut mention in the Statute of 1456 (34 Hen. VI c. 28) which ordained by the authority of the parliament that a tower and gate be erected on "the bridge of Kilmainham" to prevent Irish enemies and English rebels from crossing. There is a mention of a battle at the bridge in 1535. These bridges may have been timber bridges. However, the river is tidal along the stretch, and submerged timber in such bridges would be subject to attack by the *Toredo* (see Chapter 7), albeit less severely than further downriver.

There are many secondary references to the erection by Sir Henry Sidney of an eight-arch stone bridge at Kilmainham in 1578. There is no mention of this bridge in his memoirs,[2] the source of the specific mentions of stone bridges erected under his orders at Ballinasloe*, Athlone*, Carlow*. The principal secondary reference is given by le Harivel & Wynne,[3] namely, a note inscribed on the back of an ink and wash drawing of "Island Bridge near Dublin" painted by W.H. Barnard in 1788. The note in different handwriting from Barnard's signature states "Island Bridge, Kilmainham Dublin/built 1578 by Sir Hy Sidney became ruinous and three arches were destroyed by flood several years before 1703/A new bridge of 3 Arches was begun but abandoned. Sarah Bridge (so called from Sarah, Countess of Westmoreland who laid the first stone), a bridge of one arch was built close by the site in 1793: see *Gent. Mag.*, vol. 63, p. 311." The principal value of this mention is that it raises the question as to whether or not the bridge shown in the 1698 ink and wash drawing "Detail of Dublin from Phoenix Park, showing Island Bridge" (reproduced in miniature in the same reference) was the one built in 1578. There is a further engraving from the *Sentimental & Masonic Magazine*, reproduced in Fagan's book,[4] which, he states, shows part of the 1578 bridge through the eye of Sarah Bridge. Six spans of the old bridge are shown (two broken down and repaired by timber trestles). The full arches shown are of small span and the pier thicknesses are almost equal to the spans.

A detailed examination of the originals of the foregoing illustration might produce some additional information. My view is that Sidney's 1578 bridge survived until 1784 but that several arches had been replaced in the intervening period. There may be further information in various archives that would fill the gaps.

The bridge we are primarily concerned with here is Sarah Bridge (fig. 187). The enabling act (30 Geo. III c. 42) for this bridge has an unusual title—"An Act for extending the power of the Corporation for paving, cleaning and lighting the streets of Dublin and to enable the said Corporation to build a bridge across the River Anna Liffey at Island Bridge." The following is a summary of the relevant sections relating to the bridge: "whereas the bridge over the Liffey at Islandbridge has been destroyed and rendered impassable for carriages . . . and there do not appear any means of building a new bridge" the corporation may apply for the funds necessary for building a new bridge. The reason for this provision is the old bridge was situated in the county. The act then

Fig. 187: *Sarah's Bridge: Downriver Elevation*

specified that no toll would be permitted. The material from the old bridge was vested in the corporation and probably reused (including possibly the lost Henry Sidney plaque mentioned by de Courcy). Another section prescribed that "After 7 years the Corporation shall give up care and management and it [new bridge] shall become a county bridge to all intents and purposes and kept in repair at the charge of the county of Dublin by presentment or in such a manner as other bridges are supported and repaired." There is an interesting prescription that no main or pipe shall be laid on or within the bridge for five years unless it be cast iron. This ad hoc act paved the way for Sarah's Bridge. An earlier act, 21 & 22 Geo. III c. 1 provided under sect. 26 that "The sum of 2,000 pounds to the trustees of the Circular Road round Dublin to be expended towards building a bridge over the Liffey near Islandbridge." It would appear that this was not used. Ruddock[5] states that the bridge was designed by the elder Alexander Stephens who had designed and built Drygrange Bridge over the Tweed at Melrose in Scotland, which had a 100ft central span flanked by a 55ft span on each side and cost £2100. Stephens also designed bridges at Kelso and Montrose. In 1789 he became a full-time builder. Rennie considered him one of the best contractors. Mullins[6] stated that the dimensions of Sarah Bridge "entitled it to be considered one of the best specimens of bridge building of the period being; 7ft greater span that the Rialto".

Fig. 188: *Sarah's Bridge: Arch Springing and Haunch*

The latter is the famous segmental arch built by Antonio Da Ponte over the Grand Canal in Venice in 1591, still in use.

Sarah Bridge was measured accurately in 1990 by Brian Madden, assistant engineer, Dublin Corporation and found to have a span of 104ft 5in., a rise of 21ft 7in. and a ring thickness of 31in. An analysis of the drawing of the arch gives no combination of curves that would fit the intrados exactly. However, a segment of an ellipse with a major axis of 109ft, a semi-minor axis of 27ft 3in. gives a curve which fitted into the bottom third of the ring, the span of the segment being 104ft 5in. and the rise 21ft 7in. Perhaps this was the curve aimed at by the designer. An arc of 88ft radius passes through the soffit of the crown and follows the intrados very closely through a segmental angle of 25° each side; however, for the remaining 15° of arc it passes through the ring emerging on the extrados at the springings. Perhaps the arch was intended to be a segment of an ellipse (fig. 188), but was modified to reduce the number of voussoirs that needed to be cut to individual templates.

Sarah remained the longest span in Ireland until Lucan Bridge was completed in 1814. It is still the second longest masonry arch road bridge span in the country.

Lucan Bridges

One of the most perplexing problems encountered in the research for this book was that of tracing the sequence and dates of the many bridges erected over the Liffey in Lucan down through the centuries. The need of a solution became more acute when it emerged that the present bridge is the longest span masonry arch ever built in Ireland (see fig. 16).

The ancient Slighe Mhór ran along a route to the south of the Liffey as far as Celbridge, the correct Irish name of which is Cill-droichid, the church of the bridge. The first mention of a bridge at Lucan that I found is in the statute Rolls under 34 Hen. VI c. 28 (1456) which prescribed that "two towers with two gates be made, one upon the bridge of Kilmainham, another upon the bridge of Lucan . . . ". The object was to prevent incursions by "Irish enemies and English rebels" into Fingal by night.

The Down Survey map (1656) shows a bridge over the Liffey with the castle and village located about half a mile to the south west of it. A bridge is also marked on Moll's map (1714) which shows the principal road to the west, from Dublin and Palmerstown crossing the Liffey upriver from Leixlip (see New Bridge). It also shows a branch road crossing Lucan bridge and looping through St Catherine's and over a bridge on the Rye Water to rejoins the great west road in Leixlip.

The first Dublin to Kinnegad Turnpike Act (5 Geo. II c.16) was passed in 1731. The first sentence of it gives a clue to the line of the principal road to the west at the time as it mentions "the road leading from the city of Dublin through the towns of Kilmainham, Island-bridge, Chappel-izod, Palmerstown, Lucan, Leixlip, Monouth, Kilcock, Cloncurry . . ." and states it was in a ruinous and bad condition. Section 20 states that "the road leading from the bridge at Lucan by the causeway of St Katherine's to the town of Leixlip by the sudden and frequent overflowing of the river Liffey over the said causeway is dangerous to passengers, several persons having lost their lives and many cattle having been drowned, and it is almost impractical to raise and make the same safe and commodious, and by the building of a bridge over the river in a convenient place, and turning the road another and shorter way the like accidents will for the time to come be prevented." The act then empowers the trustees to build a bridge of stone and lime in some convenient place over the Liffey and make a new road through Lucan and the lands of Cooltreeny leading to such bridge. The quotation is long and can easily be interpreted by a glance at Map 5. It is evident from the map that the trustees built the new bridge at Leixlip and the new line of road from the present Celbridge junction to it sometime during the 21 years after 1731. Leixlip Bridge has three 30ft-span arches and was widened by a cantilevered footpath in the 1890s. It is still in good condition and will be relieved in 1994 when the Lucan to Kilcock motorway is opened.

Among the 100 or more trustees named in the 1731 act there are two Agmondisham Veseys, father and son. The Veseys had come into the Lucan estate when the father married a niece of Patrick Sarsfield in the 1720s. The importance of Lucan Bridge diminished with the building of the Leixlip road and bridge. No direct evidence of a Lucan bridge in the 1730s, was found; however Dean Swift's couplet fills the gap: "Agmondisham Vesey out of great bounty/ Built the bridge at the expense of the county.": this is generally accepted as relating to the Lucan bridge over the Liffey. Swift, who probably composed the couplet sometime in the 1730s, was one of the trustees named in the Blackbull-Trim-Athboy Turnpike Act, 1731 and was no doubt familiar with road financing pro-cedures. This evidence suggests that a bridge was built at Lucan in the 1730s.

A bridge is shown in a drawing by Mrs Delaney (Cat. no. 2722, 47 in the National Gallery) which is dated 1749. Rocque's map (c. 1756)—see Map 5—shows the bridge spanning the Liffey immediately north of the confluence of the Griffeen river and of the junction of the Coldblow road on the north bank. Positive evidence of a new bridge is given in an act 11 & 12 Geo. III c. 35 (1771-2) which prescribed:

Whereas a new bridge has been built at the expense of the county of Dublin over the river Liffey near the village of Lucan; and whereas Agmondisham Vesey esquire has consented and undertaken that the road from the said new bridge shall be carried without expense to the county through his estate in a straight line from the said bridge to Thomas Lynch's house where it will intersect the turnpike road which will be con-

Fig. 189: *Vesey Bridge: Downriver Elevation and Plaque*

siderably shortened thereby be it enacted by the King's Majestie by the Lords . . . that as soon as the said new road be finished it may be lawful to the said Agmondisham Vesey to stop and inclose that part of the old road which lies west of the little river called the Griffeen . . .

The construction of the new line of road involved the building of a new bridge over the Griffeen river. The upriver elevation of this single span bridge is shown in fig. 189a. It is a further development of the Palladian style that came into vogue with Essex* and some of the Kilkenny* bridges in the third quarter of the 18th century. The plaque erected on the top of the downriver parapet is its most interesting feature and reads: "This bridge built/by Ag/Vesey for Ye/public in Ye yer 1773" (see fig. 189b). I was puzzled by the wording, the style of lettering and the location of this plaque; it did not match the period, yet it seemed to provide the answer to the Swift satire. Eventually I noticed that the date appeared to have been altered and I concluded that it came from the 1730s' bridge over the Liffey. An examination by an archaeologist will be needed to confirm or refute this.

The Vesey act is one of the few private ones relating to bridges found in the Irish statutes. The Veseys were a very influential family, as evidenced by a provision in the 1763 act (3 Geo III c. 1), oulined in Chapter 3, Part I, which dispensed many bounties including £500 voted to Agmondisham and General Vesey "as a reward towards their expense and trouble in preparing . . . the accounts of the nation for the House."

The mention of a new bridge over the Liffey in the Vesey act strongly suggests that one had been erected by the grand jury in the latter half of the 1760s. But, where was the bridge located? The answer was found by comparing Rocque's maps with Major A. Taylor's "Map of the County Kildare" which has been dated as 1783. The latter locates Lucan bridge downriver of the Griffeen confluence and shows the new line of road outlined in the Vesey act. The scale of the strip map in Taylor & Skinner's atlas of 1778 (which also shows the line) is too small to determine the precise location of the bridge.

Re-examination of an undated painting of Lucan House by T. Roberts reproduced in the *Acquisitions Catalogue of the National Gallery 1982* in which a Liffey bridge is shown, led to the conclusion that this was not the one shown on Rocque's map. The catalogue stated that from incidental mentions of the rebuilding of Lucan House and other information the Roberts painting had been dated as early 1770s. Roberts died in 1778. There is an excellent reproduction of the painting in *The Book of the Liffey*[2] and from it one can see that the bridge was located a few hundred yards from an in-service quarry located on the Strawberry Beds road. The quarry is shown on Rocque's map. The catalogue also mentioned a Malton print of 1783 which shows a bridge; I did not examine this because an examination of the 1844 O.S. six-inch map provided the necessary clues to piece together the evidence. This map shows the remnants of an abutment and two piers

adjacent to the north bank of the Liffey marked "Piers of Br." just above the Griffeen confluence. Three hundred yards downriver the word "Piers" is also marked on the map and a further two hundred yards downriver the present bridge is shown at the quarry site. Evidently the middle bridge mentioned in the Vesey act was swept away in the floods of 1784 or 1786.

Reverting to the main question—the date of erection of the present bridge—it can be assumed that the grand jury of Co. Dublin, having lost two Lucan bridges in the space of about 20 years, gave long and careful consideration to the problem before embarking on the construction of a new bridge. They had also lost Kilmainham Bridge in the 1784 flood though it was made usable by temporary repairs in timber. They were unable to fund a new bridge at Kilmainham at the time (see Sarah Bridge), so it can be assumed that no funds were available for a replacement of Lucan which would have been a far less busy crossing-point. Sarah Bridge was opened in 1794. Due to the destruction of the grand jury records information is sparse.

There is one clear-cut and informative mention by Bernard Mullins in his presidential address to ICEI in 1859:[3] "this structure, consisting of a single arch of 111ft span and 22ft rise, like many of the same period, is of a far more expensive character than the occasion called for. Its construction was attended with no difficulty, a good foundation having been easily obtained, with suitable materials immediately at hand, and yet the cost of construction exceeded £9,000. Mr George Knowles was the architect and, probably, the contractor, an arrangement common in those days, owing to the difficulty of obtaining the services of a sufficiently competent person of the latter class, together with the want of capital, there having been no banks to assist enterprise of that description."

Mullins is a reliable authority, but his remarks are critical and suggest that the cost was high and that there was difficulty in financing the bridge and getting a suitable contractor. Surprisingly he does not give the date of erection. His one definite statement is that George Knowles was the architect. Ruddock[4] states that Knowles was the contractor for Richmond Bridge built in 1813–16 (now O'Donovan Rossa) and for Whitworth in 1816 (now Fr Mathew's) on the Liffey.

Mullins attributes Drumcondra Bridge over the Tolka, commenced in 1813 and which cost £3,000, to Knowles; he also states that the design for Richmond was given by James Savage of London.

Savage, according to Ruddock, was a London architect who won second place in the competition for the design of Union Bridge, Aberdeen. The winning bridge was not built; it was replaced by a new design by Rennie, a cast-iron one with a span of 130ft. In 1805 Savage won first prize in a competition for rebuilding Ormond Bridge, Dublin but another design was adopted. Richmond Bridge cost £25,000. From the foregoing facts, it would appear that Savage & Knowles were an architect/contractor combination and were the team responsible for the Lucan Bridge. The date of its erection was solved by de Courcy,[5] who found that the metal balustrades were made by the Phoenix Iron Works of Dublin in 1814. The date (decipherable on only one of the square base plates: fig. 190) conforms with what might be expected on the basis of the literature. In addition we have the statutory statement that the Dublin County grand jury could not afford to build the far more important Sarah Bridge (described above) in 1790. Following the Act of Union the influence of Vesey must have diminished considerably; moreover, the local authorities were preoccupied during the first decade of the 19th century with military works following the 1798 rebellion (see Laragh Bridge). The map of the Mullingar Turnpike[6] shows the bridge was there in 1829; it also outlines a proposed new line of road from the village to Edmonsbury subsequently constructed.

The inspiration for Lucan (fig. 191) obviously came from Sarah Bridge, which had outspanned Lismore by five feet. Given the decision to span the river at Lucan with a single arch, the designer could have opted for a shorter span given the rocky banks and river bed, but he probably decided to add five feet to the Sarah span and ensure it was the longest span in Ireland. The bridge looks quite similar to Sarah's and could be mistaken for it in panoramic photos; however, there is a significant structural difference. Lucan is a segmental arc with a rise-to-span ratio of 0.20, whereas Sarah is three-centred, perhaps oval, with a ratio of 0.29; Lismore is 0.22. The ashlar masonry in Lucan is superb and the see-through iron

Fig. 190: *Lucan Bridge Date Stamp (Phoenix Iron Works, 1814)*

Fig. 191: *Lucan Bridge: Upriver Elevation*

balustrade parapets and unobtrusive spandrels give it a superb overall appearance from the river. The skewback (fig. 192), resting on an impost, is formed of three stones with a springing face at 45° to the horizontal. This is unusual for such a large arch; however, the springings are backed each side by solid 6ft-thick pier abutments up the road level, giving a large vertical load; more-over, it springs from less than 3ft above the solid rock; consequently there is little risk of horizontal slippage resulting from the horizontal component of the arch thrust. This, of course, has been proved over a service life of 176 years. The actual span was checked by Dublin Co. Council in 1990 and is 110ft.

Fig. 192: Lucan Bridge: Arch Springing and Voussoir

The bridge had two problems. First, the approach gradients were too steep for horse-drawn traffic and it had poor vertical sight distance over the crown for mechanically propelled vehicles. This was rectified at some stage by raising the road surface, thereby causing an adverse visual effect on the balustrades and the road profile. The second defect is the thin arch-ring—more than adequate for 19th-century traffic but restricted for modern heavy goods vehicles (something the designer could not have foreseen in his wildest imagination). The very characteristics that so enhance its beauty now restrict its serviceability.

Lucan Bridge is the pinnacle masonry arch bridge in Ireland because it is the longest such span ever built on our island and at the same time looks like a champion greyhound in full stride.

Poulaphoucha

The design of this spectacular single-span 19th-century pointed segmental arch is generally attributed to Alexander Nimmo. It spans the Liffey at the point where it crosses the Wicklow/Kildare border, seven miles south of Blessington right over the celebrated waterfall and the puca's pool. Joyce[1] states that the puca boasts that he can "put a girdle round about the earth in forty minutes" and that the genius of Shakespeare had conferred on him a kind of immortality. Had there been an ancient

bridge here it would surely have been called Droichetanphuca in the tradition of Ahaphuca where a bridge now spans the Ounagerragh river on the Limerick/Cork border.

In 1981 Professor Sean de Courcy presented a paper[2] on Alexander Nimmo to the National Library Society. In it he explains the difficulties of obtaining objective information on a man whose engineering works are remembered in the oral tradition throughout the length and breadth of Ireland. He states that none of his personal papers are known to exist and very little is known about his family. He was born in Fife in Scotland in 1783 and died in 1832. He studied voraciously and worked with Thomas Telford in Scotland. He came to Ireland in 1812 and worked as a private engineering consultant mainly on public works. He was elected a member of the Royal Irish Academy in 1818.

Nimmo designed many bridges, but he is best remembered for the remarkable, if expensive, Wellesley (now Sarsfield) Bridge, across the Shannon and for Pollaphuca, both designed and constructed in the 1825–39 period. In 1915–16 he toured France, Germany and Holland to inspect public works and increase his engineering knowledge. He was fluent in Dutch, French, German and Italian. His design for Wellesley Bridge (fig. 193) was an exact half-scale replica of the world-famous Pont Neuilly designed by Jean Perronet, head of the Corps des Ponts et Chausses, built across the Seine in Paris in the 1780s. Ruddock[3] describes the Pont Neuilly as a masterpiece with flat segmental arch rings on the facades rising only 14.5ft in 128ft spans. The bodies of the arches were elliptical and sprang from skewbacks 17.5ft lower so that the whole intrados was above flood levels and always visible.

Sarsfield Bridge was designed by Nimmo in 1823–4. The enabling Wellesley Bridge Act was passed in 1823; the lord lieutenant, Lord Wellesley, notified a grant of £60,000 for it and for work on the docks. The foundation stone was laid on 25 October 1824 and the bridge was completed in 1831. The contractors were Clements & Son. It has five river arches plus a swivel span and two quay arches. The toll produced a return much less than predicted; eventually it was de-tolled with the aid of liberal grants from the grand juries of Limerick and Clare in 1883—an event that is surprisingly, if not uniquely, marked by a plaque.

Fig. 193: *Sarsfield Bridge: Downriver Elevation*

The best literary evidence the writer found attesting that Nimmo designed Pollaphuca Bridge is in a paper[4] by Archdeacon Sherlock "The Horse-pass bridge is now in ruins. The road to Baltinglass once passed over it, but the turnpike road over the arch at Pollaphuca drew the traffic from the precipitous road which it formerly followed. . . .Pollaphuca bridge consists of a single bold arch thrown across a chasm, above the falls of the Liffey and the whirlpool supposed to be haunted by a malignant spirit. It was built from a design by Alex Nimmo in 1820, at a cost of £4,074. The span is 65 feet, height above the bed of the river 150 feet. It is a fine structure, adding greatly to the convenience of the traveller, but, placed as it is, it detracts much from the savage grandeur of the scene, which was well represented in a drawing published in the 'Post Chaise Companion', as the romance of the place is now destroyed by the traffic of tourists and picknickers who visit the falls." De Courcy draws attention to the fact that all the attributions of the bridge to Nimmo are from secondary sources. Sherlock gives no indication of the source of his information but he gives a good clue to its origin when he linked the turnpike road with the arch.

There was no turnpike act passed before 1800 relating to any road in this area. The section of the Liffey for a distance of several miles upriver and downriver formed the boundary between the barony of Upper Cross, to the west, which was part of Dublin, and Talbotstown barony to the east, which was in Co. Wicklow. Sometime after 1850 Upper Cross was amalgamated with Kildare. Prior to that, the Kildare grand jury had no responsibility for the roads in the immediate vicinity. The road from Blessington to Baltinglass crossed the Liffey via Horsepass Bridge (now submerged in the reservoir) and from thence to Hollywood as shown on Major Taylor's map of Co. Kildare.[5] It was a precipitous and twisty road. The Dublin, Blessington, Baltinglass Turnpike Trust was set up under 10 Geo. IV c. 75 in 1829. The road was not a mail coach road. Blessington was served by a post road from Naas, and Baltinglass by one from Castledermot, as shown on Larkin's map of 1805.[6] In 1835 Sir John Burgoyne, commissioner of the Board of Public Works, gave evidence to a select committee[7] that the Blessington Trust were held up with a new line which would save seven miles on the Dublin-Waterford road, because the Kildare grand jury refused a presentment for one shilling. However, another witness said that the real purpose of the new line was to enable the existing road, which passed close to Col. Bruin's lawn and deerpark,

Fig. 194: *Pollaphuca Bridge: Downriver Elevation*

The bridge is shown in fig. 194. It is very inaccessible for measurement and examination and it is very difficult to get detailed photos; however, a 1983 Bord Failte photo shows the upriver facade of the arch, parapet walls and abutment towers almost head on and level with and in line with the centre of the span. The scale was determined by measuring the actual length of the parapet coping, which is 68ft. The estimated span worked out at 64.6ft so Sherlock's figure of 65ft seems correct. Based on this, the radii of the arch intrados segments are 40ft the centres being located on the span line joining the springing points. The rise of the arch is 39.3ft. Since the centres are located on the span line, the haunches spring at right angles to the imposts. The increase in height compared to a semi-circular arch is 6.8ft—sufficient to leave the road over it almost level with the surface of the rock on the northern approach road at a point 100ft back from the bridge.

Architecturally the arch is described as "hard gothic" which became common in churches and buildings all over Ireland from 1840 to the end of the century and which revived many of the details of medieval gothic. Fig. 194 shows a plenitude of such details on the bridge loops, slits, crenellations etc. in addition to the mouldings on the voussoirs. The intrados curve and span of the arch is almost identical to those in the five principal arches in the famous surviving 13th-century downriver section of Le Pont Vieux over the Tarn river in Albi in France. The lofty perch resembles the 14th-century Pont "Romain" du Lauzet-Ubaye which spans a 100ft-deep river gorge in Alpes-des-Haute. Nimmo would no doubt have come across these when he toured France.

There is a small arch under the roadway about 50ft back from the south abutment which provides pedestrian access between both faces. Two hundred and fifty feet back the road crossed a dry river channel at a height of about 30ft, supported on each side by masonry retaining walls, the height being necessary to achieve the 1 in 35 grade on the south approach to the main bridge. The dry channel is spanned by a small gothic arch (fig. 195) over an opening which was obviously intended as a cattle and horse cart pass. The abutments are hollow and ornamented on the face with the loops. The gothic arch has moulded cut-stone voussoirs and supports the carriageway only; the road margins are carried by higher-

to be closed. There is no indication of where the lawn is located but the seven miles must have encompassed the bridge section because two miles south of Pollaphuca the Kildare boundary turns west away from the road.

The Report of the Select Committee on Turnpike Roads[8] gives details of income and expenditure by all the surviving trusts for the years 1829, 1830 and 1831. The Blessington Trust had no income or expenditure in 1829. It spend £1,581 in 1830 and £1,797 in 1831 on the 47 miles in its charge. The act was repealed and the trust abolished under the general Turnpike Abolition Act 1855 (18 & 19 Vic. c. 69). The OS six-inch map for Co. Wicklow published in May 1840 shows the bridge; the Dublin map is dated 1844. Accepting that the bridge cost £4,070 it would appear that it was erected in the 1830s, probably after 1835. Alexander Nimmo died in Jan. 1832 in Dublin, so it would appear, that like Youghal timber bridge, he was not involved in the construction.

level Tudor arches, in rough cut stone, of larger span so as to form recesses.

Fig. 196 shows another bridge called Beala-clugga of the same style spanning the tidal estuary of the little river Annagh about one and a half miles north of Quilty on route N67 in Co. Clare. There is no information available on its origin. It is shown on the 1842 OS six-inch map. The similarity between its arch and ornamentation and Pollaphuca bridge is obvious. The road is not shown on any pre-19th century maps.

Nimmo was involved in the construction of many new roads in the west of Ireland, particularly in Connemara, after the completion of the Bog Surveys in 1813. De Courcy mentions that he had a strong regard for formal architecture and became a member of the Institute of British Architects; also that he may have been responsible for a gothic arched bridge near Torc in Co. Kerry. Ruddock states that Nimmo, after a brilliant school career at St Andrews and Edinburgh University, became second master of Fortrose Academy in the north of Scotland, teaching many engineering-related subjects. During his summer vacations he worked with Telford, who was responsible for the design and construction of many new roads and bridges in Scotland, including Tongland Bridge[9] built in 1804–8, comprising a bold segmental arch of 112ft span over the deep tidal estuary of the river Dee, which has many ornamental characteristics similar to Pollaphuca. Further north, there is the famous O'Balgownie bridge across the river Don in Aberdeen, said to date from 1320, which has a single pointed segmental arch of about 69ft span and a rise of 35ft, is founded on rock and spans a narrow deep channel. It was, no doubt, a source of inspiration for Nimmo.

The bridge erected by Nimmo at Maam Cross in Co. Galway was blown up during the War of Independence and was later replaced by a lattice girder bridge spanning from the old masonry abutments. This became dangerous in the 1980s and was replaced by a new bridge upriver. There is need of a comprehensive paper on all of Nimmo's wide-ranging civil engineering works which would undoubtedly lead to the identification of many more surviving masonry bridges that should be attributed to him. The findings from our research leave little doubt that Pollaphuca was one of his masterpieces.

Fig. 195: *Dry Bridge: Pollaphuca*

Fig. 196: *Bealaclugga Bridge: Upriver Elevation*

Newrath

In 1942, one Saturday morning a 12-ton steam-roller was plying to and fro compacting the new surfacing being laid on the section of the Kilcoole-Rathnew road just south of Hunter's Hotel. As the road ganger directed the roller across the 15ft wide cast-iron girder and jack-arch three-span bridge it collapsed suddenly and the roller fell 12ft into the river tragically killing the ganger. The county engineer, the late J.T. O'Byrne, investigated the cause of the failure and also designed the replacement bridge. I worked as an assistant engineer in Co. Wicklow in the late 1940s and early 1950s and can recollect being told to keep a close watch on a number of similar bridges that were scheduled for replacement or strengthening as soon as the necessary funds became available.

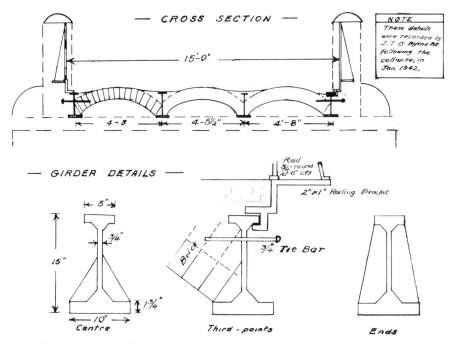

— CROSS SECTION —

15'-0"

NOTE
These details were recorded by J.T. O'Byrne BE following the collapse, in Jan. 1942.

4'-8"   4'-5½"   4'-8"

— GIRDER DETAILS —

Rail ¾" round at 6" cts
2"x1" Railing Bracket
¾" Tie Bar
Brick

5"
¾"
15"
1¾"
10"
Centre

Third-points

Ends

Fig. 197: *Newrath Bridge (1839-1942)*

In 1982 I discussed the collapse again with J.T. and he produced a copy of a drawing he had made following the accident illustrating the findings of his investigation (fig. 197). The drawing shows the construction of the deck of the failed, simply-supported span. There were four 17.5ft span cast-iron girders 15in. deep with 10in. flanges on the bottom and 5in. on top, spaced at approximately 4.5ft centres. The

Fig. 198: *Newrath Bridge: Downriver Elevation of Reconstructed Bridge*

space between was bridged with brick jack-arches which supported the 4in. to 8in. thick road surfacing. The lateral thrust on the outer "I" girders was taken by wrought iron, ¾in. diameter tie-rods, which were threaded through the girders and arches and bolted on the other side. The bar spacing is not given, but they were usually at 5ft centres, alternating between the top and bottom of the web. This was a skew bridge, the angle being 15° off square. The piers are 3ft thick, composed of solid ashlar granite blocks; the abutments were faced in a similar manner.

It will be noticed on the drawing that the tie bars do not go right through the bridge. This was how they were found in the actual bridge; the contractor had departed from the specification and put in a short stub at each end giving the impression that they went through. The defect was not noticed and, short of dismantling a jack arch, would not have been apparent subsequently even in a detailed non-destructive inspection. In 1989 Mrs Mary Scanlon, niece of the late J.T. O'Byrne, gave me some material of historic interest found among his books. They included a copy of the abstracts of presentments for the summer azzizes 1842 for Co. Wicklow[1] (now passed on to the National Archive); in this the following "resolution of the Grand jury" was found:

> Resolved—That if the Bridge on the public road from Newrath Bridge Hotel to Ashford be not completed on or before the 6th day of August next, that the Recognizance entered into by Peter Nangle and his Securities be proceeded upon, and that on the Surveyor's Report to the effect that the work has not been completed on the said day, the Secretary of the Grand Jury be hereby directed to hand over the bond to the proper Officer.

The Wicklow query books for 1817–82 and the presentment books etc. for 1813–87 were destroyed in the Four Courts fire so we shall probably never know what happened regarding the completion.

This type of bridge came into vogue with the Railway Era. Over 4,000 were built in Britain alone, carrying roads and railways. Under the Road & Rail Traffic Act 1933 (UK) a programme of research, investigation, and reconstruction was drawn up. The findings of the research which included full-scale destructive tests were given in a paper[2] to the ICE in 1944. It covers all aspects of their assessment and evaluation. In regard to tie rods it records: "the importance of tie-rods was fully realised. It seemed very desirable to take steps to keep heavy loads off the sides of bridges of the type in question [i.e. jack arch] whether of wrought iron and steel or of cast iron, because there was a tendency for the tie-rods to rust; if a heavy vehicle went on the side of the bridge the girder might be forced off by breakage of tie rods and a serious accident might result." Bad enough, not to mention dummy tie-rods. The Building Research Board published a paper[3] in 1952 supplementing the papers and other publications.

Most of the dozen or more such bridges in Co. Wicklow were either replaced or strengthened since the 1950s. All cast-iron jack arches on the CIE rail network have also been replaced. Newrath Bridge was replaced by a continuous reinforced concrete beam and slab bridge designed by J.T. O'Byrne in 1943 using the superb original piers and abutments as shown in fig. 198. It carries a plaque "Droichead An Thubraig 1943". Evidently the bridges at

Fig. 199: *Muclagh Bridge: Surviving Original Jack Arch Bridge*

Fig. 200: *Muclagh Bridge: Deck Soffit showing Wrought-iron Girders and Jack Arches*

Newrath have for centuries been called by this name. According to Joyce, Newrath's name implies "a place abounding in yews".

Figure 199 shows a two-span jack-arch bridge over the Muclagh river a few miles west of Aughavannagh, Co. Wicklow. It is believed to be one of the very few, perhaps the only, surviving examples that have not been altered. It has two 21.5ft spans and the road is 11.5ft wide. There are three simply-supported wrought iron girders and two jack arches in each span as shown in fig. 200. The thin 5ft central pier and the abutments are built in ashlar masonry. The combination of iron parapet rails, slender decks (18in.), thin pier and sparkling water, set in the Wicklow mountains make this one of the most aesthetically pleasing little bridges in the whole of Ireland. It is now load restricted (10 ton); it is to be hoped that Wicklow Co. Council will be successful in maintaining it intact as a monument for the future.

Causeway Bridge

In the early 1980s Waterford Co. Council and Dungarvan Urban District Council investigated various methods of alleviating the traffic accident problem on this busy bridge which is only 25ft wide between parapets. The aesthetic considerations were fully debated, in particular the visual effect of removing the parapet walls in order to provide footpaths. The existing single 80ft-span bridge with a semi-elliptical intrados is highly embellished and ornamental (fig. 201). It was erected in 1813–16. The ideal solution was adopted in the end when a new bridge, part of a by-pass route, was constructed, a short distance upriver. The new bridge, consisting of a central span and two cantilevered side spans, has an overall length of 160ft and is aesthetically very pleasing. It is called Shandon after the townland in which it is located and was opened in 1987. It is described in a paper[1] in 1987.

During investigation by the local authorities a manuscript report[2] by Samuel Ware on the construction of the 1816 bridge was found by the National Library among the Lismore papers (Ms. 7199). It is a most informative report from the engineering aspect and sheds much light on the problems encountered in the design

and construction of large arch bridges at the beginning of the 19th century. The most relevant extracts are quoted below. Evidently it was first intended to construct a five-span masonry arch bridge because a drawing showing the section of such a bridge, based on sketches by a Mr Atkinson, was attached to Ware's report. Ware recommended a bridge of three arches, two land arches of 49.5ft span and a middle arch of 80ft "as at present proposed". When he surveyed the state of the bridge on 24 February 1813, evidently at the request of a John Heaton who must have been an employee of the duke of Devonshire who apparently commissioned the bridge, he found "the abutment pier on the west side and the first pier erected; and the voussoirs laid to heights about 6ft above the springings of the arches". The mention of the "first pier" is puzzling because it implies that work was in progress on a bridge of at least three arches, as proposed by him, but the eventual outcome was the present single-span arch. The rest of his report throws no light on this problem, but he has some strong comments on the stone and the method of construction. He found on the quay "an immense quantity of free stone brought from England at an expense of two shillings per cubic foot". He was shown two quarries of limestone near the site of the bridge on different sides of the river. At one of these he saw "stones being got out of considerable size—sufficiently large for any purposes of the bridge" and on calculating the cost found the imported stone to be 1.3 times the local cost for worked stone and almost three times for unworked.

He provided a drawing showing a longitudinal section of "the bridge proposed to be erected". This must refer to the original five-arch bridge because that is all that is shown on the drawings attached to the report. He favoured a bridge finished with a corbel moulding having a plain parapet and stated that "all decoration beyond that seemed unnecessary and inconsistent with the situation": the drawings he had seen in Dungarvan gave the impression that the bridge was intended to be finished in a manner suited to a nobleman's park or a great city. The embellishments are shown in fig. 202.

One of the safety defects of the bridge that was built was the grade on each side which gave a hump back with inadequate vertical

Fig. 201: *Causeway Bridge: Upriver Elevation*

Fig. 202: *Causeway Bridge: Arch Ring Detail*

sight distance. Ware criticised the grade proposed (1 in 14) and stated that it should be less than 1 in 18.

His penultimate paragraph quoted in Part I of this book is important enough to be repeated here: "The arches of the proposed bridge are false ellipses being composed of segments of circles drawn from three centres: I am of opinion that they ought to be true ellipses and the voussoirs should be at right angles to the intrados requiring a mould for each voussoir in each semi-arch." This was more expensive, but, given the money wasted on imported stone, indecision etc., the extra cost would have been trivial in comparison.

There are many unsolved mysteries about the bridge. Was it built at the expense of the duke or the county? What did it cost? Is the intrados of the single arch that was built a true or false semi-ellipse? had the duke no confidence in Irish architects and engineers who a few decades before had created a superb local style, not 100 miles away in Kilkenny? At all events a durable bridge was built on very difficult ground.

Cromaboo

This is one of what Ruddock[1] describes as local (north Kilkenny) style of bridges built in the area in the last quarter of the 17th century. It is much photographed, but because of the constant high level of the water (navigation channel) it loses some of its elegant proportions (fig. 203). We find all the basic information inscribed on the plaque over the crown of the centre arch on the downriver side. It is mounted in a pediment in the parapet just above the footpath. The inscription, while weatherworn, is easily decipherable:

Crom-a-Boo
Bridge
Foundation Stone laid by his
Grace
Robt. Duke of Leinster
23 May 1796
Contract: Sir James Dulehanty
Knight of this Trowel

A few years ago the Kilkenny Co. Library received a query from the USA about the origin

Fig. 203: *Cromaboo Bridge: Upriver Elevation*

and meaning of the titles accorded James Dulehanty. Searches of the peerage lists and queries to the National Library, PRO etc. failed to identify their origin. I, who had often used the term 'Knight of the Trowel" as an elegant pseudonym for a first-class stone mason, but never considered its possible association with Sir, was then contacted. It was quite a challenging problem of considerable interest from the aspect of bridge history. The Masonic Grand Lodge, Molesworth Street, Dublin, whose archivist was intrigued by the query, confirmed that Robert, duke of Leinster, had been grand master in Ireland on three occasions, but among the records of operative masons there was no trace of a James Dulehanty nor of the use of the Knight's title. It occurred to me that the "Sir" accorded to Peter Lewys who built the old Athlone Bridge in 1567 might be of the same origin and, right enough, in a written contribution to Berry's 1909 paper on Lewys,[2] I found that the "Sir" marks a clerkly, not a knightly, dignity. Chambers's dictionary stated that there were formerly many kinds of knight e.g. "Knight of the pestle"—an apothecary; Knight of the road etc., so obviously the Athy bridge inscriptions implies a master mason and the bridge itself is indeed a testimony to his skill. "Crom-a-Boo" was the war cry of the Desmonds. This is one of the best and most intriguing bridge inscriptions in the country.

The town takes its name from the Barrow crossing Baile-ata-ooi. "The Ford of Ae" is the title of a paper by Dr Cumerford[3] in which he explains that after the battle of Mullaghmast c.111 the Munster chief Ae was slain there and the ford was called after him. In Part I it was mentioned that in Ogham writing the combination "AE" is written thus ⧻ and described as "beams for a bridge" (Book of Ballymote). Perhaps there was a ford with wickerwork on the river bed here in ancient times, an athces; this could be an alternative explanation. Cumerford sates that the town originated with the founding of two monasteries in the 13th century, and that one of the measures taken by Sir John Talbot, governor of Ireland, in 1413 was "the erection of a fortress at Athy, where he also built a bridge". In 1506 the castle was erected "on the bridge".

A 1536 reference[4] states that Lord Deputy Grey provided victuals, lime, masons and carriage intending to re-edify the castle and bridge of Athy and the manor of Woodstock. The most positive indication of a stone-arched bridge is on the ancient 1565 map of Laois[5] referred to under Monks Bridge*. The crossing marked "Athee" is delineated by a tiny sketch at the appropriate location on the river showing three arches and the castle. The number of arches is most likely purely diagrammatic and it would have needed perhaps nine with spans of that period to cross the Barrow. In 1599 the earl of Essex went to Athy with a large force, captured the castle and repaired the bridge, "which was broken down in two several places".[6] It was broken again by the confederates in the Cromwellian wars in 1649.

There is a bridge shown here on the Down Survey of 1656. On Moll's 1714 map it is shown as the principal road crossing between Carlow and Monasterevin. The Kildare Grand jury query books for 1788–1882 and various presentment papers and abstracts for the 1790s were destroyed in the 1922 fire, hence the lack of information on the present bridge and its cost. An upriver elevation is shown in fig. 203.

The Palladian-style architectural features of the bridge are discussed in general under Kilkenny Bridges* and in Chapter 9. The name of the designer of Athy was not found in any of the records. Thomas Ivory, who had prepared design for a Palladian-style bridge in the duke of Leinster's Carton estate in the 1750s, died in 1786 so it is unlikely that he was involved. The most likely source of the design was the Barrow Navigation engineers who carried out works in the area up to 1812. The arches are all segments of circles subtending an angle of 85°. The central span is 45ft. Each of the pair of arches, on both sides, has a span of 27ft, an unusual feature, but the effect is not apparent to the eye due to the overall camber of the bridge and the walls and trees at the land abutments.

There is no reference to any works carried out to the bridge in the paper[7] describing the large 1926–34 Barrow Drainage Scheme which covered the catchment from Cromaboo upriver. In all it affected 95 public road, railway and canal bridges and 170 accommodation bridges. Most of the bridges, the paper stated, did not possess any features of particular interest and all the new bridges replaced "old structures with narrow arches giving insufficient waterway and having roadways unsuitable for modern traffic".

An investigation by the Urban District Council in connection with a watermain in 1987 revealed that the barrels of the arches are composed of interlocking ashlar masonry and that the spandrels are filled with dressed stone bound with mortar. Such haunches contribute significantly to the strength of the arch rings.

Griffith's Bridges

In 1822 a potato crop failure occurred in the north west of Co. Cork centred on the 5,000 acre "Crown estate" at Pobble Ui Caoimh, and rebellion broke out in the area. This was led by the Whiteboys, who had first emerged in Munster in the 1760s in opposition to Cromwellian landlordism. The 5,000 acres had been attainted in 1641, but the inhabitants never acknowledged the confiscation and the old Gaelic system of land tenure still prevailed in 1820. The area was largely inaccessible to the large Government garrisons based in the peripheral towns of Newmarket, Listowel, Glinn etc. The Castle administration, always fearful after '98, were greatly concerned.

In June 1822 the viceroy, Lord Wellesley, who incidentally procured the massive £90,000 grant for Nimmo's bridge in Limerick city and had it called after him, sent down Richard Griffith to survey the area, designated as the Southern District, and appointed him to carry out public works, in particular the opening of direct and easy communications through the area. Griffiths had as his assistant a surveyor named Hill Clements, whom he scarcely mentions in his copious reports, for good reason evidently, because he was an important Castle spy. The local inhabitants were at starvation level, so Griffith had no problem in getting the works underway. In the succeeding 17 years, 243 miles of new roads were built in the area at a cost of £148,975. Griffith moved house from Dublin to Mallow and spent many years there between 1822 and 1839 planning and supervising the work, which was carried out by direct labour.

The act under which most of the work was financed and carried out (1 and 3 of Geo. IV) required that periodic reports be prepared for the House of Commons showing in detail the situation, object and extent of the separate roads, together with a statement of the cost of each, distinguishing the amounts paid for roads from bridges and other works of masonry.

Griffith prepared eight such reports in 1823–39. The reports are described in a paper by O Lúing.[1] I summarised the road building work including bridges in a paper[2] published in 1978.

The requirement of the act that bridge information be recorded separately was followed meticulously by Griffith, and it is reproduced in a detailed appendix to his report of 12 April 1831,[3] which gives details of 177 miles of roads built under the act up to that time. The remaining 66 miles were built under different acts and did not require reports giving the same degree of detail. It was possible by combining some of the data to extract the following information (on the 177 miles) from the Appendix: there were 128 bridges of 6ft span or greater, an average of one bridge every 1.4 miles of road on the 177 miles. Twenty-two per cent of the total expenditure of £121, 183 was on bridges, the average cost per bridge being £211 and the range from £20 for a 6ft span to £2,614 for the 70ft single-span Wellesley (Feale) Bridge. Seventy-six of the bridges were in the 6ft to 8ft span range, 33 in the 9ft to 19ft, and the remaining 19 were 20ft or more.

The foregoing are just a few data that are useful in the context of Part I of this book. The detailed information is so useful that here it is best to reproduce the "Schedule of Bridges" (fig. 204) as set out by Griffith in his 1831 report for the road from Newcastle by Abbeyfeale to Castle Island which was 26 miles 7 furlongs 8 perches in length. Thirty five per cent of the cost of this new road went on bridges.

A detailed analysis of this and the similar tables for the other roads is beyond the scope of this summary. However, a few points will indicate the nature of the information that can be drawn from them. The bridge at Barna (No. 2) has enormously high abutments, also evidenced by the supplementary provision for retaining walls. The arches are obviously flat segmental arches because the rise is only one sixth the span. There is not one semi-circular arch among the 21 as the largest rise-to-span ratios is one third; in fact most of the smaller bridges have this ratio, which enabled the shuttering to be reused. The cheapest 8ft span is No. 1, which has 3ft high abutments, whereas the dearest was No. 20, which has 11ft high abutments.

Griffith included a few observations on old bridges and on the methods then employed

Bridges	Rivers	Number of arches	Span		Rise		Height of abutments				
			F.	I.	F.	I.	F.	I.	£.	s.	d.
1. Rollinson's Bridge	Stream	1	8	0	2	8	3	0	19	16	4
2. Barna Bridge	Mountain stream	3	18	0	3	0	30	0	260	–	–
Ditto, retaining walls	–	–	–	–	–	–	–	–	57	13	9½
3. Doonakinna	Mountain stream	1	8	0	2	8	11	0	50	–	3
4. Inchabane	Ditto	1	11	0	3	8	10	0	60	9	0
5. Goulburn Br.	Ullan	1	55	0	14	0	12	0	1176	9	4
6. Ditto, retaining walls, and flood bridge)	–	3	11	0	3	8	8	0	923	–	–
7. Curragh	Mountain stream	1	8	0	2	8	9	0	52	2	9½
8. Gloshanagreve including high retaining walls	Ditto	1	8	0	2	8	14	0	91	8	2
9. Abbeyfeale	Glorough	1	11	0	3	8	12	0	297	1	–
10. Kilconlea	Mountain	1	8	0	2	8	6	0	139	10	10½
11. Wellesley Br.	Feale	1	70	0	20	0	14	0	2614	7	0½
12. Ditto, E. Bridge retaining walls and approaches	–	1	8	0	2	8	12	0			
13. Ditto, W. Bridge, and retaining walls and approaches	–	2	11	0	3	8	12	0	2037	2	–
14. Kilmanahan	Mountain stream	1	8	0	2	8	10	0	98	16	7
15. Knockbrack	Ditto	1	8	0	2	8	10	0	180	4	6
16. Cummernacolly	Ditto	1	8	0	2	8	9	0	50	14	2½
17. Headly Bridge	Owbeg	1	30	0	9	0	8	0	741	18	6
18. Ditto, flood arch, approaches, and and new river course	–	1	11	0	3	8	8	0	370	19	3½
19. Tooreenmore, East	Mountain stream	1	8	0	2	8	13	0	120	1	10
20. Tooreenmore, West	Ditto	1	8	0	2	8	11	0	92	5	7
21. Owrne	Ditto	2	8	0	2	8	7	0	121	4	2
									£9599	19	9½

Fig. 204: *Schedule of Griffith's Bridges on Newcastle-Castleisland road*

by the grand juries for building and repairing them in his report. They give rare insights, so they are worth recording here. In his report in 1824 he stated that the Feale Bridge had no foundations and that this was the principal factor that led to the frequent collapses and eventual destruction. He was quite critical of the manner in which bridges were built: "In building bridges deep foundations were never thought of as the mason working under the grand juries considered only the superstructure which meets the eye and had no objection to his bridge being carried away next flood . . . as it created more work". In this he was re-echoing a statement by McEvoy in the 1815 Statistical Survey of Tyrone. However, it is a surprisingly generalised statement for a man of his knowledge and experience, because there were indeed many survivors. He then gave his own theory on what we call scour: "in mountainous countries bridges are usually founded on rounded stones . . . above which an imperfect pavement is placed which is intended to serve as an artificial foundation; this soon gives way and the bridge which may be said to be built on castors follows it."

In the Appendix to his 1831 report he mentions that many streams crossed the line of the Newmarket-Listowel road and an unusual number of bridges were required, some of considerable size. In many cases "it was necessary to sink the foundations of the abutments to the depth of 10 to 16ft below the river bed." There was no stone in the area which could be dressed by the hammer or worked by pick, punch or chisel; consequently the whole of the arch stones and the faces of the abutments of the large bridges and the quoins of the arches and abutments of the smaller ones were brought over a 900ft mountain summit and from limestone quarries, often up to 12 miles distant, on an old track.

It might be mentioned here that the cost of Listowel Bridge which has five 50ft-span segmental arches and which he built under (Geo. IV c. 81) was £2,418. The date of erection is not given, but it was sometime in the 1820s. It gives a landmarker in evaluating the cost of other bridges of the period, such as Nimmo's Poulaphoucha Bridge, which cost £4,074.

Two bridges are selected to show the nature of Griffith's work—Wellesley (Feale) and Gouldbourne, both on the Newcastle-Castleisland road. They are still there, but the latter

Fig. 205: *Feale Bridge: Three-centred, 70ft Span*

was retired from service in the 1970s due to the bad road alignment on the approaches.

Feale Bridge

This is a semi-elliptical (three-centred) arch of 70ft span (fig. 205). The previous bridge, as Griffith states, crossing the river half a mile above the new one, was erected at the joint expense of the counties of Limerick and Kerry. It had 21 arches but no trace remained in the 1820s, "it having been abandoned to the impetuosity of the mountain torrents" by the grand juries "who became weary of the annual demands for its repair as every winter one or more of the arches were carried away by the action of the floods which frequently rise and fall 12ft in the course of six hours". These facts alerted Griffith to foundation problems early in his work and he ensured that his bridges would not suffer a like fate. In the Feale Bridge he obviously choose a long span to avoid piers in the river. He went down over 10ft with the foundations, to judge from his general remarks. He sprang the arch from the bed of the river and choose the semi-ellipse to give maximum cross-sectional area of water flow and prevent flooding of the bridge approach roads. The bridge is constructed entirely of ashlar masonry. Griffith was an expert geologist and was assiduous in the choice of stone—limestone from ten miles away. The height or length of the voussoirs on the face increases from the springing to the crown. The extrados are finished in what was then called "elbow appareil", that is, the outer edges were chamfered to match the vertical and horizontal joints in the spandrel walls. This is discontinued through the crown because edge fracture could occur from the small settlement that was inevitable as the centering was removed. The width of the road-way matches the width of the "metalled" or paved width of the approach road—21ft in the case of this road.

Gouldbourne Bridge

This is a 55ft single span segmental arch over the Ullan river (fig. 206). It has a rise of 12ft. The arch in this case springs from a level of 6ft over the bed of the river. The abutments are substantial as is the filling over the arch haunches, which provides weight to resist the horizontal thrust from the relatively flat arch. The skewbacks are well shaped with no acute angled corners. The upper edges of the vous-soirs have the same "elbow appareils" as for Feale Bridge. This feature provided the vital clue as to the source of Griffith's expertise in road and bridge building, namely Sganzin's book.[4]

Goleen

The road from Skull to Crookhaven in west Cork crosses a small tidal stream near Goleen over a multiple gullet (fig. 207), which is of particular interest because this type of clochan was very common up to the end of the 19th century when it was superseded by concrete and pipes. The Drainage Reports of the 1840s are full of references to both the construction of gullets and their replacement by small stone arches, but there is only one reference to a multiple gullet and that was "a treble" on the Parsons Green river in Leitrim townland, Co. Fermanagh. The report recommended its replacement by a "double pipe". Most gullets are covered up and the outlets obscured by hedges and bushes; not so Goleen, which is "unbattlemented", to use the ancient word, and very picturesque. Though it may not be very old, it is representative of a very ancient form of construction commonly called a "clapper bridge" abroad, from the Latin word *claperium* or pile of stones.

The area engineer in Skibbereen in 1987, Fabian O'Keeffe, kindly supplied the following information on Goleen. Number of spans: five consisting of four 0.9m and one 0.8.; height of soffit over stream bed 1.2m; thickness of span slabs 0.12m; width of piers 0.4m; overall width of bridge 8.2m. Some of the stone roof slabs have been replaced with reinforced con-crete. The general condition is good and there are no traffic load restrictions. The road align-ment vertical and horizontal is good. There are a few other surviving "groups of gullies" in west Cork, but all of them have parapet walls. No information is available on age. The flood capacity is adequate.

It should be noted that the thin masonry piers are rounded at the ends to form cut-waters and prevent weeds and other debris accumulating in front of them. Also, this little bridge is quite different from the one near Louisburg, Co. Mayo, described in Barry,[1] which is a footbridge with a paved ford along-side.

Fig. 206: *Gouldbourne Bridge: Segmental Arc, 55ft Span*

Fig. 207: *Goleen: Multiple Gullet, Downriver Elevation*

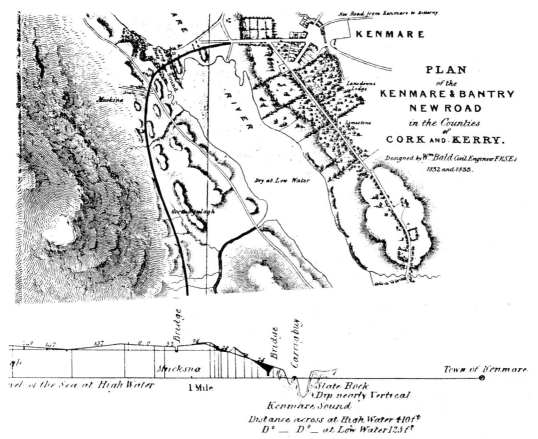

Fig. 208: *Plan and Section of Kenmare Sound by William Bald, 1833*

The Skibbereen-Crookhaven road with a branch to Bantry (total length 29 miles) was one of the "Wellesley roads" built or reconstructed under the direction of Richard Griffith in 1826–9.[2] The cost was £13,466 and the purpose to speed communications between the British Navy Stations in Crookhaven and Cork. The present multiple gullet may date from that period, though it is not on the same road.

Kenmare

In 1832 the Board of Public Works employed William Bald to investigate a new line for a road across the mountain ridge from Bantry Bay to Kenmare, at the expense of the marquis of Lansdowne.[1] He completed his survey and report in 1833. The plan and longitudinal sections accompanying the report are given in an appendix to the 1835 Report of the Commissioners of Public Works. It was a bold and daring plan by a very competent engineer,

especially the passes and tunnels through the summit ridges of the mountains in between; less well known is Bald's plan for a bridge across Kenmare Sound. This was vital to the new line which he choose to the west of the Sheen river. The old road was for the most part on the east of the river valley. It crossed the Kenmare river at the commencement of the estuary one mile upriver from the confluence of the Sheen at "Ruarty Bridge".

The crossing point selected by Bald was at "Carrig Butty", shown on the part of his plan and section (fig. 208). The distance across at high water as measured by Bald is recorded as 410ft (125ft at low water) and the channel depth is 30ft at its deepest point. The vertical scale on his section is ten times the horizontal, so the slope is exaggerated; nevertheless, allowing for building up the approaches it is evident that the choice of bridge was a most difficult task given the remoteness of the area and the economic constraints.

287

Fig. 209: *Kenmare Suspension Bridge: Postcard by J.M. Donovan*

The decision to go ahead with the road was evidently taken quickly because the Board of Public Works granted a loan of £2,737 (No. 33) to Cork County and £5,865 (No. 39) to Kerry County for it in 1833.[2] However, the bridge (fig. 209) was not mentioned and evidently not included. The next item of information regarding the bridge is a drawing in the *Civil Engineer and Architects' Journal* of 1838 showing the proposed "iron suspension bridge across Kenmare Sound, Ireland, Designed by William Bald" in elevation. The proposed is more or less identical to the actual. A loan of £890 (No. 211) was granted to Kerry Co. on 10 April 1840 for "Approaches to new Suspension Bridge, Kenmare". It is evident, therefore, that the bridge was under construction in 1840.

Mullins[3] writing in 1859, states that work on the Bantry-Kenmare road commenced in July 1833 under the direction of Richard Griffith. He also gives a description of the bridge: "The Sound . . . is divided into two channels by a rock; on this the tower of suspension [bridge] is erected with a half catenary on either side of it. The distance between the points of suspension is 313ft; the versed sine is 27.75ft; the angle of catenary is 20°; length of platform 300ft; vertical strength in tons per inch section 8.2191 assuming the load it will sustain before it begins to stretch to be 12 tons per inch section, as calculated from the original design, by Mr James B. Farrell." Remarkably, Mullins make no reference to or mention of William Bald. Confronted with this dilemma I searched farther in an effort to settle this long-standing problem as to who designed the suspension bridge—a daring and innovative solution for the period in Ireland. A similar type bridge, Ponte l'Ille Barbe, was erected over the Saone river in France in 1828.[4]

The Kenmare bridge lasted until March 1932, almost a century, when it was replaced by the present bridge (fig. 210). The construction of the new reinforced concrete bridge is fully described in a paper[5] by C.J. Buckley in December 1933. It contains additional information on the old bridge: "The bridge, believed to have been the first suspension bridge built in Ireland, was a wrought-iron structure. The suspension system consisted of eight chains in four pairs, from which were slung lattice cross girders by means of 1⅜in. diameter round rods at 5ft centres attached to the link pins by lugs . . .". He also mentions that the construction was completed in 1841 under the supervision of Captain, afterwards Sir, Samuel Brown, that the total cost was £7,280, and that it was in a dangerous condition in 1931: "Under traffic of even a light nature the bridge deck sagged and rose in a most alarming manner and on first acquaintance gave the impression of imminent collapse" (fig. 212).

The paper made no other mention of Brown and the brief mention gives the impression that he was involved only in supervising the construction. Mullins implies that a James B. Farrell did the basic design work. Buckley also states that he was unable to discover by whom the ironwork of the structure was manufactured or find any description of the actual constructional operations. He acknowledges assistance from the marquis of Lansdowne in obtaining historical materials, which meant that he had searched the estate papers. It is an important historical question, because it was an historic bridge "believed to have been the first suspension bridge built in Ireland". It has wider implications, because a man named James Finlay, who was born in Ireland in 1756 and who emigrated to the USA, is credited with being the pioneer, designer and constructor of iron suspension bridges; yet little is known of his early career before he built the first one over Jacob's Creek in Pennsylvania in 1801.

Finlay's career and some of the bridges were described in a paper[6] by Kemp published in 1979. This paper provided the clue because it also mentions the pioneering work of Samuel Brown in the development of suspension bridges in the UK. Kemp records that Brown was a captain in the Royal Navy and was involved in the manufacture and promotion of iron chains and iron standing rigging for ships. In 1812 he retired from the Navy and a year later constructed a model bridge at his factory in the Isle of Dogs. Kemp believes that Brown saw Finlay's work in the US and became interested in bridges. He made a major contribution by developing and patenting bar chain designs. In 1820 he constructed the 436ft span Union Bridge and became a leading suspension bridge builder.

From all of the foregoing it would appear that Bald consulted Brown and they evolved the suspension bridge solution. In other words the idea was conceived by Bald and the bridge was built by Brown. This conclusion is substantiated by the similarity between the 1828 suspension bridge Pont de l'Ile Barbe shown in Prade[7], and the 1838 section of Kenmare (fig. 211). Storrie states that Bald believed to have lived in France for four years between 1825 and 1830. I have not consulted Kemp's paper on Brown[7] and it may well contain some additional information. The replacement bridge (fig. 210) and its construction are described in great detail in Buckley's paper. It is a two-span rigid arch reinforced concrete bridge designed by L.G. Mouchel & Partners and constructed by A.E. Farr, whose site agent in charge of construction was, as mentioned in the preface of this book, the elder co-author. Professor Purcell was the consultant engineer to Kerry Co.

Fig. 210: *Kenmare: Rainbow Arch Reinforced Concrete Bridge, 1933*

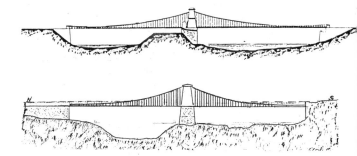

Fig. 211: *Elevations of Two "Half-catenary" Suspension Bridges (a) France, 1828; (b) Kenmare, 1838*

Fig. 212: *Kenmare Suspension Bridge: Postcard by M.O. O'Sullivan*

Council. The bridge was opened on 25 March 1933 by Sean T. O'Kelly, who later became President of Ireland. It cost £9,000.

Fig. 210 will enable the reader to reach his own decision on the aesthetics, but the verdict given at the discussion on the paper on 4 December 1933 was by Sean Keating RHA, who commended all concerned with "a work that was bound to be of great utility, not alone to Kerry but, because of its artistic appearance, to the nation as a whole."

Other Bridges

The accounts of the bridges and bridge groups in Part II include long and short descriptions of about 200 bridges. This gives an average of 25 per century over the period 1000 to 1830; however, the numbers found for some centuries, especially the 16th, are well below the average. All the medieval bridges for which early mentions and good descriptions were found have been included. From 1650 onwards the number of survivors increases rapidly but in most cases no reliable evidence was found on the period of construction.

The literature sources which were consulted are given in the references and in several chapters in Part I. They are not exhaustive and many sources, such as the journals of the Irish Historical Society, contemporary newspaper reports from the 19th century, military histories etc. remain to be explored. Inspection of existing bridges in the light of the criteria and examples in the book will undoubtedly lead to the identification of other medieval survivors which can be subjected to detailed literature searches in the hope of authenticating the estimated dates or periods of construction.

Among the counties, Cork has considerable potential for new finds and to a lesser extent Limerick, Tipperary, Cavan and the counties in east Ulster. Moll's map, reproduced in Appendix 10, will be of considerable assistance to searchers. Specific bridges which appear to date from the medieval period, but were not investigated in detail include Ballyartella on the Nenagh River, Beaumont and Dardistown on the Nanny, Golden and Knocklofty on the Suir, Rivermount and Birr in Co. Offaly, and Cardiff and Finglas-Wood in the Tolka in Dublin.

Among the bridges and arches described in the text there are several for which no definitive early mentions were found and which have been assigned tentative dates on the basis of their characteristics. In due course, these gaps may be filled by historians and antiquarians, so that eventually a typology will emerge which will compensate for the massive gaps left in our bridge records by the conflagration in the Public Records Office in 1922.

Appendixes

1: References to Bridges and Fords in the various Annals of Ireland

A. Clon.	=	*Annals of Clonmacnoise*, ed. D. Murphy, 1986
AFM	=	*Annals of the Four Masters*, ed. J. O'Donovan, 1848-51
AI	=	*Annals of Inisfallen*, ed. S. MacAirt, 1951
MIA	=	*Miscellaneous Irish Annals*, ed. S Ó hInnse, 1947

1001 "The causeway of Ath-Luain was made by Maelseachlainn, son of Domhnall, and by Cathal, son of Conchobhar. The causeway of Ath-liag was made by Maelseachlainn to the middle of the river" (AFM). A footnote by O'Donovan states that the second sentence is imperfectly given by AFM and should read: "The causeway, or artificial ford at Ath-liag [Lanesborough], was made by Maelseachlainn, King of Ireland, and Cathal Ua Conchobhair, King of Connaught, each carrying his portion of the work to the middle of the Shannon."

1001 "King Moyleseaghlyn and Cahall O'Connor of Connaught made a bridge at Athlone over Synan. Dermott O'Laghtna, prince of the land of Teaffa, was killed by some of his own men. King Moyleseaghlyn made a bridge at Athlyag to the one-halfe of the river" [A. Clon.]. The year 994 (given in A. Clon.) is equivalent to the year 1001 in AFM.

1071 "A muster of the Munstermen by Tairdelbach Ua Briain, King of Mumu, and in a fortnight they built the bridge of Ath Caille [Woodford] and the bridge of Cell Da Lua" (AI). The Irish version is: "Tinol fer Muman la Tairdelbach Hua mBriain la ríg Muman, so ndernsat drochet Átha Caille agus drochet Cille Da Lua ra cóichthiges."

1120 "The bridge of Ath-Luain, the bridge of Ath-Croich (on the Sinain) and the bridge of DunLeodha on the Suca, were made by Toirdealbhach Ua Conchobhair" (AFM)]. Footnotes explain that Ath-Chroic was near Shannon Harbour and Dun-Leodha was opposite Dunloe Street in Ballinasloe.

1126 "The bridge of Ath-Luain and the bridge of Ath-Croich were destroyed by the men of Meath" (AFM).

1129 "The Castle of Ath-Luain and the bridge were erected by Toirdhealbhac Ua Conchobhair in the summer of this year i.e. the summer of the drought" (AFM).

1153 "Ua-Lochlainn then set out with two battalions of the flower of his army across Ath-Maighae . . ." (AFM). A footnote states that Lismoyny is a townland in the parish of Ardnurcher, Barony of Moycashel, and county of Westmeath.

1154 "The wicker bridge [*cliatdroicit*] of Ath-Luain was destroyed by Maelseachlainn and its fortress was demolished. The wicker bridge of Ath-liag (Ballyleague) was made by Toirdhealbach Ua Conchobhair" (AFM).

291

1155 "A fleet was brought by Toirdhealbach Ua Conchobhair to Ath-Luain, and the wicker bridge [cliatdroicit] of Ath Luain was made by him for the purpose of making incursions into Meath. The bridge [droicit] of Ath-Luain was destroyed, and its fortress was burned by Donnchadh, son of Domhnall Ua Maeleachlainn" (AFM).

1159 "A wicker bridge was made at Ath-Luain by Ruaidhri Ua Conchobhair for the purpose of making incursions into Meath." The forces of Meath and Teathbha, under the conduct of the King of Meath, Donnchadh Ua Mealeachlainn, went to prevent the erection of the bridge; and a battle was fought between both parties at Ath-Luain . . ." (AFM). A footnote quotes from AD 1158 A. Clon.: "as they were coming to the joyste or wooden bridge over the Seanyn at Clonvicknose called Curr Clwana, they were met by the rebell Coibre the swift and his kearne. . .". A footnote in A. Clon. states that Curr Clwana is a place on the Shannon near Clonmacnoise in the King's County.

1163 "A lime-kiln, measuring seventy feet every way, was made by the successor of Colum-Cille, Flaithbeartach Ua Brolchain and the clergy of Colum Cille in the space of twenty days" (AFM). The Irish version states "lrr traigid ar gac let", which is 70ft. on each *side*.

1167 "Ui Concobhair escorted the lord of Desmond with his forces southwards through Thomond as far as Cnoc-Aine [Knockany] with many jewels and riches" (AFM).

1170 "They (the Ui-Maine) plundered Ormond on this occasion, and destroyed the wooden bridge [clárdroicit] of Cill-Dalua" (AFM).

1210 "The Justice went to Athlone, with the intention of sending his brothers to Limerick, Waterford and Wexford, that he himself might reside in Dublin and Athlone (alternately); but it happened through the miracles of God, St Peter and St Kieran, that some of the stones of the castle of Athlone fell upon his head, and killed on the spot Richard Tuite with his priest and some of his people along with him" (AFM). A footnote based on A. Clon. & Kilronan states that the above should have read: "Previous to his being called to England, this Lord Justice (John de Gray) went to Athlone to erect a castle there, that he might send his brothers (or relations) to Limerick, Waterford and Wexford and that he himself might make Dublin and Athlone his principal quarters. For this purpose he raised forces in Leinster and Meath (where Richard Tuite had been the most powerful Englishman since the flight of the De Lacys to France) and marched to Athlone where he erected a bridge across the Shannon and a castle on the site of the one which had been built by Turlough More O'Connor in the year 1129."

1210 "When the King of England saw the want of respect he was being shown he went from Droichead Sruthra to Carlingford where he made a bridge of his ships across the harbour and from thence he went to Carrickfergus with great forces on land and with a fleet at sea and so took the Castle" (AFM).

1236 "He pursued them as far as the bridge of Sligo [Droicid Sliege]" (AFM).

1249 "The Lord Justice then assembled the English of Meath and Leinster who marched a great army across [the bridge] of Athlone and thence into Munster" (AFM).

1315 "The Scots invaded Ireland . . . . Lord Richard, earl of Ulster, . . . pursued the Scots to Cúil Rathain on the [river] Banna. The latter became alarmed on his approach and burned the whole town save only the monastery of the Friars Preachers and, moreover, they destroyed the bridge [pontem destruxerant] so as to deprive him of a suitable passage as he was about to cross over. For these waters could not be forded save at two points and only when there was excessive drought which nevertheless did not occur in the above year" (AFM).

1361 "Droichit clochaelta do deanam le Catal Og O Concobain ar abainn Irra Dara. . . . A bridge of lime and stone was built by Cathal O'Connor across the river of Eas-dara [Ballysadare]" (AFM).

1478 Footnote states that "By far the greater part of the dwellings of the Irish chieftains were, at this period, constructed of wood and placed on islands in lakes."

1482 AFM contains two references to fords: "Bel-an-atha-fada", mouth of the long ford, now Ballinfad, Co. Roscommon and "Ath-na-gCeannagheadh", ford of the merchants, now Belanagranny, which is on a stream south of Oldcastle, Co. Meath.

1483 "He [O'Donnell] himself proceeded on his way through Tyrone and spoiled and burned the country on each side of him as he passed along, until he arrived at the river Abhann-Mhor; and there they (his force of pioneers) cut down and felled dense impervious woods, which impeded their progress, on the brink of that river [Blackwater], so they formed a free and open passage for the army through the woods. He ordered his army to construct a strong wicker bridge across the river [Cisaigdroicit comdaingin do déanam tar an abainn], which being done, his whole army, both infantry and cavalry, crossed the stream, without man or horse being drowned. They [then] let the bridge float down the stream, so that their enemies could only view them from the opposite side" (AFM). A footnote states that passage looks odd for if O'Donnell crossed Blackwater he would be in O'Neill country. The Four Masters may have mistaken the Mourne River at Strabane for the Blackwater between Armagh and Tyrone.

1487 "An army was led by MacWilliam of Clanrickard . . . into Hy-Many, by which he destroyed the bawn of Athliag Maenagan and destroyed much corn and many towns throughout Hy-Many. . ." (AFM). A footnote states that Athliag-Maenagan is the stony ford of St Maenagan now called Athleague in Co. Roscommon and that the river Suck frequently overflowed its banks at this ford but it is said that it never covers a certain liag, or stone therein, and whenever it did the town would be destroyed according to prophecy of Donnell Cam: "Athleague shall be drowned/Lough Glinn shall be burned/Glinsk shall be waste/And Clonalis without a man."

1489 "A great plague (raged) in this year, of which great numbers died. It was so devastating that people did not bury the dead through Ireland" (AFM).

1497 A footnote is AFM describes the Bealach-Buidhe, sometimes called the Red Earl's Road, and states it was traceable through Dunnaveeragh, Mountgafney, Ballinafad, Cartron, Ballaghboy, Garroo, Spafield (celebrated pass through the Curlew mountains). Another footnote mentions Bel-ath-daire i.e. os vadi roboreti, mouth of the ford of the oakwood and states it is probably marked by bridge on the Leanan about half a mile from Rathmelton.

1510 "An army was led into Munster by Garrett, Earl of Kildare, Lord Justice of Ireland. . . . Thence they passed into Ealla [Duhallow], and they took the Castle of Ceann-tuirc, and plundered the country. Then proceeding into Great Desmond they took the castle of Pailis and another on the bank of the River Mang [caislean eile or bru mainge] after which they returned . . ." (AFM). A footnote explains that no part of this older castle of Kanturk remained in 1851.

1547 "O'Connor and O'More crossed the Shannon, some of their sons having come for them to Ath-Croich" (AFM). A footnote states this was a ford on the Shannon near Shannon Harbour.

1565 "The Earl [of Desmond] arrived in the country and received no notice [of their designs] until he was surrounded on every side at a place called Ath-Meadhain, where he was overpowered" (AFM). A footnote states "Ath-Meadhain—The situation of this ford is still well known and vivid traditions of this battle are preserved in the neighbourhood of Cappoquin in Co. Waterford. The place is still called At Meadáin, *Anglice* Affane. It is now the name of a townland and parish in the barony of Decies without Drum, but the locality originally so called was a ford on the River Nemh, now the Blackwater, and situated about two miles to the south of Cappoquin. The life of St Carthach of Lismore gives the exact situation and a curious description of this ford under the name of Ath-medhoin (Vadum Alvei)."

1567 AFM contains a mention of Fearsad-Suilighe, passage of the Swilly, which a footnote explains is now called Farsetmore, two miles east of Letterkenny, opposite Ardingary. It could (1840s) be easily crossed at low water.

1567 "The bridge of Athlone was built by the Lord Justice of Ireland i.e. Sir Henry Sidney" (AFM). A footnote states that Charles O'Connor, translator of AFM, interpolates, Henri Mór na Beorac i.e. Big Henry of the Beer.

1586 AFM contains a reference to the Bridge of Cul-Maoile [Collooney]. "The Scots were obliged to abandon the bridge and to cross the ford on the west side of it."

2: Letter from King John to the Mayor and Citizens of London, 1202[1]

John, by the Grace of God, King of England, &c., to his beloved & faithful the Mayor & Citizens of London, greeting. Considering in how short a time the bridges of Saintes and Rochell, by divine providence and the careful diligence of our faithful Clerk, Isenbert, Master of the Schools at Saintes, a man distinguished both for his worth and learning, have been constructed, we have entreated, admonished, and even urged him, by the advice of our venerable father in Christ, Hubert [Walter], Archbishop of Canterbury, and others that, not only for your advantage, but also for the general good, he will come and use the same diligence in building your bridge; for we trust in God that the bridge so necessary, as you know, to you and all those passing over it, will, with God's assistance, by means of the industry of Isenbert, be quickly completed. And . . . we will and grant saving our right, and the indemnity of the City of London, that the profits of the edifices, which the same master of the Schools intends to erect upon the said bridge, be for ever applied to the repairing, casing, and sustaining thereof. And, since the said bridge so much required cannot be perfected without your and other assistance, we command and exhort you graciously to receive and be courteous to, as you ought, the renowned Isenbert and his assistants, your interests and your honour demanding it; and that you should unanimously afford him your counsel and assistance in what has been suggested; for indeed, every kindness and respect exhibited by you towards him, must be reflected back upon yourselves. If, however, anyone shall do injury to the said Isenbert, or his people (which we cannot suppose) cause the same to be instantly re-dressed. Witness ourself at Molineux, on the 18the day of April in the third year of our reign [1201]."

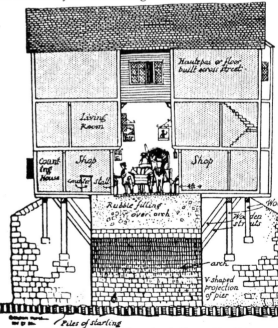

Fig. 213: *Cross Section of Old London Bridge, 1185–1830*

1. From Home, G., *Old London Bridge*, London, 1931, p. 343.

3: References to Bridges in Irish Statutes, 1310-1800

This is a copy of the "Bridges" section in the index volume of *Stat. Ire.* The style, orthography etc. are as in the original. *P.* indicates "perpetual"; *V.*, the volume of the *Statutes; Rep.*, "repealed."

1. Old acts enforcing their repair. *10 C. 1. S. 2 c. 26. V. 2. p.* 89.—*4 An. c. 6. §. 4. V. 4. p.* 80—*6 G. 1. c. 10. §. 7. V. 4. p.* 533.—*1 G. 2. c. 3. V. 5. p.* 199.—All repealed, *5 G. 3. c.* 14. *§.1. V. 9. p.* 324.

2. *5 G. 3. c.* 14. *§.* 12, *&c. V. 9. p.* 330. *Rep. by* 13, 14 *G. 3. c.* 32. *V.* 10. *p.* 511. & 13, 14, *G. 3. c.* 34. *V.* 10. *p.* 550.

3. One to be built over *Blackwater* at *Cappoquin,* at charge of certain counties, as apportioned by chief gov. and council. 17, 18 *C. 2. c.* 16. *V. 3. p.* 175. Ex.

4. Customary reasonable tolls for cattle or goods may be taken by persons obliged to repair. *4 An. c. 8. §. 2. V. 4. p.* 83.—*P. 6 An. c.* 12. *V. 4. p.* 146.

5. Removing indictment, &c. for not repairing, by *certiorari.* 8 *An. c. 5. §. 4. V. 4. p.* 219.—*P. 4 G. I. c. 9. §. 5. V. 4. p.* 462.

6. For *Baal's-bridge* in *Limerick.* 31 *G. 2. c.* 20. *V. 7. p.* 601.

7. For building 2 bridges in *Cork.* 1 *G. 3. c.* 19. *V. 7. p.* 913.—Altered, 5 *G. 3. c.* 24. *§.* 14. *V.* 9. *p.* 424. *P.*

8. 8000*l.* granted for building 6 bridges in city and co. Kilkenny. 3 *G. 3. c.* 1. *§.* 13. *V.* 9. *p.* 6.

9. 4000*l.* for bridges in co. Cork damaged by floods. 5 *G. 3. c.* 1. *§.* 7. *V. 9. p.* 270.

10. County presentments for building, rebuilding, enlarging, and repairing, and overseers wages not exceeding 1s. in the pound. 13, 14 *G. 3. c.* 32. *§.* 15. *V.* 10. *p.* 521. *P.*—How to be obtained, &c. and on what terms paid. *§.* 16. *ib.*

11. Plan and estimate annexed to affidavit, if for building or rebuilding. *ib.*—But no plan necessary for repairing. 17, 18 *G. 3. c.* 22. *V.* 11. *p.* 197. *P.*

12. Where a bridge a boundary, half on each co. 13, 14 *G. 3. c.* 32. *§.* 17. *V.* 10. *p.* 522. *P.*

13. Owner of ferry may build bridge, and take toll equal to ferry, except in cities and towns corporate. 5 *G. 3. c.* 14. *§.* 17. *V. 9. P.* 332. *P.*—13, 14 *G. 3. c.* 32. *§.* 20. *V.* 10. *p.* 524. *P.*—19, 20 *G. 3. c.* 22. *V.* 11. *p.* 569. *P.*

14. Penalty for pulling down any part of any bridge. 13, 14 *G. 3. c.* 32. *§.* 32. *V.* 10. *p.* 534. *P.*—On the circular road. 17, 18 *G. 3. c.* 10. *§.* 30. *V.* 11. *p.* 96. *P.*

15. Power given to grand juries to present bridges, to be built by private persons at their own expense, according to estimates, and in consideration of tolls agreed on; a schedule of which to be annexed to the presentment, *&c.* 19. 20 *C. 3. c.* 41. *V.* 11. *p.* 684. *P.*

16. Freeholders, persons interested, &c. may traverse, *&c. §.* 4. *p.* 685.

17. Other regulations and restrictions. *§.* 5. *&c. p.* 686, *&c.*

18. After 41 years grand jury may redeem such toll, *&c. §.* 12. *p.* 689.

19. Past parliamentary grants for bridges, &c. subjected to commissioners of imprest 23, 34 *G. 3. c.* 26. *V.* 12. *p.* 635.

20. Bridges built or repaired by parliamentary grant or presentment, protected from injury 23, 24, *G. 3. c.* 42. *§.* 3. *V.* 12. *p.* 717. *P.*

21. Presentment for accidental damage during assizes, or within 6 days. *§.* 12. *p.* 720.

22. Half presentment where bridge is a boundary between co. *Dublin* and another co. 26 *G. 3. c.* 14, *§.* 6. *V.* 13. *p.* 564. *P.*

23. Pulling down any part of bridge in co. *Dublin. §.* 70. *p.* 609.

24. Bridge over *Dodder* from *Irishtown* to *Sandymount,* to be presented for as soon as the line for the new course of that river is marked out. 26 *G. 3. c.* 19. *§.* 84. *V.* 13. *p.* 700. *P.*

25. For building a bridge over the northern channel of the *Lee* in *Cork.* 26 *G. 3. c.* 28. *V.* 13. *p.* 782. *P.*

26. Do. over the *Suir* at *Waterford*. 26 *G. 3. c.* 58. *V.* 13. *p.* 940. *P.*

27. *Dublin* bridges as far as the lamps extend within the circular road, subjected to the jurisdiction of the paving board. 26 *G. 3. c.* 61. §. 26. *V.* 13. *p.* 987. *P.*

28. How assessed for lighting tax. §. 62. *p.* 1003.

29. Bridges of inland navigations protected from violence. 27 *G. 3. c.* 30. §. 22. *V.* 14. *p.* 279. *P.*

30. For building a bridge at *Derry*, over *Lough-foyle*, 30 *G. 3. c.* 31. *V.* 15. *p.* 244.

31. The paving corporation empowered to build a new bridge at *Island-bridge*, and keep it in repair 7 years. 3. *G. 3. c.* 42. §. 3. *V.* 15. *p.* 304.

32. No toll; materials of the old bridge vested in the corporation; after 7 years to be a county bridge and repaired by co. *Dublin* presentment. §. 4, *&c. ib.*

33. Bridges put under the care of the barony constables appointed under 32 *G. 3. c.* 16. *V.* 16. *P.*

34. A newbridge eastward of *Ballybough-bridge*, called *Annesley-bridge*, to be built by trustees of road from *Dublin* to *Malahide*; and power to borrow 2000*l.* for the purpose. 32 *G. 3. c.* 37. *V.* 16.—And 2000*l,* more, 33 *G. 3. c.* 26. *V.* 16.

35. Power given to prevent for bridges on the road from *Naas* to *Maryborough* and so to Limerick. 33 *G. 3. c.* 32. §. 3. *I.* 16.

36. Presentments for bridges in co. city *Dublin* regulated. 33. *G.* 2. *c.* 56. §. 35. *V.* 16. *P.*—Protected from violence. §. 49.

37. For building bridges over the *Slaney* at *Wexford*. 34 *G. 3. c.* 26. §. 1 *& 56, &c. P. See Essex Bridge. Presentments. Highways, &c. Harristown-bridge, John's-bridge, Kilcullen-bridge, Old-bridge.*

4: The 1634 Bridge Act

The Irish House of Commons held a session from 14 July 1634 to 2 August 1634 in the tenth year of the reign of Charles I. The debates and proceedings are minuted in Volume I of the Journal of the House of Commons. A facsimile of the act in question is reproduced below.

(The word "causey" had several meanings and spellings in the context of the act; it obviously meant "a solid mounding at the end of a bridge" (OED) and to a lesser extent "a raised way formed on a mount across a hollow esp. low wet ground." See the article on Duleek Bridge in Part II of this book, for the 1587 usage.)

An Act concerning the repayring and amending of Bridges, Causeyes, and Toghers in the High-wayes.

22 *H. S. 5. Eng.* Justices of affize and peace shall inquire of broken or decayed bridges or cauſeways, and of erecting new,

BE it enacted by the King our ſoveraign lord, and the lords ſpiritual and temporall, and the commons in this preſent Parliament aſſembled, and by authority of the ſame, That as well the juſtices of affize in their ſeverall circuits, as alſo the juſtices of peace in every ſhire of this realme, franchiſe, city or borrough, ſhall have power and authority to enquire, hear and determine publickly in the generall affizes or ſeſſions of the peace reſpectively, of all manner of annoyſances of brigdes, cauſeyes, and toghers, broken or decayed in the high wayes, to the dammage of the King's liege people; and alſo of and concerning the new building, erecting and makeing of new bridges, cauſeyes, or toghers, in other places fit and neceffarie for the fame, and

and award procefs and pains upon prefentment, againft fuch as are chargeable.

to make fuch proceffe and peines upon every prefentment afore them refpectively, for the reformation of the fame, againft fuch as ought to be charged for the making or amending of fuch bridges, caufeyes, and toghers, as the King's juftices of his bench ufe commonly to doe, or as it fhall feeme by their difcretions be neceffary and convenient, for the fpeedy amendment, erecting and making of fuch bridges, caufeyes, and toghers, and every or any of them; and where in many parts of this realme it cannot be known and proved what county, barony, city, borrough, towne or parifh, nor what perfon certaine, or body politick, ought of right to make or repaire fuch bridges, caufeyes, or toghers, by reafon whereof fuch bridges, caufeyes, and toghers, for lack of knowledge of fuch as ought to make or repair them, for the moft part lye without making or repairing, to the great annoyance of the King's fubjects: For

to be made by inhabitants of the fhire or barony, or of a corporate town, if a county of itfelf;

remedy thereof, be it enacted by the authority aforefaid, That in every fuch cafe, the faid bridges, caufeyes, and toghers, if they be without citty or town corporate, fhall be made by the inhabitants of the fhire or barony within the which the faid bridges, caufeyes and toghers fhall happen to be in decay, or thought fit to be newly erected or made; and if within any citty or town corporate, which is a county of it felf, then by the inhabitants of every fuch citty or town corporate, wherein fuch bridges, caufeyes and toghers fhall happen to be in decay, or thought fit to

A. D. 1634. Chap. 26.

be newly erected and made; and if within a town corporate

or of both counties where part in one, part in another.

which is no county, then by the county or barony wherein fuch bridges, caufeyes, or toghers, fhall happen to be or thought fit to be newly erected; and if part of any fuch bridges, caufeyes, or toghers, or any of them, happen to be in one county, and the other part thereof in another county, that then in every fuch cafe, the inhabitants of both the faid counties fhall be charged and chargeable to amend, make and repair fuch part and portion of fuch bridges, caufeyes and toghers, or any of them, as fhall lye and be within the limits of the fhire wherein they be inhabiting and dwelling.

Said juftices with affent of the grand jury may tax every inhabitant reafonably.

II. And be it further enacted, that in every fuch cafe, the faid juftices of affize in their circuits, and the faid juftices of the peace in the quarter feffions refpectively, with the affent of the grand-jury, fhall have power and authority to taxe and fet every inhabitant in any fuch county, barony, citty, borrough, towne or parifh, within the limits of their commiffions and authorities, to fuch reafonable ayde and fumme of money, as they fhall think by their difcretions convenient and fufficient for the new build-

and write the names and fums in a roll indented,

ing, repayring, reedifying and amendment of fuch bridges, caufeyes and toghers; and after fuch taxations made, the faid juftices of affize, and juftices of peace refpectively, fhall caufe the names and fums of every particular perfon fo by them taxed, to be written in a role indented, and fhall alfo have power and authority to make two collectors of every barony, citty, borough, town or parifh, for collection of all fuch fumms of money by them fet and taxed, which collectors receiving the one part of the faid role indented, under the feales of the faid juftices, fhall have power and authority to collect and receive all the particular fumms of money therein contained, and to diftraine every fuch inhabitant as fhall be taxed and refufe payment thereof, in his lands, goods and chattels, and to fell fuch diftreffe, and of the fale thereof retain and perceive all the money taxed, and the refidue (if the diftreffe be better) to deliver to the owner thereof; and that the fame juftices of affize, and juftices of the peace refpectively, within the limits of their commiffions and authorities, fhall alfo have power and authority to name and appoynt two furveyors, which fhall fee every fuch bridge, caufey and togher, builded, repayred and amended from time to time, as often as need fhall require, to whofe hands the faid collectors fhall pay the faid fumms of money taxed, and by them received; and that the collectors and furveyors, and every of them, and their executors and adminiftrators, and the executors and adminiftrators of them and every of them from time to time, fhall at the publique feffions of the peace, make a true declaration and account to the juftices of peace of the fhire, citty or town corporate, wherein they fhall be appointed collectors or furveyors, of the receipts, payments, and expences of the faid fumms of money; and if they or any of them refufe that to doe, that then the juftices of the peace from time to time, by their difcretions, fhall have power and authority to make proceffe againft the faid collectors and furveyors, and every of them, their executors and adminiftrators, and the executors and adminiftrators of every of them, by attachments under their feales, returnable at the generall feffions of the peace; and if they appeare, then to compell them to account, as is aforefaid, or elfe if they, or any of them refufe that to do, then to commit fuch of them as fhall refufe to ward, there to remaine without baile or mainprife, till the faid declaration and account be truly made.

III. And be it further enacted by the authority aforefaid, That the juftices of affize, and juftices of the peace, refpectively, fhall have full power and authority to allow fuch reafonable cofts and charges to the faid furveyors and collectors, as by their difcretions fhall be thought convenient.

(marginal notes:)

make two collectors of every barony, &c. who fhall levy faid fums by diftrefs and fale.

Said juftices may alfo appoint two furveyors for fuch bridges, &c. to whom collectors fhall pay faid fums, and who fhall account at the publick feffions.

A. D. 1634. Chap. 26.

Upon refufal, procefs againft them, their executors, &c. to compel to account or be committed.

Reafonable charges allowed to furveyors and collectors.

5: Extracts from Technical Works

1. Verbatim extract from George Semple, *Building in Water*, 1776 concerning lime, mortar and grout.

I have from my Childhood, been well acquainted with the Nature of Lime and Sand made in Mortar, of all sorts, that have been used in Buildings in these Countries, and tried numerous Experiments with them; on which, together with what I have observed and learned from old experienced Workmen, during the Course of upwards of sixty Years, I think, I can safely affirm, that good Mortar, that is, Mortar made of pure and well-burnt Limestone and properly made up with sharp, clean Sand, free from any sort of Earth, Loam or Mud, will with-in some considerable Time actually petrify, and as it were, turn to the Consistence of a Stone. I remember I had one of my Remarks from an old *Scotch* Mason, which I shall give you in his own identical Words, that is, *When a hundred Years are past and gane,/Then gude Mortar is grown to a Stain*; (or a Stone.)

My Father (who was a Workman about the Year 1675) often told me, and my own repeated Observations convince me, that the Methods Masons practised in former Times, in building Churches, Abbeys, Castles or other sumptuous Edifices in this Country, was to this effect. After they laid the out-side Courses with large Stones, laid on the flat in swimming Beds of Mortar, they hearted their Walls with their Spawls and smallest Stones, and as they laid them in, they poured in plenty of boiling Grout, or hot Lime-Liquid among them, so as to in-corporate them together, as if it were with melted Lead, whereby the heat of it exhausted the Moisture of the out-side Mortar, and united most firmly both it and the Stones, and filled every Pore which (as the Masons term it) set, that is, grew hard immediately, and this Method was taught to our antient Masons, by the *Romish Clergy* that came to plant *Christianity* in these Countries, and I affirm, that in many of such old Buildings, I have seen the Mortar, as it were, run together and harder to break than the Stones were.

Now let us suppose, that a Peck of Roach-lime was slacked into White-wash, and then mixed with two or three Barrels of sharp Sand, so that every individual Particle of Sand par-took, and as it were, got a white Coat of this Liquid-lime, such Mortar, that would only appear to be mere Sand, supposing such could be wrought into Mortar, would sooner harden and petrify, either in or out of Water, than if there had been ten Times that Quantity of Lime made up with it; but nevertheless, observe, that I do not recommend that Proportion for Mortar, though it might answer for our present Purposes extremely well.

It is not within my Province to account for the petrifying Qualities of Lime-stone, Lime or Lime-water, though I have often heard, seen and read of several very remarkable Instances of each of them, but it is sufficient for my pre-sent Purpose, that they have these petrifying Qualities to great Degrees; but all sorts of Limestone have not this Quality in the same Proportion, yet I believe, no Limestone what-ever can have more excellent Qualities than such as we have in, perhaps, every County in the Kingdom: And indeed, it has some use-ful Qualities not much known among the Generality of Workmen, as for instance, our Limestone will make exceeding good Tarrass for Water-works, for which purpose you are to prepare it thus: Get your Roach-lime brought to you hot from the Kiln, and immediately pound or rather grind it with a Wooden-maul, on a smooth large Stone, on a dry boarded Floor, till you make it as fine as Flour, then without loss of Time, sift it through a coarse hair or wire Sieve, and to the Quantity of a Hod of your setting Mortar (which on this Account ought to be poorer than ordinary) put in two or three Shovels-full of this fine Flour of the Roach-lime, and let two Men for Expedition sake, beat them together with such Beaters as the Plasterers make use of, and then use it immediately. This, I can assure you will not only stand as well, but is really preferable to any Tarrass.

I will give you another Instance which will be hereafter found to come within our Subject, *i.e.* the making Cisterns in which Tarrass is generally used in ordinary Work, build all your outside and inside Rows or Courses with wet Bricks, and with Tarrass-mortar made as above directed; observing, that your Mortar is to be a little too soft for Work, and then the heat of the Lime-flour will bring it to a proper Consistence immediately; but never throw Water upon it when you are heating it, for that will chill and flack your Lime-flour, which you ought most carefully to avoid, but make the Men temper it with the utmost Expedition, and what you want in Water to make it fit for your Work, give it Elbow-grease; and this Rule ought to be observed in making all sorts of Mortar.

The Grout which you lay your Middle Row with, must be thus made (in a Tub or Bucket)[:] pour your Water on the Roach-lime, which must be pure and well burned, very leisurely; and when it is boiling, you may strain it through either a wire or hair Sieve, so as it may be tolerably free from Stones, and then let it be used directly, and be sure your Sand is sharp and clean, and when you are using it, do not take the thin that is uppermost, but stir it up and take plenty of the Sand with it; but in Masons Work, when the outside and inside Courses of cut Stone are set, pour in this boiling hot Grout, and instantly lay down your middle Course of wet Bricks between them, in double or single Rows of Stretchers, braking Joints as usual, according as the Largeness or Smallness of the Work may require, and that will press and squeeze the Grout into all the inside Pores that are next to it; and so they will all unite, and by the heat of the Grout and Dryness of the Bricks, they will all set together immediately, and become staunch and solid; but if you were making a Cistern of rough Stone, mix one fourth of the Powder of Tiles, or well-burned Bricks with your Mortar.

But with respect to the Matter in hand, I admit that Mortar will not set or grow so soon hard in Water as upon Land; but I am fully convinced, that good Mortar will in reasonable Time grow as firm and as substantial in Water as upon dry Land; but not dwelling upon mere Reports, I shall come to Facts, and I do also affirm, that in pulling down Essex-bridge, and repairing Ormond-bridge, we found the Mortar of the lower Courses of the Piers better cemented to the Stones, than it was in the upper Works, for a wet Stone or a wet Brick imbibes the Mortar, and holds it faster than a dry Stone or Brick will do; the Dust and Dryness of either crusts the Mortar immediately, and the wet Stones or Brick suck and unite with it, as for instance, take two Bricks equally well burned, wet one of them and lay it on a Bed of Mortar, and at some Distance from that lay on the other dry, let them lie so as long as you please, and then take them up, and you will find the wet Brick will bring up its Bed of Mortar with it, but the dry Brick will separate and leave its Bed of Mortar behind it.

There are several sorts of Limestone, some indeed, set much sooner and harder under Water than others, but any good Lime properly mixed, and tempered with sharp clean Sand, will bind and cement as effectually under Water as above it, as I hinted before.

What I mean by good Lime, is that which is made of clean, close-grained Limestone. All Marble is Limestone, but all Limestone is not Marble. All Marble will take a polish, but all Stones that will burn to Lime, will not take a polish. For instance, Chalk will make Lime, but it will neither polish nor make good Lime for any Purpose; therefore, I advise you to choose the closest grained, the hardest, and consequently the heaviest Limestone for any Work, but particularly for Water-works.

I need not explain what I mean by sharp, clean Sand, but I shall give this one Caution, that it is better to put too much Sand in your Mortar than too little. I know Workmen choose to have their Mortar than too little. I know Workmen choose to have their Mortar rich, because it works the pleasanter, but rich Mortar will not stand the Weather so well, nor grow so hard as poor Mortar will do; if it was all Lime it would have no more Strength in Comparison, than Clay.

2. Extracts concerning lime mortar from D.H. Mahan, *An Elementary Course of Civil Engineering*, 1845

The term *cement* is applied to certain mineral substances, found either in a natural state, or prepared artificially, which, being mixed with common lime, impart to it the property of hardening under water.

The ingredients that usually enter into the composition of mortar are *slaked lime*, and *sand*; to which sufficient water is added to bring the mixture to a proper consistence or temper before using it for the purposes to which it is to be applied. When the mortar is to be used for hydraulic works, a certain proportion of cement is to be added to the other ingredients.

Lime. When limestone is submitted to a high temperature for some length of time, the water, and nearly all the carbonic acid, which enter into its composition, are driven off, and the result obtained is known by the name of *quick lime*. The stone in this new state shows a strong avidity for water, which it absorbs even from the atmosphere; and when water is poured over the stone it swells and cracks, evolving a very considerable degree of heat, and finally, falls into a fine white powder, in which state it is denominated *slaked lime*, and belongs to that class of chemical substances denominated hydrates.

If the limestone is a perfectly pure carbonate, it will absorb about three-and-a-half times its bulk in the process of slaking, and the hydrate will be found increased in the same proportion. . . .

Owing to the great consumption of lime, its preparation has become a distinct branch of the useful arts, and the material is a common commercial article; but as the engineer is sometimes thrown into situations where it may be necessary to prepare the material himself, the following outline of the process may prove of some service. . . .

The management of the fire is a subject, in all cases, for careful experiment, as its effects are very different, varying with the quality of the stone. The lime from the pure carbonates is never injured by the most powerful heat of ordinary kilns; but the impure carbonates may be rendered almost useless, if over-burned. The effect of intense heat on the latter is to cause the stone to slake very slowly, and to fall into small lumps, instead of giving a fine impalpable powder; and, if it be used when it is only partially slaked, the mortar, after a series of years, will be found to have increased considerably in bulk; disfiguring the surface of walls, if it has been employed for plastering, or injuring the masonry by causing cracks, if used for stone-work: all of which effects arise from the gradual slaking of the small lumps by slowly absorbing moisture from the atmosphere. . . .

22. As a building material, lime is divided by engineers into two classes: 1. *common lime*; 2. *hydraulic*, or *water lime*. Common lime is also sometimes termed *fat* lime, from the appearance and feeling of the paste made from it with water; whilst hydraulic lime, with the same quantity of water, yielding a thin paste, is denominated *meagre* lime. This difference of appearance in the paste of the two, it must, however, be observed, does not serve in all cases to distinguish the two classes: for some varieties are very meagre without possessing

the slightest hydraulic properties.

The distinction between the two classes consists in the uses to which they are applicable. The mortar of common lime will never harden under water, or in very moist places, as in the foundations of edifices, or in the interior of very thick walls; and, therefore, is only suitable for dry positions and thin walls; whereas, hydraulic lime yields a mortar which sets readily, and soon becomes nearly as hard as stone in all moist situations.

23. To ascertain the properties of a limestone, direct experiment should always be resorted to; for the external appearance of the stone does not present any indication which can be relied on with certainty. The simplest method consists in calcining a small portion of the stone to be tried over a common fire on a plate of iron, slaking it and kneading it into a thick paste; this paste being placed at the bottom of a glass-vessel, and carefully covered with water, will, in a short time, give evidence of the quality of the stone. If, after several days, it is found not to have set, the stone may be pronounced as affording common lime; but if it has become firmer, or hard, it may be safely classed among the hydraulic varieties, and its excellence will be shown by the quickness with which it hardens.

24. It is only within a few years back that scientific men have come to any certain conclusions as regards the causes of this peculiar property of hydraulic lime. For a long time, it was ascribed to the presence of metallic oxides; then, to the manner of slaking the lime and mixing the ingredients of mortar; but careful analysis and experience have finally settled the question, and it is now fully ascertained that this property is owning to the presence of argile or common clay in the stone, which, after the latter is calcined, forms a compound possessing this highly important quality. It still, however, remains to be determined, whether the presence of both the elements of argile, which are silex and alumine, are necessary to impart this property. Alumine alone, it is known, does not; and an hydraulic lime has been found in France, in which it is stated that silex is alone present.

Whatever may be the solidifying principle, a most important fact to engineers is put beyond doubt, that an artificial hydraulic lime can be made equal in quality to the best natural varieties, by mixing common lime, in a slaked state, with any mineral substance of which argile is the predominant constituent, by simply exposing it to a suitable degree of heat, and afterwards converting it into a fine powder, before mixing it with the lime. . . .

27. *Puzzolano*, and *trass* or *terras*, are the most celebrated natural cements. They are both of volcanic origin, the former being found in a pulverulent state near Mount Vesuvius; the latter near Andernach on the Rhine, where it occurs in fragments, and is ground fine, and exported for hydraulic works.

The constituent elements of both these natural products are nearly the same, and as follows, in one hundred parts:

Silex.	55 to 60 parts.
Alumina . .	20 — 19 —
Iron	20 — 15 —
Lime.	5 — 6 —

28. Common potter's clay, such as is suitable for making pottery and tiles, furnishes the best artificial cement when properly calcined. The best proportions of the constituent elements are when the alumina is nearly one-third of the silex, with an addition of about five-hundredths of lime. With these proportions, the clay requires to be brought to a state of calcination somewhat inferior to that of brick, denominated cherry red. When the lime is in greater quantity than this, the calcination must not be carried so far, or the cement will be injured; when the clay is entirely free from lime, it must be submitted to a high temperature, but not to so great as to produce vitrifaction. . . .

34. Hydraulic mortar, made of natural hydraulic lime, will take about two-and-a half parts of sand. When an artificial hydraulic mortar is made, the common lime, sand and cement, should be in equal proportions.

It is not usual to add a cement to mortar made of lime naturally hydraulic, unless it is so only in an inferior degree; but experiments have shown, that a certain dose of cement improves the quality of the mortar made of the best hydraulic lime, the quantity of the cement being smaller as the quality of the lime is stronger; and in all cases, when a cement is added, it has been found that the mortar will require a smaller dose of lime than when sand and lime are alone used.

Mortar made of fine sand is superior in quality to that made from any other, and is,

moreover, the only kind suitable for cut-stone masonry, or any kind of work where close joints, and accurate finishing, are indispensable. For rubble work, a mixture of coarse and middling sand will answer all the purposes of good workmanship; and it is besides more economical than mortar of fine sand. . . .

36. *Concrete.* In preparing concrete, the following proportions have been found to succeed perfectly in some recent structures.

Hydraulic lime, (unslaked.). .	0.30 parts
Sand, (middling.).	0.30 —
Cement, (common clay.) . . .	0.30 —
Gravel, (coarse.)	0.20 —
Chippings of stone.	0.40 —

The lime, sand, and cement, are, in the first place, thoroughly worked up into a homogeneous mass of a hard temper; this mass is suffered to rest in a heap about twelve hours; it is then spread out into a layer about six inches thick, and the gravel and stone are evenly spread over it, and the whole well mixed up. The mass, before it is used, is suffered to remain until it has partially set, which will require from twelve to thirty-six hours, according to the quality of the mortar. This method is found to improve the quality of the concrete.

This material depends on the quality of the mortar for its excellence. It is not stronger than simple hydraulic mortar, but it is far more economical. The gravel, which enters into its composition, is used to fill up the voids between the fragments of stone, which would otherwise be filled by the mortar alone.

Broken brick may be used instead of fragments of stone when the latter cannot be had; or gravel alone may be used.

37. There is no subject connected with the art of the engineer upon which more ingenuity has been uselessly expended than upon that of mortar. Misled by erroneous or forced interpretations of some passages of the ancients, particularly of Vitruvius, various hypotheses have been formed to explain the superior properties of the mortar found in the remains of ancient edifices, over that of a modern date; and almost universal failure, for a long period, attended all the experiments made in conformity with these hypotheses, as they were not conducted according to the only sure method of investigation in such cases, a

careful analysis. The fallacy, both of the hypotheses adopted, and the results obtained, led scientific engineers to treat the subject in a more rational manner, and with a success which has fully repaid the care bestowed on it. The true nature both of lime and mortar—thanks to the labours of Vicat, Raucourt, and Treussart,—men who stand at the head of the professions of civil and military engineers in France—is now perfectly understood; and the results, owing to the light that they have thrown on the subject, may with certainty be predicted. It is now placed beyond a doubt, first, that neither the methods followed in slaking the lime and mixing the ingredients, nor the age, are the causes of the great strength and hardness of some kinds of mortar, although they doubtless exercise some influence; but that these qualities are attributable, almost solely, to the nature of the lime; secondly, that with common lime and sand a mortar is obtained which is suitable only for dry exposures; and that no age nor preparation will cause it to harden in moist situations, such as foundations, the interior of heavy walls, and constructions under water; thirdly, that there are natural varieties of lime-stone which possess this peculiar property of hardening under water and in moist situations, and are, therefore, alone suitable for hydraulic mortar; and that whatever this natural hydraulic lime cannot be procured, an artificial mortar can be prepared, fully equal to that made of the natural lime, by adding some natural or artificial cement to common lime and sand.

With regard to the action of the lime on the sand, the most careful analysis, thus far, has not been able to detect any appearance of a chemical combination between the two; and it is the received opinion that the union between them is simply of a mechanical character: the lime entering the pores of the sand, and thus connecting the particles much in the same way as the particles of granular stones are connected by a natural cement. The sand itself serves the important purposes of causing the mass to shrink uniformly, whilst the hardening or *setting* of the mortar is still in progress, and thus prevents any cracking, which must always be the result of irregularity in the shrinking; it promotes the rapid desiccation of the mass; and is conductive both to solidity and economy, from its superior strength, hardness and cheapness, to lime.

No perfectly satisfactory solution has yet been given for the hardening of either common or hydraulic mortar. That the former acquires strength and hardness with age, experience has very conclusively shown; and it was, for some time, supposed that this arose from a gradual conversion of the lime into a carbonate by the slow absorption of carbonic gas from the air; but, from experiments conducted with great care, it seems that only a very thin coating on the surface undergoes this change, and that no more gas can be detected in the interior of the mass than is usually retained by lime which has been submitted to the greatest heat of ordinary kilns. As to the action which takes place in the hydraulic lime, it is accounted for on the supposition that a chemical combination takes place between the lime and argile when mixed in a moist state, being a compound formed with new properties distinct from those of the constituent elements: this combination requiring a longer or shorter time, depending on the energy of the ingredients, to become complete.

3. A summary of the principal stone bridge recommendations in Alberti's *The Ten Books of Architecture*

Foundations Choose a ford where the water is not too deep. Find rock if possible. Avoid elbows. The best architects used to make a continued foundation of the whole length of the bridge. If too expensive make separate foundation for each pier in the form of a ship with one angle in the stern, another in the head. Water is much more dangerous to the stern: it forms eddies which turn up the bed. Give the foundation an easy slope, otherwise the water rushes and routs up the bottom. Dig till you come to a solid foundation or make use of piles burnt at end, driven close together.

Piers Build the piers of the biggest and longest stones which do not decay in water or crack and split under great weight. Place the stones lengthways and breadthways in alternative order so as to be binding. Absolutely reject any stuffing with small stones. Fasten with a good number of brass cramps and pins. Make extra piers on the shore and turn some arches on the dry ground in case any part of the bank be carried away.

Cutwaters Raise the head and stern angular. Let top of pier be higher than the fullest tide (flood). Make the pier thickness one fourth the height of the bridge. Some masons terminate the head and stern with an half circle. I prefer the angle not to be so sharp as to be liable to be broken and defaced by accidents, but it may end in a curve not so obtuse as to resist the force of the water. The angle is of good sharpness if it is three-quarters of a right angle.

Arches Ought to be stout and strong to resist violent shaking of carts or periodic immense weights such as an obelisk. Use very large and stout stones that withstand blows as an anvil does a hammer. All vaulted work consists of arches and stuffing and the strongest of all arches is the semicircle; if by the disposition of the piers this should rise too high make use of the scheme arch (i.e. segment < 180 deg.) but take care to make the shore piers (abut-ments) stronger and thicker. There should not be a single stone in the arch(es) of thickness less than one tenth the chord (span). Fasten the ring stones with brass cramps and pins. Cut the last wedge (keystone) slightly bigger at the top and stroke in with a light beetle. The span should be between four and six times the pier thickness.

City Bridges Make the bridge as broad as the street. Piers should equal one another on each side in number and size. The angles or heads that lie against the stream must project in length half the breadth of the bridge and be built higher than the water ever rises. The downstream heads must have the same projection but can be less acute.

4. Summary of the principal stone bridge recommendations in Palladio, *The Four Books of Architecture*

Foundations Choose rock or stone, avoid whirl-pools, also gravelly or sandy bed because they are continually moved by floods. Make banks firm and strong by art or by additional arches. If bed is gravel or sand, dig until solid ground is found, or drive piles of oak with iron points to solid bottom.

Piers Pilasters ought to be even in number and located where stream is less rapid. Should not be thinner than one sixth arch span nor thicker than one quarter. Make with large stones joined with cramps.

Cutwaters The fronts of the pilasters are commonly make angular; some are also made semi-circular so that objects carried down are thrown off and pass through the middle of the arch.

Ancient Stone Bridges Palladio does not give any recommendations on arches but names a number of stone bridges built by "the antients", and describes three of them, Rimino and two at Vicenza, together with two of his own invention. The following is a summary of his descriptions:

Rimino Bridge: "Of all the bridges I have seen" that at Rimino, a city in Flamina, seems to be the most beautiful, and the most worthy of consideration, as well for its strength as for its compartment and disposition. . . . It is divided into five arches, the three middle ones are equal, and five and twenty foot in breadth, and the two next the banks are less, that is, only twenty foot broad. All the arches are semi-circular and their *modeno* (ring) is one tenth the span of the greater and one eighth the span of the lesser. The pier thicknesses are a little less than half the span of the greater arches. The angle of the cutwater is a right one. There are niches in the spandrels and a cornice.

Vicenza Bridge (river Bacchiglione): This bridge is divided into three arches; the middle 30ft span, the others 22ft 6in. The piers are one sixth the span of the middle arch. The height (rise) is one third the spans. The *modeno* (ring) thickness is one twelfth of the middle span and one tenth of the smaller arches, and wrought like an architrave. On the pier faces near the ends, under the imposts, "some stones project forward, which, in building of the bridge, served to support the beams, upon which were made the centerings of the arches. And, in this manner, the danger of the floods carrying away the beams, to the ruin of the work, was avoided; which had it been done otherwise, it would have been necessary to drive them into the river, to make the said centerings."

Vicenza Bridge (river Rerone): This bridge has three arches, the middle greater than the other two. All the arches are a segment of a circle less than a semicircle, and without any orna-

304

ment at all. The rise of the smaller arches is one third the span, the centre one a little less. Piers are one fifth the span of the smaller arches; and stones project to support the center-ing. There are four bridges at Padua made after the same proportions; one has five arches.

Stone Bridge of Palladio's Invention: "The river was 180ft wide. I chose three spans, two 48ft and the centre one 60ft. The piers were 12ft thick: I made them very thick that they might project out and better resist the impetuosity of the very rapid river and the stone and timber that might be carried down by it. The arches would have been a segment of a circle to give easy ascent. I made the *modeno* of the arches the seventeenth part of the span for the middle arch, and one fourteenth for the other two."

6: The "Irish Bridge", *c.* 1815

Fall from *a* to *b*, of sixteen inches, should be well secured by a strong pavement, or rather thin stones, placed edgewise, especially towards *a*.

c. The flags covering the pipe or gullet.

d. The side-well, which should be well sunk, if the foundation be of a soft nature.

When the pipe is filled with flood-water, it will soon increase over the flagging, *c*, and gradually rise, till is arrives at a, from whence it will tumble over the rocks, or large stones, *a*, *e*, without doing the least injury, if the stones are securely placed, by sinking them well, and fixing the largest at bottom. The bottom should be well paved, and made a dead level, which should continue so for some distance below *e*.

One of the great secrets in building all sorts of bridges, is, that, if the water is not naturally level, or nearly so, means should be taken for that purpose.

In the section, across the pipe or gullet, the shape of the road will appear thus, and give some idea of the quantity of water that may be discharged over it.

The pipe is capable of discharging six cubical feet of water, and the segment, *a*, *b*, is equal to nearly ten cubical feet. But there is no necessity of being confined to one pipe; more may be introduced, if the case should require it, and the excavation made in proportion. Instead of flags, logs of oak may be used, which will last for ages.

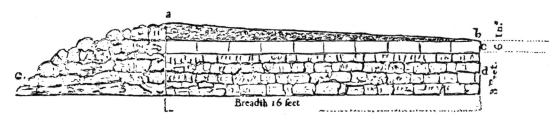

Fig. 214: *(a) "Irish Bridge" c.1815:Longitudinal Section*

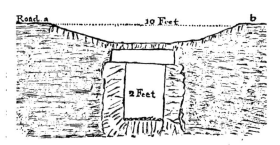

Fig. 214: *(b) "Irish Bridge" c.1815: Cross-section*

Fig. 215: *Modern "Irish" Bridge on Forest Road*

7: Killaly's Specification for a Canal Bridge, *c.*1810

SPECIFICATION of the Public Road, and Private or Accommodation Bridges, proposed to be built on the Royal Canal Extension

The *foundations* to be excavated to the solid ground in all cases, and the bridge founded at least 12in. under the bottom of canal.

The abutments are to be 5ft thick at the springing of the arch, and upright at the back— the face having a curvelineal batter as described in the drawings—the other dimensions of the bridge with the form, height, and thickness of the walls, batters, &c. &c. to correspond strictly with those figured on the plans and section: observing, however, that the private, or accommodation bridges, are to be 10ft narrower within the parapets than the public road bridges.

The *arch* to be a semi-ellipsis, as shown on the elevation, the *ring*, or *quoin stones* of which are to be of cut stone, 18in. in height, and regularly sommered, bonding into the arch 2ft and 2ft 6in. alternately.

The *sheeting* to be of good hammered stone, set in courses in the direction of the radii, 21in. deep at the springing, diminishing to 18in. at the top of the arch; no stone to be less than 6in. in breadth, or 18in. in length on the face; the back joints of the sheeting to be firmly packed with spauls, and well grouted.

The *abutments, wings, spandrels* and *parapet walls* of the bridge, together with the *water wings* and *trackway walls* (where not otherwise described) are to be built of good, sound, rubble stone, well bedded, flush in mortar, and in curses not exceeding 14in. in height, each course to be well bounded and grouted, and the joints carefully broken.

The *coping of trackway, water wings*, and *parapet walls*, also the *water line courses*, with *the quoins of the abutments*, from 6in. above water surface to the springing of the arch, to be of cut stone, as hereafter described, likewise the plynth and piers.

The trackway and water wing coping to be 12in. thick, with 2ft top bed, 18in. long on the face at least, and to be well jointed and bedded; the batter to be taken out of the face, and the top arras to be neatly rounded for the whole length.

The *water line course* to be set on the level shown in the elevation, and to consist of ashlers not less than 12in. in thickness, with bonds of corresponding height, not more than 8ft asunder; the ashlers to be 18in. in length at least, with 12in. bed, the bonds not less than 1ft long on the face, and 2ft deep in the bed; both ashlers and bonds to have 6in. square dressed joints and beds at least.

Quoins of abutments to have 18in. heads, and to be bonded in the same manner as the ring stones.

The *plynth* or *belting course* to be 6in. in thickness, and lodged 9in. in the wall, having a projection of 9in. beyond the dashing.

The *piers* which terminate the wing walls to be of cut stone, to the depth of 2ft below the plynth, and of the dimensions shown in the drawing.

The *parapet coping* to be uniformly 9in. thick, 15in. broad, and fair jointed for the whole breadth.

Where *stop gates* are required there is to be a cill of fir or oak, 12in. deep, by 9in. broad, laid at the level of 6in. above the bottom of canal, and lodged 3ft at least under the side walls, having a row of sheeting piles on each side, 4ft deep, and 3in. in thickness spiked thereto, and well puddled in front. For the distance of 5ft 6in. on each side of the cill, the space between the walls is to have a floor of square hammered pavement 12in. deep, terminated as shown in the drawing. There are to be cut stone grooves carried up from the level of the cill to the top of the side walls, in which stop gates may be put down when necessary.

The *face and joints of all the cut stone* to be neatly punched, and to have a chissel draft round the arrasses.

The parapet and front walls of the bridge to be well *dashed*, excepting such parts as are faced with cut stone or covered with earth works.

The *mortar in which the cut stone is to be set* must be composed of one part of good roach lime to three parts of clean, sharp sand; the lime when wet for slacking is to be covered with its due proportion of sand, after which they are to be mixed together and passed through a fine screen, observing not to prepare a greater quantity at once than there shall be immediate occasion for.

The *mortar for the rubble work* to be composed

of one part of good roach lime to four parts of clean sand, in proper proportions of fine and coarse, to be slacked and mixed in the manner above described, and the mortar in all cases to be well and sufficiently beaten before used.

The *grout* to consist of diluted fine mortar, with a small addition of roach lime.

The foundations of the bridge, &c. to be excavated and kept clear of water by the Contractor for Masonry, and puddles to be carried round the back of the trackway, water wing walls and abutments, for 2ft in thickness from the foundation to the height of 1ft above water surface, the arch of the bridge to be covered with a puddle 15in. in thickness.

The *backing or approach* to a public road bridge to be 27ft in breadth on the top with a descent of 1 in 14 from the puddle on the crown of the arch; the approach to a private accommodation bridge to be 17ft in width on top, with a descent of 1 in 10; the descent from the road of the trackway to be 10ft wide on top, and not quicker than 1 in 9. All the approaches to have side slopes of 1ft 6in. in base to 1ft perpendicular; the entire roadway to be covered with a coat of good binding gravel 6in. in thickness.

As the situation, &c. of the bridges are particularly pointed out in the section of the Royal Canal Extension, it will be incumbent on the Contractors to satisfy themselves with respect to the nature of the foundation, &c. as no allowance will be made beyond the amount of their contract.

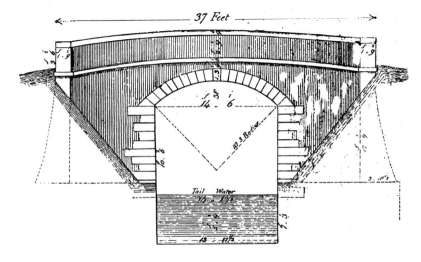

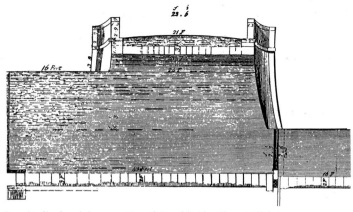

Fig. 216: *Longitudinal and Cross-section of Canal Bridge (from Killaly)*

8: Elevation of Various Bridges

The mini-elevations of bridges presented in this Appendix were compiled from information and measurements obtained from a variety of sources, including maps, drawings, engravings, sketches and photos. The scales vary depending on the overall length of the bridge. In each case a measurement is given so that approximations can be made of other dimensions. In some cases the actual spans were known and these have been inserted for each arch. Some drawings are sections, so cutwater are not shown.

The bridges have been assembled in the same chronological order as in Part II. The object is to give the reader some idea of the development in Irish arch bridge profiles down through the centuries. The elevations of the bridges on the river Shannon are based on those prepared by Thomas Rhodes under the Shannon Navigation, 1833 (see Drumheriff Bridge, fn. 2). Most of these bridges were either demolished or altered in the navigation works of the 1840s. Finally, two sketches based on 17th century maps are given, show-ing Galway and Drogheda bridges and their fortifications.

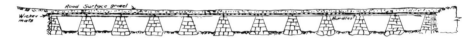

Fig. 217: *Drumheriff Bridge: in 1840s (based on Rhodes)*

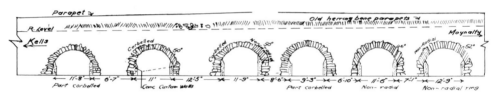

Fig. 218: *Mabes Bridge: Downriver Elevation*

Fig. 219: *Thomond (old) Bridge: Upriver Elevation in 1830s*

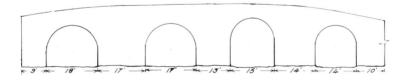

Fig. 220: *Castlemaine Bridge: in the 1970s*

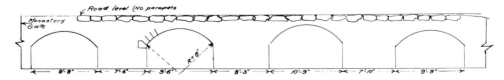

Fig. 221: *Athassel Bridge*

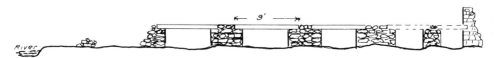

Fig. 222: *Ballybeg Clapper Bridge: Remnants in 1988*

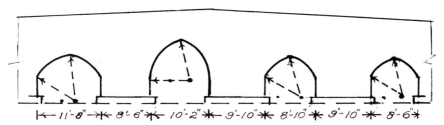

Fig. 223: *Buttevant (old) Bridge: Downriver Elevation*

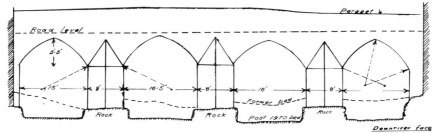

Fig. 224: *Trim Bridge: Upriver Elevation*

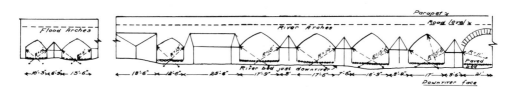

Fig. 225: *Slane Bridge: Old Bridge: Downriver Elevation*

Fig. 226: *Carrick-on-Suir Bridge: Downriver Section*

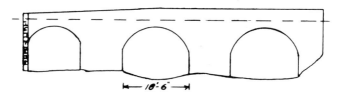

Fig. 227: *Clonmel (old) Bridge: Upriver Section*

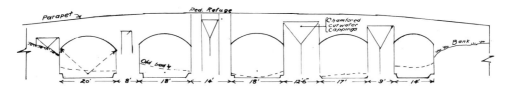

Fig. 228: *Newtown Bridge: Upriver Elevation*

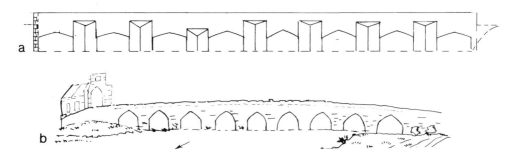

Fig. 229: *Holycross Bridge: Downriver Elevations (a) from Photos & Measurements*
(b) based on Lord Donoughmore's 18th-century Sketch

Fig. 230: *Kilcarn Bridge: Downriver Elevation*

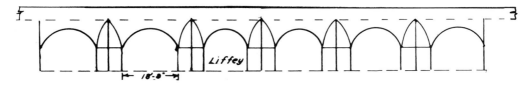

Fig. 231: *Carragh Bridge: Upriver Elevation*

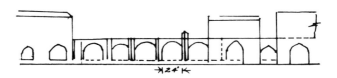

Fig. 232: *Athlone Bridge: Downriver Elevation (Rhodes in 1830s)*

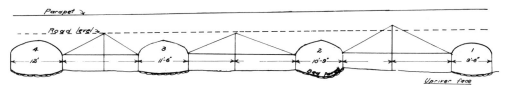

Fig. 233: *Ballinsaloe Bridge: Upriver Elevation*

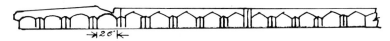

Fig. 234: *O'Briens Bridge: in 1830s (based on Rhodes)*

Fig. 235: *Sir Thomas's Bridge: Downriver Elevation*

Fig. 236: *Leighlin Bridge: Downriver Elevation*

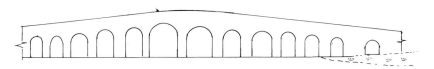

Fig. 237: *Fermoy Bridge: Profile of 1680 Bridge*

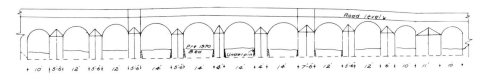

Fig. 238: *Bective Bridge: Upriver Elevation*

Fig. 239: *Old Long Bridge: Elevation based on 1834 Six-inch Map*

Fig. 240: *Banagher Bridge; in 1830s (based on Rhodes)*

Fig. 241: *Original Essex Bridge: Section looking Upriver*

Fig. 242: *Semple's Essex Bridge: Section looking Upriver*

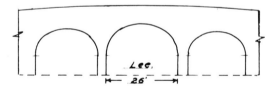

Fig. 243: *South Gate Bridge: Section looking Downriver*

Fig. 244: *Scariff Bridge: Downriver Elevation*

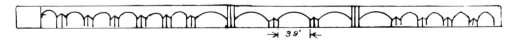

Fig. 245: *Killaloe Bridge: 1830s Section (based on Rhodes)*

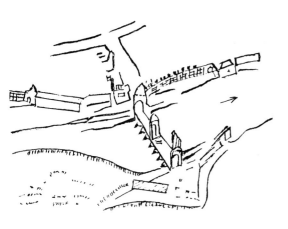

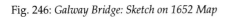

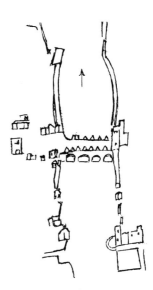

Fig. 246: *Galway Bridge: Sketch on 1652 Map*

Fig. 247: *Drogheda Bridge: Sketch based on Newcomen's 1657 Map*

9: A Typical Presentment

The proposed bridge is to be built in accordance with the above plan and following instructions.

The direction of the abutments is to form an angle of 70° with the centre line of the wall and river course is to be attired to correspond with the line of the bridge to such extent as may appear necessary.

Excavations: The rock in the bed of the river is to be excavated to the width and depth shown by the sketch.

Foundations: The masonry of the foundations for a depth of 12in. to be built with large flags closely connected and well bonded, laid in a bed of rich mortar and fully grouted.

Abutments: The masonry in abutments and retaining wall to be built in broken ashlar, in courses 12in. deep. The stones forming the face to be roughly punched or hammer dressed, squared 4in. deep all round, with bonds of good length introduced at short intervals in each course and backed up with the best rubble, well connected with the face and fully grouted.

Centres: The arch to be turned on a centre of timber framings, well supported, set on wedges and closely sheeted with planks.

Rings: The ringstones to measure 15in. uniform depth by 18in. and 2ft 3in. alternately on the soffit. To be punched and draughted neatly on the face; the beds to be formed accurately.

Sheeting: The sheeting to measure 15in. deep also, squared the full depth, provided in flags and laid with break joints of 9in. at least.

Coping: The coping to measure 12in. deep, by 15in. on beds, provided in the lengths shown in the plan, punched and draughted on face and finished with rock work on top.

Quoins: The quoins of abutment to measure 2ft long by 12in. square in the head. The quoins of retaining walls to measure the same size and both to be neatly punched and draughted.

Mortar: The abutments to measure 3ft 6in. long. The masonry to be laid in mortar made with well burnt lime and clean sharp sand in the proportion of two measures of the former to three of the latter.

The work to be finished to the satisfaction of the County Surveyor before the 1st October 1868 and preserved in good order until the presentments shall be discharged.

James Neary   Contractors
Roderick Gray

13 January 1868

10: A New Map of Ireland, by Herman Moll, 1714

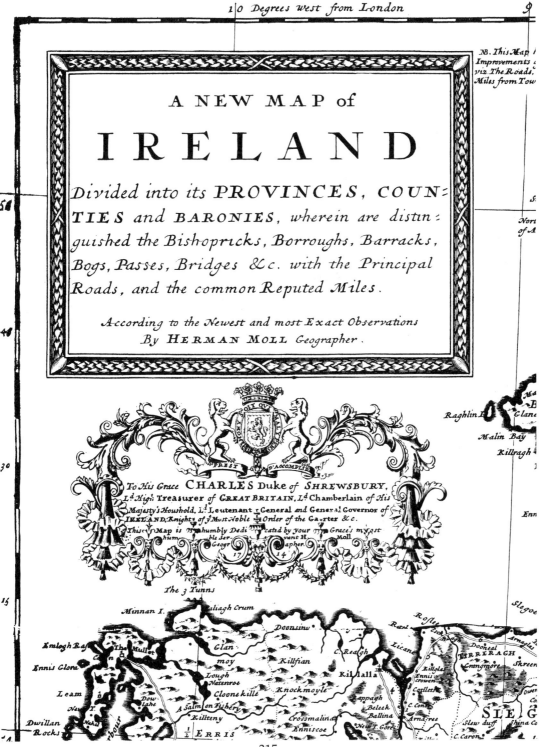

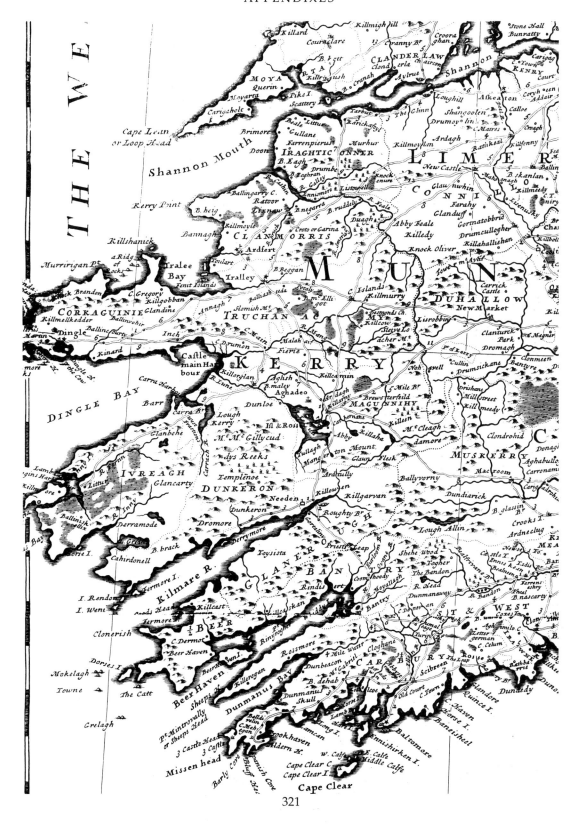

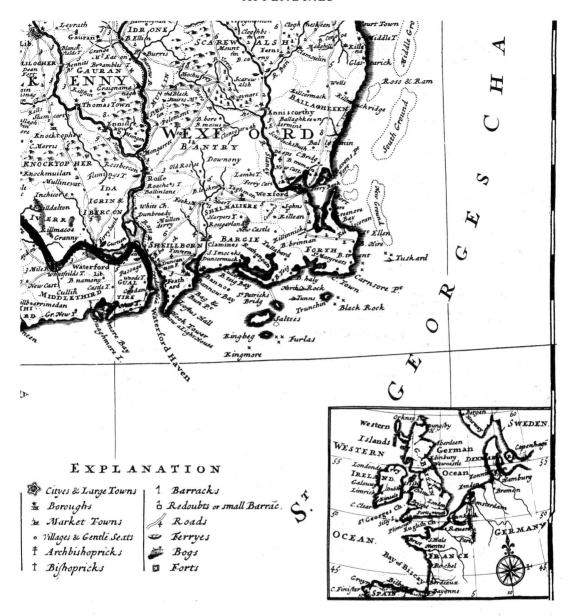

EXPLANATION

⊛	Cityes & Large Towns	1	Barracks
⚐	Boroughs	⚑	Redoubts or small Barrac.
⚐	Market Towns	⚔	Roads
∘	Villages & Gentle Seats	⚓	Ferryes
‡	Archbishopricks	⬤	Bogs
†	Bishopricks	⊠	Forts

Notes

CHAPTER 1
1   Inventory of Public Roads in Ireland at 31 December 1977; unpublished, Department of the Environment.
2   Statutory Rules and Orders 1946, No. 273, Public Bodies Order, 1946, Stationery Office, Dublin.
3   The results were printed in a *Report on Bridges*, 1918.
4   Commonly known as the "MacQuillan Act".
5   Road Inventory 1974, Reports RT 74, RT 78 and RT 94, An Foras Forbartha, Dublin 1975.
6   Stevenson, W.H.C. "Bridge Design Aspects and Their Effect on Maintenance," Symposium on Maintenance of Bridges & Highways, Inst. Highways and Transportation, Belfast, 1983.
7   *Bridge Maintenance: A Report prepared by an OECD Road Research Group*, OECD, 1981.
8   Holland, T.J., *An Estimate of the Number of Road Bridges in the Republic of Ireland*, An Foras Forbartha Report R.287, Dublin 1988.

CHAPTER 2
1   Joyce, *Places*, i, pp. 353–69.
2   Sherlock.
3   White, Col. J.G. *Historical and Topographical Notes, etc. on Buttevant, Castleroach, . . . Mallow. . .*, Cork, 1905, p. 80.
4   Bound volumes of District Drainage Reports of the Board of Public Works in the 1840s in the IEI Archive. See Chapter 6 below.
5   Lowry, T.K., "The True Position of the Ford of Belfast", in *The Ecclesiastical Antiquites of Down, Conor and Dromore*, ed. W. Reeves, Dublin, 1847, p. 260.
6   Clarke, H.B., "The Topographical Development of Early Medieval Dublin," *Journal RSAI* 107, 1977, pp. 29–51.
7   Power, P., *Place Names of the Decies*, London, 1907.
8   Jones, W., "The Clapper Bridge at Springfield, near Ballybeg Abbey," *JCHAS* XII, series 2, 1906, pp. 200f.

CHAPTER 3
1   2nd ed, ch. 5, London, 1981.
2   O'Kelly, F., *A Guide to Early Irish Law*, Dublin, 1988.
3   McCurtain, M., *Tudor and Stuart Ireland*, Dublin, 1972.
4   See *Stat. Ire. John-Hen. V*, p. 13.
5   Greig, W., *Strictures on Road Police containing Views of the Present Systems by which roads are made and repaired . . . in Great Britain and Ireland*, Dublin, 1818, p. 9.

6   *Stat. Ire. John-Hen. V*, p. 13.
7   This error originated in a wrong summary given in *Chartal. St Mary's, Dublin.*
8   25 Edw. I c. 10 quoted in Berry, op. cit.
9   Boyer, p. 93.
10 Russell, J.C. *Medieval Regions and their Cities*, Newtown Abbot, 1972, pp. 144–5.
11 Leask, *Castles*, p. 75.
12 25 Henry VIII c. 5 (England).
13 Sidney.
14 *11th Report of Deputy Keeper of Public Records in Ireland*, Dublin, 1879, p. 83.
15 *Cal. S.P. Ire. 1574–85.*
16 *Cal. pat. rolls Ire., Eliz.*
17 Moody, T.W. and Martin, F.X., eds., *The Course of Irish History*, Cork, 1967, p. 371.
18 O'Brien, G., *The Economic History of Ireland in the Seventeenth Century*, Dublin, 1919, pp. 6–7.
19 *Report on the Manuscripts of the Marquis of Ormonde*, ii, London, 1899, p. 312.
20 10 Chas. I c. 26, in *Stat. Ire*, iii., III; index 1301 AD to 1799 AD, Bridges; National Archive Office.
21 In *Natives and Newcomers*, C. Brady & R. Gillespie, eds., Dublin 1986, p. 174.
22 *Council Book Youghal*, p. 394.
23 "Manuscripts of the Old Corporation of Kinsale", *Analecta Hibernica* 15 (November 1944), pp. 163–77.
24 Andrews, "Road Planning", p. 23.
25 Young, ii, 79.
26 Townsend, H., *A General and Statistical Survey of the County of Cork*, ii, Cork, 1815.
27 *The Fourth Report of the Commissioners . . . on Bogs in Ireland*, H.C. 1813–14, (131)VI, Second Part, App. No. 10.
28 Cf. O'Keeffe, P.J., "Richard Griffith, Planner & Builder of Roads," *RDS Historical Studies in Irish Science & Tech.*, No. 1, Dublin 1980.
29 Cf. White, H.V., "County Work in Ireland considered in relation to Grand Jury Laws," *Trans. ICEI* 17, 1885, pp. 19–81.

CHAPTER 4
1   The evolution of this system summarised by D. Roche in his *Local Government in Ireland*, Dublin, pp. 27–32 and p. 45
2   C.F. Webb, J.J. *Municipal Government in Ireland, Medieval & Modern*, Dublin, 1918, pp. 5–8.
3   Young, i, p. 77.

4   McCutcheon, p. 5.
5   *The Grand Juries of the County of Westmeath from the year 1727 to the year 1853*, i, Ledestown, 1853, preface.
6   *Report of the Select Committee on Grand Jury Presentments: Ireland*; House of Commons, 1827.
7   White, H.V., 'County Works in Ireland in relation to Grand Jury Laws", *Trans. ICEI* 17, Dublin 1886, p. 23.

CHAPTER 5
1   Reprinted Shannon, 1969.
2   A set is housed in the archives of the Institution of Engineers of Ireland, Dublin.
3   Andrews, "Road Planning", p. 20.
4   Burke, F. and O'Keefe, P., "The Rehabilitation of an Ancient Bridge in Co. Meath", IEI, Dublin 1989.
5   Boyer.
6   Cooke, T. C., *The Early History of the Town of Birr, or Parsonstown*, Dublin 1875, p. 320.
7   W. Petty, *Hiberniae Delineatio rep.* Shannon, 1969.
8   Speed, J., *Theatre of the Empire* (1611): Limerick, Cork, Dublin, Galway and Enniskillen Castle in *Ireland from Maps*, Dublin 1980.
9   Ulster Maps 1609; maps of the Escheated Counties in Ireland 1609 copied by Col. Henry James 1861.
10   Hore, H., "Notes on a Facsimile of an Ancient Map of Leix, Offaly . . .", *JKSEAS*, 1863, pp. 345–72.
11   O'Hanlon, J. Canon, *A History of the Queen's County*, Dublin 1907.
12   Dunlop, A., "Sixteenth-Century Maps of Ireland", *English Historical Review*, xx, no. lxxviii, 1905, pp. 309–337.
13   Referred to in n. 8 above.

CHAPTER 6
1   Carville, G., *The Heritage of Holycross*, Belfast 1973, p. 70.
2   Colmcille, OCSO, Fr., *The Story of Mellifont*, Dublin 1953, p. 110.
3   Archdall, p. 178.
4   Morrogh, p. 178.
5   O'Brien, G., *The Economic History of Ireland in the Eighteenth Century*, Dublin, 1918, p. 323.
6   Watters, P., "The History of Kilkenny Canal", *Royal Hist. & Arch. Association of Ireland*, II, new series (1872/73), p. 98.
7   Delany, p. 103.
8   See Dooge, J.C., "Manning and Mulvaney, River Improvements in 19th century Ireland", *Hydraulics & Hydraulic Research Review*, Rotterdam 1987, II. 173–83.
9   Kelly, J.W., Report on Proposed Drainage, Nore, in Cos. Tipp & . . . 1845, in the IEI archive.
10   [Harper, S.], "Implements & Ornaments", *Transactions of the Kilkenny Arch. Soc.*, vol. 1, 1849/51, p. 30.
11   Cf., for example, Edwards, R.D. & Williams, T.D., *The Great Famine*, Dublin, 1956. Chapter 4.
12   Connellan, O., "On the Rivers of Ireland with the Derivatives of their Names", *RIA Proc.* X, Dublin 1866–9, pp. 443–58.

CHAPTER 7
1   Raftery, J., "Knocknalappa Crannog Co. Clare", *North Munster Antiq Journal*, 3, 1942.
2   Hencken, H. O'Neill, "Ballinderry Crannog No. 1," *RIA Proc.*, xliii, Section c, no. 5, 1936, p. 103–239.
3   *The Celtic Way of Life*, A. McMahon (ed.), i ,1976, p. 20.
4   Wood Martin, W.G. *The Lake Dwellings of Ireland*, London 1886, reprinted Dublin, 1983.
5   Cosgrave, A., *A New History of Ireland : Medieval Ireland, 1169–1534*, Oxford 1987, p. 8.
6   Keating G., *Foras Feasa ar Éirinn*, ed. by P.S. Dineen, iii, London, 1908, p. 269.
7   *Contributions' Dictionary of the Irish Language, based mainly on Old and Middle Irish materials*, Dublin, 1968.
8   Evans, E. Estyn, *Irish Heritage*, Dundalk, 1977, p. 126.
9   Joyce, i, p. 427; p. 224.
10   Jacob Grace, "Killenniensis," *Annales Hibernia*, ed. R. Butler, Dublin, 1842 p. 117
11   *Chartul. St Mary's, Dublin*, p. 372.
12   Semple, p. 59.
13   McCracken, E., "The Woodlands of Ireland *c*.1600", *Irish Historical Studies* XI, no. 44, 1959, pp. 271–91.
14   *Irish Penny Magazine*, Dublin, 28 Sept. 1833, p. 310.
15   Boyer, 1976.
16   Little, G., *Dublin Before the Vikings*, Dublin 1957, p. 71.
17   "Some Account of Ancient Irish Treatises on Ogham Writing", *J. Royal Historical & Archaelogical Association. Ireland*, Vol. 3, p. 211.
18   Home, G., *Old London Bridge*, London, 1931.
19   Lanchester, H.C jr. et al, *Underwater Inspection and Repair of Bridge Substructures* Washington DC, 1981.
20   Purser, J. "The Deterioration of Marine Structures", *Trans. ICEI* 62, Dublin, 1936, pp. 121–57.
21   Halliday, C., *The Scandinavian Kingdom of Dublin*, p. 237.
22   Mullins, M.B., "On Boring Animals in Connection with Structures exposed to the Sea", *Trans. ICEI* II, Dublin 1847, p. 76–97.

CHAPTER 8
1   Leask, i, p.2.
2   Champneys, A.C. *Ecclesiastical Architecture of Ireland*, London, 1910, Chapter III.
3   Vitruvius, M., *The Ten Books of Architecture*; trans. by M. Morgan, New York, 1960.
4   Casey, C. 'Architectural Books in Eighteenth-century Ireland', *Iris an dá chultúr* 3, Dublin 1988.
5   Sterpos, D., *The Roman Road in Italy*, Rome 1970, p. 43.
6   Stokes, M., *The Early Christian Architecture in Ireland*, London, 1878.
7   Bigger, Francis J., 'Some Notes in the Churches of Saint Tassach of Raholph . . .in Down', *Journal RSAI* XLVI, pt II, 1916, p. 123.
8   O'Danachair C. 'Materials and Methods in Irish Traditional Building', *Journal RSAI* 29, 1957–58.
9   Alberti, L.B. *The Ten Books of Architecture*, the 1755 Leoni edition, reprinted New York 1986, p. 36.
10   Harbison, p. 19.
11   Barrow, George Lennox, *The Round Towers of Ireland*, Dublin 1979, pp. 38–41.

12 Stokes, M., *Early Christian Art in Ireland*, London 1887, p. 167.
13 Joyce, ii, p. 228.
14 Davis, D. & Quinn, D.B., 'The Irish Pipe Roll of 14 John, 1211–12', *UJA* 4 supplement, 1941.
15 The findings are discussed in an article by Campbell in *Medieval Archaeology* 27 (1983).
16 Palladio, A., *The Four Books of Architecture,* New York 1965, book I, Chapter 5.
17 Wilkinson, p. 258.
18 *Council Book Youghal*, p. 25.
19 *Council Book Cork*, p. 364.
20 Semple, pp. 62–63.
21 Mahan, D.H.
22 De Courcy, J. 'A History of Concrete in Ireland', a paper presented to IEI, *c.* 1985.
23 Rutty, J., *An Essay towards the Natural History of Dublin*, ii, Dublin 1772, p. 98.
24 Purser Griffith, J., 'The Lowering and Widening of Essex Bridge', *Trans. ICEI* 13, 1880, p.32.
25 Cf. Stoney, Bindon, 'On the Action of Sea Water on Lime Mortar', *Trans. ICEI*, Dublin 1862, pp. 90–96.
26 Cf. Woods, K. et al., *Highway Engineering Handbook*, New York, 1960, pp. 179f.

CHAPTER 9

1   AFM, in the year 1361.
2   AFM AD 734.
3   BS 892: 1967; *Glossary of Highway Engineering Terms*, British Standards Institution, London, p. 16.
4   McEvoy, J. *A Statistical Survey of the County of Tyrone*, Dublin, 1802. p. 129.
5   Petrie, G. "Thomond Bridge, Limerick", *Dublin Penny Journal*, vol. 1, no. 19, p. 150, Dublin 1832.
6   Joyce, i, p. 368.
7   Lugli, G., *La Tecnica edilizia romani*, i, Rome 1957, pp. 337–8, quoted in Sterpos, D., *The Roman Road in Italy*, Rome, 1970.
8   *Stat. Ire., Hen. VI* p. 629.
9   Boyer.
10 Purdon, H.S., "Medieval Hospitals for Lepers near Belfast", *UJA* II, no. 4, 1896, pp. 268–71.
11 Gwynn & Hadcock, pp. 344–57.
12 Logan, "Lazar Houses", *UJA*, vol. 12, 1895/6.
13 Burke, F., O'Keeffe, P.J., "The Rehabilitation of an Ancient Bridge in Co. Meath", *Trans. IEI*, Dublin 1989.
14 Cogan, Rev. A, *The Ecclesiastical History of the Diocese of Meath, Ancient and Modern*, 3 vols, Dublin (1874), i, p. 30.
15 Leask, H., "The Characteristic Features of Irish Architecture from Early Times to the 12th Century," *NMAJ*, 1, 1936.
16 Stalley, p. 41.
17 Fitzgerald, E., "On Ancient Mason's Marks at Youghal and Elsewhere and the Secret Language for the Craftsmen of the Middle Ages in Ireland", *JKSEAS* II, new series 1858/9, p. 70.
18 Okey, T., *The Story of Avignon*, London, 1926, p. 333.
19 Orpen, G.H., *Ireland under the Normans, 1169–1216*, ii, Oxford 1911, p. 252.
20 Warren, W.L., *King John*, London, 1961, pp. 112–3.

21 Cf. Davis, O. & Quinn, D.B. "The Irish Pipe Roll of 14 John, 1211–12", *UJA* 4, supplement, 1941.
22 Cf. Leask, *Castles*, pp. 25 and 153–162.
23 Cf. Berry, H.F., "The Manor and Castle of Mallow in the Days of the Tudors", in *JCHAS* 14, 1983, p.15.
24 Palladio, A., *The Four Books of Architecture*: trans I. Wate 1738; rep. NewYork, 1986.
25 Alberti, L.B., *The Ten Books of Architecture*; the 1755 Leoni edition, rep. NewYork, 1986.
26 Casey, C. "Architectural Books in Eighteenth Century Ireland," *Iris an dá chultur* 3, Dublin, 1988.

CHAPTER 10

1   *Calendar of Documents Ireland* 1171 AD to 1251, Pat. 10, John 5.
2   Graham, B.J., "Anglo Norman Settlements in Co. Meath", *R.I.A., Trans.* 1975.
3   *Rot. pat. Hib.*, Vol I, pt. I, p.52.
4   Westropp, T.J., "St Mary's Cathedral, Limerick: its plan and growth", *Journal RSAI* 28, 1898, pp. 35–48.
5   Viollet-le-duc, *Dictionnaire Raisonné de l'Architecture François, du XI au XVI Siecles*, Paris 1864.
6   Gwynn, S., *The Famous Cities of Ireland*, London 1915.
7   Westropp, T.J., "The Antiquities of Limerick and its Neighbourhood," *Journal RSAI*, 1892.
8   Rabitte, Rev. J., "Galway Corporation MSS" *JGAHS* XV & XVI, 1931–35, p. 86.
9   "Notes on the Pictorial Map of Galway", *JGAHS* 1905–6, p. 134.
10 Cf. O'Sullivan, M.D., *Old Galway: The History of a Norman Colony in Ireland*, Cambridge, 1942, frontspiece.
11 Cf. art. cit. in n. 8 above.
12 O'Sullivan, M.D., 'The Fortifications of Galway in the 16th and early 17th Centuries,' *JGAHS*, XVI, nos. I & II, 1934, pp. 1–47.
13 *13th Report* of the Deputy Keeper of Public Records, Appendix 99, 3447 (2666) Lease, 6 Aug. XVII.
14 Story, G., *An Impartial History of the Wars of Ireland*, London 1693.

CHAPTER 11

1   Von Beek, G.W., "Arches and Vaults in the Ancient Near East," *Scientific American*, July 1987, pp. 78–85.
2   Fletcher, Sir Banister, *A History of Architecture*, 18th ed. revised by J.C. Palmes in 1975, p.1310.
3   Leask, *Castles*, p. 24.
4   *Ancient Bridges* (various volumes), London 1930–36.
5   Bressey, C.H., *The Development of Road Bridges in Great Britain*, published by the Organising Committee of the Public Works, Roads and Transport Congress, London, 1933.
6   Prade.
7   Benson, J., "An Account of the Skew Bridge built on the new Western Entrance to Cork", *Trans. ICEI*, Dublin 1849, pp. 1–2.
8   Alberti, Leon Battista, *The Ten Books of Architecture*; (English ed. 1755); rep. New York, 1986.
9   Bald, W. "Account of the Voussoirs of the four elliptic arches in the bridge erected over the Owen-more River in the West of Ireland," *Trans. ICE*, 1837/41.

10 *Bridge Collapse*, p. vii.
11 Semple.
12 *Pacata Hibernia*, opp. p. 157.
13 Thomas, D.L., "Bridges in Britain", *J. Inst. Highway Engineers*, London, 1969. p. 33.
14 Lugli, G. *La tecnica edilizia romana,* i; Rome, 1957, pp. 337f.
15 Shirley, E.P., 'Extracts from the Journal of Thomas Dinley . . .', *JRSAI*, IV, 1862–3.

CHAPTER 12
1   Semple.
2   Ruddock.
3   Hawksmoore, *Account of London Bridge*, London 1736.
4   *French Know-How in Bridge Building*. ISTED. 1989.
5   Leonhardt, F., *Bridges, Aesthetics & Design*, London 1982.
6   Andrews, "Road Planning".
7   *Fourth Report of the Commissioners on Bogs in Ireland,* House of Commons, 1813–14.
8   *The Edinburgh Encyclopaedia*, Edinburgh 1830, IV, Pt 2, Bridges (Nimmo & Telford).
10 Storrie, M.G. "William Bald: surveyor, Cartographer & Civil Engineer", *Trans. Inst. Br. Geogr. 47* (1968), 205–231.
11 Bald, W., "Account of the Voussoirs of the Four Elliptic Arches in the Bridge erected over the Owenmore River in the West of Ireland," *Trans. ICEI*, Vol. 1837/41.
12 *First & Second Reports: Public Works in Ireland,* House of Commons 1835.
13 O'Keeffe, P. '"Griffith, R. (1784–1878) Planner & Builder of Roads", in *Richard Griffith*, Dublin, 1980.
14 Sganzin, M., *An Elementary Course of Civil Engineering* (1827). Trans. from French by Davis, J.
15 Bowen, J. "Salvage of the Main Road Bridge at Ballyvoyle, Co. Waterford", *Trans. ICEI* 54, 1928.
16 Rankin, W.J. *Manual of Civil Engineering*, 1862.
17 Castigliano, C.A., *Theorie de l'equilibre des systems elastiques et ses applications*, Turin, 1879.
18 Alexander, T. & Thomson, A.W., *The Scientific Design of Masonry Arches*, privately printed in 1900 and published in 1927.
19 Lilly, W.E., "The Design of Arches," *Trans. ICEI*, 40, 1914.
20 Pippard, A.J. & Chitty, L., *A Study of the Voussoir Arch,* National Building Studies Research Paper 11, London, 1951 and *JICE* 4, 1936.
21 Heyman, J., *The Masonry Arch*, London, 1982.
22 Page, J., "Load Testing to Collapse of Masonry Arch Bridges," Transport and Road Research Laboratory, London, 1986.

General:
Ruddock, E.C., "Hollow Spandrels in Arch Bridge: A Historical Study" in *Structural Engineer*. 52, no. 8, 1974; Harvey, W.J., "Applications of the Mechanism Analysis to Masonry Arches' in *Structural Engineer* 66, no. 5, 1988; Pippard & Baker, *Analysis of Engineering Stuctures*, London, 1968; Harvey, W. "Testing Time for Arches" in *New Scientist*, 15 May 1986.

SKEAGH CAUSEWAY

1   Jones W., "The Clapper Bridge at Springfield, near Ballybeg Abbey", *JCHAS*; series 2, xii, 1906, pp. 200f.
2   Gwynn & Hadcock.
3   Commissioners for the Improvement of the Navigation of the River Shannon, *4th Report* (1839), Survey of the River Shannon, Plan No. 3.
4   Davis, O. and Quinn, D.B., "The Irish Pipe Roll of 14 John, 1211–1212", *UJA* (3rd series) 4, supplement, July, 1941, p. 45.

KNOCKAINEY CLOCHAN

1   Crawford, H.S., "Primitive Bridge or Causeway at Knockainey, Co. Limerick", *JRSAI* 47, pt. 1, 1917, p. 82.

DRUMHERIFF

1   Quoted in Lenihan, p. 50.
2   *Commons' jn*, Drumheriff, River Shannon Navigation 1833 (371) xxxiv 235, plate 14. Elevation of Bridges, T. Rhodes.
3   *The Miscellany of the Irish Archaeological Society,* (1846) i, p. 165.

GARFINNY

1   Harbison, pp. 107–114.
2   Barrington, T.J., *Discovering Kerry, its History, Heritage and Topography*, Dublin, 1976, p. 246.
3   Leask, *Churches*, p. 25.
4   Andrews, "Road Planning", pp. 31–32.
5   Wilkinson, p. 169.

ST MARY MAGDALEN

1   Note in *Journal RSAI* 46, 1916, p. 202.
2   Gwynn & Haydock, p. 354 citing Dr P.L. Logan.
3   Ibid., p. 350.
4   Andrews, J.H., *Plantation Acres*, Belfast, 1985.
5   Cuffe, P., "History of Duleek, Section II, Ecclesiastical A.D. 432–1172", *Riocht na Midhe* 2–3, 1959–66 (quotation from *Analecta Hibernia* I, p. 124).

BABES

1   Ellison, C., *The Waters of the Boyne and Blackwater*, Dublin, 1983, p. 89.
2   *Stat. Ire., 1–12 Edw. IV*, p. 207.
3   Grace, J., *Annales Hiberniae*, R. Butler, ed., Dublin, 1842, p. 117.
4   In connection with a seminar: see *Bridge Collapse*.
5   Alexander, T. and Thomson, *The Scientific Design of Masonry Arches, with Numerous Examples*, London, 1927.
6   Prade.
7   Warren, W.L., *King John*, London, 1961, p. 194.
8   *Register of the Abbey of St Thomas, Dublin*, edited by J.T. Gilbert, London, 1889.
9   Prade, M., *Les grand ponts du monde: I: Ponts remarkables d'Europe*, Poitiers, 1990.

MABE'S

1 Burke, F. and O'Keefe, P.J., *The Rehabilitation of an Ancient Bridge in Co. Meath: A Paper Presented to the Heritage Society IEI, February, 1989*, Navan, 1989,
2 Wilkinson.
3 O'Connell, Philip, "Kells—Early and Medieval, Part 1", *Rioch na Midhe* II, no. 1, 1959; Part 2, *Rioch na Midhe* II, no. 2, 1960.
4 O'Donovan, J., "The Irish Charters in the Book of Kells", *The Miscellany of the Irish Archaeological Society*, i, Dublin, 1846, pp. 127–157.
5 Healy, J., *Historical Guide to Kells (Ceanannus Mór) with Map*, Dublin, 1930, p. 12.
6 *The Assessment of Highway Bridges and Structures*, Advice Note BA 16/84, Department of Transport, (UK) 1984.

MONKS

1 O'Hanlon, J. Canon, *History of the Queen's Country*, i, Dublin, 1907, ii, 1914.
2 Stalley, p. 241.
3 Hore, H., "Notes on a Fac Simile of an Ancient Map of Leix, Ofaly, preserved in the British Museum", *JKSEAS* 1863, pp. 342.
4 *Abbey Leix Ireland; A Booklet*, Deale & Son Ltd., Dublin (undated), p. 16.

THOMOND (OLD)

1 Stalley, R., "William of Prene and the Royal Works in Ireland", *Journal of the British Archaeological Association* 81, 1978, pp. 30–49.
2 Gwynn & Hadcock, p. 90.
3 Lenihan, pp. 47f.
4 Barry, J.G. "Old Limerick Bridges" in *JNMAS* I, 1909–11, pp. 7–13.
5 Ruddock.
6 Lewis, S., ii, p. 268.
7 O'Sullivan T.F., "Limerick Harbour-Dock Extension", in *Trans. ICEI* 64, 1938, pp. 179–208.
8 *Report on Manuscripts of Marquis of Ormonde*, ii, London, 1899, pp. 316f.
9 Shirley, E.P., "Extracts from the Journal of Thomas Dineley Esq. . . . his visit to Ireland . . . (1660–1665), *Journal RSAI* 8, 1864–66, p. 428.
10 Gwynn, S., *The Famous Cities of Ireland*, Dublin, 1915, p. 203.
11 *Pacata Hibernia*.
12 Westropp T.J. "St. Mary's Cathedral, Limerick: its Plan and Growth," *Journal RSAI* 28, 1898, pp. 35–48.
13 Sweetman, P.D., "Archaeological Excavations at King John's Castle, Limerick", *RIA Proc.* 80, C, no. 11, p. 208.
14 *Rot. pat. Hib.*, Chartae, Privilegia & Immunitates AD 1325, Anno 17 Ed. II, p. 52.
15 *Histoire des Institutions religieuses, politiques, judiciaries . . . de la Ville de Toulouse* (Toulouse 1844–6), quoted in Boyer.
16 Boyer, M.N., "Rebuilding the Bridge of Albi, 1408–1410" in *Technology and Culture* 7 (1966) pp. 495–503.
17 Viollet-le-Duc, M., *Dictionnaire Raisonné de l'Architecture Française* (XI to XI centuries), Paris, 1864.

18 *Historic & Municipal Documents of Ireland 1172–1320*, ed. J.T. Gilbert, London, 1870, p. xliii.
19 Wilkinson, G.,

ABBEYTOWN

1 Gwynn & Hadcock, pp. 128–129.
2 Stalley.
3 Burke, F., and O'Keeffe, P.J., *The Rehabilitation of an Ancient Bridge in Co. Meath.*, Navan, 1989.
4 Gross, F., *The Antiquities of Ireland*, i, 1791 pl. II, p. 82.
5 Wilkinson, p. 264.

KING JOHN'S

1 Rocque, J., *An Actual Survey of County Dublin.* (surveyed in late 1750s).
2 Curtis, E., "the Court Book of Esker and Crumlin, 1592–1600," *Journal RSAI* 59, 1929, p. 45; and Simms, A., "Rural Settlement in Medieval Ireland: the example of the Royal Manors of Newcastle Lyons and Esker in South County Dublin" in *Village, Fields and Frontiers* (B.K. Roberts & R.E. Glasscock eds) Bar International Services 185, 1983, pp. 133–152.

CASTLEMANG

1 Carmody, Rev. J., "The Story of Castle Magne, Co. Kerry", *JKAS* I, 1908–12.
2 *Pacata Hibernia*, i, p. 111.
3 *4th Annual Report from Commissioners . . . for Drainage of Land in Ireland* 1846 [733] xxii. 17.

ST JOHN'S

1 *Council Book of the Corporation of Waterford 1662–1700*, edited by S. Pender, Irish Manuscripts Commission Dublin, 1964, pp. 136, 251, 277, 281, 302, 248, 358.
2 Ryland, Rev. R., *The History, Topography and Antiquities of the County and City of Waterford*, London, 1824, opp. p. 113.
3 Gwynn & Hadcock, pp. 356–357.

ATHASSEL

1 Gwynn & Hadcock p. 157.
2 Harbison, p. 219.
3 de Breffny, B. and Mott, G., *The Churches and Abbeys of Ireland*, London, 1976, p. 67.
4 *Shell Guide*, p. 194.

BUTTEVANT OLD BRIDGE

1 Joyce, i, p. 392.
2 *Shell Guide*.
3 Gwynn & Hadcock, p. 159.
4 Jones, W., "The Clapper Bridge at Springfield, near Ballybeg Abbey", *JCHAS*, series 2, XII, 1906, pp. 200f.
5 Grove White, Col. J., *Historical and Topographical Notes: Buttevant, Castletownroach, Doneraile, Mallow . . .*, 1905.
6 Harbison.

GORMANSTOWN

1 *Fourth Report of the Royal Commission on Historic Manuscripts*: Gormanstown Register ed. by J.T. Gilbert, London, 1874, p. 573.

NEW BRIDGE

1 Sherlock.
2 Craig, M., *The Architecture of Ireland*, London and Dublin, 1982, pp. 277f.
3 "Leighlin Bridge" in *Irish Penny Journal*, vol. 1, 1840.
4 Deputy Keeper Pub. Records, *17th Report* 16 to 20, 1884–88; Appendix: Calendar of Christ Church Deeds entries nos. 201 and 205.
5 De Burgo, T., *Hibernia Dominicana*, ed. of 1762, p. 192.
6 Warburton, J. et al., *History of the City of Dublin from earliest accounts to the present time*, London, 1818.
7 Mallagh, J., "City Bridges over the Liffey, Present and Future", *Trans. ICEI* 65, 1938/9, p. 225.
8 Gilbert, J.T., *Chronicles and Memorials of Ireland*, ii, 1884.
9 De Courcy, J, "The Engineering of Dublin", *Engineers Journal* 41, no. 9, 1988.
10 Conlin, S and de Courcy, J., *Anna Liffey*, Dublin, 1988.

BAAL'S

1 Barry, J.G., "Old Limerick Bridges", *JNMHS* 1 1909, p. 11.
2 Brocas, James Henry (1790–1846), Old Baal's Bridge Limerick, National Gallery of Ireland, print 1986.
3 Westropp, T., "St. Mary's Cathedral Limerick: Its Plan and Growth" *Journal RSAI* 28, 1898, p. 37.
4 *Cal. pat. rolls* quoted in Lenihan, p. 62.
5 Fleming, Rev. J., *St John's Cathedral Limerick*, Dublin 1987, p. 12.
6 Lynch, P.J., "Notes", *JNMAS* 1, no. 1, 1909, pp. 11–13.

TRIM

1 Joyce, p. 456.
2 Conwell, E., *A Ramble Round Trim*, reprinted from the *Journal of the Royal Historical Archaeological Association of Ireland*, 1873, pp. 1–2.
3 *Register of Primate Swayne, Armagh, 1418–1439*, ed. D. Chart, London, 1835, p. 39.
4 McNeil, C. "Copies of the Down Survey in Private Keeping" in *Analecta Hibernica* 8, March 1938. p. 424.
5 O'Keeffe, P.J., Notes on the History of the Multi-Span Masonry Arch Bridges over the Boyne on Trim 1976 (unpublished).
6 Barry, J.G. "Old Limerick Bridge, *JNMAS* 1, 1909, p. 10.

SLANE

1 Trench, C.E.F., *Slane*, Dublin, 1976.
2 Andrews, "Road Planning", pp. 17–41.

3 Larkin, W., *A map of the Cross and Bye, Branching, Mail Coach and Post Roads of Ireland*, Dublin, 1803.
4 Taylor, J., County of Meath (map) in R. Thompson, *Statistical Survey of County Meath*, Dublin, 1802.
5 Edwards, p. 53.

CARRICK-ON-SUIR

1 Bradley, J., "The Medieval Towns in Tipperary" in *Tipperary: History and Society*; W. Norton (ed.), 1985.
2 Morrogh, p. 175.
3 Loeber, R., "Biographical Dictionary of Engineers in Ireland 1600–1730", *Irish Sword* (issue not known).
4 Howden, G.B., "Reconstruction of the Boyne Viaduct, Drogheda", *Trans. ICEI* LX, 1934, pp. 71–92.

CLONMEL

1 Bradley, J., "The Medieval Towns of Tipperary", in *Tipperary: History and Society*, W. Norton (ed.), 1985.
2 Chetwood, W.R., *A Tour through Ireland . . .*, 1748, London, 1757.
3 Lyons, Patrick, "Norman Antiquities of Clonmel Burgh", *Journal RSAI* VI, 7th series, 1936, pp. 282, 285–294.

ADARE

1 Leask, *Castles*, p. 34.
2 *Shell Guide*, p. 35.
3 *Memorials of Adare Manor, by Caroline, Countess of Dunraven with historical notices of Adare by her son, the Earl of Dunraven*, printed for private circulation, Oxford, 1865, p. 104.
4 T. Pierce et al., *Adare—A Short Guide to the Village*, Limerick, 1976, p. 25.

ASKEATON

1 Westropp, T.J. Macalister, R.A.S., Mac Namara, G.U., "Antiquities of Limerick and its Neighbourhood", *RSAI Antiquarian Handbook*, Ser. No. VII, 1916, p. 52.
2 Spellissy, S., *Limerick the Rich Land*, Ennis, 1989 p. 107.
3 Alberti, Leon Battista, *The Ten Books of Architecture*, New York, 1986.
4 *Pacata Hibernia*, 1633, between pp. 52 and 53.
5 MacCurtain, M., *Tudor and Stuart Ireland*, Dublin, 1972.

NEWTOWN

1 R. Haworth, "Heritage of Meath", *Meath Chronicle*, 28 November 1986.
2 *The Statute Rolls of the Parliament of Ireland, Ed. IV.* edited by J.F. Morrissey, Dublin, 1939.
3 McDonald Scott, M., "Newtown Bridge", *Irish Times*, March 1976.

GLANWORTH

1 O'Sullivan, M., "Note", *JCHAS*, second series, XIX, 1913, p. 95.
2 Byrne, J., "Glanworth", *JCHAS*, second series, XVIII, no. 96, 1912, p. 165–174.

3 Gwynn & Hadcock, p. 225.
4 Moody, T.W., Martin, F.X., Byrne, F.J., *A New History of Ireland*, ix, Oxford, 1984, p. 35.
5 *British Bridges.*
6 Close Rolls of Henry III, 26 Sept. 1255 (39 Hen. III).
7 Brunicardi N., *The Bridge of Fermoy*, Fermoy, 1985.
8 *Council Book Youghal*, p. 345.
9 "Manuscripts of the Old Corporation of Kinsale", *Analecta Hibernica*, 15, Nov. 1944, p. 193.
10 Milner, L., *The River Lee and its Tributaries*, Cork, 1975, pp. 26–27.
11 Westropp, T. Johnson, "The Monastery of St. Brigid, Kilcrea, the Castle of the McCarthys", *JCHAS* XIV 1908, pp. 159–177.
12 Hall, Mr & Mrs S.C., *A Week at Killarney*, London, 1865, p. 34.

GRACE DIEU

1 Gwynn & Hadock, p. 317.
2 MacCurtain, Margaret, *Tudor and Stuart Ireland*, Dublin, 1972, p. 35.

BENNET'S BRIDGE

1 Tighe, W., *Statistical Observations relative to the Co. of Kilkenny*, Dublin 1802, p. 131.
2 Ruddock.
3 Carrigan, Fr. W., *History & Antiquities of the Diocese of Ossory*, iii, Dublin, 1905, p. 486–7.
4 *Journal RSAI* 23, pt. II, 1893, p. 231.
5 Breen, M., "The Civil Parish of Treadingstown," *In the Shadow of the Steeple* (W. Murphy ed.) Tullaherin Parish Heritage Society, 1987 pp. 21–26.
6 Hogan, J., "Topographical & Historical Illustrations of the suburbs of Kilkenny", *JKSEIAS*, III (new series) 1860–1, p. 370.
    See also: Okey, T, *The Story of Avignon*, London, 1926; and Lafort, M.F., *Travaux de l'Académie Nationale de Reims*, 1886.
7 Boyer, M.N., "The Bridge-building Brotherhoods", *Speculum* 39, No. 4 (Oct. 1964), pp. 635–50.

WATERCASTLE

1 Hore, H.F., "Notes on a Fac Simile of an Ancient Map of Leix . . . in the British Museum", in *JKSEAS*, 1863, pp. 345–372.
2 Ordnance Survey Letters Queen's Co., Letter from T. O'Connor of 28 Dec. 1838, vol. II, 1838, p. 295.

HOLYCROSS

1 Hayes, W.J., *Holy Cross Abbey*, Dublin, 1973, p. 84.
2 Carville, G., *The Heritage of Holy Cross*, Belfast, 1973, p. 34.
3 Stalley.
4 Medcalfe, L., *Discovering Bridges*, Tring, Herts, 1979.
5 *British Bridges.*

ENNISCORTHY

1 Graves, Rev. J, "Transcripts documents: presented by J.P. Prendergast", *Journal RSAI*, 1868, pp. 15–16.
2 *Council Book Cork*, p. 197.

KILCARN

1 Cogan, A., *The Diocese of Meath Ancient & Modern*, 3 vols, Dublin, 1862, 1867 and 1870.
2 Gwynn & Hadcock, p. 189.
3 Ellison, C., *The Waters of the Boyne and Blackwater*, Dublin 1983, p. 89.
4 Haworth, R., "Heritage of Meath", *Meath Chronicle*, 28 November 1986.

CARRAGH

1 Joyce, i, p. 420.
2 Taylor, A., Map of the County of Kildare, 1783.
3 Sherlock.
4 *JKAS* 7, 1912–14, p. 57.

LISSENHALL

1 Gwynn & Hadcock, p. 44.

DROGHEDA

1 Hamilton, G.V., "The Northern Road from Tara" in *Journal RSAI*, 1913, pp. 310–13.
2 Ibid., p. 310.
3 D'Alton, J, *History of Drogheda*, ii, 1844, pp. 160 and 181.
4 Columcille, Fr, OCSO, *The Story of Mellifont*, Dublin, 1958, p. 295.
5 Bradley, J., "The Topography and Layout of Medieval Drogheda", *Journal of the Louth Archaeological Society* I, 1978, pp. 98–127.
6 *Cal. Doc. Ire.*, *1171–1251*, Doc. 473, 28 July 1213, p. 76.
7 *Chronicle and memoral of of Great Britain and Ireland in the Middle Ages*, ed. J.T. Gilbert, ii, p. 372: Laud 1884.
8 Gwynn & Hadcock.
9 McNeill, C; "Copies of the Down Survey Maps in Private Keeping: Duleek Barony", *Analecta Hibernica* 8, March 1938, p. 424.
10 Boulge, D.G., *The Battle of the Boyne*, London, 1911.
11 Ellison, C., *The Waters of the Boyne and Blackwater*, Dublin, 1983, p. 91.
12 *Dublin Builder*, 15 August 1866.
13 *Dublin Builder*, 1 June 1867.
14 Strype, W.G., "Description of the Iron Lattice Girder Road Bridge, Recently Erected over the River Boyne, at the Oelisk" in *Trans. ICEI* 9, 1871, pp. 67–78.
15 McMahon, T.J., and Faherty, P.J., "The Planning, Design and COnstruction of the Boyne Bridge at Drogheda", *Trans. IEI*, March, 1976, pp. 45–52.

ATHLONE

1 Gwynn & Hadcock, p. 110.
2 Ibid.
3 Joly, Rev. J.S., *The Old Bridge of Athlone*, Dublin, 1881, p. 17.
4 Mills, J., "Peter Lewys: His work and workmen", *Journal RSAI* 26, pt. 2, 1896, pp. 99–108.
5 Berry, H.F., "Sir Peter Lewys, Ecclesiastic, Cathedral and Bridge Builder, and his Company of Masons

1564–7", *Trans. Quatuor Coronati Lodge*, XV, 1902, pp. 4–22.

6   Mills, J., "The Journal of Sir Peter Lewys 1564–65", *JRSAI* 26, pt. 2, 1896, p. 136.

7   *Report on the Manuscripts of the Marquis of Ormonde, preserved at the Castle, Kilkenny*, ii, London, 1899.

8   Leask, *Castles*, p. 24.

9   Mullins, H.B., "An Historical Sketch of Engineering in Ireland", *Trans. ICEI* 6, 1859–60–61.

10 Conlan, P., OFM., "The Medieval Priory of Saints Peter & Paul, in Athlone" in *Irish Midland Studies, Essays in commoration of N.W. English*, ed. H. Murtagh, Athlone, 1980, pp. 73–83.

11 *Analecta Hibernica*, 15 November 1944, p. 250.

12 Story, G. *An Impartial History of the Wars of Ireland . . .*, London, 1693, pp. 523–31.

13 De Vere, Aubrey (1824–90), "A Ballad of Athlone (2nd Siege); or How They Broke Down the Bridge."

14 Weld, I., *Statistical Survey of the County of Roscommon*, Dublin, 1832, pp. 536–37.

15 Otway, Caesar, *A Tour in Connaught*, Dublin 1839, pp. 65–66.
    See also *35th Report* of the Deputy Keeper of the Public Records of Ireland, 1903, Appendix 3.

BALLINASLOE

1   Sidney, *UJA* 6, p. 315.

2   Egan, Rev. P.K., *The Parish of Ballinasloe*, Dublin 1960, p. 136.

3   *Cal. pat. rolls. Ire., Eliz.*, p. 20.

4   Leask, *Castles*, p. 6.

ABINGTON

1   Barry, J. Grene, "The Cromwilliam Settlement of the County of Limerick", *Limerick Field Club* III, 1905–1908, p. 18.

2   Shirley, E.P., "Extracts from the Journal of Thomas Dineley, Esquire . . .", *Journal RSAI* 8, 1864/66, p. 278.

3   Stalley, p. 241.

4   Joyce, i, p. 427, iii, p. 224.

5   Metcalfe, L., *Discovering Bridges*, Tring, Herts, 1979.

6   *Butler's Lives of the Saints*, Thurston, Herbert and Nora Leeson eds, London, 1936, p. 201.

BALLYSHANNON

1   *Ballyshannon: its History and Antiquities*.

2   *Cal. S.P. Ire., 1584*, p. 533.

3   Jackson, P.A., "Erne Hydro-Electric Development: Reconstruction of Ballyshannon Road Bridge", *Trans. ICEI* 74, 1947/48, pp. 43–59.

4   *Ballyshannon: The Rare Old Times*, booklet, 1988.

CARRIGADROHID

1   Joyce.

2   Windele, J. *Cork and its Vicinity*, Cork, 1848, p. 250.

3   J.C., "Antiquarian Remains and Historic Spots around Cloyne", *JCHAS*, 2nd series, 19, 1913, pp. 70f.

4   Ibid.

5   Leask, *Castles*, p. 155.

6   Du Noyer, G.V., "On Early Irish & Pre-Norman Antiquities", *RIA Proc.* IX (1864–66), p. 441.

7   McCarthy, S.T., "The Clann Carthaigh", *Trans. Kerry Arch. Soc.* II, no. 10, 1913, p. 64.

8   *The Civil Survey AD 1654–56 County of Waterford*, vi, with Appendices: Muskerry Barony, Co. Cork, Kilkenny City & Liberties. . . . Prepared for publication . . . Robert C. Simmington, Dublin, 1942.

SIR THOMAS'S

1   Lyons, Patrick, "Norman Antiquities of Clonmel Burgh", *Journal RSAI* 66, pt. II, pp. 285–294.

2   Barry, M., *Across Deep Waters*, Dublin, 1985.

3   Delaney, p. 71.

4   Power, P., *The Place Names of Decies*, 2nd ed., Cork and Oxford, 1952.

LEIGHLIN

1   Hogan, J., "Topographical and Historical Illustrations of the Suburbs of Kilkenny", *Trans. Kilkenny Arch. Soc.* I, p. 370.

2   Gwynn & Hadcock, pp. 89f.

3   Ware, Sir James, *De Hibernia et Antiquitatibus ejus*, London, 1654.

4   Sherlock.

5   Hollingshed, *Chronicles of England, Scotland and Ireland*, vi, Ireland, London, 1808, pp. 320–5.

6   *Chartul. St Mary's Dublin*, ii, p. 361.

7   Harvey, J., *The Medieval Architect*, London, 1972.

8   Crofton, T. Croker ed., *The Tour of the French Traveller, M. De la Boullaye Le Gouzin, Ireland AD 1644*, London, 1837, pp. 8–9.

9   Chetwood, W.R., *A Tour through Ireland . . . 1748*, London, 1757.

10 Ryan, J., *History of the Antiquities of the County Carlow*, Dublin, 1833.

11 *Irish Penny Journal*, vol. 1, 1840.

12 Comerford, Rev. M., *Collections Relating to the Dioceses of Kildare and Leighlin*, 3 vols, Dublin, 1883–86.

13 OS Letters Co. Carlow, Letter from T. O'Connor, from Leighlin Bridge, 22 June 1839.

14 UDRONE Irelandae in Catherlagh Baronia: A c.1571 map from the Lambeth MSS, London.

15 Sidney, in *UJA* 8.

16 Delaney.

MILLTOWN

1   Ball, F. Elrington, *History of the County of Dublin*, Part II, 1903, pp. 111f.

2   P, "The Old Bridge of Miltown, County of Dublin", *Irish Penny Journal*, vol. 1, no. 36, 6 March 1841, p. 281.

3   Sidney, in *UJA* 5, p. 305.

4   Conlin, Stephen and de Courcy, John, *Anna Liffey*, Dublin, 1988, p. 27.

CAPPOQUIN

1 Morrough, p. 177.
2 Dixon Hardy, P., *Dublin Penny Journal* , vol. II, no. 93, 12 April 1834, p. 325.
3 S. Pender (ed.), *Council Books of the Corporation of Waterford 1662–1700*, Dublin, 1964, p. 101.

BECTIVE

1 Gwynn & Hadcock, p. 128.
2 *British Bridges*, p. 304.

LEABEG

1 Orpen, "Newcastle Mackinegan" in *Journal RSAI.*
2 *Cal. doc. Ire.*, ii (1252–84), p. 309f.
3 Lewis.

OLD LONG

1 Joyce, i, p. 361.
2 *Cal. S.P. Ire.*, *1509–73* xxvi, p. 391.
3 Lowry, T.K. "The True Position of the Ford of Belfast", in *The Ecclesiastical Antiquities of Down, Conor and Dromore*, W. Reeves, ed. Dublin, 1847, p. 260.

CORK CITY GROUP

1 Walsh, M. "Cork Bridges", *Engineers Journal* 34, no. 7/8 1981, p. 35.
2 *Pacata Hibernia*, 1896, facing p. 136.
3 *Council Book Cork*, p. 57.
4 Brunicardi, N., *The Bridge at Fermoy*, Fermoy, 1985.
5 Ruddock.
   See also Twiss, H.F., "Mallow and Some Mallowmen", *JCHAS*, 2nd series, 29, 1924, pp. 81–87.

CROOKED

1 Morris, H., "The Slighe Cualann", and "Where King Loighaire was killed", *Journal RSAI*, series 7, vol. 8 (vol. 68, pt. 1) June 1938, pp. 113–129.

NORTHERN IRELAND GROUP

1 McCutcheon, pp. 1–49.
2 J.J.H., "Belfast's Many Bridges and Their Historic Associations", *Belfast Telegraph*, 6 February 1931.
3 Joyce, iii, p. 534.
4 *Drainage Reports Ulster*, Report on Lough Neagh District, *c.* 1848.

ESSEX

1 Semple; also published in *Hibernia's Free Trade or a Plan for the General Improvement of Ireland*, Dublin, 1780.
2 Gilbert, J.T. *Calendar of Ancient Records of Dublin*, v, 1895.
3 Ruddock.
4 Labelye, C., *A Description of Westminster Bridge*, London 1751.

5 Belidor, R.F. de, *Architecture Hydraulique*, 4 vols, Paris, 1752.
6 Purser, Griffith, J., "The Lowering and Widening of Essex Bridge", *Trans. ICEI*, 1880, pp. 32–50.

KILKENNY GROUP

1 Tighe, W., *Statistical Observations relative to the County of Kilkenny*, Dublin, 1802.
2 Delaney.
3 *Commons' jn.* Appendix CXCIX, Report from the Committee Appointed to Enquire What Sums have been Expended Upon the Navigation & Public Works for which Money was Granted by Parliament (Mr Perry, 14 Nov. 1759).
4 Ruddock.
5 Murphy, J.C., "The Kilkenny Marble Works", *Old Kilkenny Review* II, 1949, pp. 16f.
6 Pilsworth, W.J., *History of Thomastown and District*, 2nd ed., 1972.
7 Hughes, E.W., "Discovering our Bridges and Rivers", an article in the Graiguenamanagh GAA Club's match programmes of 29 June and 19 July 1986.
8 Semple.
9 "Extracts from the Journal of Thomas Dineley", *Journal RSAI* vi, 1867, p. 78.
10 Shannon Commission *4th Report* 1838, Plan & Elevation of the Bridge over the River Fergus at Clare, Surveyed by Henry Buck: 1839 [172] xxvii 1, 1839 [208] xxviii 1 Plan no. 107.
11 Barry, M., "The Partial Collapse of an Abandoned Multi-span Masonry Arch Bridge at Dysart, Co. Kilkenny, in 1985" in *Bridge Collapse*.

KILLALOE AND O'BRIENS

1 Delaney.
2 *Commons' jn. Ire.*, 1759, App. cciii.
3 *Cal. State Paper relating to Ireland of the reigns of Henry . . . Eliz. 1509–1573* (report on the Proceedings of the Expedition to Munster of Lord de Grey), p. 21 and 42.
4 "Notes and Queries, O'Brien's Bridge", *JNMAS* 3, 1913–15.
4 Shannon Commission, *2nd Report* 1839: 1837–38 [130] xxxiv. 1, plate 34.
6 Letters from Prof. T.S. Mulvany, RHA, to his eldest son, William T. Mulvany, Royal Commissioners of Public Works Ireland (period 1825–45, source of book not stated).

AVOCA

1 *Bridge Collapse*: Paper No. 2: "Flood Damage to Ten Bridges in Co. Wicklow following a Hurricane in August 1986" by J. Forristal, Co. Engineer, Wicklow County Council; and Paper No. 4: "The Restoration of the Partially Collapsed Three Span Masonry Bridge at Avoca, County Wicklow, in 1986 by J. Solan, Senior Executive Engineer, Wicklow County Council.

SCARIFF

1 *18th Report of the Board of Public Works, Ireland*, 1850, Appendix H: 1850 [1235] xxv 509, p. 168.

KANTURK

1 *Council Book Youghal*, pp. 357f.
2 "Manuscripts of the Old Corporation of Kinsale", ed. by R. Caulfield, 1879 in *Analecta Hibernica* 15, Nov. 1944, p. 190.
3 White, Col. J. Grove, *Historical and Topographical Notes, Buttevant, Castletownroach, Mallow . . .*, 1905, pp. 208–9.
4 Ruddock, pp. 38–43.
5 *Hibernia's Free Trade*, Dublin, 1780.

CLARA

1 McCarthy, D., "The Disaster of Wicklow" in *Journal RSAI* 1859, p. 438–40.

CASHEN

1 O'Kelly, M.J., 'A Wooden Bridge on the Cashen River, Co. Kerry", *Journal RSAI* XCI, pt. II, pp. 135–152.
2 Morrough, p. 177.
3 Barry, J.G., "Old Limerick Bridges", *JNMAS* 1, 1909–11, pp. 7–13.

LISMORE

1 Joyce, i, p. 272.
2 Ryland, R.H., *The History, Topography and Antiquities of the County and City of Waterford*, London, 1824, p. 350.
3 McPartland, E.., *Thomas Ivory, Architect*, Dublin, 1973, p. 9.
4 *Irish Penny Magazine*, vol. 1, no. 11, 16 March 1833, p. 81.

LARAGH

1 Griffith, R., in Appendix 10 of *4th Report of the Commission on Bogs in Ireland*, 1814: 1813–14 (131) VI, 2nd pt., pp. 167, 169.
2 Kerrigan, P., "Military Road, Wicklow. Notes for MHSI Field Day, 24 August 1975" (unpublished) (Note from Life of Michael Dwyer by Charles Dickson, 1944).
3 Leask, H.G., *Glendalough, Co. Wicklow. Official Historical and Descriptive Guide*, Dublin, n. d. (1977).
4 *Prose writings of Thomas Davis* edited with an introduction by T.W. Rolleston, London. (The article, titled "Irish Antiquities", is on p. 85 and the sentence quoted was taken from "The Athenaeum" by Davis. No dates are given but the first number of the Nation appeared in 1842 and Davis died in 1845.)

LEMUEL COX'S

1 James, J.G., "The Evolution of Wooden Bridge Trusses to 1850: Part II", *Journal of the Institute of Wood Source* 9, 3, 1982, p. 169 (Part I, p. 119).
2 Ordnance Survey Reports: City of Londonderry (Colby Thomas), Dublin, 1837, p. 117f, 130f, 296f.

3 Hancock, H.B. and Wilkinson, N.B., "An American Manufacturer in Ireland, 1796", *Journal RSAI* XCII, 1962, p. 135.
4 Farrell, J.B., "On the Design and Details of Construction for a Proposed New Bridge over the Estuary of the Slaney, at Wexford, *Trans. ICEI* IV, p. II, 1850–1, pp. 1–7.
5 Jackson, D.C. & Sheehy, P.E., "The Design and Construction of Ferrycarrig Bridge", *IEI Trans.* 105, 1980.
6 *Cal. doc. Ire.*, 1171–1251, Writ of 21 June 1210, p. 60.
7 "Wooden Bridge find gives Medieval Data", *New Civil Engineer*, 10 Nov. 1988, p. 7.
8 Lewis, entry "Ross (New)".
9 Maconchy, J.K., "Mountgarrett Bridge", *Trans. ICEI* LVIII, 1931–32, pp. 147–231.
10 Moynan, J.O., "A Short Description of the Existing Bridges at Waterford and Portumna . . ." *Trans. ICEI* xxxvi 3, 1910, pp. 224–250.
11 Power, P., *The Place-names of Decies*, 2nd ed., Cork and Oxford, 1952, p. 381.
12 O Lochlainn, C., *Roadways in Ancient Ireland* (map).
13 Otway, J., "The Port and Harbour of Waterford", *Trans. ICEI* 17, 1887, pp. 82–95.
14 Semple, G., *Hibernia's Free Trade or a Plan for the General Improvement of Ireland*, Dublin, 1780.
15 Covey, T., *A Scheme for Building a Bridge over the River Suire at the City of Waterford*, Waterford 1770, p. 59.
16 Jones, J.E., "Account & Description of Youghal Bridge", Paper no. 8, vol. III, *ICE*, London, June 1837.
17 *Who was Who in American History—Science and Technology*, Wilmette, Ill. 1976, p. 181.

SARAH'S

1 Conlon, S. and de Courcy, J., *Anna Liffey*, Dublin, 1988, pp. 12–13.
2 Sidney.
3 Le Harivel and Wynne, in *National Gallery of Ireland: Acquisitions 1982–83*, Dublin, 1984, p. 49.
4 Fagan, P., *The Second City: Portrait of Dublin 1700–1760*, Dublin, 1986, p. 26.
5 Ruddock.
6 Mullins, M.B., "An Historical Sketch of Engineering in Ireland", *Trans. ICEI* VI, 1859/60/61, p. 115.

LUCAN

1 Le Harivel, A. & Wynne, M., *National Gallery of Ireland: Acquisitions 1982–83*, Dublin, 1989, p. 39.
2 Healy, E., Moriarty, C. & O'Flaherty, G. *The Book of the Liffey from Source to the Sea*, Dublin, 1989, p. 137.
3 Mullins, M.B., "Presidential address being an Historical Sketch of Engineering in Ireland", *Trans. ICEI* 6, Dublin, 1863, p. 122.
4 Ruddock.
5 Conlon, S. and de Courcy, J., *Anna Liffey*, Dublin, 1988, p. 9.
6 Survey Map of Mullingar Turnpike Road, 1829, Dublin Co. Council Archives.

POLLAPHUCA

1 Joyce, i, 188.
2 De Courcy, "Alexander Nimmo, Engineer, Some Tentative Notes", N. Lib. Soc. of Ireland November 1981.
3 Ruddock, pp. 196–200.
4 Sherlock.
5 Taylor, A., *A Map of Kildare*, 1783.
6 Larkin, W., *A Map of the Cross and Bye, Branching, Mail Coach and Post Roads of Ireland*, Dublin, 1803.
7 *First and Second Reports* of the Select Committee Appointed to Inquire into the Amount of Advances made by the Commissioner of Public Works in Ireland with Minutes by Evidence: 1835 (329) (573) xx 145. 169; 1835 (573) xx 191.
8 *Report of the Select Committee on Turnpike Roads*: 1831–32 (645) xvii. 397.
9 *British Bridges*, pp. 463 and 432.

NEWRATH

1 Abstract of Presentments granted at Summer Assizes 1842, Co. Wicklow.
2 Chettoe C.S. et al., "The Strength of Cast Iron Bridges", *J. Inst. C.E.* 8, 1943/44, October 1944.
3 Davey, N., "Tests on Road Bridges", *National Building Studies, Research Paper No. 16*, DSIR, London, 1953.

CAUSEWAY BRIDGE

1 Walsh, M., "Shandon Bridge Dungarvan", Institution of Engineers of Ireland, November, 1987.
2 Ware, S., Report of a Bridge Being Built at Dungarvan 91813), in Lismore Papers, MS 7199, National Library of Ireland.

CROMABOO

1 Ruddock.
2 Berry, H.F., "Sir Peter Lewys. Ecclesiastic, Cathedral and Bridge Builder", *Trans. Quatuor Coronati Lodge*, vol. 15, 1902.
3 Cumerford, Dr "The Ford of AE, some historical notes on the Tower of Athy", in *JKAS* I 1891–95.
4 *Cal. S.P. Ire. 1509. 73*, iii, 24 June 1536, p. 42.

5 Hore, H., "Notes on an Ancient Map of Leix, Ofaly," *JKSEAS* 1863, pp. 345–372.
6 *Calendar of State Papers, Ireland, Elizabeth, 1599, April-1600, February*, E.G. Atkinson (ed.) London, 1899, p. 38.
7 Hogan, T.L., "River Barrow Drainage", *Trans. ICEI* 65, 1939, pp. 137–168.

GRIFFITH'S GROUP

1 O Lúing, S., "Richard Griffith and the Roads of Kerry" *J Kerry HS* 8, 1975 pp. 89–113, and 9, 1976, pp. 92–124.
2 O'Keeffe, P.J., "Richard Griffith: Planner and Builder of Roads" in *Richard Griffith, 1784–1878*, Dublin, 1980, pp. 57–76.
3 Report on the Roads made at Public Expense in the Southern District in Ireland by R. Griffith: H.C. 1831 (119) XII, 61.
4 Sganzin, M.J., *An Elementary Course of Civil Engineering*, Boston, 1827.

GOLEEN

1 Barry, M., *Across Deep Waters*, Dublin, 1985.
2 See Griffith's Group, above, fn. 2.

KENMARE

1 Storrie, M.C., "William Bald, Surveyor, Cartographer and Civil Engineer", in *Trans Inst. Br. Geog.* 47 (1968).
2 *6th Report* from the Board of Public Works in Ireland, 1837–38 (462) xxxv 143 and *17th Report* of the Board of Public Works, Ireland, 1849 [1098] xxiii, 433.
3 Mullins, B., "An Historical Sketch of Engineering In Ireland", in *Trans. ICEI*. VI, 1859/61, pp. 113f.
4 Prade, M., *Ponts & Viaducts au XIX siecle*, Poitiers, 1987.
5 Buckley, C.J., "Kenmare Bridge" in *Trans. ICEI* 60, 1934, pp. 29–52.
6 Kemp, E.L. "Links in a Chain: The Development of Suspension Bridges 1801–70", *Structural Engineer* 57A, no. 8, August 1979.
7 Kemp, E.L., in *History of Technology*, London, 1977.

Glossary

This glossary is based largely on Ruddock[1], Harris & Lever[2], Mitchell[3], Sganzin[4] and Mahan.[5]

abutment or butment: An end support of a bridge.

acre: 4840 sq. yds. statute measure; Irish acre 8640 sq. yds. In the medieval period in Ireland an Irish acre ranged from 1.5 to 15 times statute.

arch: An arrangement of stones (bricks) sometimes wedge-shaped (voussoirs) built over an opening in the form of some curve and supported at the end by piers or abutments built to carry a load in addition to its own weight. The most usual forms: the full centre or semicircle (rise = ½ span); the segment formed of an arc less than a semicircle; the pointed segmental, formed of two arc segments meeting at a point above the span centre; the oval in which the rise is less than half the span and the tangents and the springings are vertical, generally formed of a semi-ellipse or an odd number of acres of circles of unequal radii tangential to each other. If the span and rise are given and the rise is less than half the span, an infinite number of curves can be drawn to pass through the crown and springings, in which case other conditions need to be imposed to make problem determinate. (See Addendum below.)

archivolt: Moulded projecting stones forming the rim of an arch on the extrados.

arch ring: The stones forming the arch between the intrados and the extrados and between the springing planes.

arris: The sharp edge formed by the meeting of two straight or curved surfaces.

ashlar: Masonry composed of stones that are carefully hewn and worked, usually over 12in. deep and having joints not more than ⅛in. thick.

barbican: An outer defence, sometimes in the form of a tower, to protect the entrance to a castle.

bas-relief: Lettering etc. formed in stone by cutting away the surrounding area.

bay: The part of a waterway between two points of support; and the space between the bottom of the river, the piers (abutments) and the soffit of the superstructure.

beam: A straight continuous member which supports loads and transfers them to its supports.

bonder: A stone reaching from the face into the opposite half of a wall.

caisson: A large prefabricated open topped box for sinking in water to enable the foundations of a bridge to be constructed. The masonry may be built in it before it is sunk to rest on piles or on the prevously levelled river bed.

cantilever: A beam fixed at one end, unsupported elsewhere.

carucate: 80 acres if arable land Irish measure, but variable between counties and provinces.

castellated: Coped in battlement style to look like a castle.

cast iron: Cast iron is relatively inelastic, easily fractured, strong in compression, weak in tension, 2% to 6% carbon, unforgeable.

centre: A temporary structure, usually timber, which supports an arch during erection.

centering: The temporary support on which the arch is constructed.

cesdroichet (cesaigh): A wicker bridge.

cliathdroichet: A hurdle bridge.

clardroichet: A wooden bridge.

clochdroichet: A stone bridge.

clochan: A small stone building rounded in plan with roof corbelled inwards in successive courses like a beehive. (See Addendum, below.)

corbelling: The laying of stones in oversailing or projecting courses.

cofferdam: A temporary enclosed structure formed to exclude water from its internal area.

coping: The covering course of masonry forming a waterproof top.

corne de vache: A chamfer on the edge of arch rings and piers to streamline flow.

crannog: An artificial island built in a lake by driving young trees into bed usually in a circle and filling the inside with turf and other lightweight materials.

crown: The highest part of an arch including the keystone.

cramp: An iron bar like a staple pin often used to hold coping stones together, often leaded in to stonework.

cutwater: The upstream or downstream end of a bridge pier projecting beyond the vertical plane of the spandrel walls. In French *avant-bec* (upriver or fore), *arriere-bec* (downriver, or aft). See Table 5, Chapter 11, Part I for shapes. Purpose: to improve hydrodynamics and divert floating objects.

droichet: A bridge or causeway.

droichet clochaeltra: A bridge of stone and lime (mortar).

drawbridge: A span of a bridge that could be raised or pulled back to allow passage for ships or prevent persons crossing.

elbow-appareil: Treatment of joints in arch ring above springing using elbow-shaped voussoirs to avoid placing a vertical joint over the point where the horizontal joint meets a voussoir.

ellipse: A curve on which all the points have a constant distance from two fixed points called the foci. The half above (or below) the major axis is called a semi-ellipse.

equilibrium: The state when the forces acting on a body are balanced.

extrados: The outer surface of an arch ring.

fill: Material used for topping the extrados between arches and forming a level or graded road pavement sub-base.

flange: The broad top or bottom of an I-shaped beam.

flush: To pour liquid mortar into the voids of freshly built masonry.

freestone: Stone with no perceptible laminations.

girder: A structure composed of tension and compression flanges connected by bracing or web members. N-type bracing or lattices common in 19th century.

Gothic: A style of architecture characterised by the pointed arch common from about the 13th century.

grand jury: An institution which originated in Norman times. The members were selected by the sheriff of each county; they met twice yearly before the assizes but has no continuous existence. Replaced by elected county councils in 1898.

grouting: Injecting a fluid binder into the interstices of a material *in situ* or into the voids in masonry under applied pressure.

guniting: The application of a layer of mortar or concrete by projecting it at high velocity on to a surface.

haunch: The part of an arch between the springing and the crown.

heads: The surfaces of a bridge visible from a point upstream or downstream.

herringbone: Masonry in which the stones in successive courses are tilted in opposite directions.

header: A stone reaching from the face to the back of a wall.

hewn: Stone worked to give even bedding and vertical joint faces.

hydraulics: The branch of the science of hydrodynamics that deals with the motion of water.

hydraulic lime: Lime burned from rocks containing clay (silicia, alumina, etc.) which enables it to set under water. (see Chapter 5, Part I, and Appendix 5.)

impost: The flat stone on the top of a pier or abutment from which a semicircular or semi-elliptical arch springs.

incised: Lettering etc. cut into stonework.

intrados: The interior surface of an arch.

joggle: A joint in which a portion of the side of one stone is cut to form a projection and a corresponding sinking made in the adjacent stone.

journeyman: A tradesman who travels from job to job without settling in any particular area.

keep: A tower.

keystone: The uppermost or central stone of an arch.

kiln: The building or container in which calcium carbonate materials are burned to produce lime. Two types—a flare kiln in which the material does not come in contact with the fire, and a draw kiln in which fuel and raw material are placed in alternate layers.

lamination: Small scale layering in sedimentary rocks, usually but not always parallel to the bedding planes.

lime: The material obtained by calcining sea shells, chalk, limestone, or other carbonates of lime, generally called quicklime. (See Chapter 5, Part I, and Appendix 5.)

limestone: Consists mainly of calcium carbonate ($CaCO_3$) in calcite form. Classified mainly on origin.

masonry: The art of building in stone. The stones are usually of varying dimensions, requiring skill to bond them properly. "Random rubble" when stones are irregular and uncoursed; "coursed" when arranged to form horizontal beds 12in. to 18in. high; "regular coursed" when all stones in one course are squared to some height.

masons' marks: Symbols usually of a geometrical pattern inscribed on wrought stones by stonemasons; each mason had his individual mark by which his work could be identified. None found so far on a surviving road bridge in Ireland.

masons' tools: Classified under picking and surfacing, setting, cutting, saws, hoists. (See Addendum, below, for descriptions.)

mortar: The matrix used in the beds and joints to distribute pressure, adhere and bind, fill the voids.

motte: A steep truncated cone of earth usually surrounded by a deep ditch, often surmounted by a bailey.

niches: Recesses in walls to receive statues, generally polygonal or semi-circular in plan.

offset: A horizontal projection between a higher and lower course in a wall or pier.

ogive: A broken curve with an angular point at the apex composed of two, sometimes four circular arcs.

perch: Standardised at 16.5ft by act of parliament in 1836. Prior to that it varied—Ireland 21ft (called the Petty perch), Scotland 18ft, Cheshire 24ft, etc. The perch of masonry (solid) in grand jury presentments (1650–1836) in Ireland was 21ft long 1ft 6in. broad and 1ft high (30.5 cubic ft). In 1676 a 40 cu. ft perch was used in military engineering.

pier: The support between two arches.

pile: A timber beam or pole driven into the ground to support a pier or abutment foundation. Other materials such as steel and concrete also used from mid 19th century onwards.

plateband: A lintel composed of wedge-shaped stones or an arch with a crown of such composition.

ploughland: 120 "acres" of arable land excluding rivers, meadows, moors, pastures, hills and woods (often included an allowance for cow pasturage).

pointing: The finish applied to face joints in masonry; it can be flush, struck, keyed, recessed, coved, tuck etc.

pozzolana: A natural cement of volcanic origin found in a pulverised state near Mt. Vesuvius (Silica 55%, Aluminium 20%, Iron 20%, Lime 5%, approx.).

presentment: A specific proposal for a road, bridge, goal, etc. laid before the justices at an assizes session.

puddle clay (daib): Clay worked to a suitable consistency to form a barrier to the passage of water.

quarry sap: Moisture in freshly quarried stone which renders it softer and easier to work.

query book: The book summarising the presentments approved at an assizes session and placed before the following session.

quoin: The external corners (angles) of a building, sometimes applied to the stones forming it.

refuge: A recess in the parapet wall usually built up from a cutwater.

ribs: Projecting bands of hewn stone which support the cross sheeting slabs of a vault.

rise: The perpendicular distance from the chord between the springing points to the soffit or intrados at the keystone.

roache: Trade name for beds of very pure oolitic limestone (c.95% $CaCO_3$) found on Portland Island.

Romanesque: A style of architecture in which semicircular arches predominated that emerged in the 11th and 12th centuries in Europe and of which there was a native Irish variety.

saddle: A reinforcing layer placed over the extrados of an arch.

scour: The erosive action of running water in streams in excavating and carrying away material including rock from the bed particularly at bridges, where the waterway is constricted.

segment: An arc of a circle less than a semi-circle.

shoal: A short section of a river where the bed level rises above its normal grade due to rock, deposition or artificial filling.

sheeting: Commonly used to describe the portion of an arch between the facing rings; strictly, the stones laid across the ribs in a ribbed arch. Also used to refer to the boards or planks laid between the centres during the construction or an arch.

skewback: The stones forming the slopes on the piers/abutments on which the lowest ring stones rest in segmental arches.

soffit: The underside of an arch or beam, same as intrados.

sounding: Finding the depth of water and soft material in the bed of a river or estuary by inserting a vertical bar or pole.

spall (spaul): A fragment of rock usually broken off from a larger mass.

span: The distance between the supports of an arch or beam.

spandrel: The irregular triangular space between two arches enclosed by vertical lines drawn from the springing of the extrados and the horizontal line tangent to the crown.

springings: The points from which the curves of an arch commence as seen in elevation.

starling: An artificial island formed by contiguous piles driven into the river bed and the enclosed space which is filled with stones and gravel to form a foundation for a pier. Sometimes misused to describe a cutwater.

strain: The alteration of shape or dimensions resulting from stress. Can be tensile, compressive or distortional (shear).

stress: Force per unit area can be tensile, compressive or shear.

striking: The releasing or lowering of centering.

string course: Horizontal courses sometimes projecting and moulded built into faces of walls to act as a tie and give emphasis to divisions of a structure.

superstructure: That part of a bridge which is supported by the piers and abutments.

t(a)rass: A natural cement found in rock fragments near Andernath on the Rhine.

treenail: Hardwood pins of large diameter used where iron would rust.

thrust: The forces acting towards the springing, not necessarily normal, at the abutting faces of the stones in an arch. The line of thrust is that along which the resultant of these forces acts at various points along the arch.

Tudor: A style of architecture common in the 16th century exemplified in bridges by the four-centred arch.

turnpike: A gate erected across a public road for the purpose of stopping traffic and charging a toll. A section of a public road subjected to a toll.

underpin: To excavate beneath the foundation of piers or abutments and extend them downwards in masonry or concrete.

voussoir: A wedge-shaped stone with two faces cut to slopes that are normal to the intrados curve of an intended arch. For non-circular curves stones must be cut for particular positions in each semi-arch (e.g. semi-ellipse).

waterway: The distance between the end abutments less the sum of the pier thicknesses.

wing-wall: A wall extending back from the abutment supporting the approach road.

wrought iron: The principal ferrous metal until the Bessemer process cheapened the production of mild steel. Wrought iron durable under heat, easily forged, should show long "silken fibres" at slow fracture. Very resistant to shock. Contains less than 1% carbon, liable to corrosion.

Metric Equivalents

1 inch	= 25.4 mm
1 foot	= 0.304 m
1 yard	= 0.914 m
1 perch	= 5.5 yds. = 5.03 m
1 mile	= 1.609 m
1 mile (Irish)	= 2240 yds. = 2.048 km
1 sq. ft	= 929.03 cm²
1 cubic ft	= 0.0282m³
1 sq. perch	= 30.25 sq. yds. = 25.29 m²
1 rood	= 40 sq. perches = 1011.5 m²
1 acre (statute)	= 4 roods = 4046.9 m²
1 sq. perch (Ir.)	= 49 sq. yds. = 40.97 m²
1 acre (Irish)	= 160 Ir. sq. perches = 6555 m²

1 Ruddock, T., *Arch Bridges and Their Builders 1735-1835*, Cambridge, 1979.

2 Harris, J., Lever, J., *Illustrated Glossary of Architecture 850-1830*, London, 1966.

3 Mitchell, C., *Building Construction and Drawing*, 9th ed., London, 1920.

4 Sganzin, M., *An Elementary Course of Civil Engineering*, trans. from French by J. Davis, Boston, 1827.

5 Mahan, D.H., *An Elementary Course of Civil Engineering*, Edinburgh, Dublin, London, 1845.

ADDENDUM

A Note on Arch Forms

Given the great variety of arch forms found in the bridges described in this book, it was thought advisable to include descriptions from a number of sources for the benefit of the reader. The *Illustrated Glossary of Architecture 850–1830* gives the following: "*Arch*. A curved structure formed of wedge-shaped blocks of brick or stone (voussoirs) held together by

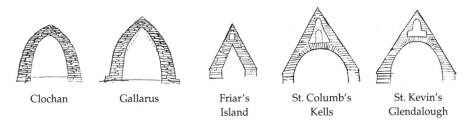

Clochan   Gallarus   Friar's Island   St. Columb's Kells   St. Kevin's Glendalough

Development of Irish Stone Roofs (Leask)

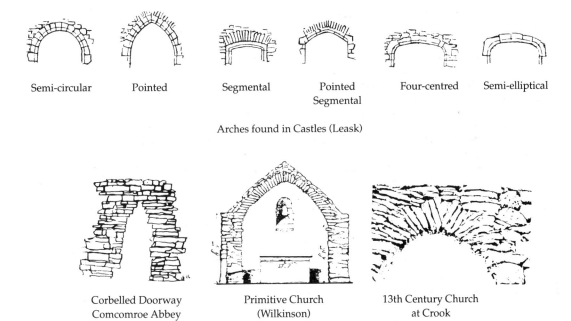

Semi-circular   Pointed   Segmental   Pointed Segmental   Four-centred   Semi-elliptical

Arches found in Castles (Leask)

Corbelled Doorway Comcomroe Abbey   Primitive Church (Wilkinson)   13th Century Church at Crook

Fig. 248: *Some Arch Forms found in Early and Medieval Irish Buildings*

mutual pressure and supported only at the sides. *Semicircular arch*: a semicircle having its centre on the springing line. *Stilted arch*: an arch springing from a point above the imposts; the vertical masonry between the imposts and springing line resembling stilts. *Elliptical arch*: a half-ellipse drawn from a centre on the springing line. *Segmental arch*: the segment of a semicircle drawn from a centre below the springing line. *Pointed arch*: composed of two arcs drawn from centres on the springing line. *Lancet arch*: a narrow pointed arch whose span is shorter than its radii. *Equilateral arch*: an arch whose span is equal to its radii. *Drop arch*: an arch whose span is greater than its radii. *Three-centred arch*: two separated arcs with centres on the springing line, surmounted by a segmental arch with centre below the springing line. *Four-centred Tudor arch*: a depressed pointed arch composed of two pairs of arcs, the lower pair drawn from two centres on the springing line and the upper pair from centres below the springing line. *Ogee arch*: a pointed arch formed of two convex arcs above and two concave arcs below." A few have been omitted here as not relevant to bridges.

Prade gives a table of arch shapes found in masonry arch bridges in France by period, which is outlined in Part I, Chapter 11 above. He defines the ogive as "a broken curve with an angular point at the summit and composed of two or sometimes four arcs of circles." He

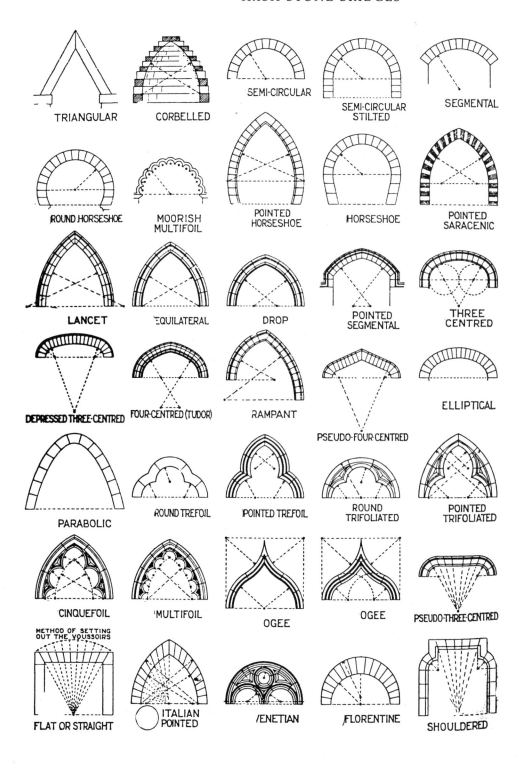

Fig. 249: *Shapes of Arches given in Early Editions of Banister Fletcher,* History of Architecture

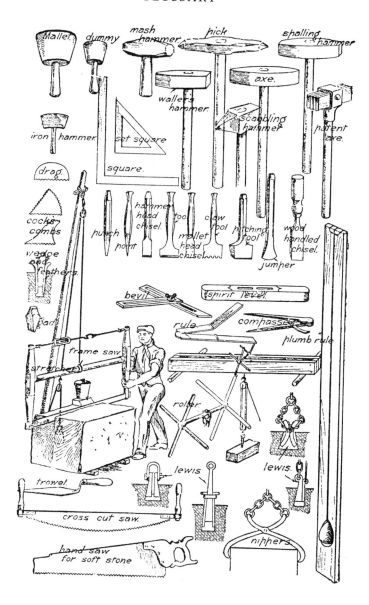

Fig. 250: *Masons' Tools from Mitchell*, Building Construction

states that it is of Roman origin, from Syria and may have been brought to Europe from the Middle East by pilgrims about the 9th century.

The development of the Irish stone roof from the clochan, as found in early stone-roofed buildings in Ireland, is fully described by Leask, *Churches*. His sketches are reproduced in fig. 248. It was these sketches that prompted me to conclude that stone arch bridges in

Ireland had evolved from the application of the principles developed in the construction of stone roof churches, such as St Columb's (Kells) and St Kevin's (Glendalough). This hypothesis is explained in Chapter 11, Part I and under St Mary Magdalen's and Mabes bridges in Part II. I was unable to trace any information on the orientation of the stones in the corbelled haunches of the arches in St Columb's or St Kevin's—whether they are

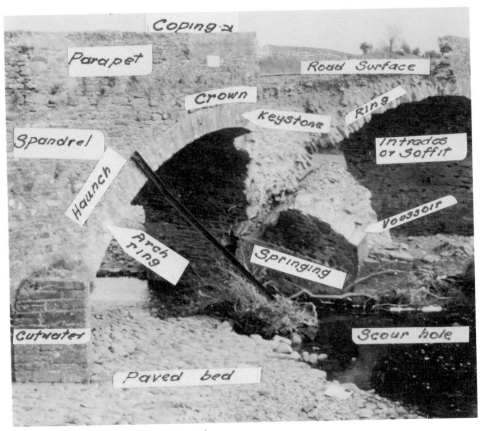

Fig. 251: *Principal Parts of a Masonry Arch*

horizontal as sketched by Leask, or progressively titled as in the bridges. Close inspection of the intrados with the aid of lights of adequate wattage should enable one to estimate the stone slopes; however, this may prove more difficult than in bridges where the mortar has been washed out leaving open joints.

Sketches of a fully corbelled doorway from Corcomroe Abbey erected between 1175 and 1180; of "a primitive church" given in Wilkinson; and of a window in the 13th-century church in Crook, Co. Waterford; have also been included in fig. 248. A photo of Crook (fig. 53) is included under St John's Bridge, Waterford, together with a discussion of its resemblance to the 13th-century surviving bridge arches.

Leask discussed the development of castle briefly in his book on Irish castles and gives small sketches of the shapes found by him; those that are relevant to bridges are included in Fig. 248.

From the foregoing it will be evident that further research is needed on arch shapes found in early and medieval buildings including bridges in Ireland. This could lead to a classification by period which would be of great value for dating purposes. Regarding the definition of an arch, the following should cover most of the examples given in this book: "An arrangement of stones built over an opening in the form of a concave curve, supported at the ends by abutments and/or piers, and of adequate strength to carry its own weight and superimposed loads."

Finally, the comprehensive set of arch shapes given in early editions of Sir Banister Fletcher's famous *History of Architecture* and the sketches of masons' tools in early editions of Charles Mitchell's *Builder Construction* are reproduced in figs. 249 and 250 respectively. In fig. 251 the principal parts of arch bridges are shown on a photo of a collapsed multi-span arch bridge.

342

Index